Sir Frank Packer

By the Same Author

The House of Packer: The Making of a Media Empire (1999)
Party Games: Australian Politicians and the Media from War to Dismissal (2003)
Changing Stations: The Story of Australian Commercial Radio (2009)

Sir Frank Packer

A Biography

Bridget Griffen-Foley

SYDNEY UNIVERSITY PRESS

Published in 2014 by Sydney University Press

Author's Note:
When Australia changed to decimal currency in 1966, £1 was equivalent to $2.

Copyright © Bridget Griffen-Foley 2000
Copyright © Bridget Griffen-Foley 2014
First published in Australia in 2000 by HarperCollins Publishers

Reproduction and Communication for other purposes
Except as permitted under the Act, no part of this edition may be reproduced, stored in a retrieval system, or communicated in any form or by any means without prior written permission. All requests for reproduction or communication should be made to Sydney University Press at the address below:

Sydney University Press

Fisher Library F03
University of Sydney NSW 2006
AUSTRALIA
Email: sup.info@sydney.edu.au

National Library of Australia Cataloguing-in-Publication entry

Author: Griffen-Foley, Bridget, 1970- author.
Title: Sir Frank Packer : a biography / Bridget Griffen-Foley.
ISBN: 9781743323823 (paperback)
ISBN: 9781743323830 (ebook : epub)
ISBN: 9781743323847 (ebook : kindle)
Notes: Includes bibliographical references and index.
Subjects: Packer, Frank, Sir, 1906-1974.
    Consolidated Press--History.
    Publishers and publishing--Australia--Biography.
    Mass media--Australia--Biography.
    Businessmen--Australia--Biography.
Dewey Number: 070.092

Cover image Providence Journal Photos
Cover design by Miguel Yamin

*In loving memory of my uncle,
Brian Jackson*

Contents

Preface ix
Acknowledgments xiii
Abbreviations xvi
Introduction xvii

1 Napoleon's Debut 1
2 His Father's Footsteps 14
3 Little Frankie's Wanderings 31
4 El Dorado 48
5 The Young Master 65
6 Mansions and Mêlées 80
7 'Political Harlots of Mammon' 103
8 Jekyll and Hyde 121
9 Powerbroking 138
10 Treading on Corns 155
11 Rumours 171
12 Setting Sail 188
13 Toasting Victory 215
14 The Sound of One Man Clapping 234
15 The King is Dead 252

Chronology 266
Endnotes 267
Bibliography 315
Index 325

Preface

Pamela Williams (a Fairfax journalist) and HarperCollins (a Murdoch company) scored a coup when the scions of the Packer and Murdoch dynasties agreed to pose for the cover of her book, *Killing Fairfax: Packer, Murdoch and the Ultimate Revenge*, about the decline of the once mighty Fairfax media group. James Packer and Lachlan Murdoch share not only a birthday, but the pressures of dynastic succession and the searing experience of the collapse of One.Tel. Fairfax, Packer, Murdoch — all sharing the spotlight at the launch of *Killing Fairfax* on 23 July 2013.

For a century, these three families have dominated the Australian media. But as the 'old' media struggles to adapt to the new, with declining audiences, converging technologies and changing business models, traditional notions of the family media dynasty are also under threat.

Since the 1980s, the Fairfax empire has been lost to the family, classified advertising has collapsed and, in 2012, 1900 job losses were announced. Fairfax is now the prism through which the Australia print media will be evaluated. Since Kerry's death in 2005, the Packer family has all but vacated its print and free-to-air television assets and transformed itself into a gaming and entertainment business. The Murdoch family business, which began spreading offshore in the 1960s, is struggling to deal with both corporate and personal scandals, while the complex issue of succession has media watchers eagerly following every breathless Tweet from the octogenarian Rupert Murdoch. In June 2013 the New News Corp launched as a 'Global Media and Information Services Company', cut adrift from the profitable 21st Century Fox.

As my biography of Sir Frank Packer documented in 2000, the issue of succession at Consolidated Press had been resolved, somewhat poignantly, before Sir Frank's death in 1974. The elder son and heir, Clyde, infuriated by yet another act of paternal interference and censorship, had resigned his management positions within the group in 1972. When Clyde's younger brother Kerry assumed the reins two years later, the *Canberra Times* remarked that Sir Frank 'was too much the individualist for any successor to truly emulate'.

By 2000, I was aware of a rumour that Sir Frank's father, Robert Clyde Packer, had sired another son. Ernestine Hemmings, who had been working as a sub-editor at *Smith's Weekly*, where R. C. Packer was manager, had given birth to a son, Robert, on 30 October 1924 in Hobart, where Packer had spent his early life. Unmarried, Ernestine had assumed the surname Hill. There were no official records to prove the paternity of Robert Hill, whose birth was unregistered. However, Hill believed that Packer was his father, and there is mounting circumstantial evidence that this was the case. The full story of journalist and travel writer Ernestine Hill and her son Robert, who died in 2003, awaits her biographer. Meanwhile, chapters 2 and 3 of *Sir Frank Packer: A Biography* must now be read in the context of a likely relationship between R. C. Packer and Ernestine Hill.

During the 1990s, R. C. Packer's daughter Kathleen (Lady Stening) had proved to be a valuable source for my biography, agreeing to be interviewed on several occasions, and carefully selecting family letters and photographs from a trunk to which I was never given access. She died shortly before the first edition was published in 2000.

Sir Frank's son Clyde had been another source, by telephone, usually very early in the morning, from his home in California. He died in 2001.

Kerry Packer died in Sydney on Boxing Day, 2005. The frenzy of media coverage proved the *Canberra Times*' prediction wrong. When Sir Frank died, his flagship magazines the *Australian Women's Weekly* and the *Bulletin* between them managed only three pages and a cover. For Kerry, there were commemorative editions of both magazines, followed by a state memorial service — a federal government initiative and an unprecedented honour for a businessman. In the last half-century at least, the death of no Australian, other than Don Bradman, has attracted such saturation coverage. In 2005, perhaps not even Consolidated Press could have predicted the level of interest in Kerry, with extensive coverage also in the pages of the Murdoch and Fairfax presses. It was as though Kerry Packer had finally taken over the *Sydney Morning Herald* by stealth. A new edition of Paul Barry's 1994 biography was published as *The Rise and Rise of Kerry Packer Uncut* in 2006, with the inclusion of material previously considered too risky from a legal perspective.

In December 2006, on the centenary of Sir Frank Packer's birth, his family donated Judy Cassab's portrait of him to the National Portrait Gallery. His widow, Lady (Florence) Packer, and Kerry's widow, Ros, were on hand, together with the Prime Minister's wife, Janette Howard, for the unveiling. Lady Packer's death in Monaco in 2012 at the age of 97 saw the curtain fall on the old media moguls of Sir Frank's generation.

The buccaneers and ideologues who made up the Australian media's first families are largely gone. In their place are private equity players and other unsentimental financiers. Even James Packer (the somewhat premature subject of another Paul Barry biography in 2009) is now lean and mean, having lost a good part of his body weight following gastric bypass surgery in 2011. He is a shadow of his literally 'larger-than-life' father and grandfather. The Packers and the Murdochs, together with their wives, girlfriends and offspring, are often now portrayed as simply rich and glamorous. They have become celebrities – usually (but not invariably) reluctant products of the media their families helped to create and control for most of the twentieth-century.

James Packer along with Elisabeth, Lachlan and James Murdoch now operate in an era of MBAs, of capital markets and shareholder value. Old-fashioned, sleeves-up media proprietors have largely gone, along with their ruthless and feudal management styles, indifference to chains of command, intuitive sense of the market and fingertip feel for numbers.

Preface

Since Kerry Packer's death, his family, and that of the Murdochs, have been ripe for nostalgic embrace. Three dramatic mini-series have focused on the Packer empire: *Paper Giants: The Birth of Cleo* (airing on the ABC in 2011), *Howzat! The Kerry Packer War* (Nine, 2012) and *Paper Giants: Magazine Wars* (ABC, 2013). Sir Frank, played by Tony Barry, appeared in the wings of the first *Paper Giants*. Now, in *Power Games: The Packer-Murdoch War*, the two dynasties go head-to-head. *Power Games* aired on Nine, the network Sir Frank himself established, and his grandson James sold. The mini-series focuses on 1960 to 1975, based in part on the second half of my Frank Packer biography. Lachy Hulme (who played Kerry Packer in *Howzat!*) delivers a compelling, uncanny performance as Kerry's father. Sir Frank can also be seen on stage, in David Williamson's new play, *Rupert*.

What would Sir Frank think of *Power Games*? Find out on Twitter, for he has made a comeback there, too: @Sir_FrankPacker.

Bridget Griffen-Foley, February 2014

Acknowledgments

My principal debt in researching and writing this book is to Lady (Kathleen) Stening. In the course of many interviews, meetings and telephone conversations, Lady Stening shared with me memories of her brother Sir Frank Packer and their father R. C. Packer, and gave me access to family papers and photographs. I am aware that there will be parts of this book that Lady Stening will not like, but I hope she will feel that I have set out to provide a balanced account of her brother's life.

Lady (Florence) Packer also kindly agreed to be interviewed for my work on her late husband. Noni E. Fitzmaurice kindly clarified a number of details about the Packer ancestry, and allowed me to reproduce the photograph of Arthur Howard Packer from the family photograph collection compiled by his niece, Marie Frieda Packer (1893-1975). E. G. Theodore's daughter Myra Rowbotham has been a generous source of information and enthusiasm over many years.

My colleagues in the Department of History at the University of Sydney, particularly Professor Stephen Garton, Associate Professor Richard Waterhouse and Richard White invariably provided encouragement and sound advice. The 'Writing Lives' workshops initiated by the Research Institute for Humanities and Social Sciences in 1998 at the University of Sydney facilitated a lively exchange of ideas.

I am grateful to Professor Geoffrey Bolton, Peter Coleman, Professor Clem Lloyd and Professor Duncan B. Waterson for their helpful and incisive comments on drafts of this manuscript.

Some of my interest in Packer undoubtedly stems from the fact that my late father John Griffen-Foley worked for him on the *Daily* and *Sunday Telegraphs* for more than twenty years. I am indebted to my mother Helen for cheerfully putting up with another family member's obsession with Sir Frank.

In Australia, many other individuals enabled me to complete this project: Pat Bancks; Paul Barry; Alex Baz; Anna Binnie; Dr Margriet Bonnin; Arthur Boothroyd; Joyce Bowden; Associate Professor Patrick Buckridge; Ita Buttrose; Sally Baker; Mary Elizabeth Calwell; Robert Campbell; Pauline Curby; the late Adrian Deamer; Nigel Dick; the late Dorothy Drain; Rita Dunstan; David Evans, federal director of the Australian–American Association; Ken Ewing; Dr Peter Gifford; Harry Gordon; Gideon Haigh; Ian Hancock; Heather Henderson; Robert Hill; Emeritus Professor Donald Horne; Dick Hughes; Alfred James; Joyce James; Stephen Keir; David S. Kent; Dr Rod Kirkpatrick; Peter Lucas of the Hutchins School Archives; Terri McCormack; the late Frank McNulty; Veronica McNulty; Barry McRae; Professor Meaghan Morris; Dr Craig Munro; Dr Maree Murray; Dame Elisabeth Murdoch; Dr Melanie Oppenheimer; Dr Jim Packer; Jack Patterson; Paddy Pearl; Major-General John Hemsley Pearn; Neville Petersen; the late Elizabeth Riddell; Graham Robertson, honorary archivist of the Royal Sydney Yacht Squadron; Jim Russell; Colin Sanders, chief executive officer of the Royal Agricultural Society of New South Wales; Professor Geoffrey Sherington; Noel Slarke; Gavin Souter; Tom Uren; Bruce Wakeling and Jack Ryan of the Boy Scout Memorabilia Centre; Eleanor Watson; Dr Anne-Maree Whitaker; Sheila Wood; and John Wynne-Lewis.

I also thank the staffs of the Archives Office of New South Wales, the *Australian Dictionary of Biography*, the Australian Stock Exchange, the Australian War Memorial, the John Fairfax Archives, Fisher Library at the University of Sydney, the History Research Section of the Central Army Records Office of the Australian Army, the Mitchell Library at the State Library of New South Wales, Moore Theological College, the National Archives of Australia, the National Library of Australia, the Noel Butlin Archives Centre, the Royal Agricultural Society of New South Wales Archives, the State Library of Victoria, and the University of Sydney Archives.

In Britain, I was assisted by Katharine Bligh, archivist (modern collections) of the House of Lords Record Office; David M. Bowcock, assistant county archivist (Carlisle) of the Cumbria Record Office; the Newspaper Library at the British Library; Robin Burgess, chief executive of the CN Group Limited; David Cliffe and Alan Hanhin of the County Reference Library, Berkshire; John G. Entwisle, manager of the Reuters Archive; Wilma Grant, county librarian of the Royal County of Berkshire; Suzanne M. Eward, librarian and keeper of the muniments at Salisbury Cathedral; Robert Hale and Katie Willis, archivists at the Berkshire Record Office; Ian Mortimer, curatorial officer of the Royal Commission on Historical Manuscripts; Bridget Palmer of the Royal Academy of Music; Lindsay Ross, secretary of the Commonwealth Press Union; David Ward, archivist at the Institute of Commonwealth Studies at the University of London; and Rachel Wells of the Central Chancery of the Orders of Knighthood.

In the United States, I was assisted by Howard B. Gotlieb, director of the Department of Special Collections at Boston University; Donna Halper; Tom Johnson; Russell Koonts and Claire M. Locke of the Special Collections Library, Duke University; John H. Livingstone, state librarian of the New Jersey State Library; Donald Matheson; and Charles St Vil, manager of the *New York Times* Archives. Lars Forsberg, secretary, his predecessor, Peter M. Ward, Richard A. von Doenhoff, archivist and protocol officer, and Joseph Jackson, librarian, helped locate relevant records preserved by the New York Yacht Club. My American research assistant, Jennifer E. Kelley, ably worked on the club's records.

In France, Meg Sordello kindly gave me access to the papers of her late uncle, George Warnecke.

I am indebted to the following individuals and organisations for their assistance with photographs: Richard Ackland; the British Library; Jennifer Broomhead of the State Library of New South Wales; Vic Cohen; A. H. Faircloth; the Fairfax Photo Library; Mitzi Finey; Noni E. Fitzmaurice; Guy Hansen; Tony Henningham of the Herald & Weekly Times Corporate Photo Sales; Kirstie McRobert of the State Library of Victoria; Sarah McSkimming of the Australian Picture Library; the National Library

Acknowledgments

of Australia; News Ltd; the *New York Times* Picture Desk; Queensland Newspapers Pty Ltd; Susan Son of Condé Nast Publications; Lady Stening; Peter Viska; *Vogue* Australia; and Christopher Warren, general secretary of the Media, Entertainment and Arts Alliance.

I thank Angelo Loukakis, formerly of HarperCollins, for buoyantly embracing this project, and Helen Littleton and Jesse Fink for seeing it through. Jacqueline Kent was a thorough, at times demanding, but always encouraging editor.

Abbreviations

AAP	Australian Associated Press
ABC	Australian Broadcasting Commission
ABCB	Australian Broadcasting Control Board
ACP	Australian Consolidated Press
AIF	Australian Imperial Force
AJA	Australian Journalists' Association
AJC	Australian Jockey Club
ALP	Australian Labor Party
ANC	Australian Newspapers Conference
ANPA	Australian Newspaper Proprietors' Association
A&R	Angus & Robertson Ltd
AWC	Allied Works Council
AWU	Australian Workers' Union
CCC	Civil Constructional Corps
DLP	Democratic Labor Party
FP	Frank Packer
HWT	Herald & Weekly Times
MLA	Member of the Legislative Assembly
MLC	Member of the Legislative Council
MP	Member of Parliament
NYYC	New York Yacht Club
PIEUA	Printing Industry Employees' Union of Australia
PKIU	Printing and Kindred Industries Union
RSYS	Royal Sydney Yacht Squadron
UAP	United Australia Party

Introduction

In the sprawling Newport mansion built by the Vanderbilt family, 300 guests gathered on 14 September 1962, the eve of Australia's first challenge for the America's Cup. The great hall of 'The Breakers', built to resemble an Italian Renaissance palace, was decorated with Australian wildflowers flown in by Qantas. An eight-piece orchestra played 'Waltzing Matilda', 'Botany Bay', 'Click Go the Shears' and 'Tie Me Kangaroo Down, Sport'.[1] Guests dined on Australian produce: West Australian crayfish tails thermidor, roast Riverina lamb, ice cream with Hawkesbury Valley passionfruit, Murwillumbah crystallised pineapple, and wine supplied by Lindemans and Penfolds.2

The banquet brought together the cream of society, politics, diplomacy, industry and sport from Australia and the United States. At the head table sat the American president John F. Kennedy and his glamorous wife Jacqueline. They were joined by the Australian treasurer Harold Holt, his American counterpart, Douglas Dillon, the Australian minister for external affairs Sir Garfield Barwick and the American secretary of defence Robert McNamara. The host was Sir Howard Beale, Australia's ambassador to the United States, but everyone knew the dinner would not have been possible without the efforts of Sir Frank Packer. The Australian media proprietor, who had spent three years and hundreds of thousands of pounds preparing Australia's challenge for the coveted America's Cup, was seated between the president and the first lady.[3]

Adrenalin was the only thing keeping Sir Frank going. His decision to mount a challenge for the America's Cup through the Royal Sydney Yacht Squadron had propelled him into a world of imperial jealousies and political intrigue. The Australians' right to challenge for the cup had been contested by the Royal Thames Yacht Club; the Menzies government had questioned the value of being associated with the challenge; when the government had finally lent some support to the bid, Labor politicians had erupted in protest; American newspapers were reporting that morale in the Australian team was low because of Packer's constant meddling. Even the banquet, which had been suggested by Packer, attracted controversy. An Australian Labor politician, Eddie Ward, declared that some people would 'always avail themselves of the opportunity to have a guzzle at public expense' and lambasted the Liberal government for allocating US$8100 for a dinner for 'the snobbocracy of America'.[4]

Sir Frank was not just tired, he was nervous. Never an accomplished speaker, he became increasingly edgy as Beale and then Kennedy proposed toasts and delivered speeches. With an eye on fostering American–Australian relations, President Kennedy declared that Australia had proved herself a great leader in sport, was one of the world's freest nations and was closely tied to the United States in war and peace. Packer drank several whiskies in an effort to steady his nerves before he himself had to get to his feet. Sweating in his tuxedo, the tall, burly Packer clutched his notes nervously as he spoke in a voice husky from years of smoking cigarettes and cigars. His address, in which he conceded that his yacht *Gretel* was the underdog, appeared disjointed after the polished presentations of Beale and Kennedy. Adrian Quist, the former Davis Cup tennis champion who had gone to Newport to see the America's Cup match, would later recall that his friend's speech had not been his 'finest hour'. Quist had to agree when Packer asked him, 'Didn't go so well, did I?' Packer ensured that reports about the glittering dinner appeared in his publications the *Australian Women's Weekly* and the *Sunday Telegraph*. But only the president's speech was broadcast on Packer's Sydney television station TCN–9.[5]

Packer's appearance at the banquet illuminated many of the elements — a desire to mix with the rich and the powerful, a curious shyness, a propensity to court controversy, a willingness to interfere with his media outlets — that were constants throughout his tempestuous life. His relationship with the social, political and business establishment was always ambivalent. He and his father Robert Clyde Packer had made their fortunes through some controversial business transactions in the 1920s and the 1930s, and they were always regarded as 'new money'. Frank Packer both cocked a snook at, and longed to be considered part of, the establishment. He was unapologetically brash and brazen in his business pursuits and his robust sense of humour was often inappropriate to the occasion. But as a young man he took up the hobbies of Sydney's élite, such as yachting and polo, and established a grand home in Sydney's Eastern Suburbs; as he grew older he emerged as a powerbroker in the Liberal Party and introduced his countrymen to the exclusive ranks of twelve-metre yachting.

Only those closest to Packer probably ever realised that his sense of humour and blustering manner hid his shyness. He performed poorly at school and was self-conscious about his hulking size; in his late teens, it became apparent that he lacked the literary flair and journalistic creativity of the father he so revered. Packer's remarkable energy and vigour, and his dogged determination to win at whatever game he was playing, seem to have stemmed from an innate inferiority complex.[6] He was a man of many contradictions: he cheated on his beautiful first wife Gretel and then named his America's Cup yachts after her; he was a deeply compassionate and sentimental son and brother but a tyrannical father; he exasperated trade unions in the newspaper industry but bestowed largesse on individual employees; he gave generously to charities and other good causes but counted the paper clips at work; he supported Australian artists and scientific research, but his own interests were philistine and he refused to allow his elder son to go to university; he fought for the freedom of the press in the Second World War but crudely manipulated his own media outlets.

Sir Frank Packer dominated the Australian media landscape for forty years and most who crossed his path found him an endless source of puzzlement and interest. Journalists and printers still dine out on stories about Packer and their memoirs are littered with colourful anecdotes about him. The fact that his younger son Kerry has emerged as the richest person in Australia has only compounded the fascination with the Packer family. And yet the story of Robert Clyde Packer's pioneering journalistic

Introduction

pursuits in the first half of this century and Frank's own diverse activities in the media, the civil service and the political and sporting arenas has never been adequately told. It is a story that takes us first to Berkshire and then to Hobart in the 1850s.

1
Napoleon's Debut

John Packer would seem a fitting patriarch to head Sir Frank Packer's family tree. He attained considerable prominence in his lifetime: he was made a clerk of the privy seal in 1604; acquired a number of estates, including Donnington Castle in Shaw, Berkshire; was given the manor of Shillingford, Berkshire, on the coronation of King Charles I in 1625; and became a member of parliament in 1628. During the English Civil War he aligned himself with parliament, and Donnington Castle was garrisoned by the king's forces; he was appointed a visitor of Oxford University in 1647; and his four sons distinguished themselves in politics, medicine and the law. Those kindly disposed to Sir Frank would think it apt that he was descended from a man who acquired significant wealth and social distinction. Those who condemned the autocratic manner in which Sir Frank wielded his power would suggest that he was just like his ancestor, 'an excellent man of business, but self-seeking, avaricious and treacherous'. The biographer of Frank Packer would contentedly begin his or her 'story' by examining the life of the individual deemed to be worthy of inclusion in that monument to Great Men, the *Dictionary of National Biography*.[1]

But unfortunately for friend and foe alike — and despite the claims of Sir Frank's previous biographer, R. S. Whitington — there is no evidence to suggest that Sir Frank was actually descended from John Packer. Genealogical investigations reveal that the male line of descent from John Packer broke down in 1746 when his descendants became the Hartley-Russells.[2]

Like so many names of the later Middle Ages, 'Packer' seems to have been coined to describe an occupation. The earliest known Packers were packers of wool: they raised sheep in the Cotswolds in south-west England, sheared them, packed their wool into sacks and transported it to markets on the backs of horses and mules.[3] The Packers who can be shown to have a direct link with the Australian Packers established themselves in Reading, Berkshire. This branch of the family goes from Charles Packer senior (died 1808) to Charles Packer junior (1786–1854), Frederick Alexander Packer (1814–62), Arthur Howard Packer (1851–1912), Robert Clyde Packer (1879–1934) and finally Frank Packer.

In about 1120, following the death of his only legitimate son, King Henry I had decided to endow a great abbey in Reading. The king was buried in this abbey and his successor, King Henry II, sometimes used it as a parliamentary chamber. Berkshire has always been closely associated with royalty, as the county includes both Windsor Castle and the Ascot racecourse, founded by Queen Anne. Reading Abbey was dissolved in 1539 and the stones were used to help rebuild St Mary's Minster. Berkshire had the Civil War (1642–51) thrust upon it when King Charles I chose nearby Oxford as his headquarters. Although the direct royal connection ended with the Civil War, Reading emerged as a trade centre because of its advantageous position at the fork of the Kennet and Thames rivers. The town's prosperity was founded on the wool trade and to a lesser extent the brewing industry.[4]

The Packers might have settled in Reading because of its importance in the manufacture of wool, but by the eighteenth century the family had moved into watchmaking. Charles Packer senior, who was apparently born in about 1747, carried on his trade from premises in Castle Street. Young men wishing to enter the trade in London usually had to be bound to watchmakers for seven years to receive training in toolmaking, watchmaking and repair work; men intending to work in provincial areas did not always undertake such long apprenticeships. While the skills learned during apprenticeships were often not used in the production of everyday watches, they were invaluable in repair work because of the lack of standardised components. Men such as Charles Packer, who established their own businesses and employed journeymen, needed considerable technical expertise and sound business sense.[5]

Watchmakers in provincial areas did not spend all their time in making and repairing watches. The advertisement that Packer placed in the *Reading Mercury* in 1789 to advise his customers that he was moving to Minster Street indicated that he made and sold all forms of silver and jewellery. Many musical pieces were operated by clock and watch mechanisms and the shop's previous occupant had manufactured musical instruments as well as watches. In 1789 Packer announced that he would sell, let and tune pianofortes and harpsichords. Extant records show that he was also employed by St Mary's to wind up and repair the church clock, solder liveries (the distinctive badges used by the retainers of high-born citizens) and erect a flag on the tower to celebrate the union between England and Ireland in 1801. This sort of work would have provided a particularly valuable source of income in 1797, when an act of parliament imposed a duty on watches and clocks and obliged those making or selling watches to take out licences. This act caused an alarming slump in business until it was repealed a year later.[6]

By 1806 St Mary's records were referring to 'Packer & Sons'. Packer and his wife Susannah (née Griffin), had five sons and a daughter between 1784 and 1797; the girl and one of the boys died in infancy. Packer's two eldest sons, John (christened 4 February 1784) and Charles junior (christened 29 January 1786), apparently joined him in the business before his death in April 1808.[7] Packer's will indicated that he was a successful and industrious businessman who liked to consider all contingencies. It showed that Packer was the mortgagee of the premises in Minster Street and another leasehold property in Reading. The will specified that Susannah was to retain the properties and enjoy the rents and profits they accrued until she died or remarried; if she decided to sell one of the properties she was to take out an investment backed by the government or another good security. The sum of £150 was to be set aside to apprentice, educate or otherwise advance in life their two youngest sons. The estate's stock, fixtures, implements and other effects were to be split four ways. The first part was to go to Susannah, the second and third to John and Charles junior, and the fourth part was to be held in trust for the two youngest boys by their older brothers so long as they continued the business and remained in partnership.[8]

Charles Packer junior maintained his father's business for some years, presumably with the help of his brother John. In 1819 the parishioners of St Mary's subscribed money to purchase an organ; the church's records indicate that one Mr Packer donated the very generous sum of £5 and another Mr Packer £2 2s. It was becoming apparent that the Packers were capable of more than simply repairing musical instruments. Charles junior was appointed the first organist of St Mary's on a stipend of £30 per annum, and he earned an additional fee from regularly tuning the organ.[9] This appointment came at a most fortuitous time. In recent years watch hands had begun to be cut by machinery rather than manually and both the quality of workmanship and the income of watchmakers had started to decline. The 1818 report of the Select Parliamentary Committee into laws relating to watchmaking depicted the trade in a depressing light.[10]

The new organist continued to involve himself in the wider affairs of the parish. As an overseer of St Mary's, Charles junior agreed in 1836 to review its charitable services. Poverty had been exacerbated by the gradual introduction of farm machinery which took away autumn and winter work from labourers; in 1830 frustrated labourers had smashed machinery and demanded fair wages; fifty-six Berkshire men tried at Reading had been transported and another thirty-six had been sent to prison. Parishes such as St Mary's had to decide whether to introduce or maintain a poor rate. Charles junior was given an important if unenviable task in 1836; he decided that the properties St Mary's had lent to families should be recovered by legal means so that other local charities could be supported and the need for a poor rate would be reduced or alleviated.[11]

Charles junior had taken as his wife Amelia Sandys, reportedly a descendant of the royal house of Stuart and a woman known as 'the beauty of Berkshire'. Between 1809 and 1816 Amelia bore him two sons and three daughters. Their eldest son, Charles Stuart Sandys Packer, studied composition, piano and singing at London's Royal Academy of Music. Charles junior's association with St Mary's waned in the 1830s and he moved to London. He died at his son-in-law's residence in Buckingsham in 1854.[12]

Charles junior's younger son, Frederick Alexander Packer, who was christened on 30 July 1816,[13] also entered the Royal Academy of Music in 1827. Frederick spent six years studying the harp and was described by an academy publication as 'a talented player'. In 1831 his future bride joined the academy as a singing student.[14] Augusta Gow was the granddaughter of Niel Gow (1727–1807), a renowned fiddler who had attracted a number of aristocratic patrons and had raised the social status of professional music. Augusta's father Nathaniel (1763–1831) was a distinguished composer, court trumpeter and proprietor of a music publishing business in Edinburgh.[15]

On 22 July 1837 Augusta, aged twenty-two, married Frederick Alexander Packer in Edinburgh. The archival record of Frederick Alexander's activities is somewhat sparse; he served as a parish overseer at St Mary's in 1841 and appears to have been church organist at Truro in Cornwall before returning to St Mary's, probably as the organist. Between 1838 and 1851 Frederick Alexander and Augusta had four sons and four daughters.[16] In the midst of this childbearing and child rearing, Augusta retained her passion for music. She and her husband taught their eldest son, Frederick Augustus Gow Packer, to sing and play the organ, and gained him presentations to the choirs of St George's Chapel, Windsor, and the Chapel Royal, St James.[17]

The precise motives, difficulties or aspirations that made Augusta and Frederick Alexander Packer decide to leave Reading and take their young brood to Hobart Town in 1852 will probably never be known. There was already a link between the Packer family and Van Diemen's Land, though not one made by choice. In 1839 Frederick Alexander's brother Charles Sandys Packer had been sentenced to life transportation for forgery; he spent four years on Norfolk Island before being transferred to Hobart Town in 1844. While still assigned, he was allowed to take music pupils and perform in concerts as a vocalist and pianist, and after receiving a conditional pardon in 1850 he leased a theatre.[18]

At around this time Frederick Alexander, who had already followed in his older brother's footsteps by studying at the Royal Academy of Music, resolved to join him in Hobart Town. Van Diemen's Land, previously known only as the island where British prisoners had been sent for fifty years, was beginning to take on the appearance of a British colony with some attractions for the immigrant. The number of churches was expanding, the colony's administrator Sir William Denison was determined to place education on a sound footing and rumours had reached Britain of convicts who had made their fortunes.[19]

Frederick Alexander and Augusta Packer decided to emigrate at a time when the colony's whole immigration system was in a state of flux. The administrators of Van Diemen's Land wanted to attract immigrants who were likely to stay in the colony and in 1851 the Colonial Office canvassed the possibility of encouraging capitalists to emigrate by providing them with free passage and allotting them land worth £400 for a deposit of half that sum.[20] Frederick Alexander probably received a bounty for himself and each of his dependents when he and his family embarked on the *Sylph* in about April 1852. As Augusta took her last look at London from their cabin, she knew she was pregnant yet again.

When the family of ten sailed into the port of Hobart Town in July 1852 after a 12 000-mile voyage,[21] they were greeted by a scene of extraordinary natural beauty. A visitor to Van Diemen's Land in 1829 pronounced that the 'view from the harbour would make the most magnificent panorama in the world'. A few years later another traveller came upon Hobart Town '... with all its white houses, churches, trees and shipping, quietly lying in a soft and warm haze. On the left of the town rises Mount

Wellington, grand and lofty … If you turn your back on this view, you see another as beautiful, but very different. The deeply indented shores with all their wondrous sinuosities, lovely coves, sweeping bays, bold rocks and long points, are below you.'[22]

The town was well laid out, with long, wide streets diverging from each other at right angles, and flagged side paths. The huts and cottages of which Hobart Town had once consisted had been converted into regular, substantial buildings, many of them two storeys high. The Convict Department had subsidised the development of many public buildings, and these handsome and commodious constructions lent an air of permanence to the colony. The cove provided sheltered and secure anchorage and the wharves and quays were sound.[23] But as Augusta was helped onto the wharves on 10 July 1852, she was probably unable to fully appreciate her new surroundings. Just five days after her arrival in Hobart Town she gave birth to her ninth child, a son. Within a few years, another two daughters and a son followed.[24]

Frederick Alexander expressed some interest in joining the civil service in 1853, but before long he was appointed organist of St David's Cathedral.[25] The cathedral was located in the main street, Macquarie Street, opposite the Supreme Court. St David's had been consecrated in 1823 and made a cathedral church in 1843 when the diocese of Van Diemen's Land was established; the organ had been erected in 1824 with donations from parishioners. The cathedral was a large, well-built brick edifice, stuccoed and painted a light stone colour, with a shingled roof and a wooden spire topped by a fine clock; the interior had broad, heavy cedar galleries in which the soldiers of the garrison sat, enclosed cedar pews and a handsome pulpit and reading desk. Services were held four times on Sundays: at 9 a.m. for the convicts and those holding tickets-of-leave, and at 11 a.m., 4 p.m. and 6 p.m. for the other residents. Frederick Alexander's role would have been most important at the 11 a.m. service, which attracted an extremely well-dressed congregation and was attended by the military.[26]

The Packer family arrived in a Hobart Town that was flourishing. Even though the discovery of gold in Victoria in the early 1850s had drawn many people to the mainland, money came back from the goldfields, Victoria offered good markets for Tasmanian timber and agricultural produce, and inflation boosted wages. This boom might have been short, lasting only a year or two, but it gave the colony a surge of self-assurance. In 1853 the transportation of convicts to Van Diemen's Land was abolished; in 1855 a Constitution Bill went through; in 1856 elections took place, the new parliament convened and Van Diemen's Land was renamed Tasmania; between 1853 and 1858 a grand new Government House was erected.[27]

For all this, however, the Tasmanian community had a large number of illiterate and semi-literate people. The political scientist F. A. Townsley has observed that Hobart Town in 1850 had homes 'which were beacons of enlightenment set against a fairly drab background of poverty and illiteracy'. The middle and upper classes of Tasmania struggled to remove the taint of convictism and make the society respectable and of good character. Improvers abounded: temperance societies multiplied, scientific societies flourished, newspapers discussed important issues of the day with an earnest sincerity and imperial sentiment was rampant.[28]

Even though they, like so many residents, had a relative who had been a convict, Frederick Alexander and Augusta Packer would have been welcomed into this world with open arms. They were both literate and musical and they had studied in London, the centre of the British empire. Frederick Alexander always wrote the initials 'R.A.M.' after his name; Augusta let it be known that she was descended from famous composers and had herself been instructed by the renowned musicians Ignaz Moscheles, Cipriani Potter and Sir Michael Costa.[29] The couple must have been pleased that music was prominent in Tasmania. With drums beating and colours flying, the band of the regiment marched to St David's Cathedral on Sunday mornings in time for the 11 a.m. service. In the summer months the band played in the Royal Society's Botanical Gardens each week.[30]

Frederick Alexander died at his residence in Davey Street on 2 July 1862, aged forty-eight. Augusta was left with a number of small children, one less than a year old. A benefit concert was apparently held at St David's to help the family and Augusta took in piano and singing students. She and her younger offspring were probably also helped by her successful eldest son. Frederick Augustus Gow replaced his father as organist at St David's, raised funds for the organ at Hobart Town Hall and became the first city organist, and composed popular songs and commemorative odes. Augusta was accorded a lengthy obituary in the *Hobart Mercury* on her death at the age of seventy-seven on 23 February 1893. The newspaper noted that although the 'deservedly loved and respected' Augusta had been stricken by paralysis in recent years, she had 'retained her faculties in singular brightness up to within two days of her decease', and had left behind a large and distinguished family.[31]

Five of Augusta's sons rose to occupy responsible positions in the civil service. As well as being a prominent musician, Frederick Augustus Gow was appointed acting chief operator of the Electric Telegraph Office in 1859 and later became the superintendent of telegraphs and clerk of the House of Assembly.[32] Four of his brothers were promoted from clerkships to senior posts in the civil service. These included John Edward, who became under-treasurer; Robert Kerr, who was a junior operator of the Electric Telegraph Office in Tasmania before joining the Queensland Telegraph Service; and Harry Effingham, who became secretary for public works.[33]

The census of 1870 revealed the hierarchical nature of Tasmanian society. At the head stood the large landowners and the leading merchants and bankers; then came the professional people; the largest group consisted of farm labourers and domestic servants; next in line came the tradesmen and mechanics. In another category were government employees ranging from the top officials, who mingled easily with the landowning and merchant class, to junior clerks. By 1887 there were just under 900 civil servants in Tasmania, and senior members were generally well-educated and recruited in Hobart.[34]

Another son of Frederick Alexander and Augusta Packer is of principal interest to us here. Arthur Howard Packer, christened in Reading on 7 May 1851, had come to Hobart Town as an infant. Following two of his brothers into the Electric Telegraph Office, he served as an assistant telegraph officer between 1873 and 1877. The first message between Hobart Town and Launceston had been sent by the *Hobart Mercury* in 1853; new developments in communications in the 1860s and the completion of the England-Australia telegraph line in 1872 brought Tasmania closer to Melbourne and London and created a huge interest in telephones.[35] As we shall see, Arthur's son and grandson were destined to play pioneering roles in another field of communications.

On 1 October 1878 Arthur married the twenty-four-year-old Margaret Fitzmaurice Clyde in Hobart Town. Margaret was the eldest daughter of Captain John Clyde, the adjutant of the 96th Regiment, and his wife Agnes. The couple settled at 28 Colville Street in the charming and fashionable area of Battery Point. They had three sons: Robert Clyde (Sir Frank's father), born on 24 July 1879; Arthur Patrick Wellesley, born on 14 December 1883; and John Stewart, born on 11 October 1886.[36]

In 1877 Arthur Howard Packer had become fourth landing waiter in the Customs Department in Hobart Town. The secretary and collector of customs presided over the department; then came the collector of customs and registrar of shipping for Launceston, a chief clerk and registrar for both Hobart Town and Launceston, landing waiters (who, later renamed examining officers, were responsible for investigating and recording the cargo of vessels that came into port), watch-house keepers and excise officers. It was a prestigious department, responsible for collecting more than half the colony's revenue.[37] With colonial self-government, British appointees looked locally to fill new vacancies, meaning that patronage was now dispensed from Hobart Town rather than London. In the 1880s the collector of customs informed a correspondent from Brisbane that he did not have the slightest chance of obtaining a position with Customs 'without a considerable amount of influence. There are so many applicants for Government appointments and most of them [are] the sons of old Colonists … who are entitled to preference'. After holding a number of clerical positions, Arthur became a statistical clerk in Hobart, as the capital city was now known, and was reappointed a landing waiter in 1891. He retained this position when the overcrowded department moved to the new Customs House in 1899 and was taken over by the Commonwealth of Australia in 1901.[38]

Possessing a fine tenor voice, Arthur served as choirmaster of the Moonah Church of England Mission Church and was a keen member of the Derwent Rowing Club. Although he did not reach the heights of some of his brothers in the civil service, he was respected by his peers and his genial disposition made him many friends. When he died in 1912, the flags of most of the offices doing business with the Customs Department were flown at half-mast.[39]

Arthur's musical abilities and love of the water were inherited by his eldest son. Robert Clyde (known simply as 'Clyde') sailed on the Derwent River and was able to play music by ear. Some of the happiest times of his childhood were spent during family holidays on the rugged west coast of Tasmania, where he and his brothers shot kangaroos.[40]

In 1890 Clyde was sent to the second oldest public school in Australia. Capital to help build the Hutchins School on land in Macquarie Street had been subscribed by members of the Church of England. The school, named after the Rev. William Hutchins, the first archdeacon of Van Dieman's Land, was founded in 1846. Public schools funded by the state were resented by Presbyterians and in 1848 Hobart High

School, intended as a non-denominational school, was established as a rival institution. The Packers aligned themselves with high Anglicanism, sending Clyde and his brothers, along with other members of the extended family, to the Hutchins School.[41]

The school's first headmaster, the Rev. J. V. Buckland, was an ardent exponent of Thomas Arnold's belief that producing 'Christian gentlemen' was the prime objective of a church school. The Hutchins School, which emphasised the values of service, honour, self-respect and self-discipline, became known for its discipline and the thoroughness of its teaching. The school's military overtones took on a renewed urgency during Clyde's attendance, which was embraced by the two Boer Wars. He might have been a member of the cadet corps, a body designed to turn out 'embryo soldiers'.[42]

The Hutchins School maintained that in Australia the best virtues of the old — the British empire — could be blended with the new — the rugged, physical individualism nurtured on the Australian frontier. A verse of one school song ran:

> *We are the stock of the men who dare*
> *When there is fame to be won.*
> *Ours is the strength of the mountain air,*
> *Ours is a potent sun.*
> *Hutchins can boast of the days that are past,*
> *E'en though the days be few.*
> *Hers is fame that shall grow to the last,*
> *Playing the game right through —*
> *Here in the Southland, land of the gum,*
> *Land of the grey kangaroo.*[43]

At the time the Hutchins School was founded, public schools in England were making the organised game an integral part of the education system. There was a feeling that team sport was a highly effective means of inculcating physical and moral courage, loyalty, leadership, a spirit of fair play and respect for authority. 'Manly piety' uniting the Arnoldian concepts of 'godliness' and 'good learning' became 'manliness' founded on sporting endeavour.[44]

Clyde's headmaster, the Rev. H. H. Anderson, was determined to maintain the school's reputation in sport as well as scholarship. Clyde played football and a little tennis and was remembered for his skill as a 'chucker-out' of intruders into school games.[45] Two of his school reports have survived, one from mid 1893 and one from the end of the year. The first report shows that Clyde leaned more to the humanities than to mathematics and science: he was fourth in his form in scripture, slightly above average in English and did poorly in mathematics. His results, particularly in English and English history, were more impressive at the end of the year and, while he still struggled with arithmetic and algebra, he did well in bookkeeping. Clyde later boasted that on the one occasion he won a school prize, he selected a bullseye lantern and a tomahawk.[46]

It was probably at the Hutchins School that Clyde was introduced to his favourite book, *Self-Help*. Written by Dr Samuel Smiles in 1859, the book of musings on personal and social industriousness was given to schoolchildren for decades. *Self-Help* aimed to inculcate in young men 'old-fashioned but wholesome' lessons: the youth must work in order to enjoy; nothing worthwhile can be achieved without application and diligence; the student must not be daunted by difficulties, but conquer them by patience and perseverance; and, above all, he must seek elevation of character, without which capability and worldly success are worthless. Smiles asserted that happiness and well-being depended on diligent self-development, self-discipline and self-control and on the honest and upright performance of individual duty that was 'the glory of manly character'.[47]

The rhetoric of self-help was suited not only to the Hutchins School but to the colony at large. In the early 1890s Tasmania succumbed to the Australia-wide economic depression: banks crashed, mines closed, trade contracted, wages fell and unemployment became entrenched. In the face of the ascendant labour movement, governments, benevolent societies and newspapers buttressed the virtues of self-help, competition, temperance and family life.

The gold boom had briefly allowed Tasmanians to feel that they occupied an important nodal point within the administrative and trading area of the southern colonies. The depressions of the 1860s and the 1890s and the maritime strike of 1891 showed Tasmanians just how much they had become part of the socio-economic region of Australia, and the people of Hobart came to realise their true place in the colonial hierarchy of cities.[48]

What Clyde Packer did immediately after leaving school is unclear, but he does not seem to have expressed any interest in entering the civil service. He was attracted instead to journalism, which by the 1890s was an increasingly respectable profession. While traditions of hard drinking and irregular lifestyles lingered from earlier generations, greater discipline was being imposed in newspaper offices due to the heavy demands of daily journalism, and journalists who were considered competent and willing were able to make a living and achieve some security.[49] Packer might have contributed to Tasmanian newspapers on a penny-a-line basis until he obtained a position on the *Tasmanian News* in about May 1900. H. H. Gill, an explorer, farmer and prospector, had founded this newspaper in Hobart in 1883. The *Tasmanian News* was the mouthpiece of advanced opinions until labour newspapers emerged in the 1890s and Gill retired in 1896. His afternoon newspaper advocated manhood suffrage, triennial parliaments, payment of members, and land and tax reform. It joined the *Hobart Mercury* in opposing federation, predicting that intercolonial free trade would make Tasmania insolvent.[50]

The political inclinations of the *Tasmanian News* were probably of little relevance to Packer, who was simply pleased to be given the opportunity to serve his journalistic apprenticeship. He had a reasonable grasp of typing and shorthand and his knowledge of music and sport, particularly rowing, made him a versatile member of staff. He also performed as a tenor in musical productions. On 11 May 1900, for instance, he sang 'On the Road to Mandalay' for *Love's Stratagem* and played a part in *The Beacon* at a Hobart theatre. By the time a sub-editor, John McIndoe, left the *Tasmanian News* in October 1900, he had concluded that Packer could easily make musical criticism his specialty; he was 'altogether a most promising and desirable reporter possessing the true journalistic instinct'.[51]

Eighteen months later, Packer decided he had progressed as far as he could in the Tasmanian newspaper industry and left for the mainland. Hobart was too small, too complacent and too old-fashioned for someone with his energy and ambition. Packer's daughter has commented that he wanted to go to Sydney because it was 'the biggest place possible on this side of the world'.[52] Legend has it that he went to the races, picked up a sovereign, put it on a racehorse and won enough to pay his fare to the mainland. Leaving Hobart in March or April 1902, Packer took with him professional and character references from the *Tasmanian News*; Thomas Reibey, a controversial clergyman and member of the House of Assembly who was a friend of Packer's grandfather, Captain Clyde; and W. F. Brownell, a leading retailer, justice of the peace and friend of the family.[53]

Packer might have been armed with excellent references, but he found himself without letters of introduction to Sydney newspaper editors. Reibey had noted that he had no intimate friends to whom he could introduce Packer in Sydney: 'You have your way to make in life', he said. Although the twenty-two-year-old had performed well in the small world of Tasmanian journalism, it was rare for individuals on the mainland to spend their early years on the staffs of capital city newspapers.[54] He was unable to find work on a newspaper in Sydney, but was apparently too proud to ask his family back in Hobart for help.

The best Packer could do at first was to pass himself off as an expert powder monkey to a quarry, even though he had never seen blasting powder in his life. Two old hands, recognising a hungry trier, showed him the ropes and kept him in food for a week until he collected his first wages. When this job finished, Packer wheeled sacks of flour around a warehouse in Sussex Street and joined a rugged road gang.[55]

During this period of loneliness and frustration, Clyde Packer began to attend a social club for young people in the city. A Miss McCrae, who had acted as a nanny to the Packer family before founding a lacemaking business in Sydney, had initiated the informal group. The club, established to provide a place for young men and women to enjoy light refreshments, to hold singsongs and take their minds off looking for work, was responsible for introducing Clyde to his future wife.[56]

Accurate biographical information on Ethel Maude Hewson's parents is scarce.[57] Her father Frank was born in Ireland's County Wicklow and seems to have obtained a doctorate of divinity in England. While serving as a Church of England minister, he married and had seven children. After his wife's death, Rev. Hewson inherited his brother's estate in Wicklow and decided to return to Ireland. While he was presiding over the wedding of one of his daughters, a bridesmaid, Francis Harriet Briscoe, captured his attention. Frank and Fanny married and settled in his grand childhood home, 'Kilquade House', in Wicklow. They had five children, one of whom died in infancy; Ethel was born on 16 January 1878 when her mother was aged about twenty-eight. Rev. Hewson, who was much older than Fanny, was all too aware that his estate was entailed to another relative. He gave his wife a generous allowance, out of which he expected her to save for her widowhood. Fanny, however, was an extravagant woman who frittered the money away on beautiful clothes and lavish dances.

On her husband's death Fanny lost 'Kilquade House'. She took her children first to England, where they lived in greatly reduced circumstances. In the 1890s Rev. Hewson's relatives advised Fanny to take her two youngest sons to Australia. While Fanny taught music in Melbourne, one of the boys went to Perth to search for gold. Ethel, worried about the strain on her mother, joined her family in Melbourne in about 1896. Arriving in the midst of a heat wave, she lent some valuable family jewellery to the person she was staying with and never saw it again.

As Melbourne was now thoroughly spoiled for poor Ethel, she moved to Sydney in 1897. She and a Miss Talbot established a typing business for lawyers in Elizabeth Street, and Ethel continued the enterprise on her own when Miss Talbot left the following year. In 1901 Ethel moved to the third floor of Vickery's Chambers at 82 Pitt Street.[58] She boarded with Miss McCrae, who had known the Hewson family in Ireland, and became a regular at her social club. When Miss McCrae introduced Ethel to Clyde Packer, he completely misheard her name and began calling her 'Miss Richards'. Finally summoning up the courage to correct his mistake, Ethel made it clear that she did not like her real name anyway. From then on he and her family affectionately referred to her as 'Dick'.[59]

Ethel and Clyde had a great deal in common. Both came from large families but knew hardly anyone in Sydney, they were well-educated, energetic and ambitious but were struggling financially, and they shared a love of music and a lively sense of humour. They married at St Matthias Anglican Church in Paddington on 13 July 1903. Marriage hardened Clyde's resolve to escape the drudgeries of labouring work. In September he secured a position on the *Dubbo Liberal*, in the central west of New South Wales. His bride remained in Sydney, where she contributed to the young couple's finances by continuing to work under her maiden name.[60]

By the end of the nineteenth century Dubbo had established itself as an important agricultural and administrative centre. Between the 1860s and 1880s a substantial bridge had been erected over the Macquarie River, the railway had been extended to Dubbo and new banks, courthouses, handsome hotels, a post office and a hospital had been constructed. When Clyde Packer arrived in Dubbo his first impression would have been of a town with broad, well-made streets, a large park with a bandstand, and numerous hotels. He would have been pleased to discover that local concerts were well supported, travelling concerts and theatrical productions visited the town and band nights were held in the bandstand during the summer. Nevertheless, he would soon have realised that Dubbo had not yet fully recovered from the financial and social effects of the devastating rural drought of 1900 to 1902. A new railway line also brought hundreds of people to Dubbo who were fleeing the typhoid fever epidemic in Coonamble.[61]

The *Dubbo Liberal*, which had been established under another name in 1874, was published every Wednesday and Saturday. It occupied a prestigious position in a large two-storey building opposite the Exchange Hotel. The *Dubbo Liberal* reported on every local council meeting, public gathering, funeral, wedding, court case, social occasion, sporting event and dog fight. It competed vigorously with the more senior *Dubbo Dispatch*, bringing out newssheets on Mondays and Thursdays to supplement the main edition.[62]

Credited with having 'no difficulty in procuring news where others may fail', Packer scored a number of scoops for the *Dubbo Liberal*. The proprietor, William White, was greatly impressed by his new charge. He recorded that Packer had quickly shown great aptitude in acquiring local knowledge, his accounts of meetings and court proceedings were thorough and prompt, he had a good grasp of pastoral and agricultural matters and his reports of the Land Appeal Court were the best he had seen in any newspaper. Packer, in short, had a great capacity for work and was 'largely gifted with the news sense'.[63]

When White sold the newspaper to Abraham Irvine, Arthur J. Ball and George T. Harrex in May 1905, he did so on the understanding that Packer had been appointed editor. For whatever reason, however, the new owners dispensed with Packer's services. He left the newspaper with glowing and percipient references: Ball forecast that 'you will soon make a name for yourself on the Sydney Press', Harrex and Irvine that 'in the large sphere of Metropolitan journalism there is no position to which you need, in time, fear to aspire'. Ethel, whose loneliness had been alleviated by a visit to Dubbo, now had her husband to herself for a short time in Sydney. She relinquished her typing business when she became pregnant in early 1906.[64]

Poor Ethel again remained in Sydney when her husband found a job on the mid north coast of New South Wales. Clyde initially appears to have worked on the *Raleigh Sun*, which had been established by William T. Campbell in Bellingen, about thirty kilometres south-west of Coffs Harbour. When Campbell's widow Elizabeth launched the *Coffs Harbour Advocate* in February 1907, Packer was appointed editor. His arrival in the area coincided with a surge in business activity. Tramways had just been established north and south of the harbour, along with a major sawmill, and the population was increasing. Packer worked out of a small office in High Street, where the weekly *Coffs Harbour Advocate* was printed on a hand-operated flatbed press. With the aid of a horse and buggy, he continued to help oversee the production of the *Raleigh Sun*. He turned his hand to everything from reporting on local council skirmishes to writing editorials and churning out serials.[65]

Back in Sydney, Ethel gave birth to a son on 3 December 1906. The baby was christened Douglas Frank Hewson Packer, named 'Douglas' in honour of a friend of his father's who captained a vessel that sailed up and down the north coast. Before long, however, the infant was being called Frank, after his maternal grandfather. On learning of the birth, one of Clyde's relatives in Hobart excitedly penned a congratulatory letter: 'Suppose "Napoleon" is a magnificent child. May he possess all the graces of his Mother and none of the *dis*-graces of his Father … Hear the [Battery] Point is to be illuminated tonight'.[66]

Before long Clyde, who had still not had an opportunity to see his first child, left Coffs Harbour and went further north. Although there is no record of the reason for this move, it is possible that Clyde was lured to Townsville by the prospect of working on a daily newspaper. On 3 March 1907 he joined the *Townsville Daily Bulletin* as a reporter. The north Queensland town had been established as a coastal depot in 1864 to ship the district's produce and unload imports. Townsville had rich natural resources, including sugar and minerals, and vast pastoral properties. The discovery of gold at Charters Towers had encouraged a massive influx of prospectors and the merchants who serviced the goldfields had stimulated growth. In the 1870s the Church of England diocese of Townsville had been created and St James's Cathedral built. A telephone exchange had been opened in 1883 and by this time the Townsville Turf Club was active and offering generous purses.[67]

When Packer arrived in 1907, then, Townsville was on a sound economic footing. Nevertheless, there were undercurrents of tension and dissent. The labour movement had emerged as a serious political and industrial force; Kanaka labour had been contributing to the town's economic growth for decades but the workers had been brutally exploited and used as a weapon in debates about the introduction of the White Australia policy; and in 1903 tropical cyclone Leonta had caused immense damage.[68] Moreover, the stiflingly humid climate must have come as quite a shock to a man who had spent the first two decades of his life in Tasmania.

The *Townsville Bulletin* had been launched in 1881; two years later, it became the first newspaper in Queensland to be published on a daily basis. The *Townsville Daily Bulletin*, as it was renamed, was for some years a prime advocate for the cause of northern separation. In the late 1880s the editor and part owner Dodd S. Clarke had narrowly escaped losing his position because of a problem with alcohol. But Clarke remained editor and the stability of the newspaper's editorship was a factor in its success. In 1897 an advanced Cox Duplex Press was installed in new premises on the corner of Flinders and Stanley Streets, boosting both circulation and advertising content.

Unfortunately, a fire in 1912 destroyed the *Townsville Daily Bulletin*'s early archival records.[69] What little evidence remains of Packer's period with the newspaper suggests that, unlike several of his contemporaries, he did not turn to the bottle to cope with the tropical climate. Instead he threw himself into his work, earning praise as a good shorthand reporter and a reliable all-round journalist. Packer was described as 'a genial and sunny-tempered comrade' who was popular in social and sporting circles. He probably boarded at the People's Palace, recently built to help solve the area's acute housing shortage and to provide accommodation in the city for the travelling family man.[70]

In 1907 Ethel travelled by train to Brisbane and then a little coastal ship to Townsville to visit her husband. When she was hoisted over the side of the ship onto the wharf, Clyde caught his first glimpse of their strapping baby boy. As Clyde was still intent on securing a job in Sydney, Ethel and Frank returned to Sydney. In 1908 Clyde accepted a position on the Sydney *Sunday Times* and left for Sydney aboard the *Peregrine*.[71] Sydney journalism would never be the same again.

2
His Father's Footsteps

As a provincial newspaper reporter, Robert Clyde Packer had proved to be energetic, versatile and resourceful. His first decade spent attached to the Sydney press was also to be an important learning period. While on the *Sunday Times* and then the *Sun* between 1908 and 1918, Packer was to be exposed to the 'New Journalism', learn about stunts designed to boost circulation and recognise the brutal, cut-throat nature of metropolitan journalism. All these lessons were eventually to be passed on to his son Frank.

At the turn of the century there were eight metropolitan newspapers in Sydney: two in the morning, two in the afternoon, and three on Sunday. Although there were links between the leading daily newspapers and weeklies — the afternoon *Sun* and the *Sunday Sun* were published by the same firm, for instance — press chains and oligopoly were as yet hardly discernible. The early history of the *Sunday Times*, which was launched in 1885, illustrates the fluidity of the Sydney newspaper market. In its first two years the title was passed from one undercapitalised proprietor to the next. The newspaper finally acquired a sound financial footing in 1888, when it was purchased by a wealthy tea importer.[1]

By the 1890s the *Sunday Times* no longer regarded itself as merely a weekly vehicle of entertainment. It emerged as a genuine newspaper, publishing the latest in news and cables, along with prominent headlines, cartoons and line drawings. It was, in short, an example of the 'New Journalism' that had emerged in Britain and the United States in the second half of the nineteenth century. This style of journalism sought to build mass circulations by appealing to the increasingly literate lower middle classes. It parcelled up news into short portions, deployed improved printing technology and typographical devices and increasingly used illustrations and photographs.[2]

In a novel development for Australia, readers of the *Sunday Times* could cut out and send in coupons to obtain free medical and legal advice. But while news reports favoured crime, violence and sex, the newspaper was very different from one of its principal competitors. Unlike the salacious *Truth*, the sleazy scandalmonger of Sydney, the *Sunday Times* pitched itself to families and 'the popular middle class'. It ran special reports on topics such as alien residents in Redfern, railway workers, the state of the poor and the lives of working girls. Like most Sunday newspapers in the English-speaking world, the *Sunday Times* preached as well as reported on the news.[3] In their subsequent newspaper careers both R. C. and Frank Packer combined populism and stunts designed to boost circulation and engender reader loyalty with more serious social and political intent.

Clyde Packer joined the staff of the *Sunday Times* at a time when it was earnestly considering ways to strengthen the moral and physical fibre of young Australian manhood. In June 1908 the newspaper published an article by Sir Robert Baden-Powell, the 'Hero of Mafeking', about the new British youth movement he had formed. Baden-Powell saw the Boy Scouts as a means for cultivating 'a sound mind in a sound body': 'In a sense, every boy is a commander, and the training he receives as a Boy Scout teaches him not only obedience to his officers, but how to develop and command his own innate forces'. The editor of the *Sunday Times*, T. R. Roydhouse, and business and civic leaders throughout Australia were already agitating to initiate a similar movement in this outpost of the British empire. Clyde Packer was an enthusiastic participant, and at a meeting in March 1908 he and Roydhouse had decided to start recruiting New South Wales patrols. Roydhouse became chairman of the Scout Committee of Control.[4]

Even though Packer had been at the *Sunday Times* for only a few months, he already stood out from his contemporaries because of his application and his sharp news sense. In April 1909 Packer was appointed chief scoutmaster of New South Wales. In an article for the *Lone Hand*, the Hutchins School graduate wrote that the Boy Scouts would improve boys mentally, morally and physically, nurture self-reliance, inculcate a spirit of obedience, develop initiative and powers of observation, and familiarise boys with the methods that would, in all probability, be called into use for a 'greater game' in the near future.[5]

At around the same time, Packer was made chief-of-staff of the *Sunday Times*. He recruited two bright young undergraduates at the University of Sydney, R. J. H. Moses and Errol G. Knox. It was not long before Moses was appointed country secretary of the Scout Committee of Control and Knox was elected interstate secretary. The three men joined Roydhouse in seeking distinguished patrons, streamlining the recruitment process and adopting the official Boy Scouts uniform. They organised field days on the outskirts of Sydney and demonstrated such activities as hut and bridge building, signalling, pioneering and first aid. Working to ensure that able-bodied men on the *Sunday Times* spent their spare time in short pants and peaked hats, they made the back page of the newspaper a 'Boy Scouts Gazette'. When Baden-Powell visited Sydney in May 1912, Packer was part of the official contingent that greeted him at the railway station, led a parade of Scouts on horseback to a rally at Centennial Park and arranged for a camp inspection at Cooks River.[6]

In 1911 Packer had launched the Wednesday *Globe* for the Sunday Times Newspaper Company. The penny newspaper did not run cable news, sports reports or editorials, instead carrying pictures, crime and accident reports, fiction, feature articles and a series called 'Discussion for Men and Women'. Packer was already developing a reputation for driving his staff hard and he was determined to stay with the *Sunday Times* until he attained editorial control. By 1913 Roydhouse had retired and Packer had become editor of the paper. Packer was also in charge of the *Globe* and two sporting weeklies, the *Referee* and the *Arrow*.[7]

The *Sunday Sun*, which was priced at only a penny, published more pages than any other newspaper in Sydney and, backed by a costly organisation, remained the market leader. But even though the *Sunday Times* carried a cover price of twopence, its circulation and profits rose dramatically under Packer's vigorous direction. Sales had stood at 30 000 when he first joined the newspaper; in the early years of the First World War circulation peaked at over 100 000 copies per week, surpassing *Truth*'s performance.[8]

The success of the *Sunday Times* attracted the attention of the sporting and theatrical entrepreneur Hugh D. McIntosh, who took over the company in May 1916. As McIntosh began restaffing the *Sunday Times*, he considered how to dispose of Packer's services. An impulsive, extroverted, coarse and aggressive hustler, McIntosh had cut out and framed Samuel Smiles's 'Ten Steps to Success' when they were published in the *Sunday Times*. McIntosh seems to have viewed Packer — talented, ambitious and also a disciple of the Smilesian gospel — as a threat to his authority. However, the new owner was unable to sack Packer outright because the latter's employment contract was still valid. Determined to drive his editor to resign, McIntosh began hurling abuse at Packer as he put the paper to bed on Saturday nights. Packer quickly realised what McIntosh was up to, and the next time the proprietor appeared in the doorway, Packer waved a big ruler at him: 'If you enter this room, I'll brain you with this', he said. Conceding defeat, McIntosh bought out the remainder of Packer's contract for some £500 (now equivalent to $31 000); his relief was such that he added a gold watch to the termination payout.[9]

Several times during the war, Packer tried to enlist in the Australian Imperial Force (AIF), but was rejected because of sinus problems. As he saw the consolidation of imperial defence as the cornerstone of the Boy Scout movement in Australia, he must have been bitterly disappointed at not being able to participate in this 'stirring story of adventure'.[10] After his sudden departure from the *Sunday Times*, he was introduced to a new line of work by a friend, Claude McKay. Born in rural Victoria in 1878, McKay had worked as a reporter for a number of newspapers and as a press agent for a circus that went bust. In about 1908 he had joined J. C. Williamson's theatrical firm as secretary and then publicity agent. When Packer found himself without a job in 1916, McKay invited him to join the newly formed Williamson–Waddington film company.[11]

Even though he was being paid a good salary, Packer still yearned for the opportunity to work on a Sydney daily newspaper. McKay recalls his friend buying a second-hand copy of J. C. Nesfield's *Manual of English Grammar and Composition* and reading it in Hyde Park to brush up on a few things he had forgotten about grammar and syntax. By year's end Packer was working as a sub-editor on the Sun.[12] In 1910 the tobacco manufacturer (later Sir) Hugh Denison had established Sun Newspapers Ltd, taken over the old protectionist *Australian Star* and renamed it the *Sun*. On 1 July 1910 the *Sun* had become the first newspaper in Australia to have news instead of advertisements on the front page. The afternoon newspaper gave a great deal of space to news of crime and human interest stories, featured a high proportion of half-tone illustrations, and had an excellent cable service.[13] The *Sun*'s colourful and flamboyant editor, Adam McCay, immediately recognised his recruit's energy and creative news values. Within weeks of joining the newspaper, Packer was appointed chief sub-editor.[14]

As R. C. Packer's career advanced, he found himself in a position to buy his first family home. After his return to Sydney in 1908 he had rented a house at 21 Craigend Street in the seedy inner-city suburb of Darlinghurst. In 1910 Clyde and Ethel began renting 'Rothsay' in Castlefield Street, Bondi, where their second child, Kathleen Mary, was born. Two years later, they moved around the corner to a slightly bigger house in Edward Street.[15]

Although Clyde was not as brilliant musically as some of his ancestors and one of his brothers, he had a fine tenor voice and could play music by ear. He adored vaudeville and the Tivoli became like a second home to him during these years; he often met his wife at an oyster bar in King Street before taking her to see a show. Living in the coastal suburb of Bondi reignited Clyde's passion for the sea. He and Ethel would go out all day on Sydney Harbour with little Frank lashed to the centreboard trunk of the fifteen-footer they rented. Clyde also struck up a friendship with Lawrence Hargrave, the aeronautical pioneer and inventor. On Saturdays Clyde frequently visited Hargrave in Rushcutters Bay to help him construct an engine that would be light and powerful enough to get the flying machines he had invented into the air. Young Frank was sometimes put into the seat when they endeavoured to make the flying machines airborne, but Hargrave went to his grave in 1915 a disappointed man.[16]

As chief-of-staff of the *Sunday Times* Clyde earned £6 10s a week (now equivalent to about $23 000 per year), and put every spare shilling aside to buy a house. In 1912 or 1913 he purchased a cottage in Waitara, twenty-four kilometres north of the city. Land had been awarded to settlers in the area in the 1830s and 1840s to meet the demand for timber, and logs had been transported to Sydney via the Lane Cove River. Once the land had been cleared, orchards were established. In 1890 a railway line between Hornsby and St Leonards had been created; the line had been extended to Milsons Point in 1893 and Waitara station had opened between Wahroonga and Hornsby in 1895.[17]

In 1908 one observer remarked that Wahroonga 'may justly claim to be the finest suburban sanatorium' as it was 190 metres above sea level. While garden suburbs expanded and some business and political leaders began building mansions on large landscaped blocks, the area remained predominantly rural. By 1911 Wahroonga, Waitara and Warrawee had a population of only 350. There were open spaces, orchards and farms, wheatfields, paddocks with livestock or simply scrub and blackberries, and poultry in the backyards. Elizabeth Evatt, who grew up in Wahroonga in the 1930s, recalled feeling that she lived in the outback.[18]

Clyde Packer now had quite a long haul to work, but at least he and Ethel were financially independent. Trains, which ran hourly from Waitara station, took roughly 35 minutes to reach Milsons Point; a return second-class ticket cost 1s 2d. Clyde would walk from home to Waitara station (a not inconsiderable distance), catch the train to Milsons Point and then get a ferry to the city. On one or two nights a week he had dinner with Moses and Knox in a restaurant in Market Street, where the cutlery was tied to the table. In these less than salubrious surroundings they dined on chops for ninepence; during their other days at work they subsisted on rock cakes.[19]

Ethel was thrilled to finally have a home that she could call her own. For years she had carried with her memories of her childhood home, 'Kilquade House'. She pictured a palatial residence with circular stairs and a gracious walled garden. The brick cottage that confronted her in Clarke Road, Waitara, was very different: it had a tin roof and verandah, gum trees and scrub grew at the side and rear of the house, and the front 'garden' consisted of overgrown grass. Ethel immediately set about transforming the house, decorating the interior with as much taste as her budget allowed. Clyde cleared the weeds in front of the house and acquired a sheep to keep the grass down. The beautiful rose garden Ethel planted was better suited to Ireland than Australia, but she assiduously maintained it during dry summers.[20]

As their relatives were interstate or overseas Clyde, Ethel and their children were a closely-knit family. Frank, a boisterous and spirited youngster who could be quite a handful at times, spent most of his spare time outdoors, swimming in a nearby dam and playing in the bush. He was not keen on reading but, like so many boys of his generation, he enjoyed the *Boy's Own Annuals*. Launched in London in 1879, the *Boy's Own Paper* and the *Boy's Own Annual* provided boys with wholesome reading that celebrated manly Christian values; one of the contributors to the publication was none other than Robert Baden-Powell. The annual, bulging with material about sport and outdoor games, practical natural history columns, instructions on how to make things, colour plates and stories about sea adventures, jungle exploits, pioneering in India and gallant soldiers, was hugely popular throughout the British empire.[21]

Given his obvious attachment to his young son, it seems curious that Clyde did not introduce Frank to the Boy Scouts. Clyde might have been happy to distance his family life from his professional attachments at this time, and Frank certainly enjoyed a carefree childhood. His principal concern was avoiding ambushes by a tribe of boys from a neighbouring apple orchard, and he was perennially disappointed that Kathleen was not a boy to help even up the numbers. Another source of frustration was having to help his father manipulate an ancient mower when the pet sheep proved inadequate to the task of keeping the grass and weeds down. The seemingly endless process of mowing, weeding and raking left Frank with a lifelong aversion to gardening.[22]

Neither Frank nor Kathleen inherited their ancestors' musical gifts, and the boy's one flirtation with music had unfortunate consequences. While opening a crate of records with a claw hammer, Frank, aged about ten, was almost totally blinded in the right eye by a splinter. What Frank did inherit was his mother's love of animals, particularly dogs. The sheep was his first pet, and he was expected to sit on the animal's head while his mother sheared it with scissors. Given the job of fattening the turkey that was sent to his family one spring, Frank became so fond of the creature that it was not served for Christmas dinner and instead became another much-loved pet. Christmas was always a joyous occasion in the small Packer household. The family would hang mistletoe, serve a traditional dinner with all the trimmings and hoe into the huge plum pudding that a Scottish friend of Ethel's sent them each year.[23]

Affectionate and sentimental, Frank took it upon himself to visit elderly people in the district during his school holidays. The apple of his mother's eye, Frank watched as she developed numerous schemes for making money. Ethel's diminutive height — she was barely 1.6 metres (five foot three inches) tall — belied her incredible determination, her enormous capacity for work and her lively curiosity. 'Dick' was a forthright and highly intelligent woman with a quick temper, but her outbursts never lasted longer than a few minutes. During her early years in Waitara, Ethel thought of a number of schemes to supplement Clyde's salary. First she acquired hens to produce eggs that could be sold, but the creatures ended up being better fed than the family. Then she decided to grow and sell cut flowers, until Clyde and Frank kept forgetting to distribute them at the train station. Next she arrived home with two drayloads of beehives, but the honey was poorly marketed.[24]

Ethel's most successful venture indicates that, like her husband, she was interested in journalism and propaganda. She decided to bring out a little newspaper outlining the activities of Sydney North Shore residents who were aiding the war effort. After Clyde had the newspaper printed, Ethel and her daughter would go into town to collect it. Kathleen and Frank, if he were home from school, would then help their mother roll up copies and distribute them to her list of subscribers. The enterprise was so remarkable that it attracted the attention of a newsreel crew.[25]

Frank's rather turbulent scholastic career began at Abbotsholme College in about 1913. Captain J. FitzMaurice, the founder and first headmaster of the school, seems to have been distantly related to Frank's paternal grandmother, Margaret Fitzmaurice Clyde. Born in Ireland, FitzMaurice had obtained a commission in the British army and fought in the Boer War. He had then come to Australia via New Zealand for health reasons. In 1908 FitzMaurice had established Abbotsholme College in Killara a few suburbs south of Waitara.[26] The boarding school boasted 'Send us the Boy and we will return you the Man' and strove for the highest development of 'Body, Mind and Character'.

The leafy suburb of Killara was celebrated for its bracing and invigorating 'mountain air' and the boys at Abbotsholme College were expected to sleep on the verandah in open-air dormitories. The Junior House, to which Frank Packer belonged, was supervised by a matron and her assistants. Pupils were not allowed to go home during term time and parents were discouraged from visiting more than once a month. The hundred or so boys who were enrolled at the school at any one time ate vegetables grown on the premises, drank milk from the school's own small herd of cows and took turns driving the headmaster to town in his horse and buggy. Wearing grey military-style uniforms and khaki hats, the pupils were marched to St John's Anglican Church in Gordon each Sunday.

Abbotsholme College, identified by the motto *Virtute non Verbis* ('By deeds not by words'), believed that a sound physical basis was necessary for full mental development. Loafing was discouraged: the boys were expected to rise at 6 a.m., do military drill and exercises after breakfast and participate in organised games — cricket, tennis and rugby union — for two and a half hours each afternoon. The school's anxiety to develop what it described as 'manly characteristics' clearly mirrored the values of the Hutchins School. Abbotsholme College developed a reputation for strictness and became known as one of Sydney's best boarding schools for boys, educating two future prime ministers, Harold Holt and William McMahon, until it was destroyed by fire in 1925.[27] Packer, however, was not on the books for long. He might have rebelled against the school's tough discipline, or perhaps his parents simply preferred to send him to school closer to home.

Frank transferred to a private school that had been established in about 1906 and later became known as Turramurra College. The school's philosophy was education 'through interest and co-operation rather than compulsion; leading to the growth of a community spirit, the motive force of which is service instead of acquisitiveness'. It was an ideal school for boys like Packer who were keen on outdoor life. Students were encouraged to concentrate on subjects and interests that appealed to them, and nature study, which entailed surveying tadpoles and frogs in the creek that ran through the school, was one of the most popular subjects. Carpentry lessons were conducted in a large shed and the boys — known in the district as 'Turramurra Tom Cats' — were expected to compete in cricket, softball, rugby union and athletics.

The school was near Waitara and accepted day students.[28] But Frank appears to have been a boarder, presumably because his father was busy at work and his mother was preoccupied with the war effort. His earliest surviving letter, which was written in 1916, indicates that this was a period of contentment.

> *Dear Mother*
> *I will be very pleas to return home a gane on Sunday. I hope you have not eat all the peaches. or hels I will be very upset with you I will not want eny [illegible] be cos I am so happy.*
> *from your*
> *loving son*
> *Frank*

Within months, however, Packer had been expelled. He would later boast that this was because he took one of his father's revolvers to school and played with it with some of the other boys.[29] Although there is no record of Clyde's reaction to the incident, he may well have regarded taking a revolver to school during the First World War as a healthy, if rather foolhardy, manifestation of manliness and a warrior spirit.

Frank then attended Eltham College, which had recently taken over the site of the old Wahroonga Grammar School. Like Abbotsholme College, the school boasted that it was located in one of Sydney's healthiest and most beautiful districts, about 215 metres above sea level, with spacious grounds for sport and games. Eltham College aimed not only at providing boys with a thorough grounding in all school subjects, but also giving careful attention to 'the preparation in character and physique which is so important'. One of the masters was an astute judge of character, commenting in a school report that Frank, while strong-willed and sometimes difficult to manage, showed good leadership potential.[30]

As Eltham College accepted boys only up to fourteen years of age, Frank moved to the prestigious Sydney Church of England Grammar School ('Shore') in 1920. He did not board at the school, as his family moved into a house in nearby Priory Road, North Sydney, at this time.[31] Frank's lack of academic prowess again became apparent at Shore; he finished 1920 placed nineteenth out of the twenty-eight pupils in the lowest-ranked class in the form. Frank channelled his energies into rugby union, cricket and rowing, but not even his sporting performance was considered worthy of mention in the school magazine; the *Torch Bearer* recorded only his confirmation by the Archbishop of Sydney in November 1921. It is unclear whether academic difficulties, disciplinary problems or general lack of interest resulted in his departure from the school at the end of the first term of 1922. Frank re-entered the school some months later, but he left permanently at the end of second term 1923, and never sat for the Intermediate Certificate.[32]

In later years Frank sometimes alluded to his association with Shore. During a television interview, he mentioned that he had had 'disagreements on occasions' with L. C. Robson, who became headmaster in January 1923. Frank was also fond of telling amusing stories about his relationship with other members of the staff, particularly E. M. Bagot, the master of School House. Like his father, Frank appears to have delighted in relating anecdotes about his behaviour at his various schools, either as a self-defensive mechanism or as a way of portraying himself as the archetypal anti-authoritarian, anti-intellectual Australian male.[33] But while his formal education came to an end in 1923, Frank's indoctrination into the world of newspaper publishing was just beginning.

As Frank experimented with schools up and down Sydney's North Shore, his father emerged as a prominent newspaper executive and proprietor. In 1918 Clyde's friend Claude McKay was seconded to serve as director of publicity for the Seventh War Loan. This brought McKay into contact with (later Sir) James Joynton Smith, the Lord Mayor of Sydney and the president of the Seventh War Loan Committee. The son of a Hackney gasfitter, Smith had run away to sea as a cabin boy. After working as a publican in New Zealand, he had come to Sydney and prospered as a hotelier and racecourse owner. McKay invited Packer to assist him in the war loan campaign and the journalist was granted leave from the *Sun*.

The war loan was promoted with much ballyhoo. McKay and Packer devised a spectacular stunt: Smith was to challenge the Lord Mayor of Melbourne to march with bands and banners towards Sydney, while he marched to Melbourne; they were to meet on the Murray bridge to see who had collected more pledges of money. Although it is unclear who won this battle of the cities, the scheme succeeded in raising a great deal of money. McKay and Packer also staged circuses in the city, travelled to suburbs on the back of a lorry at night and canvassed country towns while the sixty-year-old Smith delivered rousing and highly emotional speeches.[34]

While in the Blue Mountains with Smith, McKay casually mentioned that he hoped to start a weekly newspaper one day. When he was defeated in municipal elections in December 1918, Smith decided that newspapers supported him only when they agreed with his views. He invited McKay to edit a new weekly newspaper; McKay agreed, asking whether he could bring in Packer to act as manager. Packer was happy to leave the *Sun*, as he felt that his hopes of advancement were being blocked by the complex and obscure hierarchy being developed by Hugh Denison.[35]

When the triumvirate met over dinner one Thursday night late in 1918, Smith pledged £20 000 to the project. Mutual trust rather than a written agreement cemented the accord: McKay and Packer were each to receive £10 a week in salary and, if it succeeded, an interest in the newspaper. All three men were rugged individualists and experts at promotion. A flamboyant, buccaneering capitalist who had lost one fortune on the races, Smith supplied the finance with bold and imperturbable confidence. McKay, shrewd, witty and often cynical, had learned how to create 'news' and excite public interest during his time as a publicity agent; he dubbed himself 'Mr Puff'. Packer was not just an experienced craftsman whose drive and brains McKay recognised; he also possessed latent entrepreneurial flair and he was determined to make the most of the opportunity to become a press proprietor in his own right.[36]

The trio spent the first months of 1919 making plans for the newspaper, called *Smith's Weekly* after its proprietor. One hundred tonnes of newsprint were acquired for £8000, two small offices were leased on the top floor of Somerset House in Martin Place, and a rotary press was found in the southern suburb of Zetland. The three men agreed that the newspaper should be a tabloid, like the *Bulletin*. McKay and Packer were attracted less to the staid and strident *Bulletin* of 1919 than to the old satirical firebolt. On the day they began preparing the first issue of *Smith's Weekly*, J. F. Archibald, the elderly former editor of the *Bulletin*, appeared in the doorway to offer his services as a 'soler and heeler of paragraphs'.[37]

The poster for the first edition of *Smith's Weekly* boldly declared: 'Buy It and See the Need for It!' The newspaper, priced at twopence and twenty-four pages in length, made its debut on Saturday 1 March 1919. After putting the issue to bed, Packer and McKay went to the latter's flat in Randwick to bathe and have breakfast. Exhausted but too excited to sleep, they boarded a tram back to the city. At the first stop, Packer nudged his companion in the ribs. They both watched anxiously as a fellow passenger doubtfully turned the pages of a copy of *Smith's Weekly*. When McKay and Packer reached the Somerset House attic, a few contributors had already arrived to study their stories and illustrations.[38]

Smith later wrote that he had founded the newspaper because 'during the war, the best impulses of the people were uppermost' and 'the spirit that had been born in the nation would be best kept aglow by an all-Australian newspaper'. *Smith's Weekly* vigorously took up the cause of returned servicemen and ran a continuous series of war anecdotes known as 'The Unofficial History of the AIF'. It campaigned, too, for that mythical figure, the average, voiceless tax-paying citizen who was always the victim of some special interest group, whether government, big business or trade union. *Smith's Weekly* was unashamedly populist, publicising grievances and exposing war profiteers and slum rackrenting, and its larrikin sense of humour was usually at the expense of women, Aborigines, Asians, Jews and communists. 'Passionately egalitarian and passionately racist', the newspaper mocked the English upper class but warmly welcomed royalty and extolled the virtues of the British empire.[39]

Smith's original pledge of £20 000 was quickly consumed. Ordinary running expenses amounted to £600 a week, while only £300 was being earned as revenue, and writs for libel were coming from all directions. Smith spent vast sums of money settling or fighting suits from individuals and companies variously accused of being war profiteers, slum landlords or 'Huns'. There was talk in Phillip Street — Sydney's legal precinct — of a monument to the triumvirate.[40] Before long, *Smith's Weekly* had recorded a loss of £45 000. But when Smith invited McKay and Packer to dinner one night in his suite at the Arcadia Hotel, it was not to tell them that he was withdrawing from the project. He ordered them, instead, to recruit the best artists and writers that money could buy.

McKay and Packer, who were working on the newspaper day and night, began offering long-term highly-paid contracts to contributors on the understanding that nobody could take out in salary more than he put in in effort: 'As he sowed, so should he reap'. They used the lure of five-year contracts to attract a group of illustrators — Alex Sass, Stan Cross, George Finey, Cecil Hartt, Virgil Reilly, Syd Miller, Joe Jonsson and Frank Dunne — who reputedly became the envy of Fleet Street. Their splendid artwork carried on the black-and-white tradition established by the *Bulletin*. Literary contributors such as Kenneth Slessor, Cliff Graves, Montague Grover, G. Bartlett Adamson, Randolph Bedford and Leon Gellert were also enticed to join the enterprise, and Packer recruited his former colleagues Errol Knox and Reg Moses.[41]

After some months the newspaper's offices were moved to the balcony of one of Smith's properties, the Imperial Arcade, between Pitt and Hunter Streets. Deciding that the printer should not be the only person to make a profit out of *Smith's Weekly*, Smith purchased a four-cylinder Hoe rotary press from New York for £22 000. The new press was duly installed in the basement of the Imperial Arcade, but management failed to test it before it was due to bring out an issue of *Smith's Weekly*. Six hours after the press should have started running, printers were still tinkering with the electric switchboard because the press and the paper roll refused to budge. Exasperated, Packer cried 'Well, that's it!' and hurled a wooden mallet at the offending equipment. This was a novel and effective piece of engineering, as the press suddenly began churning out folded papers. Smith, however, was not so happy because the noise kept his guests awake at the adjacent Arcadia Hotel. He was mollified when informed that the press would only be in action for three hours one night a week as it was capable of printing 20 000 copies an hour. Circulation had already increased from 35 000 to 60 000 copies per week.[42]

Brash and forthright, *Smith's Weekly* plunged headfirst into the political arena. Both McKay and Smith were on good terms with Prime Minister W. M. Hughes, who had left the Australian Labor Party (ALP) and formed the Nationalist Party after losing the first referendum on conscription in 1916. McKay had helped promote the 'yes' case in the second conscription referendum in 1917, and this had brought him into close contact with Hughes. The prime minister also enjoyed relaxing in the company of Smith who, like himself, was a successful self-made man, a social outsider, a colourful character and a prominent supporter of patriotic causes.[43]

As the self-styled diggers' newspaper, *Smith's Weekly* threw its support behind the 'Little Digger', who was struggling to deal with internal party intrigues. In a front-page article on the eve of the December 1919 federal election, Smith offered Hughes £5000 a year to become editor of the new daily newspaper the backers of *Smith's Weekly* were considering launching. When Hughes chose to remain in office, Smith said he would keep the offer open for three years and one month from the date of the election and would meanwhile pay Hughes £2000 a year for three signed articles a week. Hughes did not take up the exceptionally generous offer and *Smith's Weekly* later turned against him, describing him as 'the political tool of the favoured few'.[44]

The newspaper also had strong views on New South Wales politics. In 1917 Packer's old nemesis, Hugh McIntosh, had become a Nationalist member of the Legislative Council (MLC). McIntosh was a close friend of Premier William Holman, who had been expelled from the ALP over the issue of conscription and now headed a Nationalist coalition. In 1918 the Holman government failed to invite public tenders before signing a £1 million contract with Henry Teesdale Smith, who had invested in McIntosh's newspapers, to build a massive wheat silo. This episode precipitated two royal commissions and when *Smith's Weekly* appeared on the scene in 1919 it began publishing exposés of wheat scandals.[45]

During the 1920 state election campaign, as the newspaper loudly proclaimed that 'Holman Must Go', Packer's latent artistic talents became apparent. The cartoonist George Finey contended that Packer possessed a degree of artistic understanding unique among newspaper executives:

> Strolling into a weekly conference, he would spread out the roughs, twenty maybe, push his hat back, glance intently at the lot, then in a matter of minutes, often seconds only, stab one with his finger — 'That's it!' Or he might place it on top of others and walk away without a word. There has never been another like him, he had talent laid on …

As the April 1920 poll approached, Packer doodled a sketch of a bulldog with McIntosh's face and a Union Jack hoisted on its tail; the politician was at that time president of the British Empire League. From then on cartoons in *Smith's Weekly* featured the 'Macindog' trailing the premier. Holman believed that the newspaper was partly responsible for his defeat at the election.[46]

McIntosh conducted a smear campaign against Smith and his newspaper, offering Smith £5000 to serialise his colourful life story in the *Sunday Times*. Turning the tables on its enemy, *Smith's Weekly* decided to milk the publicity. McKay ghosted Smith's autobiography, which became a popular serial feature in *Smith's Weekly*. Sales, meanwhile, were climbing steadily. Circulation rose from 75 769 copies per week in January 1921 to just under 100 000 in August and 150 000 by the end of the year. At the same time, the acute shortage of newsprint that had caused the price of newsprint to soar since the outbreak of war began to ease.[47]

As *Smith's Weekly*'s popularity and financial performance improved, dinners and annual picnic days where the 'top and bottom brass' could mix together were introduced. At one of these dinners Joe Jonsson decided that Packer's address, although witty, was too long-winded. Resolving to bring Packer down in a football tackle, the artist dived under the table but grabbed the wrong pair of legs. While Jonsson lay sprawled on the floor with his arms around the knees of a thinly smiling Smith, Packer flopped back in his chair convulsed with laughter.[48]

Packer might have been regarded as a good sport, but his burning ambition was obvious to all. In April 1921 a facetious in-house newspaper described him as 'very keen', a sort of 'journalistic enthusiast, has ambitions mainly to own a paper, lives for the paper, dreams of the paper'. The opportunity to become a proprietor was presented to him a few months later. By this time Smith, with the aid of a bank overdraft, had sunk £98 000 into *Smith's Weekly*. The week the newspaper finally showed a profit, Smith told Packer and McKay that his promise to give them an interest in the company would be discussed at the next board meeting.[49]

The two executives adjourned to a bar at the Hotel Australia, speculating that they might each be awarded 5 per cent of the profits. After their second drink, they thought that they might be lucky enough to get 10 per cent and a hike in salary. When the day of the board meeting finally arrived, Packer and McKay were alarmed to see that Smith had called in his solicitor. While Smith puffed on a cigar, his solicitor handed Packer and McKay individual agreements. The manager and the editor were unable to suppress their gasps of delight and astonishment when they read that they were each to receive a one-third share in the newspaper.[50]

Even before R. C. Packer found himself the co-owner of a successful Sydney newspaper, his financial situation had been improving. In about 1919 he had purchased a sophisticated British car, the Siddeley-Deasy. The car, with its sarcophagus-like hood and big brass lamps, was promoted with the slogan 'As Silent as the Sphinx' because of the quietness of its engine. Packer continued to catch the train and ferry to work, so the car was mainly used for family outings. On such occasions, Frank would don his hat back-to-front and hop into the front passenger seat to sit next to his father. Ethel and Kathleen sat in the back seats, which were stuffed with horsehair and as comfortable as armchairs. They were all so thrilled with the car that they referred to it as 'Dearly Beloved'. Frank, who was fond of tinkering with the car's engine, learned to drive while still living in Waitara.[51]

The family spent many weekends camping by the Hawkesbury River and at Whale Beach, where neighbours sometimes joined them. On one eventful holiday, the Packers drove to Gundagai. It was only after they had spent a night camping by a river that locals informed them that the spot was infested with snakes. Setting off again, they came to a bridge that was partly submerged by a swollen river. Clyde gave Frank an umbrella and deputed him to go and test the bridge; the tall teenager took only a few steps along the bridge before he himself almost disappeared. During another holiday, the family was floodbound for days in Huskisson on the New South Wales south coast. Ethel and Kathleen were given a bedroom over the garage, while Clyde and Frank were forced to share a bed over the grocery store until 'Dearly Beloved' could make its way out of town.[52]

As an adolescent, Frank grew rapidly. His father was a good looking man of medium height, with an athletic physique and a large head. It was Ethel's boundless energy and sparkling eyes, rather than her physical appearance, that attracted those who met her. She had long, thick, wavy brown hair, a determined chin and a rather pronounced nose. Frank inherited her hair, chin and nose. He had blue eyes and was hefty and well-built; when fully grown, he was 1.8 metres (six foot one and a half inches tall). Although not classically handsome, Frank had a pleasant appearance as a young man. Nevertheless, he was so self-conscious about his size that he began putting up his age.[53]

Journalists often saw the teenager when he accompanied his father to the office. Glen William ('George') Warnecke observed that Frank 'displayed a cool assurance almost as though he had come into the world middle-aged; he certainly had nothing of the timid, blushing 16 year old that one is accustomed to'. Warnecke could not have foreseen that his career would intersect with Frank Packer's for decades to come. Born in Armidale in 1894, Warnecke had expressed interest in journalism since childhood; after serving his cadetship on the Sydney *Evening News* and enlisting in the AIF, he had worked as government roundsman for the *Daily Telegraph* and chief-of-staff of the *Daily Mail*. In 1923 R. C. Packer and his associates seized on Warnecke's experience and talents and recruited him to their ranks.[54]

George Finey remembered Frank as a 'husky boy ... strong as a bear, aggressive, full of fight'. On one occasion the cartoonist became engaged in a scuffle with the fifteen-year-old on the steps of the *Smith's Weekly*'s offices, which had recently been relocated to purpose-built premises in Phillip Street. According to Finey, the scuffle terminated abruptly when Clyde Packer appeared and told him, 'George! Don't let Frank push you around — knock him down, it's the only thing he understands'.[55] Finey's recollection suggests that Clyde was a tough, as well as an attentive, parent.

Clyde was preoccupied with thinking about what the future held for his son. When the scuffle broke up, Clyde invited the cartoonist to accompany him to the Hotel Australia. Over a tankard of beer, Clyde asked Finey what he intended putting his sons to. Clyde was not impressed when his companion declared, 'Whatever they want to be, that will be it'. The newspaper executive was concerned that Frank was showing signs of wanting to go on the land rather than following in his footsteps. Clyde did not appreciate Finey's advice that he should not force the boy to go into the 'paper game' against his wishes. Warnecke believed that Frank's parents hoped that he would continue his studies at Shore in preparation for the University of Sydney.[56] Frank, for his part, just wanted an excuse to leave school. Joining the staff of Clyde's latest publishing endeavour was an ideal compromise for all concerned.

In 1921 the sponsors of *Smith's Weekly* had begun seriously considering the possibility of publishing a daily newspaper. According to McKay, Smith planned to join forces with Hugh Denison to purchase the moribund *Daily Telegraph* for £600 000. Hearing of the scheme, McKay persuaded Smith that a new morning newspaper could be launched with considerably less capital. McKay, Clyde Packer and Errol Knox then began planning the layout and features of a daily newspaper. Packer — whom his colleagues dubbed 'Mr Snippety Snip' — referred to his enormous album of strikingly arranged pages from Australian, American and English publications for inspiration.

After a few months it was decided that Knox should get some first-hand experience of the internal organisation of a morning newspaper. Packer and McKay, who had recently turned down offers to run the *Daily Telegraph*, successfully recommended the appointment of Knox as news editor in late 1921. Smith and McKay went to London to make arrangements for a new cable service, while Packer remained in Sydney. He relished pasting up pages and laying out the appropriate type for the daily newspaper. Because *Smith's Weekly* carried as its masthead 'The Public Guardian', the new paper was to be entitled the *Daily Guardian*.[57]

Evidence has recently come to light suggesting that the relationship between Packer and Smith deteriorated even before the *Daily Guardian* was launched. The papers of the journalist Quentin S. Spedding contain an undated memorandum, headed 'Why Packer left "Smith's" and how he got back', that deals with an alleged incident that took place in November 1922. A young woman was allowed to use the boardroom of *Smith's Weekly* at night to teach French classes. According to the memo, the teacher rejected Packer's amorous advances late one night, and he was confined to bed for the next few days with an acute contusion of the testicles. When the woman reported the incident to Smith, he dissuaded her from taking the matter to the police by assuring her that Packer would be sacked. The memo concludes that Packer was reinstated within a few weeks because he and 'his cronies had got the wood over Joynton'. This mysterious account is also accompanied by a note suggesting that 'Meldrum', the secretary of the Joynton Smith trust, would be prepared to reveal the full story, as he hated Packer.[58]

Short of the providential discovery of Meldrum's account of the matter, this account will probably never be substantiated. It is unclear precisely when Spedding's dossier — which also alludes to more minor indiscretions on the part of Packer and his associates — was compiled. If it was not prepared until some time after the alleged incident, political enmities might have entered into play. As Spedding's career does not appear to have crossed with Packer's, it is unlikely that he was inspired by a personal grudge. However, in 1925 he was appointed editor of the *Labor Daily*, which was the mouthpiece of Premier J. T. Lang;[59] as we shall see, Packer and Lang became bitter enemies in the second half of the 1920s.

It is impossible to ascertain what sources Spedding relied upon to prepare his memo. Nevertheless, his position in the Sydney newspaper scene suggests that he might have known something about the inner workings of *Smith's Weekly*. His account of the alleged incident in November 1922 indicates that Packer was engaged in a bitter dispute with the advertising department but was surrounded by individual 'worshippers', including the chief accountant N. Q. Bradshaw, the news editor Jack Gell and the chief-of-staff, a Mr Nicholas.[60] Early employers might have referred to Packer's sunny and genial disposition, but over the years his personality and expectations had hardened. Staff members composed ditties such as:

Packer's the man to roar like Hell,
And when he's roaring all is well,
Inky Pinky Parley-vous.[61]

The business partnership between Smith and Packer continued beyond 1922, but whether they were close at a personal level is doubtful. The sponsors of *Smith's Weekly* had other difficulties to contend with. As the time approached for the launch of the *Daily Guardian*, Errol Knox was summoned to return with the experience and the insights he had acquired from his term with the *Daily Telegraph*. However, to the consternation of Smith, McKay and Packer, he decided to remain with Hugh Denison and was appointed managing editor of the *Evening News*. To make matters worse, Knox introduced to this newspaper some of the ideas that had been intended for the *Daily Guardian*! Packer turned to the London popular press, deciding that the new paper should be modelled on Lord Northcliffe's tremendously successful *Daily Mail*. In order to obtain the level of capital needed to finance the production of a daily newspaper, the trio floated a public company. The public took up 100 000 £1 preference shares in Smith's Newspaper Ltd.[62]

Attractive salaries lured a pool of high-profile artists and journalists to the *Daily Guardian* in 1923. George Warnecke, for instance, was unable to resist the offer of £20 per week to head the cable service in Fleet Street. Nevertheless, the newspaper's debut was a fiasco. Carpenters had not yet finished putting up partitions in the offices of the *Daily Guardian*. The place was a confusion of chairs and tables and men and women, many of them inebriated. Employee after employee fell victim to influenza. Twenty-three-year-old Eric Baume, who had just arrived from New Zealand and knew nothing about Sydney, was alarmed to find himself appointed acting news editor. No dummy appeared because Packer and McKay were quarrelling about typefaces.[63]

The *Daily Guardian* was launched on 2 July 1923. The besieged editorial staff were too eager to please, overcrowding the early pages with a jumble of cabled stories that cost £4000. Baume later wrote that the newspaper was 'such a tragedy that it should have died on the day after its messy birth'. For a week or two sales lost ground each day and before long the paper was losing £20 000 a month.[64]

In both his own autobiography and that of Smith's, which he ghosted, McKay described how he and his partners reacted to the financial crisis. According to these accounts, only Smith remained unperturbed, agreeing to back the newspaper up to £200 000. According to Warnecke, however, both Smith and McKay suggested closing down the *Daily Guardian*. Packer disagreed, arguing that the only newspaper that was at all modern in Sydney was the *Sun*; the other daily newspapers were still hidebound by the nineteenth-century style of journalism. Maintaining that the *Daily Guardian* could achieve in the morning what the *Sun* had achieved in the afternoon, Packer took responsibility for the new paper while McKay concentrated on *Smith's Weekly*.[65]

After this false start the *Daily Guardian*'s circulation started to pick up slowly, but the sales were purely casual. Recalling the stunts employed by such overseas press barons as Joseph Pulitzer, Packer and McKay decided to introduce free accident insurance to encourage readers to have the newspaper delivered. While this contributed to a rise in sales, McKay buckled under years of unrelenting pressure. He had a nervous breakdown and went to California with his wife for a complete rest.[66]

Frank Packer joined the staff of Smith's Newspapers just after the *Daily Guardian*'s launch in July 1923. As his father insisted that he learn about all aspects of newspaper production, Frank unloaded newsprint, worked in the engine room and the darkroom and drove delivery vehicles. Bruce Cockburn, one of the head printers, was assigned to teach him the secrets of mechanical processes. Jim Donald, who had been a professional pugilist before becoming a boxing writer, also agreed to take the youngster under his wing. A chest X-ray had shown up a slight fuzziness on Frank's lungs, so Clyde wanted the boy to concentrate on a sport other than rowing.[67]

Frank, who was given the title of 'cadet reporter and photographer', naturally found participating in the newspapers' exploits much more fun than attending school. Unashamedly sensationalist, the *Daily Guardian* and *Smith's Weekly* sold white slaves and bought cocaine to expose corruption. In late August 1923 Frank went to a pharmacist in Elizabeth Street in the company of a *Smith's Weekly* 'investigator' and a taxi driver. After purchasing a pillbox of cocaine for £1, the two newspaper employees revealed their identities. The exposé was published on the front page of the next edition of *Smith's Weekly* under the headline 'Boy Buys Enough To Kill 20 People'.[68] Frank enthusiastically reported his activities in letters to his mother, who was overseas.

On their marriage in 1903, Clyde had promised Ethel that he would send her back to Ireland and England as soon as he could afford it. Realising that he would be preoccupied with the launch of the *Daily Guardian* in the second half of 1923, Clyde despatched his wife and daughter abroad. The trip was a sad one in many respects because it came so soon after 'The Troubles'; the Hewsons were Protestants in the south of Ireland, and Ethel and Kathleen spent much of their time visiting cemeteries. Clyde asked George Warnecke, who was courting the Irish opera singer Nora Hill, to keep an eye on his wife and daughter. George and Nora accompanied Ethel on a nostalgic pilgrimage to her childhood haunts in Wicklow. Warnecke recalls that Ethel went into every church she passed and he and Nora would have to wait for her while she knelt in prayer. He felt it was Ethel's influence that saw Clyde decree that all signs of masculinity in photographs of champion stallions and bulls should be painted out.[69]

After disappointing his parents by not continuing with his studies, Frank seems to have been anxious to impress them with his performance at work. He reassured Ethel that although he was doing 'quite a line' with two girls, he was working 'very hard' and not going out to dances; 'Dad is also working hard and we are very glad when the week end comes, so that we can have a loaf'. He described the cocaine 'yarn' as 'a real hum-dinger … Dad is very pleased with it'. Warnecke remembered Ethel reading out her sixteen-year-old son's letters and cables to her friends in London. She was especially proud of the account Frank gave of driving an old delivery van through flooded streets, all on his own in the dead of night, to distribute the first edition of the *Daily Guardian*.[70]

The pace of work was so hectic that some of Clyde's colleagues often slept over in Kathleen's bedroom. A housekeeper, Beatrice, looked after Clyde, Frank and their visitors. Frank was a tender and considerate son, writing weekly letters to his mother and eagerly waiting for hers in return: 'Dear Darling Mother … I am simply dying to hear from you'. He kept her informed about the welfare of their beloved dogs, Nigger and Spider, and asked her to bring him a bulldog pup home. Frank also discovered that he missed his 'pretty little sister': 'I do love you so only I don't know it till you go away and stop annoying me and telling me to get out of your room … Dear old Kate when you come back I shall be able to take you out to dances and so forth'.[71]

However exciting it might have been, Frank's journalistic career was brief and inglorious. It soon became apparent that his written expression was poor and he lacked his father's literary and artistic flair. Indeed, Frank was showing more promise as a heavyweight boxer than as a journalist. The *Daily Guardian*, meanwhile, was floundering. The first annual report of Smith's Newspapers revealed that the newspaper incurred a loss of £101 378 in its first thirteen months of operation. When McKay returned from overseas, he learned that sales had slipped back to 40 000. The management reluctantly decided that the least productive members of the highly paid staff would have to be dropped. Frank Packer joined the general exodus.[72]

3
Little Frankie's Wanderings

Growing up in Waitara had left Frank Packer with a fondness for animals and a hankering to live on the land. As the *Daily Guardian* struggled for survival, Frank's parents decided to allow him to go to the country as a jackeroo. R. C. Packer presumably reasoned that roughing it in the outback would either teach Frank the skills needed to run a pastoral property or a horse stud, or turn him off rural life once and for all. Ethel had rather different motives: she wanted to get her son away from the city, where he seemed to be heading towards a career in the boxing ring.[1]

Frank worked as a jackeroo on Suffolk Vale station in Boorowa in the central west of New South Wales some time between September 1923 and June 1926; it seems most likely that he arrived in late 1924 and left in mid 1926. Suffolk Vale station, incorporating hundreds of hectares of land, had been established to grow wheat and graze sheep in the 1860s. It had also moved into producing peaches in the early 1900s. After the First World War the property had become one of the first in the district to be divided privately for closer settlement. By the 1920s it was a horse stud owned by James Barnes and managed by one of his in-laws, Robert Newman.[2]

In the first half of th century it was not unusual for wealthy young men from comfortable city households and English public schools to work as jackeroos; jackerooing in Australia was regarded as a boy's finishing school. The young men were paid very little, instead undertaking their work 'for love and experience'. The jackeroo was expected to work his way up through the ranks from boundary rider, stockman, overseer and eventually to manager in preparation for the day when he would have his own property.[3]

Jackeroos arrived at their properties looking clean and pink, with unblemished hands and teeth bearing the evidence of daily care and professional attention. The young men began work wearing moleskin trousers, khaki shirts and wide-brimmed felt hats and walking uneasily in new tan boots with elastic sides. As Frank roamed the large property on horseback, the sun's brutal rays played havoc with his skin; 'my face is coming adrift in pieces: melting', he told his mother a few weeks after his arrival in Boorowa.[4]

Most jackeroos found acquiring bushmen's skills extremely difficult. They were expected to learn how to crutch sheep with handshears, shoe horses, cut fenceposts, repair fences, kill and dress sheep, muster livestock, train sheepdogs, acquire basic blacksmithing skills and make a decent damper. The new recruits' good teeth were regarded as an asset by station managers. Jackeroos were taught the deft backhand cut needed to take the top off a ram's scrotum; then they were expected to bite off and spit out the warm young testes; finally the tail would be severed with one quick blow and the struggling lamb would emerge as another bleating wether.[5]

Adjusting to packsaddle food was quite a challenge. The midday meal, known as 'crib', usually comprised four rounds of damper laden with mutton and lashings of tomato sauce. Golden syrup sandwiches were wrapped in newspaper and wedged into saddlebags, where they absorbed the sweat from the horse and took on a distinctive taste; bits of debris and suicidal insects had to be picked out of enamel mugs of billy tea. And jackeroos were unable to slip easily into the exchange of comments on weather and wool, fluke and worms, lucerne and sorghum that passed for conversation among overseers and stationhands. In Patrick White's *The Twyborn Affair*, Eddie the jackeroo 'wished he could join in, but did not think he could ever master the liturgy'.[6]

Jackeroos worked hard and were frequently derided by old hands. Frank Packer, at least, was not too soft a target: he was big and strong, enjoyed working with animals and, unlike many of his counterparts, did not have to suffer the ignominy of being a university graduate or a 'new chum' from England. And he would not have found it too difficult to adapt to a world that was aggressively masculine[7] — a world of male camaraderie, of hearty conversation and earthy smells, where men rolled cigarettes, pissed outdoors, entered buckjumping competitions and shot rabbits and kangaroos.

Jackeroos occupied a unique place in the property's rigid social hierarchy. Station hands, domestic servants, shearers and rabbiters accepted the affectionate relationship that often developed between the gentleman's son and the boss 'as a matter of caste, in its way inevitable'. The Barnes and Newman families treated Frank well and became very friendly with his parents. Ethel and Clyde visited their young son at Suffolk Vale, spoke to him regularly on the telephone and helped arrange for a new parlourmaid to be sent to the property.[8]

By the 1920s the owners of homesteads such as Suffolk Vale lived like English gentry with an Australian veneer. They wrote letters to relatives in England, waited anxiously for English newspapers and magazines to come by ship, sent their children to boarding schools with English headmasters and headmistresses, and gathered in their drawing rooms after dinner to sing and play the piano. Frank dressed for dinner with the Barnes and Newman families at the homestead and formed parties to attend local dances. In his one surviving letter from this period, Frank gently chided his mother: 'You did not put a hair brush in my case. But everything else was good-o … I think you had better send my grey suit up to me after it is cleaned and pressed as there are some visitors coming up this week'.[9]

Many famous racehorses were bred on Suffolk Vale. In the mid 1920s, for example, Satelles, the son of Sunstar who was bred in England by Lord Dewar of Scotch whisky fame, won a number of regional New South Wales cups and show awards and was mated with mares for a hefty fee; it sired horses such as Crucis, which won the 1929 Sydney Cup.[10] Frank learned how to spot and work with a good pedigree, improved his hunting skills and probably began playing polo. In May 1926 he participated in the Grenfell gymkhana, held for the first time since the war. Bob Newman, who was now working on his own property in Grenfell, entered horses in a number of events. Frank appears to have ridden Newman's Pearl Dust to victory in a six-furlong race and to third place in a five-furlong race, and to have come second in a pony race. That night the two men were loudly cheered when they were presented with the winning trophies at a large and lavish ball at the local hall.[11]

After eighteen months, however, Frank decided to leave the property. Kathleen recalls that her brother, who had hated anything to do with gardening or weeding since childhood, simply became sick of clearing paddocks.[12] There certainly was a problem with weeds on the property at this time: in March 1925 Jim Barnes was prosecuted by the municipal council for failing to destroy noxious weeds growing on Suffolk Vale; the following month, Barnes and his workers were said to be doing 'good work' in removing weeds from the property. The work was tedious, backbreaking and seemed, to young Frank, never-ending.[13] R. C. Packer must have been relieved that his son had finally gotten living on the land out of his system and was now content to resume a newspaper career.

During Frank's spell as a jackeroo, his father had been working at a relentless pace in an effort to make a success of the *Daily Guardian* and revive the value of his interest in Smith's Newspapers. George Warnecke, who returned from Fleet Street in 1924 to join the *Daily Guardian* as a sub-editor, recalled that Clyde Packer routinely worked an eighteen- or twenty-hour day. Packer would arrive at his office early in the morning to compare the *Daily Guardian* with the *Sydney Morning Herald*, the *Daily Telegraph* and the *Daily News*. After considering stories for the next day's edition and conferring with the production managers, he would wolf down a bite of lunch or spend an hour sweating at his gymnasium. In the afternoon he would meet with his partners, hold news conferences and disappear behind closed doors for an hour to digest circulation figures and advertising receipts. Following a rapid dinner with one of his cronies, Packer would return to his desk and his deep leather chair to confer with editorial executives about breaking stories and study the proofs of the next morning's edition.[14]

Eric Baume concluded that 'The Chief' had a retentive memory and an eye for newspaper display: 'His success lay in that he was never too proud to appreciate the changes in style evolved in other countries, and, throughout the long years I knew him, he used to say, "Give me my brains, Eric. I like this style of heading". His "brains" were a slim pair of scissors in Italian steel … One had to adapt as well as create. At both of these arts Robert Clyde Packer was a master'.

Baume also found that Packer was a hard taskmaster. On days when Baume thought that the *Daily Guardian* had been splendid, he would stand to attention before a withering blast of invective. On days when he thought that the newspaper was bad Packer's praise would be fulsome and Baume would have to stand at the bar in a little hotel on the corner of King Street drinking far too many whiskies as he was told what a fine fellow he was.[15]

The *Daily Guardian* was modelled on the newspapers of Northcliffe and William Randolph Hearst, with a little of the Sydney *Sun* thrown in for good measure. It initiated a range of novel features: a film section designed to coincide with the emergence of palatial new picture theatres, a shopping bureau to attract housewives looking for bargains, and a motoring section to appeal to Sunday drivers. The real estate pages kept pace with the building boom and a daily competition called 'What I Saw Yesterday' became so successful that it required a special pool of receptionists to cope with the influx of calls.

Even though circulation rose from 85 000 in July 1924 to 103 000 twelve months later, advertising revenue remained inadequate. The *Daily Guardian*'s creative news values and outspoken political views alienated some potential advertisers. Rival newspapers told advertisers who catered to men that the *Daily Guardian* 'only sells to flappers', while women's clothes stores were informed that women never read it. Moreover, the *Daily Guardian* was unable to loosen the *Sydney Morning Herald*'s stranglehold on the lucrative classified advertising market.[16]

In the second half of 1925 R. C. Packer had an idea that reversed the *Daily Guardian*'s fortunes. As a keen observer of overseas newspapers, he had watched with interest as American dailies featured photographs of beautiful young women in bathing suits. The Miss America pageant had recently been launched in the United States and Packer decided that the *Daily Guardian* should initiate a similar quest in Australia. On 18 September 1925 the newspaper announced that it was searching for Miss Australia, who would travel to Atlantic City to challenge the winner of the Miss America pageant. Packer worked like a Trojan for weeks to make a success of the competition, rarely going home and catching only odd hours of sleep in his armchair.[17]

The competition was vigorously promoted in *Smith's Weekly*, and municipalities and shires Australia-wide were invited to submit entries; one wonders whether Frank was proud or embarrassed in November 1925 when the *Boorowa News* began soliciting entrants. The *Daily Guardian* published photographs of new entrants every day for nine months and by May 1926 more than 1000 entries had been received. A distinguished panel of individuals assessed the entries: the artists Thea Proctor, Sidney Long, Raynor Hoff and Florence Rodway; Sydney Ure Smith, publisher of *Art in Australia* and the *Home*; the cartoonists Virgil Riley, D. H. Souter and B. E. Minns; and Percy Bennison. The panel drew up a series of shortlists that the *Daily Guardian* revealed with breathless excitement. On Friday 25 June Smith's Newspapers hosted a lavish function at St James Theatre for the seven finalists. Nineteen-year-old Beryl Mills, who had obtained leave from her studies at the University of Western Australia to attend the event, was crowned the inaugural Miss Australia.[18]

On the day the winner was announced, the *Daily Guardian*'s sales jumped to 275 000 copies. An elated Clyde Packer put his head around Claude McKay's door: 'Come and have lunch, Mr Fairfax! Now, if only we could get the *Herald*'s death notices!' Over lunch, McKay suggested that the slogan of the *Daily Guardian* should be 'If you want to know who's dead read the *Herald* — if you want to know who's alive, read the *Guardian*'. The master publicists made sure that the beauty pageant attracted advertising revenue as well as new sales: Mills was given swimsuits by Lasker and Lasker, handbags and luggage from the Strand Bag Shop, a diamond and platinum ring from W. C. Taylor and Co., soap from Rexona Pty Ltd, flowers from Searl's and a gramophone from the Garcia Gramophone Co.[19]

Surrounded by admirers, Mills toured retail establishments and attended civic receptions throughout Sydney and Newcastle in a blaze of publicity. Close-ups of the brunette were shown at Hoyts De Luxe and Piccadilly theatres. The selection criteria for the title had included education, sporting ability and poise, and the *Daily Guardian* and its advertisers presented the winner as the embodiment of the ideal Australian girl. Mills, who had won swimming and diving championships and captained the hockey team while studying for a Bachelor of Arts, was portrayed as 'the synthesis of brains, beauty and athletic vigour'. The 'Golden Girl of the Golden West' was to be Australia's 'fairest ambassador' abroad.[20]

Although the winner of the title was not, as the sponsors of the competition had originally intimated, eligible to compete for the Miss America title at Atlantic City, Beryl Mills still embarked on a promotional tour of the United States. George Warnecke hopefully asked Clyde Packer whether he and his wife Nora Hill could chaperone Beryl and her mother. Warnecke was told that he was needed at his desk and that in any case the tour required the theatrical skills and experience of a man such as Claude McKay. Packer also decided that his son should join the entourage. Clyde, who had not yet had the opportunity himself to go abroad, felt that Frank would benefit from travelling with the sophisticated McKay and being introduced to prominent newspaper and advertising executives in the United States.[21]

On 28 July 1926 the party left Sydney on the Matson-Oceanic liner the Sonoma. Clyde Packer and Claude McKay ensured that a group of Australian and American dignitaries and businessmen were present at Circular Quay to farewell Beryl Mills and her mother. The number of curious onlookers was so large that McKay found it almost impossible to make his way onto the ship. The *Sonoma* travelled first to Fiji, then to Honolulu, where Mills and her entourage were given the use of a Studebaker limousine.[22]

Smith's Newspapers adroitly managed the event, arranging for a group of leading American businessmen to form a 'reception committee'. The main backer of the tour was Vacuum Oil, a company affiliated with the powerful Standard Oil Company. In San Francisco the party was greeted with wild enthusiasm. The mayor, who had recently visited Sydney and spent a lot of time in the offices of Smith's Newspapers, joined forces with a publicity agent to create an appropriate degree of ballyhoo. The Australian contingent stayed at the St Francis Hotel, where they were assigned a bodyguard. McKay had met William Wrigley, the millionaire chewing gum manufacturer, on a previous visit to Los Angeles. Wrigley came over from Catalina Island to join in the gaiety and to host a party in Mills's honour.[23] As Frank Packer made his way by train from Los Angeles to Chicago, he advised his mother to read the *Daily Guardian* 'to follow the wanderings of little Frankie in a foreign country'. He joked that if she became a subscriber, Ethel would even benefit from the free insurance scheme.

Frank did not enjoy the trip across the desert as it was 'as hot as hadies [sic]. There is more sand and soot on our food than anything else. You wash your hands, and the next second they are black again'.[24] Nevertheless, he was placated when he reached Chicago. A dozen leading Wrigley executives greeted the Australians at the station and whisked them off to the Drake Hotel. Frank and McKay and Beryl and her mother were given the run of two suites that covered nearly an entire floor overlooking Lake Michigan. Frank chose a bedroom that had a shower recess with an enormous number of taps operating from every possible angle; turning them all on at once was an exhilarating experience. On the day he arrived at the hotel, he told his mother that he and McKay had invited an actress to have lunch with them in their drawing room. Frank reassured Ethel: 'He is doing quite a line with her. I don't get a look in ... don't worry over me dear I have never lead such a quite [sic] and good life'. During the five days they spent in Chicago, Frank and McKay were taken to Wrigley Tower, which topped a skyscraper that dominated the city, and sailed on Lake Michigan in the Wrigley family's yacht.[25]

Leaving Chicago, the party travelled by train to New York. Vacuum Oil appointed the public relations guru Edward L. Bernays to orchestrate publicity. On 1 September official cars and police motorcycles escorted Mills and her chaperones to City Hall, where they were greeted by the mayor, Jimmy Walker. That afternoon McKay, Frank and members of the reception committee were entertained at lunch by Adolph S. Ochs, the proprietor of the *New York Times*, and shown around the newspaper's premises. The party then made its way to the grand Biltmore Hotel, which was controlled by the Wrigley family. The next day the party travelled to Philadelphia to attend the Sesquicentennial Exhibition. McKay and Frank were invited to the home of the president of the Standard Oil Company; one of the guests at the luncheon was George Horace Lorimer, the editor of the *Saturday Evening Post*.[26]

Unfortunately, no record of how Frank reacted to meeting Ochs and Lorimer, or what they in turn thought of him, has survived. But he wrote to his mother to say that if she did not object, he would like to stay in the United States for a year or so and work on one of the papers. McKay had indicated that 'it might be possible to arrange for me to go thru (that's how the Americans spell through) the Hearst papers starting in the East' and finishing in San Francisco. Frank told his mother that he would write to his father asking him what he thought of the idea.[27] Nothing came of the proposal, possibly because Ethel did not want her nineteen-year-old son to be so far from home for such a long period. Clyde seems to have been anxious to groom his son on the staff of Smith's Newspapers, and he might have privately felt that Frank's journalistic shortcomings would become apparent if he worked on American newspapers by himself.

Bernays arranged for Mills and her contingent to see Niagara Falls and visit Washington. By 11 September 1926 they had reached Atlantic City, where Mills took a salute from the contestants in the Miss America pageant. While McKay and Frank met American newspaper executives and attended sporting events, Mills undertook an exhausting round of public engagements during her three-month tour of the United States. Smith's Newspapers and their publicity consultants arranged for her to be entertained by chambers of commerce, attend theatre parties and supper dances, start baseball matches, give swimming exhibitions, shop in exclusive department stores, visit movie studios, meet Hollywood stars, place wreaths on war graves, appear in the rotogravure pages of Sunday newspapers and make speeches with a 'modest earnestness'. The *Daily Guardian*, claiming that Beryl and her mother had been fêted like royalty in Atlantic City, announced that there would be another Miss Australia competition in 1927.[28]

Of more personal interest to the men in Mills's entourage was the battle for the world heavyweight boxing title. Jack Dempsey, a handsome silent movie star and the incumbent title-holder, and Gene Tunney, a former marine with twenty-five victories under his belt, were scheduled to meet for the first time on 23 September 1926. McKay watched Dempsey work out in Atlantic City while Frank went off to Tunney's training camp. Frank decided to put his money on Tunney; although Dempsey was the favourite, Tunney's odds shortened as the hour of the fight approached. Wynne W. ('Bill') Davies, the New York representative of the *Daily Guardian*, managed to secure Frank and McKay tickets to the fight in the vast stadium built for the Philadelphia Exhibition. As the heavens opened they joined a crowd of 120 000 people, including politicians, mayors, police chiefs, leading businessmen and actors, at ringside. Frank emerged from the stadium soaked to the skin but considerably better off because Tunney won the bout on points.[29]

At around this time Frank, McKay and Davis also attended a major polo match. When they went to leave the match, McKay and Davis realised that their companion was missing. They found Frank being used as the 'fall guy' at the invitation of three men playing cards on the top of an umbrella. As Frank left the scene with McKay and Davis he was more than $50 ahead; although associates of the three gamblers pursued him, he refused to give the money back. From that moment on McKay 'never doubted that Frank Packer was born under a lucky star'.[30]

Mills and her entourage made their way back west via the Twentieth-Century express train through Salt Lake City and over the Rocky Mountains. They sailed from San Francisco on 13 October 1926. When Mills arrived in Sydney, she decided not to complete her degree. With the backing of McKay, who was her legal guardian until she returned to her father in Perth, she embarked on a profitable lecture tour and in 1928 she married a *Daily Guardian* journalist. The grand trip across the United States might have cost some £8000, but the industry agreed that the first Miss Australia quest had been the most successful publicity stunt ever carried out by an Australian newspaper. It had attracted a plethora of new advertising accounts for the *Daily Guardian*, added at least 20 000 new subscribers permanently, and placed Smith's Newspapers on a sound financial footing. However, the happy days of adversity were gone. Over the next few years the Packers and their associates were to be beset by the tribulations of success.[31]

The Packer family had moved to Awanui Flats in Wunulla Road, Point Piper, in 1924; two years later they took up residence in a house in the same street. The family's transition from premises in Darlinghurst and Bondi to Waitara, North Sydney and then Point Piper reflected their upward social mobility. Although fishermen, pilots and signalmen had peopled the municipality of Woollahra after white settlement, by the 1820s it had become a favourite site for Sydney's *beau monde*. Each afternoon the colony's elite, dressed in their finery, had promenaded in their gigs along what is now known as Old South Head Road. In the mid nineteenth century colonial administrators, wealthy merchants and brewers had begun to settle in the district. Attracted to the coves, bays, cliffs and headlands that dominated the area, they had built grand residences as testaments to their wealth. From Wunulla Road R. C. Packer, who had so loved the sea since his early years in Hobart, looked north to Rose Bay across a spectacularly beautiful panorama. His wife was finally able to indulge her love of antiques as she sought to recreate some of the aspects of her childhood home.[32]

When Frank returned to Sydney in November 1926, he was appointed assistant business manager of the *Daily Guardian* under the supervision of Norman Q. Bradshaw. The older man quickly realised that Frank possessed a head for figures and did not need to be instructed how to handle petty cash expense accounts. Clyde, who was intent on establishing hereditary control of the company, must have been greatly relieved at his son's obvious aptitude for finance. Frank's vocation as a financier soon became an office legend, earning him the nickname of 'The Young Master'.[33]

It was at this time that simmering editorial and managerial tensions began to surface. On becoming a sub-editor of the *Daily Guardian* in 1924, George Warnecke's flair with the pen, ability to quickly trim and head a story and innovative suggestions at news conferences had impressed Clyde Packer. Their relationship was cemented when Warnecke, who had been injured in France during the war, collapsed at his desk on one particularly strenuous night. Clyde insisted on driving Warnecke home himself, referred him to his own heart specialist, Dr G. A. Smith, and instructed him not to return to work until he was completely fit. In order to ensure that the dedicated and hardworking Warnecke left the office when the midnight edition came through, Clyde became accustomed to driving him home to Edgecliff himself.

Clyde detested the beliefs of Gandhi, Shaw and Marx and was openly hostile to Roman Catholics. He took something of a paternal interest in Warnecke's intellectual and political development, hoping that his Labor sympathies were just a sign of youthful idealism. Clyde was, by inclination and upbringing, politically conservative. Introduced at an early age to Samuel Smiles's gospel of enterprise and rugged individualism, he had established his own position in society through hard work and cunning, and he was now mixing more and more with leading businessmen and financiers. Clyde presented Warnecke with a battered copy of *Self-Help*, saying that he had been brought up on its teachings; he gave him books and photographs luridly depicting Soviet atrocities in Finland and the Ukraine; and he relieved his sectarian prejudices by tearing up photographs of Catholic celebrations he found on Warnecke's desk. Nevertheless, Clyde tacitly approved of Warnecke having 'potent friends' and contacts in the Australian Workers' Union (AWU), the right-wing union most hostile to the controversial Labor premier Jack Lang.[34]

In the 1920s Labor politics in New South Wales seethed with intrigue and dissension. Voltaire Molesworth, the Labor member for Cumberland, was a senior editorial executive with the *Daily Guardian*. A sandy-haired little larrikin, Molesworth was known for his tenacity, fierce energy and sharp pen. In June 1924, with the support of the AWU, he organised Thomas Mutch's bid for the leadership of the ALP. When the belligerent and ruthless Lang survived by only one vote, he and Molesworth became bitter enemies. Molesworth did not seek preselection for the 1925 election, telling *Smith's Weekly*: 'Labour in New South Wales is torn with strife, intrigue and political corruption … One cannot be loyal to the Labour movement and be loyal to Mr Lang'.[35]

The *Labor Daily*, which was backed by the Miners' Federation, was virtually the only newspaper in Sydney to regularly support Lang. The press, which had been purveying the dangers of bolshevism since 1917, linked the reformist premier with revolution, even after communists were banned from the New South Wales ALP in 1924. Molesworth used the *Daily Guardian* to smear Lang's name and portray him as a dictator. Molesworth was the person responsible for the newspaper delving deeply, and often crudely, into politics at the local, state and federal levels. Clyde Packer himself despised Lang and the *Daily Guardian*'s level of invective increased in 1926 when the premier floated the idea of a newspaper tax. However, even Clyde sometimes felt Molesworth had gone too far: 'We shouldn't have run that story; but what can you do? The boys tell me it was right. I've got to listen to someone'.[36]

Clyde had a personal magnetism that propelled his staff into battalions and set them off as crusaders for his cause. He was committed to ensuring that executives at Smith's Newspapers would be completely loyal to both him and his son. By late 1926 Adam McCay, who had been Clyde's boss on the *Sun*, was editing the *Daily Guardian*; Molesworth was chief-of-staff; Eric Baume had been promoted from chief sub-editor to night editor; and George Warnecke had replaced him as chief sub-editor.[37]

Clyde Packer's allies and protégés, as well as his enemies, were aware that he could be extraordinarily suspicious. During the *Daily Guardian*'s early struggle for survival, Baume had casually asked, 'How are things?' when he found himself in a lift with Packer. Meeting the question with a look of anger, misery and almost hatred, Packer retorted: 'What the hell's it got to do with you? You're lucky to have a bloody job'. Half an hour later, a somewhat abashed Packer had come over to where Baume was sitting, put an arm around his shoulder and gently asked, 'Well, how're you going, son?' Packer orchestrated complex charades to sow seeds of doubt about the ambitions of other senior colleagues in the minds of Warnecke and Baume; he would try to make one executive work harder by using another as a wedge between them.[38] Although they continued to respect and admire Clyde's skills and achievements, his protégés understood that Frank was the heir apparent and that they were, ultimately, dispensable.

As he drove Warnecke through the deserted streets of the Eastern Suburbs in early 1927, Clyde confessed that his heart specialist had advised him to slow down. Dr Smith had concluded that Packer was working too hard, he said: 'My father died at his desk when he was about my age, and his father went exactly the same way before. I guess it's about time to break the chain'. He decided to retreat to Narran Lake, an isolated area between Walgett and Brewarrina in the north-west of New South Wales. Clyde, Frank and their friends often holidayed at Narran Lake, setting up an elaborate series of tents for sleeping and dining and even organising race meetings. Clyde became so popular with the locals that they eventually erected a small monument in his honour. While Packer enjoyed lashings of solid and liquid fare and went kangaroo shooting in the first half of 1927, McKay and Molesworth ran the *Daily Guardian*.[39]

Many employees were pleased to see the back of the demanding and querulous managing editor for a few weeks. Baume wrote a note to Molesworth: 'The staff has asked me to convey to you its appreciation of your control during Mr Packer's absence, and wishes to congratulate you on the harmony which was evident throughout the whole period'.[40]

This harmony was short-lived. Ironically, it was the first newspaper with which Clyde Packer had been associated in Sydney that was responsible for triggering a bizarre dispute with Claude McKay. In April 1927 Beckett's Newspapers Ltd acquired the *Sunday Times*, which was now in dire financial straits, along with the *Referee* and the *Arrow*. A few weeks later Adam McCay, who had edited the *Sunday Times* before joining the *Daily Guardian*, held forth in a hotel lounge. As the evening wore on he met Fred Watson, an old colleague from the *Sunday Times*, and W. J. Beckett. By his own admission, McCay had had 'several' drinks and was in a mood of 'jesting braggadocio'.[41]

On 22 May the *Sunday Times* ran a front-page article entitled 'The Real MacKay' [sic]. It quoted Adam McCay calling Claude McKay a 'moral assassin' who had been a 'heeler' all his life, first to J. C. Williamson and then to James Joynton Smith; McCay was also reported to have said that he would rather lose £10 000 than have Smith's moral character. As McCay did not say anything critical of Clyde Packer and mentioned Smith only in an aside, the two-page article was liberally sprinkled with editorial comments about the management of Smith's Newspapers. The *Sunday Times* alleged that Smith had 'go-got' from the public by devious methods, McKay and Packer had 'go-got' from Smith and the 'most reprehensible paper [*Smith's Weekly*] that ever was published in this state', and McKay had nothing but 'a bank roll and membership of an exclusive golf club to lift him above the worm'.[42]

On Monday an ominous pall hung over the offices of Smith's Newspapers. McCay met Smith in the boardroom and emerged without a job. In a letter to Smith published in Tuesday's *Daily Guardian*, McCay claimed that his words had been grossly distorted and exaggerated. This was not, however, the end of the matter. Warnecke claimed that Clyde Packer wrote a letter stating that McCay's comments had reflected badly on McKay. There were other sources of tension between the three proprietors. Packer believed that the *Daily Guardian* was becoming too sensational and frightening away advertisers. He was also disturbed by the appearance of a controversial book entitled *The Awful Australians*, which was published under the name of the actress Valerie Desmond but was reputed to have been written by McKay; nearly all copies of the book had fallen into Hugh McIntosh's hands.[43] McKay and Smith had recently clashed over Jim Donald's exposé of phony wrestling contests in *Smith's Weekly*, with McKay claiming that Smith had financial links with the wrestling promoter in question.

And so in late May or early June 1927 the trio that had established Smith's Newspapers collapsed. McKay decided to sell his 50 000 shares to Smith for £80 000 and Smith in turn agreed to sell half of McKay's interest to Clyde Packer. The contract stipulated that payment was to be spread over five years and McKay was not to engage in journalism in Australia during this period. At the end of heated discussions during McKay's final board meeting, Packer is reported to have exploded: 'McKay will never come through that door again as long as I am here!'[44] McKay's departure occurred on the eve of the registration of Smith's Victorian Publishing Company Ltd. Smith and Packer became the directors of the company, which was designed to print and publish *Smith's Weekly* in Melbourne for circulation in Victoria, South Australia, Western Australia and Tasmania.[45]

Packer had recently sold 10 000 of his shares in Smith's Newspapers to Lewis Deer, a Welshman who had influential contacts in government departments and the boardrooms of major companies in Sydney. Deer had been public service inspector for the New South Wales government and had contributed a weekly column on schools to the *Daily Telegraph* before joining *Smith's Weekly*. Packer retained the voting rights attached to Deer's shares.

After McKay left Smith's Newspapers, Clyde Packer gave his son a gift of 10 000 shares, entitling him to a seat on the board. This meant that boardroom control was evenly divided between the Smith and Packer families. The directors of the company were James Joynton Smith and his son Thayre, and Clyde and Frank Packer. As Joynton Smith possessed little knowledge of newspaper management, Clyde Packer had effectively secured complete editorial and administrative control of the company.[46]

Frank was also appointed advertising manager of Smith's Newspapers. The young newspaper executive was now more self-conscious than ever about his age. He was not enthusiastic when his parents suggested hosting a party to celebrate his twenty-first birthday on 3 December 1927. When the family agreed that they would simply go out to dinner to mark the occasion, Frank insisted that no candles were to appear on the birthday cake.[47]

After the departures of the two Macs — McCay and McKay — Molesworth became editor of the *Daily Guardian* and Frank Marien, an experienced journalist and artist, was chosen to edit *Smith's Weekly*. Clyde Packer was personally responsible for enticing Marien to resign from the managing editorship of *Truth*. Putting aside his sectarian prejudices, Packer agreed to pay the Irish-Italian Catholic double what anybody else was earning at Smith's Newspapers. Packer drove his team harder and harder, giving them strict instructions to preach optimism and castigate as 'knockers' economists who expressed doubt about Australia's bullish finances. When he dropped Warnecke home at about midnight, Packer became accustomed to calling in for a cup of tea or a drink with George and his wife. He would sink into a soft easy chair and listen attentively as Nora spoke about her father's newspaper career in Dublin and her concert and broadcasting commitments. George and Nora noticed that Clyde Packer looked very weary at times.[48]

Frank's interest in boxing had not, as his mother had hoped, faded away during his spell as a jackeroo. By October 1928 he was competent enough to reach the final of the New South Wales amateur heavyweight championship. However, he was beset by nerves when he walked out in front of the large crowd at the Stadium in Rushcutters Bay. Failing to see the powerful right hook of his opponent, S. Varidel, Packer was knocked to the floor of the ring in the first round. A photograph appeared in the offices of *Smith's Weekly* showing him lying flat on his back unconscious while his second, Colonel R. J. A. Travers, the circulation manager of Smith's Newspapers, waited anxiously for him to get up. Packer never forgave the poet and sub-editor, Kenneth Slessor, for writing the caption 'Mr Frank Packer fighting in the NSW heavyweight championship'.[49]

Humiliated by being knocked out, Packer resolved to contest the title again. On 12 September 1929, weighing just over 81 kilograms (12 stone 11lb), he beat the curiously named C. E. Pick Rang on points in the heavyweight final. The *Sydney Morning Herald* reported that it was 'the most disappointing bout of the evening. Packer occasionally scored with a straight left, but there was not much between the men'.[50] To Ethel's relief, this was the end of her son's boxing career. Frank probably realised that the only way forward was to turn professional. By now he had accepted that his future lay in the publishing world, and he confined his interest in boxing to promotion and administration.

Little more than a fortnight after Frank won the amateur title, his father launched a new paper. According to the notorious *Truth* (which rarely lived up to its name when commenting on the actions of rival newspapers), Smith's Newspapers had begun negotiating the sale of the *Daily Guardian* to Sir Hugh Denison in August 1929. In a clever but very risky move, Smith's Newspapers began publishing the *Sunday Guardian* on 29 September. Its appearance at this time was almost certainly designed to convince the rapacious Denison to offer a generous price for the newspapers that competed with his own morning newspaper, the *Daily Telegraph News Pictorial*, and the *Sunday Sun*.[51]

Selected to edit the *Sunday Guardian*, George Warnecke tried to distance himself from Frank Marien, who regarded himself as editor-in-chief of Smith's Newspapers, and chose a talented and diverse group of contributors. He called on the services of two relative newcomers, W. E. Pidgeon and Arthur Boothroyd, to supplement the illustrators on *Smith's Weekly*; his friend Roy Connolly, who had edited the *Daily Mail* and the *Labor Daily*; W. E. Stanner, who later became a professor of anthropology; and Vera Hamilton, known as 'machine gun Kate' because of her commanding manner. Warnecke, who was delighted by his appointment, might not have been immediately aware of the reasons for the newspaper's launch.[52]

The camps headed by Smith and the Packers on the one hand and Denison on the other began moving their titles and assets around like pawns in a chess game. On 1 October Denison's newspaper interests were merged with those of Sun Newspapers Ltd. Denison's new company, Associated Newspapers Ltd, became responsible for publishing the *Daily Telegraph News Pictorial*, the *Sun*, the *Evening News*, the *Sunday Sun*, the *Sunday Pictorial*, the *Newcastle Sun*, *Woman's Budget*, *Wireless Weekly*, *World's News* and *Sporting and Dramatic News*. Two weeks later, in an effort to increase the pressure on the directors of Associated Newspapers, the annual general meeting of Smith's Newspapers expanded its nominal capital to £1 million.[53]

Fired up by the formation of Associated Newspapers and determined to prevent other publications from competing with his interests, Denison fell for the bait. Between December 1929 and January 1930 a contract was finalised with Smith's Newspapers. Associated Newspapers agreed to give its rival company 400 000 7 per cent preference shares in itself and £175 000 cash in return for the *Guardians*. The launch of the *Sunday Guardian* had been a masterstroke, as the goodwill value of the two newspapers was estimated at £577 470. A spokesman for the Packers later conceded: 'It was a very advantageous sale … and the results exceeded in value very considerably the asset that had been parted with'. Under the agreement, Smith's Newspapers was not to publish a morning, afternoon or Sunday newspaper for twenty-one years. The issued capital of Associated Newspapers now amounted to a staggering £3.6 million.[54]

The staff of the *Guardians* gasped in bewilderment when they learned of the sale. Although the agreement specified that they were to be taken over as a package deal, they wondered what on earth Associated Newspapers would do with such a plethora of titles and employees. Molesworth was heard to exclaim bitterly: 'So this was the future we worked out our guts for!' Clyde Packer gave Warnecke a gold watch as a departing present, along with an apologetic note: 'Dear George, just something to remember us by when you are alone with the wolves. R.C.P.' Eric Baume was the only editorial executive who did not transfer to Associated Newspapers. Clyde Packer called on Eric's ill wife at their flat in Kirribilli and convinced her not to let Eric leave his employ.[55]

For the Smith and Packer families it was a very happy Christmas. All they had to do was keep an eye on *Smith's Weekly* and calculate the financial benefits of their brilliant transaction. In May 1930 Smith's Newspapers bought the *Referee* and the *Arrow* from the publishers of the *Sunday Times*, which had gone into liquidation. Baume was appointed to edit the newspapers.[56]

Now that he was no longer responsible for securing advertising for the *Guardian*, Frank had more time to socialise and play sport. In July he and his sister Kathleen decided to fly back to Sydney instead of making the usual train journey from Kosciuszko. The first air trip to Australian skiing fields had been made only a year earlier, and the flight on which Frank and Kathleen found themselves in 1930 proved both eventful and dangerous. With six other skiing enthusiasts, they had a picnic lunch in Canberra, the nascent national capital, before boarding the aeroplane to Sydney. As the party left Berrindale airstrip, they realised that they were heading into bad weather. The passengers endured a very cold and very wet flight to Goulburn, where they stopped for tea. After leaving Goulburn the aeroplane flew into another heavy bank of clouds, and the pilot, L. H. Holden, had to negotiate alternative routes with what would now be considered as primitive navigational instruments. By the time the aeroplane reached Bulli it was flying along the coast at an altitude of sixty to one hundred metres in pouring rain. Frank and his fellow passengers, who had expected to sit back and enjoy the scenery, breathed a collective sigh of relief when they finally landed at the aerodrome in Sydney. Unfortunately Captain Holden, who had handled this tense situation so ably, was killed in a flying accident not long afterwards.[57]

The first annual general meeting of Smith's Newspapers after the sale of the *Guardians* took place in October 1930. The ordinary shareholders present were James Joynton Smith, who chaired the meeting, Thayre Joynton Smith, Lewis Deer and Clyde and Frank Packer. Some preference shareholders also came, along with the company secretary Norman Bradshaw, who held both ordinary and preference shares. The meeting decided that Smith's Newspapers should retain the cash payment of £175 000 from Associated Newspapers and that the 400 000 shares in Associated Newspapers should be distributed among ordinary shareholders. This transaction entitled the Packers to approximately 173 000 shares in Associated Newspapers. The preference shareholders were not paid out and now had to look to *Smith's Weekly*, the *Referee* and the *Arrow* to produce the profits that they had anticipated would stem from the *Guardians*.[58]

Meanwhile the value of the Packers' shares in Associated Newspapers was plummeting. As the Great Depression ate into advertising receipts, the company started to pay the price for its ludicrous policy of publishing competing morning, afternoon and Sunday titles. Although Molesworth and Warnecke continued to edit the *Guardians*, F. W. Tonkin was given the title of editor-in-chief of the two newspapers. Under the new proprietorship the *Daily Guardian* lost some of its energy and verve; the cover price was increased, decreased and then increased again; the free insurance scheme was abandoned; and as unemployment worsened, the public preferred to buy the *Sydney Morning Herald* for its job advertisements. In December 1930 sales of the *Daily Guardian* dropped to 75 000, while other publications in the stable also struggled.[59]

By early 1931 only the *Sun* and the *Sunday Sun* were making profits and no dividends were being paid to ordinary shareholders. On 10 February an extraordinary general meeting criticised the excessive price paid for the *Guardians*. It also resolved to merge the *Daily Guardian* and the *Daily Telegraph News Pictorial* to create a new *Daily Telegraph*, and to incorporate the *Sunday Pictorial* into the *Sunday Guardian*. The *Evening News* ceased publication a few weeks later. On one particularly boisterous evening during this turbulent period, Molesworth went on a drinking binge with senior colleagues. In the course of a haranguing speech reminiscent of his days in parliament, he accused Clyde Packer of 'sailing him down the river', thumping on the table so emphatically that he broke its glass top. This table happened to be Tonkin's own property and the incident provided him and H. Campbell Jones, the general manager of the *Sun* and managing director of Associated Newspapers, with the excuse they had been seeking to dismiss the waspish Molesworth.[60]

A general air of discontent also pervaded the offices of Smith's Newspapers. There is no record of the circulation of *Smith's Weekly* at this time but, according to Warnecke, sales were being eroded because of the fresher style of the dailies and the competition posed by the salacious *Truth* and *Beckett's Budget*. Frank Packer became bored and restless because working as advertising manager of *Smith's Weekly* did not keep him fully occupied. Marien, who was stalking around the offices of *Smith's Weekly* like a caged tiger, seems to have held secret talks about his position with Jones. Baume was disgruntled with his lot as editor of two moribund sporting weeklies.[61]

Frank Packer and his father were also worried about the continuing decline in the value of their shares in Associated Newspapers. In March 1931 Clyde was invited to join Associated Newspapers as managing editor and a director. The idea was proposed by Fordyce Wheeler, the advertising manager of the *Sun* and a member of the board, who believed that Packer had the experience, skills and incentive needed to stave off the company's collapse. Denison swallowed hard before accepting the suggestion, while Jones, the current managing editor, was naturally horrified by the prospect. On 9 March Packer signed a provisional agreement making him managing editor for five years. However, he decided to delay joining Associated Newspapers until September as he realised that attempting to untangle the rival vested interests in the company would place an added burden on his already weakened heart.[62]

While Packer retreated to his outback camp, the board of Associated Newspapers fractured over who should take responsibility for the company's failures. There were two factions, centred around Denison on the one hand and Jones on the other. In early May Jones, the vice-chairman Sidney Snow, R. H. Gordon and Harold Baldwin resigned from the board, and Jones gave twelve months' notice of his intention to step down as managing editor. Clyde Packer, who was unable to leave the retreat due to torrential rain, received regular wires from his son informing him of the latest developments. Extant telegrams reveal a degree of financial maturity remarkable for a twenty-four-year-old. Frank dissected the implications of boardroom decisions and fissures in minute detail and monitored the way in which different newspapers were being used to advance certain interests. Clyde was initially frustrated by being trapped in the bush but, after receiving his son's detailed and shrewd wires over several days, accepted that there was no reason why he should rush back to Sydney. During a break in the rain on 18 May, Frank managed to fly in and out of Walgett, on Smith's suggestion, to discuss with his father a libel case involving *Smith's Weekly*.[63]

Clyde's holiday came to an abrupt end on 5 June when he received a telegram from Frank saying that Jones and the other outgoing directors had called an extraordinary general meeting and that Denison wanted to have a meeting with him. On returning to Sydney and talking with Denison, Clyde arranged for shareholders and proxies to stack the meeting. He also ensured that the accountants Frederick J. Smith and Wilfred E. Johnson, whose clients included Smith's Newspapers, assailed Jones for the decline in the market value of shares in Associated Newspapers. Clyde even persuaded Molesworth to attend the meeting to scold Jones for interfering with the *Daily Guardian*.[64]

On 12 June hundreds of shareholders had to be turned away because King's Hall in Sydney's Hunter Street was bursting at the seams. After all four former directors explained why they had resigned, Jones tried to defend himself against Molesworth's verbal assault. *Newspaper News* entitled its report about the meeting '1000 Shareholders Take Part in Greatest Duel in Newspaper History … Urgent, Bitter, Intriguing, Uproarious Denunciations'. At the end of the meeting, which lasted nearly three hours, an overwhelming vote of confidence was passed in Denison. Sir Graham Waddell, D. W. Roxborough and F. H. Tout, who had strong connections with the pastoral industry and the banks, were appointed to fill the vacancies on the board.[65]

Since the annual general meeting of Smith's Newspapers in October 1930, there had been murmurs in business and political circles that Smith and the Packers had a moral duty to recompense disaffected preference shareholders. On 7 September 1931 Frank wrote a long, clear letter to his father, who was still debating whether or not he should join Associated Newspapers. Frank maintained that Clyde and Joynton Smith would be 'insane' to return some of their shares in Associated Newspapers to Smith's Newspapers. The young man was adamant that there was only one thing to do: 'go to the source of our trouble and set it right'. If Clyde moved to Associated Newspapers and succeeded in 'rehabilitating' the company, Frank wrote, the shareholders in Smith's Newspapers would benefit as well. If, on the other hand, Associated Newspapers collapsed, the Packers would 'lose everything'. Even though Clyde had spent years establishing his formidable newspaper career and his family's fortune, he seems to have needed this letter to convince him that he should tackle the task of reviving the tottering Denison empire. On 9 September he signed the ratifying agreement with Associated Newspapers making him managing editor, leaving H. Campbell Jones without a job. But Clyde chose not to be appointed as a director, preferring to bide his time until he, or perhaps even Frank, was elected to the board.[66]

Clyde left *Smith's Weekly* on amicable terms. The newspaper headed its report of the move 'From the Smallest to the Biggest Job in Australian Journalism in 27 Years'. It labelled his remarkable career 'a most amazing phenomenon in the history of Australian newspaper publishing. He has touched nothing that he has not bettered'. A more independent observer, *Newspaper News*, offered a no less generous assessment: 'Essentially, R. C. Packer is a newspaper builder, as distinct from a successful manager who comes into a business merely to "carry on". One newspaper after another has leapt ahead under his hand'.[67]

Immediately after Clyde Packer joined Associated Newspapers, however, his relationship with Smith's Newspapers broke down. Claude McKay returned from England to discover that the *Guardian*s had been sold, the remaining titles in the Smith's Newspapers stable were losing money and the preference shareholders had been left in a perilous situation. Although he no longer had a financial stake in Smith's Newspapers, McKay retained a paternal interest in the welfare of *Smith's Weekly* and he agreed to rejoin the company as managing editor. Clyde Packer — still a major shareholder in Smith's Newspapers — repeated his earlier decree that he would never again work with McKay.[68]

Smith bought the ordinary shares of Clyde and Frank Packer and gave them an indemnity against any claims that disgruntled preference shareholders might make against the distribution. McKay persuaded Smith to return 80 000 preference shares in Associated Newspapers and £20 000 cash to Smith's Newspapers, but the Packers refused to do likewise.[69] It was a sad end to a remarkable partnership and, as we shall see, the Packers' controversial share dealings were to provide their political enemies with ammunition.

Clyde's influence immediately became apparent at Associated Newspapers. He ensured that the principal publications had a freer typographic display, featured more photographic material and ran optimistic financial stories. The *Sunday Guardian* was amalgamated with the *Sunday Sun*, already the most successful Sunday newspaper in Australia. Packer also appointed his allies to key executive positions: Eric Baume transferred from Smith's Newspapers to become his personal assistant and George Warnecke was chosen to edit the combined Sunday newspaper.[70]

At about this time a youngster who wanted to be a copyboy approached Packer. Since leaving school Alan Reid had held various knockabout jobs in the bush and worked as a lift driver and an office boy. One day he ran into a copyboy on the *Sun* who told him he should try to join the newspaper, as lucrative games of poker were played all day on the roof. Reid somehow managed to score himself an interview with Packer, who assumed that he was intent on obtaining a cadetship. Packer pronounced: 'Boy, I get so many applications for cadet reporterships that if the applicants stood here, they'd extend down to the [Circular] Quay. I tell you what I'll do, I'll give you a job as a copyboy'.

After a while Packer rang a bell summoning Reid into his office. The 'snotty-nosed boy' demurred when he was offered a cadetship on the *Sun*, as he was earning more playing poker than he would as a cadet. Displaying remarkable patience and forbearance, Packer asked: 'Got any people?'

> 'Yes,' replied Reid.
> 'Mother and father?'
> 'My father's dead, my mother's alive.'
> 'Do you live with her?'
> 'Yes.'
> 'Make me a promise. Before you reject this, go home and discuss it with her.'

Mrs Reid was naturally thrilled to learn that her son had been offered a permanent job at the height of the Depression, and so Alan became a cadet on the *Sun*.[71]

Clyde Packer's dealings with Reid indicate that he had a special flair for spotting and nurturing potential; as we shall see, Reid was to emerge as Australia's most influential political correspondent. Clyde's response also says something about the importance he placed on parents guiding and mentoring their children. Clyde had joined Associated Newspapers with the intention of installing his own son as an instant executive, prominent shareholder and potential director. Frank had taken an office adjoining the Stock Exchange following his departure from Smith's Newspapers.[72] He realised that it was only a matter of time before he was summoned to work alongside his father once again.

4
El Dorado

R. C. Packer decided to take a break from work before bringing his son over to join him at Associated Newspapers. One of Clyde's main sources of relaxation was sailing in the *Morna*, the magnificent twenty-one-metre cutter he had recently acquired. Sir Alexander MacCormick, a prominent surgeon, had named the yacht in honour of his daughter; J. M. Hardie had briefly owned the yacht before it passed into Packer's hands.[1]

Packer, who by 1930 was a rear-commodore of the Royal Prince Alfred Yacht Club, conducted his sailing pursuits with the same vigour as his professional endeavours. In a spectacular race on 8 November 1930, the *Morna* snatched victory in the Royal Sydney Yacht Squadron's Fairfax Cup. Clyde won other titles, including the Basin Cup and the Albert Gold Cup in 1932, and was often joined by Frank on Sydney Harbour.[2]

In early January 1932 Clyde took his yacht down to Jervis Bay, on the New South Wales south coast. Here he met E. G. Theodore, who had been treasurer and deputy prime minister in the Scullin Labor government until a few weeks earlier.[3] Although Frank might not have been on the *Morna*, over the coming months he was to find his father's acquaintance a political and business ally of considerable worth.

The son of a Rumanian immigrant, Edward Granville Theodore had spent his early years working as a gardener, farmhand, timbergetter and miner in South Australia, Western Australia and Broken Hill. In 1906 he went to northern Queensland, where he became involved with the labour movement and was appointed state president of the AWU; by 1919 he was the Labor premier. He surrendered the premiership in 1925, but failed in his bid to win the federal seat of Herbert. Theodore — intelligent, self-educated, economically astute, handsome and autocratic — then decided to seek a seat in New South Wales. Although he quickly fell foul of Jack Lang, Theodore won the federal seat of Dalley in 1927. The sitting member's decision to withdraw from preselection gave rise to allegations of bribery and culminated in a royal commission.[4] Although Theodore was found not guilty, the episode tarnished his reputation in some quarters.

In 1929 Theodore became deputy prime minister and treasurer in James Scullin's government. The following July another royal commission found that Theodore had, while Queensland premier, conspired to engineer the sale to the state government for £40 000 of mines at Mungana said to be worth only £10 000. Theodore was forced to resign from his cabinet positions, but six months later, as the economic crisis worsened, Scullin successfully pushed for his reinstatement.[5] Between February and March 1931 there was an open split between the New South Wales and federal executives of the ALP. Ever the populist, Premier Lang maintained that payments to British bondholders should be suspended altogether, while Theodore proposed that £18 million of unemployment relief works and farm assistance should be financed by an expansion of the unbacked note issue. Soon after being expelled from the New South Wales branch of the ALP, Theodore was found not guilty in civil proceedings initiated over Mungana. The Scullin government was decimated at the December 1931 poll and Theodore lost his seat to a Langite.[6]

The newspapers headed by Clyde Packer were unrelentingly hostile to Lang. When Packer left *Smith's Weekly* in September 1931, it was running headlines such as 'Fierce Burst of Power Without Balanced Mind to Control', 'Study on Border Line of Paranoia' and 'Strong Savage Passions Rage Unrestrained'. Packer had links with two of the extremist right-wing organisations that were flourishing in New South Wales at this time. He was one of a number of businessmen who, disillusioned with the Lang government and parliamentary democracy, supported Charles Hardy's Riverina Movement. Hardy, a successful timber merchant based in Wagga Wagga, advocated replacing state parliaments with provincial councils and threatened that the Riverina would secede. The historian Andrew Moore writes that Hardy's supporters championed him as 'the "Cromwell of the Riverina", a Mussolini-style Messiah, who, like another "lowly carpenter", had returned to his earthly kingdom' for judgment day. The Riverina Movement was gradually subsumed by the parliamentary Country Party and in August 1931 Hardy became chairman of the combined United Country Movement. At the federal poll a few months later he was elected to the Senate as a United Country Party candidate.

It has been suggested that the Riverina Movement might have had a secret paramilitary arm not unlike Eric Campbell's New Guard.[7] According to George Warnecke, both Clyde and Frank Packer had friends in the New Guard, and an army intelligence report in October 1931 described Clyde as a member of the organisation. The *Daily Telegraph* admired the 'patriotism' of the New Guard, reported on its rallies quite extensively and gave tacit support to those members who forcibly broke up left-wing meetings. However, it is highly doubtful that Clyde himself was ever really a member of the organisation; if he had been, there would have been no reason for him to order Eric Baume to join the New Guard to get firsthand knowledge of its operations. And the *Daily Telegraph* expressed some misgivings about the organisation's militaristic character, declaring that most Australians did not want communism, revolution or 'the Fascism of the New Guard'.[8]

When Theodore and Clyde Packer conferred below decks on the *Morna* in January 1932, they had a number of things in common. Each enjoyed a close friendship with George Warnecke; when Nora Hill appeared in the role of Gilda in a production of *Rigoletto* in May 1932, Theodore presided over a reception in her honour. Packer, Theodore and Warnecke all despised Jack Lang. Theodore, who had become a director of the Queensland *Worker* in 1914, had vowed to expend his energies in fields other than politics when he was toppled at the 1931 election. It is possible that Theodore and Packer had met previously: Theodore seems to have tried to bolster the circulation of *Smith's Weekly* while visiting London in 1923 and he might have conferred with Packer in the mid 1920s when he was looking for a seat in New South Wales.[9] Just two months after their encounter in January 1932, Theodore and the Packers were to join forces to fight a common enemy.

Clyde Packer's immediate goal was to instal his son in the headquarters of Associated Newspapers. The pair had been working closely together since Frank was a teenager, and it had always been Clyde's intention to establish his son as a newspaper executive and proprietor. Tired and ill, Clyde now needed to tap into Frank's youthful verve and drive more than ever. Frank, for his part, adored his father and revered his achievements. Although he lacked Clyde's journalistic and creative flair, Frank had an astute business mind, an ability to sniff out dissenting views and the incentive to help advance his father's interests at Associated Newspapers.

In mid January 1932 Clyde gave Frank an office, a desk and a telephone at the company's headquarters. Hugh Denison and Fordyce Wheeler were prepared to accept the appointments of George Warnecke and Eric Baume, even if they did represent 'Smithification', but they drew the line at Frank Packer. Denison and Wheeler were grooming their own sons to attain high office in the hierarchy of Associated Newspapers: Reginald Denison was a director and company secretary, his brother Leslie was head of the mechanical department, and Wheeler's son was working alongside him in the advertising section. Both families were worried about what would happen if 'The Young Master' got his foot in the door.[10]

On 18 January, a few days after Frank bobbed up at Associated Newspapers, Clyde wrote a long memo to the board. It was a wide-ranging missive, criticising the company for, among other things, distributing too many free copies of its newspapers, using extravagant stationery, refusing to close the unprofitable Newcastle office, indulging in overstaffing and not being fully committed to making the *Daily Telegraph* competitive with the great *Sydney Morning Herald*. The memo also dared to suggest that Hugh Denison should take some responsibility for the company's string of failures, and criticised waste in the departments headed by Fordyce Wheeler and Reg Denison.[11]

Not surprisingly, this highly inflammatory memo was used as a weapon against the Packers. In a letter to Clyde on 30 January, Denison remarked that it was strange that he would want his son to join the company when he claimed it was overstaffed:

> I understand that you have been using him [Frank] in the last few days helping you with certain work which affords some relief to you, but, before you take any steps towards arranging for his definitely joining our service, I would like the matter discussed in full at our next Board meeting ...

After the meeting on 3 February, Denison wrote Clyde a formal letter informing him that the directors were unanimous in their belief that no further additions should be made to the staff under 'present circumstances'.

In a handwritten letter marked 'private', Denison tried to reassure Clyde that the board was 'entirely sympathetic to you both as regards your health and the desire to help you as much as possible'. But, he went on, some of the directors felt that the idea of using Frank 'as a sort of detective' was not conducive to office harmony. Denison concluded the letter by subtly reminding Clyde that it was in his own interests to continue working for the good of Associated Newspapers: 'Though I know you will be disappointed, I am sure that it will not affect your desire to do all you can for the best interests of the company and its shareholders'.[12]

Clyde Packer had made a rare tactical error by not accepting the earlier offer of a seat on the Associated Newspapers board. When Frank was forced out of the company on 3 February 1932, his father lost his most loyal and important ally. According to the voluble Baume, relations between Clyde and Wheeler were now so poisonous that they both had to have bodyguards and carry revolvers.[13]

Frank returned to his office in Stanton House near the Stock Exchange, where he had considerable success speculating in shares, and linked up with two unknown inventors. He established a company called Seal Tite Pty Ltd, which had the patent for a waterproof nail for sealing corrugated iron roofs. He also backed an invention designed to produce normal lighting from neon tubes, which at that time were used only for colour displays. Frank even considered the possibility of launching a new Sunday newspaper in Sydney.[14] These interests were, however, ephemeral; just six weeks after leaving Associated Newspapers, Frank was called upon to help his father defeat a plot that had the potential to bankrupt his family.

In late February 1932 Jack Lang banned *Daily Telegraph* journalists from entering his office and ordered his ministers not to supply any information to the newspaper. The *Daily Telegraph* had recently suggested that the government was giving undue preference in its advertising to the *Labor Daily*, of which Lang was a shareholder and a director. G. H. Williams, chairman of the ALP's Propaganda Committee, complained of the *Daily Telegraph*'s 'mendacious reports, faked descriptions, doctored photographs, lying headlines and unfair comment'.[15]

On the evening of Thursday 17 March Lang suspended standing orders to rush a bill through the Legislative Assembly in one sitting. The Companies Amendment (Preference Shareholders) Bill was designed to prevent ordinary shareholders from disposing of their assets without the assent of preference shareholders. The bill was to be made retrospective to 1 July 1929 in order to bring the October 1930 transaction into its ambit. Lang aimed at forcing the Packers to return their shares in Associated Newspapers to the preference shareholders of Smith's Newspapers, saying that 'the smallest amount of justice that can be done to the people who supplied the preference capital for Smith's Ltd. is that Mr. [R. C.] Packer and his colleagues should restore to them what has been stolen … Here is an opportunity for members to show that they are game to make a thief return his ill-gotten gains, to make a burglar drop his loot'.[16]

Lang also alleged that Clyde Packer was an influential ally of the deputy leader of the Opposition, (later Sir) Bertram Stevens: 'the man ... has, through the agency of Mr. Stevens, become practically the leader of the Opposition'.[17] Packer might well have established links with the United Australia Party (UAP), just as he flirted with the Riverina Movement and, through his new associate E. G. Theodore, the federal ALP. Although Packer was something of an opportunist, principally interested in commercial advantage,[18] he genuinely supported private enterprise and, like so many business and publishing figures in New South Wales, regarded Lang as a dangerous socialist and megalomaniac.

In the debate on the bill, the leader of the Country Party, Lieutenant-Colonel M. F. Bruxner, argued that parliament should not be used to settle squabbles between two newspaper proprietors. *Smith's Weekly* had been markedly more sympathetic to Lang since Clyde Packer's departure and some observers believed that Sir James Joynton Smith was behind the premier's actions. Under the bill, Smith would be required to return to Smith's Newspapers the shares he had retained in Associated Newspapers. However, once the preference shareholders had been paid out, Smith and the other ordinary shareholders would be entitled to the balance.[19]

Despite the Opposition's vociferous protests, the bill passed the Legislative Assembly in the early hours of Friday 18 March. That afternoon a petition from Clyde and Frank Packer was read to the Legislative Council and their counsel, J. A. Ferguson, spoke at the bar of the house for two and a half hours. Ferguson argued that changes to company law required 'fair and deliberate consideration'; pointed out that as Clyde Packer had been out of town, Smith himself had conferred with lawyers and accountants about the terms of the transaction; and maintained that all shareholders had been entitled to attend the vital annual general meeting of Smith's Newspapers in October 1930. Ferguson's petition, which intimated that Lang was working in cahoots with Smith, insisted that the bill, if passed, would bankrupt the Packers and force Clyde to forfeit his position at Associated Newspapers. Claude McKay entered the fray, writing a long article in *Smith's Weekly* about the history of Smith's Newspapers. Readers were told that justice would be done only if the bill were passed: 'Glaring cases justify drastic remedies'.[20]

At the same time, Clyde and Frank Packer began conducting a frantic behind-the-scenes lobbying operation. Their only hope lay in the fact that the allies of Theodore and the AWU held the balance of power in the Upper House. Warnecke's close friend J. F. Higgins, a Labor MLC and former journalist, acted as an intermediary between the Packers and the members of the Upper House. Warnecke helped write the speeches of members who opposed the bill and, according to Lang, one 'leading member of the *Guardian* turned up with a suitcase in his hand'. Baume recalls that for weeks 'the happenings became like a chapter in some brightly written history of Chicago'. The bill lapsed when parliament was adjourned until 26 April, and on 13 May the Lang government was dismissed by the governor Sir Philip Game.[21]

This extraordinary piece of legislation revealed the lengths to which Jack Lang was prepared to go to punish newspaper critics. While working alongside his father in the 1920s, Frank Packer had learned how to assess and deal with shifting boardroom allegiances. In 1932 he discovered how closely the newspaper and political arenas intersected, and just how vulnerable corporate successes could be to hostile outside forces. These were lessons he did not forget.

The Lang episode might have tarnished the Packer name in some circles, but it left the family with its fortune intact. Frank and Kathleen, both young and quite good looking, began to be involved with glamorous charity and social functions. In 1932 the *Home* featured a portrait of Kathleen alongside photographic studies of other beautiful and wealthy maidens from Sydney's Eastern Suburbs. Frank's closest friends were Ralph McFadyen, who came from a large and hospitable family in Bellevue Hill; James Bancks, the creator of the *Ginger Meggs* comic strip and the husband of Jessie Tait of the Tait theatrical dynasty; and James D. MacLeod, who became managing director of the leading pastoral firm Pitt Son & Badgery Ltd. Frank played polo with MacLeod and often stayed with him in his flat in the exclusive Astor apartment block in Macquarie Street.[22]

In 1932 Frank, who during his childhood had tinkered with Lawrence Hargrave's flying contraptions, managed to combine his interest in flying with raising funds for a worthy cause. He and eleven other sportsmen and aviators agreed to sponsor the 'Lady of the Air' Tourney in aid of the Benevolent Society of New South Wales. Each sponsor was expected to raise money for five young women; the girl in each group who sent in the highest amount of money was given a seat in an aeroplane in the 'Lady of the Air' race. It is doubtful whether Frank himself flew one of the twelve aeroplanes that left the aptly named Hargrave Park at Warwick Farm on 20 August.[23]

Although Frank had been speculating in shares and flirting with inventions since his departure from Associated Newspapers, he was essentially unemployed. In the second half of 1932 he again seized an opportunity to 'go bush'. Ernestine Hill, who had worked as a sub-editor on *Smith's Weekly*, had recently begun writing travel articles for Associated Newspapers. Her series of sensationalist articles about the discovery of gold in the Granites in the Northern Territory contributed to a gold rush and a stock market boom. Clyde Packer reasoned that investors and prospectors were entitled to a more detailed and authoritative description of the field, and his readers would be interested in reports on an outback quest. Associated Newspapers, in conjunction with Melbourne's Herald & Weekly Times (HWT) group, sponsored an expedition to the Granites headed by the geologist Dr C. T. Madigan. Eric Baume joined the party to despatch reports to the *Sun* and affiliated newspapers.[24]

Frank Packer, who had recently invested in a tin mining company in Malaya, decided to join the expedition, which held out the prospect of adventure, excitement and, just possibly, great riches. Madigan was less than thrilled when Frank and a 'mining expert' from Sydney were tacked on to the expedition at the last minute. On 13 October 1932 the group boarded the train for the 1440-kilometre trip from Adelaide to Alice Springs.[25] Liquor flowed and jealous competition as well as excitement ran high. Madigan's party was regarded with suspicion when the other adventurers on the train discovered that the mining man had already been in the area before and reported on a 'show' near the Granites. The journey became a nightmare after the train left Terowrie, as passengers had to endure five hours of being jerked and rattled around due to the state of the railway gauges. Conditions improved when they passed through Quorn, 320 kilometres north of Adelaide, and the train continued through the night. However, heavy rains and frequent stops meant that the party did not reach town until after 10 p.m. They wearily collapsed into bed at the hotel, knowing that they needed their rest before embarking on the next and most arduous leg of the journey.[26]

In Alice Springs Madigan and his contingent made final arrangements for the 600-kilometre trip to the Granites. They bought and salted 45 kilograms of beef, acquired a case of oranges to prevent scurvy and packed flour, rice, oatmeal, sugar, tea, condensed and skim milk, jam, onions, ham and tinned fruit. Madigan and the head driver Simon Reiff estimated that they would not be able to get fresh water until they reached Thompson's Rockhole, 540 kilometres north-west of Alice Springs. This meant they had to take ninety litres of water, along with petrol for 1280 kilometres, on their two trucks.[27] The road party was to be accompanied by an aeroplane under the care of Frank William Follett, who had trained as an engineer and worked with the Department of Civil Aviation. The pilot appears to have been the brother of Evelyn Mary Follett, Clyde Packer's long-serving and intensely loyal secretary.[28]

But images of Frank Packer were never captured by the small camera lent to the group by the director of Cinesound, Ken G. Hall. On 23 October Frank's name was absent from the Sunday Sun's list of the four men who were preparing to leave for the Granites at dawn that day. While sweltering in Alice Springs in temperatures of about 45° Celsius (114° Fahrenheit), the group had held stormy meetings about the involvement of Frank and the mining man from Sydney in the expedition. Just at the time the two men agreed to withdraw from the party, Frank seems to have received a wire asking him to return to Sydney immediately.[29] Clyde Packer and George Warnecke had become aware that a labour newspaper was in dire financial straits. Another El Dorado beckoned.

Since the 1890s sections of the Australian labour movement had aspired to publish their own newspapers in order to counter the misrepresentations of the 'capitalist press'. In 1910 the AWU formed Labor Papers Ltd with the intention of launching a daily newspaper. The company had a number of problems to contend with over the next twenty years: unions did not subscribe enough capital; the Tasmanian *World* proved an expensive failure; and in Sydney, Labor Papers was unable to broker a compromise with Jack Lang and the publishers of the *Labor Daily*.[30]

The split between the New South Wales and federal branches of the ALP gave Labor Papers the impetus it needed to launch a newspaper in Sydney. In April 1931 Theodore and other representatives of the federal ALP asked the directors of Labor Papers to 'seriously consider the publication of a newspaper at an early date'. And so, on 26 October 1931, the *World* finally made its debut from premises in Macdonell House in Pitt Street. Theodore helped ensure that Monty Grover, one of the most experienced and able journalists in Australia, was appointed editor. Warnecke's friend, the Labor MLC J. F. Higgins, was made 'advisory editor' in order to direct the afternoon newspaper's political line.[31]

Although the *World* was bright, well illustrated and witty, it began losing money almost immediately. As the newspaper was designed to promote one section of the labour movement, it did not attract enough readers or advertising revenue. In January 1932 rumours started to circulate that Theodore, who had lost his seat only a few weeks earlier, was interested in joining the board of Labor Papers. By August the *World* had accrued losses of £120 000. Realising that severance payments could amount to £10 000, the directors desperately began looking around for another organisation to take over the publication of the newspaper. They called on Theodore, with his considerable financial experience and business contacts, to help find a solution to the crisis. On 11 October Theodore and two directors were despatched to meet with the Chamber of Manufactures to ascertain whether it would be interested in taking over the *World*. The following day Theodore reported that the organisation 'could not entertain any proposal for carrying on the newspaper'.[32]

Warnecke, who was a friend of both Theodore and Higgins and had contacts in the AWU, became aware of the *World*'s plight. Knowing only too well how anxious Associated Newspapers was to circumvent new competition, he developed a daring scheme. He decided that a syndicate should acquire the *World* and announce that it intended to convert the title into a penny newspaper. If all things went to plan, Hugh Denison, who published the *Sun* at 1½d, would panic and offer to take over the new paper.

Warnecke outlined his scheme to Clyde Packer when they met for afternoon tea at the Hotel Australia. Although he was immediately attracted by the plan's ingenuity, Clyde was in a difficult position as he was still an executive at Associated Newspapers. He decided that his son would be better placed to broker the deal, preferably in conjunction with that financial genius E. G. Theodore. While Warnecke tried to get an urgent wire to Frank on his way to the Granites, Clyde Packer played for time.[33]

On 21 October Clyde walked into Denison's office to say that he was disturbed about something that was happening in connection with the *World*. Frank, his father commented mysteriously, had joined forces with Theodore but was refusing to reveal any details of their intentions.[34] On 1 November Theodore obtained a £100 nine-day option for a one-year lease, with the possibility of an extension, on the *World* and that portion of Macdonell House occupied by it for £4000. Theodore is reputed to have met the AWU's Jack Barnes and Ted Grayndler in a pub and pulled a pound note from his pocket, which he paid as a deposit, and produced another note on which the vendors wrote out their receipt.[35]

By now Frank, after making a frantic dash halfway across the country, seems to have arrived back in Sydney to meet Theodore. To increase the pressure on Denison, Frank gave an exclusive interview to *Newspaper News*. On 1 November a front-page story reported that he and Theodore intended to launch a new afternoon paper, probably priced at a penny, modelled on the London evening dailies. Two days later, Frank's father telephoned Denison in Melbourne to confirm the news. Clyde claimed that although he 'was using every endeavour to block this move', Frank and Theodore remained committed to publishing a penny newspaper. Clyde asked Denison to return to Sydney, as matters had to be 'fixed up' quickly to prevent the launch of the new title. Denison reputedly 'blanched when informed by his managing editor, Packer Senior, that irrepressible Packer Junior, in cohorts with E. G. Theodore, legendary wizard of finance, had snatched the *World* from its deathbed and were already preparing to give it blood transfusions'.[36]

On 4 November Reg Denison, Fordyce Wheeler and Colonel Jack Travers, now the circulation manager of Associated Newspapers, conferred in Clyde Packer's office. Wheeler argued that the *Sun* should continue to be sold at 1½d because it would almost certainly be bigger than the new paper; he believed that a title supported and manipulated by Theodore so soon after his major electoral rebuff could not succeed in New South Wales.[37] However, Hugh Denison and a majority of the directors were convinced that the cover price of the *Sun* would have to be cut for it to compete with a cheaper newcomer, and estimated that this would cost the company £30 000 per year.

On Sunday 6 November the board of Associated Newspapers authorised Denison to prevent the publication of the new paper. He met Theodore that evening and scheduled a further meeting for the following day.[38] Only now, when a payout from Associated Newspapers seemed guaranteed, did Theodore and Frank Packer register a new company. On Monday Sydney Newspapers Ltd was registered with an authorised capital of £150 000; paid-up capital, however, was only £30 000. Frank, who became managing director, and Theodore, who was named chairman, invested £5000 each. Warnecke acquired 1000 £1 shares and the remainder of the paid-up capital was borrowed from friends and business associates.[39]

When he met Denison on Monday, Theodore agreed that Sydney Newspapers would not publish a new paper in return for compensation on 'certain terms'. However, negotiations were broken off the next day when Theodore and Frank demanded higher compensation payments. After returning to his office, Denison received a telephone call from Clyde Packer asking where things stood. A few minutes later the deputy chairman of Associated Newspapers, Sir John Butters, told Denison he had seen Frank Packer coming up in the lift. Denison and Butters realised that Frank must have been with his father when the latter made his telephone call.[40] Nevertheless, the directors of Associated Newspapers remained committed to circumventing the publication of a new rival to the *Sun*.

Later that afternoon Clyde Packer told Denison that it was foolish to suspend negotiations for the sake of 'a thousand or two' pounds. He remarked that Frank was 'up on his toes' and intended to go right ahead with plans for the new paper. At least one commentator has questioned whether Sydney Newspapers ever intended to launch the *Star*.[41] However, Frank seems to have felt that establishing the newspaper would provide him with an opportunity to prove his publishing abilities to his father; at the very least, making sound provisions for the *Star* would provide him with a safety net if Clyde's plotting failed.

Frank held two meetings with the secretary of the Newsagents' Association to discuss how its members would feel about handling a newspaper for a penny. He also made arrangements for a cable service to run for twelve months.[42] On Wednesday 9 November the *World* announced that 'an entirely new paper' would be launched the following Thursday. In order to counter criticisms from the likes of Fordyce Wheeler, the *World* emphasised that the new title, to be known as the *Star*, would be 'entirely free of political affiliations'. Warnecke left Associated Newspapers to edit the paper, which was advertised on B-class (commercial) radio stations.[43]

On 9 November, the day the *World* was taken over by Sydney Newspapers, Denison again conferred with his board. The directors asked their chairman to reopen negotiations with Sydney Newspapers at an increased price. Immediately after the meeting, Clyde Packer called on Denison and offered to help resolve the matter. Denison agreed that Clyde should see his son and Theodore and offer them compensation of no more than £82 500. Later that afternoon Clyde telephoned Denison at the Rose Bay Golf Club to say that he had had 'great trouble' in concluding a deal with Frank and Theodore. The pair had finally agreed not to publish an afternoon or a Sunday newspaper within 300 miles (480 kilometres) of Sydney for three years in return for £86 500; they had accepted a letter on Denison's behalf committing him to the agreement.[44]

Denison was furious when he learned that his managing editor had committed Associated Newspapers to paying Sydney Newspapers £4000 more than it had been prepared to offer. Worse was to come. When Clyde Packer produced the agreement on Thursday morning, Denison swiftly objected to two clauses. One seems to have specified that Theodore was to contribute articles to the *Daily Telegraph*, but neither he nor the Packers pursued the matter. However, Clause 9 proved to be a real sticking point. It provided that: 'Associated Newspapers Ltd. will offer to Mr Frank Packer within one month of the signing of this agreement a position in the office of Associated Newspapers Ltd. in Sydney in keeping with his general status or as an alternative Mr Frank Packer may proceed to London as the sole Advertising Representative for Associated Newspapers Ltd in London'.[45]

On 12 November Associated Newspapers paid Sydney Newspapers a first instalment of £12 000 on the understanding that the *World* would be closed down within seventy-two hours. The newspaper ceased publication two days later.[46] Meanwhile, George Waddell, Associated Newspapers' solicitor, considered the implications of Clause 9. He hoped it would soon emerge that the clause had been included in the agreement simply to soothe the wounded feelings of Frank Packer. But if Frank insisted on its literal application, Waddell concluded that the board would probably be entitled to terminate its contract with his father.[47]

On 25 November Frank met Waddell. The young man's feelings of anger and humiliation about his dismissal from Associated Newspapers, as well as his confidence in the business world, quickly became apparent. He declared,

> I am not disposed to help the Board in any way as I consider that I have been very badly treated. I would not have entered into the agreement if that clause had not been included. It has been included and I expect it to be honoured by the Board in the spirit and the letter … I reserve to myself an absolutely free hand as to whether I accept it [the offer of a position] or whether I don't.

Waddell told Frank that insisting on his legal rights under the clause could place his father in a difficult situation. Frank, however, observed that it would be a good thing if Clyde were paid out to leave the company; indeed, he felt so strongly about this point that he said he would pay half the compensation himself to see his father free of his present worries.[48]

The directors of Associated Newspapers were determined not to allow the Packers to work closely together again. On 28 November, claiming that no position was available in Sydney, Denison reluctantly offered to appoint Frank as sole advertising representative in London on a salary of £1500 per annum. Frank immediately wrote a letter maintaining that he should also be offered a position in the Sydney office. The matter was then handed over to Clyde Packer who, under the terms of the letter of agreement between Associated Newspapers and Sydney Newspapers, was responsible for acting as arbiter in the event of any dispute. On 8 December Frank curtly informed Denison that he had decided to waive his rights under Clause 9.[49]

Why had Frank suddenly backed down after digging in his heels on this issue for a month? It seems unlikely that he had ever seriously considered going to London; leaving his ailing father to work on his own in such a fraught atmosphere had probably never been an option. As Frank himself intimated, his main goal had been to assert his superior bargaining power in his dealings with the board that had treated him and his father so harshly. Clyde might well have realised that the company would never offer Frank a post in Sydney and that even if it did, the young man's working environment would be made an absolute misery. Frank might also have decided that his father's position would be completely untenable if he insisted on pursuing the claim.

In any case, Frank and Theodore had executed a deal that made them both extremely wealthy in their own right. In less than ten days they had turned a £100 option into £86 500 — now equivalent to $5 million. The 280 employees of the *World* were not so lucky, finding themselves out of work in the depths of the Depression. Sydney Newspapers paid printers two weeks' salary and members of the Australian Journalists' Association (AJA) one month's salary in lieu of notice. Labor Papers also found itself responsible for some severance payouts. Over the next few years the company, the AWU and their political allies used every possible opportunity to condemn the piratical actions of Sydney Newspapers. Unionists who felt that Frank Packer and E. G. Theodore had slighted them would find a way to exact revenge during the Second World War, and Packer was to learn that the Australian labour movement has a very long memory.

Frank Packer flirted with a number of business ventures after securing the payout from Associated Newspapers in November 1932. He announced that Sydney Newspapers would launch a 3d newspaper on Fridays beginning in February 1933. Newspaper premises, a plant and delivery vehicles had come as part of the deal with *Labor Papers*.[50] Precisely why this new title failed to materialise is unclear; perhaps Frank had announced the plan to placate industry unions, who were dismayed by the closure of yet another newspaper. It is also possible that Associated Newspapers claimed that launching a weekly newspaper would be in breach of the recent agreement with Sydney Newspapers.

Frank also became involved with the aviation company run by F. W. Follett. Formed in 1930, Adastra Airways Ltd operated an aviation school and undertook aerial conveyancing. Frank joined the board of Adastra Airways, which was incorporated in New South Wales with capital of £3000 divided into £1 shares.[51]

By the time he had completed the deal with Sydney Newspapers that made his son such a rich man, Clyde Packer was desperately weary. In December 1932 he decided to have another holiday before returning to the rigours of work at Associated Newspapers. He planned to take the *Morna* down to Tasmania, which he had apparently visited only once since his departure thirty years earlier. Several men, including Frank, withdrew from the crew at short notice because they were busy with other sporting and social commitments. Clyde, however, felt that there was no reason why he could not reach Hobart with the help of his experienced boatman, Fred, and his wife's nephew Gerald Hewson. Ethel's younger brother had settled in Hobart with his Tasmanian-born wife and their three children. After struggling to find work and make ends meet, Ethel's brother had died. Clyde and Ethel had brought the children to Sydney one by one to rear and educate them. Gerald became particularly close to the Packer family, working first for Clyde and later for Frank.[52] Ethel, Frank and Kathleen made arrangements to travel to Hobart by steamer to spend Christmas 1932 with Clyde.

The *Morna* and its three crew members encountered fierce storms as they sailed down the south coast of New South Wales. When the yacht headed into Jervis Bay to take shelter, she was blown towards the rocks by a wild gale. Clyde jumped onto the rocks and attempted to push the *Morna* to safety. His companions, meanwhile, got into a dinghy and tried to pull the yacht away from the rocks. The men's frantic efforts saved the *Morna*, but Clyde badly tore the muscles in his chest. The doctor his family sent down from Sydney strapped his chest so tightly that he was in agony for days. When the bandages were removed, Clyde resolved to continue down south as the weather had improved.

After leaving Jervis Bay Clyde and his crew ran into another storm. By the time he helped get the *Morna* into Eden, Clyde was battered and weak. Ethel and their children immediately drove down to join him. Clyde took a room at the Hotel Australasia and was ordered to stay there for at least six weeks. Ethel and Kathleen reluctantly returned to Sydney on New Year's Day to look after their pets. Frank, who had been at something of a loose end since the closure of the *World*, was able to stay a little longer.[53]

Clyde experienced terrible pain in his hips, back and chest, and a shortness of breath made him feel 'well used up'. The man who had always been so active found being bedridden a source of immense boredom and frustration. As soon as he was able, Clyde began taking short walks around Eden. The local children were attracted to the wealthy and entertaining visitor in their midst, and he consolidated his appeal when he began buying them ice creams.[54] Clyde's health improved sufficiently for him to return to Sydney and his job at Associated Newspapers, but the accident left him permanently weakened.

At Clyde Packer's insistence, the agreement with Sydney Newspapers had specified that George Warnecke should be allowed to go back to Associated Newspapers. Nevertheless, Warnecke found the summer of 1932–33 an uncertain and disquieting period. Having publicly displayed his willingness to desert Associated Newspapers, he did not relish the prospect of rejoining the company. During sick leave and then holiday leave, he developed a proposal for a new women's periodical. Clyde had often mused aloud to him about the possibility of establishing a newspaper for women and Warnecke had spent part of his early career working on *Woman's Budget*. During his time in England, he had also watched with interest as women's magazines intended for middle- and lower-class consumption replaced 'society' journals.[55]

With the help of Nora Hill, her brother John, a photojournalist, his wife, the poet Phyllis Duncan Brown, and the cartoonist W. E. Pidgeon, Warnecke created a dummy for the new periodical. The *Australian Women's Weekly* was to have two distinctive features: firstly, it would be a newspaper with an element of topicality in all its features; secondly, it would attempt to appeal to all Australian women, regardless of class, and have a national focus. Wanting the periodical to appeal to a mass audience, Warnecke hoped that it would be a material sign that Australia was coming out of depression.[56]

In a speech in 1923, Warnecke had observed that 'it was only the man who was an owner who could have the sort of paper that every newspaper man wanted to have. The owner could do what he liked with the paper'. Ten years later he reluctantly concluded that he did not have the capital necessary to execute his idea. After considering selling the idea to a number of publishers, he took the *Women's Weekly* dummy to Frank Packer in early 1933.[57] This decision was to consolidate Packer's wealth, create the foundations of a major media empire — and break Warnecke's heart.

As the decades passed and Warnecke became increasingly embittered, he wrote two differing accounts of how Packer reacted to the suggestion that Sydney Newspapers should sponsor the *Women's Weekly*. According to the earlier account, Packer responded cautiously to the proposal. He felt that the periodical would be an enormous strain on resources, particularly as E. G. Theodore was considering investing in gold mines in Fiji. His instinct was to wait until the agreement with Associated Newspapers lapsed so that Sydney Newspapers could publish a daily newspaper. It was only after consulting his father and the powerful J. Walter Thompson advertising agency that Frank Packer determined that the periodical had a reasonable chance of success. Warnecke's other account has Packer responding enthusiastically to the dummy. Warnecke — who had not received a share of the £86 500 payout — appears much more businesslike and astute in this version. He claims that he asked Packer whether he would be allocated a share in Sydney Newspapers; Packer is reputed to have placed a hand on Warnecke's shoulders and reassured him, 'You can depend on me'.[58]

Whatever the case, Frank Packer did decide to embark on this new publishing venture. A millionaire by today's standards, the twenty-six-year-old needed never to have worked again or risked his capital on a speculative publishing enterprise. After executing his stunning agreement with Associated Newspapers, he could simply have travelled the world playing polo, following boxing matches and courting beautiful young women. But Frank was never lazy or complacent. His parents were bundles of energy, he had grown up with the expectation that he would follow in his father's footsteps and pursue a publishing career, and he thrived on taking risks.

Theodore agreed that Sydney Newspapers should back the *Women's Weekly* to the amount of £25 000. In May 1933 he left Sydney to inspect a lease on Viti Levu and investigate the possibility of establishing a mining venture there. A few months earlier Theodore had heard from an old associate, Patrick Costello, that gold had been discovered near the Nasivi River.[59] Theodore's departure on 25 May, just a fortnight before the launch of the *Women's Weekly*, illustrated the confidence he had in his young partner Frank Packer. Norman Bradshaw, meanwhile, made arrangements for Sydney Newspapers to receive the balance of the payout from Associated Newspapers. According to Reg Denison, Clyde Packer engineered the opportunity for 'his friend Warnecke' to resign on inadequate notice from Associated Newspapers to become editor of the *Women's Weekly*.[60]

Like his father, Frank was determined to recruit a pool of talented and well-known contributors. Jessie Tait, for example, was appointed fashion editor. Many of the individuals who joined the new publication had worked for Clyde Packer: the advertising manager, W. J. P. ('Bill') Dowsett, had been on the staff of both Smith's Newspapers and Associated Newspapers; Lennie Lower, the author of *Here's Luck*, had been a prominent humorist on *Smith's Weekly*; the artists Bill Pidgeon ('WEP'), Arthur Boothroyd, Syd Mellor, Will Mahony and Geoffrey Turton ('Petrov') had worked for Smith's Newspapers; and George Stanbridge, who took charge of printing the *Women's Weekly*, had been head compositor on the *Sunday Guardian*.[61]

Frank Packer estimated that the *Women's Weekly* would sell about 50 000 copies per week. On this basis, he and Dowsett set the advertising rate at 5s per column inch. Packer had learned from his father the importance of conducting extensive and innovative promotional campaigns, and the *Women's Weekly* was advertised in big newspaper spaces and promoted during a specially written serial on B-class radio stations. Announcements about the title's features were made each evening, ostensibly from Warnecke's own home. The *Women's Weekly* was priced at twopence, a penny less than its principal rivals, *Woman's Budget*, the *Australian Woman's Mirror* and the fortnightly *New Idea*.[62]

The first issue of the *Women's Weekly*, dated Saturday 10 June, hit the streets of New South Wales on 8 June. Its forty-four black-and-white letterpress pages contained the traditional features of women's magazines, such as recipes, serials, social notes, advice columns and film reviews. The issue also included investigative reports, an article about the conference of the Women Voters' Federation and sports news. The strikingly illustrated fashion section caused rival publications to look staid and matronly. The bold advertising campaign, the low cover price and the range of features made the first issue a phenomenal success. Demand quickly exceeded supply: newsagents from all around the state ran out of copies and a special rush order of newsprint from Canada was needed. Frank Packer worked alongside his employees in the basement of Macdonell House loading bundles into delivery vehicles. The first issue of the *Women's Weekly* sold 121 162 copies; many more could have been sold if the presses had not been stretched to the limit.[63]

Kathleen Packer had gone overseas with a friend, Peggy Bullmore, a few months earlier. When Clyde wrote to Kathleen in London, he joked that her brother's 'effeminate' publication was performing strongly. The very success of the *Women's Weekly* enraged the Packers' enemies. In early June Clyde had an argument with Reg Denison about an advertisement and a book review. When Denison challenged Clyde to a fight, the latter ordered Denison out of his office and called for his dismissal. Denison retaliated by writing a long memo to the board of Associated Newspapers criticising Clyde's activities over the last two years. It concluded by alleging that Clyde had done nothing to improve *Woman's Budget* as the time for the launch of the *Women's Weekly* approached. When the board rejected his recommendation that Denison should be sacked, Clyde demanded an apology from Denison. Needless to say, no apology was forthcoming, and on 15 June Clyde Packer left the company.[64]

A week later Jack Lang rose from the Opposition benches to launch another savage attack on the Packer family. Clyde and Frank were labelled 'vultures' for the way in which they had stripped the assets of Smith's Newspapers and Associated Newspapers. Lang seems to have been leaked some of the correspondence that had flowed between the Packers and Associated Newspapers concerning the closure of the *World*. He observed that the letter Clyde had written agreeing to pay Sydney Newspapers £86 500 (the actual figure had not been made public) should occupy an honoured position in a volume of 'letters from a self-made merchant to his son'. Claiming that the deal between the two companies constituted 'the most barefaced robbery known in Sydney', Lang urged the government to institute a royal commission to investigate the actions of the Packer family: 'Let it probe and inquire to see how these people, the Packers and their kind, line their own pockets at the expense of their shareholders and the public … These swindling humbugs, by the use of their newspapers, destroy the characters of men whose shoes they are not worthy to black'.[65]

Frank Packer immediately put the matter in the hands of his solicitors. Allen, Allen & Hemsley challenged Lang to make his comments without the protection of parliamentary privilege: 'We are instructed to inform you that the allegations of underhand or dishonest dealings concerning the acquisition of the "World" newspaper as alleged by you are entirely groundless, and are regarded by our client and those associated with him as being malicious lies, and an attack deliberately calculated to do him serious injury'.[66] Frank Packer was of course right when he pointed out that the politician intended to damage the reputations of himself and his father. Nevertheless, it is clear that Clyde Packer had brokered the deal with Associated Newspapers in that feverish first week of November 1932 in order to secure his son's wealth.

Immediately after the launch of the *Women's Weekly*, Packer commissioned detailed market research surveys from the J. Walter Thompson agency.[67] But as circulation boomed, so too did the *Women's Weekly*'s production costs. As an in-house publication later observed, the cheap cover price of twopence 'buttered no parsnips' and the advertising rates were dangerously low. In about September 1933 Frank Packer walked into the exclusive Fairfax & Roberts jewellery store in Hunter Street. He told Roy Roberts, 'It is impossible to carry your ad. any longer for five shillings. We shall have to double the price as our circulation has trebled'. Roberts told Frank that this would be in breach of the firm's contract with Sydney Newspapers. Frank tried to explain that he would go broke if the advertising rates were not increased, but Fairfax & Roberts cancelled its advertisement.[68]

Although Theodore was delighted by the impressive sales of the *Women's Weekly*, he was worried about its financial dilemma. In a letter to his partner, he observed that when he was federal treasurer, his opponents had accused him of underestimating expenditure and overestimating receipts. In the whole of his political experience, Theodore concluded wryly, he had found that public servants usually worked with at least *one* eye on reality. Frank is reputed to have replied, with a twinkle in his eye, 'We've just got to keep on spending'.[69]

Clyde Packer, who had refused to panic when the infant *Smith's Weekly* and then the *Daily Guardian* had struggled for survival, probably advised his son that the best thing he could do in the short term was to keep on spending. Sydney Newspapers launched a Victorian edition of the *Women's Weekly* in September 1933 and a Queensland edition a month later. Frank wrote a long, optimistic memo to Theodore naming a date when the *Women's Weekly* should turn the financial corner. The chairman, who was planning a share market float for the gold mines in Fiji, replied 'go ahead and I trust you realise any extension will be disastrous'.[70]

When the publishing industry's unions began dealing with Frank Packer in 1933, they quickly realised that 'The Young Master' would be no pushover. He had had enough experience working alongside his father and had risked too much money launching the *Women's Weekly* to immediately succumb to the unions' industrial demands. Clyde Packer had, as we have seen, insisted on paying high salaries to attract prominent contributors. He believed in rewarding individual merit rather than in being confined to a rigid industrial system. During his time with Smith's Newspapers, Clyde had objected to the visits of AJA officials to inspect office time books and had angrily accused at least one journalist of sheltering behind the award.[71]

In May 1933 Frank Packer and Norman Bradshaw began talking to the AJA and the Printing Industry Employees' Union of Australia (PIEUA) about agreements to cover employees on the New South Wales edition of the *Women's Weekly*. Publishers threatened to go out on strike on the eve of the launch, feeling less than adequately provided for under Packer's proposed agreement. Sydney Newspapers used the overwhelming demand for the magazine to stall negotiations. Several months elapsed before agreements were signed with both unions.[72]

Frank Packer became increasingly confident and self-assured as his business activities expanded. After the First World War, Thomas G. Hopkins, who had been a sports editor with a number of newspapers, had launched *Turf Life*. The newspaper, which appeared twice weekly, consisted of racing news and a form guide. In 1931 *Turf Life* earned a net profit of £2320. A few months later, the Packers purchased the newspaper and registered Sporting Life Publications Ltd with an authorised capital of £10 000. Clyde held 3000 £1 shares in trust for his son. Voltaire Molesworth took up 1500 shares with £500 lent by Frank Packer, and became managing editor.[73]

In late 1932 Frank and Molesworth decided to launch an edition of *Turf Life* in Queensland. Frank was delighted that Hopkins had agreed to take charge of the Queensland edition, but relations within the company soon deteriorated. By August 1933 Frank had concluded that Hopkins was 'not playing the game' because he was trying to entice a colleague in Sydney to join the newspaper in Brisbane. Two months later, Hopkins left the company and Molesworth agreed to purchase the Packers' shares for £4500. Molesworth contracted to repay Frank eleven promissory notes, carrying an interest rate of 8 per cent, by September 1934.[74]

Frank was not, however, content to leave the running of Sporting Life Publications to Molesworth. On 22 January 1934 Frank rang Molesworth to say that a Mr East, who seems to have been involved with the editorial side of *Turf Life*, should be sacked. Molesworth objected strongly, saying 'I don't like to be a party to brutalise [sic] a man you have fallen out with'. He told Frank that he should concentrate on the *Women's Weekly* and leave him free to run *Turf Life* 'as long as I wish so long as I don't hurt the asset'. In another telephone conversation half an hour later, Frank announced that he intended to sell Molesworth's promissory notes and take possession of *Turf Life*. A furious slanging match ensued. Threatening to have Frank thrown out if he tried to enter the office, Molesworth said that 'by the time I'm finished you wont [sic] have a shred of your reputation left'. Frank yelled, 'I'm going right after you', and, 'I'll finish you'. Unfortunately, no record of how the matter was resolved has survived. Within days of the exchange, Frank had to make an emergency dash to England, and Molesworth died later that year.[75] But the *Turf Life* episode showed that Frank was already an interventionist, imperious and fiery proprietor.

5
The Young Master

Everyone agreed that Gretel Bullmore was quite a catch. She was vivacious, artistic, athletic and strikingly attractive. Her social credentials were impeccable. Frank Packer had been keen on girls since he was a teenager, and in the late 1920s he had begun to step out with a number of pretty girls. One of his earliest sweethearts was a sister of his close friend Ralph McFadyen, and there is some suggestion that he was involved with Maisie McMahon, an attractive young woman who had worked as R. C. Packer's secretary and later wrote about films and beauty for the *Women's Weekly*.[1]

But from the time Frank Packer laid eyes on Gretel Bullmore in the whirl of parties and dances frequented by the Eastern Suburbs set, he pursued her with a single-minded determination. Gretel's grandfather, Edward Augustus Bullmore, had emigrated from Cornwall to Victoria in 1853. He embarked on a varied career for the next decade or so, working first as a chemist's assistant before trying his hand at farming in the Hunter Valley in New South Wales, where he was defeated by the elements, and overseeing properties in Queensland. Settling in Ipswich in the 1870s, Bullmore profited in the sawmilling business, was appointed a justice of the peace, became a member of the Queensland Masonic Lodge, and established a fine residence, 'Rockton'. A supporter of protectionism and federation, he was defeated in his bids for the seats of Warrego and Fassifern. Before his sudden death in 1892, he served as president of the Ipswich Hospital Board and the Queensland Pastoral and Agricultural Society and chairman of the Ipswich Grammar School Trust.

Edward Augustus Bullmore and his wife Caroline had three sons and five daughters; tragically, the two eldest boys drowned.[2] Their only surviving son, Herbert Henry, excelled academically at Ipswich Grammar School and represented Queensland in rugby union. He joined a legal office and studied law for three years before deciding to enter the medical profession. Henry obtained his medical degrees at Edinburgh University between 1902 and 1904, where he was also awarded blues for rowing and football. After graduating he was appointed house physician to the Royal Infirmary, Edinburgh, served as resident surgeon at the Edinburgh Children's Hospital and practised in Bath.

Dr Bullmore seems to have married Elfride Henriette Victoria Büttner while he was overseas. Elfride, who was of German descent and had studied at the Sorbonne in

Paris, had spent some time in Melbourne. Their first child, Joan, was apparently born in Europe. On the family's return to Australia, Dr Bullmore took up practice in Woollahra. He played a leading role in founding the Australasian College of Surgeons and was honorary physician to St Vincent's Hospital. When the hospital was recognised as a clinical school by the University of Sydney, he could have taken up the lectureship in clinical medicine. Believing he lacked teaching experience, Dr Bullmore decided that the position should go to a younger man. He served instead as honorary physician to South Sydney Hospital and Prince Henry Hospital.[3]

Dr Bullmore and his wife lived in a fine residence, 'Calingra', complete with a tennis court, in Ocean Street, Woollahra. The couple had another four children: Gretel Joyce, born on 5 May 1907, followed by Peggy, Mary and James. Dr Bullmore, who had a retiring nature but a transparent honesty and friendliness, was affectionately called 'Bully' by his colleagues. Elfride's warm and gracious manner and lovely face and smile won her many friends. Fortunately her daughters inherited her looks; Dr Bullmore had an athletic build but a remarkably plain face.[4]

Gretel, who enrolled in the exclusive Ascham School, Edgecliff, in 1922, was remembered by classmates as 'one of the beauties'; she became a tall, statuesque brunette with large violet eyes. Teachers and students also discovered that she had a mind of her own. When she arrived at school one day wearing kiss-curls, she was despatched home to remove the curls and the glue. On another occasion she was caught talking to a classmate, Eileen Orford Hall, and was sent to the back row. While Gretel put her feet up on the desk in front of her, Eileen confessed that it was she who had spoken first. After Gretel refused to return to her regular seat, the teacher, Miss Saxby, primly inquired if she normally sat like that at home. 'Yes', said Gretel boldly, 'but at home I have my feet on the piano'. The girl also established an op shop to alleviate a temporary cash shortage. When she was refused pocket money to see a popular movie her father deemed unsuitable, Gretel sold off items of her wardrobe to pay for a ticket. She left school in 1923 after completing the Intermediate Certificate. A year later she was said to be studying art, and she also seems to have worked in an exclusive boutique.[5]

In 1926 Elfride hosted a dance to mark her daughter's debut into society. Like her sisters and other women of their class, Gretel began attending and helping to organise a range of social and fund-raising events: she performed in a mixed review for charity at Adyar Hall; was present at chukka balls, Sydney race meetings and Melbourne Cups; skied in Kosciuszko; served on committees which arranged mannequin parades and dances in aid of the Country Women's Association, the Royal Flying Doctor Service and the Royal Prince Alfred Hospital; helped to entertain guests at the dance hosted by her parents to raise funds for St Luke's Hospital and, with Jessie Tait, organised the Pageant of Fair Women for the 1933 Polo Ball.[6]

Dr Bullmore built a holiday house on the steep slopes and precipitous hilltops overlooking Palm Beach. In the 1920s Palm Beach became an increasingly popular spot for wealthy Sydney families to spend their summers. A fishing and golfing enthusiast, Dr Bullmore could try his hand at casting from the beach and play golf at the nine-hole golf club that opened in 1924. Members of his family surfed, loafed on the beach, held dances and invited friends as house guests. Gretel was good at outdoor sports and became a skilful surfer during her summer holidays.⁷

Gretel's aunt was married to Sir Frederick Maze, inspector-general of the Chinese Maritime Customs. In early 1934 Gretel visited her uncle and aunt in Shanghai; she helped Sir Frederick launch two ships and attended a dinner with the last emperor, who had been forced to abdicate in 1912, and his wife. Gretel's three sisters made fine matches: Joan married Douglas Henty, of the Victorian pioneering and pastoral dynasty; Mary married Anthony Hordern, a widowed grazier and member of the leading Sydney retailing family; and Peggy married George William Campbell, a Scottish grazier. On Peggy's engagement in March 1934, the *Home* observed that 'now there's only one Bullmore maiden left for the eligible bachelors to fight over, the beautiful Gretel'.⁸

Gretel did indeed have many ardent suitors, forcing Frank Packer to chase her strenuously for several years. The entire Packer family became very fond of the dashing, charming and kind young woman who had captivated Frank so completely. Shortly after Kathleen left for England with Peggy Bullmore in April 1933, she received a letter from her father saying, 'Gretel told mother she must not go [overseas] before September. I don't know what that means'.⁹ This did not, however, mean that an engagement was imminent. Another year — a turbulent and highly emotional year — was to elapse before Gretel agreed to marry Frank.

Clyde and Ethel Packer did decide to go abroad in September 1933. Clyde hoped that treatment in a London clinic would improve his chest and heart complaints, and he was delighted at the prospect of seeing his only daughter again. As Clyde had not been overseas before, a senior colleague from Associated Newspapers gave him a letter of introduction to Frank Roberts, who published the *Sunday Chronicle* in Manchester; Clyde's friend also suggested that he try to meet Max Aitken (Lord Beaverbrook) and visit advanced printing firms in London and Berlin.¹⁰

But Clyde was more than content to have a family holiday and relax after years of unrelenting work and pressure. When he was not visiting specialists or attending the clinic, Kathleen would take her father out for walks around London. Even though he was only fifty-four, Clyde sensed that he was nearing the end of his life. During one of their walks he suddenly asked his daughter, 'I suppose you'll be getting married one day? I think we'll go get you a wedding present now'. Clyde walked into a store and bought Kathleen, who was not yet engaged, a superb canteen of silver.

As London was bitterly cold, the family stayed at a seaside hotel for Christmas. When Clyde returned to London his health deteriorated sharply and in late January 1934 the family sent for Frank, who had remained in Sydney to court Gretel Bullmore and supervise the publication of the *Women's Weekly*. Over the summer Frank had also sailed the *Morna* competitively, with considerable success. On 11 November 1933 he came from behind to win the F. J. Jackson Cup and on 6 January 1934 he narrowly beat another schooner 'in a finish the like of which has not been seen for years' to take out the Norn Cup.¹¹

Leaving Sydney on 24 January, Frank managed to reach London in just nineteen days. After travelling to Adelaide by train, he flew to Fremantle, caught a steamer to

Java, flew to Amsterdam and then caught another flight to London via Paris. He was exhausted by the time he landed in Paris, and the few words of French he knew were insufficient to prevent the obsequious staff at his hotel from pestering him as he tried to sleep.[12]

When Frank arrived in London he immediately took charge of his mother and sister. Although they were very comfortable at the Cumberland Hotel near Marble Arch, Frank insisted on moving them to the grander Dorchester Hotel; Kathleen was mortified when their luggage was transferred to the Dorchester carrying Cumberland labels. Frank had become involved in staging boxing matches at the Sydney Stadium, and during his time in London he took the opportunity to line up fights for the Rushcutters Bay venue. While Clyde recuperated at the clinic, Ethel and Kathleen moved around the Dorchester escorted by pugilists with crooked noses. Frank's new friends also took the family on some hilariously unorthodox walking and driving tours of London.[13]

At the end of February Frank wired friends in Australia to say that his father's health was improving. Feeling confident about Clyde's condition, he decided to return to Sydney and his pressing business commitments. He flew to the United States on the way home to briefly meet newspaper and advertising executives. Frank's parents and sister, meanwhile, set sail for Australia aboard the *Maloja*. Everything went smoothly at first, as the Packers were delighted with their cabins and Clyde was under the care of a nurse. However, he awoke one morning feeling weak and unwell. While Ethel and Kathleen stayed by his bedside, the crew roped off their section of the ship to ensure their privacy. Clyde died of arteriosclerosis in the Gulf of Lions, off Marseilles, on 12 April. He who so loved the sea had died with the sound of its waves in his ears.[14]

Clyde's body was taken ashore and embalmed in Marseilles. His widow and daughter then accompanied the body on the long, sad journey back to Australia. Poor Frank was in the mid Pacific when he received a cable saying that his beloved father had died. In a touching gesture, Gretel Bullmore met Ethel and Kathleen in Perth and travelled with them to Sydney.[15]

On 21 May 1934 George Faunce Allman played Chopin's 'Funeral March' as Clyde Packer's coffin was carried into St James's Church in King Street. Allman had made St James a centre for church music, so it was an appropriate place to hold the funeral of someone who had been passionate about music all his life. As the Rev. Dr P. A. Micklem also noted, it was 'fitting that the man we mourn should be brought to the parish church in the city centre in which he had laboured so long'. The church was crammed with newspaper and advertising executives, journalists, politicians, senior police officers and members of the Boy Scouts Association. Although the Denisons were conspicuous by their absence, some people who had fallen out with Clyde, such as H. Campbell Jones, were present to pay their respects to the man who had left an indelible impression on the Sydney newspaper industry.[16]

Frank Packer ran a full-page obituary in the *Women's Weekly*. It stated, with just a hint of exaggeration, that Clyde Packer's influence on Australian journalism was 'as great as that of Lord Northcliffe' on British journalism, and credited him with sole responsibility for introducing the 'New Journalism' to Australia. It also made the rather startling claim that Clyde had kept his post at Associated Newspapers while his health was in decline because of 'a high sense of the duty of newspapers in guiding the public' through the difficult period of the Depression.

The *Bulletin* was the only contemporary observer to publicly question Clyde Packer's achievements: 'he had great journalistic gifts of a sort — organising ability, energy and a keen sense of what readers of the mental age of 15, or less, want in the way of news and stunts'. A more recent commentator has offered a more balanced and judicious assessment. Richard White writes that Clyde was the model 'of the modern newspaper boss, innovative, cynical, thriving on hard work, inspiring loyalty as well as enmity, politically influential but chiefly concerned with commercial advantage'.[17]

During his controversial career Clyde had exposed Frank to every facet of newspaper production, illustrated the value of spectacular promotions and tutored him in the nuances of boardroom and political intrigues. In the end, however, Clyde's relentless efforts to save his family's shareholdings in a string of newspapers had contributed to his early demise. Eric Baume said he had never known a man to work so hard for his objectives: 'He killed himself'. George Warnecke 'grieved, deeply' when his mentor was 'brutally cut down' before his time.[18]

Clyde Packer was cremated at Rookwood Crematorium and his ashes were later interred at the family vault in South Head Cemetery at Vaucluse. His wife oversaw the construction of the large and elaborate vault, which featured plaques commemorating generations of the Packer, Hewson and Clyde families and was topped by a Celtic cross. Not all members of the Packer clan approved of the result, feeling that Ethel had gone 'completely Irish'.[19] Clyde, whose estate was valued for probate at £54 306, left all his shareholdings in Sydney to Frank. Clyde's brother Arthur inherited the shares in Smith's Victorian Publishing Company Ltd. Clyde's executors were instructed to give Ethel £200 immediately, and asked to pay his secretary Miss Follett £5 a week for the rest of her life. Ethel and her daughter moved into an apartment at the Astor in Macquarie Street.[20]

In January, while Frank Packer had been making his frantic dash to his father's bedside, E.G. Theodore had visited Sydney. Frank's partner, who was planning a share market float for the gold mines in Fiji, was horrified to learn that £50 000 (now equivalent to $3 million) had been pumped into the *Women's Weekly*. After going through the books, the former federal treasurer called Warnecke into his office to say that the company did not have enough cash at hand to meet expenses. According to Warnecke, Theodore proposed cutting staff, wages and production. The editor, pleading for more time to allow the *Women's Weekly* to trade its way out of difficulties, offered £1000 to relieve the cash flow shortage. On 27 March Warnecke was allocated 1000 £1 ordinary shares in Sydney Newspapers.[21]

Frank Packer returned to Australia a few weeks later, in time to attend his father's funeral. So shattered was he by the loss that he attempted to get in touch with Clyde's spirit by using a ouija board. On his arrival in Sydney, Packer called on the Warneckes at their home in Edgecliff. George recalls that Packer was shaken and his eyes brimmed with tears. Touching his cheek with her fingertips, Nora said in her lilting Irish voice, 'I am sorry for your poor mother'. Packer undoubtedly found some solace in visiting the couple, both of whom had been extremely close to his father. Nevertheless, Packer was displeased when he learned that Warnecke had doubled his shareholding in Sydney Newspapers. Packer, who had planned to rely on a bank overdraft until advertising rates and the cover price could be increased, realised that Warnecke had now secured a seat on the board.[22]

The relationship between Packer and his editor was becoming obsessively uneasy and uncertain. Packer knew that Warnecke believed that he had been entitled to a one-third share in Sydney Newspapers since its formation. The fact that Warnecke's £1000 had come from a 'nest egg' Clyde had given him before his departure to England was particularly galling. Frank seems always to have regarded Warnecke as a rival for Clyde's affections. While working closely alongside Clyde for almost a decade, Warnecke had proved to be a much more talented journalist than Frank. Warnecke, for his part, was somewhat jealous of Frank, eleven years his junior. Frank was 'The Young Master', son of a self-made newspaper baron, shoving his way into the world with boldness and guile. Warnecke later wrote, 'Frank wanted success on his own account, not merely [to be seen as] the playboy son of a rich father, so he did not want to share credit with anybody for the *Weekly* miracle. He showed dutiful regard for his father's affection and advancement of me, but without the warmth that made RCP a constant visitor to myself and Nora in our home. Maybe Frank felt a touch of filial rivalry'.[23]

Warnecke claimed that he retained his new shareholding in Sydney Newspapers only after entering into a secret agreement to vote with Packer against Theodore in any boardroom division.[24] Was Packer trying to undermine Theodore's role in the company so soon after its formation? The most likely explanation is that Packer insisted upon the agreement because he feared that Warnecke might persuade Theodore to vote him down at some future board meeting.

All other accounts suggest that the relationship between Packer and Theodore was respectful, trusting and affectionate. Packer revered the former politician, who became something of a father figure after Clyde's death. For many years Packer called Theodore 'Sir'; in later years he still could not bring himself to call his partner 'Ted', so he addressed him as 'E. G.'. Theodore brought to the partnership financial acumen, administrative experience and a long history of dealing with unions. Packer — young, energetic, shrewd and ambitious — had observed and aided his father in his aggressive publishing endeavours. Theodore was an indulgent mentor, watching 'with interest, and maybe awe, how Packer sold himself to this black art as he gradually shaped himself'.[25]

As chairman and joint proprietor of Sydney Newspapers, Theodore shared in all the major policy decisions made in the 1930s. But in the detailed conduct of the publishing business, he played the role of elder statesman backing youthful zeal.[26] By contrast, it was Theodore who oversaw the Fijian gold mines, bringing in Packer as a minor, silent partner. In mid 1933 Theodore had paid £600 for an option held by Patrick Costello, an acquaintance from Queensland. A few months later, Theodore shifted his attention to an adjoining claim at Tavua belonging to Harry Morton and a Mr Foulis. Theodore paid £1000 for an option to purchase for £10 000 cash and 15 per cent in shares any company subsequently formed. Encouraged by the claim's prospects, Theodore decided to exercise the option. In about October 1934 the Emperor Gold Mining Co. was incorporated to work the claim with capital of £100 000 in £1 shares. The principal shareholders were Theodore, Packer, a major wine manufacturer, Patrick Cody, and one of his business associates, John Wren. Theodore had become acquainted with Wren even before the Melbourne gambling entrepreneur had bought into the Brisbane *Daily Mail* in 1915. A reputation for sleaziness clung to Wren, on whom was based the character John West in Frank Hardy's controversial novel *Power Without Glory* (1950). But Wren's numerous business partners did not doubt his integrity, and he and Packer do not seem to have had a direct association.[27]

In August 1935 the Emperor Gold Mining Co. was floated in order to equip the mine with a plant and to increase production. The syndicate, which now seems to have consisted only of Theodore, Packer, Cody and Wren, received £300 000 in cash and 600 000 fully paid shares of 10s each. Interest in the float was intense, with the public issue of 900 000 shares many times oversubscribed. On 9 August shares in Emperor Mines Ltd were trading on the Melbourne Stock Exchange for 23s each, more than double the par value.[28]

By November 1936 Theodore and an accountant, John Vincent Ratcliffe, owned 70 000 shares; Ratcliffe and a Melbourne company, Oran Pty Ltd, owned 60 000 shares; Packer owned 50 000; and L. B. Tomlins, a Melbourne accountant, owned 420 000. Over the next few years, Ratcliffe was to become one of Packer's closest financial advisers and confidantes. Ratcliffe had served as assistant commissioner of taxation in New South Wales before becoming a partner with Smith, Johnson and Co., the accountancy firm that had represented Smith's Newspapers, in 1931.[29]

Theodore floated two other mining companies in August 1935.[30] Even if Packer were not involved with these new firms, he had made an enormous profit from his partner's foray into Fiji. Their willingness to risk some of their capital during the difficult early days of the *Women's Weekly* had paid off handsomely. The public share subscription to Emperor Mines had been a lucrative exercise and then the expanded operations facilitated by the float yielded a steady stream of gold. Packer was content to leave the management of the mines to Theodore, who bought a house near Suva in 1937. Packer did not even join the board of Emperor Mines, and he seems never to have visited Fiji himself. By 1945 Theodore's companies had produced some 650 000 ounces of gold, and the total value of gold and silver mined amounted to a staggering £6 million.[31] Packer had no cause for complaint as profits soared and hefty dividends rolled in.

In 1934 Frank Packer lost his father and became worried about his editor's proprietorial ambitions. The year, however, also brought him great joy. Packer's obvious devotion to his ailing father seems to have been the factor that finally convinced Gretel Bullmore to marry him. Gretel decided that he was more intelligent and entertaining than his rivals and she sensed that he was 'going somewhere'. Putting the quarrel with the Fairfax & Roberts jewellery store behind him, Packer asked Bart Fairfax to make Gretel the finest diamond ring he was capable of producing. When the dazzling engagement ring was lost a decade later, it was valued at £475.[32]

On 20 July 1934, a few days before the wedding, friends and business associates hosted a dinner in Packer's honour at Usher's Hotel. Theodore and Jimmie Bancks shared the role of master of ceremonies. Packer was presented with a handsome cigar and cigarette box with the signatures of those present engraved on it. Guests at the dinner included Ralph McFadyen, Jim MacLeod, George Warnecke, N. Q. Bradshaw, Bill Dowsett, Senator Charles Hardy, David Yaffa, the managing director of the Yaffa Syndicate and the proprietor of *Newspaper News*, and Eric Kennedy, an advertising executive with the Sun.[33]

Archdeacon W. Leslie Langley married the couple at All Saints' Church, Woollahra, on 24 July. McFadyen was best man and Gretel's elder sister Joan matron of honour. The Bullmore and Packer families decided that the wedding should be a quiet affair so soon after Clyde's death, and the mothers of the bride and the groom wore black. After the ceremony Dr and Mrs Bullmore hosted a cocktail party at 'Calingra', now occupied by Joan and Douglas Henty. Frank and Gretel had a brief honeymoon at Oran Park, Cobbitty, before settling in 'Kismet' in Wylde Street, Potts Point.[34]

Frank's participation in sporting contests did not wane after his marriage. Sailing the *Morna* in December 1934, he won both the Alfred Milson Memorial Cup and the inaugural John Muston Memorial Cup. He pursued his interest in polo with similar vigour. In an effort to improve his form, he trained in a Sydney gymnasium. He sat in a saddle erected in the centre of a private room repeatedly hitting the ball as it rolled down the specially designed sloping floor towards him. In later years he trained at home on a custom-made wooden horse.[35]

In 1935 Packer and the other three players in the 'Nutcrackers' team overcame bad weather and an outbreak of influenza to emerge victorious in the Quirindi polo festival. On 6 August the Nutcrackers defeated the team from Tamworth, and the next day they beat the team from Scone to take out the Northern Challenge Polo Cup. The following year Packer was the only original member who played in the 'Nutcrackers' team when it again won the coveted cup. In 1936 he also competed for the Countess of Dudley Cup and began entering horses in polo pony cups.[36]

Packer had an official handicap of two in the 1936 season and, at his peak, had a rating of four. This was despite the fact that he was a right-hander with his good eye on the left. Some members of the exclusive polo circuit were less than impressed by Packer's presence. J. O. Kelly, a mining agent who was married to the children's author and illustrator May Gibbs, recorded that he had enjoyed being a spectator at a polo match: 'The only blot is the large vulgar lumbering Figure of the Packer Animal'.[37]

By 1936 Packer's brother-in-law Anthony Hordern was president of the New South Wales Polo Association and Jim MacLeod served on the executive. Polo tournaments were social events as well as sporting contests for wealthy Australian men and their wives. At the start of each polo festival, team captains were handed an envelope bulging with invitations to social and charity events. Gymkhanas were often held before the tournament proper began. Competitors could test their skills in a range of amusing activities and the women could hit polo balls around obstacle courses. They spent their nights attending cocktail parties, 'at homes' hosted by local graziers and, of course, the glamorous Polo Ball.[38]

Women such as the new Mrs Frank Packer wrapped themselves in fur coats and huddled comfortably in sedans to gossip and watch their husbands and brothers compete. Each afternoon they enjoyed luncheons and afternoon teas prepared by the local Country Women's Association. Gretel and her sister Mary Hordern helped to organise the Polo Ball to celebrate the opening of a new field at Kyeemagh, Botany, on 22 June 1935.[39] Just a month to the day later, Gretel gave birth to the couple's first child. The infant was christened Robert Clyde Packer, after his grandfather, and also became known as Clyde.

Ethel Packer was not in Sydney to celebrate the birth of her first grandchild. In March she had accompanied her daughter on a trip to England, via the United States. Kathleen brought back a wedding dress from London when they returned to Sydney in early November 1935. Her fiancé was Dr George Stening, who had achieved brilliant results in his medical degree at the University of Sydney and had studied surgery in Edinburgh before setting up private practice in Bondi.[40] On 11 November Frank and Gretel hosted a cocktail party at 'Kismet' to celebrate the imminent nuptials. The function also served to welcome Gretel's sister Peggy Campbell, who was visiting from Scotland, back to Sydney. The following day Frank, who was an affectionate, considerate and generous brother and son, gave Kathleen away at the ceremony at All Saints' Church, Woollahra, and held the reception at 'Kismet'.[41]

At the very time he was celebrating his sister's marriage, Frank was engaged in crucial and intricate business negotiations. He and Theodore had been waiting for the lapse of the November 1932 agreement with Associated Newspapers, which prevented the publication of a daily or Sunday newspaper for three years. In the second half of 1934 Sydney Newspapers had finally begun to benefit financially from the impressive sales of the *Women's Weekly*: advertising rates rose in September and the cover price increased to 3d a few weeks later to coincide with the inclusion of a free novel.[42]

The ageing press at Macdonell House struggled to cope with the demands of churning out a novel and a magazine each week.[43] In 1934 Packer and Theodore offered Labor Papers £35 000 for the plant, machinery and office equipment. This time, however, the company drove a hard bargain, and as negotiations dragged on, the board indicated that it would only be prepared to sign a long term lease.[44] As the year drew to a close, Frank Packer turned his attention to the possibility of purchasing a new press to produce the magazine and sections for the anticipated daily newspaper. Warnecke volunteered to go overseas for six months to investigate the latest advances in printing technology.

On 21 December 1934 Warnecke signed an agreement whereby the shares he had recently obtained were to be held in trust for him by Packer; in return, Warnecke was given the title of editor-in-chief of Sydney Newspapers. When George and Nora left Australia aboard the *Orama* the following day, Packer publicly announced his company's intention of entering daily and Sunday journalism in twelve months' time.[45] Packer, who must have been relieved to put some distance between himself and his disaffected employee, was probably delighted that Warnecke was actually away for most of 1935. Warnecke not only explored printing technologies in England, Europe and the United States, but also arranged new features and cabled stories about international developments for his beloved *Women's Weekly*. The competent, stern and demanding Alice Jackson, whose talents had been spotted by Clyde Packer at *Smith's Weekly* and the *Daily Guardian*, edited the magazine in Warnecke's absence.[46]

While Warnecke was overseas, one of Australia's leading newspaper publishers attempted to buy into the blossoming *Women's Weekly*. Advertisements placed by the magazine indicated that circulation rose from 210 424 copies per week in January to 307 160 in November 1935. The magazine's success in Sydney and its inroads into Melbourne impressed Sir Keith Murdoch, managing director of the HWT. In June 1935 Sydney Newspapers rejected his offer to buy into the *Women's Weekly*.[47] Packer and Theodore were determined to enter the newspaper field and they obviously realised that the magazine would play an integral role in subsidising the new venture.

At about this time Sydney Newspapers made a tentative offer to buy Ezra Norton's Truth & Sportsman Ltd, publisher of the Sunday *Truth*. When nothing came of the proposal,[48] Packer and Theodore knew that they had to settle on another strategy to move into the newspaper market. Taking on the *Sun* on its own turf was too great a challenge, as it had many retail advertisements and Associated Newspapers fiercely defended its afternoon monopoly. As a result, Packer and Theodore turned their attention to the morning newspaper field. They had two choices: they could launch a new daily newspaper to compete with the *Sydney Morning Herald*, the *Telegraph* and the *Labor Daily*, or minimise competition by taking over an existing morning newspaper.

The moribund *Telegraph* was an easy target. Since its launch in 1879, it had undergone numerous changes in ownership, direction and even name. In 1927, as it struggled to compete with the *Daily Guardian*, it had been taken over by Hugh Denison and renamed the *Daily Telegraph News Pictorial*. Four years later Associated Newspapers decided to merge the title with the *Daily Guardian*; the new paper became known as the *Daily Telegraph*. When Clyde Packer resigned in June 1933, the company was planning to relaunch the newspaper yet again. A friend who remained on the staff of Associated Newspapers privately told him that the *Telegraph*, as it was now simply known, was 'a damp rocket. They made, as it were a lovely scone, but they haven't yet tumbled to it that the carbonate of soda has been left out. In other words they have the aspirations of a Northcliffe, but have not the ability to run a prawn stall'. New features, notably a rotogravure pictorial supplement, were introduced, contributing to a modest rise in circulation. In the second half of 1934, however, Associated Newspapers decided to economise and concentrate its efforts on the *Sun* and the Sunday *Sun*. The *Telegraph*'s cartoons, the Saturday magazine section and the rotogravure supplement were discontinued.[49]

By 1935 the *Telegraph* was an industry joke. *Smith's Weekly* observed that 'no newspaper in the last 25 years has suffered so many changes of management and direction and ownership'. In July rumours that the *Telegraph* would cease publication began to circulate; just how involved Frank Packer and his associates were in spreading them is unclear. It was precisely at this time that a friend of Packer's made a decisive intervention. During a train trip from Melbourne, David Yaffa told the Associated Newspapers executive Sir John Butters that Packer was thinking of starting an afternoon newspaper. Yaffa commented that selling the *Telegraph* would keep Packer out of the field.

The encounter between Yaffa and Butters was not accidental. Some years later a Packer publication noted that 'Dave' negotiated many important newspaper deals, including the sale of the *Telegraph*.⁵⁰

The Associated Newspapers board immediately began considering ways of once again preventing a company headed by Packer from launching a newspaper to compete with the *Sun*. By September it was discussing the possibility of selling its building and plant at 168–74 Castlereagh Street, which had lain idle since the closure of the *Evening News* in 1931, to Packer. In return Associated Newspapers wanted a guarantee that Sydney Newspapers would not publish an afternoon paper for less than 1½d. Packer suspended negotiations: although his company was looking for a plant and premises, its main objective was to take over the *Telegraph* at a cheap price.⁵¹

Such was the concern of Associated Newspapers about a perceived threat to the *Sun* that it was prepared to resume talks with Packer along different lines. In mid September Packer put forward three propositions. The two main proposals entailed forming a new company to publish the *Women's Weekly* and the *Telegraph* and to acquire the *Evening News* premises and plant. The possibility of the new firm taking over Associated Newspapers' weekly magazine *Woman* was also considered but the idea fell by the wayside. Sydney Newspapers indicated its willingness to agree not to publish an afternoon newspaper and not to undercut the price of other daily and Sunday papers in Sydney.⁵²

Packer called in Theodore to help him assess the value of the *Women's Weekly* in relation to the *Telegraph*. On 15 October Theodore proposed that the goodwill of the magazine and the newspaper should be fixed at a ratio of 2¼ to 1. Although the board of Associated Newspapers was disappointed by this valuation, Hugh Denison asserted that the 'friendly discussions' between the two parties should continue. As observers noted, Associated Newspapers had always been 'a tame and copious milch cow for Theodore and Packer'.⁵³

On 29 October Denison and Packer agreed to form a new company with a nominal capital of £750 000 in £1 shares. Sydney Newspapers was to receive 265 625 shares for the goodwill of the *Women's Weekly*; Associated Newspapers was to receive 125 000 shares for the *Telegraph*, 35 000 shares for the plant and fixtures at the *Evening News* building and £95 000 cash for the actual building; Packer, Theodore and/or Sydney Newspapers were entitled to 150 000 shares. The new company was not to produce an afternoon paper for ten years, and various restrictions were imposed on the cover price of the *Telegraph* and any future Sunday newspaper. Associated Newspapers was not to produce a morning paper, nor to reduce the cover price of daily papers below 1½d and Sunday papers below 3d, more than 135 000 copies of *Woman* were not to be printed per week and *Woman* was not to undercut the *Women's Weekly's* cover price and advertising rates.

The proposed agreement also imposed restrictions on the print run, cover price and advertising rates of *Woman* in order to safeguard the market dominance of the *Women's Weekly*.⁵⁴ The Associated Newspapers board objected to this section of the agreement, maintaining that limitations should not be placed on a publication that was not involved in the deal. Packer and Theodore stood firm, arguing that the *Wo-*

men's Weekly should not be exposed to a possible challenge by *Woman* while they concentrated on building up the *Telegraph*. Butters persuaded his board to agree to limit *Woman*'s print run to 140 000 copies for three years and to maintain advertising rates at the same level until the magazine recorded sales of 100 000 or more.[55]

Packer and Theodore had successfully executed another stunning business coup. Acquiring an existing newspaper meant that they did not have to take the enormous risk of launching a new daily newspaper. In the quarter of a century since R. C. Packer had first worked in Sydney, the Australian metropolitan newspaper field had become increasingly concentrated. Independent newspapers had been squeezed out of the market, and publishing chains — most notably the HWT and Associated Newspapers — had appeared as the high price of printing technology and elaborate advertising campaigns formed a natural barrier to new entrants.

Frank Packer had every reason to be happy about the deal concluded with Associated Newspapers. The building he and Theodore had purchased for £95 000 had cost £120 000 to erect on land in an ideal location worth £62 000 a decade earlier. And *Woman* could not undermine the precious *Women's Weekly*, which was continuing to flourish. But Packer also knew that the terms of the agreement pegging cover price and circulation could result in new allegations of bribery. He asked Denison not to reveal certain aspects of the transaction when he addressed shareholders at the annual general meeting of Associated Newspapers.[56]

When George Warnecke returned to Sydney in early November, Packer was at the docks to greet him. It was here that a surprised Warnecke learned that the purchase of the *Telegraph* had just been finalised. At a welcome-home luncheon at the Hotel Australia on 6 November, the staff of the *Women's Weekly* produced a special menu to mark the occasion. It averred that 'Dear Old George' might be 'peeved to learn that our circulation has become uncontrollable since you went away. You may be assured, however, that we appreciate the fact that it was you who established us on the firm basis on which we now rock'.[57] Warnecke's employer never appreciated this fact.

Consolidated Press Ltd, the new company formed by Sydney Newspapers and Associated Newspapers, was incorporated in New South Wales on 8 January 1936. The signatories were Frank Packer; Norman Bradshaw; Bill Dowsett; Maisie McMahon; Jack Travers, who had defected from Associated Newspapers a few months earlier to become circulation manager of the *Women's Weekly*; and the accountants Frederick Llewellyn East and Sydney Charles Glencross. Theodore was appointed chairman and Packer became managing director and deputy chairman. Associated Newspapers nominated a respected accountant, T. H. Wynne-Lewis, to fill its one position on the board. The public offer of 100 000 £1 preference shares was fully subscribed.[58]

Although Bradshaw was made secretary of the new company, his relationship with Packer was deteriorating. He first earned Packer's displeasure for criticising the acquisition of the *Telegraph* during a conversation with Theodore. Then, in January 1936, Packer concocted a scheme designed to increase his own shareholdings and those of Theodore. Bradshaw, who had acquired 1000 shares in Sydney Newspapers, advanced an alternative proposal designed to improve the position of minority shareholders.

Even though nothing came of either scheme, the intervention of the company secretary angered Packer. According to Warnecke, Bradshaw also wanted the title of general manager and felt that Travers had been brought in to undermine his position.[59]

Packer spent the early months of 1936 planning how to move into the Castlereagh Street building without disrupting the production of the *Women's Weekly*. Of primary concern, however, was reviving the *Telegraph*: new features had to be acquired, arrangements for a cable service made and the editorial and advertising staff overhauled. Packer told an anxious delegation from the AJA that probably no more than 10 per cent of the existing staff would be replaced. But, as he pointed out, staff at the senior level would have to be replaced to make the *Telegraph* a discernibly better newspaper.[60]

Sydney H. Deamer, who had worked on *Smith's Weekly* and a number of other titles before becoming editor of the *Adelaide Register* and then the Melbourne *Herald*, was appointed to edit the *Telegraph*. R. C. Packer's old friend Reg Moses, who had been editing *Smith's Weekly* since 1932, became consultant editor. The other journalists who were appointed to senior editorial positions on the *Telegraph* — Harry Cox, Jack W. Bellew, C. S. McNulty, Jack Bridges, Allan Dawes, Jack G. Paton, Jean Williamson and Dorothy Baverstock — combined experience with youthful vigour and obvious potential. Bill Pidgeon and George Finey were signed up as cartoonists.[61]

Several other people who had worked with Clyde Packer were recruited or promoted. Jack Gell, formerly a *Smith's Weekly* sub-editor, became news editor of the *Women's Weekly* in 1935. F. D. McShane, who had worked at both Smith's Newspapers and Associated Newspapers, was appointed advertising manager of the *Telegraph*. Bill Davies, who had met Frank during the 1926 Miss Australia tour, took charge of the Consolidated Press New York office. Nora Hill's cousin E. W. MacAlpine, who had been foreign editor of the *Daily Guardian*, was appointed editor of the Consolidated Press London bureau.[62]

The *Telegraph* withdrew from Australian Associated Press (AAP), which had recently emerged as the country's dominant cable service. AAP, controlled by the HWT and John Fairfax & Sons Pty Ltd, was aligned with Reuters. To the consternation of some local publishers, Packer decided that the *Telegraph* should have a foreign news service unique to Australia. Consolidated Press subscribed to the London *Daily Express* and the Hearst-based International News Service. In late February articles about the launch of the new *Telegraph* began appearing in the Women's Weekly. Seeking to capitalise on the depth of editorial talent, advertisements breathlessly declared that the *Telegraph* would be produced by 'Ten Brilliant Editors'.[63]

On the night of 22 March 1936 Gretel Packer watched as her mother-in-law pressed the switch to begin printing the revitalised newspaper. Consolidated Press had decided to revert to the newspaper's original title, so the 1½d broadsheet was known as the *Daily Telegraph*. The first editorial proclaimed that the newspaper was determined to 'recapture the position of influence and esteem to which the old *Daily Telegraph* rose by honest, fearless and enterprising journalism' while being 'thoroughly modern — as modern as television, wireless and airmails'.[64]

As Frank was preoccupied with reviving the *Telegraph* and negotiating with the industry's unions, Gretel went on a holiday to Honolulu with her friends Ruth and

Ernest Watt and their young daughter. A wealthy pastoralist and racehorse owner, sixty-two-year-old Ernest Watt lived in Point Piper and was a popular man about town. Many years her husband's junior, the warm, generous and artistic Ruth was Gretel's closest friend. The two women surfed and sunbathed on the golden sands of Waikiki Beach by day, danced to the throb of the ukelele by night and bought patterned bathing costumes and presents before departing adorned with leis and to the strains of the 'Hawaiian Farewell'.[65] Frank Packer and his executives, meanwhile, ensured that the *Telegraph* featured 'exclusive' overseas reports, lively serials, comprehensive sports reports, photographic pages, a pattern department, a shopping bureau, pithy news and views columns, a daily article by Lennie Lower, competitions and special issues.[66]

At the same time, another Australian newspaper was collapsing. On Good Friday 1936, after a brave but unsuccessful bid to arrest the dominance of the Melbourne *Herald*, the *Star* ceased publication. Many of the *Star*'s bright young journalists, including Cyril Pearl, Richard Hughes, J. K. ('King') Watson and Godfrey Blunden, flocked to Sydney to join the new *Telegraph*. Richard Hughes was exactly the same age as his prospective employer, and as tall and as powerfully built. Nevertheless, the journalist found his interview with Packer — still only twenty-nine years of age — an unnerving experience. When Hughes entered his office, Packer swept aside with one huge hand a bottle of tomato sauce and some biscuits.

>'So you're Hughes?,' Packer barked, with his damaged eye remaining fixed.
>
>'Yes, sir, I am,' Hughes squeaked.
>
>'What makes you think you're a good journalist?,' Packer growled.
>
>'I don't think I'm a good journalist; I know I am,' Hughes blurted out as he sweated profusely in his suit.
>
>Packer grinned at the unexpected cockiness of the remark. 'Confident big bastard, at least. Well, we've got the best here. So good luck.'[67]

Hughes and his colleagues were fortunate that there was a buffer between them and Packer. Kathleen Maisie Faircloth had joined the staff of Smith's Newspapers as a junior secretary in 1924 and gone to Sydney Newspapers with Packer in 1932. Unassuming and bespectacled, 'Fairy' was to work for Packer for the rest of his life. She would warn her colleagues if Packer was in a bad mood and she was not afraid to jolly him up and tell him that he was being too tough on someone. Packer, for his part, valued Faircloth's tact, discretion, loyalty and business competence.[68]

Employees such as Hughes did not simply help to resuscitate the *Telegraph*. A court case in mid 1936 revealed that Packer was prepared to use his employees to look after his personal interests. A good but aggressive driver, Packer was charged in 1935 with negligent driving and failing to stop after colliding with a taxi on New South Head Road. The police officer who interviewed Packer testified that the defendant had not realised that he had hit a car and the magistrate dismissed the charges.[69]

The case Packer was involved in the following year was more serious. He was charged with driving his Auburn car in a manner dangerous to the public after hitting another car in the rear and causing it to overturn at Narrabeen on Sydney's northern beaches. The other driver claimed that he had put out his hand signalling his intention to turn right, but this evidence was refuted by Packer and two of his passengers, Gretel and their good friend Lennox Bode. Although he testified that he had been driving at only 48 to 55 kilometres per hour, Packer could not account for the skid marks that extended for 25 metres from the scene of the collision. One witness claimed that Packer had been travelling at more than 100 kilometres per hour and another witness testified that he had heard the screeching of brakes 100 metres before the point of collision. In the course of the case, Packer admitted that he had sent an employee named O'Donnell to Narrabeen to 'secure eyewitnesses'. It emerged that the two witnesses who corroborated Packer's account had been out of work at the time of the accident and had called at Consolidated Press to meet O'Donnell. The police prosecutor asked one of the witnesses whether anything had been said to him about being paid expenses to appear in court; the man claimed that no such offer had been made. The magistrate dismissed the charges because there were so many discrepancies in the evidence and he had to give Packer the benefit of the doubt. However, he noted that if he had been satisfied that Packer had been driving at around 90 kilometres per hour, he would not have had the 'slightest hesitation' in convicting him.[70] In later years Packer employed a chauffeur.

6
Mansions and Mêlées

Bellevue Hill rises about 100 metres above the waters of Sydney Harbour. In 1820 Governor Lachlan Macquarie had ordered that the 'vulgarly' named 'Vinegar Hill' should henceforth be known as 'Belle Vue'. By the 1930s Bellevue Hill, with its winding streets, commanding vista of the sea and wealth of trees and flowers, was among the most fashionable addresses in Sydney. The view in the course of the drive up the long, serpentine stretch of Victoria Road was one of the finest in Sydney, and beautiful and costly homes were set along the full distance of the run.[1] 'Cairnton', a mansion on the high side of Victoria Road, occupies one of the suburb's most elevated vantage points. It was here that Frank and Gretel Packer made their permanent home and established the basis of what became a family compound.

Packer purchased 'Cairnton', which was valued at £8000, from Isobel Garland in 1934 or 1935. Mrs Garland was the widow of John Garland, a barrister who had been attorney-general in the Holman state government and had built the house in about 1908. By the time Packer acquired 'Cairnton', it boasted rolling lawns, garages and a tennis court. He and Gretel did not move into the mansion immediately, presumably because they wanted to undertake renovations. They left 'Kismet' in early 1937 and for a few months lived at 'Greenoaks' in Darling Point.[2] On 17 December 1937, shortly after taking up residence at 'Cairnton', Gretel gave birth to their second child. The boy was christened Kerry Francis Bullmore Packer.

As he made his way to the office each day, Frank passed Craigend Street, where he himself had been born. But while the drive from Bellevue Hill to Darlinghurst took less than ten minutes, they were poles apart in socio-economic terms. By now Packer and his family and friends had colonised the Eastern Suburbs: Mary and Anthony Hordern owned the grand 'Retford Hall' in Darling Point; Joan and Douglas Henty lived in Fairfax Road, Bellevue Hill; Ethel Packer took up residence in 'Daingeen' in Victoria Road before moving into the old house her daughter and son-in-law had renovated in the same street; and Jimmie Bancks and Jessie Tait also lived in Victoria Road.[3]

An enthusiastic gardener, Gretel Packer tended to and oversaw the care of the extensive English garden that encircled 'Cairnton'. She was also a keen interior decorator who loved experimenting with new styles; sometimes rooms would be decorated in

French provincial style and at other times she would succumb to Japanese minimalism. No snob, Gretel liked nothing better than fossicking for unique *objets d'art* in junk shops. Even though she would park her car a couple of streets away in an effort to conceal her wealth, the shopkeepers invariably sensed from her elegant manner and appearance that she had money to spend.[4]

There were certain fixtures on the social calendar for wealthy Sydney residents like Gretel and Frank Packer. They holidayed at Palm Beach in January, attended the Royal Easter Show and the Easter race meetings in March or April, sometimes went skiing in June or July (the sport was not one of Frank's favourites), attended the spring race meetings at Randwick in September and October and watched the running of the Melbourne Cup in November.

Tragedy nearly struck the family at Palm Beach in 1939. The *Sun* journalist and gossip columnist Dorothy Jenner (known as 'Andrea') was sitting on the beach when she noticed a bundle, which turned out to be four-year-old Clyde Packer, floating in the water. Jenner waded in and picked up the blue-faced child by the seat of his bathers and shook him vigorously. Gretel, who had been basking in the sun covered with oil, came running when she heard her elder son coughing and yelling. She was too shaken and too busy scolding Clyde to thank Jenner for saving his life.[5]

The social pages record numerous diversions for Mr and Mrs Frank Packer. They were often guests of the Horderns at 'Milton Park' in Bowral in the Southern Highlands, where Mary created a famous garden; enjoyed holidays at the exclusive Menzies Hotel in Melbourne; hosted buffet dinners and bridge parties to farewell or welcome friends who were departing or returning to Australia; attended cocktail parties and dances put on by members of their circle; and were present at the party held at Government House in 1937 to celebrate the coronation of King George VI.[6]

In December 1938 Prince's restaurant opened in the basement of the MLC Building at 42 Martin Place. A few months later the new Romano's restaurant opened on the corner of Martin Place and Castlereagh Street opposite the Hotel Australia. The two restaurants and cabaret venues quickly became the places to be seen in Sydney and the functions they hosted provided regular fodder for the women's pages of the *Telegraph* and the *Sydney Morning Herald*. Although the Packers attended lunches, dinners, suppers and opening night parties at both venues, they preferred Prince's. Frank often dined there between the laying out and the printing of the *Telegraph*. He liked table two and his favourite dish was a prawn cocktail served in a brandy balloon. He was not really an aficionado of theatre, and he would doze through many a show if the plot did not interest him. But he enjoyed lively musicals and was happy to join his wife at the premiere of such shows as *Anything Goes*.[7]

Now that he published a Sydney metropolitan newspaper as well as a best-selling magazine, Packer had to attend numerous business functions and make frequent visits interstate. Often he was simply a guest at functions such as a luncheon for the managing director of England's Lever Bros advertising agency, who visited Sydney in 1937. Increasingly often, however, Packer was called upon to deliver speeches. In 1938, for example, he and Roy Doutreband, the general manager of Associated Newspapers, addressed the annual dinner of the Retail Newsagents' Association of New South Wales.

Never an accomplished public speaker, Packer addressed his audiences in a gruff and rather halting manner.[8]

The Australian Newspapers Conference (ANC), which represented most of the country's newspaper proprietors, held meetings every six months in different capital cities. When the ANC conferred in his home town, Packer and his Sydney counterparts were expected to entertain delegates from interstate. In May 1938, for instance, the Sydney members hosted a cocktail party at the Hotel Australia, a dinner at Usher's Hotel and an 'at home' at Elizabeth Bay House. Gretel Packer, meanwhile, entertained the delegates' wives at dinner at 'Cairnton', followed by a show in town. If Theodore happened to be visiting from Fiji, he sometimes accompanied his partner to these conferences and social events.[9]

The *Telegraph*'s performance was steadily improving. The September 1935 audit had revealed a net circulation of 110 000 copies per day; this had increased to 130 000 copies a year later and 166 000 copies in 1937. When the executives of the *Sydney Morning Herald* looked at their sales figures, they could not have been happy: the newspaper's circulation rose by only 4000 copies, from 217 000 in September 1935 to 221 000 copies two years later. The management at Fairfax was overhauled and the newspaper, which had become staid and somewhat complacent, competed more energetically for scoops and racing news.[10]

The revitalised *Telegraph* quickly emerged as a provocative champion of the liberal and the modern. Waging a steady attack on 'wowsers, old fogies and fuddy-duddies', it campaigned against six o'clock closing laws, ridiculed bans on books and attempts to regularise bathing costumes and sought to expose the petty tyranny of bureaucrats. It celebrated symbols of the city and modernity, such as the skyscraper, published annual 'Industrial Supplements', enthusiastically reported on the work of scientists and eagerly anticipated the development of television. The newspaper adopted a progressively liberal political stance rather than an obviously partisan one. It argued that the incidence of tuberculosis in tramway employees and the number of accidents in the workplace were unacceptable; it savaged Eric Spooner, the deputy leader of the New South Wales UAP, for trying to abolish relief work in 1936; and it maintained that the Country Party, representing only sectional interests, had too much influence in Joseph Lyons's federal government.[11]

There is little evidence to suggest that Packer directly intervened in his newspaper's coverage of political events during this period. It is quite possible, of course, that he — or perhaps even Theodore — instructed Deamer to advocate a vote for Bertram Stevens's UAP government at the 1938 New South Wales election. Nevertheless, the editorial that appeared on the eve of the poll was much less savage about Jack Lang than editorials in earlier organs of 'the Packer press'.[12] In the second half of the 1930s Frank Packer was more than willing to leave the editorial direction of the *Telegraph* to Syd Deamer and his talented team, while he himself concentrated on consolidating the newspaper's market share and expanding his company's business interests.

Although the *Telegraph*'s circulation was steadily improving, Packer had cause to be worried about its financial position. The regular market research surveys he commissioned consistently showed that the newspaper appealed most to C and D class readers — that is, lower-middle and lower-working-class readers — in less affluent suburbs. This meant that the *Telegraph* did not attract lucrative advertising accounts from clients such as David Jones, and the *Sydney Morning Herald* dominated the vital classified advertising market. Most readers also bought the newspaper through casual street sales rather than having it delivered.[13]

George Warnecke recalled that Packer hurriedly convened a board meeting in the second half of 1936 to propose inserting the New South Wales edition of the *Women's Weekly* into the *Telegraph* as a free supplement on Thursdays. Packer maintained that this would boost the newspaper's permanent sales and pull in major advertising accounts. The idea, according to Warnecke, was met with a stunned and bewildered silence. The editor-in-chief vehemently objected to the suggestion, arguing that the magazine itself was a rich source of revenue: 'It will carry the *Telegraph* on its back and give it a chance to find its own character', he said. Then Michael Stiver, J. Walter Thompson's managing director, offered a similar assessment, and there were murmurs of agreement. Packer, flushed and on his feet, gave an instant verdict: 'It looks like everybody is unanimous but me. You may be right at that'. Back in his office, Packer criticised Warnecke for not supporting him in front of Stiver, 'an outsider'.

While the *Telegraph* opened a classified advertising office, introduced free insurance for readers who had the newspaper delivered, and launched a Monday Home Magazine to try to attract new advertisers,[14] the *Women's Weekly* was certainly flourishing. As a result of Warnecke's overseas study tour, Consolidated Press had purchased a new, high-speed printing press that could print in four-colour rotogravure and could be attached to a black letterpress. Packer had persuaded Theodore that the *Women's Weekly* should be printed on a modern press specially suited to magazine production. Packer had estimated that the plant would cost about £50 000, but Theodore later confessed that he mentally revised the figure to £100 000. In the end, the exercise cost £130 000.[15]

The installation of the press, which became operative in December 1936, helped expose the incipient divisions within Consolidated Press. Warnecke felt that Packer was determined to loosen his paternal attachment to the *Women's Weekly*. Warnecke later maintained that Packer wanted his interest in the magazine to be primarily technical: in other words, he was to concentrate on supervising the press's installation. Alice Jackson, who had edited the *Women's Weekly* during Warnecke's absence abroad, came to be seen as a rival editor. At the same time, printers were concerned that the new technology would lower manning levels and the fumes would damage their health. Grit was applied to wear away the engraved cylinders, chemicals added to the ink gave the paper a foul odour, and there were fires in the ventilation ducts. After spending the early weeks of 1937 tracking down the saboteurs, Packer demanded more conspicuous loyalty from his employees than ever before. Despite these difficulties, the plant opened up the capacity to print cheap, glamorous publications by the million and to offer advertisers a national medium. Indeed, the type of plant installed by Packer was so advanced that it had not yet begun operating in England.[16]

By 1938 Keith Murdoch had become disturbed by the aggressive interstate tactics of the *Women's Weekly* and the way in which it was 'sucking' advertising revenue from his newspapers. In early July he offered £350 000 for a half share in Consolidated Press. Packer countered by asking for £450 000. Such a deal would have allowed Packer and Theodore to make a massive profit on their original investment of less than £30 000 and secured the *Telegraph*'s ongoing viability. When Packer proposed equal control of the proposed company, Murdoch made an outright bid of £800 000. Packer was inclined to reject the offer, cheerfully telling Warnecke: 'If it's worth that to him [Murdoch], it's good enough to keep'.[17]

The accountant Fred Smith, who had been negotiating the deal, decided that the matter was important enough to summon Theodore from Fiji. During a conference in the Consolidated Press bunker, Theodore announced that he agreed with Packer that they should not sell out of the company. 'You realise what you are doing, E. G.?', asked the cautious accountant. 'You are turning down £800 000.' Theodore replied, smiling, 'I think we'll give the young fellow his head'. As a sign of the trust that Theodore had in his partner, a special resolution was passed at the Consolidated Press annual general meeting two months later. It stipulated that the deputy chairman (Packer) could take the chair if the chairman (Theodore) was absent from future meetings.[18]

Although relations with Theodore remained warm, Packer's dealings with other executives were often tense. In September 1936 N. Q. Bradshaw finally severed his working relationship with Consolidated Press and joined the Melbourne *Age*, but he retained his shares in Sydney Newspapers. In January 1939 Packer and Theodore developed another scheme designed to curtail the rights of minority shareholders. At various times since the incorporation of the company the two men appear to have advanced monies totalling £35 000. They maintained that Sydney Newspapers was not in a position to repay this indebtedness unless it released a considerable portion of its shares in Consolidated Press. After discussing the matter at a board meeting, Packer proposed that he and Theodore should take up an allotment of £7000 each at a premium of £1 10s per £1 share. Bradshaw, estimating that the shares he had acquired for £1 were now worth £10 each, asserted that he and Warnecke should be entitled to take up proportionate allotments on the same terms as the two majority shareholders. Bradshaw also maintained that the price to be paid by Packer and Theodore was inadequate and, as a result of his protests, their attempt to improve the position of the majority shareholders was again stymied. When war broke out a few months later, Bradshaw agreed to sell his shares to Theodore rather than Packer for £3500. The disaffected Bradshaw wrote to Warnecke from Melbourne: 'They were worth £10,000 but I thought it better to sell. You could hardly get any information at all about the company'.[19]

Packer's relations with Warnecke were no better. Years of unrelenting work and tension had exacted both a physical and emotional toll on the editor-in-chief, who in 1939 announced that he was resigning from Consolidated Press. On 27 April Packer attended a farewell luncheon at the Tattersalls Club presided over by Warnecke's close friend, Justice H. V. Evatt. Although Packer must have been relieved at Warnecke's decision to pursue a newspaper career in the United States, another eight years were to elapse before the creative brains behind the Women's Weekly agreed to relinquish his shares in Sydney Newspapers. Warnecke's long, complex association with the Packer family was finally severed in the mid 1950s when he purchased Consolidated Press's rights to produce *Family Circle*. In a poignant letter to Evatt, Warnecke commented that it was 'good to feel free, even if slightly tattered'.[20]

The *Telegraph*'s editor also left the company in April 1939. A heavy drinker with a sharp mind, a biting wit and a healthy disrespect for authority, Deamer often succumbed to the urge to display his intellectual superiority. He was present at a dinner during the 1936 abdication crisis when Packer mistakenly referred to a 'morgantic marriage' between the Duke of Windsor and Mrs Wallis Simpson. The editor is reputed to have tartly corrected his employer: 'Morganatic, my dear boy, morganatic'.[21]

There is some suggestion that Deamer caught Packer in a compromising situation in 1938 or 1939. Packer's office, complete with a mini-bar, was located at the Elizabeth Street end of the third floor of the Consolidated Press building. An adjoining reception room accommodated his two secretaries, Fairy Faircloth and Mabel Gilburt, and assorted chairs and a sofa. In one wall was a door leading directly into the *Telegraph*'s offices with the lock on Packer's side. Journalistic lore contends that late one night Deamer went through this door, which Packer had forgotten to lock, to discuss something with him. When he discovered Packer attempting to seduce a woman on the sofa, Deamer did not miss a beat. 'I'm terribly sorry', he is supposed to have said. 'I'll come back later. I see Mr Packer's not in yet'. While Packer recovered from the surprise, Deamer returned to his office and did not mention the incident. However, Packer is said to have been so amused by Deamer's remark that he just had to tell someone. By midnight, despite Deamer's repeated disclaimers, the story was known to everyone on the editorial floor.[22]

Nevertheless, it is unlikely that this encounter contributed to Deamer's exit from the company a few months later. There are many versions of the events that precipitated his departure in April 1939. Some say that Deamer was out drinking when the brilliant but ruthless news editor, Brian Penton, wanted to discuss an urgent cable story with him; others that Deamer was sacked after having a row with Packer and possibly Penton. In any case, Clarrie McNulty was promoted from chief sub-editor to editor of the *Telegraph*.[23]

The year 1939 brought not only the departures of Warnecke and Deamer but several new challenges and opportunities. Consolidated Press launched another magazine, Packer had a spectacular fracas with a fellow newspaper proprietor, plans were set in place to produce a Sunday newspaper, the company made an important intervention in Australia's cultural politics and its managing director was appointed to a leading position within the publishing industry.

Packer planned to mark the third anniversary of the new *Daily Telegraph* with the launch of a Thursday afternoon newspaper. But Associated Newspapers pounced when Packer revealed his intention to begin publishing the *Evening Telegraph* on 23 March 1939. Claiming that the newspaper would breach the 1935 agreement stipulating that Consolidated Press could not produce an afternoon newspaper for a period of ten years, the company threatened to sue.[24]

Immediately after being forced to abandon its plans for the *Evening Telegraph*, Consolidated Press announced that it would begin publishing a new monthly magazine. The idea for *Fashion* was conceived by Packer's wife, who wrote the first issue's editorial and contributed a regular double-page spread called 'Models selected by Gretel'. The actual editing was done by a *Daily Telegraph* journalist, Godfrey Blunden. But, although the magazine appealed to advertisers and made good use of the *Women's Weekly*'s rotogravure press, fashion illustrators and pattern service, it was an early casualty of the wartime newsprint shortage. *Fashion* survived only a few months after its launch in June 1939.[25]

Despite the deteriorating international situation and the lack of newsprint, Packer was determined to utilise Consolidated Press's idle printing capacity. In July he despatched David Yaffa to the United States to arrange for features for a new paper to be known as the *Sunday Telegraph*. Packer reorganised his company's advertising staff[26] and on 21 September he assured Mrs C. Budd, who had developed a dummy for the women's section, that the newspaper would definitely proceed. By the end of the month, however, his commitment to launching the *Sunday Telegraph* had begun to waver. Packer told the New South Wales branch of the PIEUA, which objected to plans to include a comic supplement imported from the United States in the newspaper, that it was unlikely his company would go ahead with the launch.[27]

It was precisely at this time that Packer had a celebrated brawl with a rival newspaper proprietor. By now the Sunday newspaper market had only two players. On the one side was the *Sunday Sun*, which enjoyed a high circulation and was bloated with retail advertising. Its competitor was *Truth*, which in recent years had been trying to improve its racy reputation and become more like a family paper. It began a regular section of foreign news and comment and enlarged the women's section, film and book reviews and the motoring pages. Nevertheless, its proprietor, Ezra Norton, remained a social pariah. A coarse and hectoring employer, Norton was a lone wolf who shunned publicity and travelled around town with bodyguards.[28]

Despite Norton's dubious reputation, his dealings with Packer were civil in the early years of Consolidated Press. In 1938 a group of major Australian newspaper publishers, including Fairfax and the HWT, had joined forces to form Australian Newsprint Mills Pty Ltd. The syndicate had applied for a bounty and a levy on the cost of imported newsprint to help finance the production of Australian newsprint from a new mill in Tasmania. A small group of recalcitrants, including Consolidated Press and Norton's Truth & Sportsman Ltd, had rejected the idea of paying more for imported newsprint while waiting, perhaps for years, for an Australian industry to materialise. Packer and Norton had both appeared before the Tariff Board inquiry in March 1938 to criticise the proposal, and had even considered investing in an abortive proposal by a group of businessmen to produce newsprint in South Australia without the need for a bounty.[29]

In 1939, however, relations between the pair broke down. On 16 September the *Telegraph* criticised an article *Truth* had written about dealings between Germany and

Britain. *Truth* retaliated the next day by publishing two photographs of Packer, one bearing the caption 'Approved', the other 'Disapproved'. The article claimed that Packer had taken strong exception to the 'Disapproved' photograph that had appeared in *Truth* on a previous occasion. Packer had certainly been embarrassed by his large size as a teenager, and it is possible that he remained somewhat self-conscious about his appearance. He could not be blamed for objecting to the 'Disapproved' image, which was cruelly unflattering. *Truth* alleged that the posed portrait of Packer bearing the label 'Approved' had been retouched by artists at Consolidated Press. Not to be outdone, on Friday 29 September the *Telegraph* ran a report about a court case in which Norton was appearing as a witness. The article, entitled 'Newspaper Proprietor Buys Allegedly Stolen Brooch', was accompanied by a photograph of Norton captioned 'Hurries Away From Press Photographer'.[30]

The next day Packer and Norton, both members of the Australian Jockey Club (AJC), attended the Derby race meeting at Randwick. They encountered each other near the official stand and fisticuffs ensued. A burly man who appears to have been Norton's bodyguard intervened to hit out at Packer. By the time a crowd of about 2000 people had gathered to catch a glimpse of the fight, another man had gone to Packer's aid. Packer seems to have come off worst, emerging from the mêlée 'hatless, breathless, and bleeding from a cut over one eye and marked on both cheeks, his face puffed, hair tussled, and clothing in disorder'. He went straight to the gentlemen's retiring room to minister to his battered countenance, and no report about the unedifying spectacle appeared in either the *Telegraph* or *Truth*. When Packer appeared at the office on Monday, Richard Hughes remarked, 'I believe you had a pretty rough time at Randwick'. Packer agreed, saying that it was a pity that Roland Pullen, a *Telegraph* journalist who had gone to the races, had not been around to help. Pullen might have been a mad punter, but he was more of an aesthete than a brawler. When Hughes commented that his friend was not the pugilistic type, Packer retorted grimly: 'No, but he had an umbrella'. Packer and Norton were subsequently severely reprimanded by AJC officials.[31]

Even though war had now broken out and newsprint rationing was inevitable, the brawl seems to have renewed Packer's resolve to launch a Sunday paper. He announced that *Truth*'s new rival would make its debut on 19 November. In the weeks preceding the launch, the state and federal offices of the PIEUA furiously debated whether the *Sunday Telegraph*, which still planned to publish an imported comic supplement, should be declared black. Although the AJA and the Black and White Artists' Club also opposed the 'menace' of imported supplements, Packer stood firm. He and his executives cleverly exploited the divisions within the union movement: the father of the Consolidated Press chapel was prepared to let the supplement go ahead because he wanted the *Sunday Telegraph* to provide a new outlet of employment for his members, and the Amalgamated Printing Trades Employees' Union, which had refused to merge with the PIEUA, agreed to the importation of the supplement on the understanding that it would be printed in Australia within a year. In a close vote, the PIEUA agreed to allow the *Sunday Telegraph* to proceed.[32]

The erudite and iconoclastic Cyril Pearl, who had come to Consolidated Press from the defunct Melbourne *Star*, was appointed editor. The new paper was promoted with a comprehensive press and radio advertising campaign. Nearly 400 000 copies of the first issue of the comic supplement were distributed free in the *Women's Weekly* and the *Daily Telegraph* in the days preceding the launch. A radio personality known as 'Charlie Chuckle' was created to read the comic on radio on Sunday mornings. E. G. Theodore, on a visit to Sydney, and Ethel Packer pressed the switch to begin printing the first issue of the *Sunday Telegraph* on 19 November.[33]

It was quite a week for Frank Packer. Just a few days before the launch of his new paper, he attended the half-yearly meeting of the ANC in Melbourne and was elected president. Murdoch immediately wrote to Packer to congratulate him:

> It is the highest honor [sic] that proprietors and managers can give to one of themselves. I feel sure you will be a sound progressive leader, and I hope you will call on me for any help if there is anything I can do.

Despite the laudable sentiments, Murdoch knew that the appointment had not been a *fait accompli*. He and his good friend Sir Lloyd Dumas, the managing director of Advertiser Newspapers Ltd in Adelaide and retiring president of the ANC, had spent much of the year speculating about the presidency. Extant correspondence between the pair makes it clear that Packer had enemies other than the Denisons within the industry. Delamore McCay was said to dislike Packer 'intensely', and in January 1939 Packer had objected to the proposal that McCay should be appointed secretary of the ANC. The hostility between the two men might have been the result of the falling-out between R. C. Packer and McCay's brother Adam in 1927; it is also possible that ill-feeling arose because of Frank's ruthless dealings with Associated Newspapers during Delamore's tenure as editor-in-chief. However, Packer agreed to accept a majority decision, even though 'it was a great mistake', and McCay was appointed secretary.[34]

By mid 1939 both Murdoch and Dumas had concluded that Packer was the obvious choice for the ANC presidency. But while they were prepared to concede that the thirty-two-year-old had achieved a great deal in his short career, they were also wary of him. Murdoch observed that 'there are good points in having him wrapped closely to us' and Dumas commented that 'if we get him into the responsible position of President, he will be much less likely to be a disturbing factor than if we leave him outside'. Dumas was also encouraged by the 'good co-operative spirit' that Packer was displaying about AAP. When Packer had failed in his bid to launch the *Evening Telegraph*, he had moved to have Consolidated Press admitted to AAP. In October 1939 the application was vetoed by Geoffrey Syme, the managing editor and joint proprietor of the Melbourne *Age*. Syme deeply disliked and distrusted Packer, whom he sarcastically dubbed 'the gentleman from Elizabeth Street'. In the end, however, Syme decided that he would rather have Packer as president of the ANC than E. G. Knox, now managing editor of the *Argus*, and in 1940 Consolidated Press joined AAP.[35]

At the same time as Packer was being elected president of the ANC, his newspapers were co-sponsoring an important exhibition of French and British modern art. In November 1939 the newspapers agreed to sponsor the groundbreaking exhibition of paintings at the Art Gallery of New South Wales that Murdoch's Melbourne *Herald* had brought to Australia. Gretel Packer and Mary Hordern shared a keen interest in art, and were early patrons of (later Sir) William Dobell. Frank Packer himself seems to have had little knowledge of art, but he was more than willing to see his company enter the artistic arena. Many of the people who worked on the *Telegraph*s had links with the art world, were champions of modernism and shared a commitment to educating as well as entertaining their readers.[36]

By late 1939, then, Packer had a beautiful society wife, lived in one of Sydney's best addresses, played rich men's sports, headed the publishing industry's peak body and had emerged as a patron of the arts. Nevertheless, it is clear that some colleagues regarded him with disdain: they refused to forget or ignore his blatant exploitation of Associated Newspapers, his robust and at times aggressively isolationist business style and his unseemly brawl with Ezra Norton.

Although they often deplored Packer's business strategies, it is doubtful whether his counterparts always realised just how cunning he could be. As 1939 drew to a close, Packer appears to have told R. A. G. Henderson, the wily general manager of Fairfax, that he was thinking of selling out to the HWT. It is highly unlikely that such discussions were taking place; as we have seen, negotiations with the HWT had collapsed on two previous occasions and Consolidated Press had been looking for means to expand throughout 1939. The infant *Sunday Telegraph* was proving a considerable drain on the company's resources and Packer told Henderson that all the company needed to keep independent and out of the red was a rise in the cover price from 1½d to 2d. Knowing that Fairfax would be daunted by the prospect of the HWT moving into Sydney, Packer was anxious to ensure that the *Sydney Morning Herald* would not undercut the *Daily Telegraph*'s price. Fairfax dutifully obliged, agreeing that the cover price of the two newspapers should rise simultaneously in February 1940.[37]

The outbreak of the Second World War posed a number of problems and challenges for Packer and his company. The need to conserve shipping space and foreign exchange forced the government to ration newsprint. In mid 1940 the major daily, Sunday and weekly newspapers were required to reduce their newsprint consumption by 35 per cent. As supplies of the newspaper industry's lifeblood contracted, schisms enveloped the industry. In April 1940 cabinet agreed to grant Truth & Sportsman a newsprint licence for the publication of a new afternoon newspaper. The Sydney proprietors were understandably dismayed by this development but their interstate counterparts, who could afford to be more philosophical, refused to support their protests. As a result, Consolidated Press and Associated Newspapers withdrew from the ANC and Packer resigned from the presidency. A few weeks later, with the international situation worsening, the government revoked the licence for Ezra Norton's *Daily Mirror*.[38]

As a result of relentless lobbying by Truth & Sportsman, the situation was again reversed in January 1941. When federal cabinet announced that the *Daily Mirror* could go ahead, a delegation of newspaper proprietors went to Melbourne to meet (later Sir) Eric Harrison, the minister for trade and customs, and the deputy prime minister (later Sir) Arthur Fadden. They complained that a new paper should not be allowed to proceed at a time when newsprint was critically short for existing titles. Packer was at pains to emphasise the damaging impact that restrictions on the size of his papers was having on his company's advertising revenue. In February metropolitan daily newspaper companies, with the exception of Truth & Sportsman, reunited to form the Australian Newspaper Proprietors' Association (ANPA).[39]

The second major challenge for such companies as Consolidated Press was coping with the government's censorship regulations. The key players in the early years of Consolidated Press, including George Warnecke, Brian Penton and Cyril Pearl, passionately opposed censorship and relished attacking 'wowsers' and bureaucratic excesses. When the Department of Information was created in September 1939, it was given the authority to examine before publication any matter that dealt with the size, movement or operations of defence forces and any other matter that could be useful to the enemy or prejudicial to safety and defence, the efficient conduct of the war and the maintenance of essential supplies and services. The federal government could seize journals that contravened any censorship order, and forbade the disclosure of any suppression of, or amendment to, copy.[40]

Within weeks, the *Telegraph* was being condemned by censorship authorities for ridiculing government regulations and printing alarmist posters about the progress of Britain's war effort.[41] As news editor and then editor, Brian Penton was responsible for many of the *Telegraph*'s challenges to the intrusiveness of censorship regulations and its criticisms of the worrying deficiencies in Australia's defences.

Born in Brisbane in 1904, Penton was only two years older than Packer. He had worked on the Brisbane *Courier* before securing a position on the *Sydney Morning Herald* in 1925. His provocative and sardonic columns on the New South Wales parliament brought him to the notice of R. C. Packer, but Penton declined an invitation to join the *Daily Guardian* in 1926. In 1933, after a spell in England, Penton was enticed onto the staff of the old Sydney *Telegraph* by Warnecke and R. C. Packer.[42] Penton advanced quickly on the *Telegraph*, serving as columnist, literary editor, news editor and then, from 1941, editor. In the 1930s he also wrote two impressive novels, *Landtakers* and *Inheritors*, about the hardships experienced by Queensland settlers.

After spending time in Spain in the lead-up to the civil war, Penton had made a detailed study of Australia's defence preparedness and leadership. With the end of the phony war in March 1940, the *Telegraph*s began running double-column front-page editorials assessing military matters. They argued that people should be more fully informed about what was happening at allied war councils in order to maintain morale, and claimed that R. G. Menzies' conservative government had relied too heavily on Britain, which was now largely incapable of helping Australia, for war materials and weapons.[43] As 1940 progressed, the *Telegraph*s and even the *Women's Weekly* campaigned for the appointment of outstanding individuals to an all-party government. The newspapers' front pages featured editorials entitled 'Please Read This, Mr Menzies' that suggested how to sharpen Australia's war effort and attempted to provoke the Australian people out of their perceived complacency.[44]

Packer took the unusual step of signing the editorial that appeared on 20 September 1940, the day before the federal election. The editorial listed the candidates who had been given access to printing or broadcasting facilities by Consolidated Press: Eric

Spooner (UAP), the treasurer; Bertram Stevens (UAP), the former New South Wales premier; Dr L. W. Nott (UAP), who was opposed by Eddie Ward, a pugnacious socialist and a former Langite; Dr Frank Louat (UAP), a lawyer and civil libertarian who occasionally wrote for the *Telegraph*; William McCall, the UAP candidate for Martin; and Captain J. P. Abbott (Country Party). Packer also indicated that Dr H. V. Evatt, who had resigned from the High Court bench to stand for the ALP in a seat held by the UAP, had received secretarial assistance. The *Telegraph* championed Evatt as a future leader of the ALP and Les Haylen, the news editor of the *Women's Weekly*, was ordered to caption a photo of the Labor candidate 'Stepping Forth' and one of Menzies 'Complacency'.[45]

Professor Henry Mayer, an influential commentator on the media, observed that people object to gifts from media proprietors because of their secrecy. Packer's editorial on the eve of the 1940 poll, then, is admirable for its candour. Nevertheless, he was rather circumspect about the reasons the *Telegraph*s were supporting one particular candidate. As the election approached, *Truth* had questioned why the *Telegraph*s were advocating a vote for an 'Independent UAP' candidate, (later Sir) Norman Cowper, against the sitting UAP member, Eric Harrison, in the blue-ribbon seat of Wentworth. As *Truth* pointed out, Cowper was a partner in Allen, Allen & Hemsley, the company that handled Consolidated Press's legal matters. *Truth* also noted that Harrison was disliked by the daily newspapers because he had permitted the launch of the *ABC Weekly*, which they believed represented 'unfair competition', by the national radio broadcaster in 1939. In his editorial, Packer was unable to effectively rebut these points. Many years after losing the contest, Cowper conceded that he had been friends with Theodore and admitted that he had been 'pitchforked' into the election by Packer.[46]

The coalition hung onto power with the support of two independents. In this highly unstable political environment, Packer invariably stood by his employees in clashes with the censorship authorities. Although he left most dealings with the censors to Penton, Pearl and other senior journalists, there were times when he personally intervened. Consolidated Press was disconsolate on the rare occasions that it had to concede that one of its publications had overstepped the mark. In July 1940 the *Sunday Telegraph* reported that the chief justice of the High Court, Sir John Latham, had agreed to become Australia's first minister to Japan. After the chief publicity censor criticised this report, saying that the announcement had yet to be confirmed, Packer immediately wrote to the censor and Prime Minister Menzies to apologise. He explained that the article had arisen out of a misunderstanding because Consolidated Press had believed that Latham's appointment had been confirmed and was about to become public knowledge.

Packer was rarely so conciliatory. In January 1941 he rang a censor in 'a high state of excitement' to discuss the treatment of some photographs for the *Telegraph* and then took his complaint directly to H. S. Foll, the minister for information. When the matter was resolved to Packer's satisfaction, the bemused censor noted that he had been thanked in a 'most friendly fashion' for his 'splendid co-operation'.[47]

Packer believed that he could do more than just campaign editorially for the maintenance of public morale and the successful prosecution of the war effort. He had enlisted in the militia several months before the start of the war. The citizen army had been retained since the end of the First World War, although its resources and potential effectiveness were questionable: it lacked mortars, anti-tank and anti-aircraft guns, tanks, armoured cars, a variety of engineering and signal gear and adequate reserves of ammunition. But the disturbing events in China and Europe in 1938, culminating in the Munich crisis, renewed the Australian government's commitment to the militia. Major-General Sir Thomas Blamey directed a recruiting campaign that saw the size of the militia double from 35 000 members in September 1938 to 70 000 six months later.[48]

Both Frank Packer and Brian Penton were moved by the campaign. But when Penton announced that he intended to join the militia, his employer decreed that the *Telegraph* could not survive with both of them working part-time. A ruthless, quixotic and ambitious perfectionist, Penton played favourites and divided the *Telegraphs*' journalists into cliques. He enjoyed a close, some said conspiratorial, relationship with Frank Packer. Packer almost certainly never read Penton's harsh and at times savage novels, but he genuinely admired intellectual and cultural sophistication in others. With his sharp intellect and polemical style, Penton became, in a sense, Packer's intellectual complement. Packer instinctively believed that newspapers were weapons to be wielded by their proprietors, he was concerned about the state of Australia's defence and the torpor of the government, and he resented the idea of governmental and bureaucratic interference with his publications. Penton, with his interest in the idea of democratic propaganda, his knowledge of defence policy and his long-standing opposition to censorship, was ideally placed to articulate and advance his employer's thinking. Packer, who had a good eye for talent and a nose for what would succeed, became a facilitator for Penton's remarkable journalistic innovations. Some years later, when Penton was gravely ill, Packer told Penton's wife: 'He's my brother'.[49]

In 1939 Packer challenged Penton to a series of one-on-one 'duels' with a heavy medicine ball in a local gymnasium to decide who should join up. The champion sportsman naturally won, becoming a lieutenant in the 18th battalion of the militia on 21 April. The militia was not sufficiently well trained to meet on equal terms an army of the European type based on two or three years of conscript service. Nevertheless, the Australians were trained by highly qualified professional and citizen soldiers who had seen hard service in the war of 1914–18. The scheme produced a nucleus of officers who were capable of commanding platoons, companies and battalions in action, and a useful body of non-commanding officers.[50]

Many of the men who joined the militia were leaders in their professions. Even though he was the wealthy managing director of a newspaper and magazine publishing company and the father of two children, Packer seems to have had a genuine desire to 'do his bit'. Perhaps his education at schools like Abbotsholme College, which had placed great emphasis on the value of public service, had not been wasted after all. Militiamen were required to undergo sixteen days' training in camp each year and all officers and noncommissioned officers were to do an additional sixteen days' home training in drill halls. They undertook complicated and arduous exercises, and the men usually gave much additional time to weekend and evening classes. In January 1940 Packer was seconded to the 1st division to serve as an orderly officer.[51]

Not surprisingly, patriotic groups were eager to cultivate the support of newspaper and magazine proprietors. The executive of the New South Wales War Loan and War Savings Committee included Packer, Hugh Denison, Rupert Henderson, Claude McKay and A. E. Pratt from the *Daily News*; Packer also belonged to the publicity sub-committee. In 1940 he became an honorary organising secretary of the Red Cross race meeting held at Randwick each September. Gretel, too, was heavily involved with the Red Cross, organising art unions and serving on the executive of the New South Wales division.[52]

On one memorable occasion a Consolidated Press employee humiliated the couple at a Red Cross function. When the famous English dramatist (later Sir) Noël Coward visited Australia to make broadcasts about the British war effort and give fund-raising concerts, he agreed to help further the work of the Red Cross. On the evening of 16 November 1940 a reception welcoming him to Sydney was held at the Town Hall. Frank Packer, who was on the guest list, ordered Lennie Lower to attend the reception and report on it for the *Telegraph*. Lower, who was paid a hefty salary by Packer to contribute to the *Women's Weekly* and the *Telegraph*s, was a notorious drunk and larrikin who hated official functions. On being introduced to the guest of honour, Lower commented that he admired Coward's work and could not understand how he could have gained a reputation as a 'cissy'. Packer was dismayed by this remark, which alluded to rumours that Coward was homosexual (which he actually was), and summarily dismissed the humorist. When Lower called at the *Telegraph* the next day, the lift-driver said that Packer had ordered him not to allow Lower into the building. Poor Gretel had to face Coward three days later, as she was one of the organisers of a dinner-dance at which he was guest of honour.[53]

To the surprise of some authorities, the outbreak of the war had not seen large numbers of militiamen rushing to join the Second AIF. Members of the militia were reluctant to leave the units they knew, many were disinclined to accept three shillings less a day in a force that might not offer even the adventure of going overseas, and no effective link between the militia and the expeditionary force emerged. Packer himself did not rush to enlist in the AIF and leave the running of his publications and his company in the hands of others. But in early 1941, when good young leaders began seeking transfers to the new Armoured Brigade of the AIF, Packer decided to follow suit.[54]

Frank Packer's paternal grandfather, Arthur Howard Packer, c. 1870. (Noni E. Fitzmaurice)

Frank Packer's mother, Ethel Hewson, c. 1902. (Lady Stening)

Frank Packer's father, Robert Clyde Packer, c. 1900. (Lady Stening)

R. C. Packer, chief scoutmaster of New South Wales, at Cooks River, April 1909. (Boy Scout Memorabilia Centre)

R. C. and Ethel Packer, with Frank and Kathleen, on the steps of their first home in Waitara, c. 1913. (Lady Stening)

Frank Packer as a teenager. (Lady Stening)

Frank Packer (*top left, sitting*) and his father (*right, standing*) on board the *Morna* off Palm Beath, c. 1930. R. C. Packer jokingly wrote of this photo of his son: 'This gentleman is somewhat gone in the legs as you will observe. However, he is all right!' (Lady Stening)

R. C. Packer's protégé and Frank Packer's associate, G. W. Warnecke, 1931. (NLA: *Newspaper News*, 1 October 1931, p. 1)

Unhappy with how a stall is being run at the Royal Easter Show, Frank Packer takes over. (Lady Stening)

The extraordinary general meeting of Associated Newspapers Ltd stacked by R. C. Packer in June 1931 inspired these headlines. (Lady Stening: *Newspaper News*, 1 July 1931, p. 11)

The geological expedition at Adelaide en route to the Granites, October 1932. *From left*: Dr C. T. Madigan, Frank Packer, Eric Baume and W. I. Turner. (*Sun*, 15 October 1932, p. 1)

Peggy Bullmore (*top*) and Frank Packer's sister, Kathleen, leave for England aboard the *Orsova*, 1933.

(Lady Stening: *Home*, 1 May 1933, p. 18)

Gretel Bullmore assists her uncle, Sir Frederick Maze, and Captain Hillman at the launch of the *Hai Ping* and the *Hai Hui* at the Kiangnan Docks in Shanghai, 1934. (Lady Stening: *Home*, 1 June 1934, p. 29)

Frank Packer's wedding, 24 July 1934. *From left, standing*: Douglas Henty, Kathleen Packer, Dr H. H. Bullmore, Frank Packer, Gretel Packer, Joan Henty, James MacLeod and H. J. Bullmore. *Seated*: Elfride Bullmore, Ethel Packer and Ralph McFadyen. (Lady Stening)

The 'Nutcrackers' — Captain McDonald Jones, R. Skene, Doug Munro and Frank Packer — after winning the Northern Challenge Polo Club in Quirindi, 1936. (*Quirindi Advocate*, 7 August 1936, p. 2)

Australian Newspapers Conference 'at home' at Elizabeth Bay House, 1938. *From left*: Gretel Packer, Dulcie Sheedy, E. P. M. Sheedy, Mary Sheedy, E. G. Theodore and Thelma Sheedy. (*Newspaper News*, 1 June 1938, p. 15)

Australian Newspapers Conference 'at home' in Brisbane, 1939. *From left*: Marjorie Dunstan, Frank Packer, Margaret Davies and Helen Dunstan. (*Newspaper News*, 1 July 1939, p. 13)

Truth, owned by Frank Packer's nemesis, Ezra Norton, ridicules Frank's sensitivity about his appearance. (NLA: *Truth*, 17 September 1939, p. 23)

Gretel Packer on the terrace of 'Cairnton', 1940. (*Home*, 2 December 1940, p. 17)

7
'Political Harlots of Mammon'

On 17 February 1941 thirty employees and friends were dragooned into hosting a dinner in Frank Packer's honour at the Hotel Australia. The function was designed to congratulate Packer on enlisting in the AIF and to mark an executive reshuffle at Consolidated Press. Clarrie McNulty was appointed editor-in-chief, Brian Penton (sitting on Packer's right) was promoted to the editorship of the *Telegraph* and Jack Travers (on Packer's left) became an alternate director.[1]

In his classic novel *Scoop*, Evelyn Waugh deliciously satirised the dinners held by the proprietor of the fictional *Beast*. Packer was not yet as self-indulgent as the exaggerated character of Lord Copper and the English business and publishing worlds were somewhat more formal and hierarchial than in Australia. Nevertheless, Waugh's passage gives some sense of the relationship between a newspaper tycoon and his underlings in the first half of this century:

> Lord Copper quite often gave banquets; it would be an understatement to say that no one enjoyed them more than the host for no one else enjoyed them at all while Lord Copper positively exulted in every minute. For him they satisfied every requirement of a happy evening's entertainment; like everything that was to Lord Copper's taste, they were a little over life-size, unduly large and unduly long; they took place in restaurants which existed solely for such purposes ... the provisions were copious, very bad and very expensive; the guests were assembled for no other reason than that Lord Copper had ordered it; they did not want to see each other, they had no reason to rejoice in the occasions which Lord Copper celebrated; they were there either because it was part of their job or because they were glad of a free dinner ... [Lord Copper] had bought them, hand and foot, with consommé and cream of chicken, turbot and saddle, duck and pêche melba, and afterwards when the cigars had been furtively pocketed and the brandy glasses filled with the horrible brown compound for which Lord Copper was paying two pounds a bottle, there came the golden hour when he rose to speak at whatever length he liked and on whatever subject, without fear of rivalry or interruption.[2]

After the dinner in February 1941, Packer was made a lieutenant in the 1st Armoured Brigade and went into camp at Puckapunyal, about 80 kilometres north of

Melbourne. He was fortunate that the army camps at Puckapunyal and Ingleburn (New South Wales), which had been constructed in great haste, had improved since the early days of the war. The first recruits had been greeted by unmade roads, inadequate electrical appliances, no stables or harness rooms, inefficient drainage, unhygienic kitchens and meat houses, and butter boxes used as chairs and packing cases acting as tables.[3] By 1941 conditions had improved: there were four or five recreation halls, a post office, a dental centre, a bootmaker, a tailor and, luckily for Packer, a paper shop. But Puckapunyal was still a vast camp without a blade of grass to be seen. Most of the gravel and soil that covered the ground finished up in the huts when a strong wind blew, as the side walls of each hut had a one-foot gap. The dust caused a mild irritation that became known as 'Pucka throat'.[4]

The 1st Armoured Brigade consisted of three armoured regiments and one motor battalion. North of the camp at Puckapunyal was a suitable range area, while the rolling country further afield was lightly timbered and provided good going for tanks as well as a fair amount of cover. The objectives of the brigade, which had been established to play an offensive role by engaging in decisive tank-to-tank combat, were bound to appeal to someone like Packer. The brigade's role was to utilise surprise, speed and fire power to penetrate, disorganise and isolate enemy forces. Recruits were expected to be able to think quickly and have initiative and a first-rate physique.[5]

Nevertheless, Packer soon discovered that even in the Armoured Brigade, army life was less exciting than suggested by the *Boy's Own Annuals* he had so liked reading as a child. He went from the luxury of 'Cairnton' to sharing huts with other men, where the theft of personal effects was always a possibility. All soliders had to report to the dental centre for check-ups; one contemporary recalls that a 'butcher' masqueraded as the dentist. On Sundays members of each Christian denomination were expected to attend a service in the hut that had been made available for religious instruction. But the most mundane part of Packer's time in Puckapunyal was attending training courses and sitting for examinations. Undertaking courses in the Army School of Mechanics, the Anti-Gas School and the Training School Artillery Wing must have brought back unhappy memories of his difficult years at school. Diversions came in the form of two-up, drinking home brew in the 'wet canteen', and seeing special performances put on by Melbourne's Tivoli Theatre.[6]

Packer gave Penton a relatively free rein in developing the *Telegraph*'s editorial line and stylistic innovations during the war, and he had great faith in Alice Jackson's abilities as editor of the *Women's Weekly*. But despite his training commitments, Packer still endeavoured to oversee his company's wider pursuits. In mid 1941 the government considered tightening restrictions on newsprint to 55 per cent of base year consumption. On 10 June Packer joined other publishers at a meeting with the trade minister, Eric Harrison, in Melbourne. The Department of Trade and Customs was anxious to involve Packer in these critical discussions, as his company was a major consumer of newsprint and an often outspoken critic of government policy.[7]

In parliament Labor's Eddie Ward, whom the *Telegraph* had dubbed an 'incredible ratbag', questioned Packer's participation in the delegation. He demanded to know why Packer had been granted special leave, asked why he had been given a commission, alleged that he spent most of his time at a hotel at Broadford, and joked that the name of the camp at Puckapunyal should be changed to 'Packapunyal'. (Later Sir) Percy Spender, the minister for the army, replied that Packer had only been given two days' leave, received no other special treatment, and had made 'a very big sacrifice' when he enlisted.[8]

Refusing to let the matter rest, on 18 September Ward pointedly asked how Packer had passed the medical test, given his defective eyesight, and again questioned Packer's leave arrangements. Spender's response was short and judicious: 'If Lieutenant Packer has defective eyesight and has yet succeeded in enlisting, that redounds greatly to his credit'. *Reveille*, the official journal of the New South Wales branch of the Returned Servicemen's League, weighed into the debate: 'One may pass over [Ward's] gibe in the knowledge that while we have men of the calibre of Lieut. Packer ready to forsake the easy amenities of life, to serve their King and Country, even to death itself — then those who are content to be onlookers are indeed fortunate!'[9]

Although there can be no question that he made a sacrifice by choosing to don khaki, Packer does seem to have benefited from generous leave arrangements. In August 1941, in his capacity as retiring president of the New South Wales Amateur Boxing and Wrestling Association, he attended a reception in Sydney for a team of Tasmanian boxers; in September he was again honorary secretary of the Red Cross race meeting at Randwick; and in October he was present at a dinner held in Sydney for a visiting press delegation from the Dutch East Indies.[10] Soon, however, Packer was to be called upon to make a much bigger commitment to the allied war effort.

It was once said that E. G. Theodore's name stood for 'success, efficiency, ruthlessness, political dynamite'. By the late 1930s Packer's partner had enjoyed a remarkable career: he had risen from humble, non-Anglo-Celtic origins to become a state premier, federal treasurer, a successful businessman and one of the leading citizens of Fiji. It was a career full of ironies and contradictions: touted as a future prime minister, Theodore had ignominiously lost his seat; the one-time union organiser had emerged as a newspaper tycoon and the head of companies in Fiji that were accused of exploiting local labour; the man who had once declared that 'gold has a fictitious value because a majority of the stupid people in the world have chosen to make it their currency' had made a fortune out of gold mines.[11]

In another extraordinary reversal in 1939, J. A. Lyons called on the services of his former colleague. After Theodore had been forced to step down from his cabinet positions in 1930, Lyons had been appointed acting treasurer; when Theodore had been restored to cabinet a year later, Lyons had resigned in protest and founded the UAP. But in March 1939, with his government increasingly unstable, Menzies complaining about a lack of national leadership and war in Europe a real possibility, Prime Minister Lyons turned to his old foe for help. Possibly after dealing with Packer as an intermediary, Lyons cabled Theodore in Fiji to ask him to return to Australia and become co-ordinator of all national resources for the country's defence. Theodore was reluctant to re-enter the political arena and the offer lapsed a few weeks later when Lyons died and was replaced by Menzies.[12]

In May 1940, as the international crisis deepened, the Loan Council offered Theodore a new position as works co-ordinator. However, the suggestion was immediately attacked by Archie Cameron, who threatened to withdraw the Country Party's support from the government. When Menzies was forced to deny that he had communicated any offer to Theodore, the *Telegraph* lashed out at the 'petty-mindedness of the little group of obstructionists which Mr. Cameron leads'. The leader of the Country Party issued the author of the article, Brian Penton, with an unsuccessful libel suit.[13]

At the same time as Theodore was proclaiming that nothing would take him back to politics, the federal government was disintegrating. Throughout 1941 Consolidated Press continued to criticise the government's handling of the war effort and call for a national administration. Believing that the *Telegraph* was helping to destabilise his leadership, Menzies privately complained about the 'crapulous' actions of the newspaper and described it as a 'rag'. Returning from overseas, Menzies found himself under increasing pressure from elements in the coalition and on 28 August 1941 he resigned. His successor, Arthur Fadden, was voted down on the floor of the House of Representatives by the two independents a few weeks later.[14] The resultant Labor government, headed by John Curtin, was immediately confronted by a series of enormous challenges. In December Pearl Harbor was bombed by the Japanese and the United States entered the war; American forces and equipment began arriving in Australia; in February 1942 Singapore fell and Darwin was bombed.

On 15 February, the day Singapore capitulated, Curtin rang Theodore at his apartment in Edgecliff to ask him to take up the position of director-general of a new organisation responsible for overseeing all civil and military engineering and construction works within Australia. Theodore, realising the gravity of the situation, rang Curtin back a few minutes later to accept the position, refusing to accept a salary. The new organisation, known as the Allied Works Council (AWC), was to fund, purchase or requisition materials and provide the skilled manpower necessary to enable major civil engineering tasks to be carried out anywhere in Australia.[15]

Curtin had difficulty convincing cabinet to approve the formation of the AWC and the appointment of Theodore. Many Labor politicians found the concept of civil conscription repugnant and some government members from New South Wales, particularly Eddie Ward, Jack Beasley and Sol Rosevear, hated Theodore with a vengeance. Brisbane's *Catholic Leader* defended Theodore against the attacks of the Langites: 'Mr. Curtin must have known how many puny minds and die-hards would oppose Mr. Theodore's recall, but he knew, too, that never in its history had the Government of the Commonwealth a more able Treasurer than the much maligned ex-Premier of Queensland'.[16]

Theodore decided to create directorates of finance, mechanical equipment and materials supply, and personnel. This last position was vital as the incumbent would be required to supply and co-ordinate the manpower resources needed by the AWC. Theodore asked to have Packer seconded from the AIF to join the AWC as director of personnel. Although Packer was reluctant to leave the Armoured Brigade, he was persuaded to do so by his partner, and he joined the AWC on 14 March.[17] There were overseas precedents for such an appointment: during the First World War Northcliffe and Beaverbrook had held public office, and in 1940 Winston Churchill had convinced Beaverbrook to join the ministry. The Australian government must have realised the usefulness of involving a press proprietor in a massive recruitment and construction campaign, and Theodore saw in his thirty-five-year-old partner a unique combination of youthful vigour and entrepreneurial and industrial experience. Energetic and ruthless, Packer knew how to cut through red tape, recruit and manage staff and execute unpopular decisions.[18]

As soon as Theodore called on his trusted partner to act as director of personnel, Rosevear signalled left-wing disquiet with the appointment. On 25 March 1942 he addressed a question to the minister for the army, Frank Forde.

> In view of the long period for which Lieutenant Packer was in camp and the energy expended, now wasted, on training him, what special circumstances demanded his release? What special training has he had in handling the manpower problem to fit him for his new job?[19]

Although Theodore had wide-ranging powers over the direction of manpower, he could not actually conscript labour to work on projects under his control. The AWC decided to establish an entirely separate civilian labour force that could be called up for duty as required. Members of the force were not to be subject to military discipline or conditions of service. However, all able-bodied men between the ages of eighteen and sixty could be conscripted, with the exception of those employed in reserved occupations or those on active service in the defence forces, and members would be subject to a stringent set of rules that would govern how, where and when they worked. On 14 April the Civil Constructional Corps (CCC), to be controlled by Packer, was established. This was the first time in Australia's history that a system of civil conscription had been proposed and the scheme provoked a considerable number of dissenters among politicians and trade unionists. Over the next few months certain unions and newspapers joined some members of parliament in a campaign to pressure the government to remove Packer and Theodore from their positions.[20]

Theodore moved into a suite in the Menzies Hotel, but it is unclear whether Packer stayed there or at the Hotel Australia. The AWC initially worked out of a block of flats in South Melbourne but, as a result of its rapid expansion, soon took over three floors of a building in Collins Street. CCC recruiting centres were set up in each capital city. The organisation had as its unofficial motto 'Build for victory and build for the future'. As one politician predicted, the works undertaken were to play an extremely useful role in Australia's future industrial and economic development:

> This vast construction program will not only serve the vital needs of the nation in this its time of greatest need, but unlike most other things associated with war, will prove of utmost permanent value to our country when once more Australia is able to practise the arts of peace.[21]

But within weeks of the CCC's formation, Packer was in conflict with a senior adviser. Arthur Blakeley, a former Labor member of parliament (MP) and now the AWC's chief industrial officer, was deputed to draw up a statement on industrial policy. As awards were made at both the state and federal levels, he recommended that members of the CCC should be paid under the awards that prevailed in their industries in their states. Packer, however, wanted a uniform set of conditions drafted to cover members of the CCC. He instructed Blakeley to initiate this process by preparing a determination on awards and conditions in Victoria. On 29 May Blakeley resigned: he believed Packer should have held further consultations with the relevant unions, strongly objected to Packer's insistence that the Victorian determination should include certain penal clauses, complained about Packer's 'consistent refusal' to accept advice on industrial matters and concluded that 'our respective outlook on industrial policy was as wide apart as the poles'.[22]

In an unfortunate irony, Packer and Theodore found that they had to work with Eddie Ward, now minister for labour and national service. In May 1942, when the *Telegraph* claimed that Ward had held up work on the Warragamba Dam scheme, the minister announced that he intended to look into the cost of training Packer as a military officer and whether this money had been wasted. A few weeks later, the New South Wales branch of the AWU — which had not forgotten Packer's role in the *World*'s demise — turned up the heat. The executive asked the government to return Packer to the AIF, saying that he should be replaced by an official 'with some knowledge of industrial awards and an understanding of the industrial movement'.[23]

At the very time Packer was engaged in a struggle about industrial matters within the AWC, his own company's manpower requirements were becoming a contentious political issue. In February 1942 new manpower regulations removed journalists from the list of reserved occupations and placed newspapers in a group of industries in which production could be allowed to partially fall off without damaging the war effort. Packer immediately wrote to the Adelaide *Advertiser*'s Lloyd Dumas to say how disturbed he was about the policy: 'there is an irreducible minimum for Metropolitan daily newspapers beyond which staff cannot be reduced and the paper got out'. By now Packer had also made an enemy of one of his father's old associates, maintaining that E. G. Knox, now president of the ANPA, was displaying an 'extraordinary' lack of concern about the matter. On 9 April Theodore used his position to make a direct approach to Curtin and Ward, complaining that the new regulations would make producing Consolidated Press publications 'impossible'.[24]

Later that month, in response to a question from the UAP's Eric Harrison, Eddie Ward told parliament that he had considered prosecuting Consolidated Press for failing to provide lists of *Telegraph* employees to manpower authorities. The company, which appears to have learned of this threat through its Canberra representatives, had supplied the lists before the prosecution could be launched. Despite Packer's public duty to recruit labour for the domestic war effort, self-interest does seem to have dictated his company's manpower policies. After meeting with Consolidated Press's general manager, Jack Travers, Lloyd Dumas concluded (with some exaggeration) that the *Telegraph* 'had not reduced its editorial staff by one man below prewar strength'.[25]

Consolidated Press also continued to provoke the ire of censorship authorities. On 6 May 1942 the *Telegraph* ridiculed the policy that members of the conscripted Citizen Military Force should not be allowed to serve outside Australian territory. E. G. Bonney, the commonwealth's chief publicity censor, decreed that no copies of the newspaper should leave Australia as it could damage overseas opinion and relations with the United States. Bonney was a tough and uncompromising censor who prohibited the publication of any news or comment that the enemy might use to damage the morale of Australians or their allies. When the *Telegraph* retaliated with an article about the critical attitude of American pressmen to Australian censorship, Bonney told Curtin that it was time to serve the *Telegraph* with an order to submit all matter intended for publication.[26]

Packer realised that this represented the most serious action against a publication for breaching censorship regulations since the outbreak of the war. On 14 May he sent an urgent telegram to Bonney saying Consolidated Press was prepared to submit articles criticising or commenting on particular acts of censorship; however, it would not submit articles dealing with the broad principles of censorship and it would not forgo the right to criticise or comment on censorship of 'a political nature'. The commonwealth crown solicitor observed that Packer's stance was 'most objectionable and serious, particularly coming from a man wearing the King's uniform'.[27]

On 16 May Bonney received a priority telephone call booked in Theodore's name. The person at the other end of the line proved instead to be Theodore's partner. Bonney lashed out at Packer for using a government privilege to conduct his own business matters before telling him, 'You must decide now whether you intend to be an Army officer, a working member of the Allied Works Council, or a newspaper campaigner. You can't be all three. If you intend to still run your newspapers in Government time, you'll obey censorship or take the consequences'. Bonney accused Packer of trying to stir up trouble among American war correspondents and told him that it was not for any one newspaper to decide what should or should not be censored. According to Bonney, a dumbfounded Packer agreed that his paper had acted wrongly and at the end of the conversation was a 'very chastened man'. As Bonney believed that he had concluded the matter successfully, the *Telegraph* was not served with an order to submit.[28]

Throughout 1942 a chorus led by Eddie Ward and sections of the union movement and the press continued to make allegations about inefficiency, cronyism and corruption in the administration of the AWC and the CCC. In September the iconoclastic *Bulletin* published a cartoon captioned 'A Day in the Life of the Allied Works Council'. It depicted Theodore smoking a pipe and playing poker at one end of a table adorned with a bottle of whisky and a soda siphon. Packer, dressed in civilian clothes and surrounded by greyhounds, was shown sitting on the floor playing two-up with horse-trainers, pugilists and a jockey. He did, at least, have some defenders. Hubert L. Anthony, a Country Party MP, criticised ministers for attacking 'individuals engaged in defence work who had no right to reply in this House to such attacks'. *Reveille* again came out in support of Packer, praising his 'guts' and declaring 'it is to men of his type that the country turns in proud salute; while sorrowing for the class who chatter irresponsibly and do nothing'.²⁹

Ted Scorfield's cartoon in the *Bulletin* sends up Lieutenant Frank Packer and his associates in the Allied Works Council.
(*Bulletin*, 30 September 1942, p. 7)

Theodore clearly found working for the AWC in such trying conditions an isolating and dispiriting experience, and it is doubtful that Packer was any happier. Theodore's secretary pleaded with Don Whitington, the *Telegraph*'s political correspondent, to call at his suite any Sunday he was in Melbourne because he (Theodore) was so lonely. At the end of September, after Ward had accused Packer and Theodore of displaying a 'lack of sympathy and considerateness' for the men called up to the CCC, the exasperated pair tendered their resignations. In a letter to Prime Minister Curtin, Theodore complained that the Department of Labour and National Service — which Ward himself presided over — had denied them access to lists of strong young men who were not engaged in protected industries; as a result, they had had to conscript men more than fifty years of age who were unsuited to arduous manual labour. He also claimed that some members of the CCC were causing disaffection or going out on strike and then getting 'a sympathetic hearing' from certain ministers and members of parliament.³⁰

Curtin, H. V. Evatt, now the attorney-general and minister for external affairs, and Sir George Knowles, the solicitor-general, met Theodore on 1 October. Here they restated Theodore's powers over members of the CCC, explained what avenues of prosecution were open to him, and proposed changing the manpower regulations so that the director-general of manpower would be required to furnish the AWC with a list of persons suitable for its purposes. Believing that he had succeeded in taking a stand against political interference, Theodore withdrew his resignation. Packer was still inclined to return to the AIF, but he agreed to remain with the AWC when Theodore told him and the government that his services were indispensable.[31]

Truth and the *Daily Mirror* remained two of the most vocal critics of Packer and Theodore. While the world was at war and Australia struggled to cope with the very real threat of Japanese invasion, Frank Packer and Ezra Norton continued their feud. In 1940 one of Norton's bodyguards, John William Johnson, had been charged with assaulting a *Telegraph* photographer, Ernest Nutt, and stealing his camera. In the course of the case, it emerged that another *Telegraph* photographer, accompanied by a former pugilist, had been sent to Norton's home to get a photograph of him. Norton's chauffeur and Norton himself, who hated being photographed, became engaged in a scuffle with the photographer and the 'bruiser'. When Norton appeared in court later that day as the witness in a case involving the theft of a brooch, two former pugilists accompanied a *Telegraph* journalist, Robin Slessor, Ernie Nutt and another photographer, Harold Dick. After one of the photographers took the unprecedented step of photographing Norton through the window of the courthouse, Johnson allegedly punched Nutt and grabbed his camera. The magistrate who sentenced Johnson to three months' jail for assault deplored the actions of the rival newspaper 'factions'. He gravely observed that the situation 'can only be recorded as smacking of gangster tactics, that one sees in some of the American films. I look upon this as a very serious matter'.[32]

Norton took no notice of this reproach. In 1941 a man was charged with stealing jewellery worth £790 from 'Cairnton'. Packer had bought the jewellery — a diamond and platinum ring, an emerald and platinum ring, a zircon ring, two diamond and platinum rings, a watch, and diamond and platinum earrings — for his wife, and he had large reproductions drawn to help locate the stolen property. Even though the defendant allegedly confessed to the theft and was committed for trial, *Truth* used the case to ridicule Packer:

> Perhaps the trouble never would have occurred at all had the valuable articles not been left in the bathroom of the Packer residence, Victoria-road, Bellevue Hill; had the bathroom window not been left open; and had Packer's own ladder not been left in a handy position. Who knows?

Truth even found noteworthy the fact that Packer's chauffeur, Richard William Gray, was granted a divorce.[33]

On 11 October 1942 *Truth* described the recruitment of 'that political adventurer' E. G. Theodore and his business associate Lieutenant Packer to the AWC as 'amazing'. The article criticised the appointment of 'the notorious racecourse personality' Peter Cruise, saying he was not a fit and proper person to be employed by the AWC. Packer, who mixed with Cruise in racing circles, later explained that Cruise had written to him offering to work for the AWC. Cruise had informed Packer that he had business experience gained from working in the office of the estate of the late Samuel Hordern (Mary Hordern's father-in-law), knew how to type, had a car and was not looking for a big salary. The *Sunday Telegraph* responded to *Truth*'s attack by publishing an imaginary conversation between a group of men in Canberra discussing who was Australia's greatest hero of the week. One man, nominating 'Mr. Norton', shook his head gloomily:

> 'It's only his weak stomach that keeps him out of the fighting line. It was the same last war. He was nineteen then — game youngster. Great pity that stomach. Great break for the Japs.'
>
> There was only one nark present. 'Real reason why Norton took a poke at Cruise is that Peter refused to handle his betting', he snarled. 'Peter's got to draw the line somewhere.'[34]

At the very time that *Truth* was condemning his association with Cruise, Packer was trying to deal with another difficulty in the AWC's administration. On 11 October eight members of a construction unit at Clermont in Queensland came to Sydney to complain about conditions in their camp. They met W. S. ('Stewart') Howard, the deputy director of personnel. Packer's somewhat mysterious deputy had graduated in Economics and reviewed films and books for the *Women's Weekly* before joining *Smith's Weekly* and becoming publicity adviser to (later Sir) W. J. McKell, leader of the New South Wales Labor Opposition. At the meeting on 11 October 1942 Howard apparently satisfied the construction workers' grievances and arrangements were made for them to return to Brisbane that night. Packer, however, rang Howard from Melbourne to say he did not think it was proper for the men to leave until he was able to see them himself. When the men met Packer the next day, they were unaware that four military policemen were posted in the passage outside his office. Apparently viewing the men from Clermont as deserters, Packer was determined to ensure that the vital construction work being undertaken in Queensland was not disrupted.

Packer was so exasperated with the situation that he privately referred to the members of the CCC as 'Curtin's Clueless Cunts'. He and Howard were desperate to put an end to the 'persistent and slanderous gossip' circulating about the AWC. On 21 October Howard called the personnel staff together to tell them that any officer who spread gossip in the future would be put to work with a pick and shovel.[35] However, the political and press campaign against the administration of the AWC was about to come to a climax.

On 18 November the executive of the AWC sub-section of the Federated Clerks' Union held a meeting attended by Sol Rosevear. Although representatives from the *Daily Mirror*, the *Sydney Morning Herald* and the *Sun* were invited to attend, no invitation appears to have been issued to the *Telegraph*. Much of the discussion centred around the 'dictatorship and Gestapo methods' employed by Steward Howard, who was alleged to have insulted his personnel officers, refused to pay AWC officers for public holidays and to have been under the influence of alcohol while at work. Calling for a royal commission into the administration of the AWC, the clerks' union also alleged that bookmakers were defying call-ups to the AWC, preferential treatment was being given to residents of exclusive suburbs such as Bellevue Hill, incompetent people were being assigned to the AWC's administrative staff and men outside the public service were being appointed over the heads of experienced officers.[36]

When Norton gleefully ran a major article about this meeting in the *Daily Mirror* on 19 November, Howard interrogated members of his staff and the secretary of the clerks' union. Calling a meeting of his staff the next day, Packer pointed out the gravity of the statements that had been made, contended that they were unfair and unrepresentative of the views of most AWC employees, and said that those people who had made the statements must substantiate them. The four clerks who had moved the resolutions at the meeting two days' earlier were suspended pending an inquiry into their claims on Monday 23 November. When the clerks failed to appear at Collins House on Monday, they were dismissed. The secretary of the clerks' union responded by writing a long letter to Packer restating concerns about the administration of the AWC, asserting that the clerks had been victimised and commenting that 'whatever dictatorial rights Lieutenant Packer might possess in certain spheres, the Trade Union Movement will not surrender to him the right to determine the business it will discuss'. On 19 December, following further discussions with government ministers, the four clerks were reinstated and then suspended from duty. That same day Curtin appointed Sir Harry Brown, the co-ordinator general of public works, to conduct an inquiry into the allegations that had been raised by the *Daily Mirror* and in subsequent correspondence.[37]

The inquiry that began on 29 December ran for two months. In the course of the inquiry, the charge of using 'dictatorship and Gestapo methods' was also brought against Packer because of the way he had conducted the meeting with the workers from Clermont.[38] Packer spent three days on the witness stand in early January 1943 taking questions from his friend (later Sir) Jack Cassidy KC, who represented the AWC officers, and counsel for the clerks' union. Packer's secretary, Daisy Thrum, testified that she had worked closely with him and Howard for the last six months and considered them both very 'industrious and conscientious'. The *Telegraph*s ran articles with such headings as '"Bung" Rules at A.W.C. Clerks' Meeting'; 'Why A.W.C. Clerks Were Disciplined. Declined Invitation To Produce Facts in Proof of Allegations, Inquiry Told'; 'Charges Damaging to A.W.C. Morale'; and 'A.W.C. Investigator Rebuts Allegations. Charges Came From Only Few Men And One Newspaper, He Says'.[39]

While Brown prepared his report, Packer continued to crack the whip at the AWC. Even though he had entered the civil service reluctantly, he enacted his duties with predictable drive and determination. In February Packer asked for a weekly record of expenses and new appointments and insisted that Theodore also be provided with weekly reports on the AWC's activities.[40] But Packer was understandably exasperated by the orchestrated campaign against the administration of the AWC, and he pounced when he spotted an opportunity to escape from the pressures of his position for a short time. In early March he tried to secure leave to participate in the Australian delegation to the Imperial Press Conference in London. On being rebuffed, he asked Keith Murdoch and Lloyd Dumas to lobby the government on his behalf. Murdoch noted that 'Packer will go like a shot out of a gun' for a break from the AWC.[41]

Although nothing came of these approaches, Packer must have been consoled by two important developments. Some of his difficulties had been caused by the fact that prior to the CCC's establishment there were no national awards for men working in the construction industry. This situation was partly resolved on 5 March, when the Commonwealth Court of Conciliation and Arbitration handed down an interim award for all members employed on CCC projects.[42]

A fortnight later, Harry Brown completely vindicated the actions of Theodore, Packer and Howard. Brown's report concluded that no evidence had substantiated 'any of the allegations that had been made against the Council's administration'. He did say that Packer's decision to post military police outside his office when meeting the men from Clermont had been 'unwarranted and particularly undesirable; but it would be grossly exaggerating the actions he took to suggest that they be classified as Gestapo methods'. Brown reserved his censure for the Norton press and its allies:

> It seems incredible that so serious a situation should develop from the causes which are revealed as of almost infinitesimal account in relation to the magnitude of the task which the Department [the AWC] was expected to execute, and still more so when contrasted with the urgency and vital nature of the work to be done.
>
> ... Not only is there little justification for many of the unwholesome suggestions planted in the minds of the great body of workers controlled by the Council and also given general publicity, but there had developed gossip, tongue-wagging of a completely irresponsible kind, scandal-mongering and what might fittingly be termed an insidious whispering campaign of calumny directed against members of the organisation holding positions of responsibility.[43]

Nevertheless, while it is clear that individuals and organisations harbouring grudges against Theodore and Packer had triggered the inquiry, concerns about the wider issue of civil conscription had also entered into play. Even after Brown delivered his findings in March 1943, the carping of political, industrial and press opponents was to continue until Theodore and Packer resigned from their posts the following year.

While Packer coped with the campaign of destabilisation against his involvement with the AWC and the CCC, he dabbled in politics and tried his best to keep abreast of happenings at Consolidated Press. In July 1942 he joined Theodore and Rupert Henderson at 'an evening' with Menzies. The former leader of the UAP apparently wished to encourage the press to help rebuild him and his ailing party. This meeting was held at the very time that Packer was fretting about the impact that the Labor government's manpower policies were having on his newspapers. But his participation in the meeting stemmed from more than self-interest. The *Telegraph*s were continuing to adopt an activist and adversarial role, setting themselves up in permanent opposition to the status quo. Maintaining that Australian politicians had failed to make a 'strong, electrifying call to action', they were determined to expose military bungling and political complacency.[44] Given the stance adopted by his newspapers, it would seem that Packer thought that having a vibrant, viable Opposition would help to improve the government's performance and possibly lead to the formation of a national administration for the duration of the war.

In November 1942 Les Haylen, the *Women's Weekly*'s news editor, decided to stand for Labor preselection in the federal seat of Parkes. When Packer learned of this development he wrote to Haylen instructing him to move from the staff of the magazine to the *Telegraph*. A deputation from the AJA, believing that Haylen was being victimised for his political beliefs, met Packer on 2 December. In the course of the interview Packer explained the reasons for his actions: Haylen, who had signed a five-year contract with Consolidated Press, had indicated a willingness to break it; Consolidated Press was determined to keep the *Women's Weekly* free of party politics; Haylen had been told that the company did not want its executives engaging in politics. Packer's case was reasonable and measured, and it would be too simplistic to suggest that he attempted to transfer Haylen to a subordinate position on the *Telegraph* because he was biased against the ALP. After all, Consolidated Press's co-founders, E.G. Theodore and George Warnecke, had both had strong Labor ties. The difference was that Warnecke had not been an endorsed party candidate at the time he held editorial office.[45]

Les Haylen denied it had ever been suggested that he should not do political work in his spare time. After refusing to accept Packer's ultimatum to withdraw his name from preselection or to move to the *Telegraph*, Haylen was fired. His protests and those of the AJA were supported by the PIEUA and the Trades and Labor Council, but Curtin (himself a former journalist) declined to intervene. It was left to Arthur Calwell, a volatile and outspoken Labor backbencher, to raise the matter in parliament.[46] Calwell was no friend of Consolidated Press: his political career began and ended with libel actions against the press and, as a devout Catholic, he seems to have been repelled by Brian Penton's womanising. The *Telegraph*'s editor contemptuously described the politician, who had launched a savage parliamentary attack on him a few months earlier, as 'one of the leaders of Labor's isolationist, red-bogey-haunted, book-banning, church-ridden, anti-intellectual, anti-libertarian wing'.[47]

Within weeks of the Haylen furore, Packer had to contend with another crisis involving an executive. On the night of Saturday 9 November Clarrie McNulty left Consolidated Press to drive a woman friend to an address in George Street. On his way home he visited a men's lavatory behind Wynyard station, where he encountered a plainclothes policeman, N. W. Grigg, and was allegedly guilty of willful and obscene exposure. When taken to Phillip Street police station by Grigg and his partner, McNulty gave a wrong name ('Charles McNally') and occupation ('clerk') to protect his family. McNulty, who was denied permission to contact the deputy police commissioner, was bailed out by the *Sunday Telegraph*'s chief-of-staff, Eric Marshall.[48]

On Sunday Marshall and a distraught McNulty went to see Packer at Palm Beach. After McNulty vigorously proclaimed his innocence, Packer rang the police commissioner, William J. MacKay. The commissioner was a controversial figure in New South Wales: his force had become increasingly involved in political surveillance as unemployment and dissent had become widespread during the Depression; in the mid 1930s he had publicly praised the efficiency of the German police and the discipline of Nazi society; and his arbitrary methods of promotion were resented by the Police Association of New South Wales. MacKay had been a 'firm friend' of R. C. Packer, attending his funeral in 1934. The commissioner, who had known Frank since he was a boy, was treated sympathetically by the *Telegraphs*. After talking to MacKay on the telephone on 10 January 1943, Packer took McNulty and Marshall to the commissioner's weekend retreat on the Hawkesbury River. Early the next morning, MacKay rang McNulty to say, 'I have had inquiries made and it won't be necessary for you to appear in court'.[49]

The episode triggered a major public controversy fanned by the Norton press. The Police Association demanded a royal commission to investigate MacKay's decision to drop the charge; cabinet decided to issue McNulty with a summons; the defence alleged that the constables were 'arch plotters' who might have received money in return for recommending a solicitor to represent men charged with indecency. The magistrate ruled that the prosecution had not proved its case beyond reasonable doubt, the two arresting officers were suspended from duty, and a departmental inquiry found that they had wrongfully arrested seven men, including McNulty, on charges of indecency. The Manpower Local Appeal Board then ordered that the constables be reinstated and the policemen issued libel writs against Consolidated Press and MacKay.[50] Packer could have had no idea that these events would follow his decision to contact the commissioner on 10 January. If he had been prepared to leave McNulty to his own devices, he would have successfully distanced himself from an incident bound to bring his company embarrassing publicity. But Packer was intensely loyal to those employees who served him loyally and he remained convinced of McNulty's innocence (as did most of his colleagues) throughout the whole sordid episode.

The *Telegraphs*' provocative style perplexed and infuriated politicians at both ends of the political spectrum. On 6 February 1943 the *Telegraph* ran a cartoon suggesting that the government was not showing enough concern about Australian prisoners-of-war in Malaya. George W. Martens, the Labor member for Herbert, responded by describing Packer and Theodore as 'political harlots of Mammon' who were 'not fit to be engaged in the public service of this country'.[51]

The relationship between Eddie Ward and Consolidated Press executives was becoming increasingly poisonous. After allegedly truncating a statement to make Ward appear to be advocating a slackening of the war effort, Brian Penton was fined £20 by the AJA ethics committee.[52] In March 1943 the minister instructed the manpower authorities 'pretty bluntly' to see that Consolidated Press reduced its staff to 40 per cent of its prewar level in line with other newspaper companies. On 25 May Packer, who was about to leave for Darwin to oversee some of the CCC's projects, cabled the prime minister to complain that Ward was behind repeated calls for Penton to enlist. He also reported that Penton's wife Olga, who was outside the age range for call-ups and was engaged in war work, had been called up by manpower. An agitated Packer claimed that if journalists 'work on the *Telegraph* they are selected for special consideration. This is devastating'.[53]

As the election of 18 August approached, the *Telegraph*s ran 'Electors' Guides' on major issues and advised readers to 'vote for men before parties'. The newspapers' insistence that Curtin could not go on taking orders from 'the little men of Caucus and the Trades Hall' was motivated by anti-syndicalist rather than crudely anti-Labor imperatives; readers were told to remember that whatever 'sectional interests seem most important to you, you are also an Australian'. But although the *Telegraphs*' coverage of electoral issues was generally balanced and judicious, Packer seems to have been moving increasingly to the right. According to Don Whitington, Packer hosted a dinner to celebrate what he believed would be a conservative victory on election night. Whitington claims that when he was seen writing the front-page story accurately predicting a Labor landslide, Packer stormed through to his office without a word.[54] If Whitington's account is correct, it suggests that the government's manpower regulations and the relentless attacks of Ward, Calwell and other left-wing figures were pushing Packer further and further away from the ALP.

Another Labor politician who frequently took parliamentary swipes at Packer and Theodore was Max Falstein. Blunt and impetuous, Falstein was aligned with Calwell and forces within the ALP opposed to Curtin's leadership. The *Telegraph* was becoming increasingly concerned by communist involvement in strikes and on 12 October 1943 it ran an article blaming communists for leading boilermakers out on strike. The article inspired Falstein, who described himself as 'a workers' representative', to attack Packer's political bias. Falstein used the dismissal of Les Haylen (whom he incorrectly identified as the *Women's Weekly*'s editor) to support his lengthy diatribe. Having the proprietors of Consolidated Press occupy key positions in the civil service was, the politician averred, intolerable: 'I do not intend to rest until both Mr. Theodore and Mr. Packer are dismissed from the positions which they hold'.[55]

In such a tense environment, Packer must have been greatly relieved that the CCC's activities were beginning to slow down. After peaking at 53 859 men on the active service list in August 1943, the CCC gradually lost members as they were released back to their former jobs in industry. In March 1944 Packer himself applied for release from his duties as director of personnel in order to return to the AIF.[56]

When Sir Harry Brown had delivered his report about the AWC and the CCC, he had remarked in passing that Packer did not act like a 'normal' public servant or head of a government department. Packer might have been a reluctant recruit to the AWC, and the management style he had adopted may have been unorthodox, but he certainly delivered results. Within a year of the CCC's inception, more than 300 forward airfields and landing strips had been constructed in northern Australia and thousands of kilometres of road had been laid or upgraded. The CCC built a major repair and service facility for allied naval forces at Garden Island, pioneered the use of laminated timber beams for structural purposes and designed and built large quantities of prefabricated buildings. These techniques were subsequently employed in the housing construction industry and the vast Snowy Mountains scheme, and the use of large-scale, heavy earthmoving and construction equipment became common in the civil engineering and building industries. During the AWC's three-year existence, £144 730 620 was spent on its capital works program and a total of 77 507 men served in the CCC.[57]

While Packer was preoccupied with the army, the CCC and his company's relations with the censors, his wife was working almost full-time for the New South Wales Red Cross. Appointed to a special fund-raising auxiliary in 1941, Gretel Packer found her husband's publications useful. In 1942 the *Sunday Telegraph* introduced a weekly beach girl contest and pageant, and the *Women's Weekly* auctioned a 'Dream Home' to raise money for the Red Cross. As newsprint rationing and manpower restrictions tightened, the magazine sought to establish itself as the nation's pre-eminent morale booster. In late 1942 Gretel Packer and Alice Jackson became joint presidents of the new Australian Women's Weekly Club for Servicewomen at David Jones.[58]

The artistic interests and contacts of Gretel Packer and Brian Penton influenced Lieutenant Packer. In 1942 he summoned to his office Joe Morley, a *Telegraph* journalist who was working as his assistant and as public relations director for the AWC. Packer instructed Morley to see that William Dobell, who was serving as a camouflage artist at Bankstown aerodrome, was appointed an official artist with the AWC. The drawings and oils Dobell produced in this capacity depicted CCC men as brawny, muscular and heroic war workers, and illustrated the scale of the construction projects being undertaken.[59]

As he had yet to win the Archibald Prize, Dobell was given six months' leave from the AWC to prepare for the 1943 contest. Now at a high point of his career, much liked by the Sydney art community and by wealthy patrons such as the Packers, Dobell produced three entries for the prize: 'The Billy Boy', a marvellous portrait of a man whose only job seemed to be boiling the billy for a CCC construction gang's smoko; a portrait of Penton that captured the editor's mercurial brilliance; and an unconventional portrait of the artist Joshua Smith. When 'Portrait of an Artist' won, two unsuccessful artists brought an action to overturn the award, claiming that the exhibit was a caricature. In the sensational court case that ensued, Penton and Pearl threw the combined weight of the *Telegraph*s behind Dobell. In the end, the suit against Dobell was dismissed. Penton hoped to get enough money together to buy his portrait but when the Archibald exhibition closed Packer bought it for £150 and hung it at Consolidated Press headquarters.[60]

Gretel Packer also commissioned Dobell to paint a posthumous portrait of her only brother. In November 1942 Flight-Lieutenant Herbert James Bullmore had been killed instantly when his aircraft's Boston bomb load exploded, causing it to disintegrate in midair over Gona, New Guinea. Jimmy, who had worked as a jackeroo on Anthony Hordern's properly, had been very close to his older sisters, particularly Gretel and Mary. He had often stayed at 'Cairnton', borrowing Frank's car to take Sheila Lyle, whom he was courting, on drives. After Jimmy's tragic death the Packers took Sheila under their wing, inviting her to stay at 'Cairnton' and helping her to obtain a job on a newspaper. Sheila has recalled that Gretel hated being bothered with money and was generous to a fault, thrusting armfuls of evening gowns upon her at a time when clothing was rationed.[61]

Kerry Packer has observed that his mother was 'a woman of beauty and intellect. She was devoted to her husband. I don't mean by that that she neglected us — she didn't. She believed that her function in life was to look after my father and I don't disagree with that'.[62] Gretel stoically endured her husband's volatile temperament and the knowledge that he was not always faithful. Despite his gravelly voice, his forthright manner and his often explosive temper, Frank Packer possessed immense charm; photographs of him at social functions capture him listening solicitously to his companions, making them feel as if there was no one else in the room. Women found his sheer physical bulk, his swaggering manner and his obvious vitality attractive.[63] Packer had been intent on winning the hand of the beautiful and elegant Gretel Bullmore and in his way he probably loved her. But like so many rich men of his generation, he seems to have believed that all a husband had to do was provide for his wife and children financially. While he waited for his sons to assume the reins of his publishing empire, Packer made little effort to conceal his womanising — 'everyone', it is still said today, 'knew' about it.

Although Gretel must have been hurt and humiliated, she handled the situation discreetly and rarely talked about it with friends. But Frank nearly drove his wife to the end of her tether in 1942, when he appears to have had an affair at the very time war work was supposedly keeping him separated from his family for long periods. One day during the 'Dream Home' appeal, Gretel confided to a friend that she was thinking of leaving Frank. But she did not. It is unclear whether the illness that caused her to lose a significant amount of weight and to be hospitalised in the first half of 1943 was stress-related.[64]

At the end of the Second World War it was still common for wealthy Australian parents to employ nannies to look after their children. Clyde and Kerry Packer were under the care of Inez McCracken, only the third woman to graduate as a Tresillian mothercraft nurse in Sydney. Clyde has recalled that Miss McCracken was 'a very kind person, totally devoted to me and my brother, a surrogate mother. She taught me everything ... how to read, write, she gave me the only religious instruction I ever had'. 'Nanny Packer' took the boys to numerous children's parties, where 'Nanny Watt', 'Nanny Lloyd Jones', 'Nanny Hordern' and 'Nanny Fairfax' lined up to watch their young charges tuck into cakes, jellies and ice creams. Clyde and Kerry holidayed with McCracken at her parents' place in the Mallee: 'we stayed in a bakery, it was wonderful'. Another of Kerry's favourite pastimes was wandering across the road to visit his aunt, Kathleen Stening, and to fill up on her banana fritters.[65]

Clyde and Kerry, along with the children of several other wealthy Eastern Suburbs families, often attended Miss Claire Pile's informal morning 'school' on the verandah of the Royal Prince Edward Yacht Club near Lady Martin's Beach. The boys were instructed in more than just spelling and the multiplication tables. One day they were amusing themselves by throwing sand at a little girl who was also playing on the beach. The girl's mother told the boys that if they did not stop throwing sand at her daughter, they would have to leave. 'Why?', demanded Clyde. 'Because I own the beach', replied the society matron. After conferring for a few minutes, Clyde and Kerry returned to ask the woman, 'How much money have you got?' 'A million pounds', was the reply. This immediately silenced the young materialists, who had heard Daddy talk of a great deal of money, but never quite a million.[66]

The boys were dismayed when their nanny was called up. Clyde has observed that McCracken had made 'an unbearable childhood tolerable ... the day I lost my nanny was the unhappiest day of my life'. Kerry, despite his rather defensive comments about his mother, has conceded that he found the war years a 'fairly lonely, difficult period'. The boys were sent to board at Cranbrook School, just a few minutes down Victoria Road from 'Cairnton'. Established by the Church of England in 1918, the school catered to the sons of the Eastern Suburbs gentry.[67]

When Japanese invasion seemed a real possibility, Clyde and Kerry went to live with their aunt Mary Hordern in Bowral. As it was difficult to get into a school during the war, they attended a girls' school with their cousins. Kerry lived in Bowral for two years until one morning he got out of bed and fell flat on his face. Diagnosed as suffering from polio and rheumatic fever, he immediately returned to Sydney.[68]

After spending nine months in an iron lung, Kerry went to Canberra to recuperate. He stayed at the house in Red Hill that his mother had recently advised Consolidated Press to buy. Here, in the section of Canberra that was to become increasingly attractive to the diplomatic community, the boy was under the care of a housekeeper and a particularly grim nurse. When he was well enough Kerry attended a public school and then Canberra Grammar. As a result of his illness, Kerry had fallen behind in his schoolwork, and he proved to be, in his own words, an 'academic failure' like his father. The boy's only pleasure came when his Aunt Kate and her young children stayed with him during school holidays. Two years after his arrival in Canberra, Kerry returned to Sydney to live with his parents. In the four years that had elapsed since he had gone to Bowral, he had seen his mother no more than six times, and his father not at all.[69]

8
Jekyll and Hyde

On being granted leave to visit Sydney in April 1944, Lieutenant Packer immediately became involved in one of the most dramatic censorship disputes in Australia's history. Over the last few months, the *Telegraph* had exasperated censorship authorities. On 30 November 1943, following a report about shortages of coal and stoppages within the industry, the newspaper had been served with an order to submit all copy before publication. Clarrie McNulty and Brian Penton claimed they had not been told the reason for the order, a union journal had run an identical story about the coal situation, and E. G. Bonney had declared, 'If the censor gives an instruction he does it with the power of the law behind him and it will have to be obeyed, whether it is right or wrong'.

While Bonney asked the attorney-general's office whether a prosecution could be initiated against Consolidated Press, the company issued a writ against the commonwealth, Bonney and the state publicity censor, Horace Mansell, claiming that the order to submit was invalid. In late December the matter was stood over until after the High Court's recess. Packer himself put forward a proposal regarding the order to submit; according to H. V. Evatt the proposal, which has not survived, was viewed as objectionable by censorship authorities. Nevertheless, Evatt and some other members of the government did not want to be engaged in a protracted dispute with a major newspaper company, and Consolidated Press was naturally anxious to have the order lifted. In January, after the *Telegraph* was accused of yet another breach, Penton gave Evatt an undertaking to observe censorship instructions on certain conditions and the order to submit was revoked.[1]

Despite the *rapprochement*, editors and executives at Consolidated Press and other newspaper companies were becoming increasingly convinced that the only way to achieve reform was through an open challenge to censorship. In March 1944 Curtin finally agreed to hold an inquiry into it, but another crisis developed before the inquiry even had a chance to convene. On 13 April Rupert Henderson, speaking as president of the ANPA, made the somewhat exaggerated claim that most American correspondents had been withdrawn from Australia because of censorship. Arthur Calwell's criticisms of this statement were allowed to run in full in the press, but a rejoinder by Henderson was, as expected, heavily censored.[2]

Spoiling for a fight, Packer now made a crucial intervention. He suggested that the *Telegraph* should leave blank spaces in Henderson's statement on Saturday 15 April to indicate where it had been censored. Although Fairfax executives supported this defiant action, the *Sydney Morning Herald* did not run blank spaces, having chosen that very Saturday to begin publishing news instead of advertisements on the front page. When Henderson issued another statement explaining that his reply to Calwell had been mutilated, censorship authorities realised that the Sydney press was staging an open challenge to their authority. On Saturday evening an order to submit was served on Consolidated Press. At 9.16 p.m. Cyril Pearl submitted a proof of page one of the *Sunday Telegraph* featuring a trenchant editorial entitled 'Free Speech is the Basis of Democracy' and the Thomas Jefferson quote, 'Where the Press is free and every man able to read, all is safe'. When the state publicity censor's office was unable to make a decision on the copy within half an hour, the machines started printing newspapers with blank columns in place of Henderson's statement and the editorial.[3]

While this was going on, Packer and the other Sydney newspaper proprietors met their legal advisers to discuss a challenge to censorship. Rupert Henderson and Eric Kennedy agreed that the *Sydney Morning Herald* and the *Sunday Sun* would not try to boost sales if the *Telegraph*s were put off the street. By the time commonwealth police officers stormed into the Consolidated Press delivery bay at 11.15 p.m., some copies of the *Sunday Telegraph* were already on their way to regional New South Wales. The officers gave Packer, Pearl, Penton and their solicitor an order signed by Mansell directing them to seize all copies of the newspaper. Pearl later recalled that Packer put on a superlative performance to baulk, bluff and bamboozle the hapless police officers:

> He rumbled, 'Okay, take 'em — and get them out of here, because they're blocking the way. I've got to start printing the *Women's Weekly*'.
> Well, they hadn't counted on anything like that. Their wretched leader said, 'How can I get them out?'
> And Packer told him, 'I don't care how you do it — just move them right now or I'll sue you for obstruction'.
> So the officer tried to get a truck from the PMG [postmaster-general], but couldn't. He approached Packer in a very hangdog manner and asked, abjectly: 'Will you hire me a truck, Mr. Packer?'
> Packer snorted, 'I'm in the business of producing newspapers, not hiring out trucks. That's your problem'.
> The officer said he would throw this great mountain of papers out into the street — and, at that, Packer's solicitor stepped forward.
> The solicitor was M. W. 'Bunty' McIntyre, who worked for a law firm which just happened to represent the Sydney City Council.
> Bunty proclaimed, with all due majesty, 'You throw those papers into the street and the city will prosecute for blocking the public thoroughfares'.

Pearl and other employees took advantage of the confusion to spirit armfuls of the *Sunday Telegraph* away into the adjacent building and hand them out to people at the front door.[4]

On Sunday afternoon the newspaper proprietors, executives and barristers again conferred at Consolidated Press. They agreed that a 'one in, all in' approach would bring the matter before the High Court. Penton's account of the dispute appeared in Monday's *Telegraph* and the *Sydney Morning Herald* alongside an editorial entitled 'Calwell Challenges Your Freedom to Read, Think, Write'. In the early hours of Monday morning commonwealth police were again despatched to seize copies of the *Telegraph* and the *Sydney Morning Herald*. Packer cheekily decided to use another printing press owned by Consolidated Press to print a special edition of the *Telegraph*. The company had acquired the ailing *Labor Daily* (renamed the *Daily News*) in 1940 and nominally merged it with the *Telegraph*. A skeleton crew sneaked out of the Castlereagh Street building and took a roundabout route to the *Daily News* premises in Brisbane Street to throw police off the scent. They managed to smuggle a few armfuls of the four-page issue of the *Telegraph* out of the building before the police tracked them down. At 'Cairnton', Gretel Packer showed nine-year-old Clyde a dramatic photograph of a policeman pointing a gun at a lorry loaded with piles of the *Telegraph*.[5]

Later that morning, the Full Bench of the High Court heard applications by the newspapers for an injunction restraining the commonwealth from preventing publication of material relating to censorship on the condition that they did not carry copy prejudicial to national defence. With typical impudence Packer arranged for copies of the banned newspapers to be delivered to the judges' homes, and each of them had a morning paper tucked under his arm when he took his place on the bench. The court granted an interim injunction.[6]

The case against Consolidated Press for alleged breaches of censorship began in the Special Court of Petty Sessions on 27 April. It was adjourned a week later when the chief justice advised the parties to hold a conference to resolve the issue. At a meeting between Evatt, Packer, Henderson, Kennedy and Ezra Norton on Saturday 13 May, the parties reached broad agreement on a new code of censorship principles. The code represented a significant victory for Packer and his counterparts: censorship was to be limited to defence security and was not to be imposed merely for sustaining morale; unless there was an immediate danger to security, an infringement should be dealt with by prosecution rather than by seizure.[7]

In May 1944 E. G. Theodore hosted a dinner in Packer's honour at Usher's Hotel. Thirty Consolidated Press executives were invited to congratulate their managing director on his contribution to the AWC and the CCC. Theodore lavished praise on his partner, declaring that in the postwar period Packer's courage, ability and leadership qualities would be important not only to the newspaper world but to Australia at large.[8]

The war, however, was not yet over, and Packer was transferred to the AIF's reserve of officers. After two years of working behind a desk, his body was unprepared for the rigours of military drill. By the end of May he had been admitted to Concord Military Hospital suffering from a callus on his left foot and a nasal obstruction.[9]

At around this time Packer appears to have again dabbled directly in the political arena. According to the Fairfax historian Gavin Souter, Packer, Henderson, Kennedy and Keith Murdoch attended a dinner at the Melbourne home of James Fitzgerald, a senior executive of New Broken Hill Consolidated Ltd. The dinner was organised by the leading industrialist William S. Robinson to discuss how best to bring a new conservative party into existence.[10]

Robert Menzies, who was present at the dinner, had begun discussions with some of his parliamentary colleagues about the possibility of establishing a nationwide political movement to succeed the UAP. In the wake of the 1943 federal election the *Telegraph*s had pronounced the UAP 'dead': its policies were outdated and unimaginative, its organisational structure was not up to the task of governing the nation, and many of its principal exponents were 'old fogies'. But even after the April 1944 censorship debacle, the newspapers could not be labelled blatantly anti-Labor; in August they supported the ALP's unsuccessful 'yes' case in the Postwar Reconstruction and Democratic Rights referendum. The *Telegraph*s genuinely believed that any government would suffer without the 'corrective of a progressive, virile Opposition' and their managing director was undoubtedly pleased about being in a position to influence a new chapter in Australian political history. He was probably present at another meeting to discuss the formation of the Liberal Party that was held at Anthony Hordern's T. & G. Building in Sydney.[11]

Packer was also in town when his company precipitated a further censorship controversy. On 5 August 1944, 231 Japanese prisoners-of-war (POWs) died in a failed bid to escape from the Cowra internment camp. The government and the censors were understandably anxious to suppress the magnitude of the breakout and the nationality of the prisoners in order to avoid reprisals on allied POWs. But to the dismay of Curtin, Calwell and Mansell, the front page of the *Sunday Telegraph* on 6 August hinted at the prisoners' nationality.[12] That night Mansell spoke to Lou MacBride, editor of the *Telegraph* while Penton was overseas, and then to Packer about how they intended to cover the breakout on Monday. Although Packer maintained that the newspaper had not indicated the prisoners' nationality, he agreed to co-operate fully with the censors so as not to endanger the lives of Australian POWs.

Ten minutes later, however, Packer rang back to say he expected that any stories submitted for Monday's *Telegraph* would be given liberal treatment. He maintained that if there had been a serious riot the public was entitled to know about it; in any case, 'we would not shoot or ill-treat any Japanese prisoners of war if we learned that Japanese shot or ill-treated any Australian prisoners of war held by them'. Packer then seems to have spoken to executives at the *Sydney Morning Herald* to see how they intended to deal with the story. In the end, Packer instructed MacBride to submit all material to the censors for 'liberal' treatment and the editor agreed to make some alterations when he was convinced of the gravity of the situation.[13]

What had caused Packer to change his views so dramatically in the short time between his two conversations with Mansell? Until he was called by the state publicity censor, Packer seems to have known little about the breakout, and he does not appear to have played any role in determining the layout of the *Sunday Telegraph*'s front page. Lieutenant Packer's first instinct had been to do what he could to help protect the lives of Australian soldiers. The fact that he was capable of doing an about-face so quickly suggests that he was easily influenced by his employees in 'philosophical' matters such as censorship. His behaviour also calls into question his military, as well as his editorial, judgment. Since 1939 the editorial hierarchy of the *Telegraph*s had been chanting 'freedom of the press' like a mantra, and in April 1944 they had scored a commendable victory in their battle against the overarching and clearly political aspects of wartime censorship. But a few months later Packer, increasingly of the view that the freedom of the press meant nothing more than the freedom to run his newspapers without external interference, was unwilling or unable to recognise his employees' abject recklessness.

A month after the Cowra breakout Packer joined the 43rd Landing Craft Company of the Water Transport Section. As the Japanese no longer posed any real threat to the north or west of Australia,[14] the Armoured Brigade had been disbanded and its members were transferred to the various landing craft companies as reinforcements. The companies were designed to supply stores and equipment to areas where there were no roads; to carry troops, especially in amphibious assaults; to evacuate wounded soldiers; and to build port facilities such as jetties and landing stages to facilitate the operation of inshore water craft. Packer's nautical knowledge and his experience in co-ordinating and supervising construction projects would have been seen as valuable additions to the company. Captain Nigel Bowen, another of the company's twenty-six officers, was later to serve as a Liberal minister, and Corporal Ninian Stephen was destined to become governor-general.[15]

Packer joined the 43rd Company at its headquarters at Labu Lagoon, near Lae, at the end of September 1944, and remained in New Guinea for a month. The company was supplying food, petrol, stores and ammunition via barges to shore-based military detachments of the AIF. In mid October a different phase of operations began, when the soldiers embarked on a new training course in advanced signalling, arms training and navigation, and work intensified on the local building program. Ken Ewing, who served in the company, recalls that Packer was primarily involved in seeking timber suitable for construction work.[16]

Some Labor politicians saw Packer's overseas service as too little, too late. On 21 November R. T. Pollard, the member for Ballarat, sarcastically asked whether the lieutenant was 'discharging special functions which necessitate his constant attendance at race meetings'.[17] Packer was, at this time, doing a military engineering course at the Officers' Training School in Liverpool in Sydney's west. Once again Packer proved an easy target for political opponents. What Pollard failed to acknowledge was that all officers were given leave for the weekend at midday on Saturdays, meaning that they were free to attend weekend race meetings. To add insult to injury, Packer failed the engineering course.[18]

On 24 November the Country Party's Archie Cameron described Calwell's decision to seize Sydney's newspapers in April as 'one of the most extraordinary and inexplicable things' ever to have happened in the history of Australia. Cameron was no friend of Consolidated Press but he disliked Calwell even more, and he was a biting critic of the Curtin government. Cameron's speech provided Calwell, still smarting at his exclusion from the negotiations that had resulted in the new Code of Censorship Principles, with an excuse to launch another attack on his newspaper enemies. When the minister for information savaged Packer for his role in the coverage of the Cowra affair, Penton erupted. The editor had been hoping to go overseas again to speak at a Nobel Prize anniversary dinner in New York. On 24 November, the very day that Packer was criticised in parliament, Penton's travel authorisation was cancelled on the instructions of Calwell or Evatt. On 25 November the *Telegraph*, insisting that it had obeyed censorship instructions about the breakout, labelled Calwell 'a dishonest, calculating liar' and challenged him to sue for libel.[19]

The rigours of army life, his academic failures and the constant sniping of political opponents took their toll on Packer. His only extant personal letter from this period was written on 28 March 1945 when he was in Toorbul Point, just north of Brisbane, doing a navigation course. He informed his mother and sister that, with luck, 'I have only another two or three weeks to go at this bloody school' and at least a '50/50' chance of passing. Packer complained about the violent storms and winds of Queensland, overcrowded tents, and fleas and mosquitoes. He found solace in weekend visits to Brisbane, where he relished clean sheets, hot baths and privacy. He playfully told his sister Kathleen that her husband, now a colonel in charge of Concord Military Hospital, was his 'only claim to fame in the Army'. Packer feared that the war in the Pacific would still be running when he was called into combat: 'God how I hate being a soldier … Would have loved it ten years ago, but not today'.[20]

When Packer was granted a week's leave in Sydney in mid April, he became the subject of yet another parliamentary broadside. During a debate about army equipment, James W. Hadley, the Labor member for Lilley, described Lieutenant Packer as 'Fascist-minded', maintained that he had a permanent pass-out check which enabled him to leave any military area, and accused his newspapers of trying to deprive the people of 'their rights and liberties as Australian subjects'.[21] Although Packer must have been seething with anger, he made no public comment on Hadley's attack.

Packer continued to struggle with examinations, and after failing another engineering course he was seconded to the 2/1 Australian Amphibious Armoured Squadron. He served in Morotai and Aitape before returning to Townsville in June. His military service came to an end when he was demobbed on 13 July.[22]

Packer could not return to normal civilian or business life quickly enough. Immediately after obtaining his discharge, he attended the Consolidated Press Youth Club dance at the Australia Hall. Functions such as this were designed to engender a company spirit and enhance employee loyalty. Consolidated Press offered low-interest loans, sponsored staff sporting competitions and provided facilities for the production of *Telegus*, a newspaper produced by copyboys and copygirls. Packer and his executives donated prizes for social, sporting and literary contests and good-naturedly tolerated their employees' lampooning. At the dance in August 1945, Packer, Colonel Travers and Eamon MacAlpine, who had just replaced Clarrie McNulty as editor-in-chief, judged the 'mad hat' competition. Declaring the youth dance a great success, Packer decided that the annual staff ball, which had been abandoned in the early years of the war, should be reintroduced.[23]

The youth dance came less than a year after a dramatic twelve-day newspaper strike. While Packer had been serving in New Guinea, printers on the Sun, followed by their counterparts on the *Daily Mirror*, the *Sydney Morning Herald* and the *Telegraph*, had stopped work to demand a forty-hour week and four weeks' annual leave. When the daily newspaper companies had decided to produce a composite newspaper, their journalists had also gone out on strike, and the workers had published their own newspaper, the *News*, until a settlement was negotiated on 19 October 1944. One of the clauses had stipulated that there was to be no victimisation on either side but, according to Don Whitington, Penton flagrantly breached this undertaking. Many journalists who had played leading roles in the dispute left the *Telegraph*, and in November 1944 Penton sacked two cartoonists for refusing to sign cartoons condemning trade unions.[24] Although Packer almost certainly condoned (and might well have been behind) his editor's actions in these matters, he must have seen events such as youth dances and staff balls as a means of helping repair the damage generated by the strike.

But as the war drew to a close, Packer's principal concern was to make plans for his company's expansion. Newsprint rationing had forced the *Telegraph*s to become tabloids, the *Women's Weekly* to discontinue publication in Western Australia and some advertising contracts to be cancelled. Consolidated Press, which had always believed that a publication's influence rested in its level of popularity, had elected to convert the *Telegraph*s into tabloids rather than to reduce circulation. Another group of publishers, including Fairfax, preferred to maintain size and advertising volumes; Rupert Henderson believed that adopting the 'popular [tabloid] format' would result in the 'complete destruction' of the *Sydney Morning Herald*.[25]

The newsprint pool formed to allocate scarce resources collapsed into a series of intrigues, claims and counter-claims. In February 1943 Keith Murdoch, who was struggling to convince some recalcitrant newspaper publishers to sign a deal with Australian Newsprint Mills, privately described Packer's terms as 'atrocious': 'What a deplorable thing his Press is, and so is Norton's'. A member of the Adelaide newspaper establishment was equally contemptuous of the brash and forceful proprietors who thrived in the cut-throat Sydney market. Lloyd Dumas told Henderson, who watched Packer's manoeuvres like a hawk and had most to lose from the *Telegraph*'s success, that Packer was 'a difficult chap' who would 'always be a trouble-maker so long as he is outside'. The newsprint situation remained critical until mid 1943, when the shipping crisis began to ease.[26]

Within days of his army discharge on 13 July 1945, Packer was making plans to travel overseas to hold talks with newsprint manufacturers, secure new features and acquire a sophisticated printing press. Even now he continued to attract controversy. On 25 July William P. Conelan, a Labor MP from Queensland, asked whether Packer was planning to go abroad in his capacity as a lieutenant or a businessman. Arthur Calwell, now minister for immigration, replied that he would have the 'final say' in determining whether Packer went overseas.[27]

Despite the implicit threat in Calwell's remark, Packer managed to obtain permission to leave Australia. On 12 August he and Cyril Pearl boarded an aeroplane to New York. Atomic bombs had been dropped on Hiroshima and Nagasaki a few days earlier, helping to bring the war to an end on 14 August. Packer was angered by the fact that the British foreign office concluded an ultimatum and terms of surrender with Japan without consulting Australia. He spoke about these concerns when he arrived in London in late August. Great Britain, he told *World's Press News*, had no right to ignore Australia when she had six infantry divisions in the Pacific and one imprisoned in Malaya. 'Don't they know here yet that Australia isn't a Colony?' he demanded to know, mentioning that he had seen in Whitehall a brass plate reading 'Colonial and Dominions Office'. 'Can't they separate us? I'll give them a new brass plate if they will put it up', he snapped.[28]

World's Press News was not the only British newspaper to seek out Packer's views on imperial relations. On 19 October he accepted an invitation to write an article for the London *Daily Mirror*. Packer maintained that Australia did not want to be seen as always 'grousing' about something. Instead of acting as the 'noisy, naughty boy of the Empire', Australia should become part of a permanent council that would rationalise trade, industry and defence throughout the empire. Calling for inspiring leadership to turn the British empire into a British commonwealth of nations, Packer wrote of the need for mass postwar immigration to Australia: 'We can make patriotic English-speaking citizens out of people from Europe, who would willingly come to Australia, thus diminishing the pressure of population at one danger point, and strengthening it in our favor at another'.[29]

This was a carefully articulated argument and it is doubtful whether Packer wrote the article without the help of Penton or Pearl. The piece appeared at the same time as the *Telegraph*s began focusing on the implications of England's postwar economic malaise. Advocating a radical decentralisation of the British empire represented a neat antipodean reversal of Beaverbrook's Empire Free Trade crusade, and the opportunity to join his counterpart in commenting on imperial strategy surely inflated Packer's sense of importance.[30]

The *Daily Mirror* article revealed the rationale for Packer's involvement with the Australian-American Association. Since its formation in 1936, the association had aimed to 'anchor and mobilize public opinion behind some form of understanding with the U.S.A.'. Murdoch had been instrumental in the formation of the Australian-American Association branch in Victoria and the American-Australian Association in New York, and Penton had been associated with the organisation since 1942. Packer told the *Daily Mirror* in October 1945 that it was

> ... of no advantage to Australia to be alone, a tiny white population on the perimeter of Asia.
>
> We very much want an association with the Empire, but if Britain does not recognise our claims and rights to a voice on a permanent body, permanently associated with the planning for the Empire, it is inevitable we shall look elsewhere.[31]

At around this time another London newspaper despatched a staff writer to interview Packer in his suite at the Savoy Hotel. The journalist seemed genuinely fascinated by Packer, even if he did rather patronise the press proprietor by labelling him 'a young son of the Empire who had come to the Motherland for ideas and machinery to help him to still greater success'. The correspondent was amazed by the performance of the *Women's Weekly*, which now boasted sales of 700 000 copies per week (this figure would have been higher without newsprint rationing) in a country with only seven million inhabitants. He described his encounter with Packer thus:

> The burly hand that had knocked out hefty sheep-farmers to give him the title of amateur heavyweight boxing champion of New South Wales, tapped the ash gently from his cigarette. His black, unruly hair was as smooth as it would allow him to make it. He spoke with the rich, deep voice that Australian broadcasters have now made familiar to us here in this country. And he had a great deal to say.[32]

Much of what Packer had to say concerned Consolidated Press's plans for the future. Penton had recently developed an ambitious scheme to stage a conference in Sydney allowing international newspaper editors and executives to speak about the role and responsibilities of the press in the postwar world. Packer invited J. H. Brebner, the director of the news division of the British ministry of information, to Australia. Even though Murdoch thought highly of Brebner, he was angered by Packer's suggestion that the Australian newspaper industry should 'foot the bill'. As Packer was so unco-operative in newsprint matters, Murdoch felt that the ANPA should not be used as his tool to fund a £1000 'holiday tour'. Nothing came of the proposal, as Brebner took up a lucrative position in the transport sector and logistical difficulties made organising the international newspaper conference impossible.[33]

Consolidated Press had been negotiating the purchase of twenty-five units of a high-speed rotogravure press with the firm of Crabtrees in Leeds since 1944. Soon after his arrival in England, Packer placed an order for the press at the staggering cost of £300 000. In November 1945 he went to New York to make a close inspection of American newspaper and magazine establishments. Packer also acquired new features and held talks with newsprint manufacturers, telling a New York interviewer that he did not expect the newsprint shortage to end before 1946.[34]

Packer returned to England a month later and was guest of honour at a cocktail party hosted by Clarrie McNulty, who had recently taken over as editor of Consolidated Press's London bureau. In January 1946 the pair spoke at a dinner at the Savoy Hotel to farewell Lorne Campbell, who was stepping down as manager of the London office and returning to Sydney; Packer ensured that it was a suitably lavish affair for a man who had loyally served Consolidated Press for twenty years. But the main reason for Packer's return to England was to finalise the details of the acquisition of the press,[35] to be installed at a new factory in Ultimo. In 1946 Consolidated Press formed a major subsidiary, Conpress Printing Ltd, to take over the printing of the *Women's Weekly* and undertake commercial and book printing. Theodore became chairman of directors and Packer became deputy chairman. Their old friend John Ratcliffe, who had co-written an authoritative treatise on income taxation law and set up his own accountancy and taxation consultancy, was appointed to the board. Clarence Hamilton King Miller, a stock and share broker who had married into the McFadyen family, also joined the board.[36]

When Packer flew back to Sydney in early 1946, he returned to yet another controversy. He forwarded via ship five packages that he described as personal effects, when most of them contained toys bought by American associates for his sons and his nephews. In May, as *Truth* was only too happy to report, Packer was called to answer a charge that he had made a false customs declaration. J. Darcy, the acting collector of customs, recommended a fine of £10 and the forfeiture of the goods. However, he was overruled by the minister for trade and customs, J. J. Dedman, who halved the fine and allowed Packer to take the goods. Max Falstein's contempt for Packer was so great that he did not care that the government of which he was a member took this action. He rose from the backbench to ask whether Packer had attempted to smuggle into the country a 'quantity of furs' — which sounded much more insidious than children's toys — and to inquire whether Packer could be imprisoned for the offence.[37]

On returning from the United States, Packer had also forwarded two suitcases on another vessel care of an American official in Sydney. The suitcases contained cigars, cowboy suits for his sons, and dresses and a silk bathing suit, ostensibly belonging to his employee Maisie McMahon. When the American indicated that Packer was the real recipient, customs naturally took a keen interest. This triggered a messy and long-running dispute in which Packer personally called on the comptroller-general of customs in Canberra; the minister, Senator Richard Keane, suddenly died and was replaced by Dedman; and a hearing accepted the deputy crown solicitor's advice that the evidence would not sustain a prosecution. There can be no doubt, however, that the wily Packer had been attempting to avoid paying duty on his purchases; the hearing alluded to a previous 'unauthorised importation' of antiques. More than a year after the importation of the cargo, Packer paid the additional duty and his sons finally received their cowboy suits, which they had probably outgrown.[38]

On his return to Australia in early 1946, Packer first attended to the proposed agreement with Australian Newsprint Mills. The backers of the Tasmanian venture wanted to spread resources evenly and to present a united front to the federal government. The ongoing global shortage of newsprint and the scarcity of Australia's dollar resources had forced the government to continue rationing for daily and weekly publications. Only a team player when it proved expedient, Packer again showed himself to be an aggressive isolationist. In mid September, after months of negotiations, he agreed to sign the contract if he received assurances that any further concessions from the government would favour circulation ahead of size. Fairfax executives, however, 'violently opposed' the proposal; to their alarm, the *Telegraph* had just overtaken the *Sydney Morning Herald*'s circulation and, to their anger, Consolidated Press was trying to import tonnage from Anglo-Newfoundland in excess of its pool allocation.[39]

By 24 September Packer had written a letter to Dumas detailing his conditions and his views on Rupert Henderson's stance. Although the missive has not survived, it elicited this response from Murdoch: 'I felt outraged, but then I expected to be outraged. It is a thoroughly bad action and a bad letter'. A few days later, *Truth* and the Brisbane *Telegraph*, which had also been holding out, agreed to sign the contract. Packer, astute enough to realise that he was now totally isolated, went to Melbourne to confer with Murdoch and Consolidated Press signed the contract in late October.[40]

By this time Packer was again on his way overseas for business. In New York he unsuccessfully attempted to entice (later Sir) Douglas Copland, who had just stepped down as Commonwealth prices commissioner and as economic consultant to the prime minister, to take up a position with the ANPA. But the main purpose of Packer's six weeks in the United States and England was to stabilise his company's newsprint situation.[41]

Packer returned home to yet another storm. In December AAP and the New Zealand Press Association agreed in principle to join in the ownership of Reuters from 1 March 1947. The English, Australian and New Zealand parties believed that this would help Reuters to become a great co-operative within the British Commonwealth. The basic news service to Australia was to be known as 'AAP-Reuters', and AAP was to be entitled to a seat on the Reuters board. Inevitably, however, the Australian publishers squabbled bitterly over the finer points of the agreement. In January Henderson told Dumas that he could not 'stomach' Packer's proposals; obviously concerned that Packer might replace him as chairman of AAP, Henderson warned Dumas it was doubtful that the *Sydney Morning Herald* would ever agree to Packer representing it on the Reuters board. As Dumas commented to Murdoch, 'thoughts of Packer dominate Rupert's mind most of his waking hours' and 'Rupert on Packer is not reasonable'. At a meeting of the AAP directors in Sydney on 28 February, Murdoch induced Packer to consent to the agreement with Reuters. A compromise to appease both Packer and Henderson was reached: Henderson was despatched to London to attend his first Reuters board meeting while Packer was elected acting chairman of AAP. *Newspaper News* innocently reported that these decisions had been made 'unanimously', but Murdoch privately noted that the meeting was 'terrible'.[42]

Packer also lurched from industrial crisis to industrial crisis. After being persecuted by certain unions during his term with the CCC, he adopted an increasingly belligerent and provocative stance in his dealings with the newspaper industry's unions. Workers, for their part, realised that full employment presented them with an opportunity to make up for some of their sacrifices during the years of depression and war. When the PIEUA delivered a log of claims in January 1947 requesting improved wages and conditions, Packer told his Sydney counterparts that they should put their names in a draw to decide which office should produce a composite newspaper. Henderson was understandably horrified at the thought of another strike so soon after the damaging events of October 1944, and negotiations with the PIEUA proceeded by discussion rather than confrontation.[43]

Consolidated Press was also waging a campaign designed to undermine the authority of the AJA to deal with complaints against journalists and newspapers under its Code of Ethics. In 1946, four years after Penton had fallen foul of the infant code,[44] the *Telegraph* claimed that Frank Louat had asked that his name not be included in an interview he had given about the anti-strike organisation with which he was involved. Although this practice was consistent with Penton's disapproval of the 'name-withheld' practice, the AJA claimed that the editor had not respected confidences obtained in the course of his calling.[45]

Thus began a three-year battle against the AJA's authority in which the journalist Philip Wynter, one of Penton's golden-haired boys, and David McNicoll, who wrote the 'Town Talk' column for the *Telegraph*, became involved. By 1949 Penton, McNicoll and Wynter, backed by Packer, had failed in their successive challenges to the legality of the Code of Ethics and in their bid to have the AJA deregistered.[46] Packer held a unitarist vision of his firm, believing that he and his executives had a unilateral right to manage their employees free from outside interference. In this he came to rely more and more on David McNicoll. In 1944 Packer had invited McNicoll, who had worked on the *Sydney Morning Herald* and the *Home* before being awarded a commission in the AIF, to join the *Telegraph*. Sophisticated and urbane, McNicoll was the son of a brigadier-general and a Country Party politician who frequented fashionable nightclubs and the race track and mixed easily in networks of influence.[47]

Packer would sleep in until 9 a.m. and arrive at the office an hour and a half later. Books lined the walls, creating the impression of a gentleman's study, and gewgaws cluttered the enormous desk. Here Packer would sit, eyeing callers with the wariness of a dingo, barking out instructions and directing his sprawling enterprise with the authority and ruthless efficiency of a military general.[48] He would throw himself into the seemingly endless web of *Telegraph* power struggles, personally check petty cash receipts, and attempt to oversee the execution of every Consolidated Press venture.

When the 1947 *Sunday Telegraph* Beach Girl of the Year contest was launched, Packer despatched a lackey and an advertising representative to accompany the journalist Donald Horne as he covered the parades. This caused the disgruntled news editor to conclude that the advertising department was too prominent in the conduct of the parades. Resolving to assert the *Sunday Telegraph*'s prestige over the advertising department, he ordered an office car to take Horne to the parade in Cessnock.

The Beach Girl contest culminated in a week-long series of gala events in April 1947. The final parade was held on a Friday night at the Sydney Town Hall, where a panel of judges, including Gretel Packer, announced the winner.[49] When Home was summoned to Frank Packer's office later that night, he assumed that he was to be congratulated on the conduct of the contest. Instead, he was reprimanded for failing to take the bus to Cessnock, accused of being a smart alek and sacked when he tried to explain that he had been authorised to take a car. On Saturday Horne did the rounds of the pubs kept afloat by Consolidated Press journalists. By now many of these men liked nothing better than speculating on their irascible employer's state of mind. Horne listened to anecdotes of other famous Packer sackings and was advised to return to work on Monday to ascertain whether Packer had cooled down.

On Monday afternoon Horne met Duncan Thompson, the *Daily Telegraph*'s rather fearsome chief-of-staff and a loyal Packer apparatchik. Thompson told Horne that Mr Packer had made a concession: if the journalist paid the cost of taking the car to Cessnock (£14), he would be reinstated. Outraged by the suggestion, Horne was informed that he could not meet Packer personally because he was a busy man, and ordered to collect his back pay and leave the building. Horne spent another day earnestly discussing his situation in the office pubs before going to see the secretary of the AJA. After telling Horne that if he had really committed a misdemeanour there was nothing the AJA could do, the secretary offered to dictate a letter that Horne could sign. The union official averred that the letter, which described Consolidated Press's actions as 'most tyrannical and oppressive' and 'morally and legally unjust', used the only sort of language Packer would understand. And so Horne trotted back to the pub to show the letter to the legion of self-appointed Packer experts, who informed him that the phrases he most liked had been taken straight from a notorious letter Penton had written about the AJA's Code of Ethics. Horne, realising that the secretary had been cynically using him as part of his vendetta against Packer and Penton, knew that if he delivered the letter it would be like a red rag to a bull.

The next morning Horne received a telephone call from Thompson asking him to meet the managing director at 3 p.m. When Horne walked into his office Packer rose to his feet, all smiles, and motioned him to a chair. Still smiling, Packer told Horne that he had had the wrong picture in his mind the other night and he had since banged a few heads together and found out the truth. Packer offered Horne his old job back, commented that he had a great future at the *Telegraph*, and shook hands with the relieved but understandably bemused journalist.[50]

Horne later wrote a highly stylised account of Packer's presence at one of the Beach Girl functions at the Trocadero in April 1947:

> ... with its heavy jaws, sharp teeth and sloping forehead his head had some of the features of the Neanderthal Man, other parts had elements of the 'handsome' so that, as I watched him in the flickering lights of the Beach Girl Ball, I could see a Jekyll and Hyde alternation; while he could scowl, as if deciding on immediate decapitation, or stand in the confident posture of a conqueror about to set a city to the sword, as he moved among his guests and talked, he was also able to bestow gracious smiles, or make gestures of 'charm'. There was never any doubt that he was prince.

Gretel Packer was always present at functions like this, and always on hand to graciously entertain her husband's friends and business associates. When Horne saw Gretel at the Beach Girl function draped in mink and diamonds and wearing a perfect smile on her handsome face, she reminded him of a film star in a New York nightclub.[51]

Gretel and her sister Mary Hordern also helped Frank with some of his business endeavours. To the consternation of editor Alice Jackson, Packer invited his stylish and forthright sister-in-law to begin contributing a fashion feature to the *Women's Weekly* in late 1945. A few months later Hordern went to France to select designs and mannequins to be showcased at a series of parades hosted by the magazine. When Hordern encountered difficulties in dealing with the French bureaucracy and the temperamental fashion establishment, Gretel flew to Paris to assist her. The lavish parades staged in

Sydney and interstate were so successful that they became an annual event, and Gretel visited Paris again to help plan the 1949 series.[52]

No aesthete, Frank was probably unable to appreciate Gretel's passionate interest in gardening and design. Nevertheless, he did appreciate the value of having a charming wife and an elegant residence as he mixed in increasingly influential circles. In the late 1940s Gretel was invited to contribute a piece about flower arranging to a book compiled by Helen Blaxland. Gretel's philosophy was simple: the flowers she dispersed throughout 'Cairnton' were 'dictated entirely' by her garden:

> When, as occasionally happens, the garden obliges by flowering and behaving exactly as you have planned, you can hardly bear to ruin the effect by cutting from here and there and leaving in your wake a generally thinned-out look. Instead, if you strip one corner of the garden of every flower in sight, you can then avoid that corner for a week or so, until it has had time to recover.

The photographs of Gretel's work taken by Max Dupain illustrated her real flair for colour and symmetry and her love of *objets d'art*. Pink peonies arranged in a pink glass shell reflected on a gleaming mahogany table, pink and red rhododendrons were set off by a ruby velvet cloth, white hydrangeas were piled high in an alabaster vase against embroidered white satin curtains, and dried hydrangeas topped a marble pedestal beneath a strikingly irregular clock mounted on the wall.[53]

Sheila Lyle found Gretel kind, witty and impulsive, if a touch bossy at times. On one occasion, Gretel suddenly rang her late brother's beau and invited her on a holiday to Surfers Paradise. Determined to be fashionably attired, Sheila went to an exclusive department store and bought up the entire 'Going North' collection. Staggering into the lobby of the hotel they were staying at, the young woman slipped and fell over. Gretel burst out laughing: 'Oh get up! You're only trying to get attention'. Sheila recalls that Gretel's manner was such that she would automatically be offered the best table whenever she entered a restaurant.[54]

One fixture on Sydney's social calendar for couples like the Packers was the Black and White Ball at the Trocadero on the first Tuesday in October. The inaugural ball had been held in 1937 to raise money for the Royal Blind Society of New South Wales, and it resumed after the war under the direction of the formidable Nola Dekyvere. With the help of the *Women's Weekly*, the ball became the premier social event of Sydney's spring racing week.[55] Many couples entertained friends at buffet dinners in their mansions and clubs before setting off to the ball proper. Crowds gathered outside the Trocadero to watch the New South Wales governor and the 1500 or so glamorous guests arrive. The women dressed in exquisite concoctions of chiffon, organza and taffeta, while their male escorts wore impeccable tuxedos and bought white buttonhole carnations on their arrival. With his eye for the ladies, it was no chore for Frank Packer to help judge the best white dress at the 1947 ball. The floral decorations at the Trocadero became more elaborate each year, and by 1949 Gretel was serving on the decorating committee. A year later, she became deputy president of the ball committee.[56]

Frank Packer was extremely close to members of his immediate family. His mother had not had an easy life. After her father's death Ethel had struggled to make ends meet and maintain a veneer of social gentility. She had worked so hard on her arrival in Australia that she had had little time to make friends of her own, had been separated from her husband Clyde during the early years of their marriage and had watched as he drove himself into an early grave. Ethel was greatly loved and respected by both her children. She lived with Kathleen and her husband, and Frank and Gretel, who were only a few doors away, always included her in their social gatherings. But just as she began to enjoy life again after Clyde's death, Ethel became hard of hearing. She found being deaf immensely frustrating, but was too proud to get one of the cumbersome hearing aids available in the 1940s.[57]

Even when she contracted leukemia Ethel retained her active mind and was easily bored. In 1947, after being given a series of blood transfusions, including one from her son, she asked a younger friend to accompany her on a health trip to New Zealand. However, Ethel's condition deteriorated and she was admitted to a private hospital in Wellington. While Frank was tied up with important AAP business, his sister flew to Auckland. Kathleen arrived in the middle of the Easter break and was unable to hire a car. A taxi driver agreed to take her all the way to Wellington, but the guesthouses en route were full. Kathleen was forced to catch a few hours' sleep in a police station at New Plymouth while the driver slept in the taxi. She arrived at the hospital in time to be with her mother when she died on 1 April. Ethel had clearly made an impression on the people she had met during her short time in Wellington, as the bank manager insisted on acting as a pallbearer. The taxi driver kindly agreed to take Kathleen back to Auckland, and her mother's ashes were interned in the family vault at South Head Cemetery.[58] Distance had prevented Frank from being at the deathbeds of both parents.

As children, Frank and Kathleen had been part of a small and closely-knit family. R. C. Packer had, of course, worked long hours to make a success of his publishing enterprises. But he had not had a big house to maintain, he had not entertained lavishly, he had travelled little and his children had not been raised by a nanny. His son's life was very different. When he was in Sydney, Frank worked twelve- or thirteen-hour days and attended social functions at night, and regularly travelled interstate and overseas. As a result his young sons rarely saw him. Frank was a remote but also a strict father, firmly believing in the disciplinary benefits of corporal punishment. In his decidedly defensive memoir of his childhood, Kerry recalled that one day his father took him aside to tell him:

> Sometimes I have a bad day at the office and I'm angry. I'm going to come home, and if you believe that what you've done isn't worthy of the punishment that I decide you should have, you can have a stay of execution. All you've ever got to say is, 'Look, I think you're in a bad mood and I'd like to discuss it with you tomorrow, and that'll stop it'. He said that it may not alter the punishment — that he may decide on the next day that I was wrong and he was right — but I had that option. And for a man who was supposed to be tough I don't ever remember one occasion on which I used the stay of execution. I

got a lot of hidings, because that's the sort of person I was and the sort he was. I don't ever remember getting one I didn't deserve and there's a stack that I didn't get that I should have got.[59]

R. C. Packer had always expected his son to work in the newspaper industry, carefully introducing him to every aspect of newspaper production. But while Frank also expected his sons to succeed him, he was less nurturing than his own father had been. Perhaps remembering how his father's employees had dismissed him as a playboy in the 1920s, he was determined not to give — nor be seen to give — a soft ride to his boys. Frank Packer expected a lot from his employees, his children, and himself. Much of his drive and energy seems to have stemmed from a desire to prove his publishing mettle not just to his father's contemporaries, but to himself. 'The Young Master' fiercely defended his father's considerable creative and business achievements. In 1935, when he was first included in *Who's Who in Australia*, Frank provided a summary of his late father's career almost as long as his own.[60] Frank always remained self-conscious about his own lack of journalistic prowess. He often described himself, somewhat wistfully, as a 'journalist', rather than a company director, on official papers.

Frank Packer, the man who was unfaithful to his wife and intimidated his sons, was deeply affectionate and compassionate towards other members of his family. In 1939 he had summoned his uncle to join him in Sydney. R. C. Packer's youngest brother, John Stewart ('Jack'), had been badly wounded in the First World War before becoming a prominent trotting owner-trainer in Tasmania. Frank asked his uncle, who set up his own stables in Kogarah, to look after his dogs, polo ponies andracehorses. In the early years of the war Frank and F. J. Smith, the accountant who had been working for the Packer family for decades and who was a director of Hordern Brothers, bought a horse stud near Muswellbrook. Employing Jack Packer as head trainer, the stud produced a number of successful thoroughbreds, including Columnist, Journalist, Travel Boy and Dickens. Frank lost both his racing partners in quick succession: Fred Smith died in October 1946 and John Packer in August 1947. Both men were generously profiled by the *Sunday Telegraph*.[61]

The *Telegraphs*' highly paid turf writers were not allowed to laud a horse belonging to someone Packer disliked or to criticise an animal that Packer himself owned. It was even rumoured that more than one journalist was instructed not to dwell at any length on the winning chances of a Packer-owned horse because the odds might become too short. After the war Packer became one of the biggest punters in Australia, if not the biggest. He attended the race meetings at Randwick nearly every weekend and was often seen at the Melbourne track. His bookmaker friend Arthur Browning assisted in the planning and execution of some spectacular betting plunges. His commission agent Peter Cruise stuffed the piles of tax-free money Packer won at the races into his office safe at Consolidated Press.[62] But though Packer's stud had earned £61 000 in prize money by 1949, he often lost a great deal betting on his own horses. To his chagrin his champion chestnut, Columnist, was narrowly beaten in the Caulfield Cup in 1946 and came third in the Epsom Handicap in 1947. There was some consolation a few days after the Epsom, when Packer recouped £20 000 by backing Cervantes. The

Sunday Telegraph marked Columnist's victory in the Caulfield Cup in October 1947 by plastering photographs of the horse charging over the finish line on the front and back pages. It was rumoured that Packer backed Columnist in a double with Sweet Chime in the Melbourne Cup for £120 000.[63] Sweet Chime failed to win a place, but Packer continued to gamble for enormous stakes, both on and off the track.

9
Powerbroking

Throughout the second half of the 1940s, the critical shortage of newsprint continued to cause rifts between major Australian newspaper companies. By January 1947 Australia had lifted most restrictions on imports of British goods. But during the year Britain's balance of payments steadily worsened and the British treasury became increasingly concerned that as a result of American pressure, Australia might lift restrictions on American imports and cut its British preferences. The situation became more urgent on 15 July, when sterling was made convertible and Britain's trading partners hastened to convert sterling into dollars. When British Prime Minister Clement Attlee personally informed Australia's Prime Minister J. B. Chifley of the dire British situation, the Australian Labor government announced tight restrictions on dollar imports.[1]

Petrol and food rationing were maintained and a new round of newsprint cuts was flagged. On 27 August Consolidated Press withdrew from the newsprint pool committee's rationing recommendations, labelling them 'partisan and detrimental'. This selfish and self-indulgent action failed to acknowledge that Britain was still Australia's major source of trade and investment. In early December Packer, Keith Murdoch and executives from the Sydney *Sun* and the Melbourne *Sun News-Pictorial* travelled to Canberra to warn Ben Chifley and his advisers that further restrictions on newsprint would cause widespread dismissals within the industry.[2]

In January 1948 the comptroller-general of customs drastically reduced newsprint quotas to about 46 per cent of prewar figures. Such severe rationing entailed cutting advertising space and virtually abandoning special supplements and issues, and made it increasingly difficult for newspaper editors to strike a balance between general news, political news and commentary, sports reports, women's news, and cartoons and comic strips. Members of the ANPA disagreed on the best method of allocating available newsprint. Despite their private dislike of Packer, Murdoch and Lloyd Dumas now clearly belonged to the faction advocating concessions for companies that opted to increase the circulation, rather than the size, of their titles. On 19 February representatives of the companies that favoured circulation over size met at Consolidated Press's residence in Red Hill. Here they decided to reconstitute the Australian Newspapers Conference (ANC).[3]

For a time after the formation of the breakaway organisation, Murdoch and Dumas found dealings with Packer 'extraordinarily cordial'. Packer spent mid 1948 considering whether to involve his company in a legal test case in an effort to force the government to withdraw from all matters pertaining to newsprint derived from non-dollar sources. Packer, who had several conferences with Garfield Barwick KC about the issue, was prepared to hold discussions on both sides of the political fence to advance his case. While the Consolidated Press editor-in-chief, Eamon MacAlpine, was granted an audience with Menzies, Evatt told Packer that Chifley was 'very anxious' to prevent a court case.[4]

Murdoch and Dumas were hopeful but not terribly confident that Consolidated Press's action would be successful. A few weeks before the first half-yearly meeting of the ANC, Dumas told Murdoch that Packer had just decided that Gretel would accompany him to Adelaide. Dumas evidently felt that Frank would be less pugnacious in the presence of his wife, saying that this development provided 'evidence that all will be smooth'. At the conference, the ANC deputed the former Lieutenant Packer to be its representative on a proposed committee in Sydney to determine the character of a memorial to Australian war correspondents and photographers who had died during the war. According to Dumas, the fact that the South Australian premier (later Sir) Thomas Playford and civic leaders attended the conference dinner made Packer feel that there was value in a body like the ANC. But Dumas's optimism proved to be somewhat ill-founded. Packer, who spent most of his career feuding or anticipating feuds with supposed allies, objected to the clause in the draft constitution that compelled a member organisation to continue paying a membership fee if it had been expelled from the ANC. Dumas privately informed Murdoch that Packer 'has a natural fear that, some time or other, we will gang up on him, and, some time or other, that may happen, because it would be impossible for us to work with him'.[5]

Packer did indeed have every reason to be concerned about the activities of the HWT's proprietorship. The company was planning to launch a fortnightly magazine, known as *Woman's Day*, at the same time as Fairfax intended to relaunch the *Home* as a fortnightly. Packer naturally deduced that these magazines, scheduled to appear in alternate weeks, were designed to compete directly with the *Women's Weekly*. On 28 July 1948 he wrote to Chifley to protest about the 'weekly invasion of the Woman's magazine field'. Packer complained that the *Women's Weekly* was being unfairly discriminated against as magazines that were published monthly or fortnightly were not subject to newsprint rationing. Yet he himself had exploited this anomaly in the National Security Regulations, launching a national monthly family magazine known as *A.M.* just a few weeks earlier.[6]

Packer, who was planning to go to the United States, asked the prime minister whether he would be prepared to meet him before his departure on 4 August. By 2 August, however, no meeting had taken place, apparently because Packer had been unable to secure an interview with Chifley. All Packer could do was lobby other people in Canberra while he arranged for MacAlpine to raise the issue when he met with the prime minister on behalf of the ANC. Two days before leaving the country, Packer wrote another letter of appeal to Chifley, referring to him as 'an old newspaper man'.

(Unlike his Labor predecessor John Curtin, Chifley had never been a journalist, although he was on the board of the Bathurst *National Advocate*.) The letter accused the government of putting 'completely unjustified' controls on the *Women's Weekly*, declared that the government appeared to be unfairly penalising the magazine and facilitating the 'invasion' of its 'birthright' because the *Telegraph*s had criticised Labor policies, and warned that Consolidated Press might turn the largely apolitical *Women's Weekly* into a 'political sheet'.[7]

The letter is remarkable for its degree of arrogance and paranoia. Packer's nature, always suspicious, had been hardened over the years by a series of disturbing events. A state premier had attempted to bankrupt his family, the sophisticated press in which his infant company had invested at great expense had been sabotaged by his own employees and his wartime activities had been consistently misrepresented by trade unionists and political opponents. While demanding conspicuous loyalty from his family and his employees, Packer was increasingly inclined to view standpoints and policies that did not accord directly with his own interests as evidence of deliberate persecution.

The extraordinary letter to Chifley was also the first explicit acknowledgment by Packer of his company's mounting hostility to Labor. In the September 1946 federal election the *Telegraph*s had for the first time clearly advocated a vote for the conservatives. Reacting against years of shortages and restrictions, they had applauded the Liberal and Country parties for formulating policies that would increase the output of material for food, clothing, housing and industry, would settle industrial unrest, and lift the 'dismal burden' of taxation. The newspapers contended that the Liberal Party under Menzies had produced 'pugnacious, positive, and imaginative' ideas and disposed of many of the 'old fogies' who had dominated the UAP.[8]

But despite its clear editorial preference for the Liberal Party, the *Telegraph* was still able to run a more reflective and philosophical piece as the election approached. Brian Penton argued that both major parties needed to 'see the social problem whole'. He warned that the ALP was not really a party at all but a group of parties, each with a different philosophical basis: Lockean, Irish Catholic and Marxist socialist. Equally destructive confusions underlined the non-Labor parties: they had repeatedly disintegrated in the face of war and changing economic and geographical imperatives, and they had been too busy to work out a consistent political philosophy.[9]

After the ALP was returned to office in 1946, the *Telegraph*s moved further to the right. A number of factors account for this discernible ideological drift. After years of wage restraint during depression and war, unemployment was reaching record low levels. As workers and trade unions began agitating for shorter working hours and the abandonment of wage pegging, the number of industrial stoppages and strikes escalated. Communists assumed positions of influence in many Australian unions such as the Federated Ironworkers' Association, while at the international level the Soviet Union extended its reach throughout eastern Europe. Pressures against non-conformity and dissent in the political, literary and scientific arenas intensified because of the growing fear of communism.[10]

Immediately after writing to the Labor prime minister on 2 August 1948, Packer flew out of Australia with Consolidated Press's advertising manager Bill Dowsett. In Canada, New York and London, Packer worked closely with the Consolidated Press manager, Sydney H. Wilson, to advance Australian contacts with newsprint manufacturers. According to the waspish Rupert Henderson, Packer tried to secure newsprint from Bowater Corporation for his own company; Eric Kennedy commented that the 'negotiations with Packer were mysterious all through'. By September, however, Packer had helped to conclude a deal making an additional 27 000 tonnes of English newsprint available to members of the Australian newsprint pool. The easing of the international situation in late 1948 relaxed some of the tensions about newsprint. The cut to newsprint allocations was reduced, rationing from non-dollar areas and the threat of legal action by Packer were abandoned, and the newsprint pool was discontinued. And the early issues of *Woman's Day* and *Home* failed to make an impression on the market, prompting Consolidated Press to host a 'bang up' luncheon at the Hotel Australia.[11]

By the time Packer returned to Australia in September 1948, E. G. Theodore had had a heart attack. Packer and Theodore were partners in more than just Consolidated Press. In 1940 the two men had bought a 500-hectare property near Adaminaby. They built a fishing and hunting lodge on the isolated property, which was located on the edge of Kosciuszko National Park almost 100 kilometres from Canberra. Theodore and his two sons John and Ned often travelled by jeep to 'Platypus Lodge' to fish. Packer invited media and advertising executives and senior members of Consolidated Press to holiday on the isolated property, but rarely visited it himself. Fishing was too sedentary, too contemplative, the contest too subtle and the rewards too modest to satisfy Packer. His preferred sports were those that allowed him to skylark, to compete with gusto and to order other people around.

Theodore regarded Consolidated Press as very much a joint enterprise of the Packer and Theodore families. After his heart attack in 1948, he announced that thirty-six-year-old John would replace him as chairman the following January. A graduate of the University of Sydney, Theodore's elder son had joined the company in 1936 and become a director in 1947. John's younger brother Ned went to work in the London bureau of Consolidated Press in 1949.[12]

E. G. Theodore made one last profit out of Consolidated Press at this time. In late 1949 the Chifley government introduced legislation to amend the Income Tax Assessment Act. The amendments imposed higher taxation rates on profits placed into the reserves of private companies in an effort to prevent such companies from minimising their tax liability. While the *Telegraph* railed against the changes,[13] Packer and Theodore decided to convert Consolidated Press into a public company. Associated Newspapers accepted Sydney Newspapers Pty Ltd's offer of £1 per share for the 170 000 shares it held in Consolidated Press. This meant that Sydney Newspapers now owned 525 000 of the ordinary shares in Consolidated Press, while Packer and Theodore owned 25 000 shares each.[14]

Packer and Theodore then placed on the market the parcel of shares formerly owned by Associated Newspapers. The directors of Consolidated Press explained the reasons for the decision to become a public company at the annual general meeting on 10 November. Packer was unable to be at the meeting himself as he was in Melbourne speaking at an ANC conference and attending a conference of newspaper editors with Penton.[15] On Packer's return to Sydney, the offer of shares at 35s each was oversubscribed. This was a substantial profit on the purchase price just a few weeks earlier; as a Consolidated Press publication boasted, the beards of Associated Newspapers directors had again been singed. Twenty-five per cent of the shares were reserved for preference shareholders in Consolidated Press and Conpress Printing, including Packer and Theodore. An extraordinary general meeting on 15 December ratified the necessary changes to the articles of association.[16]

Packer and his counterparts spent much of 1949 plotting behind each others' backs. Although Murdoch hoped that a new united body would emerge to represent the newspaper industry, Packer maintained that the ANC and the ANPA should negotiate separately about newsprint and industrial matters. Murdoch was alarmed in January when Dumas indicated that he was considering retiring from the ANC presidency. Although he felt that Packer had some claims to the position, Murdoch commented that he would 'hate so much to have our papers dragged at his heels that I doubt very much whether we should ever consent to such a presidency'.[17] Dumas agreed to stay on as president.

In September 1949 the matter of Australian representation on the Reuters board was again raised. Packer and Eric Kennedy were adamant that it was time for Rupert Henderson to stand down as chairman of AAP. Dumas decided that the HWT should pay attention to 'Packer's strong and not unnatural' opinion that he was entitled to the position. Although Murdoch also had some reservations about Henderson, he finally decided that the Fairfax executive should retain the post for a fixed term. Perhaps Murdoch had heeded the not altogether disinterested claim of Henderson who, in the words of one observer, had 'had to eat Packer's dust for a number of years', that Packer 'would not be acceptable to the London directors'.[18]

Packer's counterparts occasionally saw that he did not always behave in a totally cavalier and insensitive fashion. In September 1949 Murdoch was given the unenviable task of arranging the composition of the Australian delegation to the following year's Imperial Press Conference in Canada. A week after telling Murdoch that he expected that someone would represent Consolidated Press, Packer announced that he himself wanted to go to Canada: 'on thinking it over it might be a nice break, if I can take my good lady'. An exasperated Murdoch told Packer that his letter had been 'unhelpful' and explained that no more than two people would probably be able to represent the Sydney metropolitan press. Associated Newspapers had already nominated Sir John Butters and John Fairfax & Sons Ltd had nominated (later Sir) Vincent Fairfax. Packer said that he had simply tried to be 'helpful': 'If it will help you to solve the situation & you want to drop me, do so'. However, Murdoch was anxious to avoid any further ill-feeling among the major press proprietors, concluding that Packer's inclusion would be necessary to 'retain cohesion in the Sydney team and important representation'. In

November he managed to arrange for three Sydney nominees — Packer, Fairfax and Butters — to attend the conference.[19]

Shortly after these arrangements had been finalised, Packer and Keith Martin went on a business trip to the United States and Britain to sign newsprint contracts and secure new syndicated material. Packer was entertained by executives from the International News Service and the King Features Syndicate, and Lee Falk, the creator of the hugely popular comic 'Mandrake the Magician', which appeared in the *Women's Weekly*, at the famous Stork Club in California.[20]

Although Packer's timing in business matters was usually impeccable, he had an unfortunate habit of being thousands of kilometres away when those closest to him fell gravely ill. On 9 February 1950, a few days after collapsing at his apartment in Edgecliff, E. G. Theodore died. Packer paid tribute to his partner of nearly twenty years in a cable from London:

> ... he was a wonderful man in every way. The more frequently you came in touch with him the greater became your admiration and respect for his great talents and intellect, which, combined with a lovable charm and simple manner, most people found irresistible.

Gretel Packer attended the state funeral at St Mary's Cathedral and fourteen-year-old Clyde acted as a pallbearer.[21]

When Frank Packer returned to Sydney a few weeks later, his counterparts were again holding behind-the-scenes talks about the ANC presidency. Murdoch, perhaps feeling a little red-faced about the role he had played in torpedoing Packer's bid for the AAP chairmanship, decided to placate him. This time he 'cordially' agreed with Dumas's view that they could not bypass Packer without offending him and Packer was duly elected president of the ANC at the annual meeting in April. This meeting passed a special resolution asserting that 'Freedom of thought and expression is the basic freedom of democracy'. Packer still vividly remembered his newspapers' violent disputes with censorship authorities during the war, and for years he had been listening to Penton and Pearl insist on the social significance of journalism. But he and the ANC were opposed to the proposed United Nations Declaration on Freedom of Information, arguing that if the 'freedom of the press' was defined in too much detail the term could be interpreted in dangerous ways and result in government interference. The ANC resolution concluded that:

> ... any infringement on the freedom of the Press, other than restrictions necessary to preserve the morals and health of the community and the rights of individuals, and applying in like manner to all citizens, or restrictions necessary in wartime or in time of declared national emergency to protect the nation, should be resisted by every section of the community as marking the first step towards authoritarian government.
>
> The Council recommends the Australian Government to [sic] refuse to accept any United Nations convention which compromises or weakens this principle in any way, or condones the form of Press control now operating in authoritarian countries.[22]

But the Australian government was grappling with an issue that was closer to home and considerably less abstruse. In December 1949 the Chifley administration had been defeated by the Liberal and Country Party coalition. The *Telegraphs*, alarmed by the spectre of industrial unrest and the Labor government's attempt to nationalise the banks, had thrown their weight behind the coalition, declaring the election a choice between 'Socialisation and Free Enterprise'. They were delighted in April 1950 when Prime Minister Menzies introduced a bill to outlaw the Communist Party of Australia and seize its assets. The newspapers expressed no qualms about the controversial clause that made the onus of proof rest with the defence rather than with the prosecution.[23]

Packer was not content for his newspapers to simply editorialise about the bill. In early May the *Telegraph*'s chief-of-staff, Norman Kessell, and chief sub-editor, Forbes Miller, told a number of reporters: 'Mr Packer has instructed me to ask you whether you are a member of the Communist Party'. The AJA immediately convened a special meeting to discuss Packer's 'repugnant' actions, realising that Kessell and Miller had had no option but to obey orders. The New South Wales District Committee wrote to Packer complaining that the question was 'crudely offensive' and unprecedented in the industrial history of journalism. The letter pointed out that it was against the principles of British justice to ask any citizen to incriminate and possibly render himself liable to prosecution under some future law. On 18 May Packer replied that the 'management' of Consolidated Press had simply wanted to know which employees were members of the Communist Party, as it seemed likely that the party would be declared illegal. His assertion that any information obtained by the company would remain confidential and was not designed to incriminate journalists was disingenuous, to say the least.[24] He and the *Telegraph*s were now enthusiastic red-baiters, and there can be no question that if Menzies' bid to have the party banned had succeeded, Packer would have sacked or otherwise victimised employees who had identified themselves as communists.

The man who loudly proclaimed himself a champion of freedom of thought and expression[25] had little time to dwell on the real or symbolic significance of the way he had treated his journalists. Within weeks he and Gretel were on their way to the seventh Imperial Press Conference in Canada. The Empire (later Commonwealth) Press Union had been formed in 1909 to represent the publishing interests of Great Britain and her colonies and in 1910 an Australian section had been established. Every five years or so all the sections gathered together at the Imperial Press Conference. The forum in June 1950 was held in Ottawa, with side trips to Quebec, Montreal, the Muskoka Lakes and Niagara Falls arranged for delegates and their wives.[26]

Packer joined ninety-nine other delegates from eighteen sections at the conference, which decided to focus on the notion of the freedom of the press. Before leaving Australia, he told Murdoch that the Australian delegation could 'put forward a really good case demonstrating the very vital part they are playing in the maintenance of a free Press — a Press which is free, vigorous, and independent to a point which I feel is unequalled in any part of the world, or most parts of the world'.[27]

More than a decade had elapsed since Murdoch had attempted to buy Consolidated Press, and he continued to regard Packer as a dangerous publishing rival. Nevertheless the older, Melbourne-based Murdoch still viewed Packer with a patronising, condescending and at times disdainful eye. He privately told Dumas that he had 'given' Packer the job of presenting Australia's case on the proposed United Nations Declaration on Freedom of Information. British, South African and Indian representatives joined Australia in opposing the declaration. According to Murdoch, 'Frank did poorly in his first speech but well in a second and short effort, altho [sic] as is his wont he was unnecessarily forthright. He put up some propositions that could never be argued'. Packer's first speech, delivered on 17 June, suggested that the censorship clashes and the behaviour of Arthur Calwell during the war had left an indelible impression. Packer maintained that the United Nations declaration would blur the distinction between a nation's press and its government:

> If Governments decide what is news, then our newspapers will be as dull as the Russian ones, and God save us from that!
> We must refuse to accept the type of Press that can be found in totalitarian countries.

In his address the following day, Packer declared that there was nothing wrong with newspapers because more people were buying them now than ever before; competition was the greatest influence for good and kept a paper truthful and on its toes.[28] If Murdoch had paused to reflect on Packer's business activities since 1932 — the closure of the World, the decision to take over an existing morning newspaper rather than launch a new one, the discontinuation of the *Daily News*, the outraged reaction to the launch of *Woman's Day* and *Home* — he would have added hypocrisy to his list of Packer's vices.

Although he had been dabbling in politics for the last few years, it was not until Packer received a letter from Menzies in 1950 that he realised he was now being taken seriously as a political player. Packer seized the opportunity to cultivate his relationship with the prime minister and, for the next quarter of a century, was to enjoy a close, if at times turbulent, association with the Liberal Party.

Menzies was moved to write to Packer after the *Telegraph* splashed a provocative editorial across its front page on 28 September 1950 about the impact of the inflationary pressures building up in Australia. Brian Penton's editorial, entitled 'The Australian £ is bleeding to death', urged the prime minister to ensure that the forthcoming budget gave the Australian pound a more realistic value in relation to sterling, cut unnecessary spending and helped industry to increase productivity. A few days later the prime minister despatched a 'strictly personal' letter to Packer pointing out that the Country Party was opposed to any appreciation of the currency and that he did not want to risk splitting the coalition over the issue. Menzies concluded:

> Your front page article this morning ... seems to declare war on me. If this is so, let's get on with it, while Chifley chuckles ... But I prefer understanding to dispute; and political good sense to brawling.

> Hence these lines to a man whose good sense I respect, and whose courage I have never publicly (or privately) impugned.

Packer responded immediately, writing to Menzies to explain in more detail the *Telegraph*'s financial concerns. But the real point of the letter was to reassure the prime minister that Consolidated Press had *not* declared war on him: Menzies was 'a great man of international calibre' who had the confidence of the Australian people; the editorial had certainly not intended to suggest that he lacked personal courage; 'it would be a brave member of the Liberal Party indeed' who turned Menzies out of office over the issue of appreciation.[29]

Menzies' motive in writing to Packer was to negate the criticisms of the proprietor who now controlled the morning newspaper with the biggest circulation in the most populous state of Australia. Since its formation in 1944, the Liberal Party had placed great importance on 'public relations': Menzies had realised the need for a first-class press office to match John Curtin's legendary aide, Don Rodgers; the party had organised commercial radio broadcasts and radio fireside chats by Menzies; and in 1947 the federal president, R. G. Casey, had lured the services of the Hansen-Rubensohn advertising agency from Labor. Liberal politicians and officials came to realise that if they could cultivate Packer's support, he could help to deliver them votes from lower-middle and working-class readers — people who would not normally support the conservative parties.[30]

Packer, for his part, took on board the warning that running front-page editorials criticising government policy could improve the ALP's electoral fortunes. He also realised that it would be foolish to alienate a government with which he was now in broad political sympathy. In May 1951 a *Telegraph* political correspondent, Ken Schapel, wrote to Packer quoting a letter he had received from T. M. Ritchie, the federal president of the Liberal Party. Thanking the journalist for a sympathetic profile he had written about Menzies, Ritchie had expressed concern about the prime minister's hectic lifestyle. Schapel passed on the contents of the letter to Packer 'because I think that the Prime Minister tends to take more notice of things you tell him as a friend than he does of things many other people tell him, and I thought that at some time you might find it convenient to give him a friendly ear-bashing'.[31]

Schapel's comments suggest that Packer conveyed the impression that personal as well as political factors were behind the *Telegraphs*' editorial endorsement of the Liberal Party. The available evidence indicates that Schapel rather overstated the 'friendship' between Packer and Menzies at this time, and it is clear that self-interest fuelled the prime minister's desire to cultivate the support of the press proprietor he had once held partly responsible for his losing office. But Packer, who admired men like Menzies who were bastions of the establishment, patrician and well-educated, also wanted to earn the respect and affection of the prime minister. When passing on Schapel's letter to 'Bob', Packer solicitously commented that 'I cannot help feeling ... that there may be quite an element of truth in Ritchie's suggestion that you must watch your health'.[32]

Just days after this exchange of letters, Packer was fuming about both the federal and state governments. In the Queen's Birthday honours list in June, he learned he had been awarded a CBE. Packer regarded the award as a 'toy decoration', and felt he was entitled to a knighthood. During a function at the American Club, Packer told Cyril Pearl, who was now editing *A.M.*, that he would refuse the award. Although Gretel persuaded her husband not to be a 'mug', he did not bother to go to Buckingham Palace and the insignia was sent to him by post.[33] Through gritted teeth, Packer attempted to graciously accept the congratulations of employees and supplicants. On receiving a telegram from Sylvia Ashby, whose market research company had been acquired by Consolidated Press, he replied: 'Half the pleasure of anything like this is the good wishes you receive from friends'.[34]

Packer's relationship with the prime minister remained uncertain and uneasy for some time. In 1952 he appears to have managed to secure his financial adviser John Ratcliffe a personal interview with Menzies and Arthur Fadden, now federal treasurer and leader of the Country Party. In September and October the *Telegraph*s railed against Fadden for proposed changes to income tax laws. Although the *Telegraph*s declared that they had 'no selfish interest' in the matter, Sydney Newspapers was precisely the sort of company that Fadden's tax changes were targeting. Up to this point, all private companies had been allowed to retain some of their profits, free of undistributed profits tax. Levying tax in full on any company income derived from dividends meant that Consolidated Press companies would be unable to plough profits back into the publishing business tax-free.[35]

Ratcliffe's representations to Fadden fell on deaf ears. On 30 September the treasurer rose in parliament to assert that the attacks on him had their origin in 'spleen engendered in the writers because of their failures in the past to divert me and the Government of which I am a member from policies which they believe to be inimical to their private interests, and to intimidate both the Government and myself in relation to future reforms that may be necessary'. Fadden told cabinet he had

> discovered the 'master brain' behind the largest evasion scheme — Ratcliffe, who was a Sydney taxation consultant and had netted about 250 000 pounds from this to the present. He was associated with Packer from Sydney.
>
> The Treasurer was not clear as to whether the *Daily Telegraph* had benefited financially but Ratcliffe was apparently their taxation adviser and Packer was certainly backing him to the hilt.[36]

When the *Telegraph* campaign continued, Fadden informed parliament — without identifying individuals or companies — that

> By an extremely ingenious device, the legality of which is still under consideration, a very substantial avoidance of income tax has occurred. The object of the various schemes adopted has been to enable certain private companies to success in placing current profits in the hands of their shareholders, without incurring income tax at the individual shareholder's rates.

The attacks on Fadden were ineffective, with the Senate approving only one minor amendment to the legislation.[37]

After this very public spat with the treasurer, Packer decided to cultivate his personal relationship with the prime minister. He sent Menzies photographic prints of him and his daughter Heather dancing at the Savoy Ball in London and despatched photographs of the prime minister with Queen Elizabeth on her Australian tour. The humorous and ironic notes that usually accompanied these gifts left the formal and stiffly polite Menzies at a loss for words. When informed that he looked 'real 'ansome!' in one photograph, the bemused prime minister could only say 'many thanks' and 'kindest regards' in his letter of reply. In 1954, on learning that Hannah Lloyd Jones's work for charity had been recognised, Packer sent a jocular telegram to Menzies:

HANNAHS OBE GREAT NEWS STOP WE CAN GIVE YOU BOARD AND LODGINGS FOR FEW WEEKENDS GRETEL MOST DESERVING CASE GREAT CHARITY WORKER LOOKS AFTER ME AND THE KIDS STOP[38]

As Packer's publishing empire expanded, so too did his links with the establishment. In 1950 he attended the state dinner given in honour of the visiting Archbishop of Canterbury, Dr Geoffrey Fisher, and ordered a *Telegraph* journalist to write a lengthy front-page report on Fisher's speech; in 1953 Packer was one of thousands of prominent Australians to receive a Coronation Medal; in 1954 he was invited to a garden party at Government House to farewell the Queen and her husband, the Duke of Edinburgh, on their departure from Sydney.[39]

Packer asked Alan Reid to cover a section of the royal tour. Now the *Telegraph*'s Canberra correspondent, Reid often stayed at 'Platypus Lodge' near Adaminaby. Packer thought that the journalist might find a novel angle if he were assigned to cover the royal visit to the Snowy Mountains. But Packer's idea backfired when Reid, tongue planted firmly in cheek, wrote an embarrassingly slobbering and laudatory series of articles about the visit. When Packer woke up to what his star reporter was doing, he exclaimed, 'You'll never again cover a royal tour!'[40]

Packer was an ardent royalist, but he remained convinced that Australia's economic and geographical security would only be ensured by strengthening ties between Australia and the United States. His interest in fostering relations with the United States might have played a role in one of the most notorious and mysterious episodes in the history of his company. In late 1945, as part of Brian Penton and Cyril Pearl's ambitious program for postwar reconstruction, the Telegraphs had announced a series of cultural initiatives. They offered a prize of £1000, and guaranteed publication, for the best Australian novel. A panel of judges chose *Come in Spinner* as the winner. The sprawling novel centred on a group of women working in a hotel beauty parlour in wartime Sydney and their sexual entanglements, particularly with American servicemen. The prize money was paid, but the winner was never publicly announced and Consolidated Press failed to publish the manuscript. The authors, Florence James and Dymphna Cusack, eventually obtained a deed of release from Consolidated Press and took the book to William Heinemann in London; when *Come in Spinner* was published in 1951, a vicious *Telegraph* editorial relegated it to the 'dustbin' and condemned it for muckraking. At various stages during this drawn-out episode it had been said that the book 'ruthlessly exposes some of the more obnoxious aspects of life during the American occupation', and *Come in Spinner* had been described as 'red'. It is quite possible that Americans directly or indirectly exerted considerable pressure on Packer not to associate himself with a novel that could be seen as denigrating the American war effort in Australia.[41]

Packer served as president of the New South Wales branch of the Australian-American Association in 1950–51 and remained a vice-president for much of the decade. He was an enthusiastic and committed member of the executive, but his contribution tended to be practical rather than philosophical. As vice-president he arranged for John Ratcliffe to advise the association on how Americans living in Australia should deal with the requirement that they pay tax in both countries. The *Telegraph*s publicised the association's motives and activities, while Conpress Printing produced its pamphlets and booklets. The association wanted to promote Australian-American trade and maintained that co-operation with the United States, particularly in south-east Asia, should be the cornerstone of Australian defence policy.[42]

Packer's involvement with the organisation added another round of functions to his social calendar. He participated in the Coral Sea Week celebrations each May, which the Australian government and the Australian-American Association staged to commemorate the battle of the Coral Sea that had arrested Japan's southward advance between 6–8 May 1942. Gretel Packer served as president of the organising committee of the Coral Sea Victory Ball, which usually had an American naval officer as guest of honour. Through events such as this Frank Packer mixed with American consuls-general and gained entrée to powerful military, political and business networks in the United States. In 1951 he met Admiral Thomas Kinkaid, who had commanded one of the cruisers in the battle of the Coral Sea; in 1952 he hosted a reception at 'Cairnton' for General Robert Eichelberger; in 1953 he was introduced to the visiting American vice-president Richard Nixon; and in 1954 he was one of eleven Australians invited to sail from Sydney to Melbourne on a visiting American warship.[43]

As Packer became an increasingly public figure, the demands on his resources grew. In 1955 the *Telegraph*'s music critic, Tom Mead, told Packer that Ernie Llewellyn, the concertmaster of the Sydney Symphony Orchestra, needed money to travel to the United States to take up a prestigious scholarship. Although Packer was sympathetic, he explained that if he gave Llewellyn the required £1550 he would be besieged by people whose requests for money he had recently refused. But Packer — usually a soft touch when it came to a good cause — allowed the newspaper to launch a public appeal for funds.[44]

One initiative Packer did agree to personally support was the Nuclear Research Foundation at the University of Sydney. The newly appointed physics professor Harry Messel believed that industry, private individuals, governmental and semi-governmental organisations should join the university in fostering world-class scientific research. The Nuclear Research Foundation was founded on the premise that 'Australia's survival is closely linked with our being able to use and make up via a superior and advanced technology what we lack in population'.[45]

Setting out to sell the idea of the foundation in the context of developing atomic power around Australia, Professor Messel managed to secure a fifteen-minute interview with Packer on 4 June 1953. After listening to the objectives of the foundation, Packer barked, 'Right, Messel, what do you want?'

> 'Your money', replied Messel.
> 'How much?'
> '£2000 a year.'
> 'And what will I get for it?'
> 'Nothing', said Messel, 'absolutely nothing'.
> 'You can guarantee that?'
> 'Yes.'
> 'Right', said Packer. 'Your cheque will be in the mail tomorrow morning.'

No intellectual, Packer appreciated the professor's dynamic and forthright approach. And the foundation appealed to Packer because he was a moderniser in his own field, he appreciated the importance of attracting the 'best brains' to any endeavour, he was concerned that Australia was underpopulated and he was attracted to the foundation's commitment to apply nuclear power to the development of industry. By pledging £2000 per annum (the equivalent of a professor's salary), Consolidated Press became a governor member of the foundation.[46]

Arthur Fadden, H. V. Evatt, now leader of the Opposition, New South Wales premier J. J. Cahill, prominent scientists and leaders of industry and commerce attended the inaugural dinner of the Nuclear Research Foundation at the University of Sydney's Great Hall on 12 March 1954. Rising to his feet, Packer proposed a toast to the 'important people' who were present at the dinner and had agreed to father the project with hard cash:

> ... they are people who can help and assist Australia to be at least as good as any other country, if not lead the world in nuclear science. They are people who, we believe, have the atomic-zing to help achieve this.
>
> If we are awake to our present opportunity we can look forward to the time when the young brains of other countries will come here to further their studies and research.

Packer had probably never set foot on a university campus until the previous day, when he was invited to attend a series of lectures on the Nuclear Research Foundation's aims and facilities. In his speech, he revealed that he had found the occasion somewhat overwhelming:

> I assure you visitors that being a member of this Foundation, apart from the particular financial outlay which we have to make, also imposes upon one a period of concentration which, when one is in the middle forties, or, worse, nearing the fifties as I am, calls for a

degree of concentration which one finds very hard to keep going for any length of time. Nevertheless, it was a most interesting day … [47]

At the meeting of the foundation's council on 14 April, Packer was unanimously elected chairman of the finance committee. The people with whom he mixed in professional and charitable organisations realised that he was much better at raising funds and efficiently executing plans than he was at formulating ideas. By 1952 he had been elected honorary treasurer of the Australian section of the Commonwealth Press Union, a position he was to retain until his death.[48]

As the years passed, Packer used the *Telegraph*s more and more to advance his personal and political interests. He greatly admired Brian Penton's intellectual flair and provocative editorial style and in 1950 had flown his editor to New York for specialist treatment for what was ultimately diagnosed as cancer. To Packer's dismay Penton died a year later, aged only forty-seven. Penton's premature death seems to have made his employer aware of his own mortality. Packer became increasingly troubled by the realisation that his father and his grandfather had both died in their fifties. In 1952 he covenanted to serve Consolidated Press for a further five years, in return for which the company would settle a life insurance policy for the benefit of his wife and their sons.[49]

In many ways Penton had been Packer's voice, exercising his formidable polemical gifts to express and advance his proprietor's thinking and interests. Clyde Packer has observed that the *Telegraph*s, which had been like a rapier under Penton's editorship, became a bludgeon in his father's hands as he found an increasingly confident voice to express his views.[50] One of Packer's most memorable editorial interventions occurred at the time of Joseph Stalin's death in 1953. On the night of Thursday 5 March he instructed the *Telegraph* chapel to print a poster reading 'STALIN DEAD HOORAY' and bordered in red. When the father of the chapel complained about the tasteless poster to Consolidated Press executives, they would agree only to modify the poster to read 'JOE IS DEAD HOORAY'. In further discussions with the chapel, management refused to withdraw the poster. Word of the impasse reached Packer, who was dining at Prince's while waiting for the newspaper to be printed. He returned to work and agreed to address a meeting of angry printers. However, he declined their request to leave the room afterwards so they could discuss the matter, declaring that he had more right to be there than they did and that they could get out. Later editions of the *Telegraph* did not appear, as chapel members felt that they had been ordered from the premises.

At a conference with the PIEUA at 11.30 a.m. on Friday, Packer maintained that he had a right to print and publish anything he desired and it did not matter whether his newspaper went off the streets for a few days.[51] As headstrong as ever, he was determined not to back down, even if the episode precipitated a strike and the loss of sales and advertising revenue. Consolidated Press might have been a public company but, as far as Packer was concerned, he was 'the proprietor', and his employees had to do his political bidding if they wished to remain on the payroll. On Friday afternoon the Industrial Registrar, ruling that the preparation of the poster was a lawful instruction, ordered the men back to work. But still Packer was not content to let the matter rest. Lou MacBride, who had succeeded Penton as editor, and King Watson, the assistant editor, made up the front page of Saturday's *Telegraph* depicting a weeping crocodile beneath the banner headline 'POOR OLD JOE'. The page featured a bizarre 'interview' with people executed by the Soviet dictator that a disconsolate journalist had been ordered to fabricate.[52]

Being a Consolidated Press employee meant coping with a volatile and autocratic employer, ritual sackings and frugal facilities. Although Jack Travers and David McNicoll, who became editor-in-chief in 1953, often undertook industrial negotiations, employees knew that ultimate authority rested with their managing director. In June 1953 Consolidated Press was served with a log of claims for a new printers' daily newspaper award. When Travers indicated the company's reluctance to increase wages, the chapel declared that Packer's presence was essential for the completion of negotiations as he appeared 'to be the only person who can give any direct answers'.[53]

Like Lord Beaverbrook, Packer was prepared to spend money on pioneering new technology and acquiring talented contributors when he saw obvious commercial potential, but he could not abide the suspicion that someone might be getting the better of him. Office gossip centred on the latest burst of tyranny from 'Big Brother'. In 1955 a journalist on the *Women's Weekly* told a colleague working overseas that Packer, having 'run out of people to sack', had raided the mailroom to discover who was using it to post personal letters. She conjured up a 'heavenly' vision of Packer 'sitting in the middle of the floor with a steaming kettle and brightly curious licking of lips … I only wish I'd had a juicy epistle carefully stuck down with durex. THAT would have got him in'.[54]

Packer was now making annual pilgrimages to London and New York. As 'an act of propitiation before beginning some new enterprise', he found it necessary to pay his respects to 'the two great English-speaking metropolises'. He sometimes visited parts of Europe, particularly Paris and Rome, but felt a 'pretty lost sort of soul' in Paris because he did not speak the 'lingo'. However, he reassured himself that he was better off than Gretel 'because I don't pretend to understand it whereas she makes valiant efforts to communicate her thoughts which sometimes leads to amusing or embarrassing results'. London was the centre of Packer's business and pleasure. Here he would stay in a large suite at the Savoy, hobnob with Fleet Street executives, broker deals, attend race meetings such as the English Derby, and engage in strenuous forms of pleasure. He would sit in what was known as the 'visiting executive's office' and lord it over his timorous bureau staff, who counted the days until his departure. Gretel sometimes accompanied her husband to London, hoping that her presence might encourage him to slow down and relax. But one of his greatest pleasures was his daily telephone call to Sydney, where legend has it that Consolidated Press executives would line up for his instructions.[55]

Packer was in London attending the annual general meeting of Reuters when Sydney daily newspaper employees went out on strike. In May 1954 Conciliation Commissioner A. S. Blackburn began hearing a case for a new metropolitan dailies award for journalists. A year later, as the case drew to a close, Consolidated Press retrenched fourteen artists and photographers. On 27 May 1955 McNicoll told a deputation from the AJA that he had discussed the matter with Packer over the telephone the previous evening. McNicoll advised the AJA that dismissals had been made because of the pending new award, a rise in shipping freights and the expenses associated with the *Women's Weekly*'s struggle to fight off new competitors. Newspaper staffs in Sydney were reduced even further before the award was brought down on 17 June. Consolidated Press, which had told the Blackburn hearing that it was short of journalists, retrenched twenty-one.[56]

The strike itself was precipitated by trouble at the *Daily Mirror* on 24 June. Just as they had in 1944, newspaper companies joined forces, instructing their employees to handle copy at Truth & Sportsman. On 11 July 1955, presumably after consulting Packer, McNicoll stood down journalists who refused to work on a composite newspaper. These scenes were repeated in the other newspaper offices and printers stopped work in sympathy. On 14 July the proprietors accepted the AJA's proposal that newspapers should be produced from their own offices and that there should be no victimisation of employees involved in the dispute.[57]

Relations between the AJA and the four daily newspaper companies were not improved when scores of journalists were retrenched the following month. In late August Packer, who had returned to Sydney, met with a deputation from the AJA to discuss the downgrading of twenty-five journalists, and the dismissal of several other journalists and photographers. He stood firm, refusing to overturn the downgradings or even stagger the dismissals; Consolidated Press, he maintained, had been forced to act in the way it had because of economic factors and a shortage of skilled printers to produce editorial copy. It is most likely, however, that Packer's aim was to evade the payment of increased salaries under the Blackburn award, and the actions of the four newspaper companies so soon after the strike naturally aroused suspicions of victimisation.[58]

No account of Packer's industrial negotiations during this period would be complete without reference to his constant battles with lifts. He was such an energetic, bustling type that he hated standing around waiting, and lifts made him constantly do that. The lifts at Consolidated Press were old and slow. Packer had a code for ringing the lift bell so that the drivers would know he was waiting and would hurry to his floor, regardless of those waiting on other floors or already aboard. One night an eccentric *Telegraph* columnist, Alexander MacDonald, held the door open on the third floor while he finished a conversation with someone. On reaching the ground floor he realised that the furious jangling he had been ignoring had come from Packer. Purple with rage, Packer tore strips off MacDonald and sacked him. Like so many employees who were arbitrarily fired by Packer over the years, MacDonald decided to turn up for work in the hope that no more was said about the matter. But this particular journalist could not resist the temptation to write a hilarious column about his brush with the boss entitled 'The Stair Way is the Safe Way'. (New South Wales Railways was running an advertising campaign with the slogan 'The Rail Way is the Safe Way'.) When someone in editorial authority showed the column to Packer, he snorted with laughter and said, 'Great column, very funny. Run it, of course'.[59]

An incident on Friday 21 October 1955 had more serious industrial repercussions. At 11.30 p.m. Packer and McNicoll were stranded on the third floor of Consolidated Press headquarters as the lift they were waiting for repeatedly whizzed past them. Tearing down the stairs, Packer spotted an assistant proofreader, Noel Slarke, and demanded to know whether he had been in the lift. When Slarke innocently replied, 'Yes', Packer accused him of 'playing around with the lift' and sacked him. Slarke, who was a medical technologist working a second job in order to go overseas, went to supper feeling flustered but not unduly concerned. The young man was reasonably confident that his volatile employer, nicknamed 'Packer the Sacker', would reinstate him. But when Slarke returned to the office, he found that his printing colleagues had stopped work as Packer had refused to withdraw the notice of dismissal.[60] In the chaotic scenes that ensued, some bewildered journalists left the premises that night believing that they, too, had been suspended from work indefinitely.

On Saturday morning members of the PIEUA and the chapel met Packer to demand that Slarke be reinstated. Although he rejected the printers' requests, Packer seems to have been embarrassed when he realised that he had also managed to involve the AJA in the dispute. He told an AJA deputation that there had been a mistake: 'There was a lot of confusion here last night ... AJA members are not suspended'. Even though the PIEUA was understandably angered by Packer's high-handedness in dismissing Slarke, they believed that the chapel's decision to stop work that night was illegal. The *Telegraph* failed to appear on Saturday and Monday, journalists employed on the *Sunday Telegraph* were told to take the day off and an issue of the *Women's Weekly* failed to appear. On Monday afternoon, following a compulsory conference and further discussions, Slarke was reinstated and work resumed.[61]

Thus one of the most bizarre episodes in the industrial history of Consolidated Press had ended in an ignominious defeat for Packer. His anger at a minor inconvenience had precipitated an industrial dispute involving two unions, hundreds of employees and thousands of pounds of lost revenue. And the incident, coming so soon after the industry-wide newspaper strike, further soured relations between Consolidated Press, its workers and their unions. The PIEUA and the AJA had no recourse when Packer refused to pay employees for the time they had lost during the dispute. The lift incident, which has become legendary — multiple and quite fanciful variations of the story still circulate in Sydney — is seen as emblematic of Packer's managerial style.[62] He himself was capable of seeing the humour in his often arbitrary actions. When hosting a Christmas party for employees in December 1955, Packer referred to the lift, with perhaps just a hint of chagrin, as 'Slarke's office'.[63]

10
Treading on Corns

After their years in Bowral and Canberra, Clyde and Kerry Packer had returned to Cranbrook. Their father was a generous patron, making the biggest donation (£500) to the Cranbrook School War Memorial Fund in 1950, and their mother helped Hannah Lloyd Jones staff a stall at a special fundraising fête. Gretel also loaned a painting by Justin O'Brien, later a winner of the Blake Prize for religious art, and five paintings and a large print by William Dobell for display in the school library.[1]

On completing the Intermediate Certificate in 1950, Clyde was sent to board at Geelong Grammar School. This was on the advice of the Cranbrook principal, Brian Hone, who was worried about the impact Frank's bullying was having on Clyde. Exceptionally tall and thickset, the teenager was doing well in cricket and tennis but treating his classmates roughly and constantly getting into trouble. Hone advised Frank Packer to try to get his son into Perry House, which was the house the masters chose for their own sons, at Geelong. The housemaster, V. J. H. Tunbridge, was strict, blunt but kind, and he was to remain at the helm of Perry House for some twenty-five years.[2]

At Corio in south-west Victoria, hundreds of kilometres away from his father, Clyde blossomed. He played the double bass and was a sergeant in the school cadet corps band, performed in *Macbeth*, played in the First XI hockey team and served on the executives of the golf and rugby union clubs. Secretary of the Areopagus debating club, Clyde revealed himself to be socially progressive but politically conservative. He vigorously rejected the notion 'That woman's place is in the home', argued that Australia, like the United States, should not concentrate on developing primary industry at the expense of secondary industry, and proposed the motion that his house would welcome a Liberal victory in the 1953 Senate election.[3]

The youngster also thrived academically, passing five subjects in the Leaving Certificate, winning house colours and a prize in social studies, and matriculating in 1952, coming second in his year in both social studies and British history. When Clyde won a commonwealth scholarship he was able to persuade his father to allow him to stay on at school for an extra year. Kerry followed his older brother to Perry House in 1953. The school porter, Tom Judd, has recalled that Clyde completely overshadowed his younger brother. Clyde had an outgoing personality, shone in every endeavour he undertook and never missed 'an opportunity to cut you down to size'. Judd observes that Kerry was a likable lad whose 'pleasant manner had nothing of the condescension of the elder Packer boy'.[4]

Even though most of the pupils at Geelong Grammar came from moneyed families, Kerry was considered fair game for spiteful comments about his father's wealth. Scions of the Victorian establishment, the parents of Kerry's classmates seem to have made snide remarks to their sons about the Packer family's 'new money'. Kerry was big for his age and still struggled academically, so it is no wonder that he loathed school. Just as his father had before him, the boy coped with these difficult years by throwing himself into sport. He competed in swimming, shooting and athletics events and played football, tennis and golf. Kerry recalls that he was never a great natural talent, but he did well enough to play in the rugby union First XV and the cricket First XI, be awarded school colours for football and win golf and boxing trophies.[5]

Vic Tunbridge and his wife, along with the matron at Perry House, took a liking to Kerry and treated him with greater sympathy and kindness than did his father and his classmates. Kerry and his brother usually saw their parents only during school holidays, when they were expected to help out at Consolidated Press. On one occasion Kerry was playing billiards with his father at 'Cairnton' while his mother was upstairs unpacking his bags. When Gretel kept interrupting the close contest to ask, 'Where's your so-and-sos?', it emerged that Kerry had left his tennis racquet at school. Upset at losing his concentration, Frank erupted, 'For Christ's sake, Gretel, do you want me to send him back to pick it up?' Refusing to be outdone, Gretel blurted out, 'Yes'. With neither parent prepared to back down, Kerry found himself on a train back to Victoria. Twenty-four hours later, he cabled his father: 'Arrived Melbourne safely. No love, Kerry'.[6] Frank Packer could be an exceedingly generous philanthropist, but he hated waste and he was determined to teach everyone — from his lowliest employee to his own children — the value of money.

Leaving Geelong Grammar at the end of 1953, Clyde hoped to study in the United States or at the University of Sydney. Frank, however, thought that tertiary education was for other people, and he was determined that his sons should join him at Consolidated Press. It was just as well that Professor Harry Messel did not hear the man he had handpicked to preside over the Nuclear Research Foundation decree that universities were a waste of time: 'You go to work for me. You learn far more in the school of hard knocks'. After a short stint on the *Canberra Times*, Clyde began working twelve-hour days as a *Telegraph* sub-editor.[7]

Kerry left Geelong Grammar in late 1956, a few months after being involved in a serious car accident in which three people were killed. At nineteen years of age, he had finally managed to pass the Leaving Certificate. While Kerry started work on the bottom rung of the Consolidated Press ladder, he and his brother also began joining a series of exclusive clubs in Sydney. Kerry has recalled his father saying:

> 'Son, by the time you get to 35–36 years of age they won't let you into any bloody clubs, so join early. You're going to be treading on too many corns and there'll be too many people who don't like you at that stage. You'll never get elected.'

> So he put us down for a whole series of clubs when we were 18–20 years of age so we got in before anyone didn't like us too much.[8]

Frank Packer privately worried about the financial viability of the newspapers that he expected his sons to take over one day. For any company, producing a morning newspaper without the benefit of an afternoon newspaper is ruinously expensive, and the *Telegraph* had never been able to counter the *Sydney Morning Herald*'s domination of the lucrative classified advertising market. In 1952 Colin Bednall, the managing director of the Brisbane *Courier-Mail*, passed the perceptive comment that one day Packer would be 'forced to realise that his genius and his success lies in the *Women's Weekly* and he would be better off without the worry of a daily newspaper'.[9] But as much as he cherished the magazine and attempted to take credit for its success, Frank Packer was his father's son. He relished the power that came with being a metropolitan newspaper proprietor and thrived on overseeing the production of the *Telegraph*s seven days a week. Everything would be fine if he could just find a way to make the newspapers profitable and utilise Consolidated Press's idle printing capacity.

In 1944 A. W. Wood, a member of a British press delegation visiting Australia, had privately reported to Lord Beaverbrook that it was only a matter of time before Packer, a man of 'exceptional drive and ability', reached out into other states.[10] But Packer sat tight for some years, realising that moving into the metropolitan newspaper market interstate and taking on the HWT would be an enormous gamble. In 1952 he spotted an opportunity to reach into Melbourne while sharing the risks with another company.

In 1949 the *Argus*, an ailing Melbourne morning newspaper, had been taken over by the London *Daily Mirror* newspaper group. Daily Mirror Newspapers Ltd failed to arrest the newspaper's decline and by 1952 the *Argus* seems to have lost £1 million. In April 1952 the company's chairman Cecil H. King decided to visit Australia to look into the situation. King has recalled that when he first met his Australian counterpart, Packer shook him firmly by the hand and announced: 'I am interested in girls and horses, what are you interested in?'[11] Recovering from this startling introduction, King entered into talks with Packer about forming some sort of joint venture to salvage the *Argus*. They seem to have developed a scheme whereby the London company would pump a further £1 million into the *Argus*, and inject £1 million into Consolidated Press. This would mean Packer losing some control of his Sydney enterprise but gaining a subsidised entry into Melbourne.[12]

The small and incestuous network of Australian publishers was soon abuzz with rumours about these discussions. Keith Murdoch was horrified at the thought of a revitalised *Argus* competing with the *Sun News-Pictorial* and he was also concerned that a HWT executive might defect to Packer. But it was not long before negotiations fizzled out. In July Packer, attempting to save face, told Lloyd Dumas somewhat disingenuously that the closer he got to concluding a deal with King the less it appealed to him: 'he did not see why he should take on any headaches in Melbourne'. King, however, informed Dumas that Packer was still putting up proposals at which he 'smiled benignly'. Packer seems to have written a twelve-page letter to King asking the

London *Daily Mirror* to inject £1.5 million into Consolidated Press. Murdoch believed that Packer had overplayed his hand and received an 'actual rebuff' from London.[13]

When Keith Murdoch died shortly afterwards, Packer spotted a new opportunity to diversify interstate. Sir Keith's widow Elisabeth believed that the family could not afford to keep major interests in both the Adelaide *News and* the Brisbane *Courier-Mail*. Within days Consolidated Press and Fairfax executives had announced that they would 'welcome an opportunity to be of any assistance'. In late October Packer met with Bednall to say that if probate was a problem, he would like the opportunity to discuss a merger between Consolidated Press, News Ltd and Queensland Newspapers Pty Ltd. Bednall doubted Packer's claim that he had recently discussed such a possibility with Sir Keith; given Murdoch's views on Packer, Bednall was probably right to be suspicious. Packer's approach was fruitless, with the Murdoch family deciding to sell their shares in the Brisbane newspaper to the HWT and retain their stake in News Ltd.[14]

In January 1953 Packer went on a cruise to Italy for a holiday. In early February, as he prepared to fly back to Sydney, he briefly visited London. Here he was invited to attend a dinner party with Christopher Chancellor, the general manager of Reuters. Sir Keith's son Rupert, who was studying at Oxford University, was also present at the function. The dinner was an epic affair, with Packer prevaricating for seven hours before admitting to Murdoch that he had been negotiating with Cecil King all afternoon. Packer's nocturnal comments were ambiguous to say the least: he announced that he was not interested in Melbourne, did not need money for his Sydney enterprises, but had 'big plans for the national magazine field'. A bemused Murdoch privately noted that 'Packer must be the biggest crook in Australian newspapers, but equally he is the cleverest'.[15]

By now Packer had turned his attention to taking over the company that had provided him with the capital to establish his media empire. Associated Newspapers had been short of liquid funds for decades, and its directors realised that the publication of a morning newspaper was needed to justify the enormous outlay on the Sun. Packer reduced the *Telegraphs*' advertising rates to undercut those of the *Sun* and the *Sunday Sun* and hinted that he might also lower the cover price of his newspapers. In July Rupert Henderson, who was overseas, heard rumours that Consolidated Press was interested in buying Associated Newspapers. Determined not to allow Consolidated Press to attain such market dominance, Fairfax's general manager immediately returned to Sydney. In a subsequent court case, Packer was asked to reveal what he had discussed with Henderson.

> Mr Henderson on the phone said: 'I believe you are trying to buy Associated Newspapers'. I said I would not be interested in a proposal like that. I was not going to disclose to Mr Henderson what my plans were. The conversation was carried on facetiously.
>
> What you told him was not the truth? — I did not feel called upon to tell the truth.
> It was the opposite to the truth? — Yes.[16]

The battle for control of Associated Newspapers was rancorous and convoluted. Wary that the directors of Associated Newspapers would still be bitter about the way in which he had exploited the company twenty years earlier, Packer used intermediaries to undertake his early negotiations. The subterfuge could not last for long and by early August the board had realised that there was a connection between the London accountancy firm Binder, Hamlyn and Co., which was acting on behalf of Consolidated Press, and Cecil King. Henderson was only too happy to remind the directors of Associated Newspapers that they had previously had 'very unfortunate experiences' with the management of Consolidated Press.[17]

Packer's offer entailed taking over Associated Newspapers, while Fairfax proposed a more palatable merger of interests. On 27 August the directors of Associated Newspapers agreed to sell Fairfax 39 per cent of its share capital. Tongue planted firmly in cheek, Henderson sent a telegram to Packer: 'BEST WISHES REGARDS RUPERT'. As it was still possible that the Capital Issues Board might not approve the issue of capital required by Fairfax, Packer ordered his brokers to buy Associated Newspapers shares in the names of their clerks. At 12.05 a.m. on Monday 31 August — to avoid any question of illegality by meeting on the Sabbath — the directors of Associated Newspapers issued the new shares to Fairfax and were paid for them in cash.[18]

As Consolidated Press had no equitable interest in Associated Newspapers, it was unable to bring an action against the transaction. However Gabriel S. Reichenbach, a partner in Allen, Allen & Hemsley who had been looking after Packer like a Dutch uncle for decades, owned 500 shares in Associated Newspapers. On Monday afternoon he obtained an *ex parte* injunction in the Equity Court restraining Associated Newspapers and Fairfax from acting on the capital of Associated Newspapers that had been unissued at 26 August.[19] While waiting for the suit to be heard on Monday 14 September, Henderson met a deputation from the AJA to discuss staff retrenchments at the *Sun*, the *Sunday Sun* and Woman. He became agitated when the question of the injunction was raised:

> Just along the corridor there are 10 QCs drinking whisky and saying, 'Packer can't do this' and yet he is doing it. We have been flooded with subpoenas ... I thought the case would start Monday morning and end the same day. It will now not start until Monday afternoon and is likely to last three days ... Nobody with any knowledge of the newspaper industry can consider Packer a good employer.[20]

The hearing, in fact, lasted some five days. The case centred on whether the articles of association of Associated Newspapers gave the board the power to issue the unissued capital without an extraordinary general meeting of shareholders. On 22 September Mr Justice Myers ruled that, although the shares had been allotted with undue haste, the directors of Associated Newspapers and Fairfax had not acted dishonestly. An elated Henderson sent another telegram to 'Frank Facetious Packer':

OFFER YOU THREE GUINEAS EXCLUSIVE RIGHTS YOUR UNABRIDGED UNEXPURGATED OPINION JUDGEMENT WITH ADDITIONAL GUINEA IF

ILLUSTRATED BY REICHENBACH STOP BEST WISHES WHICH YOU NEED MORE THAN EVER.

Packer addressed his reply to 'Chief General Manager Assassinated Newspapers Ltd':

CONGRATULATIONS ROUND ONE STOP BY THE WAY DID YOU PLAY GOLF WITH THE JUDGE OVER THE WEEKEND.

Despite the banter, Packer was dismayed at the thought of Consolidated Press's principal rival attaining the prized morning-afternoon newspaper combination. Reichenbach appealed against Myers's decision and kept attacking the validity of the merger for the next two years. When every legal avenue open to Reichenbach and Packer failed, the parties finally reached a settlement based on costs in 1956.[21]

Although the rivalry between the Packer and Fairfax camps was intense, the relationship was punctuated by a kind of jocularity. In 1955 the *Sunday Telegraph* launched a crossword competition, entitled 'Telewords', as a circulation-builder. The *Sun-Herald* retaliated with 'Findaword', and over the next few weeks the newspapers sought to outdo each other by increasing prize money. Annoyed at the Fairfax intrusion into his territory, Packer employed an expert university mathematician to work out how many combinations of answers would be needed to win the *Sun-Herald* competition. When the mathematician reported that it could be won if 600 entries were submitted, Packer bought up 600 copies of the *Sun-Herald* and had his staff fill them in under the direction of the expert. He even had the entries witnessed by a justice of the peace and included in the bundle of his entries a key to the different words submitted to help the checkers quickly find the correct one. But the scheme backfired because Packer slipped up on one clue. Entrants were informed that the answer to the clue 'Found on every English breakfast table' was 'marmalade', not 'margarine'. In its next puzzle, the *Sun-Herald* inserted a new rule saying that staff members of any other newspaper or magazine were automatically barred from entering.[22]

In his *Sunday Telegraph* gossip column on 14 October 1956, Jim Macdougall ridiculed the *Sydney Morning Herald* for purchasing the memoirs of a visiting English playboy, the Hon. Tony Moynihan. A few days later, the *Sydney Morning Herald*'s Column 8 described the paragraph as 'false, malicious and grossly dishonest':

But Jim Macdougall didn't write it.
   It was written by people who do not hesitate to resort to threats of blackmail and to libel and gross dishonesty — or to use their columnist's name to serve their purposes.

The next morning both the *Telegraph* and the *Sydney Morning Herald* published Packer's open letter to Fairfax executives challenging them to name the person to whom Column 8 referred: 'If you will not come out in the open, but prefer to persist in your attempt to cringe behind the curtain of identification, then both the publishers of your paper and the authors of the item must forever be branded as cowards and liars'.[23]

On 22 October the *Herald* published Rupert Henderson's unrepentant reply:

We have said plainly enough that the people who can call Mr Macdougall 'theirs' include those to whom threats of blackmail are not abhorrent, who indulge in defamation and gross dishonesty to achieve their ends. This correspondence must end at this point because neither we nor our readers are interested in cheap and vulgar challenges, nor in the exasperated vituperation of a frustrated rival.

Packer, Macdougall, three of their colleagues and Consolidated Press immediately served Henderson and Fairfax with writs for libel.[24]

By now the two companies had spent three very expensive years fighting each other in the courts. Packer and Reichenbach arranged to meet Henderson and a Fairfax lawyer, Alistair Stephen, in the boardroom of Associated Newspapers. Reichenbach agreed to transfer his contentious parcel of shares in Associated Newspapers to Fairfax, and on 21 December Packer and Henderson published a joint statement in their newspapers regretting and withdrawing all allegations against each other. In the course of the peace conference, Henderson and Stephen had withdrawn from the boardroom to allow Packer to confer privately with Reichenbach. Stephen had left his briefcase in the room, and when he returned he noticed that it had been moved. 'That's not where I left my case', said Stephen. 'Of course not, you bloody fool', laughed Packer. 'We've been through it.'[25]

One Christmas a group of carol singers gathered outside 'Cairnton' to perform 'O Little Town of Bethlehem'. After listening politely to the rendition, Packer handed the singers £5 and asked them if they knew 'Hark the Herald Angels Sing'. When the youngsters replied that they did, Packer said he would give them an extra £5 if they performed 'Hark the Telegraph Angels Sing' outside Warwick Fairfax's house. The youngsters, one of whom happened to be Penelope McNicoll, the daughter of David and Jean ('Micky') McNicoll, declined the offer. When Penny relayed the story at home, she got the feeling that her parents might have happily sung the version suggested.[26]

Packer continued to thrive on taking risks. In mid 1954, while the challenge to Fairfax's crucial deal with Associated Newspapers was still under way, he made a business trip to London. In the course of his visit, Packer summoned the English cricket writer Margaret Hughes to meet him at the Savoy Hotel. Hughes had recently written to Packer asking whether she could cover the forthcoming Ashes tour for any of his publications. When Hughes walked into his suite, she was so staggered by Packer's hulking size that she forgot everything else. She found something 'intensely likeable about this burly, enthusiastic, slightly gauche newspaper tycoon' who had the 'typical Australian "I don't give a damn for anyone" approach'. After making some polite small talk, Packer suddenly stated that in his opinion cricket was dying out; in a few years, he said, it would be dead and baseball would take its place. Hughes later realised that Packer was testing her to see if she would rise to the bait. She did, delivering a passionate and provocative exposition on the attitude of cricket authorities to players with personalities. Packer threw back his head and laughed, telling Hughes to give him an article from that perspective the next day and 'then we'll arrange terms'. Hughes was duly appointed to help cover the Ashes tour, much to the puzzlement of Consolidated Press sporting editors in Sydney. As Hughes remarked in her autobiography, not many men would have had the courage to take a chance on the Australian reaction to a woman cricket writer.[27] No feminist, Packer was obviously impressed with Hughes's talents, and he probably also liked the idea of stirring Australia's cricket establishment.

During his visit to London in 1954, Packer also made the sudden decision to launch a new weekly magazine. The impulse came not from in-depth market research indicating that there was room for such a magazine, but from secondhand gossip. Donald Horne, now a member of Consolidated Press's Fleet Street bureau, happened to mention that the British company that published the racy weekly *Reveille* was planning an Australian edition. Packer decided to retaliate by launching an Australian version of the similar *Weekly Mail*, which was produced by the London Associated Newspapers Ltd group, to be called *Weekend*.

One Friday, Packer told his staff of his intention to publish *Weekend*. On the Monday he had a long talk with Horne, who agreed to return to Australia to edit the magazine for six months. Packer insisted that plans for *Weekend* remain absolutely confidential:

> If *Reveille* gets wind of this it's all off. You're not to say you're going to Australia. We'll say you're going on holidays. When you get to Sydney we'll spread new rumours. We'll say you're starting an intellectual weekly. The *New Statesman*, we'll call it. That's a good idea.

Although Packer had to leave for New York that afternoon, he rang Horne twice a day with ideas and instructions. Horne was to go to New York himself to acquire pinups for the magazine, he was to visit the wife of a newsprint tycoon in Park Avenue and buy up her astrology notes, and the staff of the New York bureau were to give him every assistance.[28]

After a whirlwind visit to New York and San Francisco, Horne arrived in Sydney. Packer, who had returned to London, rang in to say that he would be back in Sydney in a few days. In the meantime, Horne was to stay at the Hotel Australia. Packer kept a suite at the hotel, which was just down the road from Consolidated Press headquarters and was regarded as the best in Sydney. He also maintained an apartment at Marton Hall in Sydney and a suite at the Australia Hotel in Melbourne. These suites were available for visiting media figures and politicians, and they were also useful for the romantic assignations of Packer and some of his executives.[29]

When Packer returned to the office, he sat Horne down in a brown leather chair and said, 'Watch this!' On the special intercom that wired him to his executives, Packer ordered each of them into his office. Relishing the opportunity to display his power, Packer either humoured, cajoled or frightened his employees into executing his orders. Over the next few days he helped Horne choose editorial and journalistic staff; organised office space by closing down an unprofitable venture, moving departments around and kicking feature writers out of their cubbyholes; arranged for Howard French, the editor of the London *Weekly Mail*, to come to Sydney as an adviser and troubleshooter; and allocated £10 000 to promote the first two issues.[30]

In spite of Horne's best efforts, the production staff at Consolidated Press let him down. By Friday 20 August 1954 there were only two pages with ticks against 'final proof', and the first edition had to go to press on Monday. Packer arranged for a special crew to work on Sunday afternoon. He himself went into the office that day, enjoying the anxiety as Horne and his staff tracked down the fifty individual blocks from the process engraver that were still missing. When 'Australia's Brightest Newspaper' finally hit the streets of New South Wales, Victoria, Queensland and South Australia, Packer arranged for bundles to be placed alongside the afternoon papers in the lifts of the Hotel Australia. On stepping into one of these lifts, Horne was confronted by his creation, which combined sensational overseas and Australian stories with sports features, beauty advice and comics. The front page showed a cover girl with three headings arranged around her body: 'I Married the World's Strongest Woman', 'How to Recognise the Face of Your Ideal Mate' and 'Bushranger Cut off Their Heads'.[31]

What Horne privately described as an 'extreme lowbrow general magazine' quickly achieved healthy sales. Packer so enjoyed his gamble on *Weekend* that, a few weeks after its launch, he poached another idea from Fleet Street. He decided to bring out *Junior Telegraph*, based on material bought from London's *Junior Mirror*. Horne and Peter Hastings, a journalist who had just returned from the New York bureau, were given responsibility for the new title. These two intelligent and sardonic men went off together for long lunches to gossip about Packer's moods and to laugh at their foray into children's journalism.[32]

But before long *Weekend* ran into problems. Packer decided to cut costs by reducing the weekly promotional budget to £400, and he also attempted to reduce the size of the staff. To make matters worse, a national dock strike restricted the availability of newsprint. In December 1954 Horne complained that he was finding it difficult to take more than a week-by-week view of *Weekend* and the *Junior Telegraph*. He asked Packer to tell him what would happen after January, when his six-month term with *Weekend* would expire. Packer does not seem to have responded to the memo, and when the six months were up things went on as usual. Nor was Packer still interested in the *Junior Telegraph*, which one faction within Consolidated Press was attempting to undermine because they felt that it competed with their charge, *Chucklers' Weekly*. The rather inane in-house battle over children's titles came to an abrupt halt in early 1955 when Packer issued a memo ordering the burial of the *Junior Telegraph*. Meanwhile, the cover price of *Weekend* was lifted and the lowbrow magazine found a niche for itself in the marketplace.[33]

By now Packer was preoccupied with two issues that had much more significance for his own personal wealth and the future direction of his empire. Firstly, in August 1954 his interest in Consolidated Press was restructured, partly because of the implications of Fadden's tax changes. Up to this point, the 32 108 shares in Sydney Newspapers Pty Ltd had been divided equally between the Theodore and Packer families: Packer held 9051 shares individually and another 7000 in conjunction with John Ratcliffe, the Theodores controlled 16 051 shares and the remaining six shares were held in the names of another six individuals, in accordance with corporate law. In 1954 Cairnton Ltd, a trust company controlled by Packer and Ratcliffe, was registered in the

Australian Capital Territory, as was a Theodore family trust company. They had equal interests in a new company, Sydney Newspapers (Canberra) Ltd, which was owned by Sydney Newspapers Pty Ltd.[34]

When Consolidated Press Holdings Ltd was registered with a paid-up capital of £1.825 million in December, the trusts became private companies. The new holding company acquired the preference and ordinary shares in Consolidated Press and the preference capital in Conpress Printing. It also obtained 32 100 shares in Sydney Newspapers Pty Ltd and transferred them to another trust, the Sydney Newspapers Trust.[35] Packer acquired 6895 6 per cent first preference shares, 2980 6.5 per cent second preference shares and 26 708 ordinary shares of £1 each in the holding company; some of his shares were held jointly in the names of Gretel Packer, Fairy Faircloth, Keith Martin and Bill Dowsett. Ratcliffe and one of his companies, Pactolus Investments Pty Ltd, controlled another large batch of shares in Consolidated Press Holdings. Packer became managing director, John Theodore was appointed chairman and Ratcliffe joined the board.[36]

This corporate restructuring might have been complex, but it delivered enormous benefits to the Packer and Theodore families. From now on ordinary shareholders in Consolidated Press Holdings would receive the benefits of tax-free funds in Sydney Newspapers Pty Ltd. The profits earned by the empire were not paid to the two families but went through the trusts to minimise taxation.[37]

At the same time as Packer concluded these arrangements, he embarked upon a thrilling new chase. He knew that securing one of the country's first television licences would be of immeasurable help in strengthening his company's foothold in the national media landscape. And his own television station had the potential to yield him much more in the way of profits and power than a publication like the *Junior Telegraph* ever could.

Plans to introduce television to Australia were fraught and protracted.[38] Although Consolidated Press had been one of thirty syndicates to lodge an application for a commercial licence during the war, another decade elapsed before licences began to be awarded. The complications were both financial and political. The postwar federal Labor government wanted to build a national, non-commercial television system, the new coalition government was concerned that introducing television would drain Australia's low dollar resources and boost inflation, and organisations such as churches and the Workers' Educational Association questioned the moral, educational and cultural ramifications of the new medium. But publishing companies, which had now effectively carved up most of the metropolitan newspaper market between them, leaving little room for independent players and new entrants, were naturally attracted to the possibilities of television.

In January 1953 the Liberal cabinet bowed to demands to hold a royal commission into the development of the new medium. The terms of reference, however, were narrower than lobby groups and the ALP had hoped. The government itself decided on a dual system, entailing a public station and commercial stations; the royal commission was asked only to advise the government on issues such as the number of channels, standards and hours of transmission. The six individuals selected to act as commissioners were in no way distinguished; all but one lacked any relevant experience and they guaranteed commercial interests a sympathetic hearing.

The royal commission's report in May 1954 recommended that the Australian Broadcasting Commission (ABC) should run the national system and that at least two television licences should be established in Sydney and Melbourne. On 10 September the government announced that the ABC would run the national service and that the Australian Broadcasting Control Board (ABCB) would hold public hearings to grant two commercial television licences in Sydney and two in Melbourne. The government also accepted the commission's recommendation that television transmitters should be privately owned rather than leased. Both private enterprise and the prime minister had cause to be pleased: no government monopoly would be created that could fall into Labor hands and, given the enormous cost of transmitters, commercial stations could be confident that their licences would be renewed. The ABC station would also help to placate the array of religious, cultural and educational lobby groups.

Only one issue remained to trouble businessmen like Frank Packer. In November he wrote to Menzies asking whether there would be any restrictions on newspaper and radio companies forming television syndicates. The prime minister was non-committal, saying only that the government had not yet made any decision about the question of interlocking interests.[39] As the date of the Sydney hearings approached, Packer put together a syndicate to bid for one of the licences and made a rare visit to Geelong Grammar School to talk with the headmaster, (later Sir) Dr James Darling, a member of the ABCB. Even though his younger son was still attending the school, Packer made little effort to impress the gracious and highly respected English-born, Oxbridge-educated headmaster. Although Darling could not remember the subject of the blazing row he had with Packer, he did recall that 'he's the only person ever to have rolled me out flat in my own study'.[40]

Packer astutely assembled church and labour representatives on the board of the proposed company, Television Corporation Ltd. Major-General the Rev. C. A. Osborne from the Church of England Property Trust, Rev. Fr Martin Prendergast from the Catholic radio station 2SM and R. A. King, the secretary of the New South Wales Trades and Labor Council, were to join businessmen as directors. Packer was to be chairman and John Theodore managing director of the new company.[41]

Dissension and discord surrounded the Trades and Labor Council's decision to invest in the syndicate. The labour movement was again deeply divided: leading ALP politicians had sharply different views on television policy and the party and the union movement were fracturing over the issue of communism. In January 1955 the Trades and Labor Council and its 'wireless committee', which controlled the Sydney radio station 2KY, were dominated by the anti-communist faction hostile to the ALP leader H. V. Evatt. The committee agreed to contribute £10 000 to the Packer syndicate; King reasoned that by becoming involved with television at this stage, the Trades and Labor Council would have a better chance of obtaining a licence of its own at a future date. Packer offered the council fifteen minutes of free airtime each week, presumably in an effort to counter the accusation that any television station he controlled would be as biased against Labor as his newspapers.[42]

The decision to invest in the syndicate was furiously debated at a meeting of the Trades and Labor Council on 13 January. C. T. Oliver, the New South Wales secretary of the AWU, warned his fellow delegates that 'You can't win playing Packer'. At the following week's meeting, the chairman of the wireless committee commented that it had only gone in with Packer as 'a last resort' because negotiations with another proposed syndicate had fallen through. When the AWU accused the wireless committee of selling out labour by getting into bed with Consolidated Press, King lashed out: 'If they turned back the pages of history they would find out that the AWU had sold out 60 to 70 unions' when they had disposed of the *World* to Packer and Theodore in 1932. After a stormy debate, the Trades and Labor Council endorsed the actions of the wireless committee by 128 votes to 78.[43]

Packer's group had to compete with seven other syndicates for the two licences. Applicants included Amalgamated Television Services Pty Ltd, representing Fairfax and the powerful Macquarie radio network, and Truth & Sportsman. When the ABCB began hearing applications in January 1955, (later Sir) Warwick Fairfax, Rupert Henderson and Ezra Norton let their barristers and executives advance their cases. Packer, however, had always been a hands-on proprietor, and he was not prepared to leave such a crucial issue in the care of his underlings. On 3 and 4 February he appeared at the hearing on behalf of his syndicate, putting on a bravura performance before a packed public gallery that included his son Clyde.[44]

Counsel for Television Corporation was Frank Packer's friend Antony Larkins QC. Larkins began by carefully leading his witness through his honours and public offices: 'You will forgive me for asking this. I think you are a Commander of the Order of the British Empire, are you not?' Packer averred that television was 'going to be a very important factor in building up the character of the nation', claimed that it was essential for church leaders to play a big part in television and stated that the company would give the Returned Servicemen's League special time on Anzac Day and Armistice Day. When Darling asked, 'You realise that your company is accepting a high responsibility?', Packer solemnly replied, 'And a trust'.[45]

Evatt, who with Tom Dougherty was provisional trustee of a television syndicate representing the ALP and the AWU, was one of the silks who cross-examined Packer. He began by trying to raise concerns about the way in which newspaper and radio companies were trying to take over the new medium. He said, 'You have had a long experience in the newspaper industry and your father was prominent in the newspaper world. You have been a newspaper executive almost from the beginning and you are essentially a person with special experience and skill in the conduct of newspapers. Is that correct?' To the amusement of the gallery, Packer replied, 'I hope it is correct. I am on oath and cannot deny it'. As Evatt developed his line of questioning, Packer suggested that having experience in running other media outlets would be useful to any new television company. When Packer mentioned that 2BL, the first radio station in Sydney, had begun broadcasting on the roof of the *Daily Guardian* building, Evatt sarcastically asked: 'How did they get that station away from you?' There was laughter again when Packer responded, 'I was at school and they did not take much notice of me'.[46]

Nevertheless, Packer did have some prickly moments in the stand, and a few of his comments were quite revealing. Several barristers at the hearing represented groups concerned that overseas material would dominate the new medium at the expense of local performers and productions. Packer pointed out that Consolidated Press had helped Australian writers, artists, conductors, opera and ballet companies, eisteddfods and children's art competitions. This was to some extent true, as since the 1930s his editors George Warnecke, Brian Penton and Cyril Pearl had been advancing the interests of Australian cultural expression. But, as the *Come in Spinner* episode illustrated, this impetus had now faded. When Packer was asked whether his syndicate had taken any steps to protect the interests of Actors and Announcers' Equity, he bluntly replied, 'None'. He said that in comparison with American television British television was dull, maintained that the more television licences were issued, the less valuable each one would become, and urged the board to announce the successful tenderers quickly so that the ABC did not gain too great an advantage over commercial operators. Meanwhile counsel for the Consolidated Press and Fairfax syndicates argued that licences should be granted only to financially sound companies that could guarantee the necessary amount of capital required for a television station and sustain losses for at least two years.[47]

To the relief of Packer and the dismay of Evatt and his supporters, firms that already controlled print and radio outlets succeeded in their bids for television licences in Sydney and Melbourne. In March the ABCB recommended that the two commercial licences in Sydney should be awarded to Television Corporation and Amalgamated Television Services. Their report stated that one of the things they had been looking for in consortiums was 'a good record in allied communication and entertainment fields'. The decision that no licensee should be obliged to provide special rights and privileges to specific political or religious groups released Packer from his promises of airtime to the Trades and Labor Council, the Catholic Church and the World Council of Churches. Only one real limitation affected his syndicate. Companies were not allowed to have more than 20 per cent of shares in overseas hands, forcing London's Associated Newspapers and America's Paramount Film Services to reduce their proposed shares in Television Corporation.[48]

For the next eighteen months Packer's new company worked frantically at the massive task of creating one of Australia's first television stations. Despite a considerable degree of local opposition, land was acquired at Willoughby on Sydney's lower North Shore. The new station, TCN-9, purchased comedies, westerns and crime series from the United States because domestic production was deemed too expensive. A number of employees were sent to Cleveland to study technical developments in the United States.[49]

One of these employees was a young man called Bruce Gyngell. In 1954, while working at ABC radio as a trainee announcer, Gyngell had regularly visited in hospital Gretel Packer's nephew Robert Henty, who had suddenly been stricken with paralysis. Gyngell saw a lot of Gretel during this period, and one day he was invited to a barbeque at 'Cairnton' hosted by Clyde Packer. While Gyngell was relaxing by the pool, Frank came over and said, 'They tell me you're a very loyal person, you've been to see Robert every day?' When Gyngell replied, 'yes', Frank, who, as Gretel noted, had a 'fetish' about loyalty, said that if he ever wanted a job, all he had to do was ask. After joining the Consolidated Press advertising department, Gyngell was promised a job in television. But on returning from the United States he was employed as a lowly booth announcer, apparently because he had been identified as a Packer ally rather than as a Theodore man or a diplomatic neutral.[50]

TCN-9 was determined to be the first station to go to air, and it also wanted to be in a position to cover the Olympic Games in Melbourne in October 1956. On the night of Sunday 16 September, the station began broadcasting limited programs. The *Sunday Telegraph* published a statement by Packer warning viewers that they should regard broadcasts over the next few weeks as a trial run. The real point of the article was to head off criticisms about the lack of Australian programs:

> A great deal of emphasis has been placed on the need for TV to develop Australian talent.
>
> This is true, provided sufficient Australian talent is available, and the quality of entertainment and performance can match international standards at *competitive prices* [emphasis added].
>
> But it would be unfair and, in fact, impossible to expect TV, which is, after all, a movie theatre in your own home, to be restricted by impossible demands for the use of local talent.[51]

Bruce Gyngell was in the right place at the right time. When the nascent TCN-9 experienced trouble with program links, he stepped forward at the half-finished studio at Willoughby and became the first face seen on Australian television.[52]

In early 1956, after returning from studying television in Britain, Europe and North and South America, John Theodore had been appointed managing director of Television Corporation and Packer had become chairman. No evidence has survived of the boardroom machinations that culminated in these appointments; in his evidence before the ABCB in 1955 Packer had stated that he would be managing director of the company and Theodore had not even been mentioned as a potential director. While Theodore was intimately involved in the minutiae of TCN-9's debut, Packer made more sweeping gestures, issuing decrees about the development of the station and querying the expenses of the operation. Despite recognising the potential profitability of the new medium, Packer had spent more than thirty years working on newspapers and magazines, and he had begun assuming executive positions during the Great Depression. David McNicoll has observed that television was 'something entirely new and somewhat alien, and he suspected it, to an extent'. The Fairfax station ATN-7 poured money into new cameras and sophisticated studios but TCN-9 had to manage with two cameras, two small studios, little roof space and inadequate lighting. Packer had publicly told the ABCB that television would not make profits for two years; privately, however, he was not placated by TCN-9's early ratings success and he soon started cutting costs at the station.[53]

It was during this period that Packer upset John Theodore by criticising the luxury of the executive suites. The two men had never been close; Theodore was a sensitive man who found the burden of guarding his family's interests overwhelming. He was disturbed by his partner's cavalier manner and he appears to have objected to some of Packer's dealings. In early January 1957 Theodore informed Packer that his family intended to sell their shares in Sydney Newspapers Pty Ltd. Even though the advent of television had severely stretched his resources, Packer knew he would lose control of the group unless he found the money to buy out the interests of the Theodore estate.[54]

Packer, as always oblivious to the psychological toll his volatile temperament exacted on others, was surprised and perplexed by the suddenness of Theodore's decision. He had now succeeded in driving away George Warnecke, who had created the *Women's Weekly*, and the Theodore family, which had co-founded the Consolidated Press group. On 5 February 1957, clearly unnerved by the situation, Packer wrote to John Theodore:

> It was never the intention of your father and myself, when we formed our partnership, that a sudden division of interests should take place ... I can only reiterate again how sorry I am that the Theodore partnership in this organisation is to be broken up and assure you it is not my wish, nor of my seeking and, as I told you in the Board Room, I don't think it is to your advantage. But — if there is to be a break — let it be a complete one.[55]

The break was indeed complete, and acrimonious. By the end of the month rumours had surfaced that Theodore might be prepared to sell his family's shares in the group to the HWT. On 26 March a reporter from the *Sydney Morning Herald* called at Consolidated Press headquarters to investigate whether Packer was on the verge of buying out the Theodore shareholding. Escorting the reporter to the lift, Packer snapped, 'No comment. It is purely a personal matter'.[56]

John Ratcliffe, who was on good terms with the Theodore family and was involved with the Fijian mines, tried to broker an agreement. He hired a private plane and instructed Packer and the Theodores to fly around above the clouds until they reached some sort of agreement. But Ratcliffe did not remain neutral for long, electing to align himself with Packer and mastermind a mysterious rescue operation which enabled his client to buy out the Theodore shares in Sydney Newspapers for £328 193. Needing every cent he could lay his hands on, Packer asked his accountants to assess his record at the races. Although he had won thousands of pounds in prize money or on the nose, the tally revealed that he had actually lost nearly £200 000. McNicoll, who witnessed Packer studying the racing post mortem, recalls his employer commenting: 'Dave, if ever there was a lesson in the futility of gambling, this is it'. Saying that he had had a lot of fun over the years, Packer virtually gave up big gambling for the rest of his life. He continued having occasional bets with friends, but he hated losing even small amounts of money. As a billiard game at 'Cairnton' drew to a close one night, Packer moaned loudly about the £10 he had lost. The winner, Jack Cassidy, a leading silk who had played a prominent role in the formation of the Liberal Party, laughed, 'Never mind, Frank. It's only money'. 'I know it's only money', Packer retorted, 'but this money happens to be *my* money'.[57]

When John Theodore sold his shareholding and resigned from his directorships, Packer overhauled the executive hierarchy of Australian Consolidated Press (ACP), as the company had just been renamed, and its affiliates. Like his father, Packer had always believed in the benefits of installing family and close friends in executive positions in his businesses. In 1953, for instance, Tony Inglis had become business manager of ACP, with special responsibility for company flats and suites; the silver-haired and gentlemanly Inglis married the Packers' friend Ruth Watt after she was widowed in 1954. At the same time, John Ratcliffe's son R. A. ('Alan') Ratcliffe decided to abandon accountancy as a career and join the *Telegraph* as a sub-editor.[58]

In 1957 Bruce Gyngell fulfilled his ambition of becoming program manager of TCN-9 and Packer's old friend Ken G. Hall accepted an invitation to become chief executive of Television Corporation.[59] John Ratcliffe was appointed a director of ACP and one of his associates, Leslie T. Fielding, joined the boards of the holding company and ACP. Keith Martin was promoted to assistant managing director of ACP and Consolidated Press Holdings. Packer himself replaced Theodore as chairman of Consolidated Press Holdings. Clyde Packer, now aged twenty-two, was appointed to the boards of ACP, Consolidated Press Holdings and Television Corporation. In the traumatic early months of 1957, as he further entrenched his personal control over the empire, Frank Packer had a new look at the men around him: 'Some he now regarded as rats, and their days were numbered'.[60]

11
Rumours

Frank Packer was always coming up with 'some great new adventure which might amuse him'. After his negotiations with Associated Newspapers collapsed in 1953, he had remained intent on defraying the massive costs entailed in publishing a morning newspaper. His imagination had reached its farthest boundaries when he decided that ACP should launch a new afternoon newspaper. But nothing had come of the plan, presumably because cooler heads convinced him that taking on the *Sun* and the *Daily Mirror* would bankrupt his company. When Donald Horne was suddenly asked to plan some new title, he and his cohorts would spread out dummy paper, em rulers, scissors, paste and bottles of beer and get to work, laughing all the way.[1]

One dummy that did reach publication stage was the weekly entertainment magazine *Pictorial*. Clyde Packer was appointed editor, Alan Ratcliffe became his assistant and Horne oversaw production. On the eve of the launch of the New South Wales edition in March 1957, Horne warned Frank Packer that unless *Pictorial* was promoted in publications other than the *Women's Weekly* and the *Telegraphs*, it would 'get off to a fatally lame start'. Horne requested £200 a week for radio publicity, slyly noting that this would fund 'the cheapest promotion campaign in history'. His concerns were prescient: the budget for promotion was too small, too few staff members were seconded from *Weekend* to the new magazine and *Pictorial* was suddenly renamed *Pictorial Show*.[2]

Nevertheless, Horne and Clyde Packer remained convinced that they could salvage the magazine. While Frank Packer hurried through a dinner of grilled lamb chops and treacle tart at one of his favourite restaurants, Horne attempted to convince him that *Pictorial Show* was still viable. Packer seemed preoccupied with something else, so the best Horne could do was fly to Adelaide in September 1957 and try to persuade Rupert Murdoch to take over publishing the magazine in Victoria, South Australia and Western Australia. However, the young proprietor of News Ltd was shrewd enough to recognise what a bad deal he was being offered, particularly as he would have no control over the magazine's editorial content.[3] Horne and Clyde Packer, who had a paternal interest in his first editorial charge, then had to swear a solemn oath that they would discontinue publishing *Pictorial Show* if it lost more than £200 a week. In November Clyde cabled his father at the Savoy Hotel in London to say that he did not regard the magazine as 'expendable'. But just two months later, the magazine was killed off.[4]

In 1957 Clyde showed his friend and mentor Donald Horne around the family estate. Frank Packer, who fiercely protected his privacy, was turning 'Cairnton' into a veritable family compound that was dubbed 'The Taj'. In the 1950s he acquired two neighbouring cottages, which ran through to Kambala Road, from the McPhee sisters for £19 600. At 'Cairnton' Horne saw the billiard table, the poker setup, the small office where Packer read through the files he took home with him, the servants' wing housing loyal retainers and pensioners, and the heated swimming pool where his courtiers were allowed to swim at a fixed hour each day.[5]

Horne also looked over the tennis court where Packer played with his friends on weekends. At one stage in the 1950s Packer laid a bet with a pair of regulars that he would beat them in a doubles match the following weekend. In order to improve his chances of winning Packer invited Adrian Quist, the former Wimbledon and Davis Cup champion, to play. Even with his new partner, Packer still managed to lose the match three sets to love. Although Quist became a regular player at 'Cairnton' and one of Packer's closest friends, he has recalled that the big man was 'the least co-ordinated tennis player the game has ever seen'.[6]

Packer's associates were aware that he was going through a bad stretch in the mid to late 1950s. His mind was preoccupied, he seemed dissatisfied with almost everything and he found it even more difficult than usual to relax.[7] The failed bid for control of Associated Newspapers, the financial burden of the move into television, the fissure with the Theodore family, and perhaps even the awareness that he, and he alone, was now responsible for the Consolidated Press empire were taking their toll.

The company's decision to bolster circulation rather than size helped to ensure that the *Telegraph*'s sales remained higher than those of the *Sydney Morning Herald* in the first half of the 1950s. Even so, the *Telegraph* was still losing money. The newspaper's lack of appeal to upper-class readers, and its failure to arrest its rival's stranglehold on the classified advertising market, naturally continued to worry Packer. On one occasion he offered David Jones, which traditionally advertised in the *Sydney Morning Herald*, advertising space at half price; after flooding the newspaper with advertisements, the exclusive retailer complained that the ads did not bring people into its stores. When Packer himself went to talk to the chairman, Sir Charles Lloyd Jones told him that a senior director of the store would meet him to explain the advertising policy more fully. Furious that Jones was not prepared to call on him in person, Packer lashed out, 'We will never mention your name in the paper again. We don't want your advertising'. Although the standoff lasted only a month, Packer always nurtured a grievance against Jones.[8]

Nor were things going smoothly in Packer's private life. Each Sunday night he and Gretel hosted dinner parties at 'Cairnton'. Great roasts were the standard fare, with Packer wielding the carving knife himself and splashing those seated dangerously close with meaty juices. Accompanying the meal was usually Pouilly-Fuissé and Nuits-St Georges, followed by Hine brandy, which Packer had specially imported, or forty-year-old port. The guests were drawn from a basic list including Jim MacLeod, Tony

Larkins, Sir Jack and Lady Cassidy, Lionel McFadyen's widow Beryl, Packer's ear, nose and throat specialist Sir George Halliday and his wife June, and Peter M. Reid, a leading timber merchant and keen sailor. Lennox and Joan Bode, David and Micky McNicoll and Kathleen and George Stening also attended the dinners intermittently. Clyde and Kerry avoided the occasion as often as possible, grimly referring to the ritual as the 'Sunday Night Editorial Board'. Guests would offer ideas for the *Telegraph* that their father insisted on implementing, regardless of their unsuitability for a tabloid newspaper.[9]

Nevertheless, Clyde realised that these dinners occasionally had their uses. In 1957 he decided that it was time Horne got to know his father better. Invited to one of the dinners, Horne found his host in a fearsomely uncertain mood. After arriving late, Frank Packer attempted to adopt the geniality of a good host. But as he was eating the main course, he looked down at his plate and asked rhetorically, 'What does a man do when he can't get on with his own family?', and he became meditative again over port with his male guests. As soon as the gentlemen rejoined the ladies, Packer called for his car, offered Horne a lift to the office and sat brooding in the back seat, not uttering a word.[10]

It would seem that marital woes were largely responsible for Packer's malaise. He had always had a roving eye, but in the mid 1950s he had embarked on a serious love affair. The object of his affections was Sybil Connolly, a fashion designer fifteen years his junior. The daughter of an Irish father and a Welsh mother, Connolly had been almost single-handedly responsible for making fashion an Irish export industry in the early 1950s. Although her designs were discreet rather than revolutionary and she owed a good deal of her inspiration to older designers such as Christian Dior, she introduced distinctively Irish materials — tweed, flannel and linen — into the world of *haute couture*. In 1953, only a year after being given the opportunity to design her first line of clothes, she held a showing for American buyers and fashion writers at Dunsany Castle.[11] She was then fêted in New York and visited by a representative of the Consolidated Press London bureau. The *Women's Weekly* bought up her entire collection and commissioned her to design a range of clothes exclusively for Australian women.

Connolly was invited to show her clothes at parades in Sydney and Melbourne in 1954. Packer was presumably at the Sydney premiere of the collection in October, when Irish pipers formed a guard of honour welcoming Connolly to the parade at Prince's. It is unclear whether he was already romantically involved with the tall, slender designer, who had dark eyes and hair and a soft, lilting brogue. But by the time Connolly agreed to bring out another collection for the *Women's Weekly* in August 1957,[12] they had certainly formed a liaison.

In June 1957 Packer was in London firing off salvos in all directions. His comments opening a discussion at the Commonwealth Press Union conference on the methods of production and technical problems of newspapers were inspired, more than a little, by the failure of his negotiations with Associated Newspapers. It would be extremely difficult, he declared, to make a modern newspaper pay without a solution to the problem of high production costs. After accusing powerful firms such as Bowater Corporation of exploiting publishing companies and profiteering from high newsprint prices, he took aim at another conference delegate. Outraged by Sir Alan Herbert's criticisms of the prominence of photographs, gossip columns, comic strips and advertising in newspapers, Packer revealed the basic rationale behind his commercial publishing success: 'Your fundamental task is reporting news and wrapping your news up in a package with human interest so that the customer will buy your product'.[13]

The 'Great White Chief' spent much of his time in London lording it over his Fleet Street bureau with his 'usual tact and charm and grace'. On 3 July a *Women's Weekly* journalist named Betty wrote a long, anguished letter to a colleague back in Sydney.[14] The journalist, who was based in London but temporarily working in Dublin, explained that she was acting as the intermediary between Packer, Connolly, Clarrie McNulty and Esmé Fenston, the editor of the *Women's Weekly*. She found herself in the midst of 'the most awful kuffefel [sic]':

> The confusion, lack of sleep, lack of co-ordination [and] lack of co-operation and general know how is so frightening that it makes me think that its [sic] the inefficient but ruthless Ones of this world who finish up the tycoons. God knows how much money FP and SC are making out of my sweat but it must be many thousands.

The journalist was unable to please all the members of the 'most ungracious gang of monsters' she had ever met, she was being paid a meagre £20 a week and having to struggle to have her expenses reimbursed, and she was finding Packer's 'old love' insincere and 'most unreliable'.

There was a more specific reason for Betty's distress. Summoning the journalist to his office, Packer had blithely asked how the Connolly collection was progressing. After a few minutes of small talk, Packer suddenly changed his tone and snapped across the desk at her: 'I'm told you've been going around saying that when you saw me to ask for leave of absence I propositioned you and you rejected me, Izzat right?' The stunned journalist vehemently denied that she had said such a thing and Packer eventually accepted her denial, but he refused to tell her who had spread the unsavoury rumour. They chatted for another quarter of an hour, with Betty asking about television and other matters 'in such a dazed way that I have no idea what he said in reply, [and then] he saw me out with the friendliest handshake and glowing smile'.

Although Packer did not mind being known as a womaniser, in 1957 he had cause to be sensitive about unfounded rumours of a new female conquest. His wife was aware of his relationship with Sybil Connolly, and she realised that it was longer and more serious than his previous flings. When her husband refused to break off the affair, a distraught and angry Gretel went to England for several months. She was accompanied for a time by her elder son, who obtained money for the trip from a rather unusual source. Clyde had recently struck up a friendship with the colourful Francis James, who had served as a fighter pilot, escaped from a German POW camp and worked as a journalist on the *Sydney Morning Herald* before becoming manager of the *Anglican* newspaper. James's recollections reveal the intensity of the crisis in the Packer family's affairs:

Frank Packer refused to give the boy a penny when he chose to stick by his mother instead of sticking by his old man who of course had the dough. I personally accordingly guaranteed an overdraft for Clyde Packer with the Rural Bank in the sum of £500 so as to enable him to pay his air passage to London and provide the odd bit of beer money en route.[15]

In late December 1957 Frank Packer took three months' leave from Consolidated Press, ostensibly to receive specialist treatment for an eye condition. Since losing most of the sight in his right eye as a child, he seems to have developed both cataracts and glaucoma. Even though he underwent surgery in early 1958,[16] he was forced to wear thick dark glasses for the remainder of his life. Part of the reason for his absence overseas at this time might also have been to achieve some sort of reconciliation with his wife. Packer and Connolly did finally part and Gretel returned to the family home in Bellevue Hill. The fact that Gretel was also beginning to suffer from health problems of her own might have helped to bring the couple back together.

ACP launched a new publication while Packer was overseas in early 1958. A year earlier Donald Horne, whose brilliant mind was being wasted on editing the racy *Weekend*, had risked his wild card. Laughingly mentioning that he still had a return ticket to England, Horne reminded Packer that he had told him some time earlier that he would be given an intellectual weekly to edit. Packer played his own cards cleverly, telling Horne that he could start a monthly intellectual magazine at the end of 1957, but only if *Weekend* was progressing well. While editing *Weekend* and fighting his losing battle to save *Pictorial*, Horne hired staff for the new magazine and arranged for newsprint supplies. In October 1957, a few weeks before the *Observer* was due to hit the streets, Horne sent his first memo about the magazine to Packer. Out of this, somehow, came a raft of changes: the *Observer* was to be thirty-two rather than forty-eight pages, it was to be printed on cheaper newsprint and it was to be fortnightly rather than monthly.[17]

Even so, the first issue failed to appear on 14 November. In his latest bid to outsmart his nemesis Frank Packer, Rupert Henderson decided that a Fairfax subsidiary should publish a weekly magazine called *Crowd* to take on *Weekend*. The launch of the *Observer* was postponed while ACP concentrated on improving *Weekend*'s covers and outspending *Crowd*'s promotional budget. In November 1957, not long before its demise, *Crowd* found itself the subject of a censorship imbroglio. Ezra Norton's *Truth* and the *Catholic Weekly*, loudly supported by Eddie Ward, described the magazines as sex-ridden scandal sheets, and the Literature Board of Review in Queensland banned them. Horne and Clyde Packer penned detailed defences of *Weekend* and held talks with leading Catholics, while Frank Packer arranged for Garfield Barwick to challenge the legality of the ban in the courts.[18] Clyde genuinely objected to puritanism and repression, believing that if *Weekend* and *Crowd* were banned, other popular magazines could follow. His father's mind must have gone back to the *Telegraphs*' halcyon days during the war, when they had successfully challenged a censorship regime, and he could not have been happy about the distribution of *Weekend* being curtailed.

By the time the *Observer* finally made its debut in February 1958, Packer had just appointed twenty-two-year-old Clyde as managing editor of subsidiary publications. The magazine's skeleton staff contributed articles about politics, defence and foreign affairs, letters to the editor, and reviews of the arts under a range of pseudonyms. Robert Hughes, a contributor who later became a prominent art critic and historian, believes that Packer sponsored the *Observer* 'to give his operations a certain tone which would please the moderate right-wing liberals in Sydney, while giving the moribund *Bulletin* ... some competition ... Granted the views of its proprietor, you could hardly expect its political views to be other than conservative'.[19]

Horne described the magazine's editorial policy as 'radically conservative'. The *Observer* was liberal on social issues like censorship, rights for women and Aborigines, and divorce and homosexual law reform. The Cold War and the expansion of communism, however, defined its geopolitical terms.[20]

Not long after the launch of the *Observer*, another fortnightly appeared on the scene. Edited by Tom Fitzgerald, *Nation* represented a left-liberal alternative to the *Observer*. The magazines were both printed at the *Anglican*'s premises in Chippendale. Clyde Packer was an alternate director of the Anglican Press Ltd. The managing director, Francis James, found young Clyde 'a wonderful fellow director. He knew a lot about printing. He did his homework. He was enormously helpful to us'.[21]

Even though the *Observer* was essentially uninterested in local party politics, conservative Australian politicians enthusiastically embraced it. In the course of a conversation with Robert ('Buzz') Kennedy in April 1958, Menzies praised the magazine. Kennedy, who had been working as a *Telegraph* columnist and a contributor to the *Observer*, had just been appointed to the prime minister's department. Menzies told his special assistant that the *Observer* was excellent and that ACP deserved a pat on the back for producing it. In an acid aside, the prime minister commented that as so many of his conversations with Frank Packer were about the censorship of *Weekend*, 'it would be a great pleasure to talk about the *Observer* at their next meeting!'[22]

When the *Observer* took the unusual step of devoting a whole section to the arts, Horne had to find writers capable of contributing reviews and articles on film, theatre, music and the visual arts. While waiting for the right theatre critic (who turned out to be Barry Humphries) to knock on their door, Clyde Packer concentrated on writing reviews of musicals under the pseudonym 'Johnny'. The editorial staff of the *Observer* identified and wanted to cater for a new generation of people interested in making and watching Australian films. One day a nineteen-year-old named Bruce Beresford poked his head around the door and asked Peter Coleman and his colleagues whether they were interested in the problems of Australian film-makers. Beresford wrote a manifesto about the deficiencies of Australian films for the *Observer*, and McNicoll instructed Ken Hall to buy his film *The Devil to Pay* for TCN-9. Even though Beresford now describes the film as 'dreadful', he was to emerge as a film-maker of national and international repute. Packer's main interventions in the running of the *Observer* concerned the television column. When John Croyston attempted to establish himself as an independent television critic, Packer insisted that critics on his payroll be 'objective our way'. Robert Raymond persuaded Horne to allow him to write a regular column about the press, but 'So They Say' was discontinued immediately after Raymond criticised the trend towards monopoly.[23]

Packer's principal concern in the first half of 1958, however, was the spread of television interstate. After awarding television licences in Sydney and Melbourne, the ABCB had invited applications for licences in Brisbane and Adelaide. The sponsors of the commercial television stations in Sydney and Melbourne hoped that two commercial licences would be awarded in both Brisbane and Adelaide; they were concerned that if only one licence was awarded, their capacity to make networking arrangements would be jeopardised. On 23 April 1957, some twelve months before the licence hearings were held, a meeting took place at Fairfax headquarters in Hunter Street. Here Packer, Keith Martin and other sponsors of commercial television stations in Sydney and Melbourne gathered to 'carve up the empire'. They agreed that if only one licence was awarded in each capital city, they would combine their interests to ensure an equitable program sharing agreement. When news of this meeting became public, one man told Labor's Senator J. P. Kennelly that there had not been a 'greater gathering of brigands in one spot at one time since the Kelly gang was surrendered in Victoria'.[24]

At the hearings for the interstate licences in April and May 1958, Packer made it clear why forming networking arrangements was so important. Speaking on behalf of two companies yet to be formed, he explained that being able to sell national time would be of considerable appeal to advertisers. The formation of a television network would cut advertising rates and programming costs. During the hearings in Brisbane, Packer jokingly handed his counsel Tony Larkins card after card with client's instructions: 'GET STUCK INTO IT', 'STOP THINKING ABOUT YOUR RETAINER', 'DON'T BE SO UNCTUOUS', 'PAUSE FOR LAUGHTER', 'SMILE AT THE CHAIRMAN'. In his evidence for the Adelaide licence, Packer stated that TCN-9 had lost £3000 in the first forty-five weeks of the financial year but was on track to show a small profit by June. Although Packer's bid for the licences failed, he was mollified when the government rejected the ABCB's recommendation that only one commercial licence should be awarded in each city.[25]

Throughout this period, Packer was sensitive to any slight at the hands of the prime minister. On returning from overseas in September 1958, he learned that Menzies had met Lloyd Dumas from the Adelaide *Advertiser*, Harold Campbell, editor of the Melbourne *Age*, and Angus Maude, editor of the *Sydney Morning Herald*, to discuss the government's foreign policy. Packer complained to the prime minister about the 'gratuitous insult' to the *Telegraph*: 'we can't understand why you would hit an old friend, prestige-wise, below the belt'. Menzies immediately despatched a 'personal and confidential' letter to Packer, saying he had arranged the meeting with editorial executives as a 'corrective' measure. Because the *Telegraph*s were running a 'very sound' stance on foreign affairs, there had been no need to call them into line. On 15 October, just after the decision about the television licences was announced, Packer told Menzies that 'Your letter plus the resounding good news about the Television licences greatly cheered us up … You have made this a happy little office'.[26]

Appreciating the value of Packer's support, the prime minister handled the media proprietor cleverly. His letters and telephone conversations with Packer were invariably smooth, courteous and friendly, but he kept Packer in awe of him by maintaining a certain distance. Shortly after Buzz Kennedy joined his staff, Menzies asked him, 'What sort of a man is Packer as a person? We all know he flies off the handle and publishes some odd articles and opinions, but you've worked with him for some years ... Is he a straight shooter? I mean, is he honest and not a crook in any way?' Kennedy replied that although Packer was all the things Menzies said, he had no doubt that he was honest. A relieved Menzies replied: 'I've got his name on my desk for a K[nighthood] and I just wanted some assurance on that point because I don't really know him very well'.[27]

Packer was in London when his name appeared in the Queen's Birthday honours list in June 1959. Gretel, Clyde and Kerry were with him; Clyde had been gaining work experience on the London *Daily Mail* for the last six months. Cyril Pearl, who had left ACP after falling out with Frank Packer, suspected that the family had been tipped off to expect the announcement.[28] On the night the knighthood was announced, Kennedy spotted Frank and Gretel having dinner at the Savoy. He and his companion went over to the table to congratulate the new Sir Frank and Lady Packer. When Kennedy indicated that he had learned about the knighthood in the course of his duties, Gretel exclaimed, 'You probably knew before we did and you never said a word. I think you're rotten'. The next day, she insisted that Kennedy and Clyde accompany her to Kew Gardens, saying that only a barbarian would visit London in June and not go to see the gardens.[29]

On 7 July the Queen Mother conferred the knighthood on Packer at Buckingham Palace. Tom Mead, the *Telegraph*'s chief-of-staff, sent a cable to the Packers congratulating them on behalf of the staff. Sir Frank replied that the telegram was much appreciated by himself and 'Missus Packer'. On his way back home, Packer enjoyed some frustrating golf rounds with his two husky sons on the famous Gleneagles course in Scotland.[30]

The knighthood provoked condemnation in journalistic and political circles back in Australia. Pearl privately speculated that Packer had done a deal with Menzies after realising that he would never make it onto the state list; the disaffected editor believed that Menzies hated Packer but wanted a 'new beloved and trusty knight' in the Sydney media. Given that the ALP was in power in New South Wales, it seems unlikely that Packer would ever have countenanced his name appearing on the state list of imperial honours. Packer had been yearning for a knighthood for years and Menzies had archly held him at bay. Now, in quick succession, John Williams, managing director of the Melbourne *Herald*, Ham Campbell and Packer had all been knighted. Pearl concluded that Menzies had a 'divine contempt' for public opinion. Truth's successor, the *Sunday Mirror*, intimated that Menzies had bought Packer's support by giving him a knighthood. James F. Cope, the Labor member for Watson, called the knighthood 'an outrageous example of patronage':

> Every newspaperman at Canberra and every parliamentarian in this House knows, deep down, that Packer received his knighthood in recognition of his services to the Liberal and Australian Country Parties through his newspaper and television station.... Finally,

let me say this: Despite the efforts of the "Daily Telegraph" to destroy the Labour [sic] Party, this great party will still be functioning when the Packers have passed to the Great Beyond.[31]

Not long after he returned to Sydney, a curious rumour surfaced that Packer was considering selling the *Telegraph*s. Although there is no evidence to suggest that this was a real possibility, the rumour naturally made the prime minister nervous. Asking Kennedy to investigate whether the story was true, Menzies remarked that Packer's choice of a buyer might 'create a problem'. A week later, on 10 September, both Packer and Kennedy attended the Golden Ball at the Trocadero for Princess Alexandra, who was visiting Sydney. Invited to Packer's table for a drink, Kennedy inquired about rumours of a pending sale. Packer, saying that he had also heard the gossip, told Kennedy he could reassure the prime minister that he had no plans to dispose of the *Telegraph*s. Clyde and Kerry, he said, would take over ACP in due course: 'I don't think they're ready to do that yet and maybe they never will be, but it'll be theirs, no question about that'.[32]

Although Sir Frank rode both his sons unmercifully, Clyde seems to have been treated the more harshly, perhaps because he was the heir apparent and more was expected of him. Following Sir Frank into the family business meant enduring his hectoring manner and some of his worst insults, often in front of other people. 'Is he a saint or an imbecile?', one of Sir Frank's executives was reputed to have asked after watching Clyde's smiles persist through calumnies that had put everyone else off lunch. Sir Frank had cause to be worried about both his sons. Clyde was competent and intelligent, but he had shown his independence by siding with his mother during the Sybil Connolly crisis. Kerry, on the other hand, was running up gambling debts, driving fast cars and chasing young women. Over a drink at the Trocadero, Sir Frank told Kennedy that he would have to hire a top financial controller to keep Clyde and Kerry in line and see that they did not do anything stupid, 'which they might well do'.[33]

It was at about this time that Clyde Packer exercised his initiative by forming a syndicate with a group of friends to invest in the *Wentworth News*, the *Bondi News* and the *Southern News* in Sydney's Eastern Suburbs. This brought the Packer family up against Ezra Norton, who co-owned the *Double Bay Courier*. In late 1958 sixty-one-year-old Norton had sold *Truth* and the *Daily Mirror* to a Fairfax shelf company, O'Connell Pty Ltd. Consolidated Press's editorial staff were careful to check with Sir Frank before reporting on these developments. Packer vetoed the publication of one reasonably sympathetic article about Norton in the *Observer*, describing his old foe as 'one of the most crooked people you could deal with financially'.[34]

At a news conference in 1959, McNicoll mentioned how places like Rockdale in the southern suburbs had grown. This comment, coupled with Clyde's activities, made Sir Frank think about the possibility of spreading his newspaper interests into the suburbs. Calling Tom Mead, a resident of Kogarah, into his office, Packer inquired: 'Are there any good suburban papers out your way?' When Mead replied that the *Hurstville Propeller* and the *St George Call* were solid possibilities, Packer asked him to negotiate their purchase. Mead spent the best part of a year trying to buy the *Propeller*, but Norman Wenholm and his family refused the offer of $160 000.[35]

Just when it seemed that Packer's plans to move into the suburban market were not going to materialise, News Ltd made a dramatic intervention. Since his father's death in 1952, Rupert Murdoch had rapidly extended his newspaper interests from Adelaide to Perth. Deciding to enter Sydney via the back door, Murdoch set his sights on Earl White's company, Cumberland Newspapers Pty Ltd. In February 1960 two Sydney groups — one of which was almost certainly ACP — made desperate last-minute attempts to outbid him. Murdoch succeeded in buying the chain of twenty-four suburban newspapers for £1 million. Les Haylen, now a Labor MP, astutely observed: 'One thing is certain. Murdoch is in Sydney to stay'. *Nation* predicted that in ten years' time three young men who were near contemporaries at Geelong Grammar School — Rupert Murdoch, Clyde Packer and James Oswald Fairfax — would dominate the Sydney newspaper scene.[36]

Alarmed by Murdoch's move, ACP and a Fairfax subsidiary immediately joined forces to form a rival company, Suburban Publications Pty Ltd. The group decided that the idle time of the *Daily Mirror* plant should be used to produce the new company's titles. However, in late May Clyde, the managing director of Suburban Publications, and his staff learned of an almost inconceivable happening: the Fairfax shelf company had sold Mirror Newspapers Ltd to Murdoch. Although Rupert Henderson was wary of the aggressive young proprietor's ambitions, he had accepted Murdoch's offer for the company; the *Daily Mirror* was losing money, the *Sunday Mirror* was competing with the *Sun-Herald* and Fairfax needed more cash to invest in television. It was said that after the deal was concluded, Murdoch danced a little jig at Fairfax headquarters and made a triumphant telephone call to Clyde Packer.[37]

Suburban Newspapers had to hastily find an alternative plant to produce its titles. In May an associated company, Regional Newspapers Pty Ltd, made a cash offer for the assets and Chippendale premises of the *Anglican* newspaper. The Anglican Press had appointed a receiver, Jack E. Wayland, a few weeks earlier.[38] The bid to acquire the *Anglican* printery triggered a labyrinthine series of events involving Francis James, Rupert Murdoch, Clyde Packer and, by default, Sir Frank. The friendship between Clyde and Francis James had recently cooled. Clyde and Donald Horne were among those executives at ACP who complained about the quality of the work undertaken by the Anglican Press in printing the *Observer*.[39]

By 27 May Wayland had received four tenders for the Anglican Press. He resolved to negotiate privately with two of the tenderers — Regional Newspapers and the Australian Church Press Ltd — in order to obtain the best terms possible. The board of Australian Church Press, which had just been formed, included Rupert Murdoch and the ubiquitous James. Over the weekend of 4–5 June the directors received telephone calls from people prominent in newspaper and financial circles asking whether it was true that ACP, through a nominee, had acquired the Anglican Press.

On Monday morning J. S. Moyes, the Bishop of Armidale, and the directors of Australian Church Press met Wayland. Moyes remarked that the shareholders and the trustees would prefer not to see the Anglican Press sold to a secular company if a good offer were forthcoming from a firm with a religious affiliation.[40] James advised Wayland that they were prepared to amend their original offer to make it acceptable to the shareholders in the Anglican Press. Wayland said he was in a difficult position as he had received a cheque for £42 000 from Regional Newspapers and was inclined to accept it; when pressed, however, he said he had not signed a contract and wanted to seek advice about the legality of the situation. Wayland said that if the course of action he proposed was unacceptable to the trustees and the shareholders, he should be removed as receiver. At the end of the meeting Wayland agreed not to do anything until Thursday 9 June, by which time the directors of Australian Church Press would have conferred with the trustees. Moyes immediately despatched letters about the meeting to bishops around the country, urging them to look at more than just the financial situation, and saying that an injunction should be taken out against Wayland if he went ahead and tried to conclude a deal with Regional Newspapers.[41]

That night, Wayland rang James to suggest that they meet to talk things over. 'What about the Journalists' Club?', Wayland laughingly asked, knowing that this would be the most indiscreet of places to discuss a possible deal with the Packers. Although James also laughed, he would later claim that he went on to comment, 'Seriously, I do think you ought to be careful. These people who have made you an offer are a tough and dangerous crowd. I don't want to be melodramatic and suggest they have a man posted outside your front door to see where you go, and all that; but you really should be careful, I think'. (Wayland denied that James used these words.) James said that under no circumstances was Clyde Packer to attend the meeting, but he agreed that Peter Bowen could be present. The Bellevue Hill solicitor wore two hats throughout this episode. Bowen was one of only two shareholders in Regional Newspapers — a potential purchaser — at the same time as he was acting as legal counsel for Wayland — the receiver appointed by the seller.[42]

In a meeting that lasted until the early hours of the morning, Wayland produced the cheque from Regional Newspapers, said that there was a time limit on the offer and maintained that unless a better offer were forthcoming from some other person, he would have no choice but to accept the offer of £42 000. After James finally agreed to beat this offer by £500, he became ill and made 'insulting remarks' about his former friend Clyde Packer. It was left to Bowen to go outside and break the news to F. W. Millar, a lawyer with Allen, Allen & Hemsley who had been advising ACP on taxation matters for years. Bowen returned to say, 'They are not very happy about it at all', while Wayland dictated a letter to James saying that Australian Church Press would pay £42 500 for the Anglican Press by 5 p.m. that day. In a subsequent affidavit, James would paint this meeting in a sinister light. He claimed he saw a shadow of a man from his window when the meeting was under way, and when he ushered Wayland and Bowen from the building, he found Clyde Packer standing outside the door.[43]

Deeply distressed by the meeting, James regretted signing the letter dictated by Wayland. On the morning of 7 June Moyes told an apologetic James that he had certainly not had any right to bind his colleagues to an agreement, and by 3 p.m. all but one of the trustees had agreed to remove Wayland as the receiver of the Anglican Press. An accountant, Henry James Reid, was appointed in his place. The board of Australian Church Press met at 6 p.m. and made an offer to Reid in terms identical to those agreed by Wayland and James early that morning. Representatives of the Packer family, meanwhile, were informed that Wayland had been removed as the receiver.[44]

At 9.15 p.m. Clyde and Kerry Packer and an associate arrived at the Anglican printery in Chippendale. They were accompanied by 'Fearless' Fred Millar, armed with a document stating that the assets of the Anglican Press had been sold to Regional Newspapers. They were met by Reid, who said that he did not recognise the terms of the alleged sale.[45] Before long, James received a telephone call at his Wahroonga home saying that the Packer camp had managed to enter the building via the back entrance and throw out the staff. As James was preparing to leave for Chippendale, he took another telephone call. On the end of the line was Frank Browne, who had heard from Rupert Murdoch that James was having some trouble at the *Anglican*. The rambunctious Browne published the racy newsletter *Things I Hear*, which regularly passed biting comments on Packer, 'one of the richest, and most powerful, men in Australia', and his family, political associates and, at times, unorthodox business ventures. Browne had little time for ACP generally, as his contribution to *Weekend* had been scrapped by Donald Horne. James met Murdoch on the steps of the Sydney Town Hall and was given £10 000 in notes to cover any expenses that might be incurred in taking over the running of the *Anglican*. Browne immediately put £20 to good use by hiring two heavyweight boxers from a club in George Street. The contingent made its way to Chippendale and forcibly ejected the Packer camp from the building. In a fight in the street outside the building, Kerry Packer was knocked to the ground, his shirt torn and his eyes half-closed. Clyde joined his younger brother and they left the scene.[46]

Sir Frank was unable to join his sons at Chippendale because he was recovering from surgery to remove his gall bladder. He rose from his sickbed at St Vincent's Private Hospital and made his way to the ACP boardroom, where he conferred with executives and kept in touch with developments over a two-way radio.[47] In 1939 *Smith's Weekly* had headed its report on the mêlée between Frank Packer and Ezra Norton 'Press "Magnates" and Fisticuffs. UNEDIFYING SPECTACLE'; in 1960 the front page of the *Daily Mirror* screamed 'KNIGHT'S SON'S IN CITY BRAWL'. On 8 June Murdoch's newspaper solemnly reported Bishop Moyes's comments. The violence done to 'Christian morality' was disgraceful, the good bishop declared; the James camp had been right in not tamely allowing the *Anglican* printery to slip into 'secular hands'.[48]

That afternoon Anglican Press obtained an injunction restraining Regional Newspapers and Clyde and Kerry Packer from entering the *Anglican*'s premises. For a long while James remained convinced that Murdoch was motivated solely by a 'quixotic' streak of generosity in bailing out the *Anglican*. But what the incident actually represented was another stage in the newspaper rivalry between the Packer and Murdoch families. On 15 June Sir Frank told an emissary despatched by James that he was most anxious to avoid any action or publicity that would embarrass the Church of England; it seems more than likely that Packer also wanted to circumvent any further publicity that might embarrass him in the eyes of the politicians and the socialites with whom he now mixed. Packer, however, was adamant that he must have the *Anglican* building to print his suburban newspaper titles: 'It is mine. I've paid for it'.[49]

In a letter to Murdoch on 16 June, James revealed that he now felt 'deep sorrow for poor Packer':

> Don't think I'm soft. It's just that when you've had no money, no grub, no shelter, sodden rags of clothes, only a good mate by your side and a New Testament in your pocket with two hundred kilos between you and the Rhine and the police and Hitler Jugend and others panting for the sight of you I suppose it gives you a snobbish set of values, and you can never really take soft beds or filet mignon seriously afterwards. If you see what I mean, nothing physical can thereafter touch you. For the rest of your life you are somehow alone. Free. All of which is of course shooting a hell of a line; but you may take my point; poor old Packer can never hope to. So I'm sorry for him.[50]

Packer was not adopting such a reflective stance. He was busy conferring with Donald Horne about how the *Observer* should cover the case when it was resolved, agreeing that the article should be reviewed by Fred Millar in case it went too far and libelled James.[51] By late June Packer was privately indicating that he was unwilling to contest the suit as he had been forced to make other arrangements for printing his suburban titles. James concluded that 'they were getting out of it as gracefully as they can, and causing us as much annoyance as possible in the meanwhile'. The legal proceedings arising out of the dramatic events of 7 June 1960 were eventually quietly settled out of court. But James and some of his allies were unhappy with the way the matter was resolved and became somewhat disillusioned with Murdoch, feeling that settling the case on terms not to be disclosed damaged their reputation in the eyes of the public.[52]

The enterprise that had sparked this unfortunate episode was, meanwhile, well under way. Forced to share the printing between ACP and Fairfax, Suburban Publications launched the *St George and Sutherland Shire Leader* on 29 June 1960. Sir Frank and his wife were on hand to see the first issue of what was to become the company's flagship publication. When the excited editor, Tom Mead, stepped out of the lift at ACP headquarters, he overheard Gretel say to her husband, 'Oh, Frank. It is a dear little paper'. Sir Frank worked alongside his chauffeur helping to load copies of the newspaper into delivery vehicles. They were watched over by a group of bouncers, called in by Clyde in case there was any more trouble with the backers of the *Anglican*. For the next year Suburban Publications busily bought up titles across Sydney until a truce was called with Cumberland Newspapers. In July 1961 the two 'rival' companies reached a territorial agreement whereby they agreed not to compete with each other in most areas of Sydney.[53]

While his elder son was concentrating on the intricacies of the suburban newspaper business, Sir Frank was again considering how to expand his television interests. In 1959, when the ABCB invited applications for commercial television licences in regional New South Wales, Packer wrote to Menzies to press his case. He told the prime minister that he felt it was 'very important that we start off the extension of television correctly, and [by] correctly I mean the best service to the country viewers and on a basis that will allow for future expansion as Australia grows'. What Packer really meant was that he wanted to secure affiliated television stations in order to provide an outlet for TCN–9's programs and create a national market for advertisers. He admitted as much in a letter to the chairman of a local Wollongong applicant company, Television Wollongong Transmissions Ltd: 'A shareholding interest in your station doesn't worry me very much. Whether we are in or out, what I would like to do is have a definite arrangement that you will use our programs'.[54]

In early 1960 the ABCB heard applications for the licence in the Wollongong-Illawarra area. ATN-7 executives took every opportunity to convince the board and the postmaster-general, C. W. Davidson, that they would continue to invest in local production if granted network outlets. But Packer, representing two applications lodged by Television Corporation, was more forthright. He could not resist the temptation to accuse other syndicates of talking about local live production in order to ingratiate themselves with the ABCB. He went on:

> Generally speaking, local live shows are as dull as ditchwater. I don't believe people look at television for local matter. They like to be entertained. They like to see the big events on television …
>
> Television is something more than a newspaper. People don't pay £200 or £300 for a television set to get the results of the lamb sales at Flemington.

Packer presented similar views a few weeks later when he spoke on behalf of the syndicate formed by Television Corporation to bid for the licence in the Central Tablelands.[55]

While Packer was waiting for the ABCB and the government to announce the successful applicants for country television licences, new openings arose. As K. S. Inglis commented in *Nation* after assessing Rupert Murdoch's activities, among 'newspaper proprietors over the age of thirty, Sir Frank Packer was the most frisky'.[56] Packer offered £10 000 for a six-week option to buy two ailing English newspapers, the *News Chronicle* and the *Star*. ACP indicated that if it elected to exercise the option, it would pay £2.5 million for the plant and premises, and pump another £1.5 million into stabilising and expanding the newspapers. The Scottish-Canadian newspaper financier Roy Thomson also made an offer, but in July the directors of the *News Chronicle* and the *Star* rejected both approaches.

In October London's Associated Newspapers took over the newspapers and incorporated the *News Chronicle* in the *Daily Mail* and the *Star* in the *Evening News*. A meeting of the editorial staff of the two defunct newspapers alleged that the terms of this deal had been agreed upon in 1958, and that the offers from Packer and Thomson had been unfairly rejected out of hand. The National Union of Journalists demanded that an independent inquiry be established to investigate why two offers that may have saved 3500 jobs had been turned down. Packer might well have been frustrated that his one bid to enter into the world of London publishing had been stymied by the English establishment, yet in July he himself had cabled the London directors to say that he was no longer interested in the titles anyway.[57] He was content to let the matter lapse when the opportunity to form a vital Sydney-Melbourne television network suddenly emerged.

By 1960 General Television Pty Ltd ran the most successful television station in Melbourne. GTV–9 consistently won the ratings, offering viewers first-rate news coverage as well as *In Melbourne Tonight*, a hugely popular variety show hosted by the comedian Graham Kennedy. When the English electronics firm Pye bought a controlling interest in it, Electronic Industries Pty Ltd had to divest itself of its 62 per cent interest in the television station in order to comply with the ABCB's restrictions on overseas investment. Both Packer and Rupert Henderson immediately realised the potential of formally aligning their Sydney television stations with GTV–9 in Melbourne.[58]

Henderson first learned that Electronic Industries might have to sell out of GTV-9 when he happened to be in London at the same time as the chairman and principal shareholder, Sir Arthur Warner. ATN-7 already had an agreement to share some programs with GTV-9, and Warner seems to have assured Henderson that if he sold he would do so to Fairfax. Henderson confirmed this understanding during a lunch with Warner at the Hotel Windsor in Melbourne, where he offered £4 for each £1 share.[59] There were, however, two other vitally interested onlookers. Sir John Williams was managing director of the HWT, which had a major shareholding in the other commercial television station in Melbourne, HSV-7. Williams hoped to stabilise ownership of GTV-9 among local and institutional interests in Melbourne. With his sixth sense telling him that something was afoot, Packer dashed down to Melbourne and had lunch at the HWT's headquarters in Flinders Street. Such a visit could be explained because TCN-9 and HSV-7 had a program-buying arrangement, and Packer emerged from the lunch determined to forestall the intentions of his hosts and Rupert Henderson.[60]

In early July Packer — who had made two offers for GTV-9 earlier in the year — offered Warner £6 per share. There are differing accounts of Henderson's reaction when he learned of Packer's intervention. According to Gavin Souter, Henderson telephoned Warner in Melbourne, reminded him of their earlier understanding and said he would match Packer's offer. That night, he sent a deposit to Warner by express mail. Souter writes that Henderson later discovered that Packer had been in Warner's room during the telephone conversation and that they had already concluded their deal. But David McNicoll maintains that Henderson personally went to Melbourne, where he confronted Warner and made him an offer considerably above Packer's. In this version, Packer's friend Sir Ian Potter rang Warner and convinced him he would be finished commercially in Melbourne if he reneged on his agreement with Packer.[61] A stockbroker and merchant banker, Potter was one of Australia's most influential financiers and philanthropists, playing a key role in the financing of the manufacturing and mining industries in the 1950s and 1960s.[62]

The deal between Packer and Warner meant that Television Corporation acquired majority shareholdings in GTV-9 and radio station 3AK for a cost of £3.6 million. Ian Potter & Co. underwrote a share issue by Television Corporation to finance the transaction.⁶³ The morning after the deal was concluded, Warner arrived at the home of Colin Bednall, the managing director of General Television. 'I just don't know how it happened. When Packer put his cheque on the desk in front of me, I just had to pick it up', Warner said sheepishly. Bednall had cause to be worried: he may have regarded Henderson as a 'squirt of a man', but he also knew that Packer ran Television Corporation on a shoestring. TCN-9's two studios would fit inside GTV-9's Studio One and leave room over; GTV-9's massive Studio Three, which was under construction, was designed to provide facilities for live broadcasting surpassing those at the ABC. In his unpublished autobiography, Bednall claimed that Warner told him to go and ask Menzies to block the deal from going through. Even though he had known the prime minister for years, Bednall realised that the deal was a *fait accompli*, and he only told Menzies that Warner felt uneasy about the sale. Menzies simply laughed, telling Bednall that there was no way he would do a favour for Warner at Packer's expense.⁶⁴

At the end of July the ABCB recommended that control of country television stations should be in the hands of local interests and that 50 per cent of each company's shares should be offered for public subscription. Country Party politicians had their day when the government accepted the ABCB's recommendations. There was speculation in media circles that Packer had bought into GTV-9 because he had been tipped off about the government's pending decision. Even if this was the case, Packer had long suspected that regional interests would win out, and realised the value of aligning television stations in the capital cities. When lodging his group's applications for the licence in Wollongong, he had boldly declared: 'The big money is tied up where the people are, two and a half million in Sydney, two million in Melbourne, and Adelaide and Brisbane. If you take all the rest of the country stations, they don't amount to a row of beans'.⁶⁵

When Packer's move into Melbourne was announced, HSV-7 began attempting to poach executives from GTV-9. By 12 July one leading executive, known for his toughness, had resigned, alarmed at the prospect of working for Packer. Bednall tried to ease the 'flutters' of his employees, telling them that they should avoid making 'emotional decisions'. He reassured his staff that Packer had told him he saw no reason at all to interfere with GTV-9's past policies.⁶⁶ On 4 August, as mutterings of discontent about the sale continued, Packer himself sent a telegram to Bednall. He asked Bednall to inform his staff that TCN-9 was committed to continuing the policies which had made GTV-9 the most popular station in Victoria: 'WE ARE LOOKING FORWARD TO OUR ASSOCIATION WHICH COULD BE GOOD FOR BOTH GTV AND TCN AND IN VIEW OF THE PRICE HAD BETTER BE'.

Packer told Bednall he was unable to travel to Melbourne to deliver this message in person owing to 'domestic health reasons'. Packer had managed to execute this crucial business transaction while his wife was gravely ill. Gretel Packer's decline had begun the previous year, when it became apparent that she suffered from a serious circulatory disorder. In early 1960 she had travelled to the famous Mayo Clinic in Rochester, Minnesota.⁶⁷ Those who could afford it flocked to the clinic, which was the world's largest diagnostic organisation. Sir Frank probably made contact with the clinic through the Postgraduate Medical Foundation at the University of Sydney. He had become chair of the foundation, which aimed to raise funds for medical research and teaching, on its establishment in 1958. It seems likely that he became involved with the organisation through his brother-in-law George Stening, who lectured in gynaecology at the university, and the Nuclear Research Foundation.[68]

The specialists who examined Gretel Packer at the Mayo Clinic diagnosed a condition that caused a narrowing of the main artery in the abdomen. After undergoing vascular surgery at a hospital in Rochester, she returned to Sydney. She developed complications six months later and there were fears that her leg would have to be amputated. Dr Stening, who was often called in to confer about family health problems, has recalled that his sister-in-law faced up to her painful and draining condition with great courage and fortitude.[69]

In early August 1960 Gretel again left for the Mayo Clinic, accompanied by her husband and sons, their Sydney physician Dr Frank Ritchie, and a nurse. Shortly before her departure, Gretel had a long talk with Bruce Gyngell. 'Well darling', she said, 'I don't know that I'll come back, but I want you to promise me that you'll stay with … Frank and the boys … promise me you'll never leave'. Sir Frank, meanwhile, asked David McNicoll whether he would ring around the traps and try to get some 'stuff called heroin', which he had heard was the ultimate painkiller. As Packer helped get his desperately ill wife through the airport on a stretcher, a knockabout acquaintance of McNicoll's came forward and pressed a small packet of heroin into his hand.[70]

On 15 August Gretel underwent a lengthy heart operation at St Mary's Hospital in Rochester. She died the next day, aged only fifty-three, with her husband and sons at her bedside. A private funeral service was held on 17 August and Lady Packer was cremated, in accordance with her wishes. Before leaving Sydney, she had told Fairy Faircloth that she did not want to be entombed in the gloomy family vault: 'It you dare to let them put me in that vault at South Head, I'll come back to haunt you'. Returning to Sydney a couple of days after the funeral, the Packer men scattered Gretel's ashes in Sydney Harbour. On her employer's first day back at the office, Faircloth gently remarked, 'Oh dear — life's not the same any more, is it?' Sir Frank put his head on his secretary's shoulder and burst into tears.[71]

12
Setting Sail

In mid 1959 Packer had a convivial luncheon with two fellow members of the Royal Sydney Yacht Squadron (RSYS), the vice-commodore, Richard A. Dickson, and an Olympic gold medallist and head of the Australian branch of Johnson & Johnson, William H. Northam. When Packer said that he wanted to renew his interest in sailing, his companions urged him to build a twelve-metre yacht to contest the prized America's Cup. 'We kept the grog flowing pretty fast', Northam has recalled, 'and Frank soon got excited about having a go at the Yanks'.[1]

The America's Cup is the world's oldest and most prestigious yachting challenge. John Stevens, commodore of the New York Yacht Club (NYYC), and a group of wealthy Americans had entered their schooner, the *America*, in a race around the Isle of Wight during Britain's Great Exhibition in 1851. Stevens won the prize — a remarkably unattractive silver mug — and in 1857 donated it to the NYYC to be used as a trophy in a 'friendly competition'. It was renamed the America's Cup and held in trust for a challenge from any foreign yacht club.[2]

The NYYC's rules were so strict that nobody bothered to challenge for the cup until 1870. The Royal Thames Yacht Club found its schooner up against some seventeen of the NYYC's best; unsurprisingly, the English team did not win the cup. In the 1880s, following disputes about the rules of the contest, the only surviving owner of the *America* was asked to make a new deed of gift for the cup. It stipulated that the race must be between one yacht built in the country challenging for the cup and one built in the country holding the cup, and the challenge must come from a recognised yacht club. It also laid down rules for the size of the yachts and the notice a club must give when issuing a challenge. The biggest hurdle for challengers was the fact that they had to actually sail their yachts, rather than ship them over, to the United States. This meant that yachts from Britain had to be sturdy enough to make the voyage across the Atlantic, while the American defenders could concentrate on constructing lightweight hulls.[3]

In 1888 a syndicate of Sydney yachtsmen sent a naval architect, Walter Reeks, to New York to investigate whether an Australian challenge should be made in two years' time. The venture was deemed to be impractical because the boat would have to sail by way of Cape Horn, the Cape of Good Hope or the Suez Canal. In 1956 the NYYC finally amended the cup's deed of gift to allow the challenge match to be sailed in international twelve-metre class sloops that could be shipped to the United States.[4]

Few Australians had heard of the America's Cup before 1958, when TCN-9 showed clips of England's first postwar challenge. *Spectre* lost badly to the defender, meaning that all seventeen challenges mounted by Britain and Canada since 1870 had failed. When Northam calculated that a challenge would cost hundreds of thousands of pounds he had to convince Packer to proceed with the idea. The fact that no other nation had managed to win what Packer described as the 'dilapidated, and intrinsically valueless trophy' fuelled his enthusiasm. As outgoing vice-president of the New South Wales branch of the Australian-American Association, he believed that competing in the 1962 challenge would boost Australia's profile in the United States. The amount of goodwill a challenge would generate towards Australia, he wrote in the foreword to a book by Bill Baverstock, would be more effective than a multi-million dollar public relations campaign promoting Australia and Australians to the United States.[5]

In July 1959 the RSYS agreed in principle to issue a challenge for the America's Cup in 1962. The Australian America's Cup Challenge Association was registered in Canberra with four members of the RSYS forming its management committee. Packer, who had been a member of the RSYS since 1935, became chairman and Keith Martin, his close friend and employee, was appointed general manager. Northam and Dickson also joined the committee.[6]

On 10 August Packer informed Menzies that ACP, in association with the RSYS, intended to build a twelve-metre yacht and send it, with an all-Australian crew, over to New York to challenge for the 1962 America's Cup. He advised the prime minister that his syndicate intended to purchase *Vim*, an American yacht that had trained against the defender in the 1958 contest. *Vim* would be brought out to Australia and used for training the crew while the Australian challenger was under construction.[7]

Between August and September 1959, Packer sought to obtain governmental concessions to import the yacht. John McEwen, the minister for trade, agreed to issue an import licence; Denham Henty, the minister for customs and excise, was persuaded to accord duty-free admission to *Vim*; treasury, however, believed that it would be illegal to waive sales tax. And while government ministers and bureaucrats believed that Packer's venture was of considerable national significance, Menzies was cautious. When Packer invited him to be patron of the race committee, the prime minister replied that although the project was an admirable one, 'I should like to see your plans become a little more advanced before deciding whether or not I should become Patron of the event'.[8]

Plans for the challenge advanced swiftly. On 27 October the RSYS hosted a party for its commodore, Field Marshal Sir William Slim, who was leaving Australia on relinquishing the office of governor-general. In his farewell address, Slim announced that the RSYS intended to enter a challenge for the America's Cup in the squadron's centenary year.[9]

Packer's emissaries, meanwhile, were negotiating the acquisition of *Vim*. Colin Ryrie, an Australian Olympic yachtsman who was competing in the United States, conferred with *Vim*'s owner, Captain John Matthews. The captain was uneasy about the Australian proposal, saying that his American counterparts would accuse him of being a traitor if he sold the yacht. Ryrie did his best to convince Matthews that Packer was not a 'muck-about type'. By the end of October Packer himself had arrived in New York. After some lengthy horse-trading, Matthews agreed to lease the yacht to the Australians for US$80 000 for four years. Syndicates from both Britain and Canada had also been considering chartering a trial yacht. On the morning the deal with Australia was clinched in his Wall Street office, Matthews received a telephone call from London. He told the anxious Englishman on the other end of the line that Australia had won the first leg of the race.[10]

Although the Australian syndicate tried to keep details of its bid private, *Vim*'s arrival in Sydney in January 1960 caused widespread interest in national and international sporting circles. *Vim* was entered on the books of the RSYS in Packer's name and a new mooring with heavier chains was constructed at the squadron's boatshed in Kirribilli. However, the yacht was so big that it sometimes had to be moored at the RAAF's slipway in Neutral Bay.[11]

RSYS officials were busy talking with the NYYC to ascertain whether they would accept an Australian challenge for the historic trophy. On 2 March Packer requested the secretary of the RSYS to fire the 'first shot' by formally asking whether they would be prepared to accept a challenge. On 7 April the NYYC informed the RSYS that they would accept a challenge from Australia for the America's Cup in 1962.[12]

But the exchange of formalities and pleasantries between the New York and Sydney clubs was soon complicated by a disquieting development in England. In April 1960 the Royal Thames Yacht Club learned that the Australians definitely intended challenging for the cup. Lord Craigmyle and another member of the 'Red Duster' syndicate had already put up £40 000 to stage a new British bid for the cup. In mid April the Duke of Edinburgh, Prince Philip, who was patron of the RSYS, intervened. He suggested that a commonwealth co-ordinating committee should be set up to co-ordinate any challenges.[13]

The Australians were understandably alarmed at the prospect of all of the time, energy and money they had invested in the venture going to waste. Packer contacted Captain John Illingworth, commodore of the Thames Yacht Club, who had dashed to New York to confer with NYYC officials. Packer was firm, saying that Australia was the first and valid challenger for the 1962 series and the situation called for 'no solution'. His cable concluded: 'AFTER ALL YOU HAVE HAD A LONG UNINTERRUPTED RUN STOP MAYBE WE WON'T DO ANY BETTER BUT EVERY NOW AND THEN YOU HAVE TO GIVE THE YOUNG FELLOW IN THE FAMILY HIS HEAD STOP'. This remark, which was designed to appeal to imperial sentiments in London, mirrored the comment that E. G. Theodore had made about his young business partner when Keith Murdoch had offered to buy out Consolidated Press in 1938.[14]

On 27 April 1960 Dickson cabled William Slim in London, explaining that Australia had been unaware that Britain wanted to stage another challenge and that the NYYC had already accepted Australia's challenge. Asking Slim to 'SMOOTH DOWN ANY WAVES', he concluded, 'WE THINK AND HOPE WE CAN WIN'. Matters were not helped much the next day when the NYYC ruled that it was up to Britain and

Australia to decide whether they should stage elimination trials to determine which country should challenge for the cup.[15]

An embarrassing rift in sporting and diplomatic circles had opened up and newspapers in Australia, Britain and the United States had a field day. David McNicoll, who was visiting London, wrote to the *Times* to argue Australia's right to challenge for the America's Cup. On 3 May the newspaper ran an editorial noting that the challenges had historically been confined to the United Kingdom. But the editorial went on to declare that the failure of the British challenge in 1958 had been so complete 'that it would be presumptuous for anyone in Britain to claim any special national privilege as challengers'. In the same issue, a *Times* journalist based in Sydney reported that one prominent Australian yachtsman had expressed indignation that Britain should try to 'horn in' on Australia's challenge, particularly after the *Spectre* fiasco.[16]

On 3 May Slim sent a cable to Dickson reporting that he had convened a meeting at Buckingham Palace to resolve the matter. Rear-Admiral C. Bonham Carter and Major Charles Ball, the vice-commodore of the Thames Yacht Club, had agreed that the RSYS should proceed with its challenge. Prince Philip read and approved Slim's cable, which stated that the Thames Yacht Club had no wish to 'horn in' on the Australian challenge. The cable also expressed the wish that a committee to co-ordinate challenges after the 1962 match would be formed.[17]

On 31 May Bill Northam, who was visiting London, was invited to attend a meeting of the Thames Yacht Club to discuss the formation of this committee. Northam's account of the meeting illustrated how exclusive and elevated were the circles in which Packer was now mixing. The fact that Northam was prepared to write such an irreverent letter to Packer reflects their private willingness to cock a snook at the yachting establishment:

> ... unlucky me arrived two-and-a-half minutes late and I walked into the room and there were twenty blokes, mostly Lords and Earls, and at the head of the table my old cobber the Duke [Prince Philip]. I don't mind telling you I started to feel nervous, as nobody told me he was to be present. However, he left his chair despite the stony stares at me and walked over and shook me by the hand and said he was glad I could attend and I sat down at the opposite end of the large table like a shag on a rock, facing H.R.H. at the other end.
>
> ... I chipped in when H.R.H. asked me whether we had changed our minds with regard to elimination tests and I swear you could have heard a pin drop when I took it upon myself to say NO and believe me he really grinned and asked why not. I explained that it was in my opinion too late to alter [our plans]. Owen Aisher (a big shot) and Lord Craigmyle surprised me by saying 'hear, hear'. Then we got cracking.
>
> He directed more questions at me than anyone in the room and I swear that at the finish I had 95 per cent on our side and it was unanimous that Australia was the logical challenger and we all had their good wishes and definite offers to help.
>
> ... we all had lunch and a few snorts and everyone was happy and I finished up in a corner with H.R.H. and we had a long friendly yarn.
>
> The crux of it, Frank, [is] they want a Commonwealth challenge after '62.[18]

By the end of May 1960, then, the question of the next America's Cup challenge had been resolved to the satisfaction of the Sydney committee and, apparently, to the relief of members of the Thames Yacht Club. Nevertheless, papers such as the Sydney Sun, which were being given very few details about the challenge, continued to snipe at the activities of Packer and his syndicate. While the frustrated RSYS attempted to hose down ill-informed stories about an ongoing rift with the Thames Yacht Club,[19] plans for the Australian challenge proceeded apace.

The Australian America's Cup Challenge Committee undertook financial responsibility for the challenger, training the crew and sailing the match. ACP underwrote the costs of the venture, and Ampol Petroleum Company Ltd and the British Tobacco Company (Australia) Ltd took out substantial shares in the syndicate.[20] From more than 200 applicants, twenty-eight people, including Packer and Martin, were chosen to train as crew members. They trained on *Vim*, which raced against other yachts in Sydney on handicap. Jim Perry, manager of the RSYS boatyard, made models of the challenge yacht for tank-testing purposes. English-born Alan Payne, the only naval architect in Australia engaged exclusively in yacht designing, was hired to design the challenger. Packer hoped that work on building the yacht would start at Lars Halverson and Sons Pty Ltd on the Parramatta River in October 1960 and that the yacht would be on the water by August 1961.[21]

Nevertheless, Packer's work for the America's Cup tapered off somewhat in the second half of 1960. As we have seen, he secured control of GTV-9 in July and his wife died in August. The RSYS was anxious to ensure that under no circumstances would it be left to pay for the venture. On 14 July the secretary asked Packer to guarantee that, in the event of his death, Martin or ACP would 'carry the project through'. The RSYS must have been unnerved when ten weeks elapsed before it received a response to the letter. In September Packer underwent 'quite a serious operation', and then he had more surgery to remove a cataract. At the end of the month he informed the RSYS secretary that he understood and accepted the terms of the letter of 14 July. After breezily declaring that 'at the moment, the medical fraternity are very satisfied with me', he said that, if an 'unhappy event' did occur, he would do his best to ensure that the RSYS got a 'favourable wind'. However, Packer was unable to go to New York in October, as planned, as his doctors had advised him not to travel overseas until 1961.[22]

Packer's convalescence did not cause him to suspend his business interests. On 2 October 1960 he hosted a dinner party for the managing director of Reuters, Sir John Burgess, who was visiting Australia at the invitation of AAP. Gretel Packer had asked Bruce Gyngell's young wife, Ann, to oversee functions such as this and the general running of 'Cairnton'.[23]

Packer was also busy negotiating the purchase of the *Bulletin*, which in recent years had lost both sales and élan. The politics of the eighty-year-old weekly magazine were, in the words of Peter Coleman, 'paleo-conservative' — nationalist, xenophobic, anti-Semitic and anti-communist. At the end of the war, the *Bulletin* had enjoyed a circulation of 58 000; fifteen years later, the magazine was selling only 29 776 copies per week. In 1958 and 1959 the Bulletin Newspaper Co. Pty Ltd was unable to pay shareholders dividends.[24]

By late 1960 it was well known that the company's managing director, H. K. Prior, was looking for a buyer. A companion publication, the *Australian Woman's Mirror*, was also on the market. Launched by Prior in 1924, the magazine had subsidised the *Bulletin* for many years until its own sales had begun to slide as a result of competition from the *Women's Weekly* and other new women's titles. In October 1960 negotiations for the sale of the company to Conpress Printing were conducted in the boardroom of the George Patterson advertising agency with Bill Farnsworth, head of the agency, acting as the go-between. By the middle of the month the directors and shareholders of the Bulletin Newspaper Co. had accepted the offer of £3 7s 6d for each of the 124 000 shares.[25]

Packer had now acquired Australia's most legendary and, for a time, most venerable magazine. A bonus was that the *Bulletin* building was located in George Street, where land values were on the rise. On the day of the takeover the old staff assembled in the corridors, where Packer got up on the landing and made a genial speech. He told the troops that they were not to worry, although 'there might be a few staff changes'. For Packer's executives and new employees, however, the sale posed considerable challenges. Editor Donald Horne's brief was to revitalise the magazine while preserving its character as a literary-political review with a strong Australian bias. As it was obviously futile to publish competing titles, the *Observer* was merged with the *Bulletin* in March 1961.[26]

Within a fortnight of the *Bulletin*'s purchase, Packer had embarked on yet another takeover bid. In the second half of the 1940s the ACP group had moved into book publishing, acquiring Sydney's Shakespeare Head Press Pty Ltd and London's Frederick Muller Ltd, and securing the Australian rights for the lucrative Little Golden Books series.[27] Unquestionably, however, the dominant force in Australian book-selling and publishing was Angus & Robertson Ltd (A&R). But between 1959 and 1960, the old institution was targeted by two ruthless businessmen: first Walter V. Burns, and then Sir Frank Packer.

Nicknamed the 'pocket battleship', Burns was a rapacious New Zealand-born businessman who speculated in shares and real estate. Soon after arriving in Sydney in the 1950s, Burns spotted the value of A&R's freehold, low-rise property in Castlereagh Street. Through his stockbroker Anthony Hordern, Burns began buying up parcels of shares in A&R. He successfully lobbied for a vacancy on the board in August 1959 and became managing director in March 1960. Within days of the appointment, the benign old chairman and another director resigned. Hordern took over the chairmanship of the company and another accountant, T. C. Read, filled the other vacancy. Burns claimed that there was no difference between books and carpets or cakes, all being subject to the ordinary rules of marketing. By mid 1960 the publishing department had been reduced from thirty to eighteen people, A&R was buying shops in prime locations around the country and George Ferguson, the publishing director and grandson of the firm's founder, was bitterly regretting the fact that Burns had been elected to the board.[28]

In August Burns appointed P. R. Stephensen, a controversial polemicist and former publisher, to A&R as a 'production and procurement executive'. Ferguson was naturally outraged by Burns's blatant attempt to undermine his authority. In a torrid series of meetings in September, Ferguson consistently called for Burns's resignation as managing director. It was at this point that Packer intervened in the affairs of what had until recently been a secure, close-knit, family-style organisation. He had presumably been watching A&R become increasingly unsteady in recent months, and he might have gleaned insights into the company's situation from his brother-in-law, Anthony Hordern. In October Stephensen appeared at Peter Coleman's office at the *Observer* to ask whether Packer might like to buy into A&R. Coleman instinctively replied 'yes', apparently sensing that Packer would not be able to resist vying for a prize as venerable as A&R. Stephensen scribbled Burns's telephone number on a scrap of paper and told Coleman to give it to Packer.[29]

While Packer talked with Burns about the possibility of buying out his interest in A&R, Hordern resigned as chairman, ostensibly on the grounds of ill-health. One wonders whether he was actually moved to resign to avoid allegations of a conflict of interest, or of finding himself in the middle of one of his brother-in-law's bruising takeover battles. At A&R's board meeting on 18 October, Norman Cowper was elected chairman and a letter from Packer offering to buy the company's ordinary shares was tabled. The fact that Packer had championed the lawyer's political aspirations decades earlier did Cowper little good. Cowper immediately surmised that Burns and his cohorts were destroying A&R. At the meeting, Cowper successfully moved that Arthur Swain should replace Burns as managing director. Although Burns remained a director, he lost his balance of power on the board.

While A&R's directors approached Packer for clarification of the offer,[30] he came under parliamentary attack from Arthur Calwell, Les Haylen and Dr Jim Cairns, the Labor member for Yarra. Haylen lashed out at ACP's 'cannibalism', declaring that the takeover of the *Bulletin* by Packer interests was in itself a 'tragedy'. Claiming that ACP had never shown any concern for Australian writers, they pointed to the way in which the *Telegraph*s, the *Women's Weekly* and Shakespeare Head Press sought out syndicated or cheap material. Although ACP outlets were increasingly relying on cheap overseas material, Haylen should have remembered that the company had once employed critics of some standing in the literary community and that the *Women's Weekly* and the *Telegraph*s had offered generous prizes for Australian fiction in the 1940s. Cairns deplored the prospect of ACP's conservative, 'un-Australian' line penetrating Australia's greatest book publishing firm: 'It has been bad enough to have this reactionary editorial line being taken in the newspapers published by the company in question, and for which its leading director [Packer] has received honours at the hands of this Government'. The main line of defence was run by (later Sir) William McMahon, the minister for labour and national service. McMahon was a friend of Packer, having attended Abbotsholme College and Shore, worked for Allen, Allen & Hemsley and played a minor role in the formation of the original Sydney Newspapers in 1932. To laughter and interjections, McMahon told parliament 'with no reservations at all … that the head of Consolidated Press has a real desire to give Australian authors opportunities to express themselves'.[31]

Packer modified his takeover offer at the end of October, when he proposed merging Consolidated Press Holding's publishing interests with those of A&R to form a new company. In letters to Cowper, he argued that 'a combination or merger of the two groups would give added strength and diversity' to A&R and that the *Bulletin* presses would be 'capable of producing high quality paper backs at an economical price'. As *Nation* commented, the revised takeover bid was 'couched in terms that bordered on the farcical'. Packer's attempt to appease A&R's board failed; on 28 October the directors turned down the 'merger' and sacked Stephensen.[32] But it was still clear that at the annual general meeting in December, there would be two groups vying for control of the company: one led by Cowper and Ferguson, and the other by Burns and a surprise defector to his camp, Arthur Swain. The two camps frantically began share-splitting, and the Cowper/Ferguson ticket, supported by prominent authors, emerged victorious at the meeting. Cowper adroitly managed the meeting to minimise the bitterness and recrimination. But one individual, identifying himself only as an 'old bushman', managed to speak from the floor in support of Ferguson. While Burns stared impassively at the ceiling, the man concluded his emotional address with the words: 'We should not let the forest oak be supplanted by a mushroom'.[33]

In early 1961 Packer's health and business commitments finally allowed him to travel to the United States to make arrangements for the 1962 America's Cup challenge. As he prepared to leave for New York with Richard Dickson at the end of January, a flurry of letters from the RSYS and the NYYC dealt with his accommodation and social arrangements. Although Menzies was still somewhat reluctant to become intimately involved with the Australian challenge, Packer saw himself as representing Australia's interests abroad. It is unclear whether he was being facetious on 10 January when, in a letter to the RSYS, he remarked that 'if I am not staying at the White House I shall be at the Sheraton East, Park Avenue'. In the same letter, he also accepted an invitation to attend a stag (all-male) dinner at the apartment of the NYYC's vice-commodore, Chauncey D. Stillman. Even though only a few months had elapsed since his wife's death, Packer was capable of joking that he was 'extremely sorry it is a stag party'.[34]

After installing themselves at the Sheraton, Packer and Dickson held talks with the America's Cup Committee to discuss the conditions governing the match in September 1962. At the staid quarters of the NYYC, Packer wryly observed that if he succeeded in taking away the cup after so many years, 'it would leave quite a mark on the sideboard'. Packer also visited the Stevens Institute in Hoboken, New Jersey, where Alan Payne had put twenty-eight models for the Australian yacht through the towing tanks. However, for reasons that are unclear, Packer suddenly withdrew from some of the meetings at the NYYC and left Dickson to iron out the finer details of the challenge.[35] Sir Frank was back in Sydney by March 1961, and in May he attended Clyde's wedding to Angela Money, the daughter of a doctor from Bellevue Hill.[36]

On 21 June Packer again wrote to Menzies about the America's Cup. Although the letter was ostensibly designed to show how much progress the syndicate had made, it actually revealed that Packer had underestimated what was entailed in designing and building a competitive yacht. As we have seen, he had envisaged that construction work would begin in October 1960 and that the yacht would be launched in August 1961. However, work had not begun until May 1961 and Packer was now talking about the yacht entering the waters in December. Packer skimmed over these delays, instead boasting, with typical enthusiasm, that the syndicate had trained more than two dozen crew members in twelve-metre sailing.

Packer also suggested that, even though the Pioneer Shipping Line had agreed to freight the challenger and *Vim* to the United States free of charge, an Australian aircraft carrier might be made available to transport the yachts to Newport.[37] Packer's attempts to convince the prime minister of his patriotic intentions again failed. Private government records show that Menzies' response to the proposal was 'guarded'. In August he informed Packer that although a great deal of goodwill would 'no doubt' result from an Australian carrier transporting the yachts, the navy would not be able to release a ship for eleven or twelve weeks and the cost of fuel would be prohibitive. Packer replied that he was sorry that 8000 tonnes of fuel 'should come between us': 'If the economy were more buoyant we would undertake to provide the fuel, but as things are' the syndicate would accept the offer of free carriage from the Pioneer Shipping Line. A bureaucrat realised that this oblique comment was a sarcastic reference to the government-induced credit squeeze. He scrawled on Packer's note, 'Not what I'd call a generous acknowledgement'.[38]

At the same time as he was negotiating with the Australian government and international yachting authorities, Packer was overseeing the production of his two newest publications. For some months he remained convinced that the old *Australian Woman's Mirror*, in which he had a sentimental interest, could be revamped. In July 1961, however, with the credit squeeze biting into revenue, he agreed to nominally merge the struggling title with *Weekend*. The new combined magazine, edited by the ubiquitous Donald Horne, was named *Everybody's*.[39]

But it was the fortunes of the *Bulletin* that Packer monitored most closely during this period. He issued memos demanding lists of the number of pages printed each week, the number of parcels the issues were wrapped into and the total staff employed on the magazine. Packer selected some of the employees who were to be dismissed as a result of 'reorganisation and economies' and set maximum rates of pay for contributors. Horne suggested that the *Sunday Telegraph*'s news editor, Peter Hastings, should contribute the column on the media to the *Bulletin* 'so that it is not an obvious propaganda piece and at the same time does not buy the firm into unnecessary fights'. Packer, probably wary that Hastings's intelligence and wit would still result in a column that was too independent, rejected the proposal.[40] Packer convened meetings with Horne, Kerry Packer, who had studied television developments in Cleveland and was now working in ACP's advertising department, and Robert Henty, now manager of Conpress Printing, to authorise changes to the *Bulletin*. Editorial executives learned how to sniff the political breeze. In July 1961 Horne sent a memo to Packer asking whether he could bring a builders' union organiser to Sydney to talk about his split with the Communist Party in Victoria. Horne said that the man could provide 'sensational stuff' about communist activities and good material in the lead-up to the federal election; Horne was at pains to mention that the man would, 'of course', travel tourist class. Packer said 'yes'.[41]

As the election approached, the *Telegraph* began publishing a weekly article by Arthur Calwell, now leader of the Opposition. The startled politician began his first column 'Wonder of wonders!' But Packer's reasons for agreeing to this contribution from his old *bête noire* were quite Machiavellian: he informed Menzies that each article penned by Calwell did him a 'great deal of damage' and constituted 'political hari kari'. But in July, with the credit squeeze biting into profits, Packer told Menzies that ACP could not afford to keep paying the fee. Presumably in an effort to remind the prime minister of the financial sacrifices ACP made to help the Liberal Party, Packer cheekily asked whether the Liberal Party would be willing to take it over. It did not take long for Menzies to politely but firmly reject the idea: 'I must say that it opens up some remarkable, indeed revolutionary, possibilities about the use to which Party funds might be put!'[42]

Packer lacked both the intellect and the sensitivity to realise that his audacity and his perverse sense of humour alienated Australia's longest-serving prime minister. In September, with the election just three months away, Packer again tried to entice Menzies to involve himself in the America's Cup challenge. He wrote to the prime minister inviting him to come to Sydney to look over the challenger yacht and to become patron of the syndicate. Menzies replied that he would very much like to talk about the arrangements for the challenge but that, 'with the best will in the world', he might not be able to find the time to inspect the yacht.

The prime minister did, however, attach a personal note to his letter: 'Give my love to your cartoonist over the "Fairfax-Henderson" cartoon. It was superb! BOB'.[43] This alluded to the fact that the Fairfax organisation was, for the first time in its history, publicly endorsing the ALP. Political and media observers like Menzies and Packer were aware that Rupert Henderson was Calwell's de facto campaign manager. In 1960 Packer had taken it upon himself to warn the prime minister that the *Sydney Morning Herald*'s editor, Angus Maude, was meeting Calwell, Eddie Ward and others in an effort to reunite the ALP after the disastrous split of 1955. The management of Fairfax seems, at first, to have sought a strong and viable Opposition in order to prevent the Menzies government from becoming complacent. But by 1961 the Fairfax organisation was motivated by less disinterested factors: the government's ill-judged credit squeeze had not only curtailed activity and jobs in the manufacturing sector, but revenue from classified and other advertising. While officials in the New South Wales division complained about the Fairfax press,[44] they could find some solace in the unwavering support of the Packer media.

Not long before the poll on 9 December, Packer summoned the *Telegraph*'s Alan Reid into his office to ask him who he thought would win the election. When Reid replied that he was certain Labor would be victorious, Packer inquired if there was anything the coalition could do to change the tide. Reid said that the Menzies government could only be saved if it promised to restore full employment in three to six months. Packer immediately rang Menzies, telling him, 'I want you to see Alan; I've instructed him to say to you what he said to me'. Reid was duly despatched to Canberra to deliver his message to the prime minister. On 29 November Menzies told a gathering in Bega that he would not rest until full employment was restored, although he was careful not to commit himself to a timeframe. Even so, the *Telegraph*s threw their weight behind the coalition for the remainder of the campaign. The government needed all the help it could get. Menzies and his colleagues were complacent, while Calwell campaigned effectively on the ruinous effects of the government's economic policies and advanced a financially responsible social package. Billy McMahon later claimed that ACP was instrumental in the Menzies government being returned with a one-seat majority.[45]

By this time, Packer was involved in another vigorous battle for control of A&R. The company had foolishly established an ongoing association with Packer, leasing ACP the second floor of its building in Castlereagh Street.[46] On 8 November 1961 the A&R board learned that Consolidated Press Holdings had begun buying parcels of shares in the book publishing firm. Many of these shares came from the hapless managing director of A&R, Arthur Swain, who had purchased them from Walter Burns. The following day Packer rang A&R's chairman Norman Cowper, and said that a proxy battle at the firm's annual general meeting in December could be avoided if Consolidated Press Holdings was given a seat on the board. Over luncheon in the boardroom, A&R's directors unanimously agreed to reject this proposal. Cowper and George Ferguson outlined the reasons for this decision: the previous year's general meeting had resolved that A&R should continue as an independent organisation; directors should be appointed not just because they held a certain number of shares, but because they could offer appropriate qualifications and experience; Consolidated Press Holdings operated book publishing and printing works that directly competed with those of A&R.[47]

As a result of this rejection, Packer decided to launch a full-scale takeover bid for A&R. In an open letter to shareholders on 19 November, he announced that his company had acquired 22 per cent of the issued capital in A&R and declared his intention of buying 50 per cent of the ordinary capital in the firm and securing two seats on the board.[48] A court case that happened to involve an ACP subsidiary at this time revealed how Packer conducted his business. Under cross-examination from Laurence Gruzman QC, Keith Martin admitted that he had not been consulted before Packer had launched the takeover bid. ACP's assistant managing director explained that the decision had not been made at a board meeting but during informal discussions between Packer, John Ratcliffe and Leslie Fielding. When Martin conceded that he was unaware of the details of a deal that could cost his company more than £2 million, Gruzman described ACP as a 'one-man band in which Sir Frank Packer was the whole show'.[49]

On 23 November Packer invited Cowper to dinner and pressed his case for representation on A&R's board. Two days later the A&R board put forward four alternative proposals (details of which have not survived) in an attempt to resolve the matter. But that night, at the very time Packer was purporting to negotiate with the board, he despatched Clyde to London to attempt to buy British shareholdings in A&R. On 29 November Sir Frank wrote to Cowper proposing that A&R's articles of association should be altered so that the board could consist of nine members instead of seven;

naturally, Packer wanted the two vacancies to be filled by his own nominees. As this was not one of the four options the parties had agreed to consider, it was rejected by the Cowper board.[50]

By early December the Sydney Stock Exchange, as well as A&R's board, was expressing concern that Consolidated Press Holdings was overlooking the 'takeover procedure' laid down by the Australian Associated Stock Exchanges. Meanwhile, Sir Frank was conducting a vitriolic campaign against A&R's directors and the supposedly dispassionate finance editor of the Telegraphs was calling the firms shares overpriced. The gentlemanly Cowper did not escape Packer's wrath, even though they had known each other personally and professionally for twenty years. On 3 December Packer went into print in the *Sunday Telegraph* to heatedly deny Cowper's allegations that Consolidated Press Holdings was offering differential prices for strategic parcels of shares in A&R. In a letter published in the *Telegraph* two days later, Cowper alleged that Sir Frank's 'henchmen' were visiting elderly ladies at night 'armed to the teeth with transfer forms, fountain pens and chequebooks'. Cowper said he was surprised that Packer had cast him in the role of a 'Reluctant Dragon':

> Now I have always seen him as the Dragon, shooting fire from his eyes and brimstone from his nostrils, bearing down upon the lovely and desirable Princess Ayandar and threatening to gobble her up.
>
> ... he is scratching and whining at the door, protesting that all he wants is a seat at her Board, swearing he is really a pleasant, kindly, well-intentioned and wise animal, and virtuously denying any designs on Grandma or her fortune; while she, the canny old dear, knows that once he gets inside the door it will be all over with her.[51]

Packer's standover tactics failed when Dr Colin Roderick, who was in charge of technical and educational publishing at A&R, implemented an ingenious share-splitting scheme. When the votes were tallied the night before the annual general meeting on 15 December, Packer knew he would not obtain majority control of the company. He did, however, secure a seat on the board.[52]

A few months later, Packer cabled from New York that he was planning to sell his shares to American interests. Whether he was really holding such talks is questionable; in any case, his announcement had the desired effect. The A&R board was alarmed, and a group of British publishers led by William Collins & Co. Ltd was prepared to pay above market price for Consolidated Press Holdings' shares in order to keep American publishers out of Australian publishing. As a result, Packer's company sold out of A&R for a tidy profit of £120 000. Ken Wilder, Collins's representative on the A&R board, had lunch with Cowper before attending his first board meeting. When Packer spotted the pair at the Hotel Australia, he walked over to Wilder and growled, 'I hope you and your colleagues in London are happy with your new toy. I thought you would like to know I have used the money to buy a most beautiful lady named *Gretel*'. He walked away laughing, very pleased with himself. In a grateful letter to Ian Collins, Cowper lamented the fact that the advent of Walter Burns had made A&R vulnerable to the activities of an 'irrational adventurer' like Packer.[53]

The margin of time for preparation for the America's Cup was narrowing alarmingly. Alan Payne was struck down with hepatitis and there was a shortage of designs for gear in the final stages. On 19 February 1962, just seven months before the challenge match was to be sailed, the Australian yacht *Gretel* was finally launched from Halvorsen's yard on the Parramatta River. She was towed to the Captain Cook dock at Garden Island, where her 28-metre aluminium mast was stepped-in under the supervision of navy engineers. The yacht was then towed to her moorings off the RSYS clubhouse, where she was rigged and fitted with her Dacron (synthetic) sails.[54]

The debut aroused intense interest amongst the sailing community and the general public, as the challenger's construction had been veiled in secrecy. What emerged was a yacht 69.42 feet long (21.1 metres), with overhangs of 8.40 feet (2.5 metres) forward and 11.08 feet (3.3 metres) aft, giving her a measured length of 50.20 feet (15.2 metres). She had flat stern sections and a rectangular rudder placed, unusually, in front of the counter. Yachting experts concluded that the 'beamy' hull design would make the yacht a better performer in strong winds than in light breezes.[55]

The naming ceremony took place at the RSYS landing stage on 28 February. Packer cagily decided to hold the launch at 5 p.m., too late for afternoon newspapers but in nice time for the *Telegraph*. Catholic and Protestant naval chaplains led brief prayers before the yacht was christened by Dame Pattie Menzies.[56] Packer's pivotal support in the recent federal election appears to have finally convinced the prime minister that the Menzies name should be associated with the challenge.

Sir Frank would later say that the yacht was called *Gretel* in honour of a 'very gracious' Australian. This was a grand and touching tribute to the woman who had swept him off his feet, borne his heirs, charmed his friends and entertained his business associates. A sense of guilt might have propelled Packer to name the yacht in memory of the woman who had endured his volatile temperament and his philandering for a quarter of a century. Packer made other efforts to memorialise his late wife. He commissioned William Dobell to paint a portrait of her based on old photographs, but was displeased with the result and destroyed the painting. Whenever Packer saw Sheila Lyle at a social function they would lift their glasses and, without needing to say a word, drink a toast to Gretel.[57]

After Dame Pattie named the America's Cup challenger, the governor-general and RSYS commodore, Lord de L'Isle, accompanied Packer down onto the pontoon. The 200 or so guests then watched as *Gretel*, *Vim* and a veteran schooner hoisted their sails and cruised to and fro in a gentle breeze and brilliant sunshine. 'A boat's a bit like a new bride', Packer was heard to say. 'You never really know how she'll perform until you get married.' Throughout March, April and the early part of May the two twelve-metre yachts were seen trialling and training on and around Sydney Harbour.[58]

Despite the appearance of tranquillity, things were not going so smoothly for Packer behind the scenes. In March he was part of a syndicate that made a £2 million share and cash offer for the Dairy Farmers' Co-operative Milk Co. Ltd. Members of the syndicate included W. J. Smith, a leading industrialist, and Major-General Sir Denzil Macarthur-Onslow, who mixed with Packer in polo circles and was a descendant of John Macarthur. They were forced to withdraw their bid when the New South Wales minister for co-operative societies announced he would do all he could to prevent the takeover of the historic milk co-operative.[59]

Packer was also confronted by a potential threat to the *Gretel* syndicate. On 11 April Harry S. Morgan, the America's Cup Committee chairman, reminded the RSYS that the deed of gift specified that challenging yachts must be designed and constructed in their own countries. Reports that the mast extrusions and steering gear for *Gretel* had been obtained in the United States had raised considerable comment there, Morgan claimed. It must have been with some alarm that Packer asked designer Alan Payne to provide him with a report on the components used in constructing the yacht. On a brief visit to New York in May, Packer gave Morgan a list of the components. The syndicate, he explained, had been compelled to import the extrusions because they were unavailable in Australia. However, they had been welded and taped in Australia and 'we have never considered that the word "constructed" should imply the exclusive use of home produced materials'. Morgan immediately wrote to Packer to reassure him that the America's Cup Committee was completely satisfied by this answer. Many journalists subsequently concluded that the NYYC had grown so secure in its possession of the cup that it quite overlooked the enormous potential advantages it was giving away. And the club might well have been prepared to make some concessions to the challenger in order to avoid a repeat of the embarrassing 1958 match.[60]

Packer spent his short time in New York staying at the Sheraton East Hotel and working out of ACP's office in 43rd Street. The main purpose of the trip was to finalise details for the challenge and to be guest of honour at the NYYC's America's Cup dinner on 17 May. At a press conference that afternoon, the fund of knowledge about the Australian challenger was not appreciably increased. Yachting journalists found Packer, eyes glinting behind heavy horn-rimmed glasses, a deft interviewee. He was amiable, quick with a quip and scarcely missed a puff on his curved meerschaum pipe as he talked down his syndicate's chances of taking out the cup. It was only later that journalists fully appreciated the significance of his aside: 'We might even change helmsmen during the final races'.[61]

Gretel and *Vim* were soon on their way to New York on the freighter *City of Sydney*. They arrived in New York on 14 July 1962, with just two months in hand for trials and training over the actual America's Cup course. Packer arranged for the Department of External Affairs and the Australian ambassador to the United States, Sir Howard Beale, to obtain customs-free entry and cruising licences for the two yachts.[62]

Packer was involved in a round of social engagements even before he left for the United States. On 19 June the Royal Suva Yacht Club, which must have had a particular interest in the challenge because of Packer's long association with the Fijian gold mines, presented him with a pennant and badge at ACP headquarters. A few days later Packer and the rest of *Gretel*'s squad were given a civic farewell at Sydney Town Hall. The City of Sydney officially bestowed its blue and gold flag, emblazoned with a traditional sailing ship, on the gleaming yacht, and the Australian-American Association also honoured the challenger with its flag. 'If we win', Packer warned, 'we will be the most elated people in the world and very hard to live with'.[63]

Newport is one of the principal tourist resorts in America's yachting capital and smallest state, Rhode Island. *Gretel* and most of her crew arrived there on 22 July. Applause and cheers followed the Australians through the streets of Newport to an official welcoming ceremony, which Packer described as 'stupendous', at Old Colony House. He rented the shingled Castle Hill Hotel on the cliff overlooking Rhode Island Sound to accommodate the crew until the America's Cup match was held in mid September. The rolling lawn outside the main entrance to the hotel was dotted with gifts from various firms, including a Land Rover, a station wagon, a delivery van, four convertibles and a speedboat, to be used by the Australians for the duration of the series.[64]

Bad luck dogged *Gretel* immediately after her arrival in the United States. On the first sailing day the fog was so thick that informal trials against *Vim* had to be called off. Two days later the aluminium boom almost broke apart, forcing *Gretel* to sail with a temporary wooden one while a new aluminium structure was fashioned in Massachusetts. Packer and his strategists were, however, able to keep a close eye on the observation trials that selected *Weatherly* as the American defender.[65]

Packer hired a cook and a chauffeur and imposed a strict 11 p.m. curfew on *Gretel*'s crew. The men, who had agreed not to talk publicly about the challenge until six months after the cup match, nicknamed Packer 'Big Daddy'. He was joined in Newport by a number of his friends, including Adrian Quist, Lennox Bode, Florence Vincent, Peter Reid, Sir Ian and Lady Potter and Peter and Edwina Baillieu. Resolving to return the sort of hospitality to which American multi-millionaires were accustomed, he threw the biggest parties of the social season, with Mrs Baillieu acting as hostess.[66]

The American yachting fraternity and the world's media became used to seeing this giant of a man lumbering around Newport dressed in his navy RSYS blazer and a jaunty white yachting cap. Observers began to detect what *Gretel*'s crew members already knew — that Packer could not leave well enough alone and continually made arbitrary decisions about the day-to-day running of the challenge. Packer tailed after *Gretel* and *Vim* in a tender, *Sara*, barking suggestions to the two crews — one dressed in black, the other in white — via walkie-talkie radio. Experimentation always takes place on any new yacht, but the number of changes made to *Gretel* was truly phenomenal. The layout of her cockpit was radically altered on her arrival in the United States; just two weeks before the races were due to begin, her mast was restepped 19½ inches (495 millimetres) forward to correct a weather helm; winches 'came and went like autumn leaves'. Alan Payne likened his task to digging an endless ditch through heavy clay: 'There was no end to it'.[67]

On 26 July Packer was guest of honour at a luncheon hosted by the American-Australian Association. Lord Casey, formerly Australia's minister for external affairs, Harry Morgan and other distinguished citizens and yachtsmen attended the function. In his address, Packer acknowledged that inexperience placed the Australian challengers at a considerable disadvantage:

> 'We think the boat is good and the crew is good and we sail well, but we are not too familiar with 12 metres or with match races.
> 'But if we lose we'll be back like [General Douglas] MacArthur — we'll be back.

'Win, lose, or draw, however, we hope we'll be as welcome as we are now.'

Packer also joked that the Australians were like an invading force: 'The natives are friendly at the moment — but later they may attack from the sea'.[68]

Unbeknown to Packer, native Australians were carping about his activities. In April he had suggested to the Department of External Affairs that the challenge should be used to focus attention on Australia in influential official and business circles in the United States. As his syndicate was spending more than £250 000 on the challenge, he felt that the government should be prepared to sponsor an Australian banquet in the United States and a photographic display about the challenge. Although the request was not unreasonable, officials in the departments of Trade and External Affairs initially resisted the idea. One bureaucrat feared that the proposal might be a 'raw ploy' and a 'crude sales effort'; another asked on 'what possible conceivable ground is this the concern of the Department of Trade' and sarcastically scrawled on a memo to a colleague 'Perhaps we are in the markets for exporting Gretels!'[69]

Given his volatile temper, it is perhaps just as well that Packer was blissfully unaware of these private expressions of dissent. However, he responded quickly when he learned government departments were concerned that Australian companies who had offered to sponsor the banquet might commercialise the event. Even though Lindemans and Penfolds had agreed to supply 500 cases of wine, Packer said that 'Australia' would simply be advertised as the source of the wine. This did not stop political enemies from attacking plans for the dinner, which was to be held on 14 September, the night before the first race of the series. The dinner was to be hosted by Howard Beale at 'The Breakers', the former Vanderbilt mansion which he had leased for the duration of the contest.[70]

A keen yachtsman, President Kennedy had seen every America's Cup series since 1934. On 11 September the crews of *Gretel* and *Weatherly* were entertained at the Newport home of Jacqueline Kennedy's stepfather, Hugh Auchincloss, where she and Packer reportedly enjoyed a long, animated conversation. Just hours before the lavish banquet on 14 September, Packer inadvertently sparked yet another controversy. A reporter from Associated Press bailed him up at the Port O' Call marina to ask whether he thought *Weatherly* could win four of the seven races straight. When Packer replied, 'I suppose she could', this was written up as a prediction that he tipped four straight wins to the Americans. Packer responded to the reports by saying that *Gretel* had a 'very good chance' of bringing the America's Cup back to Australia, although he again emphasised that the Americans had much more experience. He was also forced to deny reports that the Australian crew was dispirited.[71] Morale was indeed low: Packer refused to announce the make-up of the crew until just before the race, only naming the skipper, Jock Sturrock, at the 'death knock'. Then Packer suddenly replaced the crack navigator, Terry Hammond, with another crew member. But even though Packer was convinced that the odds were stacked against the Australians, the punter in him could not resist laying $22 500 on *Gretel* at 5–4 odds.[72]

A huge fleet of spectator craft delayed by an hour the start of the first race on Saturday. The coastguard desperately tried to herd back the fleet of about 3500 craft, which included President Kennedy in a destroyer. The hopes of Australian spectators were raised when Sturrock momentarily outmanoeuvred his American counterpart, Emil ('Bus') Mosbacher, at the start of the triangular 24-mile course. However, the race was at least partially lost by the Australians when the novice navigator held *Gretel* on the wrong tack for two minutes. Mosbacher won by 3 minutes, 46 seconds; for Packer and his crew, the result was disappointing but by no means disgraceful.[73]

Jacqueline Kennedy sent Packer the president's flag from the destroyer he had sailed on that day: 'It comes with the deepest admiration for the spirit and sportsmanship of you and your countrymen. The race is still on as I write this — so I say to you Good Luck'. Delighted by the gift, Packer framed and hung the flag in the billiard room at 'Cairnton' on his return to Sydney. Other members of the exclusive American yachting fraternity, however, were not so gracious after the first race. A journalist in the *Boston Herald* ridiculed the Australian challengers for using a very fractured version of the English language, suggesting that Australian newspapers might tell their readers of *Gretel*'s preliminary defeat in these terms: 'Instead of a bottler, Gretel's first race turned out to be a blue duck. All of which makes it tougher to capture the pickled biscuit'. In an article for another Boston newspaper George O'Day, the technical adviser to *Weatherly*, accused Packer of interfering with his crew:

> When he called tacks for either *Gretel* or *Vim* they tacked regardless of whether or not they would run ashore or run into one another.
>
> ...
>
> The skipper cannot be told over a walkie-talkie how to handle the boat or what to do. This just doesn't work.
>
> ...
>
> Sir Frank has given confidence to no-one and is running the show himself.

Packer tried to maintain a dignified silence, refusing to comment on O'Day's remarks. When told that O'Day had described the Australians as 'novice skiers following in the tracks of a professional', Packer publicly stated, 'I don't believe he ever said it'.[74]

Exercising their right to a day off, the Australians used the Sunday and the Monday to repair the damage to *Gretel*'s backstay in the first race. Hammond was reinstated as navigator and a new sail was installed. The strong westerly wind suited *Gretel* during the race on Tuesday 18 September. On the final leg, she found a private wave, mounted it and literally surfed past the luckless defender, which ran into trouble with her spinnaker. The Australian crew whooped with joy as *Gretel* surged over the finish line forty-five seconds ahead of *Weatherly*. After the race, so great was the crowd around *Gretel* that the pontoon where she was berthed began to sink, obliging the photographers and reporters to carry on with their work ankle-deep in water. That night yachtsmen from the two nations surrounded Packer at the Cameo Bar near where *Gretel* was docked. The Australian contingent sang 'Waltzing Matilda' and their unofficial theme song, 'Beer is Best'.[75]

Gretel had broken the course record and the win made Australia the first challenger since 1934 to beat an American defender. Reports of the stunning upset made front-page news around the world. Packer's own newspaper smugly headlined its report 'The critics eat humble pie'. Footage of the race was rushed by chartered aeroplane to New York and then back to Sydney for TCN-9 viewers. Menzies, who was attending the Commonwealth Prime Ministers' Conference in London, issued a statement saying that he was 'very pleased' with the win. Federal cabinet sent Sturrock a cable congratulating him and his crew on their 'magnificent performance'.[76]

By now, however, Packer had made a major tactical error. Without consulting Sturrock or the crew, he called for another lay day so Payne could make minor repairs to *Gretel*. This meant that the Australian could not take advantage of their psychological edge, and the yacht lay idle through a day of strong winds — her favourite conditions. When the third race was held on Thursday 20 September, *Gretel* suffered one of the most frustrating experiences that can befall a yacht. She ran out of wind and lay almost becalmed at a crucial stage in the race. At one point *Gretel* was a disastrous twenty-four minutes behind *Weatherly*, but she picked up speed in the third and fourth legs and lost by 8 minutes, 40 seconds. Determined to make the best of every day legally available to them under cup rules, the Australians asked for another lay day before the next race. This again gave them the Sunday and the Monday to reconsider their techniques and wait for stronger winds.[77]

The fourth race was a heart-stopper. Although *Gretel* closed in on her opponent in the final leg of the race, *Weatherly* held on to win by twenty-six seconds — the narrowest margin in America's Cup history. Some Australians, believing that *Gretel* was just beginning to find her form, approached their bookmakers armed with cash. But Packer knew that the chances of winning three straight races from the Americans were slim. The *Telegraph* declared that, even though Australia had proved that she had the boat designers, the builders and the yachtsmen to win the cup, victory would probably not come 'this year'.[78]

On the morning of the fifth race on 25 September, Packer conferred with Sturrock for twenty minutes in the cockpit. *Gretel* lost the race by 3 minutes, 40 seconds, dashing Australia's hopes of taking home the America's Cup. The crew members of *Weatherly* joined their tired and wet Australian counterparts at the Cameo Bar after the race. Packer, Sturrock, Mosbacher, *Weatherly*'s owner, Henry Mercer, and H. Irving Pratt, the NYYC's commodore, held a press conference later that night. After thanking the Americans for their hospitality, Packer announced: 'You were too damn good. We'll probably be back. And whether we lost or not, the sun will come up tomorrow just the same'.[79]

And so the 1962 challenge for the America's Cup ended in apparent good humour, with gracious cables of thanks and hearty congratulations circulating between the RSYS, the NYYC, Packer, Pratt and Kennedy.[80] Packer argued, and most observers agreed, that *Gretel* had not had 'quite enough time to be ready'. While American and British syndicates had spent decades designing, building, tuning and training earlier challengers, the Australians had contested a series a mere three years after first countenancing the idea. Packer had marshalled his company's money and staff to propel Australia into the world of twelve-metre yachting. But, in the final months of the 1962 challenge, Packer's persistent meddling had damaged his team's chances of winning the cup. The respected American yachting journalist Norris Hoyt concluded that Packer's 'bluster and brass was a stalking horse for a mind as devious and sly as a barrel of snakes'.[81]

The young family: Gretel and Frank Packer with Clyde and Kerry, c. 1939. (Lady Stening)

Clyde Packer, Nedra Levy, Anthony Vincent and Elspeth Vincent sunbathing at Palm Beach, 1941. Many years later, Frank Packer was to marry Elspeth Vincent's sister-in-law, Florence. (*Home*, 1 March 1941, p. 5)

Lieutenant Frank Packer and bookmaker Peter Cruise at the races, 1942.
(*Truth*, 11 October 1942, p. 12)

Pictured (*from left*) at the Consolidated Press Youth Club Dance at the Australia Hotel, August 1945: R. H. King, Frank Packer, Miss G. Hyland, 'Fairy' Faircloth, Colonel R. J. A. Travers and E. W. MacAlpine. (*Telegus*, 10 September 1945, p. 4)

E. G. Theodore, co-founder of Consolidated Press, c. 1946. (Myra Rowbotham)

Smiles of victory after Columnist wins the Caulfield Cup, 1947. *From left*: Frank Packer, jockey Harold Badger, trainer Maurice McCarten, Victorian Amateur Turf Club chairman Norman Robinson, and the governor-general, William McKell. (State Library of Victoria: *Sporting Globe*, 18 October 1947, p. 1)

Frank Packer greets Queen Elizabeth II on her visit to Australia, 1954. (*Life International*, 30 July 1962, p. 45)

Sybil Connolly, 1954. (*Australian Women's Weekly*, 25 August 1954, p. 12)

The Lord Mayor, Harry Jensen (left), hosts a civic farewell for Sir Frank Packer and the crew of *Gretel* at Sydney Town Hall, June 1962. (State Library of New South Wales)

Sir Frank Packer being welcomed to Newport, Rhode Island, by Henry C. Wilkinson, July 1962. (*Providence Journal* photos)

Sir Frank Packer takes the helm of *Gretel*, 1962. (Warren Clarke: *Life International*, 30 July 1962, p. 43).

Sir Frank Packer watches as a *Gretel* crewman carries a broken boom after an accident in training off Newport, September 1962. (Bettman/Corbis: *New York Times*, 12 September 1962)

Frank Packer's future wife, Florence Porgés, surrounded by suitors in Paris, 1935. (Condé Nast Publications: *Vogue*, New York, 1 May 1935, p. 57)

Sir Frank and the new Lady Packer shortly after their marriage, June 1964. (State Library of Victoria: Melbourne *Herald*, 16 June 1964, p. 26)

One of the last photographs of Sir Frank Packer. (*Worker's News*, 9 May 1974, p. 3)

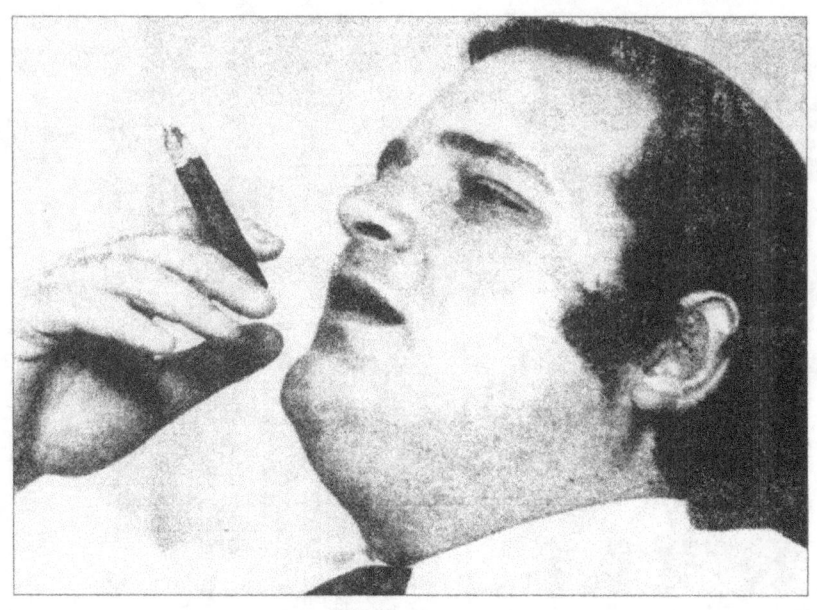

Clyde Packer giving his sensational interview to the *Australian* about life in the Packer empire.
(*Australian*, 8 November 1973, p. 1)

Kerry Packer at the helm of Australian Consolidated Press, 1977.
(*National Times*, 21–28 May 1977, p. 4)

13
Toasting Victory

Packer's unsuccessful but impressive bid for the America's Cup boosted his profile at home and abroad. Shortly after the challenge, the Melbourne *Herald* ran a full-page article about him in response to the question: 'Who is this man Frank Packer?' A few months later, Packer was guest of honour at an exclusive dinner hosted by the Reuters chairman, John Burgess, at the Dorchester Hotel in London.[1]

Easter was an important time for Sydney socialites and their country cousins. During the Royal Easter Show, crowds of graziers and horse breeders assembled in Sydney, dances and weddings dotted the calendar, mothers rescued children from boarding school for a few days and husbands and fathers retreated in heavy tweed to the Members' Bar at the Showground.[2] Packer had been involved with the Easter Show since he was a young man. In the late 1920s he had become so frustrated with the way a stall was being run that he had impetuously taken it over; in the 1930s and 1940s he and Jim MacLeod had entered polo ponies in competitions; as a child, Kerry Packer had participated in boys' riding contests; and in the 1950s and 1960s Sir Frank served as the timekeeper during the annual *Daily Telegraph* Polo Cup. The *Telegraph*s and the *Bulletin* also sponsored a range of sporting and novelty competitions, and the *Telegraph* held its Homes Exhibition at the Showground.[3]

In 1963 MacLeod successfully nominated Packer for a vacancy on the council of the Royal Agricultural Society of New South Wales, which organised the show. Almost immediately Packer joined the printing and advertising committee and the polo subcommittee. He arranged for the *Women's Weekly* and the *Telegraph*s to feature supplements and full-page advertisements about the show and for TCN-9 to tape segments from it. While the council would have been delighted by this free publicity, Packer was astute enough to realise that this material consolidated his outlets' appeal to families and to advertisers that exhibited at the show. He was also aware of the popularity of sporting broadcasts, making provisions for television stations to bid for the rights to cover football matches and other sporting events held at the Showground.[4]

In 1961 the *Daily Telegraph* had begun sponsoring the Doncaster Handicap, while the *Sunday Telegraph* had backed the Invitation Stakes. But still Packer's bid to join the AJC committee failed, for the second time, later that year. It was not until 1963 that he was accepted into the exclusive ranks of the AJC. He got great enjoyment, mixed with exasperation, out of this association. Packer thought most committee members were utter fools in the financial sense, and he would return to work after their Friday meetings spluttering with rage or throwing his hands into the air in disbelief.[5]

Packer was more than willing to defend the interests of his staff members if they came into conflict with the AJC. Mike Gibson, a *Telegraph* sports journalist, recalled the time he was cited to appear before the committee after being accused of writing an article that reflected unfairly on the AJC. Packer hardly knew Gibson, and as they drove to the AJC meeting in an air-conditioned limousine, a colleague had to remind Packer that Gibson was the young bloke who had come to the *Telegraph* 'from the university'. (Gibson had, in fact, come to Packer from the *Daily Mirror*.) When the chairman and other members of the committee began dressing down Gibson, Packer rose to his feet, put his arm around the journalist's shoulder and began a powerful oration: 'Gentlemen, I've known this young bloke, man and boy, since the day he first walked into my office from the university, and I want to tell you he's a straight-shooter — he wouldn't tell a lie'. The pair scored a runaway victory, with Gibson free to continue reporting on AJC race meetings.[6]

Even though Packer regarded some members of the committee as fools, before long he was appointed the AJC's representative on the board of the Totalizer Agency Board (TAB). In the early 1960s he also served on the board of the Royal Blind Society of New South Wales's 'Project 2000' appeal and in 1965 he was elected to the society's council. In 1967 he added an Order of St John to his list of honours.[7]

But despite his growing links with Australia's sporting and social élites, Packer still attracted and often courted controversy. To the dismay of various lobby groups, the 1954 royal commission into television had made no specific recommendations about the percentage of Australian-made material to be broadcast. In 1963 a Senate Select Committee looked into ways of encouraging Australian television production. Called to give evidence on 1 April, Packer vigorously rejected the implementation of a quota. It was 'economically impossible', he argued, for local producers to produce anything world-class at a price within the Australian advertiser's budget.[8]

At the same time, the successful applicants for the third commercial television licences in Sydney and Melbourne were announced. On 18 April Arthur Calwell told parliament that Austarama Television Pty Ltd, a subsidiary of the powerful Ansett Transport Industries Ltd, was planning to sell to another company the licence it had just been awarded in Melbourne. Even though this was only a rumour, Calwell seized the opportunity to propose a censure motion criticising the government for its handling of television policy. He declared that any system allowing companies like those headed by Packer and (later Sir) Reginald Ansett to traffic in television licences was flawed. Les Haylen opined that all Packer believed in was money-grubbing on television — 'letting the public go to hell, and making them take what he thinks they should have'. In the next day's *Telegraph*, Packer pointed out that his company had only been awarded one television licence by the ABCB and that its interest in GTV-9 had been secured through hard cash rather than by government favour. He also noted that 'Mr Calwell's personal publication', the *Sydney Morning Herald*, was itself a major shareholder in two licences, one in Sydney and the other in Brisbane. The *Telegraph* published a statement from Ansett strenuously denying that he planned to dispose of the new television licence and declaring that Calwell was 'crazy' and needed to see a doctor.⁹

Peter Viska's cartoon brilliantly captures Sir Frank Packer's eclectic interests. (*Weekend Business Review*, 19 September 1970, p. 11, by permission of Peter Viska and the National Library of Australia)

It was just as well that Packer's political enemies were unaware of the fancy footwork that was taking place in the Sydney television market. On learning that his bid for the Sydney licence had been unsuccessful, Rupert Murdoch bought a controlling interest in the Wollongong station WIN-4. By this time Packer's TCN-9 and Fairfax's ATN-7 had already joined forces to deny WIN-4 and the Newcastle station NBN-3 access to imported programs. Murdoch flew to the United States, bought up £1 million worth of programs and announced his intention of transmitting into Sydney from WIN–4. Alarmed by the prospect of the aggressive young Murdoch invading the Sydney television market, Packer brokered an ingenious compromise in June 1963. He sold News Ltd a 25 per cent interest in Television Corporation and two seats on the board in return for an agreement not to transmit from WIN–4 into Sydney. Packer had protected his television station from new competition in the short term, but he remained painfully aware that Consolidated Press Holdings, which owned only 35 per cent of Television Corporation, was vulnerable to a hostile takeover.[10]

A few months later Packer felt obliged to demonstrate a sense of the new partnership by inviting Murdoch to a Television Corporation board meeting. It had been called to consider Colin Bednall's proposal that TCN-9 and GTV-9 should secure the only two lines available for television on the new coaxial link between Sydney, Canberra and Melbourne. Bednall realised that this would ensure that Channel Nine became Australia's first truly national commercial television network. Believing the cost would be prohibitive, Packer called the meeting in Sydney to 'discuss the matter'. When Sir Frank ordered all those not in favour of allowing Bednall to spend so much money to raise their hands, the Sydney executives dutifully did so. Those at the meeting included Clyde and Kerry, who had recently followed a Packer family tradition by marrying a doctor's daughter, Rosalind Weedon. Murdoch, however, remained motionless during the vote. Swallowing noisily, Sir Frank invited Murdoch to express his opinion. In the end, the views of Murdoch and Bednall prevailed and the coaxial cable was leased for two years. Murdoch was not invited to any further board meetings.[11]

In 1964 Packer and Reg Ansett compounded the government's embarrassment about the increasing concentration of television ownership. After his application for the new Brisbane licence was passed over, Ansett made a nonsense of the ACB hearings. He and Packer joined together to buy up almost all the shares in the successful applicant company, Universal Telecasters Queensland Ltd. On 4 April, as business and political pundits speculated about the identity of the secret buyer, Packer brazenly went public in the *Telegraph*:

> I bought the Brisbane shares, but unfortunately, owing to some slip-ups by my team of skilled operatives, under the generalship of Sir Ian Potter, I got only 600,000 of the 800,000 traded.
>
> Potter will hear from me about that leakage of 200,000.
>
> I have not yet decided what to do with these shares.
>
> My present inclination is to raffle them. They are a lot cheaper than the last TV shares I bought, which cost my company £6 a time.
>
> … I refuse to reveal how my Brisbane coup was planned. This is something for the PMG [postmaster general] to find out for himself.[12]

In parliament two Labor politicians, Fred Daly and Senator James McClelland, referred to this 'strange confession' and asked the attorney-general to consider prosecuting Packer for conspiracy in trafficking in television company shares.[13] No action was taken against Packer or Ansett.

In 1960 the Broadcasting and Television Act had been amended to define ownership as the ability to control more than 15 per cent of the voting rights of a television company. The brilliance of Packer and Ansett's strategy lay in the fact that the articles of association of Universal Telecasters limited any shareholder, no matter how large his interest, to 15 per cent of the voting rights. Sir Albert Hulme, the postmaster-general, talked forlornly of the assaults of 'shrewd businessmen and lawyers' on the Broadcasting and Television Act. Later that year, after Fairfax had stymied Packer's bid for a major interest in radio 2GB and a Canberra television station, the act was again amended. The loophole in the 15 per cent clause was overcome, but the changes were not made retrospective and actually served to consolidate the holdings of companies that already had major television interests.[14]

Packer's media outlets continued to offer editorial and financial support to the Liberal and Country parties. In March 1963, on Alan Reid's initiative, the *Telegraph* photographed Calwell and his deputy, Gough Whitlam, waiting in a Canberra street while the ALP's national executive deliberated on an issue of defence policy. The resulting images, accompanied by Reid's story, led to Menzies' damaging quip about the '36 faceless men' who ran the ALP. Ongoing dissension within the ALP, an improving economy and Menzies' promise of state aid to Catholic schools saw the coalition comfortably returned to office at the November election.[15]

Rupert Henderson, mindful of his newspaper's stance only two years earlier, believed that the *Sydney Morning Herald* should offer detached criticism of both Labor and the coalition during the campaign. But a week before the poll, Warwick Fairfax ordered the *Sydney Morning Herald* to come out in support of the coalition. Satisfied that the economy was more or less back to normal, Sir Warwick felt that Menzies would follow a safer and more pro-American line than Labor in relation to developments in south-east Asia. When thanking Packer for the 'tremendous loyalty and enthusiastic help' his television stations had given the coalition during the campaign, Menzies credited him with converting the *Sydney Morning Herald* to the conservative cause. Packer, delighted by both the election result and the prime minister's gratitude, replied: 'This change was probably brought about more by your own masculine Beau Brummel charm in quarters which should not have influence but down through history have proved a force to be reckoned with'.[16]

Clyde Packer provided a direct link between his father, Menzies and the New South Wales division of the Liberal Party. In 1963 Clyde obtained preselection for the Legislative Council. Labor's Thomas P. Murphy was moved to ask sarcastically whether this was an 'extension of reward for services rendered, as indicated by the knighthood bestowed on Sir Frank Packer'.[17] Clyde maintained his executive positions within the family empire when he took his seat in the Upper House in April 1964. It was around this time that Sir Frank also approached Menzies to offer his services in some sort of political or diplomatic post. Packer said that he was looking for a change after twenty-eight years of managing the *Telegraph*; he wanted to move into a field where there was an opportunity to do something 'creative', and he would like to put his sons in control of his media empire and 'see how they go'.

In an unprecedented burst of self-analysis, Packer made a list of his 'pluses' and 'minuses' for Menzies. The attributes he listed emphasised his practical achievements and networks of influence rather than any personal or intrinsic strengths: he had a high profile in the United States as a result of the America's Cup challenge, connections with television networks, cable services and financiers in New York and London, and 'sufficient private means to entertain and no need to worry about future or saving'. Despite claiming that he got along well with staff 'as a rule' and could 'take advice', Packer acknowledged that he was more used to giving than obeying orders. His other weaknesses were that he was not a good speaker ('can get by by work and preparation in advance'), his sense of humour was often misunderstood and he would attract criticism from Labor politicians.[18]

Menzies must have known that appointing Packer to an official position would indeed provoke widespread condemnation. At the same time, he was anxious not to alienate the powerful media proprietor. By the end of May he had gently persuaded Packer that, 'for a variety of reasons', it was not possible to accept his offer. Packer appears to have been mollified by Menzies' diplomatic handling of the situation, thanking the prime minister for his 'very nice' and 'softly phrased' response. It is surely no coincidence that it was at this very time that Menzies agreed to help the twenty-nine-year-old son of his most loyal media supporter with his maiden speech. Sir Frank told Menzies that the fact he had bothered to meet with Clyde had 'given him a big lift', and Packer junior was suitably grateful that the prime minister had found the time to speak to a 'nervous young tiger'.[19]

Privately, however, Sir Frank remained restless. Although he had had romantic liaisons since Gretel's death, he liked to do the chasing and he hated to feel crowded and pressured by women. Ita Buttrose, who edited the women's pages of the *Women's Weekly* and the *Telegraph*s in the 1960s, has recalled that her employer had conservative views about how women should look and behave. Packer often commented on how nice she looked, especially if she was wearing a demure pleated skirt and twinset, was always polite to her and never used bad language in her presence.[20]

In the early 1960s Packer had an affair with Sheila Scotter, who remained a friend for the rest of his life. Born in India to English parents, Scotter edited the Australian and New Zealand editions of the fashion bible *Vogue*. She wrote of her 'romantic flirtation': 'Frank was a great courtier of women; he made sure everything was right, picked you up, the chauffeur would come ...'[21]

Even so, outrageous stories circulated about Packer's womanising. An Australian expatriate told Colin Bednall, who was holidaying at a fishing village in Tuscany, that late one night after a staff party Packer offered a female employee a lift home. According to this tale, when the woman got in the car Packer propositioned her quite insistently until she finally said that sleeping with him would be out of the question unless he 'took precautions'. Packer drove to a suburban pharmacy and hammered at the door, bringing the chemist from his bed. When Packer explained what he wanted, the chemist refused to serve him. The story ends with Packer seeing on the shop counter a jar of white jellybeans, grabbing a handful of the lollies and walking out saying, 'These look the part. They'll do me'.[22]

But Packer was now often simply content to invite old friends and colleagues to accompany him to social functions. Fairy Faircloth recalled one memorable occasion when Packer took her to see a show at the Palace Theatre. His eyesight was now so poor that they had to sit in the front stalls, where he puffed on his pipe all through the first half of the show. When Faircloth dressed him down, Packer decided not to stay past interval. It was just as well that Faircloth was used to her employer's ribbings and hair-raising pranks:

> We were walking out in the foyer. I had on a dress with a zip down the back, and he suddenly whizzed it down.
>
> There was a poor old bald-headed fellow near us — we'd never seen him in our lives — and Sir Frank abused him, and said, 'How dare you treat a lady like that!'[23]

In 1964 an old family friend, Florence Adeline Vincent, noting the team of ladies pursuing Packer, decided to leave Australia. On 26 May Packer was granted leave of absence from the Royal Agricultural Society to go overseas. He followed Florence to London, where they married in a small private ceremony a few weeks later.[24] The new Lady Packer was the daughter of a wealthy Russian businessman, Edmond Porgés, who had served as a major in the First World War, and his French wife Marcela. Born in Paris in 1915,[25] Florence maintained that her connections stretched 'from the ghetto to the Vatican'. When she made her debut in 1935, the New York edition of *Vogue* described her as 'already a great beauty ... quite blindingly so'. As the magazine noted, Parisian debutantes regarded a good marriage as their high purpose in life. In 1937 Florence married Robert Wigram Crawford at a ceremony attended by members of the English, French and Russian aristocracy.[26] It is unclear whether the elusive Crawford died or whether he divorced the young, petite brunette.

By the Second World War Florence was in London working for the Free French (La France Combattante) movement, formed by General Charles de Gaulle in defiance of Marshal Pétain's surrender to Germany.[27] In London she met Noel Vincent, a handsome Australian grazier who was serving with the RAAF. The Vincent and Packer families mixed in the same social circles and young Clyde and Kerry Packer often played with Noel's nephew Anthony. Noel Vincent introduced Florence to his friend Frank Packer when all three were in London in 1945. After marrying in New York in 1946, Florence and Noel returned to his showplace property at Exeter in the Southern Highlands of New South Wales.[28]

The couple also kept a flat in Elizabeth Street, and Sydney's social pages were soon reporting on the activities of the glamorous and sophisticated newcomer in their midst. Readers were told about the clothes Mrs Vincent bought during her overseas trips and informed when her mother sent her ball gowns from Paris. Florence compered the 1948 Christian Dior fashion parades at David Jones in a sexy French accent, attended Australian-American Association functions, helped decorate the Trocadero for the Black and White Balls, and routinely appeared on lists of Sydney's best-dressed women.[29]

But in 1958 Mrs Vincent's good fortune caused some observers to privately gasp in astonishment and indignation. On 9 November the *Sunday Telegraph* announced that she and Arthur Browning had shared the £30 000 prize in the last 'Teleword' competition. The front page featured a photograph of the ecstatic pair at Prince's toasting their win. What ACP employees knew, and readers did not, was that Florence was friendly with both Gretel and Frank Packer and that Browning was Packer's bookmaker.[30]

Florence and Noel Vincent, now a prominent company director, were divorced in 1961. Florence was in Newport the following year when Packer challenged for the America's Cup.[31] The couple married at the Caxton Hall registry office in London on 15 June 1964. Florence's cousin, Count Foy, and Jim MacLeod acted as witnesses. Jack Cassidy sent his friend a ribald cable: 'Good on you, Frank. You can take Vincent's with confidence'.[32] He could have added that Packer would now get £15 000 of his own money back.

Packer's second marriage aroused interest and some amusement in newspaper circles. In a letter to Lloyd Dumas on 19 June John Burgess wrote: 'The excitement of the past week was Frank Packer's wedding to Mrs Vincent. He was in very good form and his usual amusing self'. While in London for the wedding ceremony Frank and Florence stayed at the Savoy Hotel. They then moved on to the Sheraton East Hotel in New York.[33]

By early August Packer was back in Sydney negotiating with ACP's chapel about the dismissal of two members and complaining about increased licence fees for commercial television stations. He had spent little more than two months of a planned six months overseas. Packer hated going on holiday, and he was never able to understand why his executives who applied for leave could not be as happy as he was, day after day, sitting behind one of his beloved desks issuing orders.[34]

Packer had always been troubled by poor eyesight and susceptible to chest complaints, and the relentless pace at which he pursued his business, sporting and even social endeavours took their toll. In August 1964 he was hospitalised with a severe attack of influenza. Although he had many genuine health problems, he became something of a hypochondriac as the years passed. He would insist on trying any new pill that came on the market, usually doubling the recommended dosage in an effort to accelerate his recovery. The sort of doctor Packer liked was Frank Ritchie. He did not believe in fussy extremes of advice, counselling against too many martinis but not barring them entirely.[35]

Packer's eyesight became so bad that Florence had to describe what was happening when he watched television. Although he wore thick dark glasses most of the time, he sometimes used contact lenses. Dr George Stening recalls that his brother-in-law developed a way of putting in the lenses quickly that must have been very painful. In early January 1965 Packer visited Melbourne to consult an eye specialist.[36] By the end of the month he was in London to receive further specialist treatment from an ophthalmologist.

During their stay in London, Frank and Florence were invited to attend a small dinner party hosted by John Burgess. Sir William Slim and his wife were to attend the dinner at the Garrick Club, established in the 1830s as a dining, smoking and meeting venue for actors, artists and writers. Before the dinner, Burgess sent a guest list to one of the other guests, Major-General T. H. Birbeck from the War Office. After detailing his business and sporting credentials, the list concluded that Packer was 'a tough'.[37]

It was not just members of the London establishment who privately looked askance at Packer. There was no love lost between ACP's management and the writer Patrick White, a member of a wealthy pastoral family. David McNicoll, who had briefly courted White's younger sister, promoted the verdict of Sydney society that it was ludicrous for a grazier's offspring to live and work as he did. White was understandably angered when the *Telegraph*s assigned their humorous journalists, rather than their serious critics, to pan his novels and mock his plays. The newspapers, which in the days of Brian Penton and Cyril Pearl had fostered Australian literature, encouraged scientific endeavour, supported modern art and musical concerts, and deplored literary censorship, were becoming increasingly anti-intellectual. In October 1965 White encountered Packer — whom he had previously dubbed 'a toad' — at a state dinner for Lord and Lady Casey. In a letter to the writer and publisher Geoffrey Dutton, White wrote:

> Lady P. was all smiles and diamonds ... Have you ever seen Packer Himself? There is a putrid carcase for you. If I were Lady P. I'd hold out for a whole lot more diamonds.[38]

Packer continued to enjoy a complex and ambivalent relationship with the establishment. Members of social and business elites in Australia and overseas regarded him as brash, vulgar and very much 'new money'. But as the years passed, Packer became less inclined to flaunt the establishment. He served on the boards of Sydney's premier charitable and sporting organisations, propped up the Liberal Party and was increasingly drawn to traditional institutions like the *Bulletin* and A&R.

After joining the *Bulletin* in 1933, the historian and biographer M. H. Ellis had refined his hard-hitting journalistic style and disseminated anti-communist propaganda. Even though many old hands left the *Bulletin* on its sale to Packer, Ellis managed to hold on for five years. When Ellis retired in 1965 the magazine's editor, Peter Coleman, arranged a farewell dinner at the old baroque Belvedere Hotel in King's Cross. The guests were told that Sir Frank was not able to come, so Clyde presided over the dinner. Kerry whiled away the time by organising a sweep on how long the guest of honour would speak. Coleman, McNicoll and Donald Horne, who was now editing *Everybody's* while working at the Jackson, Wain and Co. advertising agency, all paid tribute to Ellis.[39]

As Ellis was replying, guests noticed that Sir Frank was sitting outside listening and smiling with curled lips. A seat was quickly found and Packer lumbered in, obviously under the weather, and lit his cigar while his supplicants brushed the ash from his clothes. When Ellis finished speaking, Coleman asked if Packer would like to say a few words. Packer explained that he had spent the day having treatment for a chest complaint; the same thing had been tried on one of his horses and worked well, he said, so it might just work for him. Preliminaries over, he quietly and proudly sketched the history of Australian journalism as a Packer family story. He talked about the role that his father had played in establishing *Smith's Weekly* and the *Daily Guardian* and his own success with the *Women's Weekly*, the *Telegraph*s and Channel Nine, and indicated that his sons would do a thing or two. 'And now', he said, 'we have the *Bulletin*'.

Then Packer suddenly turned on the seventy-five-year-old guest of honour, berating Ellis for 'bad-mouthing' R. C. Packer. During the fight for control of Associated Newspapers in 1953, the *Bulletin* had published an article detailing how the Packers had made their money in the 1920s and 1930s, accusing Frank of employing 'distressing' and 'strong-arm' methods and concluding that it would be preferable for Fairfax to take over the company. Although the article had been most critical of his own actions, what infuriated Packer was that it had dared to call into question the business tactics of the father he so revered. Packer and Ellis became engaged in a slanging match, with the journalist claiming that someone else had written the article and Packer thumping the table and yelling, 'It was *you*!' The party broke up in confusion, with Coleman leading the embattled guest of honour outside to a taxi.[40]

Ellis was not the only man to leave Packer's stable during this period. Since taking control of GTV-9, Packer had been complaining that Colin Bednall spent 'money like water'. Packer despatched memos to Bednall showing that GTV-9 expended much more on wages, meals, travelling, entertainment, security guards, telephone bills and stationery than did TCN-9. Although Packer was a penny-pincher when it came to the mundane operations of his media outlets, he was not the only person to notice that Bednall was inclined to spend lavishly; Keith Murdoch, Arthur Warner and Robert Menzies had also passed similar comments over the years.[41] The enormous salary Bednall paid to GTV-9's star attraction, Graham Kennedy, particularly horrified Packer. Every two years or so, Bednall would have to endure the trauma of fighting to keep the comedian and getting him more money.

Bednall might have delivered results in terms of ratings and advertising revenue but his personal relationship with his employer was uneasy. Before lunch each day Packer invited some of his executives to join him for martinis, which he described as 'mallets'. The drinks, mixed by Packer or Fairy Faircloth, were lethal, the mixture being anything from eight or ten to one. In the musty anteroom where Packer pressed the martinis on his chief lieutenants, Bednall once unwittingly made them all choke when he cracked a joke at their employer's expense.[42]

The 'rare intellectual pleasure' of working with Clyde Packer was not enough to make Bednall's working environment tolerable. He resigned in 1965 and was forced to sign an agreement that he would not manage another television station within eighty kilometres of Melbourne for two years. Just a few weeks after leaving GTV-9, Bednall received a letter from a former colleague saying that although Packer was not well, 'he still transmits all frequencies into the station's headquarters in Bendigo Street'.[43]

Packer's editors and executives did not need to be on his payroll for long before learning of his prejudices. Bednall had endured more than complaints about his extravagance and his programming decisions. Aggressively masculine, Packer had a phobia about homosexuals and insisted that he could pick one a mile off. Convinced that Graham Kennedy was homosexual, he would bring Bednall off the beach during his family holidays to scream, 'Get rid of him!'[44] Packer also supported capital punishment. In February 1967 he pulped an entire issue of the *Bulletin* that featured an editorial and cartoon criticising the Victorian Liberal premier, Sir Henry Bolte, for allowing the hanging of Ronald Ryan to proceed.[45]

Packer refused to condemn apartheid. In 1963 he was invited to sponsor the Australian branch of the Southern Africa Defence and Aid Fund, formed by leading church and business figures to raise money for the legal defence of victims of South Africa's apartheid regime. Packer rejected the invitation, arguing that Australians had no right to interfere in the affairs of another country. He claimed, further, that Australians who opposed apartheid would have an 'entirely different view' if they lived in a country with twenty or thirty million black people and eleven million white people. Three years later, Packer apparently had a meeting with a public relations consultant who had been retained by the Rhodesian government to improve the white supremacist regime's image in Australia.[46]

Packer's most memorable commentary on racial matters came in 1967 at the height of the American civil rights movement. On the night of 26 July, after three days of race riots in Detroit, he rang the *Telegraph*'s editor King Watson. Probably affected by alcohol, Packer all but dictated an editorial over the phone to Watson. It asserted: 'If every time Negro revolutionaries decided to burn and kill, those maintaining the law killed 500 Negroes, the Negroes might decide to stop burning and killing'. As Watson feared, there was a public outcry when the editorial appeared on 27 July; it was picked up by at least one London newspaper and the New South Wales ALP carried a unanimous resolution opposing the sentiments expressed in the editorial.[47]

Packer, conceding that the column was 'clumsily put', rang editor-in-chief David McNicoll, who had just returned from overseas, later that day: 'I'm afraid we've cocked things up. I want you to set to, and explain what we really wanted to say'. On 28 July the *Telegraph* denied that it had advocated shooting rioting blacks, but insisted: 'We stick firmly to this main point of the editorial — insensate violence and destruction should, when appeals to reason fail, be met with ruthless firmness even if bloodshed is involved'. McNicoll believes that Packer was more remorseful about his lack of judgment in running the original editorial than the sentiments expressed in it. In a letter to the editor of *Nation*, Packer's embittered former editor Cyril Pearl said that as the formula for ending racial trouble was so explicit, he would send a copy of the 'historic editorial' to American President L. B. Johnson by express mail.[48]

Packer's anti-labour venom became, if anything, more marked in the 1960s. He unapologetically used the *Telegraph* — the newspaper he had revived on its deathbed — as an organ of propaganda. Packer would go into the office every night except Sunday, look at the page proofs and simply say 'Kill it', 'I don't want this', 'Why are we saying this?', 'What the hell are you doing? Why has Calwell got the page three lead? Put him on page thirteen'.[49]

The intemperance of Packer's publications sometimes got them into legal hot water. In February 1963 the *Sun-Herald* and the *Sunday Telegraph* featured a story claiming that two Labor MPs had been encouraged by a Soviet diplomat to ask questions in parliament about sensitive defence matters relating to the United States North West Cape communications station. One of the politicians, Tom Uren, produced an editorial by McNicoll in the *Telegraph* and an article by Reid in the *Bulletin* that he used to help his case alleging malice on the part of ACP. In 1964 the New South Wales Supreme Court awarded Uren £30 000 damages against ACP, the highest sum ever obtained in an Australian defamation case. Fairfax reached a settlement with Uren, but Packer refused to let the matter rest. Disregarding the enormous legal costs involved, he took the matter to the full bench of the New South Wales Supreme Court and then the High Court. When ACP obtained leave to appeal to the Privy Council, Packer sent barrister Tony Larkins a cable: 'Congratulations. I take it this gives us the right to spend more money'.[50]

During the six-year legal battle, various lawyers and intermediaries attempted to negotiate a settlement between Uren and Packer. The first occasion saw the pair joined by ACP's company secretary, John Reginald Kitto, over lunch in the private dining room on the twelfth floor of company headquarters, now known as Telegraph House, in Park Street. After dining on smoked salmon and debating contemporary political issues, the pair thrashed out the terms of a settlement. Asking Kitto to leave the room, the 'tough old bird' said he would pay Uren $5000 less than the amount they had agreed upon, publish an apology and pay the balance six months later. Rightly bemused that someone in Packer's position would make this sort of offer, Uren turned it down. But when Lionel Murphy, a prominent barrister and Labor senator, persuaded him that such a public figure could not 'welch' on the deal, Uren made another appointment with Packer the following day. Packer, who had just returned from a long lunch and had a few drinks under his belt, announced that his offer had been withdrawn. Uren lashed out at Packer, 'but the more abuse I heaped on him, the more he seemed to like me'.[51]

In July 1969 Reid eventually managed to broker a deal between the warring parties whereby Packer paid Uren an undisclosed sum and agreed to publish an apology. After photocopying the cheque as a souvenir, Uren used the money to build a holiday house on the south coast which he dubbed 'Packer's Lodge'. Some time later, Uren ran into Packer at a function at Parliament House. When Uren asked him how he was, Packer replied, with a grin on his face, 'How do you bloody well think I am, having to pay you all that money?' Uren smiled back and said, 'You've got plenty of it'. The pair shook hands and parted, with Uren concluding that Packer grudgingly respected the fight he had put up against him.[52]

By this time, Packer had helped the Liberal Party to its first New South Wales electoral victory in nearly a quarter of a century. He and the Opposition leader Sir Robert Askin (who was later accused of corruption) had mixed in the same gambling circles for many years. In the lead-up to the May 1965 poll, Packer rang Askin and said, 'Look you need a supplementary campaign to get yourself into office. You need a couple of guys who can move quick, think and get their hands on some money quick'. Packer commissioned Donald Horne, who was still working with Jackson Wain, to co-ordinate a massive advertising campaign to promote the Liberal Party.[53] It was scarcely surprising, then, that in 1967 the ALP was unable to draw a statement from Askin censuring the *Telegraph* for its controversial editorial about race riots. Askin, now premier, claimed, somewhat disingenuously, not to have read the editorial and vowed that he would not be a party to gagging or tampering with the 'free press'.[54]

In 1964 Packer had penned a handwritten note to Menzies urging him to 'Take it easy old boy we need you'. Nevertheless, Menzies could see that the time for him to retire had come, and in early 1966 he stood down after winning a record seven consecutive general elections. Although Packer remained convinced for the rest of his life that Menzies was Australia's greatest prime minister, their relationship had been uneasy at times. Packer had never known quite where he stood with the patrician and autocratic Menzies. But still Packer's media outlets had played an important role in shaping Menzies' public image. The historian Ian Hancock has recently discussed how the organisational wing of the Liberal Party carefully constructed the image of the politician, first as the fatherly 'Bob Menzies' and then as the statesman 'Mr Menzies' and, finally, 'Sir Robert Menzies'.[55]

In January 1966 the treasurer Harold Holt was unanimously elected leader of the Liberal Party. The new prime minister inherited ACP's editorial and material support at the election later that year. During 1967 numerous cracks appeared in the coalition government and various Liberal MPs began eyeing Holt's job.[56] On 17 December the prime minister disappeared while swimming in Victoria. It is unclear whether Packer was already on holiday in Acapulco during one of the most dramatic moments in Australian political history. Clyde Packer has recalled that on the eve of the trip he and McNicoll were given firm instructions to look after Billy McMahon, who was now treasurer. McNicoll has claimed that Sir Frank rang from Acapulco to say that ACP should support McMahon for the Liberal leadership.

On 22 December, the day the search was scaled down, a memorial service for Holt was held in Melbourne. After the service, Clyde Packer called on McMahon at the Southern Cross Hotel in Melbourne. By this time the leader of the Country Party, John McEwen, had threatened to end the coalition if the lightweight but shrewdly cunning McMahon became leader of the Liberal Party. McMahon told Clyde that he was not going to run because of McEwen's veto. After several telephone calls, Clyde and McNicoll managed to convince Sir Frank that McMahon had no chance of succeeding Holt. McNicoll informed Packer that there was a strong body of opinion that (later Sir) John Gorton, formerly minister for the navy and now minister for education and science, was the man for the job. McNicoll admired Gorton's war record and forthright, down-to-earth manner, and he might also have leaned towards Gorton because his brother, Alan McNicoll, was an admiral.[57]

Packer ordered McNicoll to go and ask Gorton whether he would have McMahon as prime minister. After a long pause Gorton said that if he got the leadership there was no reason why he would not consider McMahon for the treasury. McNicoll reported his conversation to Packer over a crackling telephone line and received the go-ahead to give Gorton's candidacy every possible assistance. Even now, Packer remained determined to boost McMahon's image and punish his detractors. Gorton has claimed that Packer sent three emissaries to his house urging him to make a statement condemning

McEwen for interfering in the affairs of the Liberal Party and supporting McMahon's right to stand over McEwen's veto. Packer decided to stay behind Gorton even though he failed to issue the statement and Menzies tried to encourage ACP to support another leadership aspirant, (later Sir)Paul Hasluck. Gorton was supported in *Telegraph* editorials and given exposure on Channel Nine. In the end, Gorton became leader of the Liberal Party and McMahon retained the deputy leadership and the treasury portfolio.[58]

Gorton and McMahon must have thanked their lucky stars that Packer had not sold his newspaper and magazine interests to some very willing buyers earlier in 1967. On 4 April Packer and Rupert Henderson had been present at a lunch hosted by Ian Potter. In the course of the meal Packer confided to Henderson that he was thinking of disposing of the *Telegraph*s, the *Women's Weekly* and the *Bulletin*. He revealed that he had had an offer from Roy Thomson (now Lord Thomson of Fleet), who had visited Australia the previous month, and had also been talking to the HWT.[59]

Given recent developments in Packer's business and private life, it is not surprising that Henderson fell for the bait. In December 1966 Packer had learned that Fairfax was trying to buy into the Melbourne *Age* which, in terms of tradition, readership and advertising volume, was similar to the *Sydney Morning Herald*. Well aware of the value of the *Age*'s classified advertising, Packer had unsuccessfully attempted to stymie Fairfax's bid for the newspaper. Three months later, Packer had been hospitalised with pneumonia.[60]

A few days after Potter's lunch, the managing director of Fairfax, Angus McLachlan, ran into Rupert Murdoch at a dinner. Pointing at Packer, who was also on the guest list, Murdoch said to McLachlan: 'He's a sick man. If we're not careful we will have the Melbourne *Herald* in Sydney. We should do a deal. You should take the *Women's Weekly* and I should take the *Telegraph*'. On 24 April McLachlan told Packer he was going to fly to Athens, where Warwick Fairfax was on holiday, to discuss buying into ACP. Packer said that although he really was thinking of selling out, McLachlan should wait for a fortnight before 'haring across the world on a wild goose chase'. McLachlan, however, thought the matter sufficiently serious to make a quick trip to Athens. Over the next few weeks, Fairfax and News Ltd made separate offers for ACP's publications. McLachlan and Henderson developed a special code (in which Packer was known as 'Wilson') to keep Sir Warwick informed of developments by cable.[61]

In June McLachlan and Henderson nutted out a deal in London, where Murdoch was on his honeymoon. They agreed that Fairfax would take the magazines, News Ltd would run the newspapers and they would split the purchase price of $24 million. While his fellow director of Television Corporation was safely out of the way, Packer called a board meeting in Sydney. In Murdoch's absence the directors agreed that Television Corporation itself should buy the ACP publications that were purportedly on the market. Packer was able to reassure his board and the Australian Stock Exchange that $21.3 million was a fair price because ACP had already been offered $24 million by another bidder. The proprietors of Fairfax and News Ltd realised they had been taken for a ride. All McLachlan could think of in Packer's mitigation was that he had tried to stop him from haring across the world.[62]

The transaction entailed issuing 6.1 million new shares in Television Corporation to Consolidated Press Holdings. The arrangement yielded Packer and his family enormous financial and corporate benefits. It lifted the holding company's share in Television Corporation to 75 per cent and reduced News Ltd's stake to 10 per cent. Cash could now circulate freely within the group; up until this point the profits of Television Corporation had only flowed to Consolidated Press Holdings in dividends — and those dividends went to all shareholders. By dropping its ownership of ACP to 85 per cent, Consolidated Press Holdings had won majority control of TCN-9 and GTV-9. Murdoch, who had lost any influence at Television Corporation, decided to cut his losses and sell his shares to the holding company for $1.16 million less than he had originally paid. A few months later Television Corporation returned half its share capital of $9.96 million to its shareholders, so most of the capital went to Consolidated Press Holdings. In April 1968 the holding company followed suit and almost $1.65 million flowed out to ordinary shareholders — including, of course, the Packers.[63] Even his detractors had to concede that the wily old Sir Frank had executed one of the greatest coups in Australian corporate history.

A few months after bluffing his counterparts, Packer became embroiled in an industry-wide newspaper strike. Well before the strike, relations between Packer and the industry's unions had been tense. Working conditions at ACP headquarters had been shocking for years. On one occasion, after receiving complaints about the lack of ventilation in Telegraph House, Packer simply ordered square holes to be cut in the wall. A journalist later recalled that the improvised windows 'were too small to jump out of, yet large enough to allow icy winds to blast us to death'.[64]

In 1965 *Telegraph* journalists complained to the AJA about a shortage of chairs, lockers, typewriters and even ballpoint pens. ACP's management attempted to avert industrial action by assuring the AJA that new furniture was on its way. But when months passed and the furniture failed to appear, the AJA asked for permission to inspect Telegraph House. In November 1966 Packer refused to allow the inspection to proceed, telling the AJA that they should take their complaints to the Conciliation and Arbitration Commission. Packer's intransigence backfired when Commissioner McClorghy said that he himself would undertake an inspection if the parties could not reach an agreement.[65]

On 29 November Packer was present when H. G. Coleman, the New South Wales district secretary of the AJA, inspected Telegraph House. Although Coleman was impressed by some of the facilities, he discovered that there was still a shortage of typewriters, lockers and chairs. Packer refused to supply additional typewriters and lockers and to replace some of the ancient furniture; he would only agree to purchase six more chairs, three of which quickly disappeared from the general reporters' room.[66] On 15 February 1967 the AJA outlined the sorry history of working conditions at ACP to the Conciliation and Arbitration Commission. As Coleman explained, rather plaintively, Packer was a difficult man to deal with:

> We feel we can be pardoned for saying that in our opinion Sir Frank Packer — and not in our opinion alone, but also in that of other unions — is an odd character when it comes to dealing with unions. It would be an understatement to say that he does not like them.

Commissioner Portus inspected Telegraph House, recommended improvements and said he would consider the case again if there were still matters in dispute.[67]

Packer's relations with the PIEUA were little better. At 3.30 p.m. on Friday 25 February 1966 fifteen composing machine mechanics stopped work to discuss ACP's refusal to pay an increase of $4.80. This rise would have put them on a par with the over-award rate paid to their counterparts at Fairfax. At 6.15 p.m. the mechanics decided that they would resume work at their normal starting time the next morning, but this was not understood by the night staff machine compositors, who refused to operate linotype machines maintained by staff men and apprentices. ACP's foreman then stood down the machine compositors.

The situation put the PIEUA executive in a difficult position. They felt that Packer's anger at the mechanics for walking off the job in a 'cavalier manner' was justified. However, they were upset that the *Telegraph* had inflamed the situation by standing down employees, and anxious that the dispute should not spread to other newspaper offices. Four officials from the state branch of the PIEUA asked Angus McLachlan not to require Fairfax employees to handle copy for the *Telegraph*. McLachlan said that this would be up to Packer, noting that the proprietors had an agreement to assist each other in the event of any stoppage.[68]

At 10.51 p.m. the state secretary of the PIEUA, E. C. Bennett, left McLachlan's office to ring Packer and suggest that they meet to discuss the matter. Although Packer agreed to meet Bennett the following day, he was clearly confused about what staff would be available to produce the *Sunday Telegraph*. Over the last eighteen months there had been repeated stoppages and threats of stoppages at the offices of ACP, Fairfax and News Ltd in an effort to secure higher wages. Feeling decisive action was needed, Packer told Bennett that the situation was too uncertain and that ACP would have to make other arrangements to produce the *Sunday Telegraph*. When a chapel representative advised Packer he thought the mechanics intended to resume work the next day, Packer sarcastically replied, 'That's charming of them'. Just before midnight, Bennett rang Packer to confirm that all employees planned to return the next morning. By this time Packer seems to have determined that *Telegraph* copy should be sent to Fairfax and he insisted that the mechanics had gone out on strike.[69]

Saturday's *Telegraph* failed to appear, costing ACP $25 000 in lost sales and advertising revenue. When *Telegraph* staff arrived at company headquarters that morning, management informed them that there was no work for them. Keith Martin denied that the workers had been locked out, claiming that they were on strike. Packer did not return a call from Mr Justice Taylor, the president of the New South Wales Industrial Commission, later that morning. At the same time, ACP sent *Telegraph* copy over to Fairfax. Members of the Fairfax chapel refused to handle the copy and were sacked, and similar events took place at the offices of News Ltd.[70]

A mass meeting of printers was held at 2 p.m. on Saturday afternoon. When telephoned by PIEUA officials, Packer maintained he still had no work for *Telegraph* employees and that he had made 'other arrangements'. There were loud cries of derision when Packer's comments were passed on to the meeting. Further negotiations with the proprietors later that afternoon failed, and on Sunday morning reduced editions of the *Sunday Telegraph*, the *Sun-Herald* and the *Sunday Mirror* were produced by staff labour. On the morning of Monday 28 February PIEUA members accepted their branch executive's recommendation to return to work. At a compulsory conference between the union and proprietors' representatives later that day, the PIEUA's counsel argued that employees who had been stood down should not have their pay docked. The matter was set down for hearing before the Industrial Commission and Packer allowed his employees to return to work.[71]

On 13 April Packer was cross-examined by the PIEUA's counsel, C. Allen. Resenting having to explain his actions to the commission, Packer was soon criticising his interrogator's 'rude' and 'aggressive' manner. At one stage he was asked why he had not carefully read the transcripts of the evidence given by McLachlan and Bennett:

> Mr Packer: It is pretty boring stuff.
> Mr Allen: I am sorry if my cross-examination has been boring you.
> Mr Packer: Generally it is not very interesting reading.

In June 1967 Mr Justice McKeon finally ruled that the employees were not entitled to time lost during the dispute, as ACP workers had stopped work illegally and the decision to ask Fairfax and News Ltd to set *Telegraph* copy for a fee had been made in good faith and was quite reasonable under the circumstances.[72] But just a few weeks later, Packer was being condemned for his provocative role in a much more serious newspaper strike.

In October 1966 the full bench of the Commonwealth Conciliation and Arbitration Commission had begun hearing the AJA's application for a new award. The AJA's counsel, Raymond O'Dea, argued that journalism was a profession and that journalists' salaries should be brought into line with other comparative industries. On 7 July 1967 the commission handed down wage levels of a magnitude the AJA could not have hoped for; some journalists received increases approaching 30 per cent. Critically, however, the full bench rejected O'Dea's request that there should be a provision in the award to regulate downgrading. The AJA met with the proprietors at the Hotel Australia on 8 July. Packer, who was deputed to chair the meeting, failed to strike the right note with the AJA's negotiators. He bluntly indicated, among other things, that he would downgrade his own staff. (Depending on their level of skill and experience, journalists were employed on a scale from A1 to D.) At one stage the HWT's John Williams, aiming for a more conciliatory note, intervened in the discussion, only to be sarcastically asked by Packer whether he would like to take the chair.[73]

On 31 July metropolitan newspaper proprietors began downgrading their journalists. Of the 168 downgradings across the country, 109 were in Sydney. On 1 August Sydney journalists decided to stop work. Over the next two days, journalists in

Adelaide also went out on strike. The journalists' militancy surprised Packer. When the father of the ACP chapel raised the issue of the strike with Packer, he arrogantly replied, 'Forget the journalists. They won't stay out long'. The next fortnight was to show how misguided was his belief that journalists were only concerned about the size of their pay packets rather than their professional gradings.[74]

On 3 August the Printing and Kindred Industries Union (PKIU), which had recently emerged as a result of the amalgamation between the PIEUA and another union, joined the strike. On the same day Commissioner Portus called a conference between the AJA and the proprietors for 10 August. But his decision to insert a strike-ban order into the award to take effect from 4 August clouded the situation. The AJA was naturally worried that it would face heavy fines if the strike continued. The directive helped to ensure that Melbourne journalists did not go out on strike and prompted Adelaide journalists to return to work. However, a mass meeting of Sydney journalists on 3 August voted to continue the strike.[75]

While striking journalists and printers published their own newspaper, ACP executives managed to bring out small editions of the *Telegraph*. Packer himself rolled up his sleeves, donned an eyeshade and sat down to work at the sub-editors' table. At the end of each shift he insisted on bringing out Scotch and beer 'for the loyal boys'.[76]

On 10 August Portus said that although the proprietors had not acted in breach of the award, some had applied their methods unfairly by giving journalists a choice between being downgraded or dismissed. The proprietors' counsel agreed that if work resumed, they would confer with the AJA about the issue of downgrading and the notices of dismissal that had been issued to employees. A meeting of Sydney journalists that afternoon voted to return to work on 12 August.[77]

At this point Packer came blundering in again. On 11 August the *Telegraph* claimed that journalists were returning to work unconditionally and Packer announced on radio that any journalist who refused to accept a downgrading would leave their employer with no alternative but to terminate their services. By now the strike had gained a momentum the AJA could not control. On 13 August a mass meeting of 4000 newspaper workers — journalists, printers, drivers, engineers, clerks and cleaners — voted to continue the strike.[78]

On 14 August a compulsory conference between the unions and the newspaper companies was held at the New South Wales Industrial Commission. J. D. Kenny, the secretary of the New South Wales Trades and Labor Council, delivered submissions on behalf of all unions involved in the strike. The conference resolved the question of the reinstatement of certain non-journalistic employees who had gone on strike. With an eye on Packer, Kenny commented that the proprietors should be very careful what they published over the proposed resumption period. The president of the Industrial Commission, noting that the employers (including Packer) were present, asked for all parties to display commonsense, forbearance and mutual tolerance during this delicate period. The conference was adjourned and on 16 August newspaper workers agreed to return to work the next day.[79]

When the compulsory conference resumed on 17 August, Mr Justice Beattie lambasted Packer. Despite — or perhaps because of — Kenny's warnings, that morning's

Telegraph had run an editorial distorting his submissions and attacking the leadership of the AJA. Work resumed throughout the day despite several skirmishes and the threat of a walkout at ACP. Beattie described the articles that had appeared in Packer's newspaper as 'wholly deplorable', 'inflammatory in the highest degree', dishonest and intimidatory. It was just short of miraculous, he said, that the articles had not undone the work of the commission, the unions and 'some Proprietors' and led to a fresh outburst of the strike. On 18 August Packer ensured that an unrepentant statement signed 'Ed. *DT*' appeared in the *Telegraph*:

> If it were not for the fact that Mr. Justice Beattie and Mr. Justice Sheldon are members of the Judiciary and were it not for the laws of contempt which surround that position, we would have very much more to say about their statement ... which in our opinion exceeds their proper functions as members of the Industrial Commission.[80]

On 31 August Packer and McNicoll represented ACP at a stormy conference to discuss the implementation of the new journalists' award. They rejected the AJA's request to maintain the status quo and withhold payments (and therefore the allocation of regradings) pending further conferences. Packer announced that ACP would pay the new award rates and ask its employees to accept or reject regradings by 4 September. When the AJA's federal secretary snapped, 'Go off and bring out your silly little paper', Packer retorted, 'I will'. At this, McNicoll rose from his chair, opened the door for Packer and they left the meeting. That night a notice signed by McNicoll appeared on the *Telegraph*'s noticeboard announcing the company's decision. The notice said that 'if there were any injustices, real or imagined', the AJA could take them up with management. Packer's intransigence again threatened the fragile industrial truce. At the AJA's request, Mr Justice Moore and Rupert Murdoch, in his capacity as president of the ANC, held talks with Packer. ACP agreed to withdraw its notice and maintain the status quo until further meetings were held with the AJA.[81]

Although a large number of journalists gained financially from the new award, many were downgraded and there were bitter recriminations about the award and the strike during the remainder of 1967. The fact that each proprietor was also able to produce most of his newspapers during the strike showed that employers were better prepared than in 1944 and 1955 to counter industrial action with improved technology. Nevertheless, Packer and his counterparts lost an estimated $600 000 in advertising revenue during the dispute.[82]

Packer's behavior during the sixteen-day strike illustrated, yet again, his hands-on managerial style. Unable to leave the running of his publications to his executives, he had entered the fray boots and all, helping to physically produce his papers, rewarding 'loyal' employees, and provoking further industrial trouble through his bloody-mindedness. Now sixty years of age, Packer still thrived on a crisis.

14
The Sound of One Man Clapping

Even after his failed bid for the America's Cup in September 1962, Packer had remained determined to wrest custodianship of the prized trophy from the United States. However, the NYYC accepted a challenge from Britain before Australia had her second chance for a tilt at the cup. In December 1962 the NYYC tightened up the loopholes in the deed of gift that might advantage potential challengers, announcing that no future competitors would be granted concessions such as the use of American-made sails. Remembering *Gretel*'s work at the Stevens Institute, the club also decreed that other American equipment and services could not be used unless they were absolutely unobtainable in the challengers' country of origin or elsewhere outside the United States.[1]

In September 1964 the British challenger *Sovereign* lost four straight races against the American yacht *Constellation*. By this time Packer had already called on Harry Morgan, chairman of the America's Cup Committee, in New York outlining his plans to issue another challenge. Packer had ascertained that the new conditions in the deed of gift only applied to future designs and could not be made retrospective, so he invoked the 'grandfather clause', announcing that *Gretel* would be repaired below the waterline. Alan Payne redesigned the underbody completely while still retaining all the sails and equipment acquired from the United States for the 1962 challenge.[2]

This time, however, Packer had a domestic competitor to contend with. Emil Christensen, a prominent Melbourne businessman, formed an America's Cup challenge syndicate in Victoria. Payne's right-hand man Warwick Hood agreed to design a potential challenger. Jock Sturrock was retained as skipper of the new yacht. Unlike Packer, the backers of the syndicate did not interfere in any way with Sturrock's activities. Throughout 1965 and 1966, the new yacht was constructed in a shed at Berry's Bay on the north side of Sydney Harbour, while *Gretel* was rebuilt in a shed just metres away. Both camps carried out their activities in strict secrecy and yachtsmen and journalists who sought to enter the sheds were firmly turned away. The RSYS agreed to hold a series of selection trials in 1967 to determine the Australian challenger.[3]

The Victorians' new yacht came into full view for the first time when she was launched in August 1966. She was named *Dame Pattie* in honour of Dame Pattie Menzies. The prime minister, delighted by the choice of name and aware of the kudos that the 1962 challenge had brought Australia, personally christened the yacht. One can only wonder whether Menzies felt uncomfortable, and perhaps even a little guilty, about his hesitant support of Packer's first challenge. Launching *Dame Pattie*, he used the opportunity to remind spectators that his wife had christened *Gretel* at the same landing stage in 1962:

> If *Dame Pattie* wins the final selection trials, I'll be able to say to my wife, 'I see, dear, that boat I named after you is going to sail for the America's Cup'. But if *Gretel* is selected I'll say, 'That yacht you christened is going for the Cup again!'

Over the next few months, *Dame Pattie* went out on trial each weekend while *Vim* and the rebuilt *Gretel* sailed against each other over a triangular course.[4]

In January 1967 *Gretel* and *Dame Pattie* held a series of working-up trials over what had become known as the 'America's Cup course' off Sydney Heads. Archie Robertson, who had been alternate skipper in the 1962 challenge, took the helm of *Gretel*. Trygve Halvorsen replaced him after *Gretel* lost the first two races. *Dame Pattie* won the trial series 6–1, and there was speculation that the modification made to *Gretel*'s hull to enable her to go windward more smoothly had actually slowed her down. A new piquancy was added to the contest on 22 February when Rupert Murdoch's *Daily Mirror* announced that it had become part of the rival Victorian syndicate.[5]

In the weeks preceding the selection trials in late March, there was widespread speculation that *Gretel*'s team was far from happy. Yachting writers reported that one *Gretel* man first learned he had been dropped from the crew when he read a report in a Sunday newspaper, and alleged that a 'rebel group' had threatened outright mutiny unless there were changes in the higher echelon of crewmen. Halvorsen was at the helm of *Gretel* again when she lost the first three races. On the eve of the fourth race Gordon Ingate was made skipper. Asked by an evening newspaper whether he resigned from the crew because of Ingate's appointment, Halvorsen replied, 'Possibly'. Packer was forced to issue a statement denying that there was any disharmony among *Gretel*'s crew.[6]

The Packer camp was bitterly disappointed when *Gretel* lost three of the remaining four races. Even before the series finished there were plans for further alterations to *Gretel*'s hull in the hope that another trial series would be staged. Shipwrights were so scarce that the *Telegraph* ran an extraordinary front-page advertisement:

> Wanted Immediately.
>   Shipwrights for alterations to be carried out on the 12-metre yacht *Gretel*.
>   …
>
> Hurry Please!

Not surprisingly, the advertisement was ridiculed by the *Daily Mirror,* and over the next few weeks arguments for and against another series of trials raged in the two newspapers. The Victorian syndicate agreed to hold further races against *Gretel* on 5,

6 and 7 May. When *Dame Pattie* won all three races, the RSYS promptly chose her as the challenging yacht.[7]

Commendably gracious in defeat, Packer offered to lend *Gretel* to the Victorian syndicate to trial against *Dame Pattie*. The syndicate, perhaps believing that the redesigned *Gretel* was not good enough to offer more than token opposition, declined the offer. The way the finances of the syndicate were structured might also have convinced the businessmen that it would be too costly to take *Gretel* and a spare crew to Newport. *Dame Pattie* went to the United States with few crew members in reserve and no serious rival to train against. In September 1967 *Intrepid* won the best of seven races so comfortably that the Australian yacht was dubbed 'Dame Pity'. However, had she had the quality of American sails made available to *Gretel* a few years earlier, *Dame Pattie* could have been a stronger contender, particularly in light airs. And *Intrepid* was a remarkable yacht, the first of a new breed of twelves.[8]

The failures of the two Australian challenges did not cause Packer to throw up his hands in despair. By the time *Dame Pattie* had lost the fourth race on 18 September, he was already planning to build another yacht to challenge for what was now being described as the Everest of international yachting. In early October he and Ian Potter informed the NYYC that they proposed to challenge for the twenty-first America's Cup. Packer said the challenge would be issued through the RSYS, the Royal Prince Edward Yacht Club or the Cruising Yacht Club. As in 1962, he ended up issuing his challenge through the RSYS. Packer offered to build a new yacht on the understanding that he and no one else would represent the RSYS. The squadron accepted this, as no other individual or syndicate indicated their willingness to build a boat within thirty days of the end of the 1967 series.

In his preliminary correspondence with the NYYC, Packer indicated that his syndicate would be prepared to sail off against any other would-be challengers for the right to meet the American defender.[9] Eric Maxwell had already issued a challenge through the Royal Dorset Yacht Club. And, for the first time in the history of the America's Cup, a challenge had been received from a non-English speaking country. It came from the Yacht Club d'Hyères on behalf of a syndicate headed by Baron Marcel Bich, who had become a multimillionaire by manufacturing cheap ballpoint pens. In another first, there was the prospect that multiple challengers from different nations would have to sail against each other for the right to compete against the Americans.[10]

In December 1967 the NYYC concluded that negotiating with several clubs at the same time would be too unwieldy. It decided that Australia would be designated the challenger for the 1970 America's Cup, while leaving the way open for the clubs from England and France, and now the Royal Yacht Club of Greece, to sail off against Australia in elimination races three weeks before the final match. This meant that the NYYC would negotiate only with Australia but the terms of the challenge would have to be observed by whichever country won the trials.[11]

Of more immediate concern to Packer was securing the opportunity to head the RSYS challenge that would compete against the other overseas syndicates. By 1968 he was aware that he was not the only Australian interested in contesting the next America's Cup. The All States syndicate had emerged with the intention of building a new yacht and buying *Dame Pattie* as a trial horse. Reg Ansett, the Sydney accountant and publisher Norman B. Rydge junior, the Melbourne businessmen J. Birrell, Fred Moylan and G. Warner headed the syndicate.[12]

Having previously lost a chance to challenge for the America's Cup, Packer was determined not to be stymied again by another domestic syndicate. There was an added edge to the rivalry with the All States syndicate as Packer and Ansett were now competitors in other arenas. One of Ansett's companies had been awarded the third television licence in Sydney, meaning that TCN-9 had a new competitor, 0–10. Packer had already signed up Alan Payne to build a new yacht and spent a considerable sum of money on tank tests in the Department of Mechanical Engineering at the University of Sydney. *Gretel*'s impressive performance in the 1962 match also meant that Packer did not have to work hard to convince the Australian government to support his latest challenge. By 1968 the treasurer had granted those persons or corporations making contributions to the construction of America's Cup yachts double tax deductibility.[13]

In August 1968 a poorly attended meeting of the RSYS America's Cup Committee rejected the All States syndicate's request that its new twelve-metre yacht be considered a potential challenger. In a personal letter to a yachting figure in New York, Fred Moylan commented, 'Packer seems to have them [the RSYS] under his thumb — because he has threatened to pull out if the Squadron accepts our boat as a contender!! … The Squadron therefore are in a bad position whatever they do'.[14]

The decision not to hold any Australian trials aroused such widespread criticism that the RSYS decided to convene an extraordinary general meeting a few weeks later. Several people present asked Packer to agree to trial his yacht against that of the other syndicate. Turning down the request, Packer appears to have threatened to sue the RSYS if his yacht was not automatically selected as the Australian challenger. The members voted 68 to 49 in favour of accepting Packer's yacht as the challenger.[15]

The way was now clear for Packer to negotiate the terms of the international elimination match while Payne concentrated on designing the new yacht. But once again Packer's aggressive style provoked censorious gossip. When a prominent NYYC official privately reported on the outcome of the RSYS meeting to a colleague, he indicated that overseas clubs might not relish the prospect of dealing with Packer: 'I appreciate the lack of confidence that someone might have in entering any kind of a game in connection with which Sir Frank Packer was laying down the rules and interpreting those rules'. And as late as November 1968, there was still said to be tension in the Australian camp.[16]

In February 1968 Sir Frank and Lady Packer attended what Patrick White described as a glamorous 'shivoo' at Admiralty House. The governor-general Lord Casey and his wife Maie hosted the party for Nin Ryan, a prominent art collector and daughter of the New York financier Otto Kahn. White wrote in his diary that some of the guests, including the Packers, made his blood run cold. But the very qualities that alienated many of Packer's associates attracted the fascination, and sometimes the admiration, of other observers. In May 1968 Lord Casey told Garfield Barwick, now chief justice of the High Court, that 'we need more vigorous thrusting people in Australia of the sort of Bill Gunn, Frank Packer and, if you like, Reg Ansett — with the courage to get out of the rut and have a crack at things the 'respectables' haven't the fire in their bellies to do'.[17]

As Packer prepared to have another 'crack' at the America's Cup, he continued to operate as a Liberal powerbroker. The elevation of John Gorton to the prime ministership in January 1968 was initially well received by the public. But it was not long before the political instability that had been evident during the latter part of the Holt administration resurfaced and escalated. Gorton emerged as an unorthodox Australian nationalist in economic and, to some extent, defence matters. He was also impulsively outspoken, with a manner that bordered on the larrikin.[18]

Treasurer Billy McMahon, who lived in Bellevue Hill, was a frequent guest at Packer's Sunday night dinner parties. When Packer invited prominent overseas visitors like Cecil King and Henry Ford II to 'Cairnton', he always liked to have the politician at his table. Packer felt that McMahon's willingness to hold forth on economic matters greatly impressed his guests and he was determined to defend and advance his old friend's political ambitions.[19] In the early months of 1969, as the Liberal ministry and the backbench fractured over a variety of problems, McMahon concluded that he was out of favour with Gorton. On 27 March he informed Peter Howson, who had been dropped from the ministry by Gorton, that 'the knives' were out to get him. A fortnight later Packer told Gorton that he would turn his press against him if he continued to 'persecute' McMahon. By August, according to the *Bulletin*'s Canberra editor Peter Samuel, David McNicoll's support for the prime minister was alternating between acquiescence and distrust 'depending on how long has elapsed since he was last duchessed at The Lodge'.[20]

In September 1969, with wool prices falling and the market in Great Britain collapsing, the government offered finance to bring 40 per cent of Australia's annual wool clip into a controlled marketing scheme. Some wool industry leaders described this as a 'hotch-potch' idea delivered just before the election. R. W. Macarthur-Onslow said that the proposal could lead to wool stockpiling and increased costs for small growers. Packer was friends with the Macarthur-Onslow family and served on the AJC committee with a number of other men with big wool interests. By 6 October Alan Reid or Packer himself had urged the prime minister to retreat on the commitment. Gorton, who was rarely deferential to people with influence, apparently boasted that he had told Packer 'where to get off'. Samuel believed that Gorton viewed Packer as 'so bitterly anti-Labor' that he would not dare to criticise the government, no matter how deep his dissatisfaction. Samuel commented presciently that even if the *Telegraph* remained as pro-government 'as ever there may be other repercussions from this sort of behavior [sic]'.[21]

Packer did back the Gorton administration as an election was approaching and he preferred to have the coalition in rather than out of office. Maxwell Newton, the well-connected editor of the political and financial newsletter *Incentive*, understood that Packer was supporting Gorton in the short term, but that there would be a change of policy after the poll.[22] On 9 October Samuel told a correspondent that a story he thought he had 'tailored just enough to the pro-government line we are at present following' had been rejected by the *Bulletin*. Gorton was a poor television performer, and as the date of the poll neared Packer took it upon himself to redress the situation. He arranged for his 'best people' at GTV-9 to coach the prime minister and help him with his policy speech. However, the unpredictable Gorton allegedly arrived at the studio late, behaved 'boorishly and arrogantly' and made a mess of his talk.[23]

The government's majority was reduced from thirty-eight to seven seats at the House of Representatives election on 25 October. Although McMahon was anxious to challenge for the leadership, he wanted Howson to guarantee him a majority of votes before showing his hand. On Friday 31 October Howson told Clyde Packer that McMahon would have a strong chance of success if he were persuaded to throw his hat in the ring as early as possible. By Saturday morning McMahon had conferred with Sir Frank and begun to seriously consider challenging for the leadership. Later that day Clyde rang Howson to say that he would put pressure on Billy Snedden, the minister for immigration, to get him to support McMahon.[24]

The *Sunday Telegraph* declared that, in the event of a leadership spill, John McEwen must agree to serve under McMahon:

> Mr. McEwen should be able to see that if we are to have a new Prime Minister he must be chosen from among those men who command the respect of the Party, who have the capacity to rehabilitate its image in the electorate, and who — by seniority, experience and accomplishment — have proved that they have the potential for the country's most important office.

On Monday, after talking with McEwen, McMahon agreed to contest the leadership.[25]

During these crucial days Reid kept Howson informed about what his company was doing to help things along, while the *Sydney Morning Herald* also turned against Gorton. Packer gave some consideration to what would happen to his friend if Gorton held on as prime minister. Worried that McMahon might be dropped from the treasury portfolio, Packer ordered McNicoll to go and see Gorton in Canberra to discuss the issue. Accusing the irrepressibly ambitious McMahon of actively trying to undermine him, Gorton said that he could give 'Frank' no guarantee of keeping McMahon on as treasurer.[26]

At the Liberal party room meeting on 7 November Gorton was re-elected leader with an apparently wafer-thin majority. McMahon comfortably won the deputy leadership. The *Telegraph* lambasted the prime minister when he chose not to reappoint McMahon as treasurer. One front-page editorial, entitled 'Gorton needs the skills of a Houdini', warned that the prime minister might live to regret his decision. Packer's newspapers now embarked on a campaign to further destabilise Gorton's troubled leadership. Just before Christmas, McMahon and Howson agreed that the prime minister was finding the strain of the press campaign against him 'pretty tough going'. Reid was heard to say that as a result the press must redouble its efforts.[27]

While Packer dabbled in the affairs of the Liberal Party, he made another bid to extend his media interests interstate. His target was West Australian Newspapers Ltd, which published Perth's only daily newspapers, the morning *West Australian* and the afternoon *Daily News*. The Perth newspaper market was hotting up, as a new Sunday paper had just been launched and a new morning paper was being rumoured, and the share price in West Australian Newspapers was falling. An added attraction for Packer would have been aligning his interests with Perth's television station TVW-7, in which the newspaper company had a stake. ACP joined forces with an investment company, Tricontinental Corporation Ltd, of which Ian Potter was chairman and Boral Ltd the largest shareholder. On 30 June 1969 the group offered $5.50 a share on a first-come, first-served basis for a 25 per cent interest in West Australian Newspapers. But the bid quickly foundered, with the HWT announcing a takeover offer later that night and the price of shares in the Perth company skyrocketing when the markets opened the next morning. While the *Telegraphs*' financial columns proffered a partisan commentary, Packer declined to vary his syndicate's offer and on 9 July the shareholders of West Australian Newspapers accepted the HWT's takeover offer.[28] This meant that his newspaper interests remained confined to New South Wales.

Packer was also busy negotiating the terms of the elimination trials to determine the challenger for the 1970 America's Cup. By April 1969 both the Greek and British yacht clubs had withdrawn their challenges, meaning that the two contesting clubs for the trials would be the RSYS and the Yacht Club d'Hyères.[29] Throughout 1969 and 1970 the Australian, French and American parties attempted to reach agreement on the date of the elimination trials, the shape and length of the course and the placing of the windward mark.[30]

These negotiations did not always go smoothly. In October 1969 Packer asked J. B. Davies, the head of ACP's New York bureau, to find out what representation on the International Race and Protest Committee the challenger would be entitled to when sailing against the American defender. Packer wanted to do away with the committee, fearing that it would be made up solely of NYYC representatives. He proposed that a new committee should be formed consisting of either one Australian, one Frenchman and one national of another country or, more optimistically, two Australians, one Frenchman and one national of another country.[31] The approach, which indicated how aggressively Packer intended to pursue his second bid for the America's Cup, did little to enhance his reputation in international or even Australian yachting circles.

The NYYC's America's Cup Committee quickly rejected Packer's request, explaining that the Yacht Club d'Hyères had agreed that neither of the prospective challenging nations should be represented on the protest committee. The NYYC also pointed out that the RSYS itself had recommended names for inclusion on the International Race and Protest Committee. The RSYS had proposed that two prominent yachtsmen, one from West Germany and the other from Norway, should join Italy's Dr Beppe Croce on the committee.[32] The meeting of the RSYS's America's Cup Committee on 19 November resolved that Packer's proposal was 'contrary to the whole concept of the impartial international committee' and as the members had already been appointed, it was too late to add new names. In January 1970, with Packer still grumbling about the matter, the RSYS ruled that the composition of the protest committee should remain unchanged. Admitted to hospital with pneumonia, Packer finally accepted that it was pointless pursuing the matter any further.[33]

By now Packer had made a list of about fifteen men he wanted to try out as the skipper. (Later Sir) James Hardy, who had represented Australia in the Mexico Olympic regatta and had sailed on *Gretel* in 1967, was given the helm. The tall and rangy thirty-seven-year-old, who came from one of Australia's oldest winemaking firms, soon became known as 'Gentleman Jim' because of his tact and demeanour. The ebullient Dutch-born Martin Visser, who had also been an Olympic representative, was chosen as deputy skipper and tactician. Rear-Commodore W. L. Fesq, the RSYS captain and a learned, precise and authoritative figure, became navigator. The youngest member of the eleven-man crew was a twenty-three-year-old engineer, John Bertrand, who would later emerge as a key figure in Australia's America's Cup history.[34]

Meanwhile, Bill Barnett and his staff were busy building the yacht designed by Alan Payne. She had a long, low, slender bow and was U-shaped underneath, leading to a short keel well curved away from the bow section. As *Intrepid*'s designer had done, Payne avoided excess windage and maximised weight down low by having the winches below deck level. The main cockpit allowed for two steering wheels to improve the helmsman's view and overcame a problem that had troubled *Dame Pattie*. Payne also designed an unusual mast for the yacht, the elliptically shaped aluminium spar being constructed in two sections. Peter Cole made the sails, using every available type of Australian-made sailcloth. Within hours of the yacht appearing in public as she was lifted from Barnett's shed in Sydney's McMahons Point, photographs of her underwater shape were being relayed to designers in the United States. At a ceremony in Sydney in February 1970, Florence Packer christened the yacht *Gretel II*.[35]

There were early tuning problems. The yacht's mast was shifted forward 45 centimetres and 7257 kilograms of lead was shaved from her keel. But her single largest problem — the perennial one for any challenger — was a lack of opportunities for competitive racing. As *Dame Pattie* had been sold to a Canadian, the only modern trial horse available was Gretel. Packer's newspapers reported that the older boat was beating the newer one in races on Sydney Harbour, but when the time came it was *Gretel II* that was shipped to the United States. It seems that Packer was being his crafty old self, trying to divert attention from *Gretel II*'s competitive potential. The fact that her final rig had not yet been installed must have affected the yacht's performance in Australian waters.[36]

In June 1970 Payne and Barnett watched anxiously as an enormous crane picked up the white-hulled yacht from a wharf in Pyrmont. Joint Cargo Services had arranged for *Gretel II* to be shipped to the United States duty-free aboard the *New York Star*. Packer and the RSYS were naturally disturbed when delays at Queensland ports and in the Panama Canal held up the freighter. Although Gorton had little time for Packer these days, he seems to have realised that the *Gretel II* challenge had captured the Australian public's imagination. As a result of the prime minister's intervention, the *New York Star* made a special call at Rhode Island on 6 August to unload the yacht.[37]

When Packer and his crew arrived in Providence they took up residence at Chastellux Manor, a mansion that had been built in 1890. Just as he had in 1962, Packer ruled his crew members with an iron fist. A few months after the America's Cup series was over, he told a television interviewer with predictable delicacy that one of the main reasons it was difficult for a challenger to win was because 'you've got to take your crew over there and keep them away for eight or nine weeks, and the boys get homesick, love sick ... And their wives get bitchy about them being away so long, whereas the American crew [can go home]'. Mrs Earlys ('Brownie') Siegrist, the muscular cook at the popular Candy Store Hotel, had orders to turn the beer off for the Australian crew at 10.25 p.m. each night.[38]

Ted Turner, a millionaire television network owner from Atlanta, provided *Gretel II* with a trial horse in the weeks preceding the elimination series against France. Ever the entrepreneur, Packer had secured the sponsorship of clothing manufacturers for his crew members. The Australians roamed around Newport dressed in navy Anthony Squires blazers, grey Sax Altman trousers, blue Paramount shirts, Speedo Knitting Mills jumpers, Brandella track suits, Taft waterproof jackets, Dunlop shorts and shoes, and Holeproof socks.[39]

Baron Bich added even more colour to Newport than did his Australian counterpart. A contemporary observer noted that the Frenchman had 'a personality which collectively gave him the determination of a Japanese shipbuilder, the arrogance of De Gaulle, the nautical feelings of Napoleon and the possession of a million pounds to expend on his dream'. He arrived in Rhode Island with a virtual armada: the French challenger, *France*; another twelve-metre yacht, the *Chancegger*; his own luxury cruiser; and twenty-seven mainsails and fifteen spinnakers. Bich was also joined by his wife, nine children, eighty sailors and craftsmen, two pastrycooks, a cordon bleu chef and a supply of French food and wine.[40]

A few days before the elimination series was scheduled to begin, Packer indicated just how seriously he was taking the challenge. On 18 August he complained to the International Race and Protest Committee that neither challenging yacht had been measured. He claimed that while Payne had been meticulous in following twelve-metre specifications when designing *Gretel II*, the use of metal fairing strips on *France* to join the hull to the rudder illegally increased her waterline. The committee replied that the conditions governing the elimination match had been complied with and there were no reasonable grounds for any further action. At a press conference on 20 August, Packer announced that if *Gretel II* won the right to challenge for the America's Cup, Australia would protest to the International Yacht Racing Union in London over the twelve-metre measuring rule. The question upset the French, who vigorously maintained throughout the day that *France* conformed to the structural rules.[41]

Packer and Bich had only been formally introduced to each other that morning. Packer's opening line was: 'Ah, Monsieur le Baron, I've heard a lot about you'. The ballpoint pen magnate shrugged and said, 'The same for me'. That night Packer dined in shirtsleeves with his crew and cheered loudly when Jim Hardy raised a toast to 'beating the French'.[42]

The races to select the challenger took place in light winds, with Bich behaving towards his crew as capriciously as Packer had during the 1962 series. On 21 August Louis Noverraz took the helm of *France* and led the Australians for most of the way before running into a calm patch and losing the race. Bich installed another skipper for the second race, along with eight new crew members. Before long, *Gretel II* had won the first three of the best-of-seven series.[43]

Bich decided to take to the helm himself for what turned out to be the final race on 29 August. As he donned a formal yachting outfit, including white gloves, he sent a message to Hardy saying, 'Don't be too kind. Treat me as a skipper'. Fog rolled in over the course, making the race more a test of the navigator's sense of direction than of the helmsman's skill. *Gretel II* led by more than four minutes at the first mark and, under superb and uncanny guidance from navigator Bill Fesq, completed the course in almost zero visibility. In an unfortunate and almost comical end to the elimination match, *France* got hopelessly lost and dropped her sails, arriving home some six hours after *Gretel II*.

The word 'abandon' is offensive to a French sportsman, and Bich angrily accused the International Race committee of dishonouring him. He also maintained that the committee should not have allowed the race to proceed in such poor conditions. Mrs Bich slapped the face of a television cameraman after he pushed her aside to take a picture of her husband. Exhausted and despondent, Baron Bich declined the Australians' invitation to join them for a steak dinner at their residence. Packer allowed his crew to make an impression on the twenty dozen bottles of Australian wine and champagne that the Hardy family had sent over. When asked how he felt about the prospect of facing the American defender *Intrepid*, Packer simply replied, 'We are in the big league now'.[44]

The selection trials over, the French helped the Australians prepare for the challenge itself. Further races were held, with *Gretel II* winning against *France* and *Chancegger* each time. This experience was vital, as Alan Payne continued making major alterations to *Gretel II* right up until the eve of the match.[45] On 10 September Sir Frank and Lady Packer hosted a black tie buffet dinner at The Elms in Newport. A few days later the Australian ambassador to the United States, Sir James Plimsoll, presided over a reception for 350 guests at the Victorian mansion Chateau-Sur-Mer. While acknowledging Bich's generosity in helping the Australian challenge, Packer said he did not see how the International Race committee could have called off the last selection race:

> If it had, we'd have been bloody annoyed.... But the French are temperamental.
> I know, I married a Frenchwoman.
> ... He [Bich] added great color to the contest and now he is doing everything he can to help Australia.
> Maybe he's temperamental, but he's a good sport at heart.

Despite the levity, the America's Cup series was marred by further controversy. Back in Australia, Labor's Senator J. B. Keeffe asked the government to reveal the cost ($2175) of the reception hosted by the ambassador.[46] In the United States, the *Gretel II* syndicate complained that *Intrepid* did not adhere to the International Yacht Racing Union rules governing the measurement of twelve-metre yachts. When the NYYC disagreed with the Packer syndicate's interpretation of the rules, the Australians asked the International Yacht Racing Union for a ruling. On 31 August the Americans agreed to alter *Intrepid*'s stern waterline and one other minor aspect of her design. As a result, the RSYS and the NYYC agreed that the America's Cup match could begin before the International Yacht Racing Union handed down its ruling.[47]

By the time the first race was scheduled to begin on Tuesday 15 September, Newport was bursting at the seams with 25 000 visitors. The Australian crew breakfasted on steak and eggs before setting out for the shipyard. When the two yachts arrived at the America's Cup buoy, a twenty-knot wind was blowing and rain was falling. As a result of the poor conditions, only 500 yachts ventured to the race area. Packer was aboard *Pearl Necklace*, which he had chartered as a spectator yacht a few months earlier.[48]

It was to be a race of misfortune and poor judgement for the challengers. Their misfortune began when they chose a genoa too light for the prevailing winds. Then, about six minutes before the starting gun, the two yachts had to take evasive action to avoid a collision. Both immediately raised red protest flags, which had not happened in a race for nearly forty years. *Gretel II* tangled a spinnaker and became the first yacht in America's Cup history to lose a man overboard. The crew lost two minutes recovering him and *Intrepid*'s finishing margin was a massive 5 minutes, 52 seconds. Hardy requested a lay day in order to undertake repair work. Although the NYYC's race committee disallowed the protests of both yachts on Wednesday, the incident was proof of the tension in both camps. And some journalists questioned whether it was appropriate for the NYYC to be sitting in judgement on any matter in which it was directly involved.[49]

Billy McMahon, now minister for external affairs, decided to see the second race in Newport en route to a meeting in New York. However, as he and his wife made their way to the course on Thursday, the race was called off because of lack of wind. On Friday the race was abandoned at the third leg because of heavy fog, and then there was another lay day. Shortly before the race was due to be run on Sunday 20 September, *Intrepid*'s tactician reacted violently to a bee sting on the lip and was taken to hospital by helicopter. Packer, who was probably relishing the additional time available for his crew to work on *Gretel II*, radioed that if the NYYC wished he would not insist on racing that day. However, after officials decided to proceed with the race on the Sunday, the start was delayed by 1 hour, 40 minutes because an object thought to be a Second World War mine was spotted in the water.[50]

By the time the starter's gun was finally fired, there was a west-southwester of 7–8 knots, ideal for *Gretel II*. The spectators who had waited days for the race to begin in earnest saw the most controversial start in America's Cup history. Put simply, the problem was that the two yachts collided with each other and a lengthy piece of *Gretel II*'s bow was ripped off. Once again, protest flags were immediately hoisted on both yachts. After the collision, *Intrepid* crossed the starting line at good speed while *Gretel II* was almost stopped. But Hardy sailed a perfect race and, amidst wild cheering, his yacht crossed the line 67 seconds ahead of *Intrepid*. This levelled the series at one all — or so Packer and his crew thought.[51]

The Australians realised that they would still have to survive *Intrepid*'s protest. But as they saw it, their protest against *Intrepid* would have been sufficient to have the defender disqualified had she beaten *Gretel II* across the line. The NYYC race committee met to consider the protests on Sunday evening and Monday, which had been declared a lay day. Packer insisted that the hearings should be conducted formally and officially rather than in an informal and relaxed atmosphere. For five hours witnesses gave evidence and the committee studied crew drawings and aerial photographs. On Monday the committee upheld *Intrepid*'s protest and disallowed the protest from *Gretel II*. This meant that *Gretel II* was disqualified from the second race and the Americans now led the series 2–0.[52]

Racing rules are complicated and sometimes open to interpretation. A few years later B. Deveraux Barker, who chaired the race committee, commented that he remembered

> how astounded we on the committee were at the Australians' very primitive knowledge of the racing rules. Here at the very highest level of international competition, and in match racing where instinctive reactions to changing situations are vital, were men with a 'junior programme' knowledge of the rules. Bill Ficker [the American skipper] tore them apart at the hearings.

Many yachting writers, along with Hardy himself, now agree that the Australians did not have a good knowledge of the racing rules, which is ironic given Packer's earlier endeavours to try to use them to his own advantage. But in the short term, *Gretel II*'s disqualification was loudly condemned. There was a widespread feeling that the NYYC had to establish a more impartial way to deal with such disputes, and there were calls to have the result of the race declared null and void and to have it resailed.[53]

Packer dined with his dispirited crew on Monday 21 September. He told them that although they had been given a 'raw deal', they should 'get out there' and win the series. He also uttered the memorable line that 'appealing against the New York Yacht Club is like appealing to your mother-in-law about your wife'. Packer dismissed suggestions that the Australians might break off the series and return to Australia:

> Only one person says whether or not we go home — me.
> We are not going.
> We'll stay and try to win the next four races straight.[54]

Two Labor politicians in Australia, meanwhile, tried to use the controversy to their advantage. In the House of Representatives, Dr R. E. Klugman sarcastically proposed that the prime minister should pass on his government's sympathy and assure Packer that 'Liberal governments throughout Australia will continue to allow him and his companies to change the rules or suggest new ones'. Senator George Georges adopted quite a different stance, suggesting that anti-American feeling was now such in

Australia that the government should consider withdrawing Australian troops from Vietnam!⁵⁵

The third race for the America's Cup, held on Tuesday 22 September, was close but devoid of the incidents that had caused so much fuss over the previous two races. *Intrepid* won the contest by 1 minute, 18 seconds, meaning that *Gretel II* would have to take out the next race to keep the match alive. Opting for a lay day on Wednesday, Packer tried to have the protest hearing into the second race reopened.⁵⁶

On Thursday *Intrepid* seemed likely to take the fourth race and wrap up the series when she led by more than a minute at the final mark. But then the wind shifted and *Gretel II* showed how fast she was in light conditions, crossing the line 62 seconds ahead of her opponent. Packer joined skippers Hardy and Ficker at the press conference that night. Packer laughingly said that he wanted Ficker to do him a favour: 'If he does decide to lose another race, can he do it a bit earlier?' Packer, of course, knew that the chances of winning another three straight races from the Americans were slim indeed. When a journalist asked him how he felt about recording his first victory, Packer became serious:

> I don't regard it as our first victory. I regard it as our second victory.
>
> All I said to my boys this morning was, 'Whatever happens don't protest. You can't win'.⁵⁷

Requests for another lay day, followed by poor weather, saw the fifth race delayed until Monday 28 September. This meant that the twenty-first America's Cup series, which had begun a fortnight earlier, had become the longest one in its history. Shortly before the race Devereaux Barker issued a note saying that there was no right of appeal against the decisions of the NYYC race committee. Fifteen minutes before the starting gun went off, Packer radioed a message to the committee's boat: 'Mr Packer thanks you for your letter but does not agree with your point of view and wishes to take it up at a further place'. *Intrepid* won the race by 1 minute, 44 seconds. Packer stood quietly alone at the stern of *Pearl Necklace* and offered a single, seemingly grudging wave to the victorious American crew.⁵⁸

Packer now accepted that there was no point continuing to contest *Gretel II*'s disqualification. He issued another statement that evening promising that there would be no further effort to reverse the decision. Hardy tactfully commented that he thought the NYYC had acted with the utmost integrity, even though he felt that some of its rules were ambiguous. He was fortunate that, unlike in 1962, Packer had largely concentrated on citing and challenging yachting rules, rather than on undermining his authority as skipper. Gracious and humble in defeat, Hardy said he hoped that 'Sir Frank and Alan Payne don't think I let the side down as much as I do myself'.⁵⁹

Packer told his crew that even if he did not challenge for the America's Cup again, 'I have not regretted this adventure one iota'. Twenty-four hours after the end of the 1970 challenge, he announced that *Gretel II* was on the market for $175 000. Packer arrived back in Sydney on the morning of Sunday 4 October and went straight to bed. When he spoke to a reporter that night, it was clear that a bitter aftertaste still lingered in his mouth. He declared that future America's Cup challenges should be sailed in neutral waters and, as there were always two sides to any protest, the NYYC should not be the judge and jury in deciding a series. 'I've been travelling for 28 hours, and I'm still licking my wounds', he said.[60]

When Packer met his friend Billy McMahon in Newport in September 1970, the pair might have had a brief opportunity to discuss the political situation back in Australia. Prime Minister Gorton had been holding on in an unstable environment since surviving the leadership spill in late 1969. In 1970 he tried to transcend the pettiness of state loyalties, alienating premiers and the Senate in the process, and his centralism provoked hostility within his own party. At the half-Senate election in November, the Liberal Party obtained 38.2 per cent of the primary vote to the ALP's 42.2 per cent. Gorton somehow survived a meeting of the parliamentary Liberal Party on 2 February 1971.[61] But by the end of the month, he was embroiled in yet another political crisis.

On the weekend of 20–21 February, reports began to appear on the ABC and in some newspapers about difficulties that the minister for defence, Malcolm Fraser, was experiencing with army authorities. On Monday Fraser's press secretary rang the *Bulletin*'s Peter Samuel to say that the minister wanted to see him with a 'good story'. At the meeting on Wednesday, Fraser gave Samuel more details about alleged army insubordination than he had given his journalistic colleagues. This might have been because Samuel, who had visited Vietnam several times, was more capable of drawing out the defence minister than other journalists were. However, this was not the first time that the forty-year-old minister, who was already being touted as a future prime minister, had leaked material to ACP. According to Billy McMahon and Peter Howson, Fraser had for some time been giving 'background briefings' to Packer and Robert Baudino, the head of the *Telegraph*'s Canberra bureau.[62] And Packer and Alan Reid, of course, had been looking for ways to undermine Gorton's leadership for more than a year.

Samuel took Fraser's briefing on Wednesday 26 February to be 'on background': 'usable but of course no quotes'. After the meeting, Fraser arranged for people in the army and the Department of Defence to talk with Samuel. On Thursday Baudino discussed the relationship between Fraser and the army with Reid. Reid was about to go to Sydney to cover a series of meetings of the ALP federal executive and to appear on the TCN-9 panel show *Meet the Press*. He asked Baudino whether the story could wait until he (Reid) returned to Canberra. Baudino, however, said he did not think that he could delay running the story, as he believed that other journalists had been briefed by Fraser.[63]

Reid told Baudino that he should go to Gorton rather than Fraser to check the story about the military situation. As a veteran political correspondent and powerbroker, Reid must have known that Gorton loved a fight and was in a mood to take on Fraser. Samuel, by contrast, was less able to recognise the explosiveness of the situation; he had always been quite sympathetic to Gorton and, as he privately told his editor Donald Horne, 'I had no intention of getting embroiled in any political infighting'. In any case, the prime minister did indeed fall on his own sword. At a meeting with Baudino on 1 March, Gorton effectively sided with the chief of the general staff, Lieutenant-General Sir Thomas Daly. On 2 March Baudino ran a piece in the *Telegraph* about the tensions between Fraser and the army. The following day's *Bulletin* featured a more detailed account by Samuel with the inflammatory headline 'The Australian Army's "Revolt" in Vietnam'. Gorton did not attempt to discourage Alan Ramsey from writing a piece in the *Australian* on 4 August detailing Daly's charge against Fraser.[64]

Until this point, Packer could probably not have realised that his publications' revelations and his journalists' activities would have such dramatic consequences. But on 4 March he decided to swing publicly against Gorton now that he had a specific justification to publicly call for the prime minister's replacement. David McNicoll's holiday on the New South Wales south coast came to an abrupt end. He was ordered to return to Sydney and write an editorial for the *Sunday Telegraph* on 7 March saying that Gorton had to go. But despite the stridency of the piece, Packer was content to tuck it away inside the paper rather than plaster it over the front page.[65] It is possible that he still did not fully appreciate the gravity of the political crisis. On the other hand, he might have felt that to run the editorial on page one would provoke allegations of a 'Packer plot' to unseat the prime minister.

McNicoll had a second task to perform on Sunday. He was to chair the *Meet the Press* program that night featuring the journalists who had precipitated the political crisis. According to Reid, he agreed to sit alongside Baudino and Samuel only when Ramsey proved to be unavailable. Even though serendipity may have resulted in his appearance on *Meet the Press*, it is clear that Reid was actively involved in plotting Gorton's demise. Earlier in the day he had had a 'long talk' with Peter Howson, who was hoping for another leadership spill. Howson recorded in his diary:

> Now that the press is developing the crisis, the important thing is to keep it going as long as possible and to delay any discussions in the party room until the last possible moment … Altogether the decisions now are with the opposition and the press and with Malcolm Fraser.

On *Meet the Press* Reid declared that Fraser would be a puppet if he accepted Gorton's actions over the last week. On Monday morning Fraser resigned, saying that he could not tolerate the prime minister's disloyalty. Two days later, on 10 March, the parliamentary Liberal Party met in Canberra. When the meeting divided evenly on a vote of confidence, Gorton decided that it was in the best interests of the party to resign as leader. To the jubilation of Packer and his newspapers, McMahon finally fulfilled his ambition to become prime minister. But to the surprise and consternation of some of his colleagues, Gorton contested and won the deputy leadership.[66]

By the end of the month Howson had concluded that Gorton viewed McMahon's prime ministership as an interregnum. Gorton, Howson wrote, would not be a loyal deputy for long as he believed that the majority of the party was behind him and he was out of office only because of the manoeuvres of Packer and a small group of backbenchers. Although Reid and Packer had actively sought to undermine Gorton's leadership, the politician underestimated the range of forces that had amassed against him over the last two years. In a bitter irony, it was Gorton who was responsible for giving Packer his third imperial honour. In the New Year's honours list in January 1971, Packer was made a KBE for his services to Australian and international yachting. Gorton was out of office by the time the governor-general invested Packer with the honour at Government House in Canberra on 7 May 1971.[67]

Not surprisingly, at least one Labor politician demonised Packer for his role in Gorton's downfall. Kim Beazley senior criticised the 'Press king makers' who had a 'very good chance of owning the Government'. He told the House of Representatives that Gorton had refused to be a Packer prime minister: 'To Sir Frank Packer the Government of the Commonwealth is another one of his personally owned projects, like … the fight for the America's Cup'.[68]

With McMahon, Packer enjoyed a position of easier and more intimate access to the Lodge than he had with Gorton or, for that matter, Menzies. But as prime minister, McMahon soon proved to be hopelessly out of his depth. He lacked the substance to match his insatiable ambition, he had little in the way of vision or *gravitas* and many of his public utterances were jumbled and confused. In May 1971 Packer attended a function in McMahon's honour hosted by the Lord Mayor of Sydney. After the dinner the prime minister rose to his feet to talk about Australia's foreign affairs. He said that communist China was entitled to a seat in the United Nations Security Council and that it was time for Australia to build trade links with the Soviet Union. McMahon had based his speech on a set of papers from the Department of External Affairs, apparently unaware that it represented a change of policy on the part of the Australian government. At the end of the speech, Packer was said to be the only guest who clapped. The media baron did what he could to help the hapless prime minister. After McMahon spoke about tariffs to a Chamber of Manufactures dinner on 29 July 1971, Packer told him, 'Bill, that was a bloody awful speech', leading the anguished prime minister to begin talking about employing a full-time speechwriter.[69]

A fortnight later, Packer's role in the demise of Gorton's prime ministership again came under public scrutiny. Gorton was invited to write a series of articles about his administration for the *Sunday Australian*. The series was inspired by Alan Reid's account of the Gorton government, which had just been published by an ACP subsidiary, Shakespeare Head Press. In his first article on 8 August, Gorton defended the early stages of his administration and described Reid as Packer's 'hatchet man'.[70]

Packer was interviewed on ABC radio's influential current affairs show *P.M.* the following evening. When asked what was the motive behind the publication of *The Gorton Experiment*, Packer said that Reid had probably hoped to make a profit out of it; when the interviewer persisted with his line of questioning, Packer impatiently replied that his companies published employees' books on 'ordinary publishing terms'.[71] And yet there is some evidence to suggest that those close to Reid believed that his books had political implications. In 1969 Shakespeare Head Press had published *The Power Struggle*, Reid's account of the battle for Harold Holt's succession. Clyde Packer had sent a copy of what he described as the 'long-awaited epistle' to Menzies, saying that he hoped and prayed it was not defamatory. In September 1969, while Gorton was still in office, Howson recorded a conversation he had just had with Reid in his diary:

> He tells me that he's likely to publish a new book [*The Gorton Experiment*] next March dealing with the events under the Gorton leadership, also particularly examining the forthcoming election. He feels that this will have an effect on the leadership during next year.[72]

In the course of his radio interview on 9 August 1971, Packer conceded that many parts of Reid's latest book would undoubtedly annoy Gorton. After accusing Gorton of breaking cabinet confidentiality by agreeing to write his memoirs for the *Sunday Australian*, Packer described McMahon as an 'infinitely better' prime minister. Packer said that Gorton was 'a great embarrassment' to McMahon and should be retired to the backbench. Other media outlets, such as the *Age* and the Melbourne *Herald*, also maintained that Gorton deserved to be removed from office because he had breached accepted parliamentary conventions. Within a week McMahon had sought and received Gorton's resignation from cabinet.[73]

But while McMahon had needed little encouragement to roll his political opponent once and for all, Packer's public intervention attracted renewed censure. Gough Whitlam, now leader of the Opposition, detailed the long association between Packer and McMahon, saying that this explained 'a great deal about his sponsorship, protection and promotion of the Prime Minister'. Labor's Senator Don Willesee commented that although citizens had a right to put pressure on the government, governments must not allow themselves to be dominated by these people. He accused the present government of ceasing to govern and making itself subservient to 'outside bodies'.[74]

By the time Gorton resigned from cabinet, a controversial new book had hit the streets. In mid 1971 *Sir Frank: The Frank Packer Story* was published. Cassell Australia had commissioned R. S. Whitington, an ACP sports journalist, to write the book. As Packer's activities had only been dissected in newspaper and magazine profiles, the time was certainly ripe for a biography. Although Packer obsessively protected his privacy, he co-operated in the production of the book. Some years earlier, he had apparently summoned Cyril Pearl to his office, shown him a chest of records and memorabilia, and asked him whether he would be interested in doing anything with it; Packer's then editor had declined the offer. Packer obviously knew he would attract the attention of a biographer sooner rather than later, and by 1970 his public profile was higher than ever as a result of the America's Cup challenges. He gave Whitington, who was still on ACP's payroll, access to some documents in his office safe and allowed interviews to be conducted with his family and friends.[75]

On the release of the book Rohan Rivett, the former editor-in-chief of News Ltd, commented:

> Sir Frank Packer presents a popular image to many australians [sic]. Externally bluff, hearty, a former amateur heavyweight boxing champion, sponsor and controller of Australia's bid for the America's cup [sic], he has, for more than 30 years, managed to expose only broadly attractive appearances to the general public outside the newspaper industry.

But to the disappointment of industry observers and perhaps the general public, Whitington produced a hagiography that again painted Packer in a 'broadly attractive' light. The biography was excessively anecdotal and sycophantic and, in many places, factually inaccurate. The most interesting feature was Menzies' foreword, which asserted:

> I have heard him [Packer] charged with being too tough, or too rough in his treatment of people. My answer has always been, and still is, that all his faults are masculine; that he hits his opponent with a straight left; he does not stab him in the back; that he despises humbug and pretence.

The book was the subject of a derisive review by Richard Walsh, who had shot to fame after his role in publishing the controversial satirical magazine *Oz*. The iconoclastic twenty-nine-year-old told readers of the *Review* (later known as *Nation Review*):

> The life of sir [sic] Frank Packer — though this present hagiography almost disguises the fact — is that of a larrikin who almost all his life has had the kind of money that allowed him to indulge himself to the full. He is brutal in his treatment of those who cross him and power-hungry in his dealings and manipulations of men and events.
>
> Of course, as sir [sic] Robert so thoughtfully avers, such faults are 'masculine'. But so presumably were Hitler's.[76]

15
The King is Dead

In fighting against incremental increases in award wages, tussling with trade unions and indulging in ritual sackings at the same time as bestowing largesse on employees who were down on their luck, Frank Packer was like a feudal lord. Journalistic lore is full of tales of him helping out employees who had fallen on hard times, through ill-health, accident or financial misfortune. He was capable of great acts of kindness and generosity, but they were doled out in an arbitrary, rather than a systematic, fashion. It was widely acknowledged that 'The Boss' resented trade union and other interference with the way he ran his businesses. Seeing himself as the benevolent proprietor, he would bring out leftover savouries on silver platters after board meetings and hand them around to his reporters. Although he liked good food and wine, Packer had some simple tastes. Many a visitor was startled to be served sausages at office lunches and urged to hoe into the tomato sauce.[1]

By the early 1970s Packer was accustomed to inviting a small group of executives and columnists to dine with visiting tycoons and dignitaries in his personal dining room in Telegraph House. Those who sometimes joined Packer for lunch included McNicoll; King Watson, who had retired from editing the *Daily Telegraph* but was still associated with television and the *Sunday Telegraph*; Dudley Burgoyne, the *Daily Telegraph*'s new editor; John Kitto; Donald Horne; and Clyde Packer. Dr Emery Barcs, the *Telegraphs*' veteran foreign correspondent, was invited to luncheons for the likes of Alexis Stephanov, the Greek ambassador to Australia, and Lateef Kajode Takande, a Nigerian newspaper proprietor. Sir Frank used these occasions to establish and consolidate links with prominent people, hatch business plans, and solicit ideas for stories and editorial lines. After the lunch for Takande in April 1972 Barcs sarcastically recorded in his diary: 'My colleagues try to sound informed with questions which show [how] uninformed they really are. (Sir Frank asks about Mau-Mau!)'[2]

Another executive who joined Packer for many of these luncheons was H. W. B. Chester, the group finance controller of Consolidated Press Holdings. Trained as an accountant, Harry Chester had become assistant general manager of ATN-7 in 1959 and then assistant treasurer of Fairfax. In 1968 Chester informed his shocked colleagues at Fairfax that he had applied for the position in Park Street without knowing which company had advertised it. Even if this were true, Fairfax executives were not impressed to learn that their principal rival had secured the services of someone who was privy to all their financial affairs.[3]

Packer had seen Chester, nicknamed 'Hatchet Harry', at work negotiating media deals since the early 1960s. But while Chester was regarded as ruthless by some employees, senior editorial figures such as McNicoll and Ita Buttrose admired his determination to weed out inefficient practices and his 'don't pussyfoot around' attitude. Chester gradually moved ACP from its old attitude of parsimony to a new concept of ordered accounting and delegated responsibility. He managed to convince Packer that it was ludicrous for senior executives to examine staff expenses and to refuse to give higher salaries to good employees who were being headhunted by other companies. In Chester, Packer found the top financial adviser he had told Buzz Kennedy he was looking for a decade earlier. Within a short period of time, Packer became dependent on Chester to quite an extraordinary extent. No detail of finance, no investment, no new expenditure was undertaken without Chester's approval.[4]

One of Chester's main concerns was the unprofitability of the *Telegraph*s. Ever since establishing ACP, Packer had declined to give his editors details of how their publications were doing financially. The editors worked to a budget without knowing how it was worked out. And yet, even though Packer kept ledgers hidden in his desk showing how unprofitable the *Telegraph*s really were, it was widely acknowledged that the ACP group derived its profits from the *Women's Weekly* and the television stations. In the early 1970s various attempts were made to improve the *Telegraph*s' classified advertising volume and their appeal to readers in the Eastern Suburbs and on the North Shore. Chester would give Packer figures that presented the most awful picture of what was down the road if they continued to produce the *Telegraph*s at a loss. Kerry Packer, who was even more convinced than his older brother that a morning newspaper produced independent of an afternoon newspaper had no future, talked openly about offers that had been made for the papers. One such offer was rumoured to have come from Lord Beaverbrook's son Sir Max Aitken. Sir Frank became friends with Aitken when their newspapers jointly sponsored a successful London to Sydney car rally. Packer liked Aitken, who was outspoken, extroverted, dashing and a keen sailor.[5]

Watson and McNicoll tried to rebut the anti-newspaper talk at every opportunity, and no one really believed that ACP would dispose of the *Telegraph*s until Packer was dead. Horne writes that the *Telegraph* seemed like power to Packer:

> ... he would think of something and the next morning there it was in the paper. It appeared to give him political influence. It gave him interesting guests to invite to dinner, esteem when he was in London and New York, his knighthood. But I think he also loved it for itself — its racing news, the printing presses in the basement, the ledgers upstairs recording its financial failures, the comic strips, the newsagents' accounts, the sub-editors at the semi-circular desk, the attacks on the Labor Party, the teleprinters, the scruffy typography, the stereo department, the stock exchange reports, the letters to the editor, the lift-drivers (until he sacked them). Perhaps it also held for him reminders of promise — the excitements when he took it over in 1936, the improvizations [sic] and hopes of a younger man.[6]

Nevertheless, in the early 1970s a range of factors wore down Packer's resolve to cling onto the *Telegraph*s. The general economic situation was undermining business confidence. Inflation was on the rise, the mineral boom that had brought hundreds of millions of dollars of capital into Australia was collapsing and industrial unrest was widespread. In 1971 the *Sunday Telegraph* was confronted by a new competitor, Rupert Murdoch's *Sunday Australian*, ACP decided to retire employees over sixty-five years of age and the journalists' award was varied to allow a rise in wages. In September 1971 Packer withdrew his syndicate's bid for the 1974 America's Cup, explaining that it would not be fair to commit his company to an outlay of $1.5 million in the current financial environment.[7]

Packer was also under increasing pressure from the prime minister. During an official visit to the United States in November 1971, McMahon thought it appropriate to defend the Australian-American relationship in terms of the popular song *Moon River*, telling President Richard Nixon that wherever the United States was going, Australia was going the same way. In an article in the *Bulletin*, Alan Reid outlined the financial and strategic difficulties the Australian government was facing, described McMahon's speeches as 'uninspiring' and concluded that he had made only a marginal impact in official circles. Reid remarked, and historians have since agreed, that the most noteworthy event of the visit was the appearance of Sonia McMahon in a revealing dress at a White House dinner. Baffled and distressed by the poor press he was receiving back home, the prime minister called Reid a 'treacherous bastard' and said that he would complain about the article to Packer.[8]

There was a constant stream of telephone calls from McMahon to Packer early in the mornings, late at night and on weekends. The prime minister continued, of course, to confer with senior editorial figures about the coverage he was receiving. In January 1972, for example, he cabled Donald Horne to congratulate him on a 'fine article' in the *Bulletin*.[9] Just a few weeks later, McMahon was complaining to Reid about editorials in the *Telegraph*s concerning the government's taxation policies and appeals for price restraint.[10]

In his autobiography, McNicoll has suggested that Packer began to question the prime minister's credentials for the job: 'The friendship continued, slightly waning, until FP's death [in 1974]; but his disenchantment with McMahon as a politician started some time before his death'. And yet Packer probably never knew how the politician he had championed for so long looked to rival media proprietors for assistance. According to Reid, on Tuesday 1 February 1972 McMahon consoled 'himself with the thought that whatever Packer was up to he had stayed with [Warwick] Fairfax over the weekend and had one of the best and most rewarding weekends he ever had'.[11]

Sir Frank — the so-called 'king maker' — was manipulated by both Robert Menzies and Billy McMahon, albeit in very different ways. Menzies had masterfully managed to prolong the awarding of a knighthood, delay recognising Packer's America's Cup effort and discourage Packer from taking up political office, while gratefully accepting the editorial and financial support of the ACP group. Billy McMahon, a man Packer had known both personally and professionally since the early 1930s, had seemed like a very different proposition. Packer had done everything he could to get

McMahon into the Lodge, but the politician showed that he was willing to cynically cultivate the support of other media proprietors when the tide turned against his government.

In the first half of 1972 Emery Barcs, who was also a patient of Dr Frank Ritchie's, recorded in his diary that Packer was suffering from lumbago, looking 'pretty sick' and ageing fast. A holiday at Surfers Paradise could not prepare him for the harrowing months ahead.[12] On 16 April Esmé Fenston, who had secured the *Women's Weekly*'s market dominance for a record twenty-two years, died suddenly. Packer and his employees had treasured the sound common sense, the sharp mind and the dignified and unpretentious manner that Fenston had brought to the editorship of the magazine. When Sir Frank became too emotional to tell the staff the shocking news, Kerry was forced to take over. To add to Sir Frank's woes, the *Telegraph*s and the *Women's Weekly* became embroiled in a printers' strike a few weeks later.[13]

Clyde called on Phil Jones from the HWT and old Rupert Henderson from Fairfax to say that the *Telegraph*s were for sale. Jones and Henderson — who had been fooled by Sir Frank only a few years earlier — had trouble believing that the titles were really on the market. Rupert Murdoch, however, pounced at the opportunity to consolidate his position in Sydney; publishing the *Daily Telegraph* would allow him to utilise the excess capacity of the *Daily Mirror* plant and the infant *Sunday Australian* could be combined with the *Sunday Telegraph*. On Wednesday 31 May Murdoch had dinner with the Packer boys before going to a boxing match with Kerry. Sitting in the back of one of ACP's Mercedes on the way home, the pair agreed on the broad outlines of a deal.[14]

By lunchtime on Friday Kerry had convinced his father that the *Telegraph*s' future was untenable. Sir Frank, Murdoch and a bevy of legal and financial advisers spent Saturday at Telegraph House. Murdoch offered Packer $15 million for the two mastheads and by that night a contract had been drawn up. Jim Flahvin, one of Packer's senior financial executives, privately observed that Murdoch 'must have been mad' to offer $15 million for a package that did not include any plant, facilities or equipment. Sir Frank knew the offer was too good to refuse. Kerry and Frank Shaw, News Ltd's company secretary, flew down to Canberra to sign the documents in order to avoid paying stamp duty. Part of the contract stipulated that ACP was not to launch another daily newspaper for two years.[15]

On the night the agreement was signed, Billy and Sonia McMahon visited 'Cairnton', where Packer was having a drink with Murdoch. There are several versions of this encounter, so it is unclear whether the prime minister asked to see, or was summoned to meet, Packer. What is incontrovertible is that McMahon was dismayed by the sale of the *Telegraph*s. So great was his reliance on the support of the Packer media that he declared, 'Frank, I think that ends our prospects for the election'. According to McMahon, Packer suggested that he try to get an assurance that Murdoch would treat him 'fairly' in *Telegraph* editorials.[16]

ACP employees were also filled with foreboding. Some heard the brief announcement on TCN-9 on the night of Sunday 4 June, and others learned of the sale when they arrived at work the following day. Most *Telegraph* journalists were transferred to

News Ltd, but many printers lost their jobs. ACP shareholders, by contrast, had every reason to toast old Sir Frank. By the close of trading on Monday, shares in ACP had risen from $2.90 to $4.00, while shares in Television Corporation had gone from $2.75 to $3.40.[17]

On Sunday David McNicoll, who was in London, received a cable saying that the newspapers he had worked on for nearly thirty years had been disposed of. McNicoll put in a call to Packer, whose voice sounded weak and quavering. 'I'm sorry, son', said Packer. 'But it's done and it's no good looking back at it. I hope we've done the right thing.' Ita Buttrose, who was editing a *Sunday Telegraph* magazine insert and preparing for the launch of a new women's magazine, was also astonished to hear the news. As soon as she arrived in the office on Monday, an emotional Packer rang her to say: 'I haven't sold you. Goodbye'. He resigned as a director of AAP, telling the chairman that he would miss the company 'of those bright gentlemen gathered around the table bent upon taking each other down'.[18]

Silence settled on the once boisterous and bustling building. Several floors were in darkness, the Goss presses that had churned out the *Telegraph*s were still and the telephones rang only for the *Women's Weekly* and the *Bulletin*. But even though he was now a grandfather, Sir Frank maintained his thirty-six-year routine. He came into work six days a week and sat sullenly in his dark and solemn office, unable to demand that an article be rewritten, order a special editorial or complain about the appearance of a girl's navel in a photograph. It was clear to all who knew him that what Horne ironically describes as Packer's 'principled sacrifice' would be the end of him.[19] On 8 June Fairy Faircloth told Emery Barcs that the sale of the newspapers would take ten years off Packer's life. Barcs himself ran into Packer shuffling down the corridor of Telegraph House a few days later. The journalist found Packer hard of hearing and looking ghostly, like someone who did not have long to live.

On 12 July the ABC television program *This Day Tonight* interviewed McNicoll about Murdoch, Packer and the demise of John Gorton. In the course of the interview, McNicoll described Packer as one of the greatest men in Australian journalism.[20] Not long afterwards, Packer wrote to McNicoll in a shaky hand to thank him for his years of loyal service as editor-in-chief. Explaining that the *Telegraph* had not been viable without the production of an afternoon newspaper, Packer confessed that it had 'broken my heart to hand over what we built up to someone else'. Packer invited McNicoll to retain his office, remain on the board of Consolidated Press Holdings, and leave News Ltd to write a column for the *Bulletin* and have a drink with him each afternoon.[21]

Packer now spent his days fantasising about what to do with his money. At one drinks session he questioned an executive about what he knew about art: perhaps he should go to Europe and buy some art for its capital appreciation; at another session he read out a letter from someone who claimed to be experimenting with extracting oil from water. One concrete opportunity emerged in June 1972. ACP acquired a majority shareholding in K. G. Murray's interest in Publishers Holdings Ltd, which published a range of general interest and specialist magazines and had investments in street directories and ski resorts. Packer, who now controlled the biggest magazine publisher in the southern hemisphere, joined the board of Publishers Holdings in September.[22]

Packer also used his remaining media outlets to express his political preferences. In July Donald Horne requested permission to run a cover story on Margaret Whitlam, the wife of the leader of the ALP. Even though an interview had been arranged and a federal election was approaching, Packer refused to allow the story to be published.[23]

A few weeks later a rift developed between Packer and his elder son. In a profile of Sir Frank in the *Weekend Business Review* in September 1970, Richard Ackland reported that some people in the industry believed Harry Chester might one day take over the reins of the ACP group. Ackland observed that 'should the old man have to leave the scene hurriedly, for health reasons, the battle would really be on, and the blood would be flowing around those otherwise colourless corridors opposite Hyde Park'. While Kerry Packer regarded Chester as an adviser, friend and mentor, Clyde and 'Hatchet Harry' had no time for each other. It is rumoured that Clyde unsuccessfully tried to manoeuvre Chester out of the family empire in July 1972.[24]

This was a difficult and taxing period for Clyde. Sir Frank, who had never been able to draw a distinction between work and family, expected his sons to be on deck night and day. After the break-up of his marriage in 1969, Clyde began to realise that he had been suppressing part of his personality for years. At the same time as his sense of disillusionment set in, Clyde's executive duties were expanding. In 1969 he became managing director of GTV-9, and in 1970 he was appointed joint managing director of TCN-9. Feeling that he was disappearing into a kind of closed world, Clyde became irritable and concerned about losing his creativity; being a company man was, he averred, 'a combination of tedium and bullshit'. Then, in June 1972 the *Telegraph*s, which he had been groomed to take over all his life, were sold. Even though he helped to negotiate the transaction, any lingering interest he had in the family business died.[25]

Clyde later observed, somewhat ironically, that being joint managing director of TCN-9 alongside his father 'was a very equitable arrangement — I had the responsibility and he had the authority'. Clyde was enthusiastic when Michael Willesee, the former host of ABC's *Four Corners*, came to him in 1971 with a proposal for a nightly current affairs program. Sir Frank initially rejected the idea, declaring that Willesee, whose father was the Labor politician Don Willesee, was a communist. Clyde managed to convince his father that Mike Willesee was not a communist but a businessman and a first-class interviewer. Willesee's company, Trans Media Pty Ltd, began producing *A Current Affair* on TCN-9 and GTV-9 in January 1972. The program, which was hosted by Willesee and discovered the maverick brilliance of Paul Hogan, showed that current affairs could find an audience on commercial television.[26]

By early August an eight-week national petrol strike had brought industry to a standstill and forced businesses to lay off thousands of workers. Bob Hawke, the president of the Australian Council of Trade Unions, rang Eric Fisher, the chairman of GTV-9, to ask whether the ACTU could buy time to present its case. Fisher thought Hawke should be interviewed by Willesee on *A Current Affair* and Clyde Packer supported the proposal. But the plan went awry after Sir Frank saw Hawke, who had recently taken out a writ against the *Telegraph*s for damages totalling $250 000, on a regular television news bulletin. He range Clyde to say that the union official was never to appear on any Channel Nine news or current affairs program. When Sir Frank opined that the wily Hawke was too good for Nine's interviewers, Clyde ventured to suggest that this was the fault of the interviewers.[27]

Infuriated by his father's act of censorship, Clyde resigned his management positions with GTV-9 and TCN-9. On 4 August Sir Frank issued a statement refusing to give the reasons for his son's resignation, which he said he had accepted with 'great regret'. Clyde, however, later commented that his resignation was accepted with great alacrity: 'I suspect my father was as glad to get rid of me as I was to get rid of him'. While journalistic and business circles were abuzz with rumours about this dramatic development, it was agreed that Clyde should remain on the boards of Consolidated Press Holdings, Television Corporation and General Television. But Sir Frank amended his will to cut his elder son out of the succession and made Chester a joint governing director, with Kerry and Florence, of the Cairnton family trust company.[28]

Now nothing more than a silent partner in his father's empire, Clyde embarked on his own quest for personal and business fulfilment. He formed a company to produce television specials in Australia, including shows about the controversial feminist Dr Germaine Greer; joined with Willesee and Paul Hogan's producer, John Cornell, to publish an Australian edition of the sex magazine *Forum*; and crossed the floor of the New South Wales Legislative Council to prevent the passing of the government's bill on obscene publications.[29]

His elder son's new interests must have dismayed poor Sir Frank. He might have had a long history of womanising, but Packer was something of a prude when it came to public discussions of bodily functions and sex. Journalists on the *Telegraph*s had been forbidden to use the world 'lavatory' and in 1971 he had agreed with many of his viewers that the Irish comedian Dave Allen had made offensive and vulgar comments on TCN-9. Pre-empting the results of an internal inquiry into the program, Packer declared: 'I'm extremely sorry that it appeared and, if we could have seen it beforehand, it would have been cut off'.[30]

A dummy for a new magazine that Kerry Packer and Ita Buttrose were working on also bemused Sir Frank. In part a product of the women's liberation movement, *Cleo* targeted financially and sexually independent women between twenty and forty-five years of age. It aimed to talk openly about women's ambitions, emotions, desires, bodies, health and sex. On the eve of *Cleo*'s launch in November 1972 Sir Frank cabled Buttrose from Hong Kong: 'Good luck with this venture. I think you'll need it'. When the magazine, featuring Australia's first nude male centrefold, sold out within forty-eight hours, Packer sportingly sent another cable to the editor: 'Well done. You're not only good-looking but talented'. Kerry remained uneasy about his father's reaction to the more explicit stories in the magazine. A few months after the launch, Buttrose told Kerry she was working on an article about how masturbation could help female frigidity. Groaning, Kerry sank into a chair and said: 'Oh, no ... not masturbation. What will I tell the old man?' Buttrose suggested: 'Tell him it's medical'. The pair laughed and did as Buttrose suggested, and Sir Frank allowed the story to proceed.[31]

Packer was too sick and too weary to censor articles in a puzzling but profitable new magazine. At the end of November 1972 he had surgery to treat a fistula, confiding to Dr Ritchie that he was upset about the sale of the *Telegraph*s and felt unemployed. A fortnight later, Fairy Faircloth told Emery Barcs that Packer was 'a very unhappy man'. At precisely this time, Packer was forced to publicly deny a bizarre rumour that he was about to sell Channel Nine. In early 1973 he was fitted with a pacemaker, but he continued to be troubled by a bad chest and throat, bloodshot eyes and impaired hearing.[32]

One person who did bring Packer some pleasure during this sad and lonely period was Trevor Kennedy. Packer enticed to his stable the twenty-nine-year-old, who had been editing Fairfax's new weekly newspaper, the *National Times*, in November 1972. Kennedy replaced Clyde Packer's friend Donald Horne as editor of the *Bulletin*. A combination of naivete, brashness and sincerity made Kennedy attractive to Sir Frank. Packer regarded his new recruit as a rabid left-winger, and Kennedy never hesitated to express his views, to the amazed delight of his employer. Packer installed Kennedy on some ACP boards and showed great pleasure as the *Bulletin*'s sales, which had been stagnating, began to improve.[33]

But still controversy dogged Packer. In October 1972 a Labor senator alleged that TCN-9 had edited out comments made by John Gorton and Dr Jim Cairns, a vocal critic of Australia's commitment to Vietnam, during a television debate. It was rumoured that Packer, at McMahon's request, then banned Gorton from appearing on *A Current Affair*.[34]

The Australian people went to the polls on 2 December. After twenty-three years of conservative rule, it seemed that Australians might finally be ready for a change of government. Running the most professional campaign ever mounted by the ALP, Gough Whitlam's camp courted the voters — the anti-Vietnam protesters, the feminists, the activists for Aboriginal rights, and the migrants — with the slogan 'It's Time'. As polling day loomed, Packer's media outlets went into bat for McMahon. At 7 p.m. on 15 November an 'editorial' went to air over Channel Nine. The three-and-a-half minute spiel, which was written by McNicoll and read by Michael Ramsden, asserted that the ALP's platform sounded like 'marijuana dreams in a utopian Disneyland'. On 22 November Channel Nine broadcast another editorial advocating a vote for the coalition. The script of the ALP's reply to the first editorial, which arrived at TCN-9's Willoughby headquarters that evening, was not broadcast.[35] To Packer's dismay, the ALP won the election.

Not surprisingly, relations between Packer's company and the new administration were strained. On Monday 4 June 1973 *A Current Affair* broadcast a pre-recorded interview with the prime minister. During the interview, in which he criticised the performance and actions of some premiers and cabinet ministers, Whitlam passed a comment about a Catholic bishop. On Packer's instructions, the four words about the bishop were bleeped out. The show's producer, Phil Davis, said that he and his colleagues had 'strenuously disagreed' with management's alteration: 'We didn't want to be the first people to censor the Prime Minister'. Even though Packer appears to have censored the footage so as not to involve his television station in a libel action, he should have consulted Whitlam's office before the interview went to air. Labor politicians like Senator Arthur Gietzelt predictably railed against 'one man' having the power to censor and censure prime ministers.[36]

Within days, Packer's actions were again under scrutiny. On Thursday 7 June a book about the 1972 election was published. Edited by Professor Henry Mayer, the book contained a chapter about Packer's role in the coverage of the election campaign. After discussing the two controversial television editorials in the lead-up to the poll, Mayer claimed that Packer had given the Democratic Labor Party (DLP) free advertising on TCN-9. Since its formation in 1955 when the ALP split over the issue of communism, the DLP had been directing its preferences to the coalition. Mayer published a letter from an advertising executive to the DLP's Senator Jack Kane indicating that the party had received free advertising worth $18 980. The article, which appeared to provide the first direct evidence of Packer's political machinations, caused a sensation. When Kane denied that the DLP had done a deal with TCN-9, Mayer claimed that he had further, unpublished evidence of the transaction. Packer issued a statement saying that TCN-9 had not helped the DLP: 'We don't give anything away free here'.[37]

Ever more cantankerous, Packer turned the table on his accusers in the lead-up to the New South Wales election on 17 November 1973. After consulting his lawyers, Packer decided that TCN-9 would charge the two major political parties $5000 each to broadcast their policy speeches. Robert Askin, who had benefited from Packer's largesse in the past, went ahead and appeared in a paid broadcast during prime-time viewing. But the ALP, under the leadership of Pat Hills, refused to pay a fee to appear on the television station. Senator Douglas McClelland, the chairman of the Senate Standing Committee on Education, Science and the Arts, believed that charging political parties to broadcast their policy speeches was undemocratic and not in the public interest. However, on 2 November he was forced to concede that the Broadcasting and Television Act was drafted too vaguely to allow any disciplinary action to be taken against Television Corporation.[38]

It did not take Packer long to precipitate yet another controversy. Over the last few months, Willesee had been attempting to negotiate a new contract for the production of *A Current Affair*. In early November these negotiations broke down, ostensibly because Willesee was asking for $18 000 a week to produce the show. The issue of the *Bulletin* dated 10 November published correspondence between Packer, Willesee and other TCN-9 executives. One piece of correspondence cited was a memo that Packer had sent to George Chapman, TCN-9's general manager, on 30 April. The memo had criticised Willesee for bias in its coverage of domestic politics and the Vietnam War. It also condemned *A Current Affair* for featuring a segment about *Forum*, the sex magazine published by Clyde Packer and Willesee, in a 7 p.m. timeslot.[39]

The publication of this internal correspondence, together with the gibe about *Forum*, raised Clyde Packer's hackles. When the *Bulletin* hit the streets on 7 November, Graham Williams, a journalist from the *Australian*, asked Clyde for a response. 'He'll say "No comment"', predicted one of Williams's colleagues, 'you don't shit on your Dad'. How wrong he was. Puffing on a cigar, Clyde gave an exclusive interview to Rupert Murdoch's *Australian*. He described the release of private correspondence as 'completely unethical', claimed that Willesee had been manoeuvred into a position where alleged demands for money could be used in a false light against him, accused TCN-9 of making 'an incredibly stupid blunder' in not allowing Pat Hills free time for his policy speech, revealed the events which had triggered his resignation from executive positions in his father's empire and refuted Sir Frank's claim that they had parted with regret.[40]

Sir Frank must have been devastated by this outburst, which violated a family tradition that restrained the sons and muzzled the women. But even now he could not resist the temptation to push his political barrow one last time. Willesee was still contracted to produce *A Current Affair* for Channel Nine until January 1974. A few weeks before the poll, the federal government held a referendum seeking the authority to regulate prices and wages. In an interview on 3 December, Willesee asked Whitlam to outline the reasons for the referendum, explain why some sections of the labour movement were opposed to the 'yes' case, and comment on the chances of the referendum succeeding. At Packer's behest, all references to the referendum were deleted before the interview went to air. This action did nothing to improve the Opposition's case, and only served to reinforce the image of Packer as an interventionist and autocratic media baron and leave Willesee feeling rightly bemused.[41]

This was the last time Packer used one of his outlets for overtly political purposes. The traumas of the past eighteen months, coming on top of years of ill-health, sapped his strength and vitality. He reduced his circle of friends and rejected nearly all invitations to social gatherings.[42] One of the few functions he did attend at this time was the grand opening of the Sydney Opera House in October 1973. Here he met Dame Pattie Menzies, who was wearing a brooch he had given her as a gift. He sent his love to Sir Robert, now in his late seventies, and deplored 'the lack of coherent thought and planning' under Labor. Packer also managed to preside over a party for his employees, from the cleaners up, on Christmas Eve.[43]

Increasingly, however, Packer declined invitations to cocktail parties and openings, sending apologies about the pressure of work. He went to selected dinner parties but often arranged for David McNicoll to telephone him at 9 p.m. to say that he was urgently needed at the office. Packer was lured to the cinema only occasionally, where he generally had a good sleep. He spent most nights dozing in front of the television until his devoted butler and helper, Alfred Thomas, insisted that he go to bed.[44]

Sir Frank found solace in the companionship of his wife and his beloved dogs. He had an array of pets because he could not bear to see a dog lost. 'Cairnton' was home to a black labrador and a bordie collie, as well as Florence's two Siamese cats. A large salivating dog sprawled in an armchair would sometimes greet employees summoned to Packer's office to receive a dressing down. Sir Frank was very keen on a special breed of dog, a cross between the alsatian and the doberman, of which he had two, Denzil and Macarthur, named after his old friend, Denzil Macarthur-Onslow, who bred the line. But Packer's favourite dog was Henry, a white alsatian he had found wet and homeless as he drove home from work through the rainswept streets of Sydney. The Packers would often receive a call from a pub near Centennial Park saying that Henry had gone walkabout yet again, and a chauffeur would be despatched to pick him up.[45]

George Finey's whimsical caricature of his former boss, n.d.
(Dixson Galleries, State Library of New South Wales,
by permission of Mitzi Finey)

Sir Frank went to an Anglican church now and then. He liked talking to priests and parsons and trying to shock them, and joked so much about death and dying that McNicoll felt it had an awesome fascination for him.[46] One of Packer's greatest fears was that he would be buried alive. He asked his brother-in-law Sir George Stening (now a prominent gynaecologist) to inject him with strychnine if people thought he was dead to make sure that he did not come round in his coffin.

Never reluctant to diagnose his physical complaints, Packer prescribed a treatment for his psychological malaise. He knew that the second anniversary of the sale of the *Telegraph*s in June 1974 would free him to publish another daily newspaper. He placed an order for new offset presses for a cost of approximately $2 million and in January 1974 rumours that he was planning to launch a twenty-four-hour daily newspaper began to circulate. But in March Packer was bedridden with influenza. When Packer managed to stagger into the office on 3 April, Emery Barcs recorded in his diary: 'He looks emasculated and complains about his "flu". Doesn't walk but shuffles very slowly. How this bomb of energy has deteriorated, the poor man. Feel very sorry for this poor rich man'.[47]

On 25 April Packer was admitted to the Page Chest Pavilion at Royal Prince Alfred Hospital for a minor operation. A few days later, George Stening telephoned Clyde Packer to say that Sir Frank's death was imminent. Clyde visited his father in hospital and the pair reached some sort of reconciliation. At 7.30 a.m. on 1 May, while gale-force winds battered Sydney, Sir Frank died of pneumonia. He was aged just sixty-seven, but his numerous ailments meant that his death was not unexpected. Nevertheless, employees found it difficult to believe that 'The Master', who had seemed omnipotent and invincible, was no more. Fairy Faircloth remarked: 'You felt he was perpetual and eternal. You just thought he'd go on forever'.[48]

In 1959 Packer had been called upon to deliver the eulogy at the funeral of Lionel McFadyen, the brother of the best man at his first wedding. McFadyen, a father of four who had served on the executive of the Red Cross, had risen to become the youngest ever chairman of the Sydney Stock Exchange. Packer had told the packed congregation:

When the good Lord decides that He needs my services in another place, if I can shuffle off with the same reputation for integrity, with the same record of achievement, with the same record of public service, and — most important of all — with as many people as genuinely sorry I have gone and loving me as is the case with Lionel, then I and my family will be very proud ...[49]

So what then, was said of Packer on his death? Publicly, politicians, yachting officials and sporting organisations lined up to pay tribute. Premier Askin, who had so much to thank Packer for, maintained that the late media proprietor was 'widely admired for his robust Australianism and his intimate touch with his newspapers and their staff'. Robert Menzies repeated the sentiments he had expressed in his foreword to Whitington's biography: 'Sir Frank was a real man of positive views ... never neutral, sometimes difficult, always masculine and he never pretended'. Billy Snedden, now leader of the federal Opposition, said that Australia had lost 'a tough, distinctive and distinguished individual'. Prime Minister Whitlam acknowledged that Packer had had 'very great influence' on the New South Wales media and his opposition to Labor had been well known. Trying to sound statesmanlike, Whitlam said that despite their differing political views, he personally had always respected Sir Frank and believed that Sir Frank had respected him. In fact, Packer had viewed the Labor prime minister as a self-serving lightweight.[50]

McNicoll managed to pen obituaries for the *Sunday Telegraph*, the *Bulletin*, the *Women's Weekly* and the *Sydney Morning Herald*. Gavin Souter told the latter's readers that Packer 'was tough, shrewd, rumbustious, and as game as they come ... He was a great Australian individualist, one of a dying breed'.[51] The *Telegraph* described its former proprietor as 'waspish, aggressive and a rugged individualist'. Alan Trengove wrote in the *Sun News-Pictorial* that, like Lord Beaverbrook, Packer 'was obsessively anti-socialist and a would-be king-maker and breaker'. The London *Times* commented that Packer 'was in a real sense a colourful figure, but his colours were always primary ones'. The socialist *Workers' News*, remembering how Packer had covered Stalin's death, ran a savage obituary entitled 'Packer is dead — Hooray'.[52]

On 3 May the dean of St Andrew's Cathedral, the Very Rev. L. Shilton, conducted the funeral. One thousand mourners filled the pews or stood outside in abominable weather. Donald Horne recalls that at the entrance to the cathedral:

> ... the old millionaire's two riderless Mercedes mourned him. Inside, his body was carried down the aisle, followed by celebrities from the Age of Menzies; the occasion recalled generations of rich, uncultured Australians, great sportsmen, patrons of the turf, members of jockey clubs, diners at governors' tables, honoured by English monarchs for the service they rendered the public by making themselves rich.[53]

In his diary, Emery Barcs recorded that 'if a funeral can be "beautiful" this one is. Dignified. Again the impression how small coffins are'.

The Anglican Archbishop of Sydney, the Most Rev. Dr Marcus Loane, read the lesson from Paul's First Letter to the Corinthians.[54] Vincent Fairfax, a director of John Fairfax Ltd and president of the Royal Agricultural Society of New South Wales, delivered the funeral oration. Packer had always been on good terms with Vincent, who was much less involved in the day-to-day running of the *Sydney Morning Herald* and its stablemates than his cousin Warwick. Describing Packer as a 'great, strong and boisterous Australian', Sir Vincent conceded that his 'ruggedness of approach, his gambling instinct, his satisfaction in confusing and defeating competitors sometimes got a little mixed up in their application'. Nevertheless, Fairfax opined, Australia would not make its proper contribution to the world if it ran out of buccaneer businessmen like Packer who played the game to win as well as for fun.[55]

After the funeral service Clyde quietly asked his uncle whether he had followed Sir Frank's orders and administered strychnine. George Stening said 'no', and both men laughed affectionately. Sir Frank's body was cremated and the ashes were interred at South Head Cemetery.[56] The family vault that housed the remains of R. C. and now Frank Packer was in the exclusive Eastern Suburbs, an area of Sydney that they had made their own half a century earlier. Just a few short kilometres away were the city buildings that had ensconced their popular creations, *Smith's Weekly*, the *Daily* and *Sunday Guardians*, the *Australian Women's Weekly*, the *Sunday Telegraph* and *Cleo*.

The *Canberra Times*, wondering about the line of succession, wrote 'whatever transpires will be quite different to what he [Sir Frank] might have achieved himself. He was too much the individualist for any successor to truly emulate'. Kerry Packer replaced his father as chairman of Consolidated Press Holdings. Apparently aware that embarking on the publication of another metropolitan daily newspaper would be ruinously expensive, one of his first actions was to cancel the order for the new offset presses.[57] The company Kerry inherited published a plethora of general interest and niche-market magazines; controlled the powerful Nine television network; produced a number of provincial and suburban newspapers; ran commercial printing and book publishing firms; and had interests in gold mines, tourist resorts, racehorses and a piggery. R. C. Packer had played a role in closing and merging newspaper titles in the 1920s and the 1930s, and his son had helped to ensure that the Australian media market became more concentrated, and let in fewer new players, throughout his own career. Sir Frank's achievements had been largely due to two exceptional mentors (R. C. Packer and E. G. Theodore), financial cunning, bravado, prodigious energy, and an ability to identify and facilitate the creative genius of others such as George Warnecke and Brian Penton.

While Kerry took over the reins of the family empire and quickly embarked on a process of modernisation and aggressive expansion, his elder brother remained 'sick of lugging this Packer persona around'. Clyde would later say that he was afraid of his father until 'I heard he was dead, then I wasn't afraid of him anymore'. In 1976 he moved to Los Angeles, where he produced television documentaries, published a surfing magazine and remarried. He remained chairman of the conservative Australian quarterly *Quadrant* but sold his shares in the family business to his brother. The terms of the amicable agreement were never made public, but it is believed that Clyde received about $4 million.[58]

In February 1975 Sir Frank's estate was sworn for probate at $1 340 526. He left cash gifts totalling $18 000 to his three secretaries, Fairy Faircloth, Mabs Gilburt and Maisie McMahon, and $5000 for his 'friend and servant', Alfred Thomas. Even in death, Sir Frank Packer attracted controversy. It was well known in business, political and journalistic circles that elaborate tax minimisation schemes had caused Packer's estate to be greatly undervalued. Senator Arthur Gietzelt questioned how the head of 'a vast propaganda empire' and a web of more than sixty corporate identities had managed to ensure that his estate was valued at only $1.3 million.[59]

The last word is perhaps best left to two journalists who had been on Sir Frank's staff. Clearly surprised by how affected he was by news of the death, Barcs privately commented, 'I was fond of that strange buccaneer'. Elizabeth Riddell, who had worked for both R. C. and Frank Packer, wrote in the *Australian*:

> Nobody would be foolish enough at this stage to try to assess either the man or the myth. Ten years, twenty years from now there will be an account of his life and works, the writer having first sieved the truth, or as near as anyone can get to the truth, from the massive slagheap of third hand report and wishful anecdotage.[60]

Chronology

R. C. and Frank Packer's Principal Media Interests

1919 Sir James Joynton Smith, Claude McKay and R. C. Packer launch *Smith's Weekly*.

1923 Smith's Newspapers Ltd incorporated. *Daily Guardian* launched.

1929 *Sunday Guardian* launched.

1930 Associated Newspapers Ltd acquires the *Daily* and *Sunday Guardians*.

1931 R. C. Packer becomes general manager of Associated Newspapers Ltd.

1932 Sydney Newspapers Ltd incorporated.

1933 *Australian Women's Weekly* launched.

1936 Consolidated Press Ltd incorporated. Takes over the publication of the *Australian Women's Weekly* and the Sydney *Telegraph*.

1939 *Sunday Telegraph* launched.

1946 Conpress Printing Ltd incorporated.

1954 Consolidated Press Holdings Ltd incorporated in the Australian Capital Territory.

1956 Consolidated Press Ltd becomes Australian Consolidated Press Ltd (ACP).

Television Corporation Ltd's TCN-9 goes to air in Sydney.

1960 Television Corporation Ltd acquires a controlling interest in Melbourne's GTV-9.

Conpress Printing Ltd acquires the *Bulletin*.

Suburban Publications Pty Ltd incorporated.

1972 Australian Consolidated Press sells the *Daily* and *Sunday Telegraphs* to News Ltd.

Endnotes

Introduction

1. *Women's Weekly*, 26 September 1962, p. 15. See also New York Yacht Club Archives (NYYCA): 'Newport on a grand scale', newspaper clipping, n.d. (September 1970).
2. National Archives of Australia, Australian Capital Territory (NAA/ACT): A1838/386; 1525/3/266 Part 1; America's Cup Race Dinner, 14 September 1962.
3. *Women's Weekly*, 26 September 1962, p. 15, 15 May 1964, p. 3; *Newport Daily News*, 14 September 1962.
4. *Commonwealth Parliamentary Debates (CPD)*, House of Representatives, vol. 36, 23 August 1962, pp. 745–6; vol. 37, 23 October 1962, pp. 1851–2. See also Bridget Griffen-Foley, 'Playing with princes and presidents: Sir Frank Packer and the 1962 challenge for the America's Cup', *Australian Journal of Politics and History*, vol. 46, no. 1, 2000, pp. 51–66.
5. R. S. Whitington, *Sir Frank: The Frank Packer Story*, Cassell Australia, North Melbourne, 1971, p. 247; *Sunday Telegraph*, 16 September 1962, p. 3; *Daily Telegraph*, 19 September 1962, p. 3; *Women's Weekly*, 26 September 1962, p. 15.
6. Whitington, *Sir Frank*, p. 292.

1 Napoleon's Debut

1. *Dictionary of National Biography*, vol. 15, pp. 31–2.
2. Whitington, *Sir Frank*, p. 46; Donna Smith Packer, *On Footings from the Past: The Packers in England*, Bookcraft, Salt Lake City, 1988, pp. 184, 189; *International Genealogical Index (IGI)*, pp. 9323–31.
3. Packer, *On Footings from the Past*, p. 4.
4. Valerie G. Scott and Eve McLaughlin, *County Maps and Histories: Berkshire*, Quiller Press, London, 1984, pp. viii-ix, xviii, xxi, xxix.
5. Leonard Weiss, *Watch-making in England, 1760–1820*, Robert Hale, London, 1982, pp. 34–6, 41.
6. ibid. p. 47; E. J. Tyler, *The Craft of the Clockmaker*, Crown Publishers, New York, 1973, p. 69; *Reading Mercury*, 16 February 1789, p. 3, 26 December 1791, p. 3. See also Berkshire Record Office (BRO): DP98/5/1, Churchwarden's Accounts, 20 May 1792, 11 May 1800, Visitation 1801 — Visitation 1802, Visitation 1804 — Visitation 1805, Visitation 1805 — Visitation 1806.
7. BRO: DP98/5/1, Churchwarden's Accounts, 1806–07 Bills. See also IGI, pp. 9324, 9327; information from Noni E. Fitzmaurice.

Endnotes

8   BRO: DA1/159/63, Charles Packer will.
9   BRO: DP98/5/1, Churchwarden's Accounts, July 1814, May 1819; DP98/8/6, Vestry Minutes, 4 June 1819.
10 Weiss, *Watch-making in England*, pp. 233–45; Muriel Goaman, *English Clocks*, The Connoisseur and Michael Joseph, London, 1967, pp. 103–4.
11 BRO: DP98/8/1, Vestry Minutes, 28 March 1833, 8 March 1834, April 1835, 27 September 1835, 31 March 1836. See also Scott and McLaughlin, *County Maps and Histories: Berkshire*, p. xxiv.
12 Whitington, *Sir Frank*, p. 47; IGI, pp. 9323–5, 9328; E. J. Lea-Scarlett, 'Charles Sandys Packer', *Australian Dictionary of Biography, (ADB)*, vol. 5, p. 387. See also *Hobart Town Courier*, 4 December 1854, p. 2 (my thanks to Noni E. Fitzmaurice for this reference).
13 Information from Noni E. Fitzmaurice. Frederick Alexander Packer was christened with one of his sisters on 30 July 1816; see *IGI*, p. 9325.
14 *A List of the Students Received at the Royal Academy of Music Since its Establishment in 1823*, pp. 15, 29.
15 *Hobart Mercury*, 24 February 1893, p. 1; Francis Collinson, *The Traditional and National Music of Scotland*, Routledge & Kegan Paul, London, 1966, pp. 2, 214–16; John Purser, *Scotland's Music: A History of the Traditional and Classical Music of Scotland From Earliest Times to the Present Day*, Mainstream Publishing, Edinburgh and London, 1992, pp. 157, 203–6; Henry George Farmer, *A History of Music in Scotland*, Da Capo Press, New York, 1970, pp. 343–4.
16 Information from Noni E. Fitzmaurice; *IGI*, pp. 9323–6, 9328. See also BRO: DP/98/8/6, Vestry Minutes, 25 March 1841.
17 R. L. Wettenhall, 'Frederick Augustus Gow', *ADB*, vol. 5, p. 387.
18 *Hobart Town Courier*, 4 October 1845, p. 2; E. J. Lea-Scarlett, 'Charles Sandys Packer', *ADB*, vol. 5, p. 387.
19 Lloyd Robson, *A History of Tasmania*, vol. I, *Van Diemen's Land From the Earliest Times to 1855*, Oxford University Press, Melbourne, 1983, pp. 462–3.
20 ibid. pp. 463–6.
21 Archives Office of Tasmania (AOT): MB2/39/15, Hobart Marine Board passenger list, p. 136. See also P. F. Bolger, 'The changing role of a city: Hobart', *Tasmanian Historical Research Association Papers and Proceedings*, vol. 16, no. 1, July 1968, p. 7.
22 Mrs Augustus Prinsep and Robert Elwes cited by Carolyn R. Stone and Pamela Tyson, *Old Hobart Town and Environs, 1802–1855*, Pioneer Design Studio, Lilydale, 1978, pp. 176, 180, 182.
23 George William Evans, David Burn, James Syme and Robert Elwes cited by Stone and Tyson, *Old Hobart Town*, pp. 147, 126, 154, 180; Bolger, 'The changing role of a city: Hobart', p. 8.
24 *Tasmania Pioneers Index*, 1803–89.
25 AOT: General Index Card, A. Packer, 1853. See also R. L. Wettenhall, 'Frederick Augustus Gow', *ADB*, vol. 5, p. 387.
26 Anon., David Burn, James Syme and Peter Benson Walker cited by Stone and Tyson, *Old Hobart Town*, pp. 90, 92, 130, 154; *Year Book of the Church of England in the Diocese of Tasmania*, 1891, p. 6.

Endnotes

27 Robson, *A History of Tasmania*, vol. I, pp. 466-7; Bolger, 'The changing role of a city: Hobart', p. 8; Michael Roe, 'Introduction' to Stone and Tyson, *Old Hobart Town*, p. 16; W. A. Townsley, *Tasmania From Colony to Statehood, 1803-1945*, St David's Park Publishing, Hobart, 1991, p. 79.

28 Townsley, *Tasmania from Colony to Statehood*, pp. 78-9; Bolger, 'The changing role of a city: Hobart', p. 7; Lloyd Robson, *A History of Tasmania*, vol. II, *Colony and State from 1856 to the 1980s*, Oxford University Press, Melbourne, 1991, pp. 12, 15-16, 72-3.

29 *Hobart Mercury*, 3 July 1862, p. 1, 24 February 1893, p. 1.

30 Anon., Peter Benson and Henry Butler cited by Stone and Tyson, *Old Hobart Town*, pp. 92, 158, 190.

31 *Hobart Mercury*, 22 August 1861, p. 2, 3 July 1862, p. 1, 5 July 1862, p. 1, 24 February 1893, pp. 1, 2; R. L. Wettenhall, 'Frederick Augustus Gow Packer', *ADB*, vol. 5, pp. 387-8. See also Richard Lord (comp.), *Inscriptions in Stone: St David's Burial Ground, 1804-1872*, St George's Church, Hobart, 1976, p. 195.

32 *Tatler*, 9 April 1898, p. 5; R. L. Wettenhall, 'Frederick Augustus Gow Packer', *ADB*, vol. 5, pp. 387-8.

33 *Hobart Mercury*, 2 August 1902, p. 5. See also Hutchins School Archives: Hutchins School Enrolments from 1846 to 1993, no. 755.

34 Townsley, *Tasmania*, pp. 98, 179.

35 *IGI*, p. 9323; Townsley, *Tasmania*, p. 181; Robson, *A History of Tasmania*, vol. II, pp. 77, 306. See also AOT: *Statistics of Tasmania*, 1873-76.

36 *Tasmania Pioneers Index, 1885-1889*; *Sydney Morning Herald (SMH)*, 27 December 1915, p. 4; F. B. Manning's *Tasmania Directory, 1881-1882*, p. 97; Bolger, 'The changing role of a city: Hobart', p. 8; Amy Rowntree, *Battery Point Today and Yesterday*, Adult Education Board of Tasmania, no place, n.d., p. 52.

37 AOT: *Statistics of Tasmania*, 1877-1901. See also Townsley, *Tasmania*, pp. 103, 180; Henry Reynolds, 'The Island Colony. Tasmania: Society and Politics 1880-1900', M. A. thesis, University of Tasmania, 1963, p. 179.

38 AOT: *Statistics of Tasmania*, 1881-1901. See also David Day, *Smugglers and Sailors: The Customs History of Australia 1788-1901*, Australian Government Publishing Service, Canberra, 1992, pp. 177, 245, 252 and *Contraband and Controversy: The Customs History of Australia from 1901*, Australian Government Publishing Service, Canberra, 1996, p. 7; *Tasmania Post Office Directory*, 1890-91, p. 414.

39 A. H. Packer newspaper obituary, n.d. (Packer Family Papers).

40 Richard White, 'Robert Clyde Packer', *ADB*, vol. 11, p. 117; interview with Lady Stening, 30 January 1996.

41 Townsley, *Tasmania*, pp. 77-8; Peter Benson cited by Stone and Tyson, *Old Hobart Town*, pp. 190, 192. See also AOT: N36, Hutchins School Admission Register, pp. 73, 121. Much of the following is drawn from Bridget Griffen-Foley, 'The Young Master and his old man: Sir Frank and R. C. Packer', *Media International Australia (MIA)*, no. 77, August 1995, pp. 36-7.

42 E. M. Dollery, 'John Richard Buckland', *ADB*, vol. 3, p. 287; *The Hutchins School Centenary Magazine, 1846-1946*, Hutchins School, Hobart, 1946, pp. 8, 19.

43 Basil W. Rait, *The Official History of the Hutchins School*, J. Walch, Hobart, n.d. (1935), p. 136.

Endnotes

44 J. A. Mangan, *Athleticism in the Victorian and Edwardian Public School*, Cambridge University Press, Cambridge, 1981, p. 9; Geoffrey Sherington, *Shore: A History of the Sydney Church of England Grammar School*, Allen & Unwin, St Leonards, 1983, p. 29; Bridget Griffen-Foley, *The House of Packer: The Making of a Media Empire*, Allen & Unwin, St Leonards, 1999, p. 2.

45 *The Hutchins School Centenary Magazine*, p. 20; Geoffrey Stephens, *The Hutchins School: Macquarie Street Years, 1846–1965*, Hutchins School, Hobart, 1979, p. 138; *Newspaper News (NN)*, 1 May 1934, p. 2.

46 Hutchins School reports, 1893 (Packer Family Papers); *NN*, 1 May 1934, p. 2.

47 C. R. Lawe Davies, 'New Women, New Culture: *The Women's Weekly* and Hollywood in Australia in the Early 1930s', M.Phil. thesis, Griffith University, 1988, Appendix III, p. 1; Samuel Smiles, *Self-Help: With Illustrations of Conduct and Perseverance*, John Murray, London, 1910 edn, passim.

48 Reynolds, 'The Island Colony', pp. 98–9, 219–23, 108; Robson, *A History of Tasmania*, vol. II, pp. 183–4; Bolger, 'The changing role of a city: Hobart', pp. 7, 14.

49 Clem Lloyd, *Profession: Journalist. A History of the Australian Journalists' Association*, Hale & Iremonger, Sydney, 1985, pp. 25–7.

50 E. R. Prettyman, 'Henry Horatio Gill', *ADB*, vol. 4, p. 248; Reynolds, 'The Island Colony', pp. 61–2, 276–7; Robson, *A History of Tasmania*, vol. II, pp. 117, 135–6.

51 Theatre program, 11 May 1900; reference, 31 October 1900 (Packer Family Papers).

52 Interview with Lady Stening, 30 January 1996.

53 Reynolds, 'The Island Colony', pp. 13–14, 43–4, 48; George Blaikie, *Remember Smith's Weekly?*, Rigby, Adelaide, 1966, p. 40; references, 1902 (Packer Family Papers).

54 Letter from Thomas Reiby to R. C. Packer, 25 February 1902 (Packer Family Papers); Lloyd, *Profession: Journalist*, p. 21.

55 Blaikie, *Remember Smith's Weekly?*, p. 40; NN, 1 May 1934, p. 2.

56 Interview with Lady Stening, 30 January 1996.

57 Much of the following is drawn from interviews and telephone conversations with Lady Stening, 30 January 1996, 18 February 1996, 4 March 1996, 14 August 1997, 11 June 1999. Lady Stening believes that her grandfather served as an archdeacon at Salisbury Cathedral, but the cathedral archivist has been unable to find his name in diocesan records. *Crockford's Clerical Directory* lists several 'Frank' or 'Francis' Hewsons from the 1830s to the 1890s, but it is difficult to match their educational qualifications and geographical movements with Lady Stening's recollections. The Rev. Frank Hewson is referred to in Ethel Packer's (née Hewson) obituary in the *Daily Telegraph*, 3 April 1947, p. 5.

58 *Sand's Sydney and New South Wales Directory*, 1897–1901.

59 Interview with Lady Stening, 30 January 1996.

60 *Sand's Sydney and New South Wales Directory*, 1903–1906.

61 Marion Dormer, *Dubbo–City on the Plains, 1901–1988*, Macquarie Publications, Dubbo, 1988, pp. 24, 26, 28, 48–9.

62 ibid. pp. 28, 30, 35–6, 327.

63 Reference from William White, 29 June 1905 (Packer Family Papers).

64 References from Arthur J. Ball, 24 June 1905, George T. Harrex and Abraham Irvine, 24 June 1905, William White, 29 June 1905 (Packer Family Papers); Dormer, *Dubbo–City on the Plains*, p. 327. Also *Sand's Sydney and New South Wales Directory*, 1906; interview with Lady Stening, 14 August 1997.

65 *NN*, 1 May 1934, p. 2; *Bellinger Courier-Sun*, 27 September 1989, p. 16 (my thanks to Dr Rod Kirkpatrick for providing me with this reference, and for information about the history of the region's press). See also Rod Kirkpatrick, 'Packer, a country newspaper and a female proprietor', *PANPA Bulletin*, May 1999, pp. 63–5; Neil Yeates, *Coffs Harbour*, vol. I, *pre-1880 to 1945*, Coffs Harbour City Council, Coffs Harbour, 1990, pp. 67–8, 122–3; *The Coffs Harbour Story*, Central North Coast Newspaper Company, Coffs Harbour, 1976, p. 32.

66 Interview with Lady Stening, 11 June 1999. See also letter from 'F. A. P.' [Frederick Augustus Gow Packer], n.d. (Packer Family Papers).

67 *Townsville 100, 1864–1964*, T. Willmett & Sons, Townsville, n.d. (1964), pp. 3, 9, 27, 37, 61, 81; James Manion, *Paper Power in North Queensland*, North Queensland Newspaper Company, Townsville, 1982, p. 10.

68 *Townsville 100*, pp. 29, 109.

69 ibid. p. 103; Manion, *Paper Power in North Queensland*, pp. 16, 122–6.

70 *Townsville Daily Bulletin* clipping, n.d. (Packer Family Papers); Townsville 100, p. 107.

71 Interview with Lady Stening, 14 August 1997; Manion, Paper Power in North Queensland, p. 11; *Townsville Daily Bulletin* clipping, n.d. (Packer Family Papers).

2 His Father's Footsteps

1 R. B. Walker, *The Newspaper Press in New South Wales, 1803–1920*, Sydney University Press, Sydney, 1976, pp. 116, 258.

2 ibid. p. 116; Joel H. Wiener (ed.), *Papers for the Millions: The New Journalism in Britain, 1850s to 1914*, Greenwood, New York, 1988.

3 Walker, *The Newspaper Press in New South Wales*, pp. 116–17; Memoirs (Warnecke Papers).

4 *Sydney Mail*, 14 July 1909, p. 26; *Scouting in New South Wales*, vol. 49, January-February 1982, p. 20; Donald MacDonald, *Baden-Powell: Soldier and Scout*, Lake, Sons & Cowell, Melbourne, 1912, no pagination. See also Boy Scout Memorabilia Centre: 'The First Fifty Years', typescript, n.d.

5 *Scouting in New South Wales*, vol. 49, pt 2, March 1982, p. 14; R. C. Packer, 'The Boy Scouts', *Lone Hand*, 2 August 1909, pp. 380–91.

6 *NN*, 1 May 1934, p. 2; *Scouting in New South Wales*, vol. 49, March 1982, p. 14; Blaikie, *Remember Smith's Weekly?*, p. 40; *Telegraph*, 17 May 1912, p. 11, 20 May 1912, p. 11; *Sunday Times*, 19 May 1912, p. 26; Memoirs (Warnecke Papers).

7 *NN*, 1 May 1934, p. 2; Walker, *The Newspaper Press in New South Wales*, p. 229.

8 Walker, *The Newspaper Press in New South Wales*, p. 117; *NN*, 1 July 1930, p. 14, 1 May 1934, p. 2.

9 Chris Cunneen, 'Hugh Donald McIntosh', *ADB*, vol. 10, p. 285; R. B. Walker, *Yesterday's News. A History of the Newspaper Press in New South Wales From 1920 to 1945*, Sydney University Press, Sydney, 1980, p. 5; Claude McKay, *This is the Life: The Autobiography of a Newspaperman*, Angus &

Endnotes

Robertson, Sydney, 1961, p. 142; Blaikie, *Remember Smith's Weekly?*, p. 41; Memoirs (Warnecke Papers).

10 Interview with Lady Stening, 14 August 1997; Packer, 'The Boy Scouts', pp. 381, 390.
11 McKay, *This is the Life*, pp. 7–112; Blaikie, *Remember Smith's Weekly?*, pp. 37–9.
12 McKay described the book as *Nesfield's English Grammar* (*NN*, 1 May 1934, p. 2). He was almost certainly referring to the *Manual*, first published in 1898.
13 Richard White, 'Robert Clyde Packer', *ADB*, vol. 11, p. 117; Walker, *The Newspaper Press in New South Wales*, pp. 106–9.
14 *NN*, 1 July 1930, p. 14, 1 May 1934, p. 2.
15 *Sand's Sydney and New South Wales Directory*, 1908–1913.
16 Interviews with Lady Stening, 30 January 1996, 14 August 1997; *Life International*, 30 July 1962, p. 45; Amirah Inglis, 'Lawrence Hargrave', *ADB*, vol. 9, p. 197.
17 *NN*, 1 May 1934, p. 2; *Sand's Sydney and New South Wales Directory*, 1913; Ian A. Ramage, *Wahroonga–Our Home*, Ian A. Ramage, Waitara, 1991, pp. 5, 10, 16, 31.
18 See Ramage, *Wahroonga–Our Home*, pp. 17, 345, 351, and *One Hundred Years Ago: Life on Sydney's Upper North Shore*, Ian A. Ramage, Waitara, 1996, pp. 12–14.
19 Ramage, *Wahroonga–Our Home*, p. 346; interview with Lady Stening, 14 August 1997; *NN*, 1 May 1934, p. 2.
20 Interviews with Lady Stening, 18 February 1996, 14 August 1997; Whitington, *Sir Frank*, p. 67.
21 Interview with Lady Stening, 18 February 1996; Jack Cox, *Take a Cold Tub, Sir! The Story of the Boy's Own Paper*, Lutterworth Press, Guildford, 1982, pp. 9, 12, 13, 18, 34, 39, 50, 56, 58–9, 92–3.
22 Interview with Lady Stening, 18 February 1996; Whitington, *Sir Frank*, p. 69.
23 Interviews with Lady Stening, 18 February 1996, 11 June 1999; *Life International*, 30 July 1962, p. 45; Whitington, *Sir Frank*, p. 67.
24 Interview with Lady Stening, 18 February 1996, 14 August 1997; Whitington, *Sir Frank*, pp. 66–7.
25 Interviews with Lady Stening, 18 February 1996, 14 August 1997.
26 *SMH*, 29 January 1924, p. 14. Much of the following is drawn from Griffen-Foley, 'The Young Master and his old man', pp. 38–9.
27 Ku-ring-gai Local History Centre (KLHC): Abbotsholme College prospectus, c. 1925. See also *Sydney Tatler*, 11 January 1923, p. 6; *Sun-Herald*, 24 December 1967, p. 5.
28 KLHC: 'The school that lasted thirty years', typescript by Irene Phipps, 1989; 'Reminiscences of Turramurra College' by Malcolm O'Reilly, 26 April 1983.
29 Letter from FP to Ethel Packer, 1916 (Packer Family Papers). See also Whitington, *Sir Frank*, p. 70.
30 KLHC: 'Wahroonga Grammar School for Boys', n.d. See also Kerrin Cook, *The Railway Came to Ku-ring-gai*, Genlin Investments, Sydney, 1991; interview with Lady Stening, 30 January 1996.
31 *Sydney Church of England Grammar School Register 1889–1994*, Shore Old Boys' Union Incorporated, Sydney, 1994, no. 2981; *Sand's Sydney and New South Wales Directory*, 1921.
32 *Torch Bearer*, May 1920, pp. 87–8, December 1920, pp. 11–12, December 1921, p. 138, September 1922, pp. 53, 66, December 1923, p. 96.

Endnotes

33 Television interview, May 1961, pp. 3–4 (McNulty Papers); *Torch Bearer*, June 1974, pp. 15–16; Peter Taylor, *A Celebration of Shore*, Allen & Unwin, St Leonards, 1988, p. 32; Griffen-Foley, 'The Young Master and his old man', pp. 39–40.

34 Chris Cunneen, 'Sir James John Joynton Smith', *ADB*, vol. 11, pp. 650–1; *Theatre Magazine*, 1 January 1919, p. 18; *Smith's Weekly*, 26 March 1932, p. 1; McKay, *This is the Life*, pp. 124–6; James Joynton Smith, *My Life Story*, Cornstalk Publishing Company, Sydney, 1927, pp. 243, 250–9; Memoirs (Warnecke Papers).

35 McKay, *This is the Life*, pp. 126–7; Smith, *My Life Story*, pp. 260–2; Memoirs (Warnecke Papers).

36 McKay, *This is the Life*, p. 127; Blaikie, *Remember Smith's Weekly?*, p. 31; Walker, *Yesterday's News*, pp. 7–8; *NN*, 1 July 1930, p. 14; Memoirs (Warnecke Papers).

37 McKay, *This is the Life*, pp. 128–9; Smith, *My Life Story*, pp. 262–3; Memoirs (Warnecke Papers).

38 McKay, *This is the Life*, pp. 131–2.

39 Smith, *My Life Story*, p. 260; Walker, *Yesterday's News*, p. 8; *NN*, 1 May 1934, p. 2; McKay, *This is the Life*, pp. 132–48; Dennis Haskell, 'The heroism of comedy: *Smith's Weekly* in the 1930s', in Bruce Bennett and Dennis Haskell (eds), *Myths, Heroes and Anti-Heroes: Essays on the Literature and Culture of the Asia-Pacific Region*, Centre for Studies in Australian Literature, University of Western Australia, Nedlands, 1992, pp. 110–19; Peter Kirkpatrick, *The Sea Coast of Bohemia: Literary Life in Sydney's Roaring Twenties*, University of Queensland Press, St Lucia, 1992, p. 116.

40 McKay, *This is the Life*, pp. 134–5, 143–8; *Nation*, 27 February 1960, p. 17.

41 Smith, *My Life Story*, pp. 264–5, 271–4; Kirkpatrick, *The Sea Coast of Bohemia*, pp. 112–15.

42 McKay, *This is the Life*, pp. 133, 139–40; Blaikie, *Remember Smith's Weekly?*, p. 14.

43 McKay, *This is the Life*, pp. 88–100; L. F. Fitzhardinghe, *William Morris Hughes: A Political Biography*, vol. 2, Angus & Robertson, Sydney, 1979, pp. 431–2.

44 McKay, *This is the Life*, p. 143; Fitzhardinghe, *William Morris Hughes*, p. 432; Memoirs (Warnecke Papers).

45 McKay, *This is the Life*, pp. 140–2; Bede Nairn, 'William Arthur Holman', *ADB*, vol. 9, p. 346; G. C. Bolton and Jenny Mills, 'Henry Teesdale Smith', *ADB*, vol. 11, p. 648.

46 McKay, *This is the Life*, pp. 141–2; George Finey, *The Mangle Wheel*, Kangaroo Press, Kenthurst, 1981, pp. 129–30.

47 McKay, *This is the Life*, p. 142; Blaikie, *Remember Smith's Weekly?*, p. 14.

48 Finey, *The Mangle Wheel*, p. 82.

49 *Daily Squeaker*, 23 April 1921, p. 3; McKay, *This is the Life*, p. 149.

50 McKay, *This is the Life*, pp. 149–50; Smith, *My Life Story*, pp. 264–5; *Smith's Weekly*, 26 March 1932, p. 1.

51 Interviews with Lady Stening, 14 August 1997, 11 June 1999; Nick Baldwin et al., *The World Guide to Automobiles: The Makers and their Marques*, Macdonald & Co., London and Sydney, 1987, p. 444.

52 Interview with Lady Stening, 11 June 1999.

53 ibid. 30 January 1996.

54 Memoirs (Warnecke Papers); Bridget Griffen-Foley, 'A biographical profile of George Warnecke', *Australian Studies in Journalism (ASJ)*, no. 3, 1994, pp. 69–75.

55 Finey, *The Mangle Wheel*, p. 132; Blaikie, *Remember Smith's Weekly?*, p. 15.
56 Finey, *The Mangle Wheel*, p. 133; Memoirs (Warnecke Papers).
57 McKay, *This is the Life*, pp. 150–63, 173; Smith, *My Life Story*, pp. 275–7; Memoirs (Warnecke Papers).
58 Mitchell Library, State Library of New South Wales (ML): MSS 2922, Spedding Papers; Box 6; [File] *Smith's Weekly;* 'A few items', n.d. and 'Re Packer', n.d.
59 Clem Lloyd, 'An acute contusion: News management in the 1920s', *ASJ*, no. 3, 1994, pp. 139, 141.
60 ML: MSS 2922, Spedding Papers; Box 6; [File] Smith's Weekly; 'A few items', n.d. and 'Re Packer', n.d.
61 ML: MSS Set 71, Molesworth Papers; Box 8; *re Daily Guardian* 1922, *Smith's Weekly* 1922–28; untitled verse, n.d. See also p. 17.
62 McKay, *This is the Life*, p. 171; Walker, *Yesterday's News*, p. 20.
63 Eric Baume, *I Lived These Years*, George G. Harrap & Co., London, 1941, pp. 104–5.
64 ibid. p. 105; McKay, *This is the Life*, p. 173; Smith, *My Life Story*, pp. 278–9.
65 Smith, *My Life Story*, p. 279; McKay, *This is the Life*, p. 173; Memoirs (Warnecke Papers).
66 McKay, *This is the Life*, p. 174–6.
67 Interview with Lady Stening, 30 January 1996; television interview with FP, May 1961, p. 4 (McNulty Papers); Memoirs (Warnecke Papers); Baume, *I Lived These Years*, p. 112.
68 Walker, *Yesterday's News*, p. 20; Richard White, 'Robert Clyde Packer', *ADB*, vol. 11, p. 117; *Daily Guardian*, 30 August 1923, p. 1; *Smith's Weekly*, 1 September 1923, p. 1.
69 Interview with Lady Stening, 14 August 1997; Memoirs (Warnecke Papers).
70 Letters from FP to Ethel Packer, 29 August 1923 and n.d. (Packer Family Papers); Memoirs (Warnecke Papers).
71 Letters from FP to Ethel Packer, 29 August 1923 and n.d.; FP to Kathleen Packer, n.d. (Packer Family Papers).
72 Memoirs (Warnecke Papers); *SMH*, 23 October 1924, p. 11; Smith, *My Life Story*, p. 281; McKay, *This is the Life*, p. 185; Baume, *I Lived These Years*, pp. 109–10; Whitington, *Sir Frank*, p. 75.

3 Little Frankie's Wanderings

1 Memoirs (Warnecke Papers).
2 Interview with Lady Stening, 14 August 1997; Helen V. Lloyd, *Boorowa: Over 160 Years of White Settlement*, Toveloam, Panania, 1990, pp. 21–4, 46.
3 David Marr, *Patrick White: A Life*, Random House Australia, Milsons Point, 1991, pp. 93, 94, 99.
4 Maslyn Williams, *His Mother's Country*, Melbourne University Press, Carlton, 1988, p. 91; letter from FP to Ethel Packer, 'Sunday' (Packer Family Papers).
5 Sydney Buttrose, 'The life of a Jack was not an easy one', *This Australia*, vol. 3, no. 4, Spring 1984, pp. 49, 51.
6 ibid. p. 49; Williams, His *Mother's Country*, p. 206; Patrick White, *The Twyborn Affair*, Penguin, Harmondsworth, 1981 edn, p. 250.
7 White, *The Twyborn Affair*, pp. 179, 188.

Endnotes

8   Marr, *Patrick White*, p. 96; Buttrose, 'The life of a Jack was not an easy one', p. 49; interview with Lady Stening, 14 August 1997; letter from FP to Ethel Packer, 'Sunday' (Packer Family Papers).
9   Williams, *His Mother's Country*, p. 26; interview with Lady Stening, 14 August 1997; letter from FP to Ethel Packer, 'Sunday' (Packer Family Papers).
10 Lloyd, *Boorowa*, p. 281; *Boorowa News,* 14 November 1924, p. 3, 2 October 1925, p. 5.
11 Whitington, *Sir Frank*, pp. 54, 79; *Boorowa News*, 9 January 1925, p. 2; *Grenfell Record*, 31 May 1926, p. 2.
12 Interview with Lady Stening, 14 August 1997.
13 *Boorowa News*, 16 January 1925, p. 3, 13 March 1925, p. 4, 24 April 1925, p. 3; Marr, *Patrick White*, p. 95.
14 Memoirs (Warnecke Papers).
15 Baume, *I Lived These Years*, p. 113.
16 Memoirs (Warnecke Papers); *Daily Guardian*, 2 July 1927, p. 8; McKay, *This is the Life*, p. 186; Smith, *My Life Story*, p. 283.
17 McKay, *This is the Life*, pp. 186–7; Baume, *I Lived These Years*, p. 115.
18 *Boorowa News,* 20 November 1925, p. 1; *Daily Guardian*, 19 June 1926, p. 1, 26 June 1926, pp. 1, 5.
19 McKay, *This is the Life*, pp. 187–8; *Daily Guardian*, 29 June 1926, p. 9.
20 *Daily Guardian*, 26 June–27 July 1926; *Miss Australia: A Quarterly Magazine*, n.d. (December 1926?), pp. 4, 8–10.
21 Memoirs (Warnecke Papers).
22 McKay, *This is the Life*, p. 189; *Daily Guardian*, 29 July 1926, pp. 1, 16; *Miss Australia: A Quarterly Magazine*, n.d. (December 1926?), p. 17.
23 *New York Times*, 21 August 1926, p. 17; Edward L. Bernays, *Biography of an Idea: Memoirs of a Public Relations Counsel*, Simon & Schuster, New York, 1965, pp. 400–3; McKay, *This is the Life*, pp. 189–90.
24 Letter from FP to Ethel Packer, 29 August 1926 (Packer Family Papers).
25 *Miss Australia: A Quarterly Magazine*, n.d. (December 1926?), pp. 5–6; McKay, *This is the Life*, pp. 191–2.
26 McKay, *This is the Life*, pp. 192–5; Bernays, *Biography of an Idea*, pp. 402–3; *New York Times*, 2 September 1926, p. 7; *Miss Australia: A Quarterly Magazine*, n.d. (December 1926?), p. 6.
27 Letter from FP to Ethel Packer, 29 August 1926 (Packer Family Papers).
28 Bernays, *Biography of an Idea*, p. 403; McKay, *This is the Life*, p. 196; *Miss Australia: A Quarterly Magazine*, n.d. (December 1926?), *passim*; *Daily Guardian*, 9 September 1926, p. 1, 11 September 1926, p. 1, 17 September 1926, p. 9.
29 McKay, *This is the Life*, pp. 196–8; Jack and Barbara Piattelli Dempsey, *Dempsey*, W. H. Allen, London, 1977, pp. 178, 199–201.
30 McKay, *This is the Life*, pp. 196–8.
31 McKay, *This is the Life*, pp. 199–200; *Smith's Weekly*, 29 January 1927, p. 10; *NN*, 1 May 1928, p. 1.
32 *Sand's Sydney and New South Wales Directory*, 1924–6; *SMH*, 6 September 1913, p. 8, 3 April 1947, p. 5; Elaine Cassidy et al. (eds), *Impressions of Woollahra Past and Present*, Allen & Unwin, St Leonards,

Endnotes

1988, x, p. 12; Municipality of Woollahra, *The History of Bellevue Hill*, no place, no publisher, n.d. (1930s).

33 Memoirs (Warnecke Papers).

34 ibid.; Griffen-Foley, 'A biographical profile of George Warnecke', pp. 72–3, 77–8.

35 Walker, *Yesterday's News*, pp. 20, 23; Bede Nairn, *The 'Big Fella': Jack Lang and the Australian Labor Party 1891–1949*, Melbourne University Press, Carlton, 1986, pp. 71–2; *Smith's Weekly*, 6 December 1924, p. 10

36 McKay, *This is the Life*, p. 137; Nairn, *The 'Big Fella'*: pp. 85–7; Baume, *I Lived These Years*, pp. 124–5.

37 Diane Langmore, 'Adam Cairns and Delamore William McCay', *ADB*, vol. 10, p. 223; *Biographical Register of the New South Wales Parliament, 1901–1970*, eds Heather Radi, Peter Spearritt and Elizabeth Hinton, Australian National University Press, Canberra, 1979, p. 200; Baume, *I Lived These Years*, p. 102; Memoirs (Warnecke Papers).

38 Baume, *I Lived These Years*, pp. 105, 107, 110; Memoirs (Warnecke Papers).

39 Memoirs (Warnecke Papers); Whitington, *Sir Frank*, pp. 68, 85; interview with Lady Stening, 11 June 1999.

40 ML: ML MSS Set 71, Molesworth Papers; Box 8 (10); re *Daily Guardian* 1922–30, *Smith's Weekly* 1922–28; Baume to Molesworth, 16 June 1927.

41 Walker, *Yesterday's News*, pp. 37, 39–40; Memoirs (Warnecke Papers).

42 *Sunday Times*, 22 May 1927, pp. 1–2.

43 Memoirs (Warnecke Papers); *Daily Guardian*, 24 May 1927, p. 2; Valerie Desmond, *The Awful Australians*, no publisher, Sydney, 1911.

44 McKay, *This is the Life*, p. 200; Memoirs (Warnecke Papers).

45 *'Digest' Year Book of Public Companies of Australia and New Zealand*, 1928, pp. 156–7.

46 *Punch* (Melbourne), 18 September 1919, p. 459; *NN*, 2 August 1948, p. 16; Memoirs (Warnecke Papers).

47 *Who's Who in Australia*, 1935, p. 834; interview with Lady Stening, 30 January 1996.

48 Blaikie, *Remember Smith's Weekly?*, p. 16; Walker, *Yesterday's News*, p. 71; Memoirs (Warnecke Papers).

49 Finey, *The Mangle Wheel*, p. 132; *SMH*, 24 October 1928, p. 20; Douglas Stewart, *A Man of Sydney: A New Appreciation of Kenneth Slessor*, Nelson, West Melbourne, 1977, p. 29.

50 *SMH*, 13 September 1929, p. 15; *Daily Guardian*, 13 September 1929, p. 31; *Sun*, 13 September 1929, p. 9.

51 *Truth*, 10 November 1929, pp. 1, 10; Walker, *Yesterday's News*, p. 24.

52 Memoirs (Warnecke Papers); Gavin Souter, *Company of Heralds*, Melbourne University Press, Melbourne, 1981, p. 155.

53 *SMH*, 19 October 1929, p. 13.

54 *NN*, 1 February 1930, p. 1, 1 January 1932, p. 9; *New South Wales Parliamentary Debates (NSWPD)*, vol. 132, Council, 18 March 1932, p. 8768; Walker, *Yesterday's News*, pp. 24–5, 43.

55 Memoirs (Warnecke Papers); Baume, *I Lived These Years*, p. 133.

56 ibid.; Walker, *Yesterday's News*, pp. 40, 51.

57 *Australian Ski Yearbook*, 1956, pp. 55–7; Carl Bridge, 'Leslie Hubert Holden', *ADB*, vol. 9, pp. 332–3.
58 *NSWPD*, vol. 132, Council, 18 March 1932, pp. 8770–2.
59 Walker, *Yesterday's News*, p. 44; Memoirs (Warnecke Papers).
60 Walker, *Yesterday's News*, p. 45; Memoirs (Warnecke Papers).
61 Memoirs (Warnecke Papers); Walker, *Yesterday's News*, p. 73.
62 Memoirs (Warnecke Papers); Whitington, *Sir Frank*, pp. 83–4.
63 Walker, *Yesterday's News*, p. 46; *NN*, 1 July 1931, p. 11; Whitington, *Sir Frank*, pp. 85–9.
64 Whitington, *Sir Frank*, pp. 89–90; Memoirs (Warnecke Papers).
65 Walker, *Yesterday's News*, p. 46; *NN*, 1 June 1931, p. 1, 1 July 1931, p. 7.
66 Whitington, *Sir Frank*, pp. 90–1, 93, 95–6; Memoirs (Warnecke Papers).
67 *Smith's Weekly*, 19 September 1931, p. 15; *NN*, 1 September 1931, p. 1, 1 October 1931, p. 1.
68 McKay, *This is the Life*, pp. 222–3; Memoirs (Warnecke Papers).
69 *Smith's Weekly*, 26 March 1932, p. 2; *NN*, 1 October 1931, p. 1.
70 *NN*, 1 October 1931, p. 1.
71 NLA: TRC 121/40, interview with Alan Reid, 4 October 1972, tape 1, track 1, pp. 9–10.
72 Memoirs (Warnecke Papers).

4 El Dorado

1 P. R. Stephensen (comp.), *Sydney Sails: The Story of the Royal Sydney Yacht Squadron's First 100 Years (1862–1962)*, Angus & Robertson, Sydney, 1962, pp. 175, 181.
2 *SMH*, 20 October 1930, p. 3, 10 November 1930, p. 14, 18 January 1930, p. 6, 1 February 1932, pp. 12–13.
3 Ross Fitzgerald, *'Red Ted': The Life of E. G. Theodore*, University of Queensland Press, St Lucia, 1994, p. 321.
4 Neville Cain, 'Edward Granville Theodore', *ADB*, vol. 12, pp. 197–9.
5 Fitzgerald, *'Red Ted'*, pp. 214, 228, 243–76, 285.
6 Neville Cain, 'Edward Granville Theodore', *ADB*, vol. 12, pp. 200–1.
7 Memoirs (Warnecke Papers); Andrew Moore, 'Charles Downey Hardy', *ADB*, vol. 9, p. 195, and *The Secret Army and the Premier*, New South Wales University Press, Kensington, 1989, pp. 104–5.
8 National Archives of Australia, New South Wales (NAA/NSW): SP1141/1; 13; Intelligence Report, 26 October 1931. See also Memoirs (Warnecke Papers); Walker, *Yesterday's News*, pp. 50–1; Baume, *I Lived These Years*, pp. 154–6.
9 *SMH*, 16 May 1932, p. 4; Memoirs (Warnecke Papers).
10 Memoirs (Warnecke Papers).
11 ibid.; Whitington, *Sir Frank*, pp. 97–9.
12 Whitington, *Sir Frank*, p. 101.
13 Baume, *I Lived These Years*, pp. 137–8.
14 Whitington, *Sir Frank*, p. 117; *Truth*, 13 March 1932, p. 12; Memoirs (Warnecke Papers).

Endnotes

15 *NN*, 1 March 1932, p. 11; *NSWPD*, vol. 132, Assembly, 17 March 1932, p. 8751; *Labor Daily*, 1 March 1932, p. 5.
16 *NSWPD*, vol. 132, Assembly, 17 March 1932, pp. 8745-8. See also *NN*, 1 April 1932, p. 2.
17 *NSWPD*, vol. 132, Assembly, 17 March 1932, p. 8748.
18 Richard White, 'Robert Clyde Packer', *ADB*, vol. 11, p. 117.
19 *NSWPD*, vol. 132, Assembly, 17 March 1932, pp. 8745-66.
20 *NSWPD*, vol. 132, Assembly, 18 March 1932, pp. 8766-77; *NN*, 1 April 1932, p. 2; *Smith's Weekly*, 26 March 1932, p. 2. See also Chris Lawe Davies, 'George Warnecke and the Packers: A dynasty denied', *MIA*, no. 79, February 1996, p. 96.
21 Lawe Davies, 'New Women, New Culture', pp. 7, 10; J. T. Lang, *I Remember, Invincible Press*, Sydney, n.d. (1956?), p. 391; Baume, *I Lived These Years*, p. 137.
22 *Home*, 1 June 1932, p. 31; interview with Lady Stening, 30 January 1996.
23 *Home*, 1 July 1932, p. 6.
24 Margriet R. and Nancy Bonnin, 'Mary Ernestine Hill', *ADB*, vol. 14, p. 452; Eric Baume, *Tragedy Track: The Story of the Granites*, North Flinders Mines and Hesperian Press, 1994 edn, pp. viii, 1; *Sun*, 12 October 1932, p. 11.
25 Memoirs (Warnecke Papers); Whitington, *Sir Frank*, p. 117; *Sun*, 15 October 1932, p. 1; *Sunday Sun*, 16 October 1932, p. 2; Baume, *Tragedy Track*, p. 4; C. T. Madigan, *Central Australia*, Oxford University Press, Melbourne and London, 1944 edn, pp. 232-3.
26 Madigan, Central Australia, p. 233; Baume, *Tragedy Track*, pp. 7-8, 15; *Sun*, 17 October 1932, p. 7.
27 Baume, *Tragedy Track*, pp. 24-5; *Sunday Sun*, 23 October 1932, p. 1.
28 *Sun*, 12 October 1932, p. 11; *Who's Who in Australia*, 1944, pp. 348-9; *NN*, 1 September 1934, p. 17.
29 Baume, *Tragedy Track*, pp. 25, 27; *Sunday Sun*, 23 October 1932, p. 1; Madigan, Central Australia, p. 233; Whitington, *Sir Frank*, p. 117.
30 Griffen-Foley, *The House of Packer*, pp. 9-10.
31 Noel Butlin Archives Centre (NBAC): N117/1531, Labor Papers Ltd Minutes, 18 April 1931, pp. 264-5. National Library of Australia (NLA): MS 7222, Theodore Papers; Box 1; Folder 2; Grover to Theodore, n.d.
32 *Truth*, 17 January 1932, p. 13; *NN*, 1 February 1932, p. 1. See also NBAC: N117/1531, Labor Papers Ltd Minutes, 1 August 1932, p. 306; 11-12 October 1932, pp. 308-9.
33 Memoirs (Warnecke Papers).
34 John Fairfax Archives (JFA): Sale of Goodwill of *Telegraph*, 1935; Re "The World", p. 1; [200.20/3].
35 NBAC: N117/1531, Labor Papers Ltd Minutes, 1 November 1932, p. 310. See also Clyde Cameron, 'When incompetence and corruption merge: The AWU and the *World* newspaper', *Labour History*, no. 70, May 1996, pp. 177-8.
36 *NN*, 1 November 1932, p. 1; E. G. *Theodore: A Profile*, Consolidated Press, Sydney, 1949, p. 14. See also JFA: Sale of Goodwill of *Telegraph*, 1935; Re "The World", p. 1; [200.20/3].
37 JFA: Sale of Goodwill of *Telegraph*, 1935; Wheeler to Hugh Denison, 4 November 1932; [200.20/3].
38 JFA: Sale of Goodwill of *Telegraph*, 1935; Re "The World", p. 1; [200.20/3].

Endnotes

39   Australian Securities Commission (ASC): 000 025 721; Fiche A; Memorandum of Association, 7 November 1932. Flinders University Library (FUL): Evatt Collection; Warnecke File; memorandum of Mr G. W. Warnecke, n.d., section 1.

40   JFA: Sale of Goodwill of *Telegraph*, 1935; Re "The World", p. 2; [200.20/3].

41   ibid.; Peter Cook, 'The end of the *World*', *Labour History*, no. 16, May 1969, p. 57.

42   JFA: Sale of Goodwill of *Telegraph*, 1935; R. J. A. Travers to R. E. Denison, 4 November 1932; [200.20/3]. See also Sydney Newspapers (25) No. 13; agreement with PMG, n.d.; [6201.1/1].

43   *World*, 9 November 1932, p. 1, 10 November 1932, p. 4; *NN*, 1 April 1933, p. 1.

44   JFA: Sale of Goodwill of *Telegraph*, 1935; Re "The World", p. 2; [200.20/3].

45   ibid.; letter from G. W. Waddell to Hugh Denison, 22 November 1932; [200.20/3].

46   JFA: Packet 7, Associated Newspapers and Sydney Newspapers Bundle; G. W. Waddell to Hugh Denison, 14 November 1932; [6201.1/6]. See also *World*, 14 November 1932, p. 1.

47   JFA: Sale of Goodwill of *Telegraph*, 1935; Waddell to Hugh Denison, 22 November 1932; [200.20/3].

48   JFA: Sale of Goodwill of *Telegraph*, 1935; memorandum of interview with FP, 25 November 1932; [200.20/3].

49   JFA: Packet 7, Associated Newspapers and Sydney Newspapers Bundle; correspondence, 28 November-8 December 1932; [6201.1/1].

50   *NN*, 1 December 1932, p. 1.

51   ASC: 013 36 243; Fiche A; Memorandum of Association, 8 August 1930. *Who's Who in Australia*, 1935, p. 833, 1944, pp. 348–9; *NN*, 1 September 1934, p. 17.

52   Interviews with Lady Stening, 30 January 1996, 11 June 1999.

53   ibid.; *NN*, 2 January 1933, p. 10.

54   Interview with Lady Stening, 30 January 1996; letter from R. C. to Ethel Packer, n.d. (Packer Family Papers).

55   JFA: *Telegraph* 1; Main complaints against R. C. Packer in Denison memo to board, 6 June 1933; [300.70]. See also Griffen-Foley, 'A biographical profile of George Warnecke', pp. 87–8; Denis O'Brien, *The Weekly*, Penguin, Ringwood, 1982, p. 13; Cynthia L. White, Women's Magazines, 1693–1968, Michael Joseph, London, 1970, pp. 95–6, 116–18.

56   O'Brien, *The Weekly*, p. 14; Lawe Davies, 'New Women, New Culture', pp. 39–42.

57   *Journalist*, 13 August 1923, p. 124; Lawe Davies, 'New Women, New Culture', pp. 15–16.

58   O'Brien, *The Weekly*, p. 14; Lawe Davies, 'New Women, New Culture', pp. 17–18, Appendix I.

59   *E. G. Theodore: A Profile*, Consolidated Press, Sydney, 1949, p. 16; *Pacific Islands Monthly* (*PIM*), 24 June 1933, p. 10; Donald Chaput, 'The Queenslanders get Fiji gold', *Journal* (*Historical Society of Queensland*), vol. 12, no. 5, August 1986, p. 392.

60   JFA: Packet 7, Associated Newspapers and Sydney Newspapers Bundle; Bradshaw to R. E. Denison, 1 May 1933; [6201.1/6]; *Telegraph* 1; Main complaints against R. C. Packer in Denison memo to board, 6 June 1933; [300.70].

61   *NN*, 1 June 1933, p. 2; *Printer*, 16 June 1933, p. 63; *Journalist*, 26 June 1933, p. 46.

62   *E. G. Theodore: A Profile*, p. 17; *NN*, 1 July 1933, p. 2.

63   *Women's Weekly*, 10 June 1933, 17 June 1933, p. 2; *E. G. Theodore: A Profile*, p. 17.

Endnotes

64 Interview with Lady Stening, 30 January 1996. See also JFA: *Telegraph* 1; Main complaints against R. C. Packer in Denison memo to board, 6 June 1933; 'Sep. 1931 R. C. Packer came'; [300.70].
65 *NSWPD*, vol. 137, Assembly, 22 June 1933, pp. 26–8.
66 *NN*, 1 July 1933, p. 11.
67 John W. Hartman Center for Sales, Advertising and Marketing History, Special Collections Library, Duke University: J. Walter Thompson Collection; Reel 227, Proposed Investigation for *Australian Women's Weekly*, July 1933; Reel 222, *Australian Women's Weekly* Investigation, August 1933.
68 *E. G. Theodore: A Profile*, p. 18; Whitington, *Sir Frank*, p. 130.
69 *E. G. Theodore: A Profile*, p. 18.
70 ibid.; *Women's Weekly*, 23 September 1933 (Melbourne edn), p. 2, 7 October 1933 (Queensland edn), p. 2.
71 *Journalist*, 15 July 1925, p. 106; Lloyd, *Profession: Journalist*, pp. 146–7.
72 Griffen-Foley, *The House of Packer*, pp. 28–9.
73 ML: ML MSS 243, Molesworth Papers; Box 4; xiii Newspaper career papers, 1928–31; East to FP, 5 February 1932; notes, 1 October 1933; Merchants and Traders' Association Ltd report no. 50724.
74 ML: ML MSS 243, Molesworth Papers; Box 4; xiii Newspaper career papers, 1928–31; Packer to Molesworth, 27 October 1932; Packer to Hopkins, 31 January 1933; Packer to Molesworth, 28 August 1933; notes, 1 October 1933; 'Net Sales of "Turf Life"', n.d.
75 ML: ML MSS 243, Molesworth Papers; Box 4; xiii Newspaper career papers, 1928–31; transcript of telephone conversations, 22 January 1934. See also Peter Spearritt, 'Voltaire Molesworth', *ADB*, vol. 10, p. 540.

5 The Young Master

1 Interviews with Dorothy Drain, 17 March 1994; Pat Bancks, 28 November 1999.
2 *Queensland Times*, 28 July 1892, p. 2; *Brisbane Courier*, 28 July 1892, p. 6; Frederic Morrison, *The Aldine History of Queensland*, vol. II, Aldine Publishing Co., Sydney, 1888, p. 525.
3 Interview with Sheila Wood, 9 January 1998; *SMH*, 29 December 1937, p. 12; *Medical Journal of Australia*, 5 March 1938, p. 462.
4 *New South Wales Pioneers Index, Federation Series 1889–1918*; interview with Lady Stening, 18 February 1996; *Medical Journal of Australia*, 5 March 1938, p. 462.
5 *Ascham Charivari*, April 1922, p. 1, May 1924, pp. 2, 19; Caroline Fairfax Simpson, Annette Fielding-Jones Dupree and Betty Winn Ferguson (eds), *Ascham Remembered 1886–1986*, Fine Arts Press, Sydney, 1986, p. 46; interview with Lady Stening, 14 August 1997.
6 *Home*, 1 November 1926, p. 30, 1 December 1926, p. 29, 1 September 1927, p. 60b, 2 April 1928, p. 96, 1 April 1930, p. 4, 1 May 1930, p. 4, 1 April 1931, p. 8, 1 December 1931, p. 29, 1 April 1932, p. 4, 1 August 1932, p. 6, 1 October 1930, p. 6, 1 July 1933, p. 4; *Sydney Mail*, 15 April 1931, p. 20, 4 October 1933, p. 20.

Endnotes

7   *Home*, 1 December 1928, p. 35, 1 February 1929, p. 13; *Medical Journal of Australia*, 5 March 1938, p. 462; Joan Savage (ed.), *Palm Beach 1788–1988*, The Palm Beach Association, Palm Beach, 1984, pp. 46, 113, 116.

8   *Home*, 1 May 1926, p. 5, 1 April 1932, p. 4, 3 April 1934, p. 6, 1 May 1934, p. 6, 1 June 1934, p. 29.

9   *Home*, 1 May 1933, p. 18; letter from R. C. to Kathleen Packer, 22 April 1933 (Packer Family Papers).

10 Interview with Lady Stening, 18 February 1996; letter from E. Ashley to R. C. Packer, 18 September 1933 (Packer Family Papers).

11 Interview with Lady Stening, 18 February 1996; *SMH*, 13 November 1933, p. 15, 8 January 1934, p. 13.

12 *NN*, 1 February 1934, p. 1, 1 March 1934, p. 1; interview with Lady Stening, 18 February 1996.

13 Interview with Lady Stening, 18 February 1996.

14 *NN*, 1 March 1934, p. 1, 1 May 1934, p. 2, 2 December 1935, p. 4; interview with Lady Stening, 18 February 1996.

15 Interview with Lady Stening, 18 February 1996; *Women's Weekly*, 21 April 1934, p. 14.

16 *NN*, 1 June 1934, p. 6; K. J. Cable, 'George Faunce Allman', *ADB*, vol. 13, p. 25.

17 *Women's Weekly*, 21 April 1934, p. 14; *Bulletin*, 18 April 1934, p. 14; Richard White, 'Robert Clyde Packer', *ADB*, vol. 11, p. 117.

18 Baume, *I Lived These Years*, p. 135; Memoirs (Warnecke Papers).

19 *NN*, 1 June 1934, p. 6; interview with Lady Stening, 11 June 1999.

20 *NN*, 1 September 1934, p. 17; interview with Lady Stening, 30 January 1996.

21 O'Brien, *The Weekly*, p. 30.

22 Lawe Davies, 'New Women, New Culture', pp. 20–1; O'Brien, *The Weekly*, p. 30.

23 Lawe Davies, 'New Women, New Culture', p. 21, and 'George Warnecke and the Packers', p. 99. See also Donald Horne, *Into the Open*, HarperCollins, Pymble, 2000, p. 7.

24 Memoirs (Warnecke Papers).

25 Ronald McKie, *We Have No Dreaming*, Collins Australia, Sydney, 1988, p. 157; *E. G. Theodore: A Profile*, pp. 8, 31.

26 *E. G. Theodore: A Profile*, p. 20.

27 *PIM*, 24 October 1933, p. 14, 21 February 1935, p. 15, 25 June 1935, pp. 6–7. See also Fitzgerald, 'Red Ted', pp. 72, 345; James Griffin, 'John Wren', *ADB*, vol. 12, p. 581.

28 *SMH*, 9 August 1935, p. 12.

29 University of Melbourne Archives: Stock Exchange of Melbourne—Mining Companies; Box 83; Emperor 2; letter from Emperor Mines Ltd to Stock Exchange, 12 November 1936. See also *Telegraph*, 3 October 1952, p. 11.

30 Fitzgerald, 'Red Ted', pp. 359–60.

31 *PIM*, 22 October 1937, p. 4, September 1945, p. 30.

32 Interview with Lady Stening, 30 January 1996; Whitington, *Sir Frank*, p. 80; *Truth*, 8 August 1943, p. 8.

33 *NN*, 1 August 1934, p. 2.

Endnotes

34 *SMH*, 25 July 1934, p. 5; *Telegraph*, 25 July 1934, p. 15; *Home*, 1 August 1934, p. 4, 2 December 1935, p. 6.
35 *SMH*, 10 December 1934, p. 15, 17 December 1934, p. 14. Also newspaper clipping, n.d. (Packer Family Papers); interview with Lady Stening, 30 January 1996.
36 *SMH*, 10 December 1934, p. 15, 17 December 1934, p. 14; *Quirindi Advocate*, 6 August 1935, pp. 2, 7, 9 August 1935, pp. 3, 6–7, 7 August 1936, p. 1–2, 14. See also Sally Weedon, *Countess of Dudley Cup Tournament, 1985*, New South Wales Polo Association (Kyeemagh) Ltd, 1986, p. 15.
37 Weedon, *Countess of Dudley Cup Tournament, 1985*, p. 16; *Life International*, 30 July 1962, p. 45. See also *'Nutcote' History Report*, Howard Tanner & Associates, Sydney, 1992, Appendix A.
38 Weedon, *Countess of Dudley Cup Tournament, 1985*, p. 16; Alan Deans, *Australia's Polo Heritage. The Hardern Polo Team 1912–1930*, Hamilton Publishing, Sydney, 1991, p. 52.
39 *Quirindi Advocate*, 6 August 1935, p. 2, 9 August 1935, p. 3; *Home*, 1 July 1935, p. 6.
40 *Home*, 1 March 1935, p. 4, 1 August 1935, p. 6; *SMH*, 8 November 1935, p. 4, 25 July 1996, p. 44.
41 *Home*, 2 December 1935, pp. 4, 6, 7.
42 *NN*, 1 August 1934, p. 11; *Women's Weekly*, 6 October 1934.
43 O'Brien, *The Weekly*, p. 44. For the *Women's Weekly's* evolution from a newspaper to a magazine, see Griffen-Foley, *The House of Packer*, p. 37.
44 NBAC: N117/1531, Labor Papers Ltd Minutes, pp. 321–5, 13–15 February 1934.
45 O'Brien, *The Weekly*, p. 44; Lawe Davies, 'New Women, New Culture', p. 21. See also FUL: Evatt Collection; George Warnecke; memorandum for Mr. G. W. Warnecke, n.d., section 1(c).
46 Griffen-Foley, *The House of Packer*, pp. 42–4.
47 *NN*, 2 September 1935, pp. 1, 7, 1 February 1936, p. 15; O'Brien, *The Weekly*, p. 43; Griffen-Foley, *The House of Packer*, p. 41.
48 *E. G. Theodore: A Profile*, p. 20.
49 *Journalist*, 15 July 1922, p. 145; *Telegraph*, 2 July 1979, pp. 3, 5, 9, 11; Walker, *Yesterday's News*, pp. 3, 12–14, 48, 53–4. See also letter from E. Ashley to R. C. Packer, 18 September 1933 (Packer Family Papers).
50 *NN*, 1 August 1935, p. 12; *Smith's Weekly*, 9 November 1935, pp. 1–2; *Telegraph*, 10 August 1935, p. 1, 14 August 1947, p. 5. See also NBAC: Z270 Box 30, AJA Federal Minutes, p. 116, 16 July 1935.
51 JFA: Sale of Goodwill of *Telegraph*, 1935; letter from Vero Read to Hugh Denison, 19 September 1935, 'Confidential statement made by the chairman', 28 November 1935, p. 2; [200.20/3].
52 JFA: Sale of Goodwill of *Telegraph*, 1935; letter from Denison to Read, 26 September 1935; 'D. F. P.'s proposals', n.d.; [200.20/3].
53 JFA: Sale of Goodwill of *Telegraph*, 1935; letters from Denison to Packer, 3 October 1935, 16 October 1935; [200.20/3]. See also *E. G. Theodore: A Profile*, p. 21.
54 JFA: Sale of Goodwill of *Telegraph*, 1935; letter from Packer to Denison, 30 October 1935; [200.20/3].
55 JFA: Sale of Goodwill of *Telegraph*, 1935; correspondence, 31 October–5 November 1935; [200.20/3].
56 *Smith's Weekly*, 2 November 1935, p. 1, 14 December 1935, p. 13. JFA: Sale of Goodwill of *Telegraph*, 1935; letter from FP to Denison, 30 November 1935; [200.20/3].

57   Lawe Davies, 'New Women, New Culture', p. 27; luncheon menu, 6 November 1935 (Warnecke Papers).
58   ASC: 000 031 747, Fiche A, Memorandum of Association of Consolidated Press Ltd. See also *Jobson's Investment Digest*, 1 February 1936, pp. 50–1, 1 December 1937, p. 551.
59   Memoirs (Warnecke Papers).
60   NBAC: N59/19, AJA NSW Minutes, p. 61, 23 December 1935.
61   Gavin Souter, 'Sydney Harold Deamer', *ADB*, vol. 13, p. 598; *Women's Weekly*, 30 November 1935, p. 4; Griffen-Foley, *The House of Packer*, pp. 50–2.
62   *NN*, 1 March 1936, p. 15, 1 May 1937, p. 15, 1 April 1944, p. 10; *Sunday Telegraph*, 2 August 1959, p. 22.
63   *NN*, 2 March 1936, p. 15; *Women's Weekly*, 29 February 1936, p. 4, 7 March 1936, pp. 2, 4, 14 March 1936, p. 4, 21 March 1936, pp. 2, 44–5; *Telegraph*, 17–21 March 1936. See also NLA: MS 4849, Dumas Papers; Box 8; Peter Kennedy to Dumas, 8 October 1935; Dumas to Murdoch, 14 October 1935; Murdoch to Dumas, 8 November 1935.
64   *NN*, 1 April 1936, p. 1; *Telegraph*, 23 March 1936, p. 8.
65   *Home*, 1 June 1936, p. 7, 1 August 1936, p. 7; *NN*, 1 August 1936, p. 32; Martha Rutledge, 'Ernest Alexander Stuart Watt', *ADB*, vol. 12, p. 410; Susan Rankine, *Being Ernest: The Life of Ernest Watt, 1874–1954*, SGR Press, Double Bay, 1998, pp. 121–5, 142–4, 175.
66   Griffen-Foley, *The House of Packer*, pp. 56–7.
67   *SMH*, 9 March 1987, p. 14; Dick Hughes, *Don't You Sing! Memories of a Catholic Boyhood*, Kangaroo Press, Kenthurst, 1994, pp. 21, 34; Norman Macswan, *The Man Who Read the East Wind: A Biography of Richard Hughes*, Kangaroo Press, Kenthurst, 1982, pp. 23–4.
68   *Women's Weekly*, 24 August 1977, p. 9.
69   *Truth*, 22 September 1935, p. 14.
70   *Truth*, 23 August 1936, p. 19.

6 Mansions and Mêlées

1   Municipality of Woollahra, *The History of Bellevue Hill*, no pagination; *Sunday Times*, 12 May 1918, p. 3.
2   Woollahra Local History Centre: Valuation Books, Bellevue Hill, 1908; Edgecliff, 1934. See also *SMH*, 24 February 1921, p. 8, 27 April 1991, p. 2; *Home*, 1 May 1937, p. 7.
3   *Home*, 1 April 1932, p. 4, 2 November 1936, p. 4, 1 December 1936, p. 10; Commonwealth of Australia New South Wales Electoral Roll, 1937; interview with Lady Stening, 30 January 1996.
4   Interview with Sheila Wood, 9 January 1998.
5   Dorothy Jenner and Trish Sheppard, *Darlings I've Had a Ball*, Ure Smith, Sydney, 1975, pp. 161–2.
6   *Home*, 1 April 1936, p. 6, 1 October 1936, p. 6, 1 February 1937, p. 4, 1 April 1937, p. 4, 1 May 1937, pp. 6, 7.

Endnotes

7   Valerie Lawson, *Connie Sweetheart: The Story of Connie Robertson*, William Heinemann, Melbourne, 1990, pp. 180, 185, 201; David McNicoll, *Luck's a Fortune*, Wildcat Press, Sydney, 1979, p. 290; *Home*, 2 March 1936, p. 6.
8   *NN*, 1 March 1937, p. 1, 1 November 1938, p. 15; Memoirs (Warnecke Papers).
9   *NN*, 1 June 1938, pp. 1–2, 10, 15.
10 Murray Goot, 'Newspaper circulation in Australia', Media Centre Paper 11, Centre for the Study of Educational Communication and Media, La Trobe University, Bundoora, 1979, Table 2; Souter, *Company of Heralds*, pp. 159–69.
11 Donald Horne, *The Education of Young Donald*, Penguin, Ringwood, 1988 edn, p. 116; *Telegraph*, 31 March 1936, p. 6, 25 March 1935, p. 6, 31 March 1938, p. 6. See also Griffen-Foley, *The House of Packer*, pp. 56–60.
12 *Telegraph*, 22 March 1938, p. 6.
13 Griffen-Foley, *The House of Packer*, pp. 64–5.
14 ibid.; Memoirs (Warnecke Papers).
15 *E. G. Theodore: A Profile*, p. 19; *NN*, 1 October 1936, p. 17, 1 January 1937, p. 8.
16 Memoirs (Warnecke Papers); White, *Women's Magazines*, pp. 97, 271; Anthony Smith, *The Newspaper: An International History*, Thames & Hudson, London, 1979, p. 149.
17 NLA: MS 4849, Dumas Papers; Box 7; correspondence, 10 February 1937, 13 August 1937–14 February 1938, 12 August 1938. See also *E. G. Theodore: A Profile*, p. 28; Memoirs (Warnecke Papers).
18 *E. G. Theodore: A Profile*, pp. 28–9. See also Australian Stock Exchange (ASX): I-A132 BS, Fiche 1, Notice of Annual General Meeting, 22 September 1938.
19 *NN*, 1 October 1936, p. 1; Memoirs (Warnecke Papers).
20 *NN*, 1 May 1939, p. 1. FUL: Evatt Collection; George Warnecke; Warnecke to Evatt, 18 February 1956.
21 *NN*, 1 May 1939, p. 17; interview with Adrian Deamer, 5 December 1994.
22 Buzz Kennedy, *It Was Bloody Marvellous!*, Kangaroo Press, Kenthurst, 1996, p. 167.
23 Patrick Buckridge, *The Scandalous Penton*, University of Queensland Press, St Lucia, 1994, p. 191; interview with Adrian Deamer, 5 December 1994.
24 *NN*, 1 March 1939, p. 1, 1 April 1939, p. 15; *Truth*, 19 March 1939, p. 24, 26 March 1939, p. 28.
25 *NN*, 1 April 1939, p. 1, 1 June 1939, p. 15; *Truth*, 16 April 1939, p. 26; O'Brien, *The Weekly*, p. 71.
26 NLA: MS 4849, Dumas Papers; Box 8; F. Thompson to Dumas, 4 August 1939.
27 NBAC: N59/23, AJA NSW Minutes, 10 October 1939, p. 66, Secretary's Report. See also T39/1/18, PIEUA NSW Minutes, pp. 442–8, 4 September-3 October 1939.
28 Walker, *Yesterday's News*, pp. 79–81.
29 Souter, *Company of Heralds*, pp. 158–9; *Tariff Revision: Tariff Board's Report on Newsprinting Paper*, pp. 5–9; *NN*, 1 April 1938, p. 2. See also NLA: MS 4849, Dumas Papers; Box 7; Dumas to Murdoch, 25 July 1938.
30 *Telegraph*, 16 September 1939, p. 6, 29 September 1939, p. 5; *Truth*, 17 September 1939, p. 23.
31 *Smith's Weekly*, 7 October 1939, pp. 1–2; Neville Penton, *A Racing Heart: The Story of the Australian Turf*, Collins, Sydney, 1987, p. 118; interview with Dick Hughes, 29 November 1999.
32 Griffen-Foley, *The House of Packer*, pp. 81, 83–4.

Endnotes

33 *NN*, 1 December 1939, pp. 1, 3; *Telegraph,* 13 November 1939, p. 4.

34 *NN*, 1 December 1939, p. 1. NLA: MS 2823, Murdoch Papers; Series 1; Folder 11; Murdoch to FP, 21 November 1939. NLA: MS 4849, Dumas Papers; Box 8; Dumas to Murdoch, 18 January 1939, p. 1, 27 April 1939.

35 NLA: MS 4849, Dumas Papers; Box 8, Murdoch to Dumas, 2 August 1939, Dumas to Murdoch, 19 September 1939, Murdoch to Dumas, 24 October 1939; Box 7, Murdoch to Dumas, 1 May 1940.

36 *Telegraph*, 11 November 1939, p. 4; Griffen-Foley, *The House of Packer,* pp. 87–8; interview with Lady Stening, 30 January 1996.

37 Souter, *Company of Heralds*, p. 179; *NN*, 1 February 1940, p. 1.

38 Paul Hasluck, *The Government and the People, 1939–1941*, Australian War Memorial, Canberra, 1952, p. 211; W. K. Hancock and M. M. Gowing, *British War Economy*, His Majesty's Stationery Office, London, 1949, p. 114; W. J. Reader, *Bowater: A History*, Cambridge University Press, Cambridge, 1981, p. 159; Souter, *Company of Heralds*, pp. 187–8; *NN*, 1 May 1940, p. 1, 1 June 1940, p. 1.

39 NAA/NSW: SP221/3; Box 2 Newsprint rationing file; Notes of a deputation on Friday, 7 February 1941. See also *NN*, 1 February 1941, pp. 1, 4, 1 March 1941, p. 1.

40 Griffen-Foley, *The House of Packer*, p. 92; D. A. Bourke, 'The Department of Information and Censorship in Australia during World War II', B.A. (Hons) thesis, University of Newcastle, 1976, pp. 12–13, 16.

41 NAA/NSW: SP106/1; PC22 Part 1; E. L. Burke to Mr Croll, 3 November 1939.

42 Buckridge, *The Scandalous Penton*, pp. 57, 190.

43 ibid. pp. 165, 201–3; *Sunday Telegraph*, 17 March 1940, p. 1; *Daily Telegraph*, 31 May 1940, p. 8. For a recent assessment of the neglect of Australia's defences in the second half of the 1930s, see David Day, *John Curtin: A Life*, HarperCollins, Pymble, 1999, p. 376.

44 *Telegraph*, 30 May 1940, p. 1, 2 June 1940, p. 1, 9 September 1940, p. 6; *Women's Weekly*, 14 September 1940, p. 14, 21 September 1940, p. 14.

45 *Telegraph*, 20 September 1940, p. 8; *Women's Weekly*, 21 September 1940, p. 11.

46 Henry Mayer, 'Two editorials and a modest gift: *Sir Frank* Packer and the election', in Henry Mayer (ed.), *Labor to Power: Australia's 1972 Election*, Angus & Robertson, Sydney, 1973, p. 200; *Truth*, 8 September 1940, p. 23; *National Times*, 24–29 October 1977, p. 2.

47 NAA/NSW: SP 109/3; 322/12; FP to P. B. Jenkin, 7 August 1940. See also SP 106/1; PC 22 Part 1; folio 134, telephone conversation, 2 January 1941.

48 Gavin Long, *To Benghazi*, Australian War Memorial, Canberra, 1952, pp. 1, 9, 20, 24, 25–6.

49 Griffen-Foley, *The House of Packer*, p. 77; Buckridge, *The Scandalous Penton*, p. 189. See also NAA/NSW: C1777/T1, *NN* ABC scripts, tape 2, interview with Olga Penton, p. 16.

50 Buckridge, *The Scandalous Penton*, p. 190; Long, *To Benghazi*, p. 31.

51 Long, *To Benghazi*, pp. 11, 30–1. See also Australian Army, Soldier Career Management Agency (SCMA): NX203748, Lieut. Douglas Frank Hewson Packer; Officer's Record of Service.

52 *NN*, 1 June 1940, p. 6; *Red Cross Record*, 1 August 1940, p. 14, 1 November 1940, pp. 6, 13.

53 Bill Hornadge, *Lennie Lower: He Made a Nation Laugh*, Angus & Robertson, Pymble, 1993, pp. 114–24, 131; Cole Lesley, *The Life of Noël Coward,* Penguin, Harmondsworth, 1976, p. 106; *Red Cross*

Record, 1 December 1940, pp. 4–5. See also NBAC: N59/24, AJA NSW Minutes, p. 102, 26 November 1940.
54 Long, *To Benghazi*, pp. 45, 54, 61; Lionel Wigmore, *The Japanese Thrust*, Australian War Memorial, Canberra, 1957, pp. 164, 418. See also SCMA: NX203748; Officer's Record of Service.

7 'Political Harlots of Mammon'

1 *NN*, 1 March 1941, p. 13.
2 Evelyn Waugh, *Scoop*, Chapman & Hall, London, 1951 edn, p. 234.
3 *NN*, 1 March 1941, p. 1; Long, *To Benghazi*, pp. 59–61. See also SCMA: NX203748; Officer's Record of Service.
4 Australian War Memorial (AWM): MSS 1245, 'Live Cowards and Dead Heroes' by Will Hungerford, p. 4. MSS 874, 'The 2/7th Australian Infantry Battalion 1939–1946' by J. G. Littlewood, pp. 7–8.
5 AWM: Australian Armoured Corps Pamphlet No. 6, *The Armoured Brigade*, May 1941, pp. 9–10, 20. See also *Armour to Anchors*, 2/8th Australian Armoured Regiment Association, Karingal, 1991, part 1.
6 AWM: MSS 1245, 'Live Cowards and Dead Heroes' by Will Hungerford, pp. 4–20. SCMA: NX203748; Officer's Record of Service.
7 NAA/NSW: SP221/3; Bundle 2; Deputation on Newsprint Rationing, 10 June 1941, p. 1.
8 *CPD*, vol. 167, House of Representatives, 20 June 1941, p. 233.
9 CPD, vol. 168, House of Representatives, 18 September 1941, p. 359; *Reveille*, 1 July 1941, p. 1.
10 *Home*, 1 September 1941, p. 6b; *Red Cross Record*, 1 November 1941, p. 10; *NN*, 1 November 1941, p. 13.
11 *SMH*, 5 September 1945, p. 7.
12 ibid.; P. R. Hart and C. J. Lloyd, 'Joseph Aloysius Lyons', *ADB*, vol. 10, p. 188.
13 *SMH*, 5 September 1945, p. 7; *Telegraph*, 31 May 1940, p. 9; *NN*, 1 January 1941, p. 4.
14 La Trobe Library, State Library of Victoria: MS 10375, Lindsay Papers; Menzies to Lionel Lindsay, 14 May 1942, p. 2, 24 October 1942, p. 2.
15 Fitzgerald, *'Red Ted'*, p. 387; Day, *John Curtin*, p. 449; Tony Rigley, 'The Civil Constructional Corps, 1942–1945', *Journal of the Australian War Memorial*, no. 25, October 1994, p. 5.
16 Fitzgerald, *'Red Ted'*, p. 391; *Age*, 6 June 1959, p. 18; *Catholic Leader*, 5 March 1942.
17 *Report of the Activities of the Allied Works Council for the Period February 26, 1942 to June 30, 1943*, p. 6; *CPD*, vol. 171, House of Representatives, 2 June 1942, p. 1831. See also SCMA: NX203748; Officer's Record of Service.
18 Reginald Pound and Geoffrey Harmsworth, *Northcliffe*, Cassell, London, 1959, ch. 22; Anne Chisholm and Michael Davie, *Beaverbrook: A Life*, Hutchinson, London, 1992, *passim*, pp. 374–6; Griffen-Foley, *The House of Packer*, p. 106.
19 CPD, vol. 170, House of Representatives, 25 March 1942, p. 370.
20 Rigley, 'The Civil Constructional Corps, 1942–1945', p. 5; 'Australian Army behind the Army', *Rydge's*, 1 November 1942, p. 671; Fitzgerald, *'Red Ted'*, p. 391.

Endnotes

21 Fitzgerald, 'Red Ted', p. 391; *Report of the Activities of the Allied Works Council for the Period February 26, 1942 to June 30, 1943*, p. 6; J. A. Morley, 'The Allied Works Council', *Rydge's*, 1 November 1942, p. 669; 'Men of the CCC are our shock-workers', *Salt*, vol. 4, no. 2, 24 August 1942, p. 5; Rigley, 'The Civil Constructional Corps, 1942–1945', p. 6.

22 NLA: MS 2396, Ward Papers; Series 10; item 598, Blakeley to Theodore, 29 May 1942; item 599, Blakeley to Ward, 30 May 1942.

23 *Truth*, 3 May 1942, p. 18; Whitington, *Sir Frank*, p. 155.

24 Lloyd, *Profession: Journalist,* pp. 206–7. NLA: MS 4849, Dumas Papers; Box 7; Packer to Dumas, 25 February 1942. See also MS 2396, Ward Papers; Series 10; item 1, memo from Theodore, 9 April 1942.

25 *CPD*, vol. 170, House of Representatives, 29 April 1942, p. 596; Griffen-Foley, *The House of Packer*, pp. 106–7. See also NLA: MS 4849, Dumas Papers; Box 7; Dumas to Murdoch, 4 June 1942.

26 *Telegraph*, 6 May 1942, p. 1, 11 May 1942, p. 1; John Hilvert, 'Edmund Garnet Bonney', *ADB*, vol. 13, p. 215. NAA/NSW: SP106/1; PC22 Part 2; folio 169, Horace Mansell to *Telegraph*, 7 May 1942. NAA/ACT: SP195/2; 365/25; Bonney to Curtin, 14 May 1942.

27 NAA/ACT: SP195/2; 365/25; Packer to Bonney, n.d. (14 May 1942); 'H. W. E.' to Bonney, 15 May 1942.

28 NAA/ACT: SP195/2; 365/25; Lieut. Packer and Censorship, n.d. See also SP109/3; 365/01; Bonney to Curtin, 19 May 1942.

29 Fitzgerald, 'Red Ted', p. 396; *Bulletin*, 30 September 1942, p. 7; Whitington, *Sir Frank*, p. 396; *CPD*, vol. 172, House of Representatives, 17 September 1942, p. 444; *Reveille*, October 1941, p. 1.

30 Don Whitington, *Strive to be Fair,* Australian National University Press, Canberra, 1977, p. 91. NLA: MS 2396, Ward Papers; Series 10; item 2, Theodore to Curtin, 28 September 1942.

31 NAA/ACT: A5954/1; 199/1; Allied Works Council, 1 October 1942. See also *NN*, 2 November 1942, p. 12.

32 *Truth*, 25 February 1940, p. 23, 21 April 1940, p. 25.

33 *Truth*, 9 February 1941, p. 20, 13 December 1942, p. 15.

34 *Truth*, 11 October 1942, p. 12, 10 January 1943, p. 20, 17 January 1943, p. 10; *Sunday Telegraph*, 18 October 1942, p. 8.

35 Dennis Minogue, 'Packer's $15 million deal', *New Times*, September 1977, p. 6. See also NAA/ACT: A1608; AK27/1/2; Inquiry under the National Security Regulations, pp. 20–26.

36 NAA/ACT: A1608; AK27/1/2; Inquiry under the National Security Regulations, pp. 2–7. See also *Telegraph*, 28 January 1943, p. 9.

37 NAA/ACT: A1608; AK27/1/2; Inquiry under the National Security Regulations, pp. 1–2, 7–14.

38 *Daily Mirror* (country edn), 19 November 1942, p. 6. See also NAA/ACT: A1608; AK27/1/2; Inquiry under the National Security Regulations, p. 20.

39 *Telegraph*, 5 January 1943–25 February 1943, especially 6 January 1943, p. 7, 7 January 1943, p. 9, 8 January 1943, p. 7, 29 January 1943, p. 7.

40 NAA: MT7/28/0; F. Packer Figures Submitted; L. V. Bartlett to Mr Kirkham, 8 February 1943.

41 NLA: MS4849, Dumas Papers; Box 7; Murdoch to Dumas, 17 March 1943, pp. 2–3.

42 Rigley, 'The Civil Constructional Corps, 1942–1945', p. 8.

Endnotes

43 NAA/ACT: A1608; AK27/1/2; Inquiry under the National Security Regulations, pp. 25, 63.
44 NLA: MS 4849, Dumas; Box 7; Murdoch to Dumas, 13 July 1942. See also *Telegraph*, 23 January 1942, p. 1.
45 NBAC: N59/26, AJA NSW Minutes, pp. 153–204, 3 December 1942–11 January 1943. See also Leslie Haylen, *Twenty Years' Hard Labour*, Macmillan of Australia, Melbourne, 1969, p. 26; Griffen-Foley, *The House of Packer*, p. 125.
46 NBAC: N59/413, Curtin to George Godfrey, 18 January 1943. See also *CPD*, vol. 173, House of Representatives, 10 February 1943, pp. 448–9.
47 Colm Kiernan, 'Arthur A. Calwell's clashes with the Australian press, 1943–1945', *University of Wollongong Historical Journal*, vol. 2, 1976, pp. 74–111; Brian Penton, *Censored!*, Shakespeare Head Press, Sydney, 1947, p. 58. See also *CPD*, vol. 171, House of Representatives, 21 May 1942, pp. 1458–61, 1493–5; 27 May 1942, pp. 1618–19.
48 *Truth*, 28 February 1943, p. 10; interview with Frank McNulty, 7 February 1995.
49 *Truth*, 28 February 1943, p. 10, 3 September 1944, p. 15; Frank Cain, 'William John MacKay', *ADB*, vol. 10, p. 296; *NN*, 1 June 1934, p. 6.
50 Griffen-Foley, *The House of Packer*, pp. 115–17.
51 *Telegraph*, 6 February 1943, p. 1; *CPD*, vol. 173, House of Representatives, 10 February 1943, p. 490.
52 NBAC: Z270 Box 8, Penton Case 1943; Box 30, AJA Federal Minutes, pp. 38–208, 1 March–8 November 1943. AJA NSW Minutes, N59/26, pp. 209–395, 14 January–22 June 1943; N59/27, p. 50, 3 November 1943.
53 NBAC: N59/26, AJA NSW Minutes, pp. 257–8, 277–8, 5 March 1943. See also NLA: MS 2396, Ward Papers; Series 10; item 280, Packer to Curtin, 25 May 1943.
54 *Telegraph*, 7–17 July 1943, p. 6, 23 July 1943, p. 1, 3 August 1943, p. 6, 6 August 1943, p. 6, 16 August 1943, p. 6, 19 August 1943, p. 6, 21 August 1943, p. 1; *Sunday Telegraph*, 4 July–15 August 1943, p. 24; Whitington, *Strive to be Fair*, pp. 88–9.
55 J. W. Shaw, 'Sydney Max Falstein', *ADB*, vol. 14, p. 136; *Telegraph*, 12 October 1943, p. 5; *CPD*, vol. 176, House of Representatives, 12–13 October 1943, pp. 322, 376–9.
56 Rigley, 'The Civil Constructional Corps, 1942–1945', pp. 7, 9, 10; *CPD*, vol. 178, House of Representatives, 30 March 1944, p. 2280.
57 NAA/ACT: A1608; AK27/1/2; Inquiry under the National Security Regulations, p. 26. Rigley, 'The Civil Constructional Corps, 1942–1945', pp. 6–10.
58 *Red Cross Record*, 1 February 1941, p. 15, 1 March 1942, p. 7, 1 March 1942, p. 9; *NN*, 2 November 1942, p. 13; *Telegus*, 1 January 1943, p. 1.
59 Interview with J. A. Morley, 15 November 1994; Prue Davidson, 'Return to Sydney and the war years', in Barry Pearce and Hendrik Kolenberg (eds), *William Dobell: The Painter's Progress*, Art Gallery of New South Wales Press, Sydney, 1997, p. 74.
60 *Telegus*, 30 March 1944, p. 2; Brian Adams, *Portrait of an Artist: A Biography of William Dobell*, Hutchinson of Australia, Richmond, 1983, p. 17–18, 93, 96.

61 J. C. Waters, *Valiant Youth. The Men of the R.A.A.F.*, F. H. Johnston, Sydney, 1945; interview with Sheila Wood, 9 January 1998. See also NAA/ACT: A705/15; 163/24/348; Charles C. Learmoth to Mary Hordern, 9 December 1942.

62 Kerry Packer in Terry Lane (comp.), *As the Twig is Bent: The Childhood Recollections of Sixteen Prominent Australians*, Dove Communications, Sydney, 1979, p. 148.

63 'The man behind the desk', *Holiday and Travel*, vol. 2, no. 7, July 1949, p. 20.

64 Interview with Pat Bancks, 28 November 1999; *Truth*, 8 August 1943, p. 8.

65 *SMH*, 13 March 1982, p. 38; interview with Lady Stening, 30 January 1996.

66 Rankine, *Being Ernest*, p. 149; newspaper clipping, n.d. (Packer Family Papers).

67 *SMH*, 13 March 1982, p. 38; Kerry Packer in Lane (comp.), *As the Twig is Bent*, p. 146; *Cranbrookian*, August 1942, p. 19, December 1943, p. 23; *Cranbrook, 1918–1928*, no publisher, Sydney, n.d. (1928?), pp. 7, 9.

68 Lane, *As the Twig is Bent*, pp. 146–7.

69 ibid.; interview with Lady Stening, 30 January 1996.

8 Jekyll and Hyde

1 NAA/ACT: A472/1; W10525; 30 November–31 December 1943. See also A5954; 609/8; Advisory War Council Minute, 22 December 1943.

2 NAA/ACT: SP195/7; *NN* General — Correspondence with Minister for Information; Bonney to Minister for Information, 8 March 1944, 11 March 1944. See also Souter, *Company of Heralds*, pp. 243–4.

3 Penton, *Censored!*, pp. 62, 65; Souter, *Company of Heralds*, p. 244; *Telegraph*, 16 April 1944, p. 3. See also ML: ML MSS 3106, Cassidy Papers; Vol. 6; folios 177–83, statement by Pearl, 24 April 1944. NAA/ACT: SP195/7; *NN* High Court Case Material; File Record, 17 April 1944.

4 Penton, *Censored!*, pp. 66–8, 71; *Telegraph*, 2 July 1979, p. 22. See also ML: MSS 3106, Cassidy Papers; Vol. 6; folios 185–9, statement by Pearl, 24 April 1944.

5 JFA: Censorship April/May 1944; File 7; Special Conference *D.T.* Office, 16 April 1944; [200.24/2]. See also Penton, *Censored!*, pp. 72–5; *Telegraph*, 17 April 1944, p. 1, 2 July 1979, p. 22; 'Big daddy is no longer watching him', *Pol*, June 1974, p. 8.

6 Souter, *Company of Heralds*, p. 248; Penton, *Censored!*, p. 83; John Hilvert, *Blue Pencil Warriors*, University of Queensland Press, St Lucia, 1984, pp. 181–2.

7 *Telegraph*, 27 April 1944, p. 6, 5 May 1944, p. 9, 19 May 1944, pp. 1, 5; Souter, *Company of Heralds*, p. 245. See also JFA: Censorship April/May 1944; File 4 Settlement; Heads of Agreement reached … on Saturday, 13 May 1944; [200.24/1].

8 *Telegus*, 2 June 1944, p. 2.

9 SCMA: NX203748; Officer's Record of Service.

10 Souter, *Company of Heralds*, p. 271. I have been unable to find the file in the John Fairfax Archives that documents this meeting.

Endnotes

11   Gerard Henderson, *Menzies' Child. The Liberal Party of Australia 1944–1994*, Allen & Unwin, St Leonards, 1994, p. 67; *Sunday Telegraph*, 28 May 1944, p. 1; *Telegraph*, 7 September 1946, p. 11; Souter, *Company of Heralds*, pp. 271–2.

12   Harry Gordon, *Voyage From Shame: The Cowra Breakout and Afterwards*, University of Queensland Press, St Lucia, 1994, pp. 227, 229; *Sunday Telegraph*, 6 August 1944, p. 1. See also NAA/ACT: A472; W23628; Cowra Prisoners of War Camp — Request for Prosecution against "Sunday Telegraph" for Censorship Breach, Enclosures 1 and 2.

13   NAA/ACT: SP195/1; 73/23/32; Conversations between the SPC and Chief Executives of the "Daily Telegraph", Sunday, 6 August 1944.

14   SCMA: NX203748; Officer's Record of Service. AWM: MSS 1245, 'Live Cowards and Dead Heroes' by Will Hungerford, pp. 125–6.

15   *Armour to Anchors*, 2/8th Australian Armoured Regiment Association, Karingal, 1991, parts 2 (d), 3; John Hemsley Pearn, *Watermen of War*, Amphion Press, Brisbane, 1993, pp. x, 7.

16   SCMA: NX203748; Proceedings for Officer's Certificate of Service. See also Pearn, *Watermen of War*, pp. 33, 41, 107–11; interview with Ken Ewing, 8 November 1999.

17   *CPD*, vol. 169, House of Representatives, 21 November 1944, p. 72.

18   SCMA: NX203748; Officer's Record of Service. See also AWM: MSS 1408, 'The Rough Infantry: Tales of World War II' by A. C. Bennett, p. 16.

19   *CPD*, vol. 180, House of Representatives, 24 November 1944, pp. *2134–47*. See also Buckridge, *The Scandalous Penton*, p. 273; *Telegraph*, 25 November 1944, p. 1.

20   Letter from FP to Ethel Packer and Kathleen Stening, 28 March 1945 (Packer Family Papers).

21   *Telegus*, 23 April 1945, p. 4; *CPD*, vol. 181, House of Representatives, 27 April 1945, p. 1178.

22   SCMA: NX203748; Officer's Record of Service.

23   *Telegus*, 10 September 1945, p. 4; Griffen-Foley, *The House of Packer*, pp. 72–3.

24   Griffen-Foley, *The House of Packer*, p. 135–9; Whitington, *Strive to be Fair*, pp. 101, 103.

25   Griffen-Foley, *The House of Packer*, pp. 114, 170. See also NAA/ACT: A1608; C23/2/11 Part 2; Rupert Henderson to John Curtin, 14 September 1942.

26   NLA: MS 4849, Dumas Papers; Box 7; Murdoch to Dumas, 17 February 1943; Dumas to Henderson, 24 March 1943. See also Griffen-Foley, *The House of Packer*, pp. 117–18.

27   *CPD*, vol. 184, House of Representatives, 25 July 1945, pp. 4518–19.

28   Hughes, *Don't You Sing!*, p. 108; *NN*, 1 September 1945, p. 1.

29   Reprinted in *Telegraph*, 20 October 1945, p. 3.

30   See Griffen-Foley, *The House of Packer*, p. 150; Chisholm and Davie, *Beaverbrook*, p. 273 ff.

31   David S. Kent, 'A History of the Australian-American Association', History IV thesis, University of Sydney, 1980, pp. 28, 54–5; Buckridge, *The Scandalous Penton*, p. 226; *Telegraph*, 20 October 1945, p. 3.

32   'The man' newspaper clipping, n.d. (Packer Family Papers).

33   NLA: MS 4849, Dumas Papers; Box 3; Murdoch to Dumas, 5 September 1945. See also *NN*, 1 February 1946, p. 1; Griffen-Foley, *The House of Packer*, p. 157.

34   ASC: 000 053 789, Fiche B, Prospectus, 28 June 1946, p. 4. See also *NN*, 15 December 1945, p. 1.

Endnotes

35 *NN*, 15 December 1945, pp. 1, 8, 1 February 1946, p. 1.
36 Griffen-Foley, *The House of Packer*, pp. 145–6. For Ratcliffe, see *Telegraph*, 6 December 1963, p. 11; Horne, *Into the Open*, p. 6.
37 Day, *Contraband and Controversy*, pp. 270–1; *Truth*, 19 May 1946, p. 31; *CPD*, vol. 187, House of Representatives, 5 July 1946, p. 2289, 17 July 1946, p. 2668.
38 Day, *Contraband and Controversy*, pp. 270–1.
39 NLA: MS 4849, Dumas Papers; Box 3; Dumas to Murdoch, 9 April, 16 September 1946; Murdoch to Dumas, 19 September 1946.
40 NLA: MS 4849, Dumas Papers; Box 3; correspondence with Murdoch, 24 September-30 October 1946.
41 *NN*, 1 November 1946, p. 17, 1 December 1946, p. 22. See also NLA: MS 4849, Dumas Papers; Box 8; Dumas to Murdoch, 13 January 1947.
42 Donald Read, *The Power of News: The History of Reuters*, Oxford University Press, Oxford, 1992, pp. 258–9; *NN*, 1 April 1947, p. 13. See also NLA: MS 4849, Dumas Papers; Box 8; Murdoch to Dumas, 4 March 1947.
43 Tom Sheridan, *Division of Labour: Industrial Relations in the Chifley Years, 1945–49*, Oxford University Press, Oxford, 1989, p. 1. NLA: MS 4849, Dumas Papers; Box 8; Dumas to Murdoch, 13 January 1947, p. 5.
44 See p. 115.
45 *Telegraph*, 16 December 1942, p. 7, 9 May 1946, p. 1, 10 May 1946, p. 1; Buckridge, *The Scandalous Penton*, p. 285; Griffen-Foley, *The House of Packer*, pp. 167–8. See also NBAC: Z270 Box 8, The Penton Case.
46 NBAC: Z270 Box 7, D. R. McNicoll. See also AJA NSW Minutes, N59/28, 29 November 1945–3 January 1946, 23 August 1946, p. 2; N59/29, 12 December 1946–30 January 1947; N59/31, 31 March-28 April 1949.
47 Griffen-Foley, *The House of Packer*, pp. 165–6.
48 'The man behind the desk', p. 20; *Life International*, 30 July 1962, p. 45; Donald Horne, *Confessions of a New Boy*, Penguin, Ringwood, 1985, p. 322.
49 Horne, *Confessions of a New Boy*, p. 320; *NN*, 1 May 1947, p. 19.
50 Horne, *Confessions of a New Boy*, pp. 322–5.
51 ibid. p. 321.
52 O'Brien, *The Weekly*, p. 98; *Women's Weekly*, 3 September 1949, p. 19.
53 Helen Blaxland, *Collected Flower Pieces*, Ure Smith, Sydney, n.d. (1948?), pp. 46–9.
54 Interview with Sheila Wood, 9 January 1998.
55 *SMH*, 3 August 1996, pp. 6s–7s; *Sunday Telegraph*, 11 August 1996, p. 45.
56 *Telegraph*, 8 October 1947, p. 14, 5 October 1947, p. 17, 4 October 1950, p. 15.
57 Interview with Lady Stening, 18 February 1996.
58 ibid; Whitington, *Sir Frank*, p. 21; *Telegraph*, 3 April 1947, p. 5. For AAP, see *Newspaper News*, 1 April 1947, p. 13; *SMH*, 13 May 1947, p. 4.
59 Kerry Packer in Lane, *As the Twig is Bent*, pp. 144–5, 148.

60 *Who's Who in Australia*, 1935, pp. 833–4.
61 Interview with Lady Stening, 18 February 1996. See also *Sunday Telegraph*, 24 November 1946, p. 18, 3 August 1947, p. 23; Whitington, *Sir Frank*, pp. 70, 286.
62 Whitington, *Strive to be Fair*, p. 103; McNicoll, *Luck's a Fortune*, p. 298; newspaper clipping, c. October 1947 (Packer Family Papers).
63 Newspaper clipping, c. October 1947 (Packer Family Papers); *Sporting Globe*, 18 October 1947, p. 1; 'The man behind the desk', p. 48.

9 Powerbroking

1 Gianni Zappalà, 'The decline of economic complementarity: Australia and the sterling area', *Australian Economic History Review*, vol. 34, no. 1, March 1994, p. 8; David Lee, 'Protecting the sterling area: The Chifley government's response to multilateralism, 1945–9', *Australian Journal of Political Science*, vol. 25, 1990, pp. 182–3.
2 Griffen-Foley, *The House of Packer*, p. 170. See also NLA: MS 4849, Dumas Papers; Box 8; correspondence with Murdoch 3 November–4 December 1947.
3 *NN*, 1 March 1948, p. 1, 1 April 1948, p. 1; Souter, *Company of Heralds*, p. 269.
4 NLA: MS 4849, Dumas Papers; Box 8; Dumas to Murdoch, 2 June 1948; Murdoch to Dumas, 7 June 1948; Dumas to Murdoch, 8 June 1948; FP to Dumas, 11 June 1948; Dumas to Murdoch, 7 July 1948.
5 NLA: MS 4849, Dumas Papers; Box 8; Dumas to Murdoch, 17 June and 22 July 1948. See also *NN*, 2 August 1948, p. 17.
6 NAA/ACT: CP208/1; A37; FP to Chifley, 28 July 1948. See also *NN*, 1 June 1948, p. 16; Griffen-Foley, *The House of Packer*, p. 171.
7 NAA/ACT: CP208/1; A37; FP to Chifley, 2 August 1948. See also NLA: MS 4849, Dumas Papers; Box 8, Dumas to Murdoch, 16 August 1948.
8 *Telegraph*, 7 September 1946, p. 11.
9 *Telegraph*, 14 September 1946, p. 11.
10 Sheridan, *Division of Labour*, pp. 1, 82–3; Geoffrey Bolton, *The Oxford History of Australia*, vol. 5, Oxford University Press, Melbourne, 1990, p. 68.
11 *NN*, 2 August 1948, p. 16, 1 October 1948, p. 1, 10 December 1948, p. 1.; *Things I Hear*, 30 August 1948, pp 2–3. See also JFA: Newsprint Pool Correspondence:- 1947–1949; Kennedy to Henderson, 27 and 28 August 1948; Henderson to W. T. Turner, 30 August 1948; ANPA Circular to Members, 8 September 1948; [200.15/5].
12 Fitzgerald, *'Red Ted'*, pp. 407, 409; *PIM*, October 1948, p. 86; *NN*, 1 February 1949, p. 18; *Who's Who in Australia*, 1955, p. 747.
13 *SMH*, 19 October 1948, p. 3, 20 October 1948, p. 3; *Telegraph*, 28 October 1948, p. 8.
14 *E. G. Theodore: A Profile*, p. 38; *NN*, 10 December 1948, p. 27. See also ASX: I-A132 CP, Fiche 1, records, 10 November 1948.
15 ASX: I-A132 BS, Fiche 1, Directors' Report, 10 November 1948. See also *NN*, 10 December 1948, p. 2.

Endnotes

16 *E. G. Theodore: A Profile*, p. 38; *NN*, 10 December 1948, p. 27. See also ASX: I-A132 BS, Fiche 1, Notice of Extraordinary General Meeting, 10 November 1948.

17 NLA: MS 4849, Dumas Papers; Box 1; Folder 1; FP to Dumas, 29 December 1948; Dumas to Murdoch, 4 and 11 January 1949; Murdoch to Dumas, 12 January 1949.

18 NLA: MS 4849, Dumas Papers; Box 1; Folder 1; Dumas to Murdoch, 5 September 1949; Murdoch to Dumas, 11 October 1949; Dumas to Murdoch, 29 October 1949; Murdoch to Dumas, 2 and 7 November 1949; Dumas to Murdoch, 8 November 1949; *Things I Hear*, 13 September 1949, p. 2.

19 NLA: MS 2823, Murdoch Papers; Series 3; Folder 24, Empire Press Union Conference 1950; correspondence between FP and Murdoch, 13–28 September 1949; Murdoch to C. P. Smith, 11 October 1949; Murdoch to Warwick O. Fairfax, 15 November 1949; Murdoch to Oswald Syme, 18 November 1949; Murdoch to Smith, 18 and 28 November 1949; Smith to Murdoch, 29 November 1949; Murdoch to FP, 30 November 1949.

20 *NN*, 1 February 1950, p. 16, 1 March 1950, p. 14, 1 April 1950, p. 2.

21 Fizgerald, *'Red Ted'*, pp. 409–12; *Sunday Telegraph*, 12 February 1950, p. 4.

22 NLA: MS 4849, Dumas Papers; Box 1; Folder 1; Dumas to Murdoch, 21 December 1949; Murdoch to Dumas, 23 December 1949. *NN*, 1 May 1950, p. 2, 1 July 1950, p. 17.

23 Griffen-Foley, *The House of Packer*, p. 188.

24 NBAC: N59/32, AJA NSW Minutes, 9 May 1950, pp. 1–2, 25 May 1950, p. 3.

25 See *NN*, 1 May 1950, p. 2.

26 Institute of Commonwealth Archives, University of London (ICA): Commonwealth Press Union Records; Box 10; *CPU Quarterly Bulletin*, November 1968, pp. 14–15. See also Press Cuttings; Item 6, Seventh Imperial Press Conference, Canada, 1950.

27 NLA: MS 2823, Murdoch Papers; Series 3; Folder 24, Empire Press Union Conference 1950; FP to Murdoch, 13 September 1949.

28 NLA: MS 4849, Dumas Papers; Box 1; Folder 2; Murdoch to Dumas, 10 July 1950. *Sunday Telegraph*, 18 June 1950, p. 13; *Daily Telegraph*, 19 June 1950, p. 2; *NN*, 1 July 1950, p. 17.

29 *Telegraph*, 28 September 1950, p. 1. See also NLA: MS 4936, Menzies Papers; Series 1; Folder 201; Menzies to FP, 5 October 1950; FP to Menzies, 6 October 1950.

30 Ian Hancock, *National and Permanent? The Federal Organisation of the Liberal Party of Australia 1944–1965*, Melbourne University Press, Carlton, 2000, pp. 20–1, 56, 90–1. See also ML: ML MSS 2385, Liberal Party (NSW Division) Papers; Box Y4626; Item 9; public relations officer to president and general secretary, 31 August 1949.

31 NLA: MS 4936, Menzies Papers; Series 1; Folder 201; Schapel to FP, 25 May 1951. This would not be the last time that Liberal officials expressed concerns about Menzies' punishing schedule. See Hancock, *National and Permanent?*, pp. 146–7.

32 NLA: MS 4936, Menzies Papers; Series 1; Folder 201; FP to Menzies, 29 May 1951. See also p. 128.

33 NLA: MS 7995, Fitzgerald Papers; vol. 2; Cyril Pearl to George Munster, n.d. (July 1959?). See also *NN*, 2 July 1951, p. 14.

34 ML: ML 1243/91, Ashby Papers; Box 57; File: Mr Packer Personal; FP to Ashby, 27 June 1951.

35 *Telegraph*, 3 October 1952, p. 1; Paul Barry, *The Rise and Rise of Kerry Packer*, Bantam and ABC Books, Sydney, 1993, pp. 64–6, 498–9n; Griffen-Foley, *The House of Packer*, p. 195.
36 *CPD*, vol. 219, House of Representatives, 30 September 1952, pp. 2314–20; Barry, *The Rise and Rise of Kerry Packer*, p. 64.
37 *CPD*, vol. 220, House of Representatives, 9 October 1952, p. 2882; *Telegraph*, 31 October 1952, p. 1.
38 NLA: MS 4936, Menzies Papers; Series 2; Folder 116, FP to Menzies, 19 August 1953; Folder 218, FP to Menzies, 19 March 1954, Menzies to FP, 7 April 1954; Folder 282; FP to Menzies, 31 December 1954.
39 Tom Mead, *Breaking the News*, Dolphin Books, Sydney, 1998, pp. 102–4; *Telegus*, August 1953, p. 1; *Telegraph*, 19 February 1954, p. 7.
40 NLA: TRC 2172, interview with Alan Reid, October 1986, pp. 72–3.
41 See Bridget Griffen-Foley, 'Revisiting the "Mystery of a Novel Contest": The *Daily Telegraph* and *Come in Spinner*', *Australian Literary Studies*, October 2000; Buckridge, *The Scandalous Penton*, pp. 295–9.
42 NLA: MS 6455, White Papers; Series 2; Folders 3–7. See also *NN*, 1 September 1951, p. 17.
43 *Daily Telegraph*, 5 May 1951, p. 9, 8 May 1951, p. 11, 28 April 1952, p. 3; *Sunday Telegraph*, 27 April 1952, p. 31, 8 May 1952, p. 20, 3 May 1954, p. 7.
44 Mead, *Breaking the News*, p. 143.
45 D. D. Millar (ed.), *The Messel Era*, Pergamon, Sydney, 1987, p. 13. See also NAA/ACT: A10663/1; CAU/SCI/7; Summary of oral evidence, point 2.
46 Millar, *The Messel Era*, pp. 13, 139.
47 *Inaugural Proceedings of the Nuclear Research Foundation*, no publisher, Sydney, 1954, pp. 69–70.
48 University of Sydney Archives (USA): G3 22 1; Nuclear Research Foundation Minute Book, 14 April 1954, p. 14.
49 Buckridge, *The Scandalous Penton*, pp. 304–5. See also ASX: I-A132 BS, Fiche 2, Directors' Report, 1 September 1952.
50 Griffen-Foley, *The House of Packer*, p. 192; Minogue, 'Packer's $15 million deal', pp. 4–5.
51 *Printer*, March 1953, p. 29; *Printing Trades Journal*, March 1953, p. 26; *Journalist*, April 1953, p. 3; Whitington, *Sir Frank*, pp. 1–8.
52 Horne, *Money Made Us*, p. 56; *Telegraph*, 7 March 1953, p. 1; *Journalist*, April 1953, p. 3. NBAC: N59/32, AJA NSW Minutes, 12 March-2 April 1953.
53 *Printer*, June 1953, p. 51, July 1953, p. 58.
54 ML: ML MSS 5770, Barcs Papers; Box 7; 'Betty' (Best?) to Emery Barcs, 12 April 1955. See also Chisholm and Davie, *Beaverbrook*, pp. 291, 513.
55 Donald Horne, *Portrait of an Optimist*, Penguin, Ringwood, 1988, pp. 120–1, 126; *Things I Hear*, 10 May 1949, p. 1. See also ML: ML MSS 3525, Horne Papers; MLK 2146; ACP-Proj 2; FP to L. R. Coleman, 14 June 1960.
56 NBAC: N59/38, AJA NSW Minutes, 19 May 1955, pp. 3–4; 2 June 1955, pp. 3–5. See also *NN*, 1 July 1955, p. 8; Lloyd, *Profession: Journalist*, pp. 251–3.

57 *Journalist*, July 1955, pp. 1, 3; *Printer*, July-August 1955, pp. 57–60. See also NBAC: N59/900, 1955 Printers' Strike.
58 NBAC: N59/38, AJA NSW Minutes, 25 August 1955, pp. 8–9. See also Lloyd, *Profession: Journalist*, p. 253.
59 Kennedy, *It Was Bloody Marvellous!*, pp. 162–3.
60 *Printer*, November 1955, p. 95; interview with Noel Slarke, 4 August 1999.
61 *Printer*, November 1955, p. 95. See also NBAC: N59/37, AJA NSW Minutes, 22–24 October 1955.
62 See, for example, Whitington, *Sir Frank*, pp. 10–11; Barry, *The Rise and Rise of Kerry Packer*, pp. 76–7; Kennedy, *It Was Bloody Marvellous!*, p. 163.
63 Interview with Noel Slarke, 4 August 1999.

10 Treading on Corns

1 *Cranbrookian*, August 1950, pp. 6, 7, December 1950, pp. 8, 11, 20.
2 *Cranbrookian*, December 1950, pp. 28, 30, May 1951, p. 36; Barry, *The Rise and Rise of Kerry Packer*, p. 94; Tom Judd, *Fifty Years will be Long Enough!*, The National Press, Melbourne, 1971, pp. 143–4.
3 *Corian*, December 1951, p. 164, May 1952, pp. 25–7, 36, August 1952, pp. 98, 124, May 1953, pp. 34–5, 41, 44, August 1953, pp. 105, 128, 129.
4 *Corian*, May 1952, p. 21, December 1952, p. 166, May 1953, pp. 21, 23; Judd, *Fifty Years will be Long Enough!*, p. 136.
5 Barry, *The Rise and Rise of Kerry Packer*, pp. 96–7; Kerry Packer in Lane, *As the Twig is Bent*, p. 147; *Corian*, August 1953, p. 133, August 1954, p. 121, August 1955, p. 109, May 1956, p. 47, May 1957, p. 42.
6 Barry, *The Rise and Rise of Kerry Packer*, pp. 96–9.
7 *Age*, 19 November 1984, p. 11.
8 Barry, *The Rise and Rise of Kerry Packer*, pp. 105–7; *Corian*, May 1957, p. 42; *National Times*, 23–28 May 1977, p. 5.
9 MS 5546, Bednall Papers; Box 1; Folder 8; Bednall to Rupert Murdoch, 25 November 1952.
10 House of Lords Record Office: Beaverbrook Papers; BBK H/116; draft notes by A. W. Wood.
11 Cecil H. King, *Strictly Personal*, Weidenfeld & Nicolson, London, 1969, pp. 174–5, 180.
12 NLA: MS 4849, Dumas Papers; Box 1; Murdoch to Dumas, 22 May 1952, p. 2. See also *Journalist*, July 1952, p. 3; Griffen-Foley, *The House of Packer*, p. 203.
13 NLA: MS 4849, Dumas Papers; Box 1; correspondence, 22 May 1952–4 August 1952. MS 5546, Bednall Papers; Box 1; Folder 8; Murdoch to Bednall, 22 July 1952, 4 August 1952. See also letter from Rupert Murdoch to Rohan Rivett, 13 February 1953 (Rivett Papers).
14 NLA: MS 5546, Bednall Papers; Box 1; Folder 8; Bednall to H. D. Giddy, 3 November 1952; Bednall to Murdoch, 25 November 1952, p. 1; Murdoch to Bednall, 4 December 1952, p. 1. See also William Shawcross, *Murdoch*, Pan Books, London, 1993 edn, p. 77.
15 Letter from Murdoch to Rohan Rivett, 13 February 1953 (Rivett Papers). See also *NN*, 2 February 1953, p. 13.

Endnotes

16   JFA: Associated Newspapers; Negotiations, Agreement, Court Case; statement, 29 August 1953; Chairman's Address, 2 December 1953, pp. 2, 10; Henderson affidavit, n.d., p. 3; [200.20/1]. See also Souter, *Company of Heralds*, p. 303; *Telegraph*, 16 September 1953, pp. 7, 12.

17   JFA: Associated Newspapers; Negotiations, Agreement, Court Case; FP affidavit, 31 August 1953, p. 1; H. N. F. MacDonnell affidavit, 11 September 1953, pp. 1–2; Chairman's Address, 2 December 1953, p. 6; Henderson affidavit, n.d., pp. 4–5; [200.20/1]. See also House of Lords Record Office: Beaverbrook Papers; BBK/164; 'R.C.B.' to Beaverbrook, 28 August 1953; E. J. Robertson to Beaverbrook, 31 August 1953.

18   JFA: Associated Newspapers; Negotiations, Agreement, Court Case; Chairman's Address, 2 December 1953, p. 6; Henderson affidavit, n.d., pp. 4–5; [200.20/1]. Associated Newspapers; Sale of Goodwill of *Telegraph*, 1935; Henderson to FP, 27 August 1953; [200.20/3]. See also Souter, *Company of Heralds*, pp. 304–6.

19   *Telegraph*, 4 September 1953, p. 1, 15 September 1953, pp. 7, 11; *NN*, 1 October 1953, p. 2; Souter, *Company of Heralds*, pp. 307–7; Valerie Lawson, *The Allens Affair*, Macmillan, Sydney, 1995, pp. 55, 67.

20   NBAC: N59/36, AJA NSW Minutes, 14 September 1953, pp. 4–5.

21   JFA: Associated Newspapers; Sale of Goodwill of *Telegraph*, 1935; telegrams between Henderson and FP, 23 September 1953; [200.20/3]. See also Souter, *Company of Heralds*, p. 307; *Telegraph*, 23 September 1953, pp. 1, 2, 7–8, 12; *Bulletin*, 30 September 1953, p. 14; *NN*, 1 October 1953, p. 3.

22   *Australian*, 9–10 November 1991, p. 27; *West Australian*, 5 October 1955, p. 5.

23   *Sunday Telegraph*, 14 October 1956, p. 1; *SMH*, 19 October 1956, p. 1.

24   *SMH*, 22 October 1956, p. 3; *Telegraph*, 24 October 1956, p. 3.

25   Souter, *Company of Heralds*, p. 308; *Telegraph*, 21 December 1956, p. 1; *SMH*, 21 December 1956, p. 1.

26   *Australian*, 9–10 November 1991, p. 28; Penelope Nelson, *Penny Dreadful*, Random House Australia, Milsons Point, 1995, pp. 82–3.

27   Margaret Hughes, *The Long Hop*, Stanley Paul, London, 1955, pp. 11–14 (my thanks to Gideon Haigh for this reference).

28   Horne, *Portrait of an Optimist*, pp. 121–6.

29   ibid. pp. 133–4; David McNicoll, *Luck's a Fortune*, Wildcat Press, Sydney, 1979, p. 291.

30   Horne, *Portrait of an Optimist*, pp. 136–8.

31   ibid. pp. 139–41; *Telegraph*, 26 August 1954, p. 1.

32   Horne, *Portrait of an Optimist*, pp. 145, 146. See also ML: ML MSS 3525, Horne Papers; MLK 2146; ACP-Proj 2; typescript notes, n.d., p. 4.

33   Horne, *Portrait of an Optimist*, pp. 145–8. See also ML: ML MSS 3525, Horne Papers; MLK 2147; ACP-FP1; Horne to FP, 30 December 1954; FP to Horne, 16 February 1955.

34   JFA: *Telegraph* 1, 1957–1960; Sydney Newspapers Pty Ltd, n.d., pp. 1–3; [300.70].

35   ibid.; *Telegraph*, 16 December 1954, p. 3; *NN*, 1 January 1955, p. 3.

36   ASC: 008 394 509, Consolidated Press Holdings Ltd List of Allottees, n.d., pp. 42, 46; Statement in lieu of Prospectus, 23 December 1954. For Faircloth, see *Bulletin*, 12 November 1977, p. 24.

37   Barry, *The Rise and Rise of Kerry Packer*, p. 141.

38 The following is drawn from Ann Curthoys, 'The getting of television: Dilemmas in ownership, control and culture, 1941–56', in Ann Curthoys and John Merritt (eds), *Australia's First Cold War*, vol. 2, Allen & Unwin, Sydney, 1986, pp. 126–54.
39 NLA: MS 4936, Menzies Papers; Series 2; Folder 218; Menzies to FP, 9 December 1954.
40 Barry, *The Rise and Rise of Kerry Packer*, p. 99; K. S. Inglis, *This is the ABC*, Melbourne University Press, Carlton, 1983, p. 249.
41 Sandra Hall, *Supertoy: 20 Years of Australian Television*, Sun Books, Melbourne, 1976, p. 21; *NN*, 1 March 1955, p. 1, 1 May 1956, p. 15.
42 *SMH*, 14 January 1955, p. 4; Margot Kerley, 'Commercial Television in Australia: Government Policy and Regulation, 1953 to 1963', Ph.D. thesis, Australian National University, 1992, p. 48.
43 *SMH*, 21 January 1955, p. 3.
44 *NN*, 1 February 1955, p. 1; Hall, *Supertoy*, p. 21; Minogue, 'Packer's $15 million deal', p. 6.
45 Hall, *Supertoy*, pp. 21–2; *SMH*, 5 February 1955, p. 4.
46 *SMH*, 5 February 1955, p. 4.
47 ibid.; Kerley, 'Commercial Television in Australia', p. 43. See also Griffen-Foley, *The House of Packer*, ch. 3–9.
48 Hall, *Supertoy*, p. 23; Kerley, 'Commercial Television in Australia', p. 50; *SMH*, 4 February 1955, p. 4.
49 *Bulletin*, 3 February 1987, pp. 18–19; *NN*, 1 August 1955, p. 1, 1 October 1955, p. 1, 2 January 1956, p. 18; Kerley, 'Commercial Television in Australia', pp. 83–4.
50 NLA: TRC 2144, interview with Bruce Gyngell, 1 December 1983, pp. 32–44.
51 *Sunday Telegraph*, 16 February 1956, p. 7.
52 Hall, *Supertoy*, pp. 28–9.
53 *NN*, 1 May 1956, p. 15; *SMH*, 4 February 1955, p. 4; *Bulletin*, 3 February 1987, pp. 18–19.
54 Fitzgerald, 'Red Ted', pp. 411–12; *Bulletin*, 3 February 1987, p. 19; Whitington, *Sir Frank*, pp. 219–20.
55 Whitington, *Sir Frank*, p. 221.
56 *NN*, 1 March 1957, p. 1; *SMH*, 27 March 1957, p. 3.
57 Horne, *Into the Open*, pp. 6–7; Whitington, *Sir Frank*, p. 221; McNicoll, *Luck's a Fortune*, pp. 298–9; Kennedy, *It Was Bloody Marvellous!*, p. 159.
58 *NN*, 1 January 1953, p. 12, 4 October 1957, p. 10; Horne, *Portrait of an Optimist*, pp. 133, 134. See also ASX: I-A132 CP, Notice of Extraordinary General Meeting, 9 November 1956.
59 Hall, *Supertoy*, pp. 29–30; Ken G. Hall, *Directed by Ken G. Hall: Autobiography of an Australian Film Maker*, Lansdowne Press, Melbourne, 1977, p. 196.
60 McNicoll, *Luck's a Fortune*, p. 284; *NN*, 1 November 1957, p. 2; Consolidated Press Holdings Ltd Directors' Report, 15 November 1957. Fielding was on the board of Bonds Industries Ltd with Ratcliffe; see *Business Who's Who of Australia*, 1964, no. 780.

11 Rumours

1 Griffen-Foley, *The House of Packer*, p. 204; Horne, *Portrait of an Optimist*, pp. 158, 191.

Endnotes

2   ML: ML MSS 3525, Horne Papers; MLK 2147; ACP-FP1; Horne to FP, 5 March 1957. See also *NN*, 1 March 1957, p. 1; Griffen-Foley, *The House of Packer*, p. 220.
3   Horne, *Portrait of an Optimist*, pp. 188–9. See also ML: ML MSS 3525, Horne Papers; MLK 2150; ACP-Misc 3; File: Pictorial; Murdoch to Horne, 6 September 1957.
4   ML: ML MSS 3525, Horne Papers; MLK 2147; ACP-FP1; Clyde Packer to FP, n.d. See also Horne, *Portrait of an Optimist*, p. 189; *NN*, 24 January 1958, p. 2.
5   Horne, *Portrait of an Optimist*, p. 188; *SMH*, 27 April 1991, p. 2. See also Woollahra Local History Centre: Valuation Books, 1955, 1959.
6   Whitington, *Sir Frank*, p. 288.
7   Horne, *Portrait of an Optimist*, p. 187.
8   Lawson, *Connie Sweetheart*, pp. 279–80.
9   McNicoll, *Luck's a Fortune*, pp. 291, 294.
10 Horne, *Portrait of an Optimist*, p. 188.
11 *Times* (London), 9 May 1998, p. 25.
12 *Women's Weekly*, 11 August 1954, p. 12, 25 August 1954, p. 12, 13 October 1954, p. 21, 21 August 1957, p. 4.
13 *Telegraph*, 27 June 1957, p. 9.
14 See ML: ML MSS 5770, Barcs Papers; Box 5; File 14; 'Betty' to Emery Barcs, 3 July 1957.
15 James to W. Deane, 1 September 1961 (James Papers). See also Barry, *The Rise and Rise of Kerry Packer*, p. 114.
16 *NN*, 10 January 1958, p. 1. See also USA: G3 22 1; Nuclear Research Foundation Minute Book, 22 January 1958, p. 105; 27 March 1958, p. 106.
17 Horne, *Portrait of an Optimist*, pp. 189, 196, 198, and *Into the Open*, p. 2.
18 Horne, *Portrait of an Optimist*, pp. 199–204. For the outcome of the case, see Griffen-Foley, *The House of Packer*, pp. 219–20.
19 K. S. Inglis, *Nation. The Life of an Independent Journal of Opinion 1958–1972*, Melbourne University Press, Melbourne, 1989, pp. 22–3; Hughes quoted by Edward Spring, 'Don't Go Mining For Truth, Son: Cold War Ideological Perspectives of the Radical Right in Australia Through an Analysis of "The Observer", 1958–1961', B.A. (Hons) thesis, Australian National University, 1975, p. 2.
20 ML: ML MSS 3525, Horne Papers; MLK 2151; ACP-O1; Policy and Practice in "The Observer", p. 5. See also Peter Coleman, *Memoirs of a Slow Learner*, Angus & Robertson, Pymble, 1994, pp. 118, 121.
21 Coleman, *Memoirs of a Slow Learner*, p. 130; Nation, 25 July 1964, p. 14.
22 Coleman, *Memoirs of a Slow Learner*, p. 130: *Journalist*, June 1958, p. 4. See also ML: ML MSS 3525, Horne Papers; MLK 2151; ACP-02; Kennedy to Horne, 7 April 1958. See also *Journalist*, June 1958, p. 4.
23 Coleman, *Memoirs of a Slow Learner*, pp. 100, 103, 108; letter from Bruce Beresford, 1 December 1999; Robert Raymond, *Out of the Box*, Seaview Press, Adelaide, 2000, pp. 65–6.
24 Kerley, 'Commercial Television in Australia', p. 108. See also *CPD*, Senate, vol. 14; 11 March 1959, pp. 301–2.

Endnotes

25 *Telegraph*, 29 April 1958, p. 3, 7 May 1958, p. 9, 8 May 1958, p. 9; Whitington, *Sir Frank*, p. 278; Hall, *Supertoy*, p. 26.
26 NLA: MS 4936, Menzies Papers; Series 1, Folder 13, FP to Menzies, 29 September 1958, Menzies to FP, 3 October 1958; Series 2, Folder 384, FP to Menzies, 15 October 1958.
27 Minogue, 'Packer's $15 million deal', p. 6; Kennedy, *It Was Bloody Marvellous!*, p. 168.
28 NLA: MS 7995, Fitzgerald Papers; vol. 2; Cyril Pearl to George Munster, n.d. (July 1959?).
29 Kennedy, *It Was Bloody Marvellous!*, p. 168.
30 Mead, *Breaking the News*, p. 147; *Life International*, 30 July 1962, p. 45; Minogue, 'Packer's $15 million deal', pp. 4–5.
31 NLA: MS 7995, Fitzgerald Papers; vol. 2; Cyril Pearl to George Munster, n.d. (July 1959?). See also *NN*, 26 June 1959, p. 1; *Sunday Mirror*, 11 December 1960, p. 12; *CPD*, vol. 26, House of Representatives, 24 March 1960, p. 635.
32 Kennedy, *It Was Bloody Marvellous!*, pp. 159–60.
33 ibid.; 'Big daddy is no longer watching him', p. 8; Barry, *The Rise and Rise of Kerry Packer*, pp. 101–4.
34 Souter, *Company of Heralds*, p. 348. See also ML: ML MSS 3525, Horne Papers; MLK 2147; ACP-FP3; Horne to FP, 16 February 1960.
35 Mead, *Breaking the News*, pp. 147–8; Griffen-Foley, *The House of Packer*, p. 246.
36 Mead, *Breaking the News*, pp. 148–9; *SMH*, 27 September 1984, p. 9; *Things I Hear*, 25 February 1960, p. 2; *Nation*, 12 March 1960, p. 13. See also NLA: MS 7995, Fitzgerald Papers; vol. 2; letter to Cyril Pearl, 29 February 1960.
37 Mead, *Breaking the News*, p. 149; Nation, 4 June 1960, p. 14; Souter, *Company of Heralds*, p. 346.
38 Affidavit of A. F. James, 9 June 1960, pp. 1–2 (James Papers).
39 ML: ML MSS 3525, Horne Papers; MLK 2151; ACP-04. See also Horne, *Into the Open*, pp. 9–10.
40 'Statement of Facts', n.d., point 22; Lord Bishop of Armidale to Lord Bishop of Tasmania, 6 June 1960; Francis James affidavit, 9 June 1960; R. S. Walker affidavit, 21 June 1960 (James Papers).
41 Lord Bishop of Armidale to Lord Bishop of Tasmania, 6 June 1960; Francis James affidavit, 9 June 1960; J. E. Wayland affidavit, 14 June 1960 (James Papers).
42 Francis James affidavit, 9 June 1960; J. E. Wayland affidavit, 14 June 1960 (James Papers).
43 Lord Bishop of Armidale to Lord Bishop of Tasmania, 6 June 1960; Francis James affidavit, 9 June 1960; J. E. Wayland affidavit, 14 June 1960 (James Papers). For Millar, see Lawson, *The Allens Affair*, pp. 69–70.
44 J. S. Moyes affidavit, 11 June 1960; letter from James to Rupert Murdoch, 16 June 1960; 'Statement of Facts', n.d., point 37; memo re The Anglican Press Limited by L. W. Street, n.d. (James Papers).
45 Statements by L. J. Eather and V. H. Roberts, n.d.; affidavits by T. J. G. Willis and H. J. Reid, 9 June 1960 (James Papers).
46 Clem Lloyd, *Parliament and the Press: The Federal Parliamentary Press Gallery, 1901–1988*, Melbourne University Press, Melbourne, 1988, p. 199; *Things I Hear*, 21 March 1949, p. 5, 17 March 1960, p. 4, 9 June 1960, p. 2; *Daily Mirror*, 8 June 1960, pp. 1, 3; *Sun-Herald*, 20 December 1981, p. 11. See also ML: ML MSS 3525, Horne Papers; MLK 2149; ACP-WE5; Horne to FP, 16 June 1960.

Endnotes

47 Barry, *The Rise and Rise of Kerry Packer*, p. 122. See also Royal Sydney Yacht Squadron Archives (RSYSA): 25/3/14; R. A. Dickson to Sir William Slim, 23 May 1960.
48 *Smith's Weekly*, 7 October 1939, p. 1; Daily Mirror, 8 June 1960, pp. 1, 3; *NN*, 24 November 1961, p. 3.
49 James to Murdoch, 16 June 1960 (James Papers).
50 ibid.
51 ML: ML MSS 3525, Horne Papers; MLK 2149; ACP-WE5; Horne to FP, 16 June 1960; FP to Horne, 16 June 1960.
52 *NN*, 24 November 1961, p. 3; Anglican, 14 November 1963. See also James to R. T. St John, 23 June 1960; 'Aide Memoire', 16 October 1961; John Armidale to Murdoch, 22 November 1961; T. J. G. Willis to Messrs Lane and Lane, 28 September 1962 (James Papers).
53 Mead, *Breaking the News*, pp. 151, 155–6; Barry, *The Rise and Rise of Kerry Packer*, pp. 122–3.
54 NLA: MS 4936, Menzies Papers; Series 2; Folder 454; FP to Menzies, 20 April 1959. See also Kerley, 'Commercial Television in Australia', p. 128; *SMH*, 20 February 1960, p. 8.
55 Kerley, 'Commercial Television in Australia', p. 128; *SMH*, 25 February 1960, pp. 13, 53; *Telegraph*, 25 February 1960, pp. 13, 53, 6 April 1960, p. 14, 7 April 1960, p. 13.
56 *Nation*, 14 January 1961, p. 7.
57 *NN*, 28 October 1960, p. 1; *Journalist*, November 1960, p. 7.
58 Hall, *Supertoy*, pp. 25, 33; *Bulletin*, 3 February 1987, p. 19.
59 Souter, *Company of Heralds*, pp. 511–13.
60 *Nation*, 2 December 1961, p. 5.
61 NLA: MS 4738, Calwell Papers; Folder 356; memo from Arthur Warner, 7 November 1962. See also Souter, *Company of Heralds*, p. 512; *Bulletin*, 3 February 1987, p. 19.
62 *SMH*, 26 October 1994, p. 45.
63 *NN*, 8 July 1960, p. 1; *Daily Mirror*, 20 July 1960, p. 42; *Telegraph*, 5 August 1960, p. 2; ABCB Annual Report, 30 June 1961, pp. 12, 28.
64 NLA: MS 5546, Bednall Papers; Box 5; Folder 38; Autobiography, pp. 241, 271–2. See also *Nation*, 16 July 1960, pp. 9–10; Hall, *Supertoy*, p. 35; W. F. Mandle, 'Colin Bednall, 1913–1976', *Australian Journal of Communication*, vol. 24, no. 3, 1997, p. 132.
65 ABCB Annual Report, 30 June 1961, pp. 31–2; *Nation*, 16 July 1960, p. 9.
66 NLA: MS 5546, Bednall Papers; Box 1; Folder 4; Bednall to staff, 12 July 1960.
67 NLA: MS 4936, Menzies Papers; Series 2; Folder 495; FP to Bednall, 4 August 1960. Also interview with Sir George Stening, 30 January 1996.
68 *Telegraph*, 17 September 1962, p. 10; Medical Journal of Australia, 17 January 1959, pp. 83, 88–9; John Atherton Young, Ann Jervie Sefton and Nina Webb (eds), *Centenary Book of the University of Sydney Faculty of Medicine*, Sydney University Press, Sydney, 1984, p. 514; *SMH*, 19 December 1959, p. 20, 24 June 1960, p. 7. See also USA: G313 26800 Box 326; FP to M. A. Telfer, 9 July 1958.
69 NLA: TRC 2144, interview with Bruce Gyngell, 1 December 1983, p. 52. Interview with Sir George Stening, 30 January 1996.
70 NLA: TRC 2144, interview with Bruce Gyngell, 1 December 1983, pp. 52–3. See also McNicoll, *Luck's a Fortune*, pp. 180, 273.

Endnotes

71 McNicoll, *Luck's a Fortune*, p. 298; *Telegraph*, 18 August 1960, p. 3; *NN*, 19 August 1960, p. 1; *Women's Weekly*, 24 August 1977, p. 9.

12 Setting Sail

1 NLA: TRC 391/3-7, interview with William H. Northam, 4 May 1975, pp. 81-3. See also David MacDonald, 'Frank Packer sets sail for the race of his life', *Reader's Digest*, August 1970, p. 50.
2 Max Tennison, 'History of the America's Cup', *Prime Time*, October 1986, pp. 12-13; Jon Simonds, 'The business of winning the cup', *Australian Business*, 24 March 1983, p. 45.
3 ibid; W. Baverstock, *The America's Cup: Challenge from Down Under*, K. G. Murray, Sydney, 1967, pp. 21-2; Ian Dear, *The America's Cup: An Informal History*, Stanley Paul, London, 1980, pp. 41-2.
4 Baverstock, *The America's Cup*, pp. 39-42, 44; Peter Campbell, '21 years of challenge: The America's Cup race', *This Australia*, vol. 2, no. 4, Spring 1983, p. 23.
5 *Bulletin*, 11 October 1983, p. 99; *Sydney Sails*, p. 229; Frank Packer, 'Foreword' to Baverstock, *The America's Cup*. NLA: TRC 391/3-7, interview with William H. Northam, 4 May 1975, pp. 83-4.
6 *Sydney Sails*, pp. 239, 244.
7 NLA: MS 4936, Menzies Papers; Series 2; Folder 404; FP to Menzies, 10 August 1959.
8 NLA: MS 4936, Menzies Papers; Series 2; Folder 404; FP to Menzies, 10 August 1959; McEwen to Menzies, 3 September 1959; Henty to Menzies, 7 September 1959; Menzies to FP, 17 September 1959.
9 *Sydney Sails*, p. 229.
10 *Bulletin*, 15 September 1962, p. 13.
11 *Sydney Sails*, p. 230. NLA: MS 4936, Menzies Papers; Series 2; Folder 404; minister for the air to Menzies, 24 December 1959.
12 *Sydney Sails*, p. 231. RSYSA: 25/3/14; FP to RSYS secretary, 2 March 1960; W. Mahlon Dickerson to Lloyd T. Burgess, 7 April 1960. NYYCA: Dickerson to Burgess, 28 April 1960.
13 RSYSA: 25/3/14; Slim to Dickson, 3 May 1960.
14 *Bulletin*, 15 September 1962, pp. 14-15. See also p. 110.
15 RSYSA: 25/3/14; Prince Philip to Australian Yachting Federation, 19 April 1960; Dickson to Slim, n.d. (27 April 1960?); W. Mahlon Dickerson to Lloyd T. Burgess, 28 April 1960.
16 Baverstock, *The America's Cup*, p. 54; *Times* (London), 29 April 1960, p. 12, 30 April 1960, p. 7, 3 May 1960, p. 13.
17 RSYSA: 25/3/14; Slim to Dickson, 3 May 1960.
18 Baverstock, *The America's Cup*, pp. 56-7. See also RSYSA: 25/3/14; minutes of meeting and press release, 31 May 1960.
19 RSYSA: 25/3/14; Dickson to Charles Ball, 31 May 1960.
20 Baverstock, *The America's Cup*, p. 61. NLA: MS 4936, Menzies Papers; Series 2; Folder 513; FP to Menzies, 21 June 1961, p. 2.
21 *Sydney Sails*, pp. 232-3, 240-1, 244. RSYSA: 25/3/14; FP to RSYS secretary, 24 June 1960. NLA: MS 4936, Menzies Papers; Series 2; Folder 513; FP to Menzies, 21 June 1961, p. 1.

Endnotes

22   RSYSA: 25/3/14; Lloyd T. Burgess to FP, 14 July 1960; Burgess to W. A. W. Stewart, 26 September and 6 October 1960; FP to RSYS secretary, 29 September 1960; Burgess to W. Mahlon Dickerson, 6 October 1960.
23   Cumbria Record Office: Burgess Papers; DB20/309; Managing Director's Tour, 25 September–8 November 1960, p. 5. NLA: TRC 2144, interview with Bruce Gyngell, 1 December 1983, pp. 53–4.
24   Coleman, *Memoirs of a Slow Learner*, p. 139, and 'The Bulletin, the editor and the Cherry Orchard: A tale of the 1960s', *Voices*, vol. 7, no. 1, Autumn 1997, p. 88; Patricia Rolfe, *The Journalistic Javelin: An Illustrated History of the Bulletin*, Wildcat Press, Sydney, 1979, p. 301.
25   Rolfe, *The Journalistic Javelin*, p. 301; *SMH*, 11 October 1960, p. 18; *NN*, 14 October 1960, p. 1.
26   NLA: TRC 336, interview with Douglas Stewart, 21 March 1975, tape 1, track 1, p. 19. See also Coleman, 'The Bulletin, the editor and the Cherry Orchard', p. 88; Griffen-Foley, *The House of Packer*, pp. 234–6.
27   Griffen-Foley, *The House of Packer*, pp. 146, 153–4.
28   Craig Munro, 'The A&R war: Profits, personalities, and paperbacks', *Publishing Studies*, no. 1, Spring 1995, pp. 22–5; *Nation*, 23 April 1960, p. 21, 3 December 1961, p. 21; *Bulletin*, 14 December 1960, p. 6. Also NLA: TRC 221, interview with A. G. Smith, 11 September 1973, tape 1, track 2, pp. 11–18.
29   Munro, 'The A&R war', pp. 21, 26; Coleman, *Memoirs of a Slow Learner*, p. 142.
30   Munro, 'The A&R war', pp. 25–6; *SMH*, 13 October 1960, p. 12; *NN*, 28 October 1960, p. 1. See also ML: ML MSS 3269, A&R Papers; Box 4; Minute Book 1954–62, pp. 184–8, 18 October 1960.
31   *CPD*, vol. 29, House of Representatives, 19 October 1960, pp. 2187–98. See also *Nation*, 3 December 1960, p. 21; Griffen-Foley, *The House of Packer*, pp. 98, 146–7, 267.
32   Munro, 'The A&R war', pp. 26–7; *Telegraph*, 5 November 1960, p. 31; *Nation*, 2 December 1961, p. 5. ML: ML MSS 3269, A&R Papers; Box 4; Minute Book 1954–62, pp. 189–90, 28 October 1960. ML MSS 2184, Stephensen Papers; Box 54; File: Papers, 1960; Stephensen to Laurence Pollinger Ltd, 3 November 1960. Also NLA: TRC 221, interview with A. G. Smith, 11 September 1973, tape 1, track 2, pp. 18–19.
33   Munro, 'The A&R war', p. 27; *Bulletin*, 21 December 1960, p. 7; *Nation*, 16 December 1961, p. 10. NLA: MS 1578, Roderick Papers; Folder 79; item 3471, Swain circular to shareholders, 8 December 1960. Also TRC 221, interview with A. G. Smith, 11 September 1973, tape 1, track 2, pp. 18–19.
34   RSYSA: 25/3/14; Henry S. Morgan to Lloyd T. Burgess, 5 January 1961; FP to Burgess, 10 January 1961.
35   RSYSA: 25/3/14; Charles Ball to Lloyd T. Burgess, 17 February 1961; illegible signature to Burgess, 21 February 1961. NLA: MS 4936, Menzies Papers; Series 2; Folder 513; FP to Menzies, 21 June 1961, p. 1. See also *Life International*, 30 July 1962, p. 45.
36   *Telegraph*, 26 May 1961, p. 34; *Women's Weekly*, 7 June 1961, p. 17.
37   NLA: MS 4936, Menzies Papers; Series 2; Folder 513; FP to Menzies, 21 June 1961.
38   NLA: MS 4936, Menzies Papers; Series 2; Folder 513; A. L. Moore to John Gorton, 2 August 1961; Gorton to Menzies, 15 August 1961; Menzies to FP, 16 August 1961; FP to Menzies, 18 August 1961.
39   Horne, *Into the Open*, pp. 36–8, 55; Griffen-Foley, *The House of Packer*, p. 237.

Endnotes

40   ML: ML MSS 3525, Horne Papers; MLK 2147, ACP-FP2, Horne to FP, 20 February 1961; FP to Horne, 6 March and 14 June 1961; MLK 2152, ACP-B2, FP to Horne, 6 July 1961, Horne to Keith Martin, 14 August 1961.

41   ML: ML MSS 3525, Horne Papers; MLK 2147, FP-3, Horne to FP, 20 and 28 July 1961; MLK 2152, ACP-B2, A. V. Toose to W. Travers, 25 July 1961. For Kerry Packer and Henty, see *NN*, 1 September 1961, p. 3, 14 September 1962, p. 11; *Bulletin*, 3 February 1987, p. 19.

42   *Nation*, 14 January 1961, p. 7. See also NLA: MS 4936, Menzies Papers; Series 1; Folder 201; FP to Menzies, 11 July 1961; Menzies to FP, 14 July 1961.

43   NLA: MS 4936, Menzies Papers; Series 2; Folder 513; FP to Menzies, 29 September 1961; Menzies to FP, 4 October 1961.

44   NLA: MS 4936, Menzies Papers; Series 1; Folder 201; FP to Menzies, 7 January 1960. See also Souter, *Company of Heralds*, pp. 379–84; Hancock, *National and Permanent?*, pp. 198, 200.

45   NLA: TRC 2172, interview with Alan Reid, October 1986, pp. 73–4. See also *Telegraph*, 30 November 1961, p. 1; Griffen-Foley, *The House of Packer*, p. 245; Hancock, *National and Permanent?*, pp. 199–202; Whitington, *Sir Frank*, p. 270.

46   ML: MSS 3269, A&R Papers; Box 4; Minute Book 1954–62, pp. 224–5, 3 May 1961; p. 245, 1 August 1961.

47   NLA: MS 1578, Roderick Papers; Folder 77; item 3431, 'A&R Events'; item 3434, 'Diary'; item 3436, Cowper circular to shareholders, 22 November 1961. ML: ML MSS 3269, A&R Papers; Box 4; Minute Book 1954–62, p. 263, 13 November 1961. See also *Nation*, 18 November 1961, p. 5.

48   *Sunday Telegraph*, 19 November 1961, p. 47; *Daily Telegraph*, 20 November 1961, p. 5; *Things I Hear*, 29 November 1961, pp. 3–4. See also ML: ML MSS 3269, A&R Papers; Box 4; Minute Book 1954–62, p. 271, 21 November 1961.

49   For the journalist Ross Campbell's observations on this point, see Whitington, *Sir Frank*, p. 52.

50   NLA: MS 1578, Roderick Papers; Folder 77; item 3431, 'A&R Events', item 3448, FP to Cowper, 29 November 1961; item 3451, Cowper circular to shareholders, 1 December 1961. See also *Telegraph*, 5 December 1961, p. 10.

51   Munro, 'The A&R war', pp. 25–6. See also NLA: MS 1578, Roderick Papers; Folder 80; item 3476, A&R Interim Report to shareholders, 28 April 1962; item 3479, Cowper to Collins, 25 July 1962.

52   See NLA: MS 1578, Roderick Papers; Folders 77–8, 80.

53   Munro, 'The A&R war', p. 28; Ken Wilder, *The Company You Keep*, State Library of New South Wales Press, Sydney, 1994, p. 68. See also NLA: MS 1578, Roderick Papers; Folder 80; item 3479, Cowper to Collins, 25 July 1962.

54   *Motor Boating*, August 1962, p. 110; Baverstock, *The America's Cup*, pp. 66, 68; *Sydney Sails*, pp. 248–9.

55   *Sydney Sails*, p. 248.

56   RSYSA: 25/3/14; R. A. Dickson to W. E. Crowder, 7 February 1962; Dickson to L. K. Martin, 12 February 1962; Naming Ceremony, 28 February 1962. See also MacDonald, 'Frank Packer sets sail', p. 50.

57   Packer, 'Foreword' to Baverstock, *The America's Cup;* interview with Sheila Wood, 9 January 1998.

Endnotes

58 RSYSA: 25/3/14; R. A. Dickson to W. E. Crowder, 7 February 1962; Naming Ceremony, 28 February 1962. See also *Sydney Sails*, p. 250; MacDonald, 'Frank Packer sets sail', p. 50.

59 *Telegraph*, 22 March 1961, pp. 9, 11; *Things I Hear*, 16 March 1961, p. 4.

60 RSYSA: 25/3/14; Morgan to Lloyd T. Burgess, 11 April 1962; Morgan to FP, 18 May 1962; Morgan to Burgess, 21 May 1962. NYYCA: FP to Morgan, 16 May 1962. See also Dear, *The America's Cup*, p. 134.

61 *New York Herald Tribune*, 18 May 1962, p. 23; *New York Times*, 17 May 1962, p. 46.

62 NAA/ACT: A1838/386; 1525/3/266 Part 1; Department of External Affairs savingram no. 413, 12 April 1962; savingram no. 445, 19 April 1962; J. B. Davies to G. Hartley, 17 July 1962. See also Baverstock, *The America's Cup*, p. 68.

63 RSYSA: 25/3/14; L. K. Martin to RSYS, 14 May 1962; Goodwill Presentation, 19 June 1962. See also *Christian Science Monitor*, 12 July 1962, p. 9.

64 *Providence Sunday Journal*, 22 July 1962, pp. 1, 14; *Sunday Telegraph*, 15 July 1962, p. 2, 29 July 1962, p. 31; *Daily Telegraph*, 14 September 1962, p. 46.

65 *Providence Sunday Journal*, 25 July 1962, pp. 12; *Daily Telegraph*, 27 July 1962, p. 5, 12 September 1962, p. 5; *Sunday Telegraph*, 29 July 1962, p. 31.

66 *Newport Daily News*, 14 September 1962; *New York Times*, 15 September 1962, p. 17; *Women's Weekly*, 26 September 1962, p. 15; Whitington, *Sir Frank*, p. 246; MacDonald, 'Frank Packer sets sail', p. 50; interview with Lady Packer, 25 January 1996.

67 Whitington, *Sir Frank*, p. 246; MacDonald, 'Frank Packer sets sail', p. 50; Dear, *The America's Cup*, p. 137; *Sydney Sails*, p. 70; *Sunday Telegraph*, 2 September 1962, p. 21. NLA: TRC 3236, interview with Jock Sturrock, April 1995, p. 57.

68 *Telegraph*, 27 July 1962, p. 5; *Thirty Years of Service: The American Australian Association, 1948–1978*, no publisher, New York, 1978, p. 52.

69 NAA/ACT: A1838/386; 1525/3/266 Part 1; Department of External Affairs memos, 9 April 1962, 12 April 1962, 16 July 1962.

70 NAA/ACT: A1838/386; 1525/3/266 Part 1; Department of External Affairs savingram no. 570, 22 May 1962; G. Hartley to Mr Forsyth, 22 June 1962. See also *CPD*, House of Representatives, vol. 36, 23 August 1962, pp. 745–6; vol. 37, 23 October 1962, pp. 1851–2.

71 *Telegraph*, 11 September 1962, p. 5, 15 September 1962, p. 1.

72 Dear, *The America's Cup*, p. 137; *Motor Boating*, August 1962, p. 110; *Newport Daily News*, 14 September 1962. NLA: TRC 326, interview with Jock Sturrock, April 1995 pp. 57, 62.

73 Dear, *The America's Cup*, pp. 138–40; *Sydney Sails*, pp. 253–5.

74 Whitington, *Sir Frank*, pp. 247–8; *Herald* (Melbourne), 18 September 1962, p. 28; *Telegraph*, 19 September 1962, pp. 1, 3.

75 *Sydney Sails*, pp. 254–6, 258; Dear, *The America's Cup*, p. 140; *Telegraph*, 27 September 1962, p. 5.

76 *Sydney Sails*, p. 255; *Telegraph*, 14 September 1962, p. 29, 20 September 1962, pp. 1, 5. See also NAA/ACT: A4940/1; C3691; Prime Minister's Department note for file, 20 September 1962.

77 NLA: TRC 3236, interview with Jock Sturrock, April 1995, p. 63. MacDonald, 'Frank Packer sets sail', p. 51; *Sydney Sails*, pp. 257–8; Dear, *The America's Cup*, p. 140.

78 Dear, *The America's Cup*, p. 140; Baverstock, *The America's Cup*, p. 89; *Telegraph*, 24 September 1962, p. 5.
79 *Telegraph*, 26 September 1962, p. 5, 27 September 1962, p. 5.
80 RSYSA: 25/3/14; cables, 26 September 1962; Pratt to FP, 9 November 1962; FP to Pratt, 10 November 1962. See also *Telegraph*, 27 September 1962, p. 1.
81 Packer, 'Foreword' to Baverstock, *The America's Cup* and p. 90; Dear, *The America's Cup*, p. 137.

13 Toasting Victory

1 *Herald* (Melbourne), 22 September 1965, p. 5. Cumbria Record Office: Burgess Papers; DB20/312; dinner menu, 13 February 1963.
2 Marr, *Patrick White: A Life*, p. 3.
3 Royal Agricultural Society of New South Wales Official Catalogues, 1938–1974.
4 Royal Agricultural Society of New South Wales Archives: RAS Minute Book, no. 157, pp. 234–5, 29 October 1963; p. 274, 25 November 1963; p. 258, 25 February 1964. See also no. 158, pp. 5, 12, 25, 28 April 1964; p. 54, 26 May 1964; pp. 87–91, 30 June 1964.
5 AJC Annual Reports, 1961, 1963, 1966. See also *Things I Hear*, 11 December 1951, p. 4; 8 January 1952, pp. 2–3; 19 January 1961, p. 4; McNicoll, *Luck's a Fortune*, p. 302.
6 *Telegraph*, 2 May 1974, p. 4.
7 AJC Annual Report, 1966; Royal Blind Society of New South Wales Annual Reports, 1961, p. 4, 1965, p. 3; *Workers' News*, 9 May 1974, p. 3.
8 *Radio Television News*, 5 April 1963, pp. 1–2.
9 *CPD*, vol. 38, House of Representatives, 18 April 1963, pp. 697–743; *Telegraph*, 19 April 1963, p. 6.
10 *Nation*, 29 June 1963, pp. 5–6; Shawcross, *Murdoch*, pp. 112–13; Griffen-Foley, *The House of Packer*, pp. 276–7.
11 NLA: MS 5546, Bednall Papers; Box 5; Folder 38; Autobiography, pp. 301–3. *NN*, 1 November 1963, p. 2. For Kerry Packer's marriage, see Barry, *The Rise and Rise of Kerry Packer*, p. 144.
12 Hall, *Supertoy*, p. 42; *Telegraph*, 4 April 1964, p. 5.
13 *CPD*, House of Representatives, vol. 41, 7 April 1964, p. 748; Senate, vol. 25, 7 April 1964, pp. 430–1.
14 Hall, *Supertoy*, pp. 41, 43; Souter, *Company of Heralds*, pp. 359–63.
15 NLA: TRC 2172, interview with Alan Reid, 1986. See also Rodney Tiffen, 'The Packer-Labor alliance, 1978–95: RIP', *MIA*, no. 77, August 1995, p. 21; Hancock, *National and Permanent?*, pp. 217–18; Bolton, *The Oxford History of Australia*, vol. 5, p. 148.
16 Souter, *Company of Heralds*, pp. 394–7. NLA: MS 4936, Menzies Papers; Series 1; Folder 201; Menzies to FP, 23 December 1963; FP to Menzies, 28 December 1963.
17 *NSWPD*, vol. 48, Assembly, 23 October 1963, p. 5917.
18 NLA: MS 4936, Menzies Papers; Series 1; Folder 201; FP's notes, 4 May 1964.
19 NLA: MS 4936, Menzies Papers; Series 2; Folder 704; Clyde Packer to Menzies, 31 March and 12 May 1964; Menzies to FP, 25 May 1964. See also Series 1; Folder 201; FP to Menzies, 26 May 1964.

Endnotes

20 McNicoll, *Luck's a Fortune*, p. 286; Ita Buttrose, *Early Edition: My First Forty Years*, Macmillan, South Melbourne, 1985, p. 103.
21 Sheila Scotter, *Snaps, Secrets and Stories from My Life*, Random House Australia, Milsons Point, 1998, pp. 45, 231; *SMH*, 14 March 1998, p. 4s.
22 NLA: MS 5546, Bednall Papers; Box 5; Folder 38; Autobiography, pp. 262–3.
23 *Women's Weekly*, 24 August 1977, p. 9.
24 McNicoll, *Luck's a Fortune*, p. 286. See also Royal Agricultural Society of New South Wales Archives: RAS Minute Book, no. 158, p. 44, 26 May 1964.
25 Marriage certificate, 1964 (courtesy of *ADB*). Also interview with Lady Packer, 25 January 1996.
26 Lawson, *Connie Sweetheart*, p. 279; *Vogue* (New York), 1 May 1935, pp. 55–7, 126; *Times* (London), 28 October 1937, p. 19.
27 Interview with Lady Packer, 25 January 1996; H. R. Kedward, *Occupied France: Collaboration and Resistance 1940–1944*, Basil Blackwell, Oxford, 1985, pp. 47–8, 57–8, 67.
28 Interview with Lady Packer, 25 January 1996; *Home*, 1 March 1941, p. 5; *SMH*, 16 June 1964, p. 19.
29 Lawson, *Connie Sweetheart*, p. 262; Royal Blind Society of New South Wales Annual Reports, 1956–57. See also, for example, *Telegraph*, 8 October 1947, p. 14, 3 October 1956, p. 19; *SMH*, 13 March 1947, p. 14, 18 September 1947, p. 15, 8 October 1947, p. 9, 1 January 1950, p. 8, 20 January 1950, p. 5.
30 *Sunday Telegraph*, 9 November 1958, p. 1. See also p. 168.
31 *SMH*, 16 June 1964, p. 19; interview with Lady Packer, 25 January 1996.
32 Marriage certificate, 1964 (courtesy of *ADB*); Kennedy, *It Was Bloody Marvellous!*, p. 159.
33 Cumbria Record Office: Burgess Papers; DB20/312; Burgess to Dumas, 19 June 1964. See also NLA: MS 4936, Menzies Papers; Series 2; Folder 704; Menzies to FP, 16 June 1964; FP to Menzies, 3 July 1964.
34 *NN*, 21 August 1964, p. 12; *Printing Trades Journal*, September 1964, p. 152; McNicoll, *Luck's a Fortune*, p. 297.
35 *NN*, 21 August 1964, p. 1; 1; McNicoll, *Luck's a Fortune*, pp. 273–4; interview with Lady Stening, 30 January 1996.
36 Interviews with Lady Packer, 25 January 1996; Sir George Stening, 30 January 1996. NLA: MS 5546, Bednall Papers; Box 1; Folder 6; FP to Bednall, 30 December 1964.
37 Cumbria Record Office: Burgess Papers; DB20/313; Burgess to FP, 22 January 1965; Burgess to Birbeck, 22 January 1965. See also Richard Hough, *The Ace of Clubs: A History of the Garrick*, Andre Deutsch, London, 1986, p. 13.
38 David Marr (ed.), *Patrick White Letters*, Random House Australia, Milsons Point, 1994, pp. 209, 241, 286–7. See also Griffen-Foley, *The House of Packer, passim*.
39 B. H. Fletcher, 'Malcolm Henry Ellis', *ADB*, vol. 14, p. 96; Coleman, *Memoirs of a Slow Learner*, p. 144; Rolfe, *The Journalistic Javelin*, p. 299.
40 Coleman, *Memoirs of a Slow Learner*, pp. 144–5; Rolfe, *The Journalistic Javelin*, p. 299; *Bulletin*, 2 September 1953, p. 14.

Endnotes

41 NLA: MS 5546, Bednall Papers; Box 1; Folder 6; FP to Bednall, 30 December 1964. See also W. F. Mandle, 'Colin Bednall: 1913–1976', *Australian Journal of Communication*, vol. 24, no. 3, 1997, pp. 137–8.
42 NLA: MS 5546, Bednall Papers; Box 5; Folder 28; Autobiography, pp. 312, 328. See also McNicoll, *Luck's a Fortune*, pp. 294–5.
43 NLA: MS 5546, Bednall Papers; Box 1; Folder 6; Bednall to Clyde Packer, 8 June 1965; Keith L. [Martin] to Bednall, 26 July 1965. See also Mandle, 'Colin Bednall: 1913–1976', p. 130.
44 NLA: MS 5546, Bednall Papers; Box 5; Folder 28; Autobiography, pp. 311–12.
45 *NN*, 3 February 1967, p. 1; Rolfe, *The Journalistic Javelin*, p. 305.
46 ML: ML MSS 6630, SADAF Records, FP to E. St John, 8 August 1963; St John to FP, 19 August 1963. See also ML MSS 5770, Barcs Papers; Box 8; Andrew Wise to Emery Barcs, 22 April 1966.
47 *Telegraph*, 27 July 1967, p. 1, *Workers' News*, 28 April 1977, p. 6; McNicoll, *Luck's a Fortune*, pp. 134–5; *NSWPD*, vol. 67, Assembly, 15–16 August 1967, pp. 410–12, 486–8.
48 *Telegraph*, 28 July 1967, p. 1; FP in Robert Moore (comp.), *Profiles of Power*, Australian Broadcasting Commission, Sydney, 1970, pp. 101–2; McNicoll, *Luck's a Fortune*, pp. 134–5; *Nation*, 27 April 1968, p. 15.
49 Clyde Packer in Minogue, 'Packer's $15 million deal', pp. 5, 8.
50 Tom Uren, *Straight Left*, Random House Australia, Milsons Point, 1994, pp. 138–41; *SMH*, 12 March 1964, p. 5, 1 May 1969, p. 7; Whitington, *Sir Frank*, p. 282.
51 Uren, *Straight Left*, pp. 142–3. NLA: MS 6055 Uren Papers; Series 20; Folder 9; letter from Uren, 22 August [1968?].
52 Uren, *Straight left*, pp. 143–4.
53 Barry, *The Rise and Rise of Kerry Packer*, pp. 51–2, 498; John Singleton, *True Confessions*, Cassell Australia, Stanmore, 1979, p. 97; Horne, *Into the Open*, pp. 96–9.
54 *NSWPD*, vol. 67, Assembly, 15–16 August 1967, pp. 410–12, 486–8.
55 NLA: MS 4936, Menzies Papers; Series 2; Folder 704; FP to Menzies, 3 July 1964. Hancock, *National and Permanent?*, pp. 146, 231.
56 Griffen-Foley, *The House of Packer*, p. 266; Henderson, *Menzies' Child*, p. 199.
57 Clyde Packer in Minogue, 'Packer's $15 million deal', p. 8; McNicoll, *Luck's a Fortune*, p. 233.
58 McNicoll, *Luck's a Fortune*, pp. 233–5; *Sunday Australian*, 15 August 1971, pp. 10–11. Also NLA: TRC 121/44, interview with Mungo McCallum, 6 April 1973, tape 1, side 1, pp. 39–40.
59 Souter, *Company of Heralds*, p. 421.
60 ibid. pp. 412, 419; Judy Cassab, *Diaries*, Alfred A. Knopf, Sydney, 1995, p. 177.
61 Souter, *Company of Heralds*, pp. 421–2.
62 ibid. p. 424; Barry, *The Rise and Rise of Kerry Packer*, p. 126; Griffen-Foley, *The House of Packer*, p. 280; *Nation*, 18 November 1967, pp. 5–6.
63 *SMH*, 15 June 1967, pp. 4, 14; *NN*, 23 June 1967, p. 19, 4 August 1967, p. 19, 24 November 1967, p. 23; *National Times*, 23–28 May 1977, p. 56; Griffen-Foley, *The House of Packer*, pp. 280–1.
64 *Daily Mirror*, 1 May 1974, pp. 24–5.

65 NBAC: N59/165; letter to H. G. Coleman, 12 May 1965; AJA NSW Bulletin, no. 172, 24 November 1966; Coleman to FP, 1 December 1966.
66 NBAC: N59/165; AJA NSW Bulletins, no. 173, 1 December 1966, no. 178, 17 February 1967; FP to Coleman, 5 December 1966.
67 Barry, *The Rise and Rise of Kerry Packer*, p. 71. See also NBAC: N59/165; AJA NSW Bulletin, no. 178, 17 February 1967; Commonwealth Conciliation and Arbitration Commission transcript, no. 2129 of 1966.
68 *Printing Trades Journal*, March 1966, p. 46, May 1966, p. 86.
69 ibid. March 1966, p. 46, July 1967, pp. 118–19.
70 ibid. March 1966, p. 46.
71 ibid. pp. 46–7, May 1966, p. 87.
72 ibid. May 1966, pp. 86–7, July 1967, pp. 118–19.
73 Lloyd, *Profession: Journalist*, pp. 258–64; Souter, *Company of Heralds*, p. 443; *Journalist*, July 1967, pp. 1–3; *Nation*, 6 August 1966, p. 6.
74 Lloyd, *Profession: Journalist*, pp. 264–6.
75 *Printing Trades Journal*, August 1967, pp. 126, 134–5; Lloyd, *Profession: Journalist*, p. 265.
76 *Journalist*, August 1967, p. 1; *Weekend Business Review*, 19 September 1970, p. 13.
77 *Telegraph*, 11 August 1967, pp. 1, 3; *Printing Trades Journal*, September 1967, p. 148; *Journalist*, August 1967, p. 6.
78 *Telegraph*, 11 August 1967, pp. 1, 3; *Printing Trades Journal*, September 1967, p. 149; Lloyd, *Profession: Journalist*, p. 266.
79 *Printing Trades Journal*, October 1967, p. 166; *Telegraph*, 18 August 1967, p. 12.
80 *Printing Trades Journal*, October 1967, pp. 166–7; *Journalist*, August 1967, p. 5; *Telegraph*, 17 August 1967, p. 3, 18 August 1967, p. 12.
81 *Nation*, 9 September 1967, pp. 6–7; *Journalist*, September 1967, pp. 1–4.
82 Lloyd, *Profession: Journalist*, pp. 267, 269; Souter, *Company of Heralds*, p. 445; *Journalist*, September 1967, p. 4.

14 The Sound of One Man Clapping

1 Campbell, '21 years of challenge', p. 23. See also NYYCA: Resolution adopted by the Board of Trustees, 7 December 1962.
2 NYYCA: H. S. Morgan to America's Cup Committee, 2 July 1964; Morgan to L. M. Hinchliffe, 28 September 1964. See also Dear, *The America's Cup*, p. 143.
3 Dear, *The America's Cup*, p. 143; Baverstock, *The America's Cup*, pp. 110, 113. NLA: TRC 3236, interview with Jock Sturrock, April 1995, p. 70.
4 Baverstock, *The America's Cup*, pp. 110, 113.
5 ibid. pp. 108, 113–14.
6 ibid. pp. 129–30, 134.
7 ibid. pp. 134, 136, 138.

Endnotes

8   Alan Marks, *Quest for the Cup: The America's Cup Challenges, 1851–1987*, Australian Broadcasting Corporation, Sydney, 1987, pp. 206–7; Campbell, '21 years of challenge', pp. 23, 24.
9   NYYCA: H. S. Morgan to Ian Potter, 10 October 1967; FP to Morgan, 11 October 1967; memo from W. Mahlon Dickerson, 7 October 1968, p. 1.
10 Marks, *The America's Cup Challenges*, pp. 216–17.
11 *New York Times*, 3 October 1968, p. 66.
12 NYYCA: *SMH* clipping, n.d. (mid August 1968); 'Cup ruling defied', newspaper clipping, n.d. (September 1968).
13 NYYCA: memo from W. Mahlon Dickerson, 7 October 1968, pp. 1–2. See also Marks, *The America's Cup Challenges*, p. 219; Hall, *Supertoy*, p. 45.
14 NYYCA: Fred Moylan to Julian K. Roosevelt, n.d. (early September 1968).
15 NYYCA: memo from W. Mahlon Dickerson, 7 October 1968, p. 1; Jock Sturrock to Julian K. Roosevelt, 25 September 1968. See also *New York Times*, 3 October 1968, p. 66.
16 NYYCA: memo from W. Mahlon Dickerson, 7 October 1968, p. 3; Dickerson to Percy Chubb, 13 November 1968.
17 Marr, *Patrick White Letters*, p. 322; W. J. Hudson, *Casey*, Oxford University Press, Melbourne, 1986, p. 315.
18 Henderson, *Menzies' Child*, pp. 201–3; Bolton, *The Oxford History of Australia*, vol. 5, pp. 176–7, 181.
19 McNicoll, *Luck's a Fortune*, p. 273.
20 Peter Howson, *The Howson Diaries. The Life of Politics*, Penguin Books, Melbourne, 1984, pp. 502, 505, 509. See also NLA: MS 3863, Samuel Papers; Folder 31; typescript headed 'Media', 18 August 1969.
21 Bolton, *The Oxford History of Australia*, vol. 5, p. 183; *Telegraph*, 22 September 1969, pp. 1, 3. See also NLA: MS 3863, Samuel Papers; Folder 31; typescript headed 'Money Market', 6 October 1969.
22 Howson, *The Howson Diaries*, p. 546; Sarah Newton, *Maxwell Newton: A Biography*, Fremantle Arts Centre Press, South Fremantle, 1993, p. 155.
23 NLA: MS 3863, Samuel Papers; Folder 31, Samuel to Robert J. Lovell, 9 October 1969; Folder 41, confidential despatch, 20 September 1970. See also Mr Y (pseud.), 'A Packer plot?', *Australian Quarterly*, vol. 43, no. 2, June 1971, p. 5.
24 Howson, *The Howson Diaries*, pp. 564–8.
25 ibid. p. 572; *Sunday Telegraph*, 2 November 1969, p. 2.
26 Howson, *The Howson Diaries*, pp. 572–3; McNicoll, *Luck's a Fortune*, p. 273.
27 *Telegraph*, 8 November 1969, p. 3, 12 November 1969, p. 1; Howson, *The Howson Diaries*, pp. 573–4, 588.
28 *SMH*, 1 July 1969, p. 17; 2 July 1969, p. 18; 10 July 1969, pp. 1, 10.
29 RSYSA: 25/3/1; R. A. Dickson to Beppe Croce, 30 April 1969.
30 See RSYSA: 25/3/3; correspondence and minutes, 29 September 1969–15 April 1970. See also 25/3/5.
31 NYYCA: memo to H. S. Morgan, 7 October 1969. RSYSA: 25/3/1; I. H. S. Irwin to FP, 2 October 1969.
32 RSYSA: 25/3/1; I. H. S. Irwin to FP, 2 October 1969.

Endnotes

33 RSYSA: 25/3/3; minutes, 19 November 1969, 3 December 1969, 8 January 1969. See also *B&T Advertising, Marketing and Media Weekly*, 5 February 1970, p. 18.
34 NLA: TRC 2554, interview with Sir James Hardy, 18 January 1990, pp. 28–9. Marks, *The America's Cup Challenges*, pp. 220–1; *Telegraph*, 15 September 1970, pp. 25, 30.
35 Marks, *The America's Cup Challenges*, pp. 219–20; Dear, *The America's Cup*, p. 153; *Telegraph*, 15 September 1970, p. 24; interview with Lady Packer, 25 January 1996.
36 Dear, *The America's Cup*, p. 153.
37 *Telegraph*, 15 September 1970, p. 33; Marks, *The America's Cup Challenges*, p. 223. See also RSYSA: 25/3/3; minutes, 2 July 1970.
38 FP in Moore, *Profiles of Power*, p. 92; *Telegraph*, 12 September 1970, p. 9. See also NYYCA: 'Newport on a grand scale', newspaper clipping, n.d. (September 1970).
39 Dear, *The America's Cup*, p. 153; *Telegraph*, 15 September 1970, p. 31.
40 *Telegraph*, 15 September 1970, p. 33; Campbell, '21 years of challenge', p. 24; Dear, *The America's Cup*, pp. 152–3.
41 NYYCA: FP to International Race and Protest Committee, 18 August 1970; Beppe Croce to FP, 19 August 1970; FP to International Racing Union, n.d. (23 August 1970). See also *Telegraph*, 22 August 1970, p. 7.
42 *Telegraph*, 22 August 1970, p. 7.
43 Marks, *The America's Cup Challenges*, pp. 224–5; Dear, *The America's Cup*, p. 153.
44 ibid; John Rousmaniere, *The America's Cup 1851–1983*, Pelham Books, London, 1983, p. 110; *Sunday Telegraph*, 30 August 1970, p. 2; *Daily Telegraph*, 15 September 1970, p. 25.
45 Dear, *The America's Cup*, pp. 153–4; Rousmaniere, *The America's Cup 1851–1983*, p. 110.
46 *Telegraph*, 15 September 1970, p. 3; *CPD*, vol. S45, Senate, 16 September 1970, p. 594. See also NYYCA: invitation issued by *Sir Frank* and Lady Packer for 10 September 1970.
47 NYYCA: letter to Henry S. Morgan, 1 September 1970; Alan Payne to Morgan, 1 September 1970. See also *Telegraph*, 4 September 1970, p. 3.
48 *Telegraph*, 16 September 1970, p. 3, 17 September 1970, p. 3; Marks, *The America's Cup Challenges*, p. 226.
49 Marks, *The America's Cup Challenges*, pp. 226–8; Dear, *The America's Cup*, p. 155; *Telegraph*, 18 September 1970, p. 1.
50 *Telegraph*, 19 September 1970, p. 7; Marks, *The America's Cup Challenges*, pp. 228–30. See also NYYCA: article by Alan Payne, Jim Hardy and Martin Visser entitled 'Collisions Apart', p. 66.
51 Marks, *The America's Cup Challenges*, pp. 230–1; Dear, *The America's Cup*, p. 156.
52 Marks, *The America's Cup Challenges*, p. 232; *Telegraph*, 23 September 1970, p. 1.
53 Dear, *The America's Cup*, p. 156; Rousmaniere, *The America's Cup*, pp. 113–14; Marks, *The America's Cup Challenges*, pp. 233–5. NLA: TRC 2554, interview with Sir James Hardy, 18 January 1990, p. 32.
54 *Telegraph*, 23 September 1970, pp. 1, 7.
55 *CPD*, House of Representatives, vol. 69, 22 September 1970, p. 1414; Senate, vol. 45, 22 September 1970, p. 727.
56 Marks, *The America's Cup Challenges*, pp. 235–7.

57 Dear, *The America's Cup*, p. 157; *Telegraph*, 26 September 1970, p. 3.
58 Marks, *The America's Cup Challenges*, pp. 238–9; *New York Times*, 29 September 1970, p. 53.
59 *New York Times*, 29 September 1970, p. 53; *Telegraph*, 30 September 1970, p. 3.
60 *Telegraph*, 1 October 1970, p. 7; *New York Times*, 29 September 1970, p. 53; *SMH*, 5 October 1970, p. 6.
61 Henderson, *Menzies' Child*, pp. 203–4; Bolton, *The Oxford History of Australia*, vol. 5, pp. 176, 180.
62 NLA: MS 3863, Samuel Papers; Folder 68; Samuel to Horne, 4 March 1971. See also Mr Y, 'A Packer plot?', p. 3; Bolton, *The Oxford History of Australia*, vol. 5, p. 186; Howson, *The Howson Diaries*, pp. 429, 697–8.
63 NLA: MS 3863, Samuel Papers; Folder 68; Samuel to Horne, 4 March 1971. See also Alan Reid, *The Gorton Experiment*, Shakespeare Head Press, Sydney, 1971, pp. 416–17.
64 Reid, *The Gorton Experiment*, pp. 417–24; Mr Y, 'A Packer plot?', pp. 4–5; *Australian*, 4 March 1971, p. 1. See also NLA: MS 3863, Samuel Papers; Folder 68; Samuel to Horne, 4 March 1971.
65 Howson, *The Howson Diaries*, p. 708; Mr Y, 'A Packer plot?', pp. 4–5; *Telegraph*, 2 July 1979, p. 19.
66 Reid, *The Gorton Experiment*, pp. 426–7; Howson, *The Howson Diaries*, pp. 699, 703.
67 Howson, *The Howson Diaries*, p. 710; *NN*, 8 January 1971, p. 8.
68 *CPD*, House of Representatives, vol. 71, 15 March 1971, pp. 840, 842.
69 NLA: MS 7796, Reid Papers; Box 1; File: 'Lib-CP-McMahon PM'; entries for 12 May 1971, 29 July 1971. See also *Telegraph*, 14 May 1971, pp. 1, 3.
70 *Sunday Australian*, 8 August 1971, pp. 1, 10–11.
71 *Review. The Independent Quality National Weekly*, 20 August 1971, p. 1274.
72 NLA: MS 4936, Menzies Papers; Series 2; Folder 825; Clyde Packer to Menzies, 20 December 1968. See also Howson, *The Howson Diaries*, p. 545.
73 *Review. The Independent Quality National Weekly*, 20 August 1971, pp. 1274–5; *Telegraph*, 11 August 1971, p. 3.
74 *CPD*, House of Representatives, vol. 72, 17 August 1971, pp. 19–20; Senate, vol. 49, 18 August 1971, pp. 132–3.
75 Letter from Dick Hughes, 24 November 1999; Whitington, *Sir Frank*, pp. xii, 294.
76 *Review. The Independent Quality National Weekly*, 20 August 1971, pp. 1274–5; Robert Menzies, 'Foreword' to Whitington, *Sir Frank*, p. x.

15 The King is Dead

1 McNicoll, *Luck's a Fortune*, p. 294; *Weekend Business Review*, 19 September 1970, p. 13.
2 ML: ML MSS 5770, Barcs Papers; Box 1; diary entries, 2 March 1972, 11 April 1972, 13 April 1972. See also Horne, *Into the Open*, p. 147.
3 Souter, *Company of Heralds*, p. 424.
4 ibid. p. 362; Buttrose, *Early Edition*, p. 122; McNicoll, *Luck's a Fortune*, pp. 284–5, 296; Horne, *Into the Open*, p. 183. See also p. 223.

Endnotes

5   Buttrose, *Early Edition*, p. 122; Griffen-Foley, *The House of Packer*, pp. 287–92; McNicoll, *Luck's a Fortune*, pp. 277, 302–3.
6   Donald Horne, *Money Made Us*, Penguin, Harmondsworth, 1976, pp. 54–5.
7   Bolton, *The Oxford History of Australia*, vol. 5, pp. 184–7; Griffen-Foley, *The House of Packer*, pp. 289–90; Lloyd, *Profession: Journalist*, p. 271; *Telegraph*, 21 September 1971, p. 3; *SMH*, 21 September 1971, p. 1.
8   *Bulletin*, 13 November 1971, p. 23; Henderson, *Menzies' Child*, p. 208. See also NLA: MS 7796, Reid Papers; Box 1; File: 'Lib-CP-McMahon PM'; 14 November 1971 entry.
9   Minogue, 'Packer's $15 million deal', p. 9. See also ML: ML MSS 3525, Horne Papers; MLK 2152; ACP-B4; McMahon to Horne, 7 January 1972.
10 NLA: MS 7796, Reid Papers; Box 1; File: 'Lib-CP-McMahon PM'; entries 1 February 1972, 15 February 1972, 9 March 1972.
11 McNicoll, *Luck's a Fortune*, p. 273. NLA: MS 7796, Reid Papers; Box 1; File: 'Lib-CP-McMahon PM'; 1 February 1972 entry.
12 ML: ML MSS 5770, Barcs Papers; Box 1; diary entries, 16 February 1972, 1 June 1972. NLA: MS 5852, Perkin Papers; Folder 6; Packer to Perkin, 17 January 1972.
13 *Women's Weekly*, 3 May 1972, p. 3; interview with Joyce Bowden, 2 November 1994; Lloyd, *Profession: Journalist*, pp. 269, 271.
14 Minogue, 'Packer's $15 million deal', p. 10; *Nation*, 10 June 1972, p. 5; Horne, *Into the Open*, p. 191.
15 *Nation*, 10 June 1972, p. 5; Minogue, 'Packer's $15 million deal', pp. 5, 10. See also ML: ML MSS 5770, Barcs Papers; Box 1; diary entry, 6 June 1972.
16 Tiffen, 'The Packer-Labor alliance, 1978–95: RIP', p. 21; Barry, *The Rise and Rise of Kerry Packer*, p. 129. NLA: TRC 121/44, interview with Mungo McCallum, 6 April 1973, tape 1, track 1, p. 72.
17 Griffen-Foley, *The House of Packer*, pp. 293–4; *Australian Financial Review*, 6 June 1972, p. 1.
18 McNicoll, *Luck's a Fortune*, p. 304; Buttrose, *Early Edition*, pp. 104–5. NLA: MS 5852, Perkin Papers; Folder 6; Packer to Perkin, August 1972.
19 Minogue, 'Packer's $15 million deal', p. 5; Buttrose, *Early Edition*, pp. 104–5; Horne, *Money Made Us*, p. 55.
20 ML: ML MSS 5770, Barcs Papers; Box 1; diary entries, 8 June 1972, 12 June 1972, 12 July 1972.
21 McNicoll, *Luck's a Fortune*, pp. 305–6.
22 Horne, *Into the Open*, p. 191; *NN*, 7 July 1972, p. 1, 15 September 1972, p. 7.
23 ML: ML MSS 3525, Horne Papers; MLK 2152; ACP-B4; Horne to FP, 17 July 1972, 26 July 1972; memo to Horne, 9 August 1972.
24 *Weekend Business Review*, 19 September 1970, p. 11; Buttrose, *Early Edition*, p. 122; Barry, *The Rise and Rise of Kerry Packer*, p. 150.
25 *Age*, 19 November 1984, p. 11; Minogue, 'Packer's $15 million deal', p. 5; *NN*, 16 March 1973, p. 11.
26 *Australian*, 8 November 1973, p. 1; *Bulletin*, 10 November 1973, p. 32; Hall, *Supertoy*, pp. 98–100.
27 Barry, *The Rise and Rise of Kerry Packer*, pp. 133–4; *Australian*, 8 November 1973, p. 1; *SMH*, 1 May 1971, p. 9.

Endnotes

28   *SMH*, 5 August 1972, p. 3; *Australian*, 8 November 1973, p. 1; Barry, *The Rise and Rise of Kerry Packer*, pp. 133–4.
29   *Telegraph*, 4 January 1973, p. 37; *NN*, 16 March 1973, p. 10; *Pol*, June 1974, p. 8.
30   *Pol*, June 1974, p. 9; *SMH*, 20 September 1971, p. 8.
31   Buttrose, *Early Edition*, pp. 108–11.
32   ML: ML MSS 5770, Barcs Papers; Box 1; diary entries, 29 November 1972, 30 November 1972, 13 December 1972. See also *SMH*, 14 December 1972, p. 3; McNicoll, *Luck's a Fortune*, p. 286.
33   Souter, *Company of Heralds*, pp. 485–6; McNicoll, *Luck's a Fortune*, p. 285; Griffen-Foley, *The House of Packer*, pp. 295, 297.
34   *CPD*, Senate, vol. 54, 19 October 1972, pp. 1702–3, 1712.
35   Bolton, *The Oxford History of Australia*, vol. 5, pp. 213–4; Mayer, 'Two editorials and a modest gift', pp. 198–9.
36   *SMH*, 5 June 1973, p. 1, 6 June 1973, p. 6; *CPD*, House of Representatives, vol. 56, 5 June 1973, p. 2286.
37   Mayer, 'Two editorials and a modest gift', p. 199; *SMH*, 8 June 1973, p. 3.
38   *Telegraph*, 3 November 1973, p. 5; *CPD*, Senate, vol. 58, 6 November 1973, p. 1520.
39   *Bulletin*, 10 November 1973, pp. 32, 35–6.
40   *Australian*, 8 November 1973, p. 1; *Pol*, June 1974, p. 9.
41   *Pol*, June 1974, p. 9; *SMH*, 4 December 1973, p. 8.
42   McNicoll, *Luck's a Fortune*, pp. 286, 288.
43   NLA: MS 4936, Menzies Papers; Series 2; Folder 986; FP to Menzies, 23 December 1973. ML: ML MSS 5770, Barcs Papers; Box 1; diary entry, 24 December 1973.
44   McNicoll, *Luck's a Fortune*, p. 286.
45   ibid. p. 288; *Weekend Business Review*, 19 September 1970, p. 13; *Australian*, 2 May 1974, p. 10; interview with Lady Packer, 35 January 1996.
46   McNicoll, *Luck's a Fortune*, pp. 297–8.
47   ML: ML MSS 5770, Barcs Papers; Box 1; diary entries, 7 May 1973, 31 January 1974, 25 March 1974, 28 March 1974, 3 April 1974.
48   *SMH*, 2 May 1974, p. 1; *Women's Weekly*, 24 August 1977, p. 9. See also ML: ML MSS 5770, Barcs Papers; Box 1; diary entry, 1 May 1974.
49   *Telegraph*, 28 August 1959, p. 13.
50   *SMH*, 2 May 1974, p. 12; Clyde Packer in Minogue, 'Packer's $15 million deal', p. 7.
51   *Sunday Telegraph*, 5 May 1974, p. 45; *Bulletin*, 11 May 1974, pp. 12–13; *Women's Weekly*, 15 May 1974, p. 2; *SMH*, 2 May 1974, p. 7.
52   *Telegraph*, 9 May 1974, p. 3; *Sun News-Pictorial*, 2 May 1974, p. 8; *Times* (London), 2 May 1974, p. 20; *Workers' News*, 9 May 1974, p. 3.
53   *Wentworth Courier*, 8 May 1974, p. 3; *SMH*, 4 May 1974, p. 3; Horne, *Money Made Us*, p. 12.
54   ML: ML MSS 5770, Barcs Papers; Box 1; diary entry, 3 May 1974; FP funeral program.
55   Souter, *Company of Heralds*, p. 319; interview with Lady Stening, 30 January 1996; *SMH*, 4 May 1974, p. 3; *Age*, 4 May 1974, p. 5.

Endnotes

56 Interview with Lady Stening, 11 June 1999.
57 *Canberra Times*, 2 May 1974, p. 2; *Australian Financial Review*, 2 May 1974, p. 1; *NN*, 10 May 1974, p. 1; Minogue, 'Packer's $15 million deal', p. 10.
58 *Age*, 19 November 1984, p. 11; *SMH* Good Weekend Magazine, 27 October 1984, pp. 68–71; *B&T Advertising, Marketing and Media Weekly*, 12 May 1983, pp. 22–3, 26.
59 *SMH*, 6 February 1975, p. 2; *CPD*, Senate, vol. 63, 13 February 1975, p. 139.
60 ML: ML MSS 5770, Barcs Papers; Box 1; diary entry, 3 May 1974. *Australian*, 2 May 1974, p. 10

Bibliography

Manuscripts

Archives Office of Tasmania (AOT)
MB2/39/15, Hobart Marine Board passenger list
N36, Hutchins School Admission Register
Statistics of Tasmania, 1873–1901
Australian Army, Soldier Career Management Agency (SCMA)
NX203748, Lieut. Douglas Frank Hewson Packer
Australian Securities Commission (ASC)
000 025 721, Sydney Newspapers Pty Ltd
008 394 509, Consolidated Press Holdings Ltd
013 36 243, Adastra Airways Ltd
Australian Stock Exchange (ASX)
I-A132, Australian Consolidated Press
Australian War Memorial (AWM)
Australian Armoured Corps Pamphlet No. 6, *The Armoured Brigade*, May 1941
MSS 874, 'The 2/7th Australian Infantry Battalion 1939–1946' by J. G. Littlewood
MSS 1245, 'Live Cowards and Dead Heroes' by Will Hungerford
MSS 1408, 'The Rough Infantry: Tales of World War II' by A. C. Bennett
Berkshire Record Office (BRO)
DA1/159/63, Charles Packer will, 1808
DP98/5/1, St Mary's Minster Churchwarden's Accounts
DP98/8/1-6, St Mary's Minster Vestry Minutes, 1725–1868
Boy Scout Memorabilia Centre
Cumbria Record Office
DB20, Sir John Burgess Papers
Flinders University Library (FUL)
H. V. Evatt Collection
Fryer Library, University of Queensland
Collection 18, Ernestine Hill Papers
House of Lords Record Office
Beaverbrook Papers
Hutchins School Archives
Hutchins School Enrolments from 1846 to 1993
Institute of Commonwealth Archives, University of London (ICA)
Commonwealth Press Union Records
John Fairfax Archives (JFA)
Chief Executive; ANPA; Newsprint Pool Correspondence:-1947–1949; [200.15/5]
Chief Executive; Associated Newspapers; Negotiations, Agreement, Court Case; [200.20/1]
Chief Executive; Associated Newspapers; Sale of Goodwill of *Telegraph*, 1935; [200.20/3]

Bibliography

General Manager; Censorship April/May 1944; File 4 Settlement; [200.24/1]
General Manager; Censorship April/May 1944; File 7; [200.24/1]
Chief Financial Executive; *Telegraph* 1, 1957–1960; [300.70]
Associated Newspapers; Agreements; Sydney Newspapers (25) No. 13; [6201.1/1]
Associated Newspapers; Agreements; Packet 7, Associated Newspapers and Sydney Newspapers Bundle; [6201.1/6]

John W. Hartman Center for Sales, Advertising and Marketing History, Special Collections
Library, Duke University, North Carolina
J. Walter Thompson Collection

Ku-ring-gai Local History Centre (KLHC)
Abbotsholme College prospectus, c. 1925
'The school that lasted thirty years', typescript by Irene Phipps, 1989
'Reminiscences of Turramurra College' by Malcolm O'Reilly, 26 April 1983
'Wahroonga Grammar School for Boys', n.d.

La Trobe Library, State Library of Victoria
MS 10375, Lindsay Family Papers

Mitchell Library, State Library of New South Wales (ML)
ML 1243/91, Ashby Research Service Papers
ML MSS Set 71, Voltaire Molesworth Papers
ML MSS 2385, Liberal Party (NSW Division) Papers
ML MSS 2922, Q. S. Spedding Papers
ML MSS 3106, Sir Jack Cassidy Papers
ML MSS 3269, Angus & Robertson Papers
ML MSS 3525, Donald Horne Papers
ML MSS 5770, Barcs Family Papers
ML MSS 6630, Southern Africa Defence and Aid Fund in Australia Records

National Archives of Australia, Australian Capital Territory (NAA/ACT)
Attorney-General's Department, A472; W23628, Cowra Prison Camp
Attorney-General's Department, A472; W10525, "Daily Telegraph" Sydney—Breaches of press censorship order
Department of Air, A705/15; 163/24/348, BULLMORE, Herbert James
Prime Minister's Department, A1608; AK27/1/2, Allied Works Council: Inquiry
A10663/1; CAU/SCI/7, Summary of oral evidence to be presented on Foundation,
A10663/1; CAU/SVD/54, Evidence to be presented to the committee on
Australian Universities by Nuclear Research Foundation
Department of External Affairs, A1838/386; 1525/3/266 Part 1, Shipping—America's Cup challenge, Gretel
Cabinet Secretariat, A4940/1; C3691, Congratulatory Message to Crew of "Gretel" on Performance in America's Cup Race
Department of Defence, A5954/69; 1923/50, "Gretel" Yacht Challenge in USA-Cost of Dinner
Department of Defence Co-ordination, A5954/1; 199/1, *Daily Telegraph* and the War
Department of Trade and Customs, CP208/1; A37, Newsprint—Request by Consolidated Press
Department of Information, SP109/3; 322/12, Censorship "Daily Telegraph" and "Sunday Telegraph" General File
Department of Information, SP195/1; 73/23/32, "Telegraph" (Sydney) Daily and Sunday
Department of Information, SP195/2; 365/25, Cables Treatment and D.T.
Department of Information, SP195/7; NN General — Correspondence with Minister for Information

National Archives of Australia, New South Wales (NAA/NSW)
Australian Broadcasting Commission, C1777/T1; NN ABC scripts, tape 2
Department of Information, SP106/1; PC22 Part 1, *Daily Telegraph* batch 1
Department of Information, SP106/1; PC22 Part 2, *Daily Telegraph*

Bibliography

General Correspondence of the Comptroller-General relating to newsprint rationing, SP221/3; Box 2 Newsprint rationing file; Notes of a deputation on Friday, 7 February 1941
General Correspondence of the Comptroller-General relating to newsprint rationing, SP221/3; Bundle 2
Internal Security Correspondence, Headquarters Eastern Command, SP1141/1; 13, Intelligence Reports

National Library of Australia (NLA)
MS 1578, Colin Roderick Papers
MS 2396, Edward J. Ward Papers
MS 2823, Sir Keith Murdoch Papers
MS 3863, Peter Samuel Papers
MS 4738, Arthur Calwell Papers
MS 4849, Sir Lloyd Dumas Papers
MS 4936, Sir Robert Menzies Papers
MS 5546, Colin Bednall Papers
MS 5852, Graham Perkin Papers
MS 6055, Tom Uren Papers
MS 6455, Sir Ernest K. White Papers
MS 7222, E. G. Theodore Papers
MS 7995, Tom Fitzgerald Papers

New York Yacht Club Archives (NYYCA)

Noel Butlin Archives Centre (NBAC)
N59/16–36, AJA NSW Minutes, 1932–54
N59/165, Australian Consolidated Press Ltd Accommodation and Facilities
N59/413, Australian Consolidated Press Ltd and Leslie Haylen
N59/900, 1955 Printers' Strike
N117/1531, Labor Papers Ltd Minutes of Directors' Meetings
T39/1/18, PIEUA NSW Minutes
Z270 Box 8, Penton Case 1943
Z270 Box 30, AJA Federal Executive Minutes

Royal Sydney Yacht Squadron Archives (RSYSA)
25/3/1, America's Cup 1970: International Race and Protest Committee and Squadron Officials
25/3/3, America's Cup 1970: General Correspondence
25/3/5, America's Cup 1970: Details for RSYS Conducting Elimination Match at Newport
25/3/14, America's Cup 1962: *Gretel* v. *Weatherly*

University of Melbourne Archives
Stock Exchange of Melbourne—Mining Companies

University of Sydney Archives (USA)
G3 22 1; Nuclear Research Foundation Minute Book
G313 26800 Boxes 326–8; Post-Graduate Medical Foundation

Woollahra Local History Centre
Valuation Book, Bellevue Hill, 1908
Valuation Books, Edgecliff, 1934–68

Private Holdings
Francis James Papers (in possession of Joyce James and Alfred James, Sydney)
C. S. McNulty Papers (in possession of the McNulty family, East Sussex and Sydney)
Packer Family Papers (in possession of Lady Stening, Sydney)
Rohan Rivett Papers (in possession of Nancy Rivett, Melbourne; extract kindly supplied by Dr Peter Gifford)
George Warnecke Papers (in possession of Meg Sordello, Paris)

Bibliography

Newspapers and Periodicals

Australia: *Age, Ascham Charivari, Australian Women's Weekly, Boorowa News, Brisbane Courier, B&T Advertising, Marketing and Media Weekly, Bulletin, Catholic Leader, Corian, Cranbrookian, Daily Guardian, Daily Squeaker, Daily Telegraph, Grenfell Record, Hobart Mercury, Hobart Town Courier, Home, Jobson's Investment Digest, Journalist, Labor Daily, Medical Journal of Australia, Miss Australia: A Quarterly Magazine, Nation, National Times, Newspaper News (NN), Pacific Islands Monthly (PIM), Printer, Printing Trades Journal, Punch* (Melbourne), *Queensland Times, Quirindi Advocate, Red Cross Record, Review: The Independent Quality National Weekly, Scouting in New South Wales, Smith's Weekly, Sporting Globe, Sun, Sunday Sun, Sunday Times, Sun-Herald, Sydney Mail, Sydney Morning Herald (SMH), Sydney Tatler, Tatler, Telegus, Theatre Magazine, Things I Hear, Torch Bearer, Truth, West Australian*

Britain: *Reading Mercury, Times* (London)

United States: *Christian Science Monitor, Life International, Motor Boating, Newport Daily News, New York Herald Tribune, New York Times, Providence Sunday Journal, Sports Illustrated, Vogue* (New York)

Interviews

Author

Pat Bancks, Arthur Boothroyd, Joyce Bowden, Sally Baker, the late Adrian Deamer, the late Dorothy Drain, Harry Gordon, Ken Ewing, Dick Hughes, the late Frank McNulty, Joe Morley, Lady (Florence) Packer, Paddy Pearl, the late Elizabeth Riddell, Myra Rowbotham, Lady (Kathleen) Stening, Eleanor Watson, Sheila Wood, John Wynne-Lewis

NLA

Ross Campbell, Dorothy Drain, Bruce Gyngell, Sir James Hardy, Mungo McCallum, Donald Horne, Ronald McKie, William H. Northam, Cyril Pearl, Alan Reid, A. G. Smith, Douglas Stewart, Jock Sturrock

Reference Works

Australian Dictionary of Biography (ADB)
Australian Ski Yearbook
Business Who's Who of Australia
Commonwealth of Australia New South Wales Electoral Roll
Commonwealth Parliamentary Debates (CPD)
Dictionary of National Biography
'Digest' Year Book of Public Companies of Australia and New Zealand
International Genealogical Index (IGT)
F. B. Manning's Tasmania Directory, 1881–1882
New South Wales Parliamentary Debates (NSWPD)
New South Wales Pioneers Index, Federation Series 1889–1918
Radi, Heather, Peter Spearritt and Elizabeth Hinton (eds), *Biographical Register of the New South Wales Parliament, 1901–1970*, Australian National University Press, Canberra, 1979
Sand's Sydney and New South Wales Directory
Tasmania Pioneers Index

Bibliography

Tasmania Post Office Directory
Who's Who in Australia
Year Book of the Church of England in the Diocese of Tasmania

Books

Adams, Brian, *Portrait of an Artist: A Biography of William Dobell*, Hutchinson of Australia, Richmond, 1983
Armour to Anchors, 2/8th Australian Armoured Regiment Association, Karingal, 1991
Atherton Young, John, Ann Jervie Sefton and Nina Webb (eds), *Centenary Book of the University of Sydney Faculty of Medicine*, Sydney University Press, Sydney, 1984
Baldwin, Nick et al., *The World Guide to Automobiles: The Makers and their Marques*, Macdonald & Co., London and Sydney, 1987
Barry, Paul, *The Rise and Rise of Kerry Packer*, Bantam and ABC Books, Sydney, 1993
Baume, Eric, *I Lived These Years*, George G. Harrap & Co., London, 1941
— *Tragedy Track: The Story of the Granites*, North Flinders Mines and Hesperian Press, 1994 edn
Baverstock, W., *The America's Cup: Challenge From Down Under*, K. G. Murray, Sydney, 1967
Bernays, Edward L., *Biography of an Idea: Memoirs of a Public Relations Counsel*, Simon & Schuster, New York, 1965
Blaikie, George, *Remember Smith's Weekly?*, Rigby, Adelaide, 1966
Blaxland, Helen, *Collected Flower Pieces*, Ure Smith, Sydney, n.d. (1948)
Bolton, Geoffrey, *The Oxford History of Australia*, vol. 5, Oxford University Press, Melbourne, 1990
Braddon, Russell, *Roy Thomson of Fleet Street*, Collins, London, 1965
Buckridge, Patrick, *The Scandalous Penton*, University of Queensland Press, St Lucia, 1994
Buttrose, Ita, *Early Edition: My First Forty Years*, Macmillan, South Melbourne, 1985
Cassab, Judy, *Diaries*, Alfred A. Knopf, Sydney, 1995
Chisholm, Anne and Michael Davie, *Beaverbrook: A Life*, Hutchinson, London, 1992
The Coffs Harbour Story, Central North Coast Newspaper Company, Coffs Harbour, 1976
Coleman, Peter, *Memoirs of a Slow Learner*, Angus & Robertson, Pymble, 1994
Collinson, Francis, *The Traditional and National Music of Scotland*, Routledge and Kegan Paul, London, 1966
Cook, Kerrin, *The Railway Came to Ku-ring-gai*, Genlin Investments, Sydney, 1991
Cox, Jack, *Take a Cold Tub, Sir! The Story of the Boy's Own Paper*, Lutterworth Press, Guildford, 1982
Cranbrook, 1918–1928, no publisher, Sydney, n.d. (1928?)
Day, David, *Smugglers and Sailors: The Customs History of Australia 1788–1901*, Australian Government Publishing Service, Canberra, 1992
— *Contraband and Controversy: The Customs History of Australia from 1901*, Australian Government Publishing Service, Canberra, 1996
— *John Curtin: A Life*, HarperCollins, Pymble, 1999
Deans, Alan, *Australia's Polo Heritage. The Hardern Polo Team 1912–1930*, Hamilton Publishing, Sydney, 1991
Dear, Ian, *The America's Cup: An Informal History*, Stanley Paul, London, 1980
Dempsey, Jack and Barbara Piattelli Dempsey, *Dempsey*, W. H. Allen, London, 1977
Desmond, Valerie, *The Awful Australians*, no publisher, Sydney, 1911
Dormer, Marion, *Dubbo — City on the Plains, 1901–1988*, Macquarie Publications, Dubbo, 1988
E. G. Theodore: A Profile, Consolidated Press, Sydney, 1949
Fairfax Simpson, Caroline, Annette Fielding-Jones Dupree and Betty Winn Ferguson (eds), *Ascham Remembered 1886–1986*, Fine Arts Press, Sydney, 1986
Farmer, Henry George, *A History of Music in Scotland*, Da Capo Press, New York, 1970
Finey, George, *The Mangle Wheel*, Kangaroo Press, Kenthurst, 1981
Fitzgerald, Ross, *'Red Ted': The Life of E. G. Theodore*, University of Queensland Press, St Lucia, 1994

Bibliography

Fitzhardinghe, L. F., *William Morris Hughes: A Political Biography*, vol. 2, Angus & Robertson, Sydney, 1979

Goaman, Muriel, *English Clocks*, The Connoisseur & Michael Joseph, London, 1967

Gordon, Harry, *Voyage From Shame: The Cowra Breakout and Afterwards*, University of Queensland Press, St Lucia, 1994

Griffen-Foley, Bridget, *The House of Packer: The Making of a Media Empire*, Allen & Unwin, St Leonards, 1999

Hall, Ken G., *Directed by Ken G. Hall: Autobiography of an Australian Film Maker*, Lansdowne Press, Melbourne, 1977

Hall, Sandra, *Supertoy: 20 Years of Australian Television*, Sun Books, Melbourne, 1976

Hancock, Ian, *National and Permanent? The Federal Organisation of the Liberal Party of Australia 1944–1965*, Melbourne University Press, Carlton, 2000

Hancock, W. K. and M. M. Gowing, *British War Economy*, His Majesty's Stationery Office, London, 1949

Hasluck, Paul, *The Government and the People, 1939–1941*, Australian War Memorial, Canberra, 1952

Haylen, Leslie, *Twenty Years' Hard Labour*, Macmillan of Australia, Melbourne, 1969

Henderson, Gerard, *Menzies' Child. The Liberal Party of Australia 1944–1994*, Allen & Unwin, St Leonards, 1994

Hilvert, John, *Blue Pencil Warriors*, University of Queensland Press, St Lucia, 1984

Hornadge, Bill, *Lennie Lower: He Made a Nation Laugh*, Angus & Robertson, Pymble, 1993

Horne, Donald, *Money Made Us*, Penguin, Harmondsworth, 1976

— *Confessions of a New Boy*, Penguin, Ringwood, 1985

— *The Education of Young Donald*, Penguin, Ringwood, 1988 edn

— *Portrait of an Optimist*, Penguin, Ringwood, 1988

— *Into the Open*, HarperCollins, Pymble, 2000

Hough, Richard, *The Ace of Clubs: A History of the Garrick*, Andre Deutsch, London, 1986

Howson, Peter, *The Howson Diaries. The Life of Politics*, Penguin Books, Melbourne, 1984

Hudson, W. J., *Casey*, Oxford University Press, Melbourne, 1986

Hughes, Dick, *Daddy's Practising Again: An Australian Jazzman Looks Back and Around*, Hutchinson of Australia, Richmond, 1977

— *Don't You Sing! Memories of a Catholic Boyhood*, Kangaroo Press, Kenthurst, 1994

Hughes, Margaret, *The Long Hop*, Stanley Paul, London, 1955

The Hutchins School Centenary Magazine, 1846–1946, Hutchins School, Hobart, 1946

Cassidy, Elaine et al. (eds), *Impressions of Woollahra Past and Present*, Allen & Unwin, Sydney, 1988

Inaugural Proceedings of the Nuclear Research Foundation, no publisher, Sydney, 1954

Inglis, K. S., *This is the ABC*, Melbourne University Press, Carlton, 1983

— *Nation: The Life of an Independent Journal of Opinion 1958–1972*, Melbourne University Press, Melbourne, 1989

Jenner, Dorothy and Trish Sheppard, *Darlings I've Had a Ball*, Ure Smith, Sydney, 1975

Judd, Tom, *Fifty Years Will be Long Enough!*, The National Press, Melbourne, 1971

Kedward, H. R., *Occupied France: Collaboration and Resistance 1940–1944*, Basil Blackwell, Oxford, 1985

Kennedy, Buzz, *It Was Bloody Marvellous!*, Kangaroo Press, Kenthurst, 1996

King, Cecil H., *Strictly Personal*, Weidenfeld & Nicolson, London, 1969

Kirkpatrick, Peter, *The Sea Coast of Bohemia: Literary Life in Sydney's Roaring Twenties*, University of Queensland Press, St Lucia, 1992

Lane, Terry (comp.), *As the Twig is Bent. The Childhood Recollections of Sixteen Prominent Australians*, Dove Communications, Sydney, 1979

Lang, J. T., *I Remember*, Invincible Press, Sydney, n.d. (1956?)

Lawson, Valerie, *Connie Sweetheart: The Story of Connie Robertson*, William Heinemann, Melbourne, 1990

— *The Allens Affair*, Macmillan, Sydney, 1995

Lesley, Cole, *The Life of Noël Coward*, Penguin, Harmondsworth, 1976

Bibliography

Lloyd, Clem, *Profession: Journalist. A History of the Australian Journalists' Association*, Hale & Iremonger, Sydney, 1985
— *Parliament and the Press: The Federal Parliamentary Press Gallery, 1901–1988*, Melbourne University Press, Melbourne, 1988
Lloyd, Helen V., *Boorowa: Over 160 Years of White Settlement*, Toveloam, Panania, 1990
Long, Gavin, *To Benghazi*, Australian War Memorial, Canberra, 1952
Lord, Richard (comp.), *Inscriptions in Stone: St David's Burial Ground, 1804–1872*, St George's Church, Hobart, 1976
Macswan, Norman, *The Man Who Read the East Wind: A Biography of Richard Hughes*, Kangaroo Press, Kenthurst, 1982
Madigan, C.T., *Central Australia*, Oxford University Press, Melbourne and London, 1944 edn
Mangan, J. A., *Athleticism in the Victorian and Edwardian Public School*, Cambridge University Press, Cambridge, 1981
Manion, James, *Paper Power in North Queensland*, North Queensland Newspaper Company, Townsville, 1982
Marks, Alan, *Quest for the Cup: The America's Cup Challenges, 1851–1987*, Australian Broadcasting Corporation, Sydney, 1987
Marr, David, *Patrick White: A Life*, Random House Australia, Milsons Point, 1991 — (ed.), *Patrick White Letters*, Random House Australia, Milsons Point, 1994
Martin, A. W., *Robert Menzies: A Life*, vol. 1, Melbourne University Press, Carlton, 1993
— *Robert Menzies: A Life*, vol. 2, Melbourne University Press, Carlton, 2000
MacDonald, Donald, *Baden-Powell: Soldier and Scout*, Lake, Sons & Cowell, Melbourne, 1912
McKay, Claude, *This is the Life: The Autobiography of a Newspaperman*, Angus & Robertson, Sydney, 1961
McKie, Ronald, *We Have No Dreaming*, Collins Australia, Sydney, 1988
McNicoll, David, *Luck's a Fortune*, Wildcat Press, Sydney, 1979
Mead, Tom, *Breaking the News*, Dolphin Books, Sydney, 1998
Millar, D. D. (ed.), *The Messel Era*, Pergamon, Sydney, 1987
Moore, Andrew, *The Secret Army and the Premier*, New South Wales University Press, Kensington, 1989
Moore, Robert (comp.), *Profiles of Power*, Australian Broadcasting Commission, Sydney, 1970
Morrison, Frederic, *The Aldine History of Queensland*, vol. II, Aldine Publishing Co., Sydney, 1888
Municipality of Woollahra, *The History of Bellevue Hill*, no publisher, no place, n.d. (1930s)
Nairn, Bede, *The 'Big Fella': Jack Lang and the Australian Labor Party 1891–1949*, Melbourne University Press, Carlton, 1986
Nelson, Penelope, *Penny Dreadful*, Random House Australia, Milsons Point, 1995
Newton, Sarah, *Maxwell Newton: A Biography*, Fremantle Arts Centre Press, Fremantle, 1993
'Nutcote' History Report, Howard Tanner & Associates, Sydney, 1992
O'Brien, Denis, *The Weekly. A Lively and Nostalgic Celebration of Australia Through 50 Years of its Most Popular Magazine*, Penguin, Ringwood, 1982
Packer, Donna Smith, *On Footings From the Past: The Packers in England*, Bookcraft, Salt Lake City, 1988
Pearl, Cyril, *Pantaloons and Antics*, F. W. Cheshire, Melbourne, 1964
Savage, Joan (ed.), *Palm Beach 1788–1988*, The Palm Beach Association, Palm Beach, 1984
Pearn, John Hemsley, *Watermen of War*, Amphion Press, Brisbane, 1993
Penton, Brian, *Censored!*, Shakespeare Head Press, Sydney, 1947
Penton, Neville, *A Racing Heart: The Story of the Australian Turf*, Collins, Sydney, 1987
Pound, Reginald and Geoffrey Harmsworth, *Northcliffe*, Cassell, London, 1959
Purser, John, *Scotland's Music: A History of the Traditional and Classical Music of Scotland From Earliest Times to the Present Day*, Mainstream Publishing, Edinburgh and London, 1992
Rait, Basil W., *The Official History of the Hutchins School*, J. Walch, Hobart, n.d. (1935)
Ramage, Ian A., *Wahroonga — Our Home*, Ian A. Ramage, Waitara, 1991
— *One Hundred Years Ago: Life on Sydney's Upper North Shore*, Ian A. Ramage, Waitara, 1996
Rankine, Susan, *Being Ernest: The Life of Ernest Watt, 1874–1954*, SGR Press, Double Bay, 1998

Bibliography

Raymond, Robert, *Out of the Box*, Seaview Press, Adelaide, 1999
Read, Donald, *The Power of News: The History of Reuters*, Oxford University Press, Oxford, 1992
Reader, W. J., *Bowater: A History*, Cambridge University Press, Cambridge, 1981
Reading, Geoffrey, *High Climbers: Askin and Others*, John Ferguson, Sydney, 1989
Report of the Activities of the Allied Works Council for the Period February 26, 1942 to June 30, 1943
Robson, Lloyd, *A History of Tasmania*, vol. I, *Van Diemen's Land From the Earliest Times to 1855*, Oxford University Press, Melbourne, 1983
— *A History of Tasmania*, vol. II, *Colony and State From 1856 to the 1980s*, Oxford University Press, Melbourne, 1991
Rolfe, Patricia, *The Journalistic Javelin: An Illustrated History of the Bulletin*, Wildcat Press, Sydney, 1979
Rowntree, Amy, Battery Point Today and Yesterday, Adult Education Board of Tasmania, no place, n.d
Scott, Valerie G. and Eve McLaughlin, *County Maps and Histories: Berkshire*, Quiller Press, London, 1984
Shawcross, William, *Murdoch*, Pan Books, London, 1993 edn
Sheridan, Tom, *Division of Labour: Industrial Relations in the Chifley Years, 1945–49*, Oxford University Press, Oxford, 1989
Sherington, Geoffrey, *Shore: A History of the Sydney Church of England Grammar School*, Allen & Unwin, Sydney, 1983
Singleton, John, *True Confessions*, Cassell Australia, Stanmore, 1979
Smiles, Samuel, *Self-Help: With Illustrations of Conduct and Perseverance*, John Murray, London, 1910 edn
Smith, Anthony, *The Newspaper: An International History*, Thames & Hudson, London, 1979
Smith, James Joynton, *My Life Story*, Cornstalk Publishing Company, Sydney, 1927
Souter, Gavin, *Company of Heralds*, Melbourne University Press, Melbourne, 1981
Stephens, Geoffrey, *The Hutchins School: Macquarie Street Years, 1846–1965*, Hutchins School, Hobart, 1979
Stephensen, P. R. (comp.), *Sydney Sails: The Story of the Royal Sydney Yacht Squadron's First 100 Years (1862–1962)*, Angus & Robertson, Sydney, 1962
Stewart, Douglas, *A Man of Sydney: A New Appreciation of Kenneth Slessor*, Nelson, West Melbourne, 1977
Stone, Carolyn R. and Pamela Tyson, *Old Hobart Town and Environs, 1802–1855*, Pioneer Design Studio, Lilydale, 1978
Sydney Church of England Grammar School Register 1889–1994, Shore Old Boys' Union Incorporated, Sydney, 1994
Tariff Revision: Tariff Board's Report on Newsprinting Paper
Taylor, Peter, *A Celebration of Shore*, Allen & Unwin, Sydney, 1988
Thirty Years of Service: The American Australian Association, 1948–1978, no publisher, New York, 1978
Townsley, W. A., *Tasmania From Colony to Statehood, 1803–1945*, St David's Park Publishing, Hobart, 1991
Townsville 100, 1864–1964, T. Willmett & Sons, Townsville, n.d. (1964)
Tyler, E. J., *The Craft of the Clockmaker*, Crown Publishers, New York, 1973
Uren, Tom, *Straight Left*, Random House Australia, Milsons Point, 1994
Walker, R. B., *The Newspaper Press in New South Wales, 1803–1920*, Sydney University Press, Sydney, 1976
— *Yesterday's News. A History of the Newspaper Press in New South Wales From 1920 to 1945*, Sydney University Press, Sydney, 1980
Waters, J. C., *Valiant Youth. The Men of the R.A.A.F., F. H. Johnston*, Sydney, 1945
Waugh, Evelyn, *Scoop*, Chapman & Hall, London, 1951 edn
Weedon, Sally, *Countess of Dudley Cup Tournament, 1985*, New South Wales Polo Association (Kyeemagh) Ltd, no place, 1986
Weiss, Leonard, *Watch-making in England, 1760–1820*, Robert Hale, London, 1982
White, Patrick, *The Twyborn Affair*, Penguin, 1981 edn
Whitington, Don, *Strive to be Fair*, Australian National University Press, Canberra, 1977

Whitington, R. S., *Sir Frank: The Frank Packer Story*, Cassell Australia, North Melbourne, 1971
Wiener, Joel H., (ed.), *Papers for the Millions: The New Journalism in Britain, 1850s to 1914*, Greenwood, New York, 1988
Wigmore, Lionel, *The Japanese Thrust*, Australian War Memorial, Canberra, 1957
Wilder, Ken, *The Company You Keep*, State Library of New South Wales Press, Sydney, 1994
Williams, Maslyn, *His Mother's Country*, Melbourne University Press, Carlton, 1988
Yeates, Neil, *Coffs Harbour*, vol. I, *pre–1880 to 1945*, Coffs Harbour City Council, Coffs Harbour, 1990

Articles

'Australian Army behind the Army', *Rydge's*, 1 November 1942, pp. 671–2
'Big daddy is no longer watching him', *Pol*, June 1974, pp. 6–9
Bolger, P. F., 'The changing role of a city: Hobart', *Tasmanian Historical Research Association Papers and Proceedings*, vol. 16, no. 1, July 1968, pp. 6–15
Buttrose, Sydney, 'The life of a Jack was not an easy one', *This Australia*, vol. 3, no. 4, Spring 1984, pp. 49–51
Cameron, Clyde, 'When incompetence and corruption merge: The AWU and the *World* newspaper', *Labour History*, no. 70, May 1996, pp. 169–82
Campbell, Peter, '21 years of challenge: The America's Cup race', *This Australia*, vol. 2, no. 4, Spring 1983, pp. 19–30
Chaput, Donald, 'The Queenslanders get Fiji gold', *Journal (Historical Society of Queensland)*, vol. 12, no. 5, August 1986, pp. 388–400
Coleman, Peter, 'The Bulletin, the editor and the Cherry Orchard: A tale of the 1960s', *Voices*, vol. 7, no. 1, Autumn 1997, pp. 88–95
Cook, Peter, 'The end of the *World*', *Labour History*, no. 16, May 1969, pp. 55–7
Curthoys, Ann, 'The getting of television: Dilemmas in ownership, control and culture, 1941–56', in Ann Curthoys and John Merritt (eds), *Australia's First Cold War*, vol. 2, Allen & Unwin, Sydney, 1986, pp. 123–54
Davidson, Prue, 'Return to Sydney and the war years', in Barry Pearce and Hendrik Kolenberg (eds), *William Dobell: The Painter's Progress*, Art Gallery of New South Wales Press, Sydney, 1997, pp. 73–4
Goot, Murray, 'Newspaper circulation in Australia', Media Centre Paper 11, Centre for the Study of Educational Communication and Media, La Trobe University, Bundoora, 1979
Griffen-Foley, Bridget, 'A biographical profile of George Warnecke', *Australian Studies in Journalism (ASJ)*, no. 3, 1994, pp. 67–108
— 'The Young Master and his old man: Sir Frank and R. C. Packer', *Media International Australia (MIA)*, no. 77, August 1995, pp. 35–44
— 'Playing with princes and presidents: Sir Frank Packer and the 1962 challenge for the America's Cup', *Australian Journal of Politics and History*, vol. 46, no. 1, 2000, pp. 51–66
— 'R.C. Packer: Founder of a dynasty', in Graeme Osborne and Deborah Jenkins (eds), *Australian Communication Lives 1999*, University of Canberra, Canberra, 2000, pp. 40–6
— 'Revisiting the "Mystery of a Novel Contest": The *Daily Telegraph* and *Come in Spinner*', *Australian Literary Studies*, October 2000 (forthcoming)
Haskell, Dennis, 'The heroism of comedy: *Smith's Weekly* in the 1930s', in Bruce Bennett and Dennis Haskell (eds), *Myths, Heroes and Anti-Heroes: Essays on the Literature and Culture of the Asia-Pacific Region*, Centre for Studies in Australian Literature, University of Western Australia, Nedlands, 1992, pp. 107–20
Kiernan, Colm, 'Arthur A. Calwell's clashes with the Australian press, 1943–1945', *University of Wollongong Historical Journal*, vol. 2, 1976, pp. 74–111
Kirkpatrick, Rod, 'Packer, a country newspaper and a female proprietor', *PANPA Bulletin*, May 1999, pp. 63–5

Laurie, Victoria, 'Unfinished business: The legacy of the Durack dynasty', *HQ Magazine*, no. 57, March/April 1998, pp. 50–60

Lawe Davies, Chris, 'George Warnecke and the Packers: A dynasty denied', *MIA*, no. 79, February 1996, pp. 95–102

Lee, David, 'Protecting the sterling area: The Chifley government's response to multilateralism, 1945–9', *Australian Journal of Political Science*, vol. 25, 1990, pp. 178–95

Lloyd, Clem, 'An acute contusion: News management in the 1920s', *ASJ*, no. 3, 1994, pp. 136–42

MacDonald, Donald, 'Frank Packer sets sail for the race of his life', *Reader's Digest*, August 1970, pp. 45–51

'The man behind the desk', *Holiday and Travel*, vol. 2, no. 7, July 1949, pp. 20–1, 48

Mandle, W. F., 'Colin Bednall, 1913–1976', *Australian Journal of Communication*, vol. 24, no. 3, 1997, pp. 129–44

Mayer, Henry, 'Two editorials and a modest gift: Sir Frank Packer and the election', in Henry Mayer (ed.), *Labor to Power: Australia's 1972 Election*, Angus & Robertson, Sydney, 1973, pp. 198–200

'Men of the CCC are our shock-workers', *Salt*, vol. 4, no. 2, 24 August 1942, pp. 1–7

Minogue, Dennis, 'Packer's $15 million deal', *New Times*, September 1977, pp. 4–5

Morley, J. A., 'The Allied Works Council', *Rydge's*, 1 November 1942, pp. 668–70

Mr Y (pseud.), 'A Packer plot?', *Australian Quarterly*, vol. 43, no. 2, June 1971, pp. 2–7

Munro, Craig, 'The A&R war: Profits, personalities, and paperbacks', *Publishing Studies*, no. 1, Spring 1995, pp. 21–8

Packer, R. C., 'The Boy Scouts', *Lone Hand*, 2 August 1909, pp. 380–91

Rigley, Tony, 'The Civil Constructional Corps, 1942–1945', *Journal of the Australian War Memorial*, no. 25, October 1994, pp. 5–11

Simonds, Jon, 'The business of winning the cup', *Australian Business*, 24 March 1983, pp. 44–5

Tennison, Max, 'History of the America's Cup', *Prime Time*, October 1986, pp. 12–15

Tiffen, Rodney, 'The Packer-Labor alliance, 1978–95: RIP', *MIA*, no. 77, August 1995, pp. 20–34

Zappalà, Gianni, 'The decline of economic complementarity: Australia and the sterling area', *Australian Economic History Review*, vol. 34, no. 1, March 1994, pp. 5–21

Theses

Bourke, D. A., 'The Department of Information and Censorship in Australia during World War II', B.A. (Hons) thesis, University of Newcastle, 1976

Kent, David S., 'A History of the Australian-American Association', History IV thesis, University of Sydney, 1980

Kerley, Margot, 'Commercial Television in Australia: Government Policy and Regulation, 1953 to 1963', Ph.D. thesis, Australian National University, 1992

Lawe Davies, C. R., 'New Women, New Culture: The *Women's Weekly* and Hollywood in Australia in the Early 1930s', M.Phil. thesis, Griffith University, 1988

Reynolds, Henry, 'The Island Colony. Tasmania: Society and Politics 1880–1900', M.A. thesis, University of Tasmania, 1963

Spring, Edward, 'Don't Go Mining For Truth, Son: Cold War Ideological Perspectives of the Radical Right in Australia Through an Analysis of "The Observer", 1958–1961', B.A. (Hons) thesis, Australian National University, 1975

Video and Audio Tapes

Interviews with Sir Frank Packer for ABC radio, 1 September 1970, 9 August 1971, 5 June 1973

Interview with Sir Frank Packer for *Profiles of Power*, ABC Television, 11 October 1970

Index

A&R *see* Angus & Robertson Ltd (A&R)
AAP *see* Australian Associated Press (AAP)
Abbotsholme College 19–20, 92, 194
Abbott, Captain J. P. 91
ABC *see* Australian Broadcasting Commission (ABC)
ABC Weekly 91
ABCB *see* Australian Broadcasting Control Board (ABCB)
Ackland, Richard 257
ACP *see* Australian Consolidated Press (ACP)
Actors and Announcers' Equity 167
ACTU *see* Australian Council of Trade Unions (ACTU)
Adamson, G. Bartlett 23
Adastra Airways Ltd 58
Adelaide Register 77
Advertiser (Adel) 108, 177
Advertiser Newspapers Ltd 88
Age (Melb) 84, 88, 177, 228, 250
AIF *see* Australian Imperial Force (AIF)
Aisher, Owen 191
Aitken, Sir Max (son of Lord Beaverbrook) 253
AJA *see* Australian Journalists' Association (AJA)
AJC *see* Australian Jockey Club (AJC)
Albert Gold Cup (yachting) 48
Alfred Milson Memorial Cup (yachting) 72
All Saints' Church (Woollahra) 72, 73
Allen, Allen & Hemsley 62, 91, 159, 181, 194
Allen, C. 231
Allen, Dave 258
Allied Works Council (AWC)
  allegations about 109–112, 114, 117
  civilian labour force established *see* Civil Constructional Corps (CCC)
  Dobell paintings 118
  E. G. Theodore appointed as director-general 106–107
  established 106, 107, 108
  FP appointed 106, 123
  industrial conflict 112–113
  inquiry 113, 117
Allman, George Faunce 68
ALP *see* Australian Labor Party (ALP)
A.M. 139, 147
Amalgamated Printing Trades Employees' Union 87
Amalgamated Television Services Pty Ltd 166–167
America (yacht) 188
American-Australian Association 202; *see also* Australian-American Association
America's Cup (yachting) 215, 220, 250
  1962 challenge xvii–xviii, 194–196
  1962 preparations 188–192
  1964 challenge 234
  1967 challenge 234–236
  1970 challenge 236–238, 240–247
  1974 challenge 254
  All States syndicate 236
  America 188
  Australian v British bid 190–191
  Constellation 234
  Dame Pattie 235–237
  Dame Pattie v *Intrepid* 236, 241
  Gretel 199–206, 234–236, 237, 241
  Gretel II
  Gretel II v *France* 241, 242–243
  Gretel II v *Intrepid* 243–247
  Gretel v *Dame Pattie* 234–236
  Gretel v *Weatherly* 203–206
  international elimination match 237–238, 240–243
  Newport and the French 242–243
  Newport and the Kennedys 201–204, 222
  Sovereign 234
  Spectre 189, 191
  Victorian syndicate 234
  Vim 189–190, 192, 196, 200, 201, 202, 204, 235
  Weatherly 202, 203–205
America's Cup Committee 195, 201, 234, 237, 240
Ampol Petroleum Company Ltd 192

Index

ANC *see* Australian Newspapers Conference (ANC)
Anderson, Rev. H. H. 8
Anglican 174, 176, 180, 182
Anglican Press Ltd 176
   fight to acquire printery 180–184
Angus & Robertson Ltd (A&R) 223
   takeover bid by ACP 193–195
   and again 198–200
ANPA *see* Australian Newspaper Proprietors' Association (ANPA)
Ansett, Sir Reginald 216, 237–238
   Universal Telecasters 218–219
Ansett Transport Industries Ltd 216
Anthony, Hubert L. 109
Archibald, J. F. 22
Archibald Prize (art) 118
Argus (Melbourne) 88, 157–158
Arnold, Thomas 8
Arrow 16, 40, 43, 44
Art in Australia (book) 34
Ascham School 66
Ashby, Sylvia 147
Askin, Sir Robert 226, 260, 263
Associated Newspapers Ltd (London) 162, 167, 184
Associated Newspapers Ltd (Sydney) 42–46, 47, 48, 50–52, 53, 55–56, 58, 59–60, 62, 67, 68, 77, 81, 85, 88, 89, 141, 142, 224
   acquires *Daily* and *Sunday Guardians* 42
   R. C. Packer joins 45–46
   negotiations with Sydney Newspapers 56–57
   Consolidated Press takeover of *Telegraph* 73–76
   takeover bid by Consolidated Press 158–160, 161, 171, 172, 173
Associated Press 203
ATN-7 (TV station) 168, 184, 185, 217, 252
atomic bombs (1945) 128
Attlee, Clement 138
Auchincloss, Hugh 203
Austarama Television Pty Ltd 216
Australian 248, 260, 265
Australian-American Association 128, 149–150, 189, 201, 221; *see also* American-Australian Association
Australian America's Cup Challenge Association 189
Australian America's Cup Challenge Committee 189, 192
Australian Associated Press (AAP) 77, 88, 131, 135, 142, 143, 192, 256; *see also* Reuters

Australian Broadcasting Commission (ABC) 165, 167, 186, 247, 249
Australian Broadcasting Control Board (ABCB) 218
   Melbourne/Sydney TV licences 165–167, 168, 216
   Brisbane/Adelaide TV licences 177
   regional TV licences 183–184, 186
Australian Church Press Ltd 180–182
Australian Consolidated Press (ACP) 240, 250, 254, 259
   acquisition of Shakespeare Head Press 193, 194
   America's Cup *see* America's Cup (yachting)
   and Little Golden Books 193
   bid for West Australian Newspapers 234–240
   bid to enter UK publishing 184
   Consolidated Press reborn as ACP 169–170
   corporate coup 228–229
   Everybody's 196
   fight to acquire *Anglican* printery 180–184
   first bid for A&R 193–195
   Frederick Muller (UK) 193
   Harry Chester 252–254, 257, 258
   move into suburban markets 179–184
   move to book publishing 193
   Observer 174–177
   Publishers Holdings 257
   Regional Newspapers 180–184
   sale of *Telegraph* s 252–254, 255–257
   second bid for A&R 197–200
   Suburban Publications 180
   succession 179, 258, 264–265
   supporting the Liberals 196–198, 219, 226–228, 259
   takeover of *Bulletin* 192–193
   Uren case 225–227
Australian Council of Trade Unions (ACTU) 257
Australian Imperial Force (AIF) 16, 26, 93, 103, 106, 108, 111, 117, 123, 125, 132
   Armoured Brigade (1st) 93, 103–105, 106, 125
   Australian Amphibious Armoured Squadron 126
   Landing Craft Company of the Water Transport Section (43rd) 125–126
Australian Jockey Club (AJC) 87, 238
   FP elected to committee 216
Australian Journalists' Association (AJA) 58, 63, 77, 87, 159
   ACP working conditions 229–230
   award and gradings (1967) 231–233
   Blackburn award (1954) 152–153
   Code of Ethics 131, 133
   communism 144

Index

Ethics committee 116
Les Haylen affair 115
Slarke lift incident 154
Australian Labor Party (ALP) 23, 38, 49, 52, 54, 91, 115, 117, 124, 146, 164, 166, 178, 197, 219, 247, 259, 260; *see also* labour movement
   FP's hostility toward 140, 226, 253, 256
   NSW Branch 38–39, 49, 54, 225
   Propaganda Committee 51
Australian Newspaper Proprietors' Association (ANPA) 90, 108, 121, 129, 131, 138, 142
Australian Newspapers Conference (ANC) 82, 88, 233
   FP elected president 88–89
   then resigns 89
   FP bypassed for presidency 142
   reconstituted 138–140
   then elected 143
Australian Newsprint Mills Pty Ltd 86, 127, 130
Australian Star see Sun
Australian Woman's Mirror 61, 193
   merged with *Weekend* 196
Australian Women's Weekly xviii, 64, 67, 68, 71, 73, 75, 83–84, 85, 86, 88, 90, 93, 104, 112, 115, 122, 127, 129, 134, 139, 143, 152, 153, 154, 157, 169, 171, 173, 174, 193, 194, 215, 224, 228, 253, 264
   establishment and launch 60–63
   George Warnecke 60–61, 69–70, 76
   Alice Jackson 74, 83, 104, 118, 133
   Esme Fenston 174, 255
   Les Haylen 91, 115, 117
   Dream Home auction 118, 119
   Ita Buttrose 256
Australian Women's Weekly Club for Servicewomen 118
Australian Workers' Union (AWU) 38, 48, 52, 55, 108, 166
   Labor Papers 54–55, 58, 73
AWC *see* Allied Works Council (AWC)
Awful Australians, The (book)
AWU *see* Australian Workers' Union (AWU)

Baden-Powell, Sir Robert 15, 18
Bagot, E. M. 21
Baillieu, Edwina 202
Baillieu, Peter 202
Baldwin, Harold 45
Ball, Arthur J. 10
Ball, Major Charles 191
Bancks, James 53, 72, 80
Barcs, Dr Emery 252, 255, 256, 259, 263, 265
Barker, B. Deveraux 245, 246
Barnes, Jack 55
Barnes, James 31, 32–33
Barnett, Bill 241
Barwick, Sir Garfield xvii, 139, 175, 237
Basin Cup (yachting) 48
Baudino, Robert 247–249
Baume, Eric 28, 46, 49, 50, 51, 52, 53, 69
   Arrow 43, 44
   Daily Guardian 39, 42
   impressions of R. C. Packer 33
   Referee 43, 45
Baverstock, Bill 189
Baverstock, Dorothy 77
Beach Girl contests 118, 132–133
Beale, Sir Howard xvii, 201, 203
Beasley, Jack 106
Beattie, Justice 232
Beaverbrook, Lord 67, 107, 128, 152, 264
Beazley, Kim, Snr 249
Beckett, W. J. 40
Beckett's Budget 44
Beckett's Newspapers Ltd 40
Bedford, Randolph 23
Bednall, Colin 157, 158, 186, 218, 220
Bellew, Jack W. 77
Benevolent Society of New South Wales 53
Bennett, E. C. 230–231
Bennison, Percy 34
Beresford, Bruce 176
Bernays, Edward L. 36
Bertrand, John 241
Betty (journalist with *AWW*) 174
Bich, Baron Marcel 242–243
Bich, Baroness 243
Binder, Hamlyn and Co. 159
Birbeck, Major-General T. H. 223
Birrell, J. 237
Black and White Artists' Club 87
Black and White Balls 134, 222
Blackburn, A. S. 152
Blake Prize (art) 155
Blakeley, Arthur 108
Blamey, Major-General Sir Thomas 92
Blaxland, Helen 134
Blunden, Godfrey 78, 86
Bode, Joan 173
Bode, Lennox 79, 173, 202
Boer Wars 8
Bolte, Sir Henry 225
Bondi News 179
Bonney, E. G. 109, 121
Boorowa News 34

Index

Boothroyd, Arthur 42, 61
Boral Ltd 240
Boston Herald 204
Bowater Corporation 141, 173
Bowen, Captain Nigel 125
Bowen, Peter 181
Boy Scout movement 15–16, 18, 68
Boy's Own Annual 18, 104
Boy's Own Paper 18
Bradshaw, N. Q. 27, 38, 43, 63, 72, 76, 84
'Breakers, The' (residence) xvii, 203
Brebner, J. H. 129
Bridges, Jack 77
Briscoe, Francis Harriet *see* Hewson, Francis Harriet (Briscoe)
British Empire League 24
British Tobacco Company (Aust) Ltd 192
Broadcasting and Television Act 219, 260
Brown, Phyllis Duncan 60
Brown, Sir Harry 113–114, 117
Browne, Frank 182
Brownell, W. F. 10
Browning, Arthur 136, 222
Bruxner, Lieut-Col. M. F. 52
Buckland, Rev. J. V. 8
Budd, Mrs C. 86
Bulletin 22, 23, 69, 109, 176, 195, 215, 223, 225, 226, 228, 238, 239, 247, 248, 256, 260, 263
  takeover by ACP (1961) 192–193, 194
  and merged with *Observer* 193
  Donald Horne 193, 196–197, 254, 259
Bulletin Newspaper Co. Pty Ltd 192
Bullmore, Caroline 65
Bullmore, Dr Herbert Henry 65, 66, 72
Bullmore, Edward Augustus 65–67
Bullmore, Elfride Henriette Victoria (Büttner) 65, 66, 72
Bullmore, Gretel Joyce *see* Packer, (Lady) Gretel Joyce
Bullmore, Herbert James 66, 118
Bullmore, Joan *see* Henty, Joan (Bullmore)
Bullmore, Mary *see* Hordern, Mary (Bullmore)
Bullmore, Peggy *see* Campbell, Peggy (Bullmore)
Burgess, Sir John 192, 215, 222, 223
Burgoyne, Dudley 252
Burns, Walter V. 193–195, 198, 200
Butters, Sir John 74, 76, 142
Büttner, Elfride Henriette Victoria *see* Bullmore, Elfride Henriette Victoria (Büttner)
Buttrose, Ita 220, 253, 256, 258–259

Cahill, J. J. 150
Cairns, Dr Jim 194–195, 259
Cairnton Ltd 163, 258
'Cairnton' (residence) 80–81, 82, 104, 111, 118, 120, 123, 134, 149, 156, 161, 167, 169, 172, 192, 204, 238, 255, 261
'Calingra' (residence) 66, 72
Calwell, Arthur 115, 117, 121, 124, 125, 127, 145, 194, 197, 198, 216, 219, 225
Cameron, Archie 106, 125
Campbell, Elizabeth 12
Campbell, Eric 49
Campbell, George William 67
Campbell, Harold 177, 178
Campbell, Lorne 129
Campbell, Peggy (Bullmore) 62, 66, 67, 73
Campbell, William T. 12
Canberra Grammar School 120
Canberra Times 156, 264
Carter, Rear-Admiral C. Bonham 191
Casey, Lady Maie 223, 237
Casey, Lord 146, 202, 223, 237
Casey, R. G. *see* Casey, Lord
Cassell Australia (publishing company) 250
Cassidy, Lady 173
Cassidy, Sir Jack 113, 169, 173, 222
Catholic Leader (Brisb) 106
Catholic Weekly 175
Caulfield Cup (horse racing) 136
CCC *see* Civil Constructional Corps (CCC)
censorship 91, 121–123, 124–125, 175, 176
  Code of Censorship Principles 123, 126
Cervantes (racehorse) 136
Chancegger (yacht) 242, 243
Chancellor, Christopher 158
Channel 10 *see* O-10 (TV station)
Channel 7 (TV station)
  Melbourne *see* HSV-7 (TV station)
  Sydney *see* ATN-7 (TV station)
Channel 9 (TV station)
  Melbourne *see* GTV-9
  Sydney *see* TCN-9 (TV station)
Chapman, George 260
'Charlie Chuckle' (comic) 88
Charters Towers 13
Chastellux Manor 242
Chester, H. W. B. ('Harry') 252–253, 257, 258
Chifley, J. B. ('Ben') 138, 139, 141, 144, 145
Christensen, Emil 234
Chucklers' Weekly 163
Church of England Property Trust 165
Churchill, Sir Winston 107
Citizen Military Force 109

Index

City of Sydney (freighter) 201
Civil Constructional Corps (CCC) 112, 114, 123, 131; *see also* Allied Works Council (AWC)
   established 107
   controlled by FP 108
   criticism of FP 108
   allegations about 109–111, 114, 117
   achievements 117
   release of FP 117
   Dobell paintings 118
Clarke, Dodd S. 13
Cleo 258–259, 264
Clyde, Captain John 7, 10
Clyde, Margaret Fitzmaurice *see* Packer, Margaret Fitzmaurice (Clyde)
Coalition (Liberal and Country Party) 144, 197, 219
Cockburn, Bruce 29
Code of Censorship Principles 123, 126
Code of Ethics (AJA) 131, 133
Cody, Patrick 71
Coffs Harbour Advocate 12
Cole, Peter 241
Coleman, H. G. 229
Coleman, Peter 176, 192, 194, 223–224
Collins, Ian 199
Columnist (racehorse) 136, 137
Come in Spinner (book) 148, 167
Commonwealth Press Union 144, 173–174; *see also* Imperial Press Conferences
   FP elected honorary treasurer 151
Commonwealth Prime Ministers' Conference 205
communism 117, 140, 260
Communist Party of Australia 144, 196
Companies Amendment (Preference Shareholders) Bill (1932) 51–53
Conelan, William P. 127
Connolly, Roy 42
Connolly, Sybil 173, 174–175, 179
Conpress Printing Ltd 129, 142, 149, 164, 193, 196
Consolidated Press Holdings Ltd 164, 175, 194, 218, 258
   FP split with John Theodore and reorganisation 164, 168–170
   bid for representation on A&R board 198–199
   corporate coup 228–229
   Harry Chester 252–254, 257, 258
Consolidated Press Ltd 89, 90, 91, 103, 106, 114, 118, 120, 123, 126, 127, 129, 132, 142, 144, 145, 146, 147, 150, 151, 152, 156, 168, 173, 190
   establishment 76–77
   renamed *see* Australian Consolidated Press (ACP)
   corporate restructuring 163–164
   Junior Telegraph 163
   Weekend 162–163
   Margaret Hughes 161–162
   libel writ against John Fairfax 160–161
   takeover bid for Associated Newspapers 158–160, 161
   bid for interstate markets 157–158
   Kerry Packer joins 156
   communism 144
   conversion to public company 141
   changes to tax laws 141, 147, 163
   A.M. 139
   Conpress Printing Ltd 129
   industrial action *see* industrial action
   police controversy 115–116
   Les Haylen 115
   manpower regulations *see* manpower regulations
   censorship *see* censorship
   PIEUA *see* Printing Industry Employees' Union of Australia (PIEUA)
   joins AAP 88
   newsprint *see* newsprint
   Sunday Telegraph see Sunday Telegraph
   Fashion 86
   proposed *Evening Telegraph* 85–86, 88
   Norman Q. Bradshaw 84–85
   E. G. Theodore 84
   Keith Murdoch bid 84
   George Warnecke 83–84
   Daily Telegraph see Daily Telegraph
   Australian Journalists' Association *see* Australian Journalists' Association (AJA)
Constellation (yacht) 234
Cope, James F. 178
Copland, Douglas Sir 131
Coral Sea battle, commemoration of 149
Cornell, John 258
Coronation Medal 148
Costa, Sir Michael 6
Costello, Patrick 61
Countess of Dudley Cup (polo) 72
Country Party 49, 52, 82, 91, 106, 109, 125, 132, 140, 145, 147, 178, 186, 219, 227; *see also* Coalition (Liberal and Country Party)
Country Women's Association 66, 73
Courier see Courier-Mail (Brisb)
Courier-Mail (Brisb) 157, 158
Coward, Sir Noël 93
Cowper, Sir Norman 91, 194–195, 198–200

Index

Cowra breakout 124–125, 126
Cox, Harry 77
Craigmyle, Lord 190, 191
Cranbrook School 120, 155
Crawford, Robert Wigram 221
Croce, Dr Beppe 240
Cross, Stan 23
Crowd 175
Croyston, John 176
Crucis (racehorse) 32
Cruise, Peter 111, 112, 136
Cruising Yacht Club 236
Cumberland Hotel (London) 68
Cumberland Newspapers Pty Ltd 180, 183
Current Affair, A (TV program) 257–258, 259, 260–261
Curtin, John 106, 108, 109, 110, 112, 115, 117, 121, 124, 126, 140, 146
Cusack, Dymphna 148

Daily Express (London) 77
Daily Guardian 45, 63, 74, 90, 166, 224, 264
  launched 26–28
  Claude McKay 26–29, 39–41
  financial crises 28, 30, 31
  sensationalism 28–29
  George Warnecke 33, 38–39, 40, 41
  style and content 34
  Miss Australia quest 34–37
  FP employed 38
  Voltaire Molesworth 38–40, 41, 43, 44, 45
  Eric Baume 39, 43
  Adam McCay 39–40
  sale to Associated Newspapers 42–43, 44
  merged with *Daily Telegraph News Pictorial see Daily Telegraph*
Daily Mail (Brisb) 71
Daily Mail (Sydney) 26, 28, 42, 178
Daily Mirror (London) 128, 241
Daily Mirror (Sydney) 89, 111, 112, 113, 127, 171, 179, 182, 235
Daily Mirror Newspapers Ltd (London) 157–158
Daily News (Perth) 240
Daily News (Sydney) 33, 93, 123, 145; *see also Labor Daily*
Daily Telegraph 26, 28, 33, 41, 44, 49, 50, 51, 57, 74, 81, 110, 113, 124, 140, 145, 147, 148, 149, 154, 157, 158, 160–161, 171, 172, 176, 177, 178–179, 194, 197, 200, 205, 216, 219, 220, 224, 225, 227, 238, 239, 240, 247–248, 252, 258, 262, 263
  recreated in 1931 44
  rename and revival in 1936 76–78
  S. H. Deamer 77, 82, 85
  C. S. McNulty 77, 85, 103, 115–116, 121, 126, 129
  modernity 82, 89
  circulation 82–83
  Monday Home Magazine 83
  profitability 84
  Brian Penton *see* Penton, Brian
  feud between FP and Ezra Norton 86–87, 111–112, 179
  newsprint *see* newsprint
  censorship *see* censorship
  manpower regulations *see* manpower regulations
  industrial action *see* industrial action
  David McNicoll
  Donald Horne 132–134
  anti-communism 144
  death of Stalin 151–152, 264
  Clyde Packer joins 156
  sports and competitions 215
  working conditions 228–229
  sale of 253, 255–256, 257
Daily Telegraph News Pictorial 42, 74
  merged with *Daily Guardian see Daily Telegraph*
Daily Telegraph Polo Cup 215
'Daingeen' (residence) 80
Dairy Farmers' Co-operative Milk Co. 200
Daly, Fred 218
Daly, Lieutenant-General Sir Thomas 248
Dame Pattie (yacht) 234
Darcy, J. 130
Darling, Sir James 165, 166
David Jones (department store) 83, 118, 172, 221
Davidson, C. W. 184
Davies, J. B. 240
Davies, Wynne W. ('Bill') 37, 77
Davis, Phil 259
Dawes, Allan 77
de Gaulle, Charles 221
de L'Isle, Lord (governor general) 200
Deamer, Sydney H. 77, 82, 85
Dedman, J. J. 130
Deer, Lewis 41, 43
Dekyvere, Nola 134
Democratic Labor Party (DLP) 260
Denison, Leslie 50, 68, 88
Denison, Reginald 50, 56, 61, 62, 68, 88
Denison, Sir Hugh 16, 22, 26, 42, 44–45, 46, 50–51, 55–58, 68, 74, 75, 76, 88, 93
Denison, Sir William 4
Department of Customs (Tasmania) 7

Index

Department of Defence 247
Department of External Affairs 201, 203, 249
Department of Information 90
Department of Labour and National Service 110
Department of Trade and Customs 104, 203
Desmond, Valerie 40
Devil to Pay, The (film) 176
Dewar, Lord 32
Dick, Harold 111
Dickens (racehorse) 136
Dickson, Richard A. 188, 189, 190–191, 195
Dillon, Douglas xvii
DLP *see* Democratic Labor Party (DLP)
Dobell, Sir William 89, 118, 155, 200
Donald, Jim 29, 40
Doncaster Handicap (horse racing) 215
Dorchester Hotel (London) 68
Double Bay Courier 179
Dougherty, Tom 166
Doutreband, Roy 81
Dowsett, W. J. P. ('Bill') 61, 72, 76, 141, 164
Dream Home auction 118, 119
Dubbo Dispatch 12
Dubbo Liberal 11–12
Duke of Edinburgh *see* Prince Philip, Duke of Edinburgh
Dumas, Sir Lloyd 88, 108, 113, 127, 130, 138–139, 142, 143, 145, 157, 177, 222
Dunne, Frank 23
Dupain, Max 134
Dutton, Geoffrey 223

East, Frederick Llewellyn 76
Eichelberger, General Robert 149
Electronic Industries Pty Ltd 185
Ellis, M. H. 223–224
Eltham College 20
Emperor Gold Mining Co. 71
Emperor Mines Ltd 71, 169
Empire Free Trade crusade 128
Empire Press Union *see* Commonwealth Press Union
English Civil War 1
Epsom Handicap (horse racing) 136
Evatt, Dr H. V. 84, 91, 110, 121, 123, 126, 139, 150, 165, 166, 167
Evatt, Justice Elizabeth 17
Evening News (London) 184
Evening News (Sydney) 26, 28, 42, 44, 75
Evening Telegraph 85–86, 88
Everybody's 196, 223
Ewing, Ken 125

Fadden, Sir Arthur 89, 106, 147–148, 150, 163
Faircloth, Kathleen Maisie ('Fairy') 78, 85, 164, 187, 221, 224, 256, 259, 263, 265
Fairfax & Roberts (jewellers) 62, 71
Fairfax, Bart 71
Fairfax company *see* John Fairfax & Sons Pty Ltd
Fairfax Cup (yachting) 48
Fairfax, James Oswald 180
Fairfax, Sir Vincent 142, 264
Fairfax, Sir Warwick 161, 166, 219, 228, 254, 264
Falk, Lee 143
Falstein, Max 117, 130
Family Circle 85
Farnsworth, Bill 193
Fashion 86
Federated Clerks' Union 112–113
Federated Ironworkers' Association 140
Fenston, Esmé 174, 255
Ferguson, George 193–195, 198; *see also* Angus & Robertson Ltd (A&R)
Ferguson, J. A. 52
Fesq, W. L. 241, 243
Ficker, Bill 245, 246
Fielding, Leslie T. 170, 198
Finey, George 23, 24, 26, 77
First World War 16, 20, 31, 63, 92, 106, 136, 221
Fisher, Dr Geoffrey 148
Fisher, Eric 257
Fitzgerald, James 124
Fitzgerald, Tom 176
FitzMaurice, Captain J. 19
F. J. Jackson Cup (yachting) 67
Flahvin, Jim 255
Fleet Street (London) 23, 28, 33, 152, 162
Foll, H. S. 91
Follett, Evelyn Mary 54, 69
Follett, Frank William 54, 58
Ford, Henry 238
Forde, Frank 107
Forum 258, 260
Foulis, Mr (partner, Fijian mines) 70
Four Corners (TV program) 257
Foy, Count 222
France (yacht) 242–243
Fraser, Malcolm 247–248
Frederick Muller Ltd (UK) 193
French, Howard 162

Game, Sir Philip 52
Garden Island (naval base) 117
Garland, Isobel 80
Garland, John 80

Index

Geelong Grammar School 155–156, 165, 180
Gell, Jack 27, 77
Gellert, Leon 23
General Television Pty Ltd 185–186, 258; see also GTV-9
George Patterson agency 193
Georges, George 245
Gibbs, May 72
Gibson, Mike 216
Gietzelt, Arthur 260, 265
Gilburt, Mabel 85, 265
Gill, H. H. 9
Glencross, Sydney Charles 76
Globe 15
Gordon, Sir R. H. 45
Gorton Experiment, The (book) 249–250
Gorton, Sir John 241, 259
   succeeds Holt as PM 227–228
   fights off McMahon leadership challenge 238–239
   then loses 247–248
   and resigns from cabinet 248–250, 256
Gow, Augusta *see* Packer, Augusta (Gow)
Gow, Nathaniel 4
Gow, Niel 3
Granites, The 53–54
Graves, Cliff 23
Gray, Richard William 111
Grayndler, Ted 55
Great Depression 44, 47, 115
'Greenoaks' (residence) 80
Greer, Dr Germaine 258
Gretel (yacht) xviii, 199–205, 234–236, 237, 241
Gretel II (yacht) 241–246
Griffin, Susannah *see* Packer, Susannah (Griffin)
Grigg, N. W. 115
Grover, Montague 23, 54
Gruzman, Laurence 198
GTV-9 185–186, 192, 216–218, 224, 229, 239, 257–258
Gunn, Bill 238
Gyngell, Ann 192
Gyngell, Bruce 167, 170, 187, 192

Hadley, James W. 126
Hall, Eileen Orford 66
Hall, Ken G. 54, 170, 176
Halliday, Sir George 173
Halliday, (Lady) June 173
Halvorsen, Trygve 235
Hamilton, Vera 42
Hammond, Terry 203, 204

Hancock, Ian 227
Hansen-Rubensohn agency 146
Hardie, J. M. 48
Hardy, Frank 71
Hardy, Charles 49, 72
Hardy, Sir James 241, 242, 243–246
Hargrave, Lawrence 17, 53
Harrex, George T. 12
Harrison, Sir Eric 89, 91, 104, 108
Hartley-Russell family 1
Hartt, Cecil 23
Hasluck, Sir Paul 228
Hastings, Peter 163, 196
Hawke, Bob 257–258
Haylen, Les 91, 115, 117, 180, 194, 216
Hearst, William Randolph 34, 36, 77
Henderson, R. A. G. 89, 93, 114, 121, 123, 127, 130–131, 141, 142, 158–159, 161, 166, 175, 180, 185–186, 197, 219, 228, 255
   AAP-Reuters agreement 131
Henty, Denham 189
Henty, Douglas 67, 72, 80
Henty, Joan (Bullmore) 66, 67, 72, 80
Henty, Robert 167, 196
Herald & Weekly Times (HWT) 53, 74, 76, 77, 86, 89, 139, 142, 157, 158, 169, 185, 228, 231, 240, 255
Herald (Melb) 77, 78, 88, 160, 178, 215, 228, 250
Herbert, Sir Alan 174
Here's Luck (book) 61
Hewson, Ethel Maude *see* Packer, Ethel Maude
Hewson, Francis Harriet (Briscoe) 10, 29
Hewson, Gerald 59
Hewson, Rev. Frank 10–11, 29, 270
Higgins, J. F. 52, 54
Hill, Ernestine 53
Hill, Nora 29, 35, 41, 49, 60, 69, 73, 77
Hills, Pat 260, 261
Hiroshima 128
Hobart High School 7
Hobart Mercury 6, 9
Hoff, Raynor 34
Hogan, Paul 257, 258
Holden, Captain L. H. 43
Holman, William 24, 80
Holt, Harold xvii, 20, 227, 238, 249
Home 34, 67, 132, 141, 145
Hone, Brian 155
Hood, Warwick 234
Hopkins, Thomas G. 63
Hordern Brothers (company) 136
Hordern, Anthony 67, 72, 80, 118, 193, 194

Index

Hordern, Mary (Bullmore) 66, 67, 73, 80, 89, 111, 118, 120, 133
Hordern, Samuel 111
Horne, Donald 173, 175, 226, 247, 252, 253, 256, 257, 264
   Daily Telegraph 132–133
   Weekend 162–163, 175–176, 182
   Pictorial 171–172
   Observer 175–176, 180, 183
   Bulletin 193, 196–197, 254, 259
   Everybody's 196, 197
Hotel Australia
   Sydney 81, 107, 141, 162, 199, 231
   Melbourne 162
Howard, W. S. ('Stewart') 112–114
Howson, Peter 238, 239, 247, 248, 249
Hoyt, Norris 206
HSV-7 (TV station) 185, 186
Hughes, Margaret 161
Hughes, Richard 78, 87
Hughes, Robert 176
Hughes, W. M. 23
Hulme, Sir Albert 219
Humphries, Barry 176
Hurstville Propeller 179
Hutchins, Rev. William 7
Hutchins School 7–9, 15
HWT *see* Herald & Weekly Times (HWT)

Ian Potter & Co. 185
Illingworth, Captain John 190
Imperial Press Conferences 113, 142, 144; *see also* Commonwealth Press Union
In Melbourne Tonight (TV program) 185
Incentive 238
Income Tax Assessment Act 141
industrial action
   strike (1944) 127
   PIEUA log of claims (1947) 131
   death of Stalin poster 151–152, 264
   Blackburn award (1954) 152–153
   Slarke lift incident 154
   ACP working conditions 228–229
   PIEUA pay increase (1967) 230–231
   AJA award and downgradings (1967) 231–233
   PKIU joins fray 232–233
Ingate, Gordon 235
Ingleburn (army camp) 104
Inglis, K. S. 184
Inglis, Tony 170
Inheritors (book) 90
International News Service 77, 143

International Race and Protest Committee 240–241, 242, 243
International Yacht Racing Union 242, 244
Intrepid (yacht) 236, 241, 243, 244–247
Irvine, Abraham 12

J. Walter Thompson agency 60, 62, 83
jackeroos 31–32
Jackson, Alice 74, 83, 104, 118, 133
Jackson, Wain and Co. 223, 226
James, Florence 148
James, Francis 174, 176
   fight to acquire *Anglican* printery 180–183
Jenner, Dorothy ('Andrea') 81
John Fairfax & Sons Pty Ltd 77, 82, 86, 89, 122, 127, 130, 139, 142, 158–160, 166–167, 168, 175, 177, 179, 180, 183, 217, 219, 224, 228, 230–231, 252, 264; *see also Sydney Morning Herald (SMH)*
   libel writ from Consolidated Press 160–161
   support for ALP 197
John Muston Memorial Cup (yachting) 72
Johnson & Johnson (Aust) 188
Johnson, John William 111
Johnson, L. B. 225
Johnson, Wilfred E. 45
Joint Cargo Services 241
Jones, H. Campbell 44–46, 68
Jones, (Lady) Hannah Lloyd 148, 155
Jones, Phil 255
Jones, Sir Charles Lloyd 172
Jonsson, Joe 23, 25
Journalist (racehorse) 136
Judd, Tom 155
Junior Mirror (London) 163
Junior Telegraph (Sydney) 163, 164

Kahn, Otto 237
Kane, Jack 260
Keane, Richard 130
Keeffe, J. B. 243
Kelly, J. O. 72
Kennedy, Eric 72, 122, 123, 124, 141, 142
Kennedy, Graham 185, 224–225
Kennedy, Jacqueline xvii, 203–204
Kennedy, John F. xvii, 203–204
Kennedy, Robert ('Buzz') 176, 178, 179, 253
Kennedy, Trevor 259
Kennelly, J. P. 177
Kenny, J. D. 232
Kessell, Norman 144
'Kilquade House' 10

Index

King Charles I 1, 2
King Features Syndicate 143
King Henry I 2
King Henry II 2
King, Cecil H. 157, 159, 238
King, R. A. 165
Kinkaid, Admiral Thomas 149
'Kismet' (residence) 72, 73, 80
Kitto, John Reginald 226, 252
Klugman, Dr R. E. 245
knighthood 178, 219, 253, 254
Knowles, Sir George 110
Knox, Errol G. 15, 18, 23, 26, 28, 88, 108

Labor Daily 27, 39, 42, 51, 54, 74, 123; *see also Daily News* (Sydney)
Labor Papers Ltd 54–56, 58, 73
labour movement 54
Landtakers (book) 90
Lang, J. T. 27, 38–39, 48, 49, 51–53, 54, 62, 82, 91, 106
Langley, Archdeacon W. Leslie 72
Larkins, Antony 166, 172, 177, 226
Lars Halverson and Sons Pty Ltd 192, 200
Latham, Sir John 91
Lever Bros agency 81
Liberal and Country Party Coalition *see* Coalition (Liberal and Country Party)
Liberal Party 124, 140, 146, 169, 178, 197, 219, 223, 226–228; *see also* Coalition (Liberal and Country Party)
  McMahon v Gorton for PM - pt1 227
  McMahon v Gorton - pt2 238–239
  finale 247–249
Lindemans (winemaker) 203
Literature Board of Review (Qld) 175
Little Golden Books 193
Llewellyn, Ernie 149
Loane, Dr Marcus 264
Lone Hand 15
Long, Sidney 34
Lorimer, George Horace 36
Louat, Dr Frank 91, 131
Lower, Lennie 61, 78, 93
Lyle, Sheila 118, 134, 200
Lyons, Joseph 82, 105

MacAlpine, Eamon W 77, 126, 139
Macarthur, John 200
Macarthur-Onslow, Major-General Sir Denzil 200, 261
Macarthur-Onslow, R. W. 238

MacBride, Lou 124, 152
MacCormick, Sir Alexander 48
MacDonald, Alexander 153
Macdonell House 54, 55, 73
Macdougall, Jim 160
MacKay, William J. 115
MacLeod, James D. 53, 72, 172, 215, 222
Macquarie radio network 166
Madigan, Dr C. T. 53–54
Mahony, Will 61
Maloja 68
'Mandrake the Magician' 143
Manpower Local Appeal Board 116
manpower regulations 108, 116–118
Mansell, Horace 121, 122, 124
Marien, Frank 41, 42, 44
Marshall, Eric 115
Martens, George W. 116
Martin, L. K. ('Keith') 143, 164, 170, 177, 189, 192, 198, 230
Marton Hall 162
Matthews, Captain John 189
Maude, Angus 177, 197
Maxwell, Eric 236
Mayer, Professor Henry 91, 260
Mayo Clinic (US) 186
Maze, Sir Frederick 67
Maze, Lady 67
McCall, William 91
McCay, Adam 17, 88
  Daily Guardian 39–41
McCay, Delamore 88
McClelland, Douglas 260
McClelland, James 218
McClorghy, (Commissioner) 229
McCracken, Inez 119
McCrae, Miss (friend of Ethel Packer) 10, 11
McEwen, John 189, 227, 239
McFadyen, Beryl 173
McFadyen, Lionel 173, 263
McFadyen, Ralph 53, 65, 72
McIndoe, John 9
McIntosh, Hugh D. 16, 24, 40
McIntyre, M. W. ('Bunty') 122
McKay, Claude 16, 52, 93
  Smith's Weekly 21–25, 40–41
  Daily Guardian 27–29
  Miss Australia quest 34–37
McKell, W. J. 112
McKeon, Justice 231
McLachlan, Angus 228, 230–231
McMahon, (Lady) Sonia 254, 255

Index

McMahon, Maisie 65, 76, 130, 265
McMahon, Sir William 20, 194, 244, 247, 255
   relationship with FP 194, 227, 249–250, 259
   loses leadership to Gorton 227
   challenges again 239
   wins 247–248
   seeks Gorton's resignation 250
McNamara, Robert xvii
McNicoll, David 132, 152–153, 161, 168–169, 173, 176, 179, 185, 187, 223, 227, 233, 238, 239, 248, 253, 254, 256, 259, 261, 262, 263
McNicoll, Jean ('Micky') 161, 173
McNicoll, Penelope 161
McNulty, C. S. 77, 85, 103, 115, 121, 126, 129, 174
McPhee sisters 172
McShane, F. D. 77
Mead, Tom 149, 178, 179, 183
Meet the Press (TV program) 247–248
Melbourne Cup (horse racing) 66, 81
Mellor, Syd 61
Menzies, Sir Robert 90, 91, 105, 106, 114, 124, 139, 140, 144, 165, 183, 186, 224, 228, 249, 251
   relationship with FP 114, 176–179, 177, 197, 219–220, 227, 249, 254, 261, 263
   America's Cup 189, 195, 197, 200, 205, 235
Menzies, Dame Pattie 200, 234, 261
Menzies, Heather 148
Mercer, Henry 205
Messel, Prof Harry 149, 156
Micklem, Rev. Dr P. A. 68
Millar, F. W. 181, 182
Miller, C. H. K. 130
Miller, Forbes 144
Miller, Syd 23
Mills, Beryl 34–37
'Milton Park' (residence) 81
Miners' Federation 39
Minns, B. E. 34
Mirror Newspapers Ltd 180
Miss America quest 34, 35
Miss Australia quest 34–37
Molesworth, Voltaire
   Daily Guardian 38–45
   Turf Life 64
Money, Angela *see* Packer, Angela
Moore, Andrew 49
Moore, Justice 233
Morgan, Harry S. 201, 202, 234
Morley, Joe 118
Morna (yacht) 48, 49, 59, 67, 72
Morton, Harry 70
Mosbacher, Emil ('Bus') 204, 205
Moscheles, Ignaz 6
Moses, R. J. H. 15, 18, 23, 77
Moyes, Bishop J. S. 180–182
Moylan, Fred 237
Moynihan, Rt Hon. Tony 160
Murdoch, Dame Elisabeth 158
Murdoch, Rupert 158, 171, 180–183, 184, 218, 228, 233, 235, 254, 260
   buys the *Telegraph* s 255
Murdoch, Sir Keith 74, 84, 88, 113, 124, 127, 128, 129, 131, 138–139, 142–145, 157–158, 180, 190, 224
Murphy, Lionel 226
Murphy, Thomas P. 219
Murray, K. G. 256
Mutch, Thomas 38
Myers, Justice 159

Nation Review 251
Nation 176, 180, 184, 195, 225
National Advocate (Bathurst) 140
National Security Regulations 139
National Union of Journalists (UK) 184
Nationalist Party 23
NBN-3 (TV station) 217
New Broken Hill Consolidated Ltd 124
New Guard 49
New Idea 61
'New Journalism' 14, 68
New York Star (freighter) 241
New York Times 36
New York Yacht Club (NYYC) 188
   America's Cup *see* America's Cup (yachting)
New Zealand Press Association 131
Newcastle Sun 42
Newman, Robert 31, 33
News (Adel) 158
News (strike newspaper) 127
News Ltd 158, 171, 180, 218, 228, 230, 250, 256
   acquisition of *Telegraph* s 255–256
Newspaper News 45, 46, 55, 72, 131
newsprint *see also* Australian Newsprint Mills Pty Ltd
   levy on importation 86
   rationing 87, 89, 104, 118, 127, 129, 130, 138–141
Newton, Maxwell 238
Nicholas, Mr (chief of staff, *Smith's Weekly*) 27
Nixon, Richard 149, 254
Norn Cup (yachting) 67
Northam, William H. 188, 189, 191
Northcliffe, Lord 28, 34, 68, 74, 106

Index

Northern Challenge Polo Cup 72
Norton, Ezra 74, 86, 87, 89, 113, 116, 123, 127, 166, 175
  feud with FP 86–87, 111, 179, 182
Nott, Dr L. W. 91
Noverraz, Louis 243
NSW Amateur Boxing and Wrestling Association 105
NSW Industrial Commission 230, 232
NSW Polo Association 72
NSW Trades and Labor Council 115, 165, 167, 232
NSW War Loan and Savings Committee 93
Nuclear Research Foundation 149–151, 156, 187
'Nutcrackers' (polo team) 72
Nutt, Ernie 111
NYYC *see* New York Yacht Club (NYYC)

O-10 (TV station) 237
O'Brien, Justin 155
Observer 175–177, 179, 180, 183
  merged with *Bulletin* (1961) 193
Ochs, Adolph S. 36
O'Connell Pty Ltd 179
O'Day, George 204
O'Dea, Raymond 231
O'Donnell (employee of FP) 79
Oliver, C. T. 166
Olympic Games (1956) 168
Orama (ship) 73
Oran Pty Ltd 71
Osborne, Major-General the Rev. C. A. 165

Packer, Amelia (Sandys) 3
Packer, Angela 195
Packer, Arthur Howard (1851-1912) 1, 6
Packer, Arthur Patrick Wellesley (born 1883) 7, 69
Packer, Augusta (Gow) 3–6
Packer, Charles Jnr (1786-1854) 3–4
Packer, Charles Snr (born c.1747-1808) 2
Packer, Charles Stuart Sandys 3
Packer, Sir Douglas Frank Hewson ('Frank') (1906-1974)
  AIF 16, 26, 93, 103, 106, 108, 111, 117, 123, 125, 132
  Allied Works Council *see* Allied Works Council (AWC)
  America's Cup *see* America's Cup (yachting)
  ancestry 1–13
  Armoured Brigade (1st) 93, 104, 106, 125
  art 88, 118
  attitude to
    apartheid 225
    capital punishment 225
    civil rights movement 225
    communism 140
    homosexuality 224
  Australian Amphibious Armoured Squadron 126
  Australian-American Association *see* Australian-American Association
  Australian Consolidated Press *see* Australian Consolidated Press (ACP)
  birth 12
  'Cairnton' *see* 'Cairnton' (residence)
  CBE award 147, 166
  Civil Construction Corps *see* Civil Constructional Corps (CCC)
  Conpress Printing *see* Conpress Printing Ltd
  Consolidated Press Holdings *see* Consolidated Press Holdings Ltd
  Consolidated Press *see* Consolidated Press Ltd
  Coronation Medal 148
  courtship of Gretel Bullmore 65, 67
  customs imbroglios 130
  Daily Guardian see Daily Guardian
  Daily Telegraph see Daily Telegraph
  death 263
  editorial interventions 151, 257–261
  education 19–21
  elected to AJC 215
  estate 265
  eyesight deteriorates 175, 192, 221
  family holidays 25–26
  family life compared with father 135–136
  Fijian gold mines 70–71, 169, 201
  honorary treasurer of Commonwealth Press Union 151
  GTV-9 *see* GTV-9
  health declines 255
  hostility to Labor 140, 225, 253, 257
  impressions of 26
  jackerooing 31–33
  KBE 249, 253
  knighthood 178, 219, 253
  Landing Craft Company of the Water Transport Section (43rd) 125
  loyalty 115, 129, 233
  marriage 72
  militia 92
  obituaries and funeral 263
  Order of St John 216
  physical appearance 26, 129
  playing politics 90–91, 115, 124, 227
  polo and other sports 72–73, 215–216
  Project 2000 appeal 216

Index

pugilism 41–42, 105
punting - the horses 136–137, 169
relationship with E.G. Theodore 61, 63, 70, 143
relationship with sons 179
relationship with Warnecke 26, 60, 70, 73, 76, 84
romantic liaisons 119, 173–175, 179, 220
sale of *Telegraph* s 253–257
Sir Frank: the Frank Packer Story 250
split with John Theodore and reorganisation 168–170
succession 179, 258, 264
Sunday Telegraph see Sunday Telegraph
supporting the Liberals xviii, 197, 219, 226–228, 259
TCN-9 *see* TCN-9 (TV station)
Television Corporation *see* Television Corporation Ltd
temperament xviii, 64, 152, 153–154, 174, 224, 233
youth 18–19
Packer, Ethel Maude 31, 32, 35, 36, 42, 59, 67, 73, 80
 background 10–11
 birth of Frank 12
 birth of Kathleen 17
 family life and holidays 17–19, 25–26
 marriage to RC Packer 11
 trip to Ireland 29
 death of Clyde 68
 own death 135
Packer, (Lady) Florence Adeline (Porgés) (FP's second wife) 202, 223, 241, 243, 258, 261
 background 221–222
 marriage to FP 222
Packer, Sir Frank *see* Packer, Sir Douglas Frank Hewson ('Frank') (1906-1974)
Packer, Frederick Alexander (1814-1862) 3, 4–6
Packer, (Lady) Gretel Joyce xviii, 68, 73, 77, 123, 143, 144, 147, 149, 152, 156, 164, 167, 172, 174, 183, 192, 222
 background 65–67
 courtship by FP and marriage 65, 67, 72
 fashion 66, 86, 133
 birth of Clyde 73
 birth of Kerry 80
 Cairnton *see* 'Cairnton' (residence)
 social calendar 80–81, 134
 art 89, 118
 'Lady' Packer 178
 illness and death 175, 186–187, 192, 220
 Gretel and *Gretel II see* America's Cup (yachting)
Packer, Harry Effingham 6

Packer, John (born c. 1784) 2
Packer, John (no relation) 1
Packer, John Edward 6
Packer, John Stewart ('Jack') 7, 136
Packer, Kathleen Mary *see* Stening, (Lady) Kathleen Mary (Packer) (FP's sister)
Packer, Kerry Francis Bullmore (FP's son) 80, 173, 178, 182, 215, 221, 253, 255, 257
 birth (1937) 80
 Gretel Packer 118
 'Nanny Packer' 119
 school years 120, 155–156
 starts working for Consolidated Press 156, 196
 relationship with FP 179
 marriage to Rosalind Weedon 218
 Cleo 258
 succession 179, 258, 264
Packer, Margaret Fitzmaurice (Clyde) 7, 19
Packer, Robert Clyde (Clyde) (1879-1934) (FP's father) xviii, 1, 74, 88, 90, 116, 135, 224, 265
 birth 7
 Boy Scout movement 15
 Daily Guardian see Daily Guardian
 death and funeral 67–68
 education 7–9
 estate 69
 family holidays 25
 family life 17, 135
 health declines 67
 hostility towards J.T.Lang 49
 marriage to Ethel Hewson 11
 relationship with E.G. Theodore 48–49
 Seventh War Loan campaign 21
 Smith's Newspapers see Smith's Newspapers
 Smith's Weekly see Smith's Weekly
 Sunday Guardian see Sunday Guardian
 Sydney Newspapers *see* Sydney Newspapers Ltd
 upward mobility 37
 Victorian Publishing Company 41
Packer, Robert Clyde (Clyde) (FP's son) 81
 birth (1935) 73
 'Nanny Packer' 119
 school years 119, 155–156
 begins working at *Canberra Times* 156
 moves to *Daily Telegraph* 156
 Pictorial 171
 ACP subsidiary publications 176
 Daily Mail (London) 178
 relationship with FP 179, 263
 fight for *Anglican* printery 180–183
 marriage to Angela Money 195
 elected to NSW Legislative Council 219

Index

rift with FP 257–257
A Current Affair 257
the Willesee affair 257–258
succession 179, 258, 264
a new life 258, 265
Packer, Robert Kerr 6
Packer, Rosalind (Weedon) 218
Packer, Susannah (Griffin) 2
Pactolus Investments Pty Ltd 164
Paramount Film Services 167
Paton, Jack G. 77
Payne, Alan 192, 195, 200, 201–205, 234, 237–237, 241–246
Pearl Dust (racehorse) 33
Pearl Harbor 106
Pearl Necklace (yacht) 244, 246
Pearl, Cyril 78, 87, 90, 91, 118, 122, 128, 143, 147, 148, 167, 178, 223, 225, 250
Penfolds (winemaker) xvii, 203
Penton, Brian 85, 90–92, 104, 106, 115–118, 121, 122–128, 129, 131, 133, 140, 143, 145, 148, 151, 167, 223
Penton, Olga 116
Peregrine (ship) 13
Perry, Jim 192
Pétain, Marshal 221
Pictorial Show 171
Pictorial 171, 175
Pidgeon, Bill ('WEP') 42, 60, 61, 77
PIEUA *see* Printing Industry Employees' Union of Australia (PIEUA)
Pile, Claire 119
Pioneer Shipping Line 196
Pitt Son & Badgery Ltd 53
PKIU *see* Printing and Kindred Industries Union (previously PIEUA)
'Platypus Lodge' (property) 141, 148
Playford, Sir Thomas 139
Plimsoll, Sir James 243
P.M. (radio program) 249
Police Association of NSW 116
Pollard, R. T. 125
Polo Balls 66, 72
Porgés, Edmond 221
Porgés, Florence Adeline *see* Packer, (Lady) Florence Adeline (Porgés) (FP's second wife)
Porgés, Marcela 221
Portus, (Commissioner) 230, 232
Postgraduate Medical Foundation 186
Postwar Reconstruction and Democratic Rights referendum 124
Potter, Cipriani 6

Potter, Lady 202
Potter, Sir Ian 185, 202, 218, 228, 236, 240
Power Struggle, The (book) 249
Power Without Glory (book) 71
Pratt, A. E. 93
Pratt, H. Irving 205
Prendergast, Rev. Fr Martin 165
Prince Philip, Duke of Edinburgh 148, 190, 191
Princess Alexandra 179
Prince's (restaurant) 81, 151, 173, 222
Printing and Kindred Industries Union (previously PIEUA) 232
  joins AJA strike 232–233
Printing Industry Employees' Union of Australia (PIEUA) 63
  NSW Branch 86, 87
  Consolidated Press chapel 87, 151, 154
  strike (1944) 127
  log of claims (1947) 131
  death of Stalin poster 151
  Slarke lift incident 154
  pay increase (1967) 230
  ACP chapel 222, 232
  merges to bcome PKIU *see* Printing and Kindred Industries Union (previously PIEUA)
Prior, H. K. 193
Proctor, Thea 34
Publishers Holdings Ltd 256
Puckapunyal (army camp) 103
Pulitzer, Joseph 28
Pullen, Roland 87
Pye (company) 185

Qantas xvii
Quadrant 265
Queen Anne 2
Queen Elizabeth II 148
Queen Mother 178
Queensland Newspapers Pty Ltd 158
Quist, Adrian xviii, 172, 202

Raleigh Sun 12
Ramsden, Michael 259
Ramsey, Alan 248
Rang, C. E. Pick 42
Ratcliffe, John Vincent 71, 129, 147, 149, 163, 169, 198
Ratcliffe, R. A. ('Alan') 170, 171
Raymond, Robert 176
Read, T. C. 193
Red Cross (NSW) 93, 105, 118, 263
Reeks, Walter 188

Index

Referee 16, 40, 43
Regional Newspapers Pty Ltd 180–183
Reibey, Thomas 10
Reichenbach, Gabriel S. 159–161
Reid, Alan 46, 148, 197, 219, 226, 238, 247–250, 254
   The Power Struggle 249
   The Gorton Experiment 249
Reid, Henry James 181
Reid, Peter M. 173
Reiff, Simon 54
Reilly, Virgil 23, 34
Retail Newsagents' Association of NSW 81
'Retford Hall' (residence) 80
Returned Servicemens' League (RSL) 105, 166
Reuters 77, 131, 142, 152, 158, 192, 215; *see also* Australian Associated Press (AAP)
Reveille 105, 109, 162
Review 251
Riddell, Elizabeth 265
Ritchie, Dr Frank 187, 222, 255, 259
Ritchie, T. M. 146
Riverina Movement 49, 52
Rivett, Rohan 250
Roberts, Frank 67
Roberts, Roy 62
Robertson, Archie 235
Robinson, William S. 124
Robson, L. C. 21
'Rockton' (residence) 65
Roderick, Dr Colin 199
Rodgers, Don 146
Rodway, Florence 34
Romano's (restaurant) 81
Rosevear, Sol 106, 112
'Rothsay' (residence) 17
Roxborough, D. W. 45
Royal Academy of Music 3, 4
Royal Agricultural Society of NSW 215, 264
Royal Blind Society of NSW 134
   Project 2000 appeal 216
Royal Dorset Yacht Club 236
Royal Easter Show 81, 215
Royal Prince Alfred Hospital 66, 263
Royal Prince Alfred Yacht Club 48
Royal Prince Edward Yacht Club 119, 236
Royal Suva Yacht Club 201
Royal Sydney Yacht Squadron 48
   America's Cup *see* America's Cup (yachting)
Royal Thames Yacht Club xvii, 188, 190–192, 240
Royal Yacht Club of Greece 236, 240
Roydhouse, T. R. 15

RSL *see* Returned Servicemens' League (RSL)
RSYS *see* Royal Sydney Yacht Squadron
Ryan, Nin 237
Ryan, Ronald 225
Rydge, Norman B. 237
Ryrie, Colin 189

Samuel, Peter 238, 247–248
Sandys, Amelia *see* Packer, Amelia (Sandys)
Sara (yacht) 202
Sass, Alex 23
Satelles (racehorse) 32
Saturday Evening Post 36
Savoy Hotel (London) 129, 161, 222
Schapel, Ken 146
Scoop (book) 103
Scotter, Sheila 220
Scullin, James 48
Seal Tite Pty Ltd 51
Second World War 58, 89, 106, 119, 128, 221, 244
Self-Help (book) 8, 38
Seventh War Loan Committee 21
Shakespeare Head Press 193, 194, 249
Shaw, Frank 255
Sheraton East Hotel (New York) 195, 222
Shilton, Rev. L. 264
'Shore' *see* Sydney Church of England Grammar School ('Shore')
Siegrist, Mrs Earlys ('Brownie') 242
Sir Frank: The Frank Packer Story (book) 250
Slarke, Noel 154
Slessor, Kenneth 23, 42
Slessor, Robin 111
Slim, Field Marshal Sir William 189, 190–192, 223
SMH see Sydney Morning Herald (SMH)
Smiles, Dr Samuel 8, 38
Smith, Frederick J. 45, 84, 136
Smith, Dr G. A. 38
Smith, Henry Teesdale 24
Smith, Sir James Joynton 21–27, 40, 43, 45, 52
Smith, Johnson and Co 71
Smith, Joshua 118
Smith, Sydney Ure 34
Smith, Thayre Joynton 41, 43
Smith, W. J. 200
Smith's Newspapers 33, 35, 39, 41, 43, 46, 47, 51, 61, 62, 71, 77, 78
   incorporation of company 28
   FP's employment at 29
   change of ownership 40
   Packer leaves 46
   sale of *Guardian* s 43

Index

Smith's Victorian Publishing Company Ltd 41, 69
Smith's Weekly 22–27, 34, 40–47, 49–53, 61, 63, 74, 77, 112, 182, 224, 264
  R.C. Packer leaves 46
Snedden, Billy 239, 263
Snow, Sidney 45
Snowy Mountains scheme 117
Sonoma (ship) 35
Souter, D. H. 34
Souter, Gavin 124, 185, 263
South Head Cemetery 69, 135, 187, 264
Southern News 179
Sovereign (yacht) 234
Spectre (yacht) 189, 191
Spedding, Quentin S. 27
Spender, Sir Percy 105
Spooner, Eric 82, 91
Sporting and Dramatic News 42
Sporting Life Publications Ltd 63
St David's Cathedral (Hobart) 5
St George and Sutherland Shire Leader 183
St George Call 179
St Mary's Minster (Reading) 2
Stalin, Joseph 151, 264
Stanbridge, George 61
Standard Oil Company 35
Stanner, W. E. 42
Star (London) 184
Star (Sydney) 56, 78
Stening, Dr George 73, 126, 173, 187, 222, 262
Stening, (Lady) Kathleen Mary (Packer) (FP's sister) 17, 18, 25, 29, 33, 43, 53, 59, 62, 67, 73, 119, 126, 135, 173
Stephanov, Alexis 252
Stephen, Sir Ninian 125
Stephen, Alistair 161
Stephensen, P. R. 193
Stevens Institute (US) 195, 234
Stevens, Sir Bertram 52, 82, 91
Stevens, John 188
Stewart, John (Jack) 136
Stillman, Chauncey D. 195
Stiver, Michael 83
strikes *see* industrial action
Sturrock, Jock 203–205, 234
Suburban Publications Pty Ltd 180, 183
Suffolk Vale (property) 31
Sun 14, 16, 21, 28, 34, 39, 42, 44, 46, 53, 55, 72, 74, 81, 112, 127, 138, 158, 159, 171, 192
Sun News-Pictorial 138, 157, 264
Sun Newspapers Ltd 16, 42
Sun-Herald (Sydney) 160, 180, 225, 231

Findaword v Telewords 160
Sunday Australian 249, 254
Sunday Chronicle (London) 67
Sunday Guardian 43, 44, 46, 61, 264
  sale to Associated Newspapers 43
  subsumes *Sunday Pictorial* 44
  merged with *Sunday Sun* 46
Sunday Mirror 178, 180
Sunday Pictorial 42
Sunday Sun 14, 16, 42, 44, 54, 74, 86, 158, 159
Sunday Telegraph xviii, 86, 111, 115, 122, 124, 136, 154, 168, 171, 177, 194, 196, 199, 220, 222–225, 228, 230, 239, 248, 252, 255, 263
  establishment 86
  industrial action *see* industrial action
  anti-communism 144
  election campaigning 198
  sports and competitions 215
  sale of 253, 255, 257
  Telewords v Findaword 160
Sunday Times (Sydney) 13, 14–17, 24, 40, 40
Sunstar (racehorse) 32
Swain, Arthur 194, 198
Sweet Chime (racehorse) 137
Sydney Church of England Grammar School ('Shore') 21, 26, 194
Sydney Cup 32
Sydney Morning Herald (SMH) 33, 42, 44, 50, 74, 81, 89, 90, 112, 122, 124, 127, 130, 157, 160, 169, 172, 174, 177, 197, 216, 219, 228, 239, 263; *see also* John Fairfax & Sons Pty Ltd
Sydney Newspapers (Canberra) Ltd 164
Sydney Newspapers Ltd 59–63, 69, 73–76, 78, 84, 141, 147, 163, 164, 194
  incorporated 56
  negotiations with Associated Newspapers 56–58
  tax laws 141, 147, 163
  FP split with John Theodore 169–170
Sydney Newspapers Trust 164
Sydney Opera House 261
Sydney Stadium 41, 68
Sydney Symphony Orchestra 149
Sylph (ship) 4
Syme, Geoffrey 88

TAB *see* Totalizer Agency Board (TAB)
Tait, Jessie 53, 61, 66, 80
Takande, Lateef Kajode 252
Talbot, Miss (friend of Ethel Packer) 11
Tasmanian News 9, 10
Taylor, Justice 230

Index

TCN-9 (TV station) 176, 184, 185, 189, 205, 215, 217, 224, 228, 237, 247, 255, 257–261
  establishment and launch 167–168
Telegraph House 226, 229, 252, 255, 256
Telegraph, Brisbane 131
Telegraph
  takeover by Consolidated Press 74–76
  rename and revival in 1936 *see Daily Telegraph*
Telegus 126
television
  introduction to Australia 164–165
  royal commission 164, 216
  award of licences *see* Australian Broadcasting Control Board (ABCB)
  ownership and control 216–219
Television Corporation Ltd 170, 256
  award of licence 166
  corporate coup 228; *see also* TCN-9 (TV station)
  establishment 165
  Brisbane/Adelaide licence hearings 177
  GTV-9 *see* GTV-9
  John Theodore 165, 168
  networking arrangements 177, 185–186
  paid political broadcasting 260
  regional TV licence hearings 184
  succession 258, 264
  TCN-9 *see* TCN-9 (TV station)
  wheeling and dealing 217
Television Wollongong Transmissions Ltd 184
Theodore, Edward Granville (Ted) 48, 49, 52, 55, 58, 61, 82, 91, 105, 106, 107, 114, 116, 123, 163, 164, 168, 190, 265
  Fijian gold mines 60, 69, 70, 105, 169, 201
  heart attack and death 141, 143
  takeover of *Telegraph* 73–76
  relationship with FP 61, 63, 70, 84, 143
Theodore, John 141, 165, 168
  Consolidated Press Holdings 164
  Television Corporation 165, 168
  split with FP 168–170, 172
Theodore, Ned 141
Things I Hear (newsletter) 182
This Day Tonight (TV program) 256
Thomas, Alfred 261, 265
Thompson, Duncan 132
Thomson, Roy (Lord Thomson of Fleet) 184
3AK (radio station) 185
Thrum, Daisy 113
Times (London) 191, 264
Tomlins, L. B. 71
Tonkin, F. W. 44
Torch Bearer 21

Totalizer Agency Board (TAB) 216
Tout, F. H. 45
Townsley, F. A. 5
Townsville Daily Bulletin 12
Trades and Labor Council (NSW) *see* NSW Trades and Labor Council
Trans Media Pty Ltd 257
Travel Boy (racehorse) 136
Travers, Colonel R. J. A. (Jack) 41, 56, 76, 103, 108, 126, 152
Trengove, Alan 263
Tricontinental Corporation Ltd 240
Trocadero (ballroom) 133, 221
Truth & Sportsman Ltd 74, 86, 90, 153, 166
Truth 14, 41, 44, 74, 86–87, 91, 111–112, 130, 175, 178
Tunbridge, V. J. H. 155
Tunney, Gene 37
Turf Life 63
Turner, Ted 242
Turramurra College 20
Turton, Geoffrey ('Petrov') 61
TVW-7 (TV station) 240
2BL (radio station) 166
2KY (radio station) 165
2SM (radio station) 165
Twyborn Affair, The (book) 32

UAP *see* United Australia Party (UAP)
United Australia Party (UAP) 52, 82, 91, 105, 108, 114, 124, 140
United Country Movement 49
United Nations Declaration on Freedom of Information 143
United Nations Security Council 249
Universal Telecasters Queensland Ltd 218
Uren, Tom 226
Usher's Hotel 72, 123
United States North West Cape communications station 226

Vacuum Oil 35, 36
Varidel, S. 41
Vietnam War 259
Vim (yacht) 189–192, 196, 200–204, 235
Vincent, Anthony 221
Vincent, Noel 221
Visser, Martin 241
Vogue 220

Waddell, George 57
Waddell, Sir Graham 45

Index

Walker, Jimmy 36
Walsh, Richard 251
Ward, Eddie xvii, 91, 104, 106, 108–110, 116, 175, 197
Warnecke, Glen William (George) 26, 33, 44, 49, 52, 54, 55–59, 69, 72, 77, 115, 167
  relationship with R.C. Packer 26, 35, 38, 39, 43, 55, 70
  relationship with FP 26, 60, 69, 73, 76, 84
  impressions of Ethel Packer 29
Warnecke, Nora *see* Hill, Nora
Warner, G. 237
Warner, Sir Arthur 185, 224
Warragamba Dam scheme 108
Watson, Fred 40
Watson, J. K. ('King') 78, 152, 225, 252, 253
Watt, Ernest 78
Watt, Ruth 77, 170
Waugh, Evelyn 103
Wayland, Jack E. 180
Weatherly (yacht) 202–205
Weedon, Rosalind *see* Packer, Rosalind (Weedon)
Weekend Business Review 257
Weekend 162, 171, 175, 182
  censorship 175–176
  merged with *Australian Woman's Mirror* 196
Weekly Mail (London) 162
Wenholm, Norman 180
Wentworth News 179
West Australian Newspapers Ltd 239
West Australian 240
Wheeler, Fordyce 44, 50, 56
White, Earl 180
White, Patrick 32, 223, 237
White, Richard 69
White, William 12
Whitington, Don 110, 117, 127
Whitington, R. S. 250, 263
Whitlam, E.G. (Gough) 219, 250, 259, 261, 263
Whitlam, Margaret 257

Who's Who in Australia 136
Wilder, Ken 199
Willesee, Don 250, 257
Willesee, Mike 257, 260
William Collins & Co. Ltd 199
William Heinemann (publisher) 148
Williams, G. H. 51
Williams, Graham 260
Williams, Sir John 178, 185, 231
Williamson, J. C. 16, 40
Williamson, Jean 77
Williamson–Waddington (film company) 16
Wilson, Sydney H. 141
WIN–4 (TV station) 217
Wireless Weekly 42
Woman 75, 159
Woman's Budget 42, 60, 61
Woman's Day 139, 141, 145
Women's Weekly *see* Australian Women's Weekly
Wood, A. W. 157
Worker (Qld) 49
Workers' Educational Association 164
Workers' News 264
World (Hobart) 54
World (Sydney) 54, 55–59, 62, 108, 145, 166
World Council of Churches 167
World War II *see* Second World War
World War I *see* First World War
World's News 42
World's Press News 128
Wren, John 71
Wrigley (family) 36
Wrigley, William 35
Wynne-Lewis, T. H. 76
Wynter, Philip 132

Yacht Club d'Hyères 236, 240
Yaffa Syndicate 72
Yaffa, David 72, 86

www.ingramcontent.com/pod-product-compliance
Lightning Source LLC
Chambersburg PA
CBHW080611230426
43664CB00019B/2862